CW01466323

HINESE QUESTION

KYOTO CSEAS SERIES ON ASIAN STUDIES 12
Center for Southeast Asian Studies, Kyoto University

the Chinese Question

Ethnicity, Nation, and Region in and Beyond the Philippines

Caroline S. Hau

NUS PRESS

Singapore

in association with

KYOTO UNIVERSITY PRESS

Japan

© 2014 Caroline S. Hau

All rights reserved. No part of this publication may be reproduced or transmitted in any form or by any means, electronic or mechanical, including photocopy, recording, or any information storage or retrieval system, without permission in writing from the publisher.

NUS Press
National University of Singapore
AS3-01-02, 3 Arts Link
Singapore 117569
www.nus.edu.sg/nuspress

ISBN 978-9971-69-792-1 (Paper)

Kyoto University Press
Yoshida-South Campus, Kyoto University
69 Yoshida-Konoe-Cho, Sakyo-ku
Kyoto 606-8315
Japan
www.kyoto-up.or.jp

ISBN 978-4-87698-360-5

National Library Board, Singapore Cataloguing-in-Publication Data

Hau, Caroline S., 1969-
   The Chinese question: ethnicity, nation, and region in and beyond the Philippines / Caroline S. Hau. – Singapore: NUS Press, [2014]
         pages cm
         ISBN: 978-9971-69-792-1

   1. Chinese – Philippines – Ethnic identity.   2. National characteristics, Chinese – In motion pictures.   3. National characteristics, Chinese – In literature.   4. Chinese – Philippines – Social life and customs.   I. Title.

   DS732   OCN 862700926
   305.800951-- dc23

Book and cover design by Karl Fredrick M. Castro

Printed by: Markono Print Media Pte Ltd

CONTENTS

ACKNOWLEDGMENTS

I would like to thank my parents, Hau Chiok 施荣宣 and Sy Chiu Hua 林玉琦, and my sisters Cat, Carr, and Sandy for their loving encouragement, and my *ninong* and *ninang*, Mr. and Mrs. Lyonel Ty, and family friend Auntie Julie Hing, for their warm support over the years. I thank Alfonso Ang (Tu Yiban), Teresita Ang-See, Bai Ren, Aileen Baviera, Felipe Dy, Go Bon Juan, Herman Tiu Laurel, Ricky Lee, Aurora Roxas-Lim, Benito Lim, the late Lin Bin, Armando Malay Jr., Gyō Miyahara, Charlson Ong, Daniel Ong, the late Onghokham, Benny Subianto, Nariko Sugaya, Joaquin Sy, and Wang Gungwu for graciously sharing their insights and stories with me. I thank Andrew Abalahin, Jojo Abinales, Pio Andrade, Grace Pe-Bacani, Chris Baker, Pheng Cheah, Richard Chu, Beng Espinosa, Edel Garcellano, Bomen Guillermo, Reynard Hing, Kasian Tejapira, Khoo Boo Teik, Bliss Cua Lim, Liu Hong, Pasuk Phongpaichit, Vince Rafael, Tesa Encarnacion Tadem, Ed Tadem, Tan Pek Leng, and Wu Xiao An for their friendship and for helping me figure out what questions to ask and how to look for answers. Ben Anderson gave extensive comments on the draft manuscript, and his intellectual rigor and comparative breadth are a constant source of inspiration. Jun Aguilar's pioneering scholarship and warm friendship—like Ben's—have been my armor and my anchor, and his exemplary editorship of the *Philippine Studies* journal gave me the intellectual stimulation, succor, and space in which to test the major ideas of this book. The two anonymous reviewers offered thoughtful suggestions for improving the manuscript, for which I am most grateful. Ina Cosio was an excellent research assistant and a good friend throughout the preparation of the manuscript. I thank Nobu Aizawa, Nate Badenoch, Elizabeth Chandra, Tatsuki Kataoka, Yumi Kitamura, Junko Koizumi, Mari Kondo, Jafar Suryomenggolo, Takeshi Onimaru, Wahyu Prasetyawan, and Nobuto Yamamoto for their camaraderie and for generously sharing their research on the Chinese in other parts of Southeast Asia, and Daniel A. Bell, Allen Carlson, David Leheny, Peter Katzenstein, and Shih Chih-yu for their comments on chapter 7. I thank Maricor Baytion for her continuing support over the years, her faith in this project, and her patient shepherding of the manuscript through publication. I thank Yoko

Hayami, Rica Santos, Peter Schoppert, and Paul Kratoska for their great help in arranging for the co-publication of the book in Japan and Singapore. This book would not have been possible without Takashi Shiraishi, whose work and thinking about the region inform each chapter, and whose generosity, encouragement, and unstinting support at all levels of everyday life and endeavor have sustained me over the years.

Chapters 1 and 2 are expanded versions of the article, "Blood, Land and Conversion: 'Chinese' Mestizoness and the Politics of Belonging in Jose Angliongto's *The Sultanate*," *Philippine Studies* 57, no.1 (2009): 3–48. Chapter 3 is a revised version of an article, "Kidnapping, Citizenship, and the Chinese," *Public Policy: Quarterly Journal of the University of the Philippines* 1, no. 1 (Oct.–Dec. 1997): 62–89, with two slightly revised versions: "'Who Will Save Us from the Law?': The Criminal State and the Illegal Alien in Post-1986 Philippines," in *Figures of Criminality in Indonesia, Philippines and Colonial Vietnam*, ed. Vicente L. Rafael (Ithaca: Cornell University Southeast Asia Program, 1999), 128–51; and "The Criminal State and the Chinese in Post-1986 Philippines," in *Geopolitics of the Visible: Essays on Philippine Film Cultures*, ed. Rolando B. Tolentino (Quezon City: Ateneo de Manila University Press, 2000), 217–41. Chapter 4 is based on "'The Chinese Question': A Marxist Interpretation," in *Marxism in the Philippines: Continuing Engagements*, ed. Teresa Encarnacion Tadem and Laura Samson (Manila: Anvil Publishing and University of the Philippines Third World Studies Center, 2010), 156–87; and "Du Ai, Lin Bin and Revolutionary Flows," in *Traveling Nation-Makers: Transnational Flows and Movements in the Making of Modern Southeast Asia*, ed. Caroline Hau and Kasian Tejapira (Kyoto and Singapore: Kyoto University Press and Singapore Press, 2011), 153–87. A shorter version of chapters 5 and 6 appeared as "Conditions of Visibility: Resignifying the 'Chinese'/'Filipino' in *Mano Po* and *Crying Ladies*," *Philippine Studies* 53, no. 4 (2005): 491–531. A version of chapter 6 was published as "Ethnicity, Ideology, and the 'Chinese'/'Mestizo' Family in the Philippines," in *The Family in Flux in Southeast Asia: Institution, Ideology, Practice*, ed. Yoko Hayami, Junko Koizumi, Chalidaporn Songsampan, and Ratana Tosakul (Singapore and Kyoto: Singapore University Press and Kyoto University Press, 2012), 227–47. Chapter 7 was first published as "Becoming 'Chinese' in Southeast Asia," in *Sinicization and the Rise of China: Civilizational Processes Beyond East and West*, ed. Peter J. Katzenstein (London and New York: Routledge, 2012), 175–206; a shortened version appeared as chapter 5 of Shiraishi Takashi and Caroline Hau, *Chūgoku wa higashi Ajia wo dō kaeru ka?: 21 seki no shin chiiki shisutemu* [How is China Changing East Asia?: The New Regional System in the 21st Century] (Tokyo: Chūokoron, 2012), 167–212. Unless otherwise indicated, all translations are mine, and all errors of fact and interpretation are my sole responsibility.

A note on the Chinese text

All Chinese terms are rendered in simplified script form, and most use the pinyin romanization system. The exceptions are names like Hong Kong, Guomindang (which is romanized as Kuomintang), and the personal names of authors or historical and contemporary figures such as Chiang Kai-shek (Jiang Jieshi), which follow the system of romanization used in their respective territories (Wade-Giles in Taiwan, for instance) by way of acknowledging the idea of multiple sites of Chineseness. For romanization of Hokkien words, I have eschewed using the Bodman and other systems, since they are largely unfamiliar to Hokkien speakers in the Philippines, and instead rely on words as they are romanized by young Philippine Chinese in everyday usage.

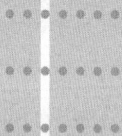

INTRODUCTION

Between August 22, 2011, and January 20, 2012, the primetime romantic comedy-drama teleserye[1] *My Binondo Girl* was aired on ABS-CBN channel, one of the Philippines' leading television networks. The series focused on a young mestiza (a female of mixed parentage or ancestry) named Jade, who was raised by her Filipino mother Zheny Dimaguiba and grandmother Amor, but still yearned for the love of her absent Chinese father, Chen Sy, now married to her mother's former best friend. Jade assumed the identity of her deceased brother Yuan in order to get close to her father. Although her masquerade was eventually exposed, she was able to vindicate the family name by becoming a successful businesswoman, opening a restaurant, ZhenChu Topps, in partnership with entrepreneur Andy Wu, whom she eventually married.

Filmed in "Chinatown" Binondo, Manila, and in Hong Kong and China, the big-budget production, the final episode of which obtained a 30.7 percent viewer share in the national household ratings of primetime television programs (Santiago 2012), featured one of the Philippines' rising young stars, Kim Chiu. In a press conference held a few months before the premiere, Kim Chiu told reporters that the "series is really close to her heart since it will showcase the life of a Chinese family," and revealed that she "will be speaking Chinese in some scenes of the series" (Buan-Deveza 2011).[2]

My Binondo Girl is not the first major media project to focus on the adventures and travails of a "Chinese Filipino" and her family. Beginning in the 1970s, Filipino films such as *Dragnet* (Manila Dragnet, 1973) and *Ganito Kami Noon, Paano Kayo Ngayon?* (This is How We were Then; What about You Now?, 1976) painted a more positive, empowering portrait of the Chinese that stood at variance with the proverbial alien and exploitative

Kim Chiu as Jade Dimaguiba and Yuan Sy in *My Binondo Girl* (courtesy of ABS-CBN)

Chinese merchant-capitalist of popular imagination. From the 1980s onwards, creative writing by Charlson Ong and Du Ai added substantially to the body of literature on the ethnic Chinese published in the Philippines and in so-called Greater China (mainland China, Hong Kong, Macau, and Taiwan). At the turn of the twenty-first century, the strong domestic box-office return of the first *Mano Po*³ film (Wen Shou, 吻手 2002) spawned five thematically unrelated "sequels" featuring different aspects of Chinese-Philippine life.

More than just weather vanes that indicate changes in public attitude and identification, literature and film have also played an active role in bringing about these changes. The *Mano Po* franchise, in particular, highlighted—and helped cement—an important shift in public attitudes toward the Chinese in the Philippines. Aristotle Dy, a Chinese-Filipino Jesuit priest who ran Ateneo de Manila University's Chinese Studies Program in 2006, stated that "[i]n the last ten years, we have witnessed great progress in outward expressions of Filipino acceptance of Filipino-Chinese as part of Filipino society. The success of Chinese-themed films is one indicator" (quoted in Seno 2006). Dy attributed this change in public perception of the Philippine Chinese to the rise of China as a superpower and to the growing popularity of Asian popular cultural products in the Philippines and the region.

What distinguishes *Binondo Girl* from the *Mano Po* films is its choice of a "Chinese Filipino" actress for the starring role. Produced by the Chinese-Filipino Monteverde[4] family's Regal Entertainment, the *Mano Po* films have been headlined by some of the Philippines' most bankable leading actresses, including Maricel Soriano, Vilma Santos, Sharon Cuneta, and Kris Aquino. But none of these lead actresses,[5] not even Kris Aquino (who is of Chinese mestizo ancestry), consider themselves, or are considered by the Filipino public, as "Chinese Filipino." By contrast, not only does Kim Chiu identify herself as "Chinese"[6]; she has done so despite the fact that she herself, like Kris Aquino, is technically a mestiza. Born to a Chinese father and a Filipina-Spanish mestiza mother, Kim Chiu is routinely tagged by the press and Internet fan sites as "the Chinese Cutie from Cebu." Her *Wikipedia* article helpfully provides her Chinese name, Zhang Jinzhu (张金珠) ("Kim Chiu" 2011).

Another instructive example—albeit one with a negative slant—of the growing visibility of the "Chinese Filipino" in Philippine popular culture is the sex scandal involving print ad model and medical doctor Hayden Kho and model-actress Katrina Halili. Like Kim Chiu, Katrina Halili and Hayden Kho are "mestizos" whose "Chineseness" is publicly known.

Interviewed by columnist Ricky Lo (2008) of *The Philippine Star*, Halili described herself this way:

> I am part-Chinese, *sa* mother [*sic*] side *ko* [on my mother's side]; her surname is Pe. I spent part of my childhood in Palawan and I studied in a Chinese school, St. Stephen [*sic*] in Binondo, Manila, until grade 5. I can speak a little Chinese. I was brought up in a mix of Filipino and Chinese customs but I think *mas* Chinese *ako sa ugali* [I'm more Chinese in terms of temperament]. I and my only brother had a *yaya* [nanny] at home but in school, *mga kasama at kaklase ko lahat* Chinese [my companions and classmates were all Chinese].
>
> Halili is my real surname. After finishing grade school at St. Stephen [*sic*], I moved to another Chinese school (on Tomas Mapua Street, Sta. Cruz, Manila) for high school. I never made it to college because after high school, I landed in *StarStruck* [a popular talent show on television]."

Hayden Kho, on the other hand, was introduced by Lo in an interview (2007) published a year before the Halili interview in this way:

He was born in Manila on May 20, 1980, to a pure-Chinese doctor-father, Hayden Kho, and a Spanish-Filipina businesswoman-mother, Irene dela Santa; one of five children. "I'm a Taurus-Gemini because I was born at 11 P.M., boundary of Taurus and Gemini." He describes his family as "above average." He speaks fluent Chinese (he studied at the Grace Christian School in Binondo, Manila [*sic*], for fourteen years).[7]

Both Kho and Halili achieved notoriety when a sex videotape of the two, allegedly filmed by Kho, went viral on the Internet and pirated compact-disc versions were peddled all over Manila and other Philippine cities in 2009. Kho subsequently accused a friend, Eric Chua, of leaking and selling the tape. Although the scandal quickly became a hot topic of national discussion and the subject of a Senate hearing, the ethnicity of Kho and Halili, as well as that of the alleged culprit Chua, was largely a nonissue. There were a few exceptions, however, as in this telling comment posted by an Internet user under the account name "jcc 34" (Gagelonia 2009):

> [If] I have to fan my Chinese bias, [t]his is how I smell this sordid scenario. Distribution of pirated DVDs/CDs and sex videos are [*sic*] big business. People who are into it are the business-minded people. Ms KH, according to her bio, is a Chinese; so is Kho and her [*sic*] frat[ernity] brod [brother] who is being made the fall guy to create some aura of innocence on the "trysters."...
>
> All these onscreen drama is [*sic*] designed to raise-up [*sic*] the pot. The more salacious gossips the sex video generates the more would be the demand for this video. Off-screen you could see these [*sic*] trio laughing their hearts out for being able to put up a grand-drama at the expense of the gullible media and the gullible Pinoys. The "Chinese" have the entire affair figured out, but some decent Pinoys are scandalized and outraged by the lowest depth that our morality had sunk [*sic*].

This blog repeats the stereotype of the "Chinese" as "business-minded people," whom the commentator accuses of cynically exploiting the publicity generated by the sex scandal to advance their careers and make money. But what makes the comment interesting is that, after a string of sentences alleging the masterminding of this entire affair by the profiteering "Chinese," the author concludes that "The 'Chinese' have the entire affair figured out, but some decent Pinoys are scandalized and outraged by the lowest depth that *our* morality had sunk" (italics added).

Two points stand out here. First, the word "Chinese" in the final sentence is enclosed in quotation marks, most likely because Kho and Halili, despite their being considered "Chinese," are actually of mixed Filipino, Chinese, and Spanish ancestry. Second, and more telling, is the statement that "decent Pinoys are scandalized and outraged by the lowest depth that our morality had sunk." The author apparently takes the actions of these "Chinese" as reflecting badly on "our" (presumably Filipino) morality, an idea that makes sense only if one assumes that the "Chinese" are, after all, one of "us." In two short paragraphs, "jcc 34"'s comment manages to locate the "Chinese" simultaneously inside and outside the "Filipino" community.

This double move of inclusion and exclusion highlights the unsettled and shifting meanings not only of "Chinese" and "Chineseness," but of mestizoness, "Filipino," and "Filipinoness" as well. The fact that Kim Chiu, Katrina Halili, and Hayden Kho are "mestizos"—that is, not "pure Chinese," to use a common expression in the Philippines—and yet identify themselves or are identified by others as "Chinese" and/or "Chinese Filipino," would seem to go against the grain of the historical trajectory of the "Chinese mestizos" in the Philippines. The common understanding of the historical fate of the Chinese mestizo is encapsulated in a sociological narrative of intermarriage, acculturation, and assimilation that resulted in the "disappearance" of the Chinese mestizo into the emergent "Filipino" nation by the end of the Spanish colonial era (outlined in Wickberg 1964, 1965; Skinner 1996). This narrative of mestizo "disappearance" is, in fact, an important subplot of the larger, grand narrative of the making of the Filipino people and nation, one that posits Filipinoness as constitutively hybrid yet also distinctly particular.[8] This particularity is spelled out not only through the country's history and its culture, economy, politics, and society, but, as with any nation-state, its specific terms for membership in the Filipino "imagined community" (Anderson 1991). In the first few decades of postwar Philippines, it was the Chinese "alien" who served as the exemplary foreigner against which Filipino national identity was negatively inferred (Hau 2000b, chap. 4).

While the historical narrative of the becoming-Filipino of the Chinese mestizo can account for why Kris Aquino, for example, is considered a "mestizo," but not "Chinese," it has little to say about why Kris's mother, former president Corazon Cojuangco Aquino, made a great show of (re)claiming her Chinese ancestry and visiting her family's "ancestral hometown" in Hongjian, Fujian Province, China, in 1988, and why Kris Aquino became involved in a film project that she herself credited with reviving her movie career and a Chinese-Filipino role for which she would win a Best Supporting Actress award at the Metro Manila Film Festival in 2002 (*Manila Bulletin*, 2002). How do we account for the revival of "Chinese" identification[9] among mestizos in the late twentieth and early twenty-first centuries?

This book is about the cultural politics of Chineseness and hybridity[10] in the postwar Philippines. It examines how terms relating to the "Chinese" and "Chinese mestizo" migrated between and across a spectrum of connotations ranging from the negative to the positive. It attempts to explain how and why this happened, and what its implications are. Its aim is to map the constellation of perspectives, policies, and practices that make up the "Chinese Question," that is, the idea that "Chinese" migrants and their descendants constitute a "foreign" group who pose political, economic, cultural, and social "problems" for the postcolonial Philippine nation-state. This book documents the political, economic, social, and cultural transformations of the past decades that spurred the reformulation of the "Chinese Question," as state imperatives and public priorities in the Philippines underwent rethinking and reorganization in the wake of geopolitical developments, intellectual change, and de facto economic regionalization and globalization.

In America, the "Chinese Question" had been posed mainly as a "Coolie Question" (see, for example, Meade 1877): Chinese labor immigration was a "problem," the resolution of which necessitated the enactment of the Chinese Exclusion Act of 1882. Applied to colonial Philippines in 1902, this act prevented Chinese labor from entering the colony while effectively sealing the occupational identity of the "Chinese" as merchant (Alejandrino 2003, esp. 40–44; Chu 2010, 281–332). In the Philippines, therefore, it was not the Chinese laborer, but the Chinese merchant, who became the specific target of postcolonial official nationalism. The economic importance of the Chinese in the Spanish and American colonial eras became a "problem" that had to be addressed through Commonwealth and postwar legislation aimed at breaking Chinese "dominance" over certain economic activities, such as retail trade, and barring Chinese entry into the professions by limiting the right to exercise professions, such as law and medicine, to Filipino citizens. This strain of decolonizing nationalism viewed economic and political rights as the privilege of "Filipinos" whose patrimony had to be secured against competition from "foreigners." The historical conflation of Chinese ethnicity with commerce and capital found expression in the stereotypical image of the rich, avaricious, and (often sexually) predatory Chinese merchant and capitalist—almost always men—whose economic activities, bordering on the illicit because they involved collusion with, if not *corrupting* of, officials of the state, had to be curbed in order for wealth to accrue to its rightful owners, the Filipino people.

Moreover, in the first two decades of the postwar period, a China that had gone Communist became a global and regional "problem" that encompassed the sizeable ethnic Chinese populations in areas in "Southeast Asia"[11] that were part of the American-led "Free Asia" ("free" here meant "anticommunist" rather than "democratic") security and trade system, which included the Philippines, Thailand, Malaysia, and South Vietnam (and later New Order Indonesia).[12] The threat of Communist subversion stoked fears of Chinese "fifth columns" in Southeast Asia, even as the ethnic Chinese population came under increasing pressure to de-sinicize in the name of assimilation or integration into "mainstream" Southeast Asian societies. The term "Chinese Question" was a convenient abbreviation for all three economic, political, and cultural concerns relating to the "national interest," and a way of posing them as problems and challenges for the national consolidation and modernization projects of the Philippine state in the name of the "Filipino people."

This book follows the checkered trajectory of post-independence Philippine state policies on the Chinese Question, and explores the ways in which changing notions of a "Filipino" bounded community are shaped by, and in turn shape, not only these policies, but also public attitudes towards the ethnic Chinese and everyday social relations and cultural interactions in the Philippines. It does so by tracing the variegated meanings and shifting conceptual boundaries not only of the words "Chinese" and "mestizo," but the national signifier "Filipino" itself. *Chinese Question* presents the history and analyzes the language, logic, and practice(s) of selective inclusion and exclusion that underpinned these terms of appellation, while also showing how the meanings of these terms evolved over the last hundred years in response to changing global and regional historical and material contexts, and changing perceptions, policies, and practices on the part of both the Philippine state and Filipino society.

A quick look at the historical and current terminology relating to the "Chinese" and "Chinese mestizo" suffices to bring out the difficulties in pinning down people once and for all by recourse to such criteria as place of birth, blood, ancestry, race (or ethnicity), and self-identification—legal and sociological concepts that have had an important bearing on the concept of belonging to the Philippine nation as well as elsewhere in the world in the post-World War II era.

The "Chinese meztizo" (meztizo de sangley) was a legal category created in 1760, when the mestizo population had become sufficiently sizeable, in the eyes of the Spanish colonial state, to warrant a separate category from "native." Although the category was abolished in the late 1880s, "mestizo" continued to be used administratively in some areas and endured as a social category well into the twentieth century (Chu 2010, 69–70). Nevertheless, there was a general decline in the use of mestizo categories in the late nineteenth century, suggesting not only political and bureaucratic changes in the colonial Philippines, but an important shift in the consciousness of people who in earlier times might have been counted as "mestizo" (Doeppers 1994, 84; Aguilar 2012a, 135–36). The word "mestizo," therefore, encodes different kinds of ascribed (or externally imposed) as well as self- (or internally generated) identifications. While "Chinese mestizo" originated as a legal category, mestizo de sangley, which referred to children of intermarriages between "sangley" (a term later changed to "chino") fathers who were migrants mainly from Fujian and "indio" ("native") mothers in Spanish colonial Philippines, its referents have encompassed, at certain points in time, the following kinds of people: inhabitants of the Philippines who were partly of Chinese ancestry and were counted as "mestizo" by the state; inhabitants of Chinese ancestry who identified themselves as "Chinese mestizo" and preferred to marry either "Chinese" or "Chinese mestizos"; those of Chinese ancestry who did not identify themselves as mestizo, but rather, as "indio," "natural," and later "Filipino"; those of Chinese ancestry who, generations removed from this ancestry, had their legal classification changed to "indio"; those of Chinese ancestry who were Hispanized in terms of education, language, and other cultural markers; those of Chinese ancestry who thought of themselves as "Filipino" and were, in some cases, vocal about their anti-Chinese sentiments; those of Chinese ancestry who thought of themselves as "Chinese" or were raised as "Chinese," whether born in the Philippines or raised in China; those who maintained links with both "Chinese" and "Filipino" communities; and those of Chinese and white American/ European ancestry who were not considered "Chinese" by other people, and who had forgotten or chosen not to acknowledge their Chinese ancestry while emphasizing their Spanish/American/European "blood" or connections.

Conversely, the word "Chinese," in its contemporary usage, has encompassed the following kinds of people: those who were born of non-Chinese parents in the Philippines but were adopted by a Chinese parent and brought up as "Chinese"; those who were born of non-Chinese parents and were adopted by a Chinese parent, and raised in Hong Kong or China or Taiwan; and mestizos raised and educated as "Chinese" in the Philippines or Hong Kong or China or Taiwan or elsewhere.

"Filipino," on the other hand, includes the following kinds of people: Chinese born in China, Chinese born in the Philippines, mestizos born in the Philippines, and mestizos born in China. The term "Filipinos" has historically encompassed the following categories of people: anyone born in the Philippines; foreigners residing in the Philippines for at least two years and paying taxes; Chinese mestizos, whether raised in China or the Philippines; and Chinese. But at certain times and depending on the circumstances, the term has also excluded all four categories.

Other terms used to refer to the "Chinese" have lineages that are just as old as, if not older than, *mestizo*. According to Anthony Reid (2010, 53–54), words such as *Chijs, Cina,* and *sangley* were already in use during the sixteenth century to refer to migrant or sojourning traders and artisans from Guangdong and Fujian, regardless of the regional or linguistic variations among them. Sangley, in particular, was used in the Philippines as well as South Celebes (Sulawesi), appearing in Makassar and Bugis dictionaries as "sanggalea," and centuries later, in Ifugao as "hanglay" (see Cense 1955, 107[13]). But the etymology of the term is uncertain (Fuchikawa 1934). Edgar Wickberg (1965, 9n14; drawing on Chang 1937 and Fuchikawa 1934), the foremost historian of the Chinese in the Philippines, stated that the term was derived from the classical Chinese *shanglü* (商旅 merchant traveler). But the historian William Henry Scott, citing the late sixteenth-century manuscript now known as the Boxer Codex (c. 1590; see Boxer 1950), traced *sangley* to *changlai* (常来, *sionglai* in Hokkien, literally "frequently coming") (Scott 1994, 190, 279; both Fuchikawa 1934, 336; and Purcell 1965, 508, discuss this). Scott's contention would appear to be borne out by sixteenth-century contemporary Francisco de Sande's (1576, 50) explanation that "Thoughout [sic] these islands they call the Chinese 'Sangleyes,' meaning 'a people who come and go,' on account of their habit of coming to these islands to trade—or as they say there, 'the regular post.'" The commonsensical understanding among the Philippine Chinese is that the word derives from *sengdi,* the Hokkien term for "business" (Purcell 1965, 508; concurs with Laufer 1907, 268). The current Mandarin term for sengdi is *shengyi* (生意), but an eighteenth-century Tokugawa Japanese government official edict (1715) explained that the term *shengli* (生理, pronounced "sengdi" in Hokkien) meant "trade" (商卖 shōbai) (Fuchikawa 1934, 343). In this case, "sangley" might have been an abbreviation of *sengdi lang* (生理人 traders).[14]

While shanglü and shengli/sengdi identify ethnicity with occupation (the latter term quite literally), changlai/sionglai is a non-ethnic marker that stresses the idea of external origins, that is, the idea of "coming" from somewhere else (somewhere that happens to be nearby and, until the late nineteenth century, home to a succession of regionally hegemonic dynastic states), as well as mobility (coming frequently). This mobility, however, is still glossed as having been for the purpose of trade. Although the word "sangley" increasingly came to be replaced by the word *chino* in bureaucratic usage during the second half of the nineteenth century—as can be seen in one of Jose Rizal's most memorable characters, "el chino Quiroga," in his masterpiece *El filibusterismo* (1891, chap. 16)—it managed to survive into the twentieth century. In his study of Chinese elements in the Tagalog language, E. Arsenio Manuel (1948, 50) provided the following definitions of "sangley": "Chinese; Chinaman; Chinese half-breed, or Chinese mestizo; term also refers to ill-bred or stupid person in Batangas." Michael Tan (2001) notes that as late as 1972, Jose Villa Panganiban's *Tagalog-English Dictionary* still contained an entry on sangley, although the term was increasingly replaced by "intsik."

Like sangley, the Tagalog term *intsik* (*inchic, insic, insik*) has regional reach and salience. Its etymology can be traced to the Hokkien[15] (福建) word for "his uncle," 引叔 *in tsiak,* which may have originally been used "as a way of introducing a Chinese newcomer to another person" (Chu 2010, 69). The word may have been used in the same way as the still commonly used *"in pe"* (his father) and *"in pê"* (his uncle), when a male speaker—in this case an elder male sangley/chino immigrant—refers to himself in the third person when speaking to a son or to a younger cohort. The word "intsik" also circulated within Nanyang (南洋, i.e., countries traversed through the South China Sea; see Wang 1992c, 11) Southeast Asia in its Malay form *encik,* which is now used as a term of respect for addressing a man or woman, regardless of his or her ethnicity, and in the Thai form *jek*. In its Tagalog usage, *intsik* came to acquire a negative connotation[16] in connection with racist chants like the Spanish-Filipino phrase *intsik viejo, tulo laway* (lit., "old drooling Chinese"), a reference that is also loaded with class baggage, since it refers not only to aged Chinese, but Chinese whose hard labor results in premature aging. Filipinos, however, are known to use the term in a non-pejorative way, while others, circumventing the potentially loaded term, prefer to use the "neutral" English word "Chinese" instead.[17]

Despite its negative connotation, at least to many (but not all) "Chinese," intsik has been reclaimed in recent years by Chinese Filipinos like Charlson Ong (2000a, xiii–xiv), who argues that

> The Chinese Filipino writer is often engaged not only in recovery but also reconstruction. He has to fill in gaps left by lost traditions, failing memories and his own inability to comprehend the harsher, crueler world of his elders. He has to redeem the images of his past foisted upon society by the media, images he himself grew up with. And to replace the irredeemable with those he finds more valid and concise.
>
> I have, for instance, always argued against the penchant of some Chinese Filipinos to replace *Intsik* with the Spanish *Chino* in every

situation. The word *intsik*, like *impe*, is derived from the Amoy terms for uncle, while *ingkong* and *akong* are derived from the Amoy word for grandfather. They were originally terms of respect. That they later acquired pejorative meanings is a result of historic racism. And in seeking to purge them from popular lexicon we, in effect, capitulate to racism by denying its history instead of facing up to it and purging its residual effects by recovering such words it had abused. Chinese Filipinos should take to *Intsik* in the manner that Afro-Americans and other Negroes now call themselves Blacks and [national hero Jose] Rizal and his gang chose to name themselves Indios Bravos.

"Chinese" migrants refer to non-Chinese Filipinos as *huanna* (番仔 fanzi), a term that, like intsik, is considered as racist/ethnocentric because it is routinely translated as "barbarian."[18] The term also has regional salience since it is used by Hokkien-speaking communities in Southeast Asia and Taiwan. But it must be noted that *fan* appears in some Qing texts as the equivalent of "westerners": the term *fanyin* 番银, for example, is glossed as yangyin 洋银 (western bank).[19] Like intsik, it may or may not be used with a derogatory intention in everyday speech. Equating huanna with barbarian, like equating intsik with the racist "chink," is an artifact of history and ideology. Just as some Filipinos have taken to using the English term "Chinese" to refer to the intsik, some Chinese have taken to calling Filipinos *huilipin lang* (菲律宾人, Filipinos) in an effort to avoid using names whose referents are entangled in a dense traffic among several tongues, namely, Tagalog, English, Hokkien, and Mandarin Chinese.

Immigrant Chinese in turn call themselves *huanke* 番客 (fanke), literally "foreign guests," or those who live in a foreign land (Tam 2006, 148). They most often use the word *lanlang* (咱人, "our people," sometimes spelled as "lannang," or "langlang") to refer to themselves and their kin, their fellow Hokkien-speakers, and more generally, "Chinese." William Henry Scott (1994, 190) notes that sixteenth-century sangley were called *langlang*—but here meaning pirate—by elder Tagalogs, most likely because of the activities of corsairs[20] like Limahong (Li Tao Kiem) who, it must be noted, commanded multi-ethnic (including Japanese *wako*) crews that raided the Spanish settlements in Filipinas. It should also be noted that, unlike the national-cultural term *Tiongkok lang* (中国人 Zhongguoren) of late nineteenth- and early twentieth-century vintage, lanlang is a we-group marker that does not necessarily specify either ethnicity or nationality. Philippine lanlang refer to their Southern China hometown(s) as *Tengsua* (唐山 Tangshan, "Tang mountains"), a term of identification with a dynastic state (C.E. 618–907) that was founded by Li Yuan, who was of mixed Han and Xianbei (Turkish) ancestry, and famous for its extensive contacts with the world—particularly Central Asia and what is now called the Middle East—and the syncretism of its cosmopolitan culture.[21]

In the twentieth century, the word *huaqiao* (华侨)became a powerful umbrella concept by means of which the mainland Qing state attempted to turn the ethnic Chinese migrants (including their mestizo offspring) in Southeast Asia and elsewhere in the world from *peranakan* (lit. "child of," referring to locally born "Chinese" or children of mixed Chinese and native ancestry; the word is now used in Indonesia, Malaysia, Singapore, and parts of Thailand), *totok, baba* ("pure-blooded Chinese"), sangley, chino, intsik, *lukjin*, and *jek* into "Overseas *Chinese*" (Wang 1992b) who could be called upon or mobilized to "contribute" to "China." This form of huaqiao-ization, underpinned by the Qing government's enactment of the 1909 law on citizenship claiming any child born in China or abroad of a Chinese father or mother as a Chinese citizen by invoking the principle of jus sanguinis (lit., "law of blood"),[22] would have an impact not only on the citizenship status of the Philippine Chinese, but on "Chinese" attitudes toward mestizos. The Hokkien term for the Chinese mestizo, *tsut-si-a* (chushizi, 出世仔, lit., "child born into the world"),[23] as Richard Chu (2002a; 2002b; and 2010) has shown, did not necessarily carry negative connotations prior to the twentieth century; it only took on negative associations once "Chinese" itself became linked to the mainland nation-state, and an idea of "pure Chinese" was used to denigrate intermarriages between "Chinese" and "Filipinos" and their offspring (Miyahara 2008a).

Ideas of assimilation and integration that originated in the social sciences and academia have served as intellectual ballast for the policies and practices of postcolonial national(ist) consolidation and nation-building. These, too, would have a strong impact on the terminology used by the "Chinese." Terms such as *huaren* (ethnic Chinese) and *huayi* (descendants of Chinese, but already politically integrated into other nation-states), and, in the Philippine case, "Chinese Filipino" (distinguished from first-generation, China-oriented "Filipino-Chinese"), *sinpino* and *pinsino* (amalgamations of Pili*pino* and *Sino*), and Tsinoy (amalgamation of *Tsino* and the colloquial term for Filipino, *Pinoy*) have been coined as part of attempts to stress a wide range of links to, as well as distance from, both "Chinese" and "Philippine" imagined communities.

The Chinese-Filipino civic organization Kaisa para sa Kaunlaran (discussed in chaps. 2 and 3), for example, distinguishes "Filipino-Chinese" from "Chinese Filipino" (note the absence of a hyphen in the latter) this way: "*Filipino-Chinese* refers to the traditional or older Chinese who are predominantly Chinese in identity but Filipino in citizenship. When used in names of organizations, it means that these groups have members who are either Chinese or Filipino citizens, such as, Filipino-Chinese Chambers of Commerce, Filipino-Chinese Fire Prevention Association, among others. *Chinese Filipino* refers to the young, mostly native-born ethnic Chinese who identify themselves as Filipinos first, but still maintain their Chinese cultural identity" (Kaisa para sa Kaunlaran 2005). Tsinoy (often spelled as Chinoy by the Philippine mass media), on the other hand, was popularized by Kaisa during the late 1980s and the 1990s and proved flexible enough to encompass even Filipinos of Chinese descent who may not have identified themselves as "Chinese" (see chap. 5). "Chinese Filipinos" have been known to differentiate themselves from recent or new Chinese migrants by pejoratively referring to the latter as TDK (Hokkien for "Tai Diok Ka," 大陆仔 or Chinese mainlander; a joking allusion to the Japanese electronics company), *chekwa*,[24] and "G.I." (genuine intsik).

An essay by Teodoro Agoncillo and Domingo Abella looks back at the crucial period of the turn of the twentieth century, and lists the names by which the inhabitants of the Philippines were called. The essay points out that the word "mestizo" in fact referred to different groups of people, depending on who was talking about them:

> As far as the *indio* ["native"] was concerned, the *mestizos* looked, talked, and behaved like Spaniards and so were considered *kastila*. The only mestizo the *indios* identified with were those which had resulted from inter-marriage with foreign Asians, specifically the Chinese. The Chinese *mestizo* identified himself with the *indio*, while the Spanish *mestizo* identified himself with the Spaniard. In Spanish records, incidentally, the term *mestizo*, unless otherwise modified, always referred to the *mestizos de sangley,* or Chinese mestizos. When they wanted to speak of the Spanish mestizos, Spaniards always wrote *"mestizos de español."* The natives, on the other hand, referred to the Spanish *mestizos* simply as *"mestizo"* while the Chinese half castes were *"mestizong intsik.* (Agoncillo and Abella 1978 [1990], 11)

While the history of the naming of mestizo and sangley/chino/intsik/ Chinese goes back more than five hundred years, the political, social, and intellectual uses of these terms from the twentieth century into the twenty-first have been closely intertwined with the material fortunes and intellectual conundrums of Philippine nationalism and the newly established nation-state. The post-independence period from 1946 onwards witnessed perhaps the most dramatic reversal of policies on the "Chinese," from a period of nationalist protectionism that constructed the Chinese as the preeminent foreigner, Other, and "alien" of the Philippine nation, to a period of "integration" of the Chinese into the Philippine national community and nation-state, to a period of resignification of "Filipinoness" to highlight "Chinese contributions" to its making, to a period of revival of Chinese identification among mestizos and Filipinos wishing to forge regional connections with rising East Asia and mainland China.

Chinese Question addresses the concrete manifestations of these national, regional, and global developments by looking closely at the strategies of accommodation, evasion, appropriation, reinvention, and resistance on the part of Philippine Chinese as they respond to ground-level changes affecting ethnic Chinese in state policy and practice as well as public perception and national imagination. Tracking the history, logic, course, impact, and reformulation of the "Chinese Question" in the postwar Philippines, the book pays special attention—but without limiting itself—to issues of ethnicity, class, nation, and region as they are worked through in literary and cinematic works on "the Chinese" by "Chinese"/"Filipinos." As representational practices, not only do literature and film allow us glimpses into the intellectual and artistic labor on the part of "Chinese" and "Filipinos" that goes into thinking through the "Chinese Question" as a problem of self, community, nation, state, and the world. The historicity of these literary and cinematic works, that is, their rootedness in a particular time and context, makes them at once sources and forms of history in their own right, shedding light on, and generating insights into, everyday life and experiences, as well as political and cultural projects and possibilities (whether realized or not), across time and space. More, their concern with the relationship between "Chinese" and "Filipino" and their attempts to pose the Chinese Question within a wider field of public debate underscore the fraught relationship between "roots" and "routes" (Clifford 1997): they show when and how people remain in place or move around, how ideas and practices travel and circulate and how they are reworked or transformed, and how people, ideas, and practices themselves contribute to remaking the world. These works are revealing of the history, discourses, and practices of inclusion and exclusion that construct the "Chinese" as foreign to, and as, "Filipino." Just as crucial is the construction of the "Chinese" not only as "Chinese," but also foreign to "Chinese."

The literary and cinematic works discussed in this book are by no means an exhaustive or even representative sampling of the creative labor in various media by Chinese and Filipinos in Filipino, Chinese, English, and other languages.[25] *Chinese Question* also departs from the standard practice in literary and cultural criticism of focusing almost exclusively and narrowly on a given text, often at the expense of elucidating the ever-crucial context in (or perhaps against) which both artistic creation and critical practice take place. This book draws on the power of art to make sense of, as well as intervene in, the historical, material, and intellectual issues that inform the Chinese Question. But it also recognizes that these creative works are products of their time and can only be understood in terms of the historical, material, and intellectual conditions under which they assumed the form and shape that they did and worked through the questions that they themselves posed.

The perspectives that literature and film offer on the Chinese Question may not necessarily be representative of the thinking of the majority of the Chinese and Filipinos in the Philippines. The works discussed in this book were chosen precisely because they belong in specific times and places, because they tell us something about their creators' (not uncomplicated) sentiments and experiences of attachment and belonging to particular "places," and because of their specific engagements with the Chinese Question. The people who created them dwelt in the interfaces of cultural (including linguistic), social, and political communities, moving within, between, and beyond "Chinese" and "Filipino" imaginaries—not just within the Philippines and between the Philippines and China, but also across the Nanyang region, America's Asia, and the world. Deeply informed by, but not always or necessarily bound up in, a concept of "nation," their stories represent individual glimpses into Philippine Chinese lives and in so doing, help illuminate the broader social, economic, and political milieu in which both "Chinese" and "Filipinos" are intertwined in intimate but fraught ways. These stories expose the power and ideologies that structure the societies in which they were produced, but reveal, as well, the cultural, social, political, and economic means and stakes involved in the making and remaking of these societies and the larger world.

In focusing on the Chinese, these works also grapple with the closely related issue of hybridity, of mestizo and mestizoness, in other words. Not only did mestizos play an important role in the making of the Filipino nation; as protagonists and antagonists in Philippine history and contemporary affairs, they were instrumental in formulating as well as interrogating the Chinese Question. A key product and agent of historical transformation in the Philippines, the mestizo and his/her story are intimately braided with the story of the "Chinese" and the "Filipino," and neither mestizo nor Chinese nor Filipino can be understood, let alone analyzed, without the other.

Ideas of mestizoness are fueled by racial-biological fantasies of "purity" and "mixing," but they derive their real force from claims (particularly by the Filipino elite) to *cultural* hybridity—claims of access to, and the ability to mediate, different cultures and "worlds," whether Philippine, Chinese, Spanish, or American. Not only do mestizos form an important subcategory of the contemporary Filipino elite (Cullinane 2003, 2, 9; Hau 2011). Their political and economic clout is matched, if not enabled, by their cultural, social, and intellectual capital. Vince Rafael (2000, 165) makes a compelling argument about the power of fantasy and identification in shaping mestizo consciousness:

> To be mestizo/a is to imagine one's inclusion in a circuit of substitutions. It is to cultivate a relationship of proximity to the outside sources of power without, however, being totally absorbed by them. In the context of neocolonial Philippine society, such requires a heightened sense of alertness to what comes before and outside of oneself. As such, mestizoness comes to imply a perpetual and... privileged liminality: the occupation of the crossroads between Spain and the Philippines, Hollywood, and Manila.

Rafael further argues that

> [M]estizo/a identity is perforce split along shifting lines of identification. Such lines (like those of a train or telegraph) allow mestizos/as to travel in and out of particular social locations, linking them to those below as well as those above and outside...We can think of the mestizos/as as the traces of the hybrid origins of the nation-state. But we should also recall that this hybridity seems always already organized, at least within Philippine neo-colonial society, along a social hierarchy. (166)

Mestizo/a "power" does not simply derive from mestizo identification with Spain and especially America and apparent "mastery" of the cultural codes—language, values, modes of behavior and socialization, among others—of the erstwhile colonizers. Just as crucial are the mestizo's familiarity with, and ability to appropriate, Philippine languages, cultural codes, and norms in their bid to install themselves as "rightful" representatives—in both senses of speaking for and speaking of[26]—of Philippine society and "the" Filipino people. Reynaldo Ileto (1998a) argues that the success of Filipino politicians during the early American colonial period depended on their ability to appropriate the "rhetoric of revolution and mass action" (137) in public oratory that called for independence and invoked the Philippine revolution, couching their speeches in language that the "masses" understood, as well as responded to (140).[27]

In Philippine cinema, the elite-mestiza actress Sharon Cuneta was able to attain "megastardom" by playing working-class women, screen roles that specifically tapped into superstar actress Nora Aunor's "populist, *kayumanggi* [brown-skinned]-identified appeal" (Lim 2009, 323).

The racial ambiguity and social flexibility of the mestizo are delineated through the memorable character of Capitan Tiago in Jose Rizal's classic novel, *Noli me tangere* (1887, 25). Here is Rizal's physical description of the man:

> Bajo de estatura, claro de color, redondo de cuerpo y de cara gracias á una abundancia de grasa, que, segun sus admiradores, le venía del cielo, de la sangre de los pobres segun sus enemigos, Cp. Tiago aparecía más joven de lo que realmente era: le hubieran creido de treinta á treinta y cinco años de edad. La espresion de su rostro era constantemente beatífica en la época á que se refiere nuestra narracion. Su cráneo, redondo, pequeñito y cubierto de un pelo negro como el ébano, largo por delanto y muy corto por detrás, contenía muchas cosas, segun dicen, dentro de su cavidad; sus ojos pequeños, pero no achinados, no cambiaban jamás de espresion; su nariz era fina y no chata, y si su boca no hubiese estado desfigurada por el abuso del tobacco y del buyo, cuyo sapá reuniéndose en un carrillo alteraba la simetría de sus facciones, diríamos que hacía muy bien en creerse y venderse por un hombre bonito. Sin embargo de aquel abuso, conservaba siempre blancos sus propios dientes y los dos que le presto el dentist, á razon de doce duros pieza.

> Short, light-skinned, round of body and of face, thanks to an abundance of fat that, according to his admirers, came from heaven, and according to his enemies, the blood of the poor, Capitan Tiago appeared younger than he really was: he might have been taken to be thirty to thirty-five years of age. At the time of our narrative, the expression on his face was permanently beatific. His skull, round, tiny, covered by hair black as ebony and cut long in front and very short at the back, was said to contain many things in its cavity; his eyes, small but not Chinese-looking, never changed expression; his nose was thin and not flat, and if his mouth had not been disfigured by the abuse of tobacco and *buyo* [betel-nut], the *sapa* [chewed betel] of which, gathering in one cheek, altered the symmetry of his features, we would say that he could very well have considered and touted himself as a handsome man. Notwithstanding that abuse, he kept very white his natural teeth as well as the two that the dentist provided him for twelve pesos a piece.

Capitan Tiago defies racial categorization. The narrator explicitly notes the fact that Tiago has a light complexion and his eyes are not slanted ("Chinese-looking"), but far from clarifying his origins, these details only reinforce the ambiguity of his racial status. His socioeconomic background, too, remains unclear, with rumors circulating that he had been born poor. What matters is that he is, or has become, extremely wealthy: at the opening of the novel, he is known as the richest man in San Diego. Tiago relies mainly on his talent for making money, aided in no small measure by his enterprising wife, Doña Pia Alba. His success grants him, like the Chinaman Quiroga of *El filibusterismo*, access to the highest social circles. But while "el chino Quiroga" remains only ever "el chino," Capitan Tiago is able to ally himself with, or else distance himself from, the legally defined categories of chino, indio, and mestizo, as he sees fit. The narrator of *Noli* cattily observes (29) that

> [S]i oía hablar mal de los naturales, él, que no se consideraba como tal, hacía coro y hablaba peor; si se criticaba á los mestizos sangleyes ó españoles, criticaba él tambien, acaso porque se creyese ya ibero puro.

> [I]f he heard the natives spoken ill of, he, who did not consider himself one, echoed the opinion and spoke worse; if anyone criticized the Chinese or Spanish mestizos, he also criticized them, perhaps because he already considered himself a pure-blooded Spaniard.

Tiago's wealth and social mobility enable him to claim—and achieve—a higher racial classification. He, in fact, served as president of the guild (gremio) of mestizos, even though many of these (presumably Spanish) mestizos resisted the appointment because they did not think of him as one of themselves (30). Scholars like Gregorio Zaide (1970, 117) have identified Capitan Hilario Chanuangco Sunico y Santos of San Nicolas as the real-life model for Rizal's Capitan Tiago. Born to a Chinese father (Chan Uan Co) and a Spanish mestiza mother from Tondo, Sunico operated a foundry on Jaboneros Street, where he cast bells (including the ones for Binondo Church) and created window grills. Sunico's claim to both Chinese- and Spanish-mestizo ancestry may explain why a character like "Capitan Tiago" could successfully aspire to head a mestizo guild, even a Spanish mestizo one. But the absence of provenance in the *Noli* needs to be understood in light of the terms of the novel itself and its artistic project, rather than in the real-life models of the fictional characters.

Is Capitan Tiago "indio," as one of his Spanish guests calls him at his own dinner party? After all, in the eyes of the Spaniards, everyone else— even the mestizo—is indio. Padre Damaso's airy response is that "Santiago does not consider himself an indio" (*Santiago no se considera como indio* [Rizal 1887, 6]), a remark that simultaneously underscores Tiago's social pretensions and Damaso's presumption of Spanish social superiority. Is Tiago, then, notwithstanding his un-Chinese eyes, "Chinese"? This may explain how he can have ready access to opium in the sequel, *El filibusterismo*, and dies an opium addict. In Spanish Philippines, the consumption of opium was officially limited to the Chinese. Tiago's success in securing, along with a Chinese, a monopoly on opium farming does not automatically indicate that he is Chinese himself, since Chinese mestizos were known to have competed for government contracts for tax farms (only toward the end of the Spanish regime did the chino Carlos Palanca gain monopoly over opium tax-farming). Moreover, access to opium, while limited mainly to Chinese, did not automatically signify that Tiago was Chinese. It is true that opium consumption was generally confined to the Chinese in the Philippines because of the poverty factor that made opium a luxury item (Trocki 1999, 89), and because of Spanish concerns about preventing large-scale opium addiction among "natives." In later years, American moves to restrict opium smoking to the ethnic Chinese also helped fix the idea that "opium smoking was a sign of Chinese status and therefore of not being a real Filipino" (Foster 2009, 97; see also Foster 2003). Nevertheless, given Tiago's wealth and connections with high officials, he would have had no problems circumventing the race-based restrictions on opium consumption.

As Benedict Anderson has argued, the absence of surnames for characters like Capitan Tiago in Rizal's *Noli* and *Fili* deliberately leaves the question of their ancestry—*particularly* Chinese ancestry—vague, in effect occluding the "Chineseness" of the Chinese mestizo (Anderson 2008, 45).[28] Tiago's uncertain, possibly Chinese and mixed, racial origins do not stand in the way of his financial success or his social ambitions; on the contrary, they may well have been the condition of his economic and social achievements. His wealth allows him to attain the presidency of the mestizo guild whose members do not think of him as one of their kind. He is in the good graces of the Spanish powers-that-be, and under the thumb of Padre Damaso, whose affair with Tiago's wife results in a miracle (at least in Tiago's eyes)—a light-haired baby daughter who physically embodies the realization of Tiago's social aspirations to be considered "Spanish" or, failing that, (Spanish) "mestizo," at the apex of the Philippine social hierarchy.

Tiago's racial ambiguity makes him the preeminent example of a man whose wealth enables him to cross racial boundaries and inhabit a variety of social spaces with relative ease, from the indio society whose women he seduces and disgraces, to the mestizo guilds and Chinese stores, to playing host to no less than the governor general himself on the latter's visit to San Diego. His subservience to the colonizers is the condition of his flourishing in colonial Filipinas, as he accrues a modicum of influence and social respectability through his proximity and access to "white" Spanish society. His relative power and prestige also derive from a capacity for mobility unmatched by anybody in the novel, not even the highly itinerant Elías, whose fugitive status and decision to turn his back on his privileged upbringing impose constraints on his freedom of movement among the spaces inhabited by the elite. Far more than Elías, then, Capitan Tiago has the ability to appear in all kinds of spaces, some of which are normally barred to, or avoided by, specific social groups:

> [E]l frac y el sombrero de copa en el Ayuntamiento, en Malacañang
> y en el cuartel; el sombrero de copa y el frac en la gallera, en el
> Mercado, en las procesiones, en las tiendas de los chinos, y el debajo
> del sombrero y dentro del frac, Cpn. Tiago sudando con la esgrima del
> baston de borlas, disponiendo, arreglando y descomponiéndolo todo
> con una actividad pasmosa y una seriedad más pasmosa todavía. (Rizal
> 1887, 30)

> [T]he dress-coat and the top hat in the Town Hall, in Malacañang
> [the governor-general's palace], and in the barracks; the top hat and
> the dress-coat in the cockpit, in the market, in the processions, in the
> Chinese shops, and underneath the hat and inside the coat, Capitan
> Tiago, sweating, with the fencing sword of a tasseled cane, arranging,
> fixing, and taking apart everything with incredible activity and an even
> more incredible seriousness.

El chino Quiroga, by contrast, remains curiously immobile in the *Fili*, even though his residence is just as luxurious and his connections, reaching as far as China and Europe and into the "underground," as extensive as Tiago's. He is depicted in his element within the confines of his house, through which different classes of Philippine society pass, some not bothering to hide their contempt or criticism (see Hau 2000b, 140–52). Tiago, too, is subject to "racist" remarks in his own home, but unlike "el chino" Quiroga, who remains bound to his ethnicity, Capitan Tiago has the luxury of deluding himself into thinking he can be "Spanish" and not one of those "natives" or "mestizos" to whom the Spanish condescendingly refer.

This obfuscation of origins and ethnic or legal markers is made possible by a combination of upward social mobility and intense social ambition on the part of enterprising segments of the population in a late-colonial Philippines that was itself undergoing profound socioeconomic and political changes. A series of administrative reforms had brought about the transformation of the Philippines from a Galleon Trade-based colony that received subsidy from Mexico into an agricultural export economy, a transformation that reformulated the relationship between the Spanish metropole and the Philippine colony (see the essays in McCoy and Alegre 1982; Legarda 1999; Larkin 1982; Fradera 2001). While the changes in colonial society transformed the lives of everybody who lived in that particular time and place, mestizoness in its cultural, if no longer necessarily biological, senses acquired the potentiality to breach racial boundaries and forge links across socially, economically, and politically demarcated communities. "Indios," "mestizos," and "chinos" could, by means of education and wealth, afford to send their sons to Europe, particularly to Spain, or have them educated in Manila. Indios, mestizos, and chinos were already moving and interacting among themselves and with different kinds of people both inside and outside colonial Philippines, including the Spaniards. The blurring of social boundaries in everyday life in both the Philippines and Spain was already a reality, and precisely because of this, was met by rising anxiety and the hardening of racist attitudes on the part of the Spanish authorities back in the colony.[29]

Philippine nationalism would be inextricably bound up with the aspirations and self-understanding of a class of Chinese mestizos whose wealth (accumulated through trade and later landholding) and education granted them entry into the ranks of the Philippine elite, and who would go on to accumulate both political and economic power during the American colonial period and the postindependence years (Go 2008).[30] Colonial policies and socioeconomic changes during the late Spanish period in effect laid the foundation for the merging of the mestizo and indio categories while maintaining chino as a separate category, thus leading to a triangulation involving "whites," "natives," and "Chinese." Competition between Chinese mestizos and Chinese in retail trade, as well as the acculturation and selective Hispanization of Chinese mestizos to the urban, hybrid culture of provincial centers, Manila, Spain, and Europe in the late nineteenth and early twentieth centuries fueled the Chinese mestizos' (especially those who were already several generations removed from their Chinese origins) sense of themselves as distinct from the culture and ethnicity of their "Chinese" forefathers while laying claim to being "native" to their country of birth, Las Filipinas. "Filipino" was itself a term denoting hybridity since it originally referred to Spanish who were born in the colony. Mestizos, along with their nonmestizo counterparts, helped imagine "Filipino" as constitutively hybrid in that it included elements of "Chinese" culture, but it was also a term that, while inclusive of both indio and mestizo, considered the "Chinese" as its Other (Aguilar 2005). This influential dichotomy between Filipino and Chinese was founded on the mestizos' "forgetting" or occlusion of their Chinese ancestry. The "disappearance" of the Chinese mestizo into Filipino would, however, take place against the sharpening of the distinction between Filipino and Chinese. The principle of citizenship by descent (jus sanguinis) that the Philippine state adopted during the Commonwealth and postcolonial era as the most important condition of membership in the national community basically legislated a form of hybridity that drew on elements of Chinese culture and ancestry while simultaneously occluding these elements as a means of distinguishing "Filipino" from "Chinese."

In other words, the economically ascendant and politically assertive mestizos were able to articulate their interests with those of "indios" in the act of reclaiming the term "Filipino." By appropriating "Filipino," they succeeded in expanding its scope and meaning beyond its narrow referent of Spaniards who were born in the Philippines. But the partial breakdown of barriers between mestizo and indio took place alongside the concomitant hardening of conceptual (if not always social) boundaries between "Filipino" and "chino." It is this legacy of "alienation" of the "Chinese" that would come to shape the statutes of citizenship in the 1930s that sought to bar Chinese from entry into the Filipino community. Nevertheless, it should be noted that even as many Chinese mestizos "disappeared" into the Filipino national community, some of them identified themselves with, and lived among, the now *huaqiao*-ized "Chinese."

The transition from colonial to postcolonial Philippines may have upset the hierarchy that privileged the colonizing "whites," but the hierarchy that obtained in postwar Philippines was one which, now led by Filipinos, served to reinforce elite (and to some extent popular) identification with "white" power. In the mid- to late twentieth century, "mestizo" came to refer not to Filipinos of Chinese ancestry who constituted the majority of mestizos in the country, but rather, to those of Spanish/American, or "white," ancestry (see Chu 2010, 240n2). However, whiteness— and its politics of skin tone— remained ambiguous enough to encompass mestizos who did not have Euro-American ancestry, so long as they could claim "mastery" of European (mainly Spanish) and, increasingly, American languages, codes, and cultures through travel to the metropoles, adoption of behavior and lifestyle, and through ownership of things "Western," especially American.

Filipinos of Chinese-mestizo ancestry were part of a powerful and influential national elite with strong economic bases in landholding, import-substitution manufacturing, finance, and real estate in the postcolonial era. The "myth" of Chinese economic dominance, in fact, belies the important fact that from the 1970s to the 1990s, non-Chinese Filipinos (a category that includes mestizos *desaparecidos*) owned most of the top thirty corporations in the country, and controlled strategic industries, such as utilities, transportation and railway, and manufacturing (see the data provided by Yoshihara 1985 for 1970; and Palanca 1995 for 1990). More important, unlike the ethnic Chinese, they possessed the necessary political clout to define state interests in terms of their personal, familial, and class interests because of their ability to dominate local, provincial, and national electoral politics and the legislative and judicial process (including laws that sought to restrict Chinese participation in the Philippine economy). Indeed, as Eva-Lotta Hedman and John Sidel (2000, 72) have argued, "it was only through their control over elective office and access to state resources that they were able to accumulate so much land and capital."[31] And yet it is the disproportionate role of the "Chinese" in the Philippine economy that has singled out this "foreign" minority and rendered it vulnerable to nationalist criticism.

In the past two decades or so, however, there have been a number of well-publicized attempts by Filipinos to (re)claim their "Chinese" heritage, the most prominent being President Corazon Cojuangco Aquino and Jaime Zobel de Ayala (see chap. 6), the latter a patriarch of *the* most prestigious clan (at least in Filipino eyes) in the Philippines, a family noted for its "Spanish" ancestry.[32] Chinese mestizoness has "reappeared" in public discourse after decades of being either "de-glamorized" (discussed in chap. 1) or else rendered indistinguishable from "Filipino."[33] Whereas mestizo had come to signify mainly European/American ancestry for much of the postcolonial period, mestizoness has now been "resinified" as mestizos become more publicly vocal about their Chinese origin and ancestry. It is also worth noting that Chinese mestizos like Ricardo "Ricky" Lee, Teresita Ang-See, and Lily Yu-Monteverde (see chaps. 2 and 5) who came of age in the first three decades of the postwar period have played an important role in promoting public awareness of the "Chinese" and "Chinese Question" through literature, advocacy work, and film, respectively.

The ongoing resi(g)nification of Chinese mestizoness is possible precisely because both "Chinese" and "Filipino" have undergone resignification in the past few decades. Kim Chiu and her "Chinese Filipino" cohort (whether mestizo or "pure Chinese") in popular entertainment have the ability to appear as *both* Chinese and Filipino, allowing them to connect not only with Philippine audiences, but to embody the fantasies and aspirations associated with "Chinese" regional and global capitalism, exemplified in the 1980s and 1990s by the three "Chinese" members of the Dragon Economies (Taiwan, Singapore, and Hong Kong), and from the mid-1900s onwards, by mainland China. Whereas official nationalism in the postwar Philippines had exerted pressure on the ethnic Chinese to "Filipinize" themselves and their institutions (such as schools and chambers of commerce) and to distance themselves especially from Communist China, global and regional geopolitical and economic developments in the past few decades have reinvented the notion of Filipinoness to integrate the "Chinese" into the Filipino national imaginary (discussed in chap. 5), while opening up the possibility for ethnic Chinese as well as Filipino elites to forge regional alliances with the elites of the rising mainland China and the region more generally.

But what does it mean to identify oneself as "Chinese" and with "China"? Is "China" the mainland state known as the People's Republic of China, as the Philippine government has officially acknowledged since the establishment of diplomatic relations in 1975? Is it the Republic of China based in Taiwan, which had been an anticommunist ally of the Philippines during the Cold War era and whose Kuomintang branch had played an active role in Chinese-community affairs in the Philippines? Is it a "Greater China" defined in terms of the combined markets of China, Hong Kong, and Taiwan (plus Macau and perhaps Singapore)? Is "China" a civilization or a nation-state? Or is it "Cultural China" (Tu 1991), a way of expanding the definition of "Chinese" beyond a single nation-state by including those who identify themselves as Chinese; those who are called Chinese; those who subscribe to "Chinese" values, ideas, "traditions," and patterns of behavior (in whatever ways these are defined); and also those who study Chinese and China (see chap. 7)? What does it mean to say that one is "pure Chinese" if one means not only ancestry, based on the "myth of blood" (Dikötter 1992, 116), but also access to something called "Chinese culture"? In what ways are the intellectual and political debates in Philippine nationalism shaped by what Liu Hong (2011) calls the "China Metaphor," that is, the ideas and fantasies of an imagined "China" circulating within and beyond the Philippines?

The Philippine case shows how boundaries between Chinese mestizo, Filipino, Chinese, and mestizo in general, have shifted over decades, even centuries, from a time when Chinese mestizos were thought to be (and accused of being) naturally "allied" with their Chinese fathers during the Chinese insurrections of the early seventeenth century,[34] to a time when Chinese mestizos defined themselves as Filipino while occluding their Chinese ancestry at the end of the nineteenth century, to a time when some Chinese mestizos identified themselves and were raised and educated as "Chinese" from the end of the nineteenth century to the latter half of the twentieth century, to a time when "mestizo" meant primarily having "white" Spanish/European and American ancestry despite the fact that a majority of the mestizos were in fact descended from Chinese mestizos, to a time when even self-avowed Spanish mestizos began to publicly acknowledge, if not actively reclaim, their "Chinese heritage." Such conceptual slippages reveal the extent to which "mestizo," "Chinese," and "Filipino" are eminently useful and exploitable terms of (self-)identification, which can be appropriated, reinvented, or deployed for different political, economic, cultural, and personal projects and under different historical contexts. These changes in terminology and shifts in meaning attest to the evolution and contest of meaning over "Chinese" and "Filipino," what they mean, who they refer to, who can use these terms, and for what purpose.

While hybridity has been a fundamental, though not unproblematical, feature of Philippine national—or, to be more specific, elite—self-definition (see, for example, Zialcita 2009, 174), there have been periods in Philippine history when one form of hybridity (white) was privileged while the other one ("Chinese") was denigrated or occluded.[35] Over the past decade, Chinese hybridity has become fashionable and desirable among the very mestizos/ Filipinos who had hitherto tended to valorize their connections with the Spanish/American "West." The politics of strategic hybridity in which mestizos, as well as Chinese and other Filipinos, have engaged during the post-independence era illuminates the aporia of Philippine nationalism: the appropriation and contestation by different social groups of the hybrid term "Filipino" took place alongside the simultaneous exclusion *and* inclusion of large segments of the Philippine population. Neither natality nor territory nor class nor culture nor race, or even a combination thereof, has provided definitive or even sufficient grounds for a foundational concept of "Filipino," a "lack" that, far from reducing Philippine nationalism to a bad copy of western nationalism, is largely responsible for fueling the considerable energies that have made Philippine nationalism a major site of political and intellectual contestation and debate.

The main institutional fulcrum on which the policies and practices of inclusion and exclusion of the ethnic Chinese hinge is citizenship. Citizenship is basically a concept that specifies the terms of membership in a political (that is often also national) community. Although citizenship is universal in the sense that it is deployed all over the world, the human association that it both presupposes and creates is a particularistic one—the "imagined community" is by definition bounded, even when its territorial boundaries are in question and its sociocultural and ideological unity cannot readily be assumed (Anderson 1991, chap. 1). What matters is that, as Rogers Brubaker has cogently argued (1992, 31), "[c]itizenship is not only an instrument of closure, a prerequisite for the enjoyment of certain rights, or for participation in certain types of interaction. It is also an object of closure, a status to which access is restricted."

Modern conceptions of citizenship straddle the line between involuntary ascription (the fact that one is born a citizen of a certain place and community) and voluntary self-identification (the fact that one can choose or feel or make oneself to be part of a community). This line is particularly difficult to draw in cases not only of "interracial" marriages and long-term "alien" residents and their children, but also in the case of "foreigners" whose presence, whether authorized or not, within a given territory constitutes a "problem" for the state, even as their migration is "simultaneously enabled, covertly courted, often managed, and certainly tolerated" by the state (Honig 2001, 97). Voluntary self-identification is, above all, almost always circumscribed by a particular state's "administrative apparatus of closure" (Brubaker 1992, 24), one that determines to an important extent the range of life choices and opportunities available to citizens and noncitizens (ibid.; see also Joppke 2010, 34–35, 84–85; and the conservative take of Schuck and Smith 1985).

As with Southeast Asian and other countries, setting the legal, conceptual, and ideological boundary between citizen and foreigner has been the most important means by which the Philippine state in its various regime manifestations throughout what Giovanni Arrighi (1994) calls the "long twentieth century" has sought to regulate the inhabitants within "its" own territory as well as the movements of people across its borders. In controlling the "gate of citizenship" (to use Filomeno Aguilar's term [2011a, 433]), the Philippine state, at least until the mid-1970s, had made the process of acquiring citizenship difficult and expensive for foreigners. Control over this gateway allows the state to assign a set of rights, privileges, and obligations to its citizens, but it also entitles the state to discriminate against the "alien," who by definition remains in principle, if not in actual fact, outside the bounds of the national community (Brubaker 1992, x). In this way, citizenship becomes, in the words of Rogers Brubaker (chap. 1), both "externally exclusive" and "internally inclusive"—that is, citizenship confers equal membership on its "people" while withholding equal membership from "aliens."

The fact that, although making up no more than approximately 1.3 percent of the total population as of 1990 (Suryadinata 1997, 21),[36] the "Chinese" nevertheless constituted the largest "foreign" population in the Philippines meant that the rules and conditions of Philippines citizenship were specifically formulated with this particular "alien"—and his (or her) history, attributes, and activities—in mind. In this sense, the Chinese was not simply an alien, but the exemplary, emblematic *other* against which the postwar Filipino national community defined itself.

A peculiar consequence of the mestizo-mediated strategic hybridity[37] (as opposed to the strategic essentialism argued by Spivak [1987, 205]) and selective amnesia in national imagining, coupled with the limited reach and capacity of the Philippine state, is that if a Chinese is able to attain Philippine citizenship, he or she can "disappear" from the view of the Philippine state. There are, of course, a number of other ways in which these Filipinos of Chinese ancestry can be counted or policed. A notorious example is the requirement, in place since the 1990s, that Filipinos with Chinese surnames who wish to apply for a Philippine passport must present themselves for ocular inspection and possible interview at the Department of Foreign Affairs.[38] This shows that institutional racism can make itself felt in everyday life. But it also shows that the state has a different vision of nationness and national belonging, one in which "Chinese" ethnicity serves as the principal category for distinguishing the Filipino citizen from the foreigner at the gate of citizenship, but becomes less salient once an individual legally becomes "Filipino."

This policing of the gate of citizenship for the purpose of establishing and maintaining the boundary between "Chinese" and "Filipino" differs from the strategies adopted by neighboring island Southeast Asian countries to deal with their "Chinese Question." Malaysia and Indonesia have extended citizenship to ethnic Chinese, while simultaneously developing a number of official procedures to enable them to differentiate "Chinese" from "native" Malaysians (*bumiputera*) and Indonesians (*pribumi*) *within* the bounds of the national community. Chinese Malaysians are compelled to be unambiguous about their ethnic identities as *Chinese* in Malaysia. The racial category of "Chinese" (regardless of dialect group) is established and reinforced via a number of quotidian bureaucratic measures:

> The first, and most critical, one is self-referential: an inscription in the birth certificate—when parents tell those who record such things (all the way back to the Registrar of Births and Deaths, I think) what their (child's) ethnicity or "race" is. This is retained when a preschool kid has to be registered for schooling. Then, it is included in an

Identity Card (now called MyKad) issued at age 12, and reissued at
adulthood... Once this "chain of ethnicity" is forged and maintained,
the Census (every ten years) totes up the numbers, this time
depending on respondents' answers. For the Chinese, it's quite easy
to "determine" their "race" by name alone. In between those steps, at
practically every point in official or bureaucratic dealings, one has to
tick a box for "bangsa" (and "agama") for "race," not nationality.

In documents of different kinds, such as an application for
passports—partly for security in the past, I believe, but that could be
just one of the reasons—a Chinese name in Mandarin is required to
accompany a Chinese name romanized (from Hokkien, Cantonese,
Hakka, etc., but, rarely until recently, Mandarin). But the current
passport does not carry a category for race (not sure if it used to), to
my knowledge, since the "old" Singapore would have adopted the
same set of procedures and assumptions. (Khoo 2011)

In the Malaysian case, this institutionalized separation of populations
by "race"—a legacy of British colonial rule—has provided the basis for
postcolonial state promotion of the National Economic Policy and its
successor policies aimed at empowering *bumiputera* by a form of affirmative
action on behalf of the majority that attempts to reverse the historical
"economic dominance" of the Chinese in Malaysia by giving priority to
bumiputera enterprises.[39]

Indonesian Chinese who had taken Indonesian citizenship were in
principle granted equal rights as Indonesians but in practice not granted
equal treatment. Indonesian Chinese were required to register with the
Ministry of Home Affairs, and were then issued a certificate of citizenship
(79). This, along with the Surat Ganti Nama (the certificate of change
of name), became the principal means for distinguishing Indonesians
of Chinese descent from the *asli* (native) Indonesians. The issuing of
the Surat Bukti Kewarganegaraan Republik Indonesia (SBKRI), the
certificate of Indonesian citizenship, in 1967, was backed by discriminative
policies enacted in 1978 and 1980, and specifically targeted at the Chinese
Indonesians (Winarta 2008, 63–64; see also Effendi and Prasetyadji 2008).

The irony is that the state is able to identify the Indonesian Chinese as
"Chinese" once the Chinese Indonesian is enjoined by the state to acquire
an Indonesian name and "proof" of Indonesian citizenship. This web
of certification[40] serves the state purpose of forcibly "assimilating" the
"Chinese" while also giving the Indonesian state bureaucracy an instrument
by which to *document* these "Indonesians" as a *different* kind of Indonesian.
This documentation then allows the government to make interventions in

Indonesian society in the name of the Indonesian nation and its imperatives. Although the SBKRI lost its importance after 1999, there remains a "web of papers" used by the Indonesian state to identify the ethnicity of "Indonesians" (Jafar 2011), most notably the national identification card (ID), which encodes the ethnicity of the bearer. In cases where an ID is not required, document forms have included boxes wherein applicants are required to tick their ethnicity.

In this way the Malaysian and Indonesian states are able to keep a more or less accurate record of the "Chinese" in their territories. The Philippine state, by contrast, lacks the same capacity as the Malaysian and Indonesian states to develop such extensive surveillance mechanisms based on bureaucratic procedures and documentation. Equally important, its legalistic tradition—shaped by Spanish-, revolutionary-, and American-era legislation and Philippine nationalist concerns—operates on a different logic from that at work in other parts of island Southeast Asia, since it puts a premium on citizenship as the major line of demarcation between "Filipino" and "foreigner." In Indonesia, both the state and the criminals operate in the murky twilight between state and society. This holds true for the Philippines as well: words like *remontados*, "those who go to the mountains," and the Tagalog *mamumundok*, "to go to the mountains" attest to the existence of spaces that in a literal sense are outside the reach of the state, spaces that have continued to nurture the Moro and Communist antistate movements. The crucial point is that certain elements of the state can exploit for their personal gain the gap between the law and its implementation precisely by exploiting the gap between the letter of the law and its interpretation(s).

Given the specific nature of the Philippine legal system's interpretation and practice of citizenship, the place that the Chinese occupy in the Philippines is at once clear-cut and ambiguous, defined yet also indeterminate. Not surprisingly, postwar nationalist thinking about the foreign is concerned first and foremost with *placing* the Chinese—that is, the main logic of its thinking is anchored in the fundamental issue of *fixing* the "proper" place of the Chinese within the Philippine nation-state. In the postwar period, the idea of the Chinese as economically dominant (see chap. 3), politically subversive (with alleged connections to Communist China, see chap. 4), and culturally different (see chaps. 1 and 2) made them the specific targets of economic nationalism, political surveillance and repression, and assimilation policies and practices.

More important, the effort to fix (in all senses of the dictionary meaning of "fix") the Chinese is also accompanied by a crucial *displacement* of the Chinese within the discourse of nationalism. This displacement is tellingly evident in two historical accounts, written by two of the most important nationalist historians who worked during the postwar period (Ileto 1998b, 185–86, 189–91), of the "nationalist awakening" of the 1950s and 1960s that culminated in the passing of laws aimed at breaking the "foreign stranglehold" over the Philippine economy. In the influential textbook, *History of the Filipino People,* principal author Teodoro Agoncillo (coauthored with Milagros Guerrero [1977, 493]), for example, speaks of "the predominant role of aliens in Philippine economy and their growing influence in the political sphere," citing the "fact that about 70 percent of the domestic trade and about 80 percent of the foreign trade are in the hands of aliens, principally Chinese and Americans," in their discussion of the genesis and subsequent evolution of Carlos Garcia's "Filipino First" policy. Agoncillo here lumps the Chinese together with the Americans under the general category "alien." In a preceding section, where he discusses the "nationalization laws," which included the Market Stalls Act of 1946 and the Retail Trade Nationalization Law of 1954, he uses the phrase "alien hold on domestic trade" without even bothering to sort out the Americans from the Chinese.

Similarly, Renato Constantino, in referring to the "[s]uppressed feelings of nationalism" unleashed by the "initially limited expression of nationalism" of the "First Filipino Policy," comments on the reaction against the Garcia administration voiced by "foreign business quarters, notably American and Chinese" (coauthored with Letizia Constantino [1978, 304]). Tellingly, the sample passage that Constantino quotes in order to illustrate the foreign business quarters' opposition to Garcia's policy is taken from an editorial written by an American, A. V. H. Hartendorp of the *American Chamber of Commerce Journal.* Of the Retail Trade Nationalization Act of 1954 (see Agpalo 1958), and the Corn and Rice Industry Nationalization Act of 1961, Constantino does not say a word.

Agoncillo and Constantino's conjoining of Chinese to American business interests in their histories of postwar Philippines, however, elides the historical specificity of the issues that are central to economic nationalism in the 1950s and 1960s. The displacement of the Chinese arises because, by lumping the Chinese with the Americans under the general category of "aliens," Agoncillo and Constantino do not really confront the question of *who* the laws were being legislated against; in other words, the question of whether these laws were meant to be remedial measures directed against all aliens or only against certain aliens.

The Retail Nationalization Act (Republic Act [R.A.] No. 1180) and the Corn and Rice Industry Nationalization Act (R.A. No. 3018)—laws that receive scant attention from both Agoncillo and Constantino—were the most significant manifestations of economic nationalism and, arguably, the ones with the most impact on the Chinese (Jiang 1974; Omohundro 1981, 35).[41] These laws were important precisely because they singled out the Chinese as the specific targets of economic nationalism. In fact, Agoncillo neglects to point out that the Retail Trade Nationalization Act of 1954 specifically *exempts* "citizens and juridical entities of the United States" (i.e., Americans) from the nationalization law.[42] Moreover, the enactment of these nationalization laws took place against the general economic backdrop painted by the Bell Trade Act and its successor, the Laurel-Langley Agreement, which had effectively tied the economy of the Philippines to that of the United States.[43] The Bell Trade Act provided for a preferential tariff system that favored U.S. capital, and contained a "parity" amendment that gave American citizens equal rights in the development of public utilities and the exploitation of natural resources in the Philippines. In addition, until the early 1990s, the U.S. retained exclusive and unrestricted use of extensive military facilities for a term of ninety-nine years. A year after the Retail Trade Nationalization Act was passed in 1954, the Bell Trade Act was replaced by the Laurel-Langley Agreement, which gave the Philippines an advantage through changes in the schedule of raising tariff duties and allowed the Philippines to impose tariffs on imported U.S. goods. The agreement also formally ended U.S. control over Philippine currency. The Agreement, however, extended equal treatment to American investors in *all* areas of the economy, not just the development of public utilities and the exploitation of natural resources—areas from which, not incidentally, the Chinese had been barred by legislation formulated during the American and the Commonwealth periods. While it is true that Americans (and to some extent Spaniards) were also targets of economic nationalism and political critique in the twentieth century, the relationship of "neocolonial" dependency between the Philippines and the U.S. afforded some degree of protection to American interests in the Philippines in the name of the "special relationship" between the Philippines and the United States.

That such a discrepancy should exist in the application of the "nationalization" laws tends to be glossed over by nationalist historiography. The resulting elision of an entire history of differential treatments of the "alien" stands as an important example of the general displacement of the Chinese from within Philippine history insofar as the villain in Philippine history is posited as *any* or *all* alien. The term displacement invokes a number of arguments here: displacement refers to the removal of the Chinese from Philippine history through a denial of the specificity of their place in it, but it also suggests the supplanting of the term "alien" by the Chinese, such that the Chinese come to stand in for all that is "foreign," or "alien," or "external." Moreover, in psychoanalysis, displacement also means the redirection of emotion or impulse away from its original object, whether an idea or a person, toward something that is more acceptable.

The construction of the Chinese as "alien" rested on the dichotomy between "Chinese" and "Filipino" and the concomitant disappearance—conceptually, politically, and culturally—of the "Chinese mestizo" into either "Chinese" or "Filipino." While mestizoness itself was a testament to the fluidity and ambiguity of social and ethnic identity, those with multiple senses of belonging found themselves under pressure to define if not declare themselves as "Chinese" or "Filipino." The construction of the Chinese as the preeminent "alien" reached its apogee in the 1935 Commonwealth Constitution, which defined Philippine citizenship on the basis of blood (jus sanguinis), and in the early postwar years, when economic nationalist legislation of the 1950s and 1960s sought to bar Chinese citizens from participation in retail trade in order to loosen their "stranglehold" over the Philippine economy. Chapter 1 of this book discusses the impact of anti-Chinese official nationalism on Chinese-Filipino thinking about citizenship and national belonging in the context of the Cold War in the 1950s and 1960s.

The subsequent dramatic reversal by the Philippine state of the citizenship policy that led to the mass naturalization of the Chinese in the 1970s, a move that enabled a large number of Chinese to acquire Philippine citizenship, is discussed in chapter 2, which also tackles the legacy of scholarly (especially sociological) language in providing the conceptual terms for thinking about Chinese "integration" into the Philippine body politic and national culture. Despite the "integration" of the Chinese by mass naturalization, the persistent linking of Chinese ethnicity with capital was forcefully articulated by the phenomenon of kidnapping in the 1980s and 1990s. This question of the relationship between ethnicity and class is addressed in chapter 3.

And for all their seeming immutability, the terms and conditions of citizenship—ideas of what the Philippine nation is, and who counts as Filipino, and who can and cannot become Filipino—were and are, in fact, historically mutable (Aguilar 2011a). While jus sanguinis has been the main organizing principle of postcolonial Philippine citizenship, it is not the only principle that was applied in the Philippines throughout the long twentieth century. Although the Americans applied the Chinese Exclusion Act (legislated in America to control the inflow of Chinese labor), judicial interpretation in the Philippines also selectively applied the jus soli (citizenship by place of birth) to Chinese mestizos who "returned" to the Philippines from China. Moreover, while territoriality (the question of place of origin) and nativity (the question of the place of birth) have long been the basis for distinguishing "us" from "them" in countries all over the world, neither origin nor birth has been sufficient to determine the status of the "foreigner" vis-à-vis the "citizen." The Malolos Constitution, enacted by the revolutionary government of Emilio Aguinaldo in 1899, embodied perhaps the most liberal idea of citizenship, one that included not just anybody who was born in Philippine territory or born of either a Filipino father or mother abroad (or on Philippine vessels), but, quite radically, those who had resided for two years or more in the Philippines.

More than a hundred years ago, the revolutionary government was already drawing on a third principle, jus domicile (citizenship by residency), which defined national belonging in terms of the social, economic, and political bonds that a resident forges in the course of his or her extended stay in a place (ibid.). This principle of domicile would gain traction from the 1970s onward as countries in the First World dealt with challenges arising from the massive influx of foreign migrants (Austin and Bauder 2010, 9). Domicile, however, is today still understood in terms of permanent residency as opposed to short-term stay, and based on the fact of living in a place (factum) as well as on the conscious choice to live in that place indefinitely or permanently (animus) (Kostakopoulou 2008, 113–14). The two-year residency requirement, formulated within the context of revolution and state consolidation, makes the Malolos Constitution quite radical in its inclusiveness. The idea that even short-term residents can contribute to the nation would come up again in the context of the reevaluation in the 1990s of Chinese (leftist) guerrilla participation in the Philippine anticolonial movement against the Japanese occupation forces during World War II, as will be discussed in chapter 4.

An equally dramatic development was the large-scale migration of Filipino professionals to America in the wake of immigration reform initiated by the Kennedy administration that resulted in the 1965 Immigration Act, which enabled more people from the Third World to enter the United States. Filipino labor migration to the Middle East, and then to East Asia and the world from the 1970s onwards also cleared the grounds for rethinking the relationship among territory, nation, and belonging, as the Philippine state sought to re-ethnicize (Joppke 2003) the Filipino diaspora by appealing to bonds of kinship and affection, encapsulated in the concept of balikbayan (return to the country), as a means of tapping into the earnings and skills of Filipinos who are working abroad and Filipinos who had already acquired other citizenships. The fact that the de-ethnicization of the Chinese Question by mass naturalization took place alongside the re-ethnicization of Filipino migrants abroad indicates that the evolving citizenship regime in the Philippines is shaped not only by domestic concerns and imperatives, but also by a larger global trend toward functionalization of citizenship to accommodate multiple attachments and belongings in the wake of large-scale postwar migration to the First World. This has led to the coining of the term "postnational membership" (Sosyal 1994), even as states continue to play an important part in regulating membership in particular territories and communities (Joppke 2010, 85).

The economic rise of East Asia and the emergence of mainland China as regional and global economic powerhouse and geopolitical superpower would also be instrumental in reinventing the image of the Southeast Asian Chinese, in ways that would prove to be boon and bane for the Chinese in the Philippines, as will be discussed in chapters 5 and 6. Such regional and global developments affirm, rather than refute, the persistent association of "Chinese" with commerce and capital. What has changed, however, is the attitude toward this conflation of ethnicity and commerce-and-capital. Public perception has swung from nationalist censure of Chinese economic dominance and political subversion to the regional identification of the Philippines with capitalist Asia (including Taiwan, Japan, and South Korea) as the leading growth center of the world, and (far more ambivalently) with the ascendant mainland China as a regional and global superpower. This growing regional identification has recast the terms by which "Filipinos" view themselves, and the Filipino nationalism that reflects the changing needs and aspirations of Filipinos themselves. Like their ethnic Chinese counterparts, "overseas Filipino workers" (OFW) have an ambiguous status in relation to the Philippine national imaginary because they have also come to be equated with "money."[44] In a time when citizenship has become commodified, with the state itself actively colluding in this process, questions of belonging continue to matter in public debates over not just the Chinese but Filipino overseas workers and migrants as well.

Filipino regional identification with affluent East Asia and rising China is, however, fraught with unresolved issues. Continuing tensions over the Spratly Islands and, more recently, Scarborough Shoal, coupled with China's recent assertive behavior on the regional stage, have stoked anti-China sentiments that have occasionally spilled over into racial rants against the ethnic Chinese in the Philippines, particularly over the Internet, with some bloggers going so far as to call for the expulsion, massacre, and confiscation of property of the Philippine Chinese (Ong 2011).[45] More seriously, while the growing affluence of the region has reshaped the economy and society of the Philippines, and has changed public perception of the Chinese in the country, it has failed to translate into the wholesale upliftment of the majority of the Filipino people from poverty into middle-class status. This situation has been blamed on predatory elite Filipino families, with which a small number of wealthy ethnic Chinese have a complex relationship (see chap. 6).

In studies on the ethnic Chinese, "China" and "Chinese" are often treated as self-evident, if not essentialized, categories (Yao 2008). Far less attention has been given to the broad, historical patterns of hybridization that were crucial to the making of "China" and "Chinese" in the modern era. The rise of mainland China has provoked questions about the changing regional and global order, particularly in light of the phenomenon in recent decades of the revival of "Chineseness" in the Southeast Asian public spheres. What are the cultural implications of the emergence of China as an economic powerhouse and geopolitical superpower? Are we, as David Kang (2007) and Joshua Ramo Cooper (2004) have argued, witnessing the remaking of East Asia in terms of a Sinocentric order founded on a "Beijing Consensus"? Or is there a more nuanced way of looking at current affairs and developments without falling into the trap of unthinking admiration of, or else blind opposition to, "China" and the "Chinese"?

Chinese Question analyzes the ways in which changing configurations of politics, economy, society, and culture shaped and reformulated the "Chinese Question" at the local, national, regional, and global levels. In particular, this book argues that "region" can be a useful and important unit of analysis for understanding the changing parameters of the Chinese Question. Characterized by fluid and shifting boundaries, the "region" is a historical and intellectual construct that has played no small role in the construction of the Chinese Question. The nation-state itself can be considered an apparatus of capture (to borrow a term from Deleuze and Guattari [1983]) that seeks to channel material flows from outside, as well as the sentiments and attachments of its inhabitants inside, into purposive use in the name of the "nation." As much as local, national, and global flows, regional flows and connections from the area now called East Asia/(Anglophone) Asia-Pacific have been an important component of the material and ideational flows and affective ties that have gone into the making of the Philippine nation-state. Whether it was the Hokkien trading networks and sojourning communities that traveled between China and Southeast Asia, Japan, and Korea in maritime Asia from the tenth century to the early colonial period (Chin 2010; see the classic studies by Wang Gungwu 2003a [1958]; and 2003d), or the Asianist network (Hau and Shiraishi 2009) that the Philippine revolutionary government tried to tap for material aid and symbolic succor, or the Comintern's Far Eastern Bureau, through which activists in the region connected and worked together (Onimaru 2011), or the U.S.-led postwar "Free Asia" regional system that sought to contain Communist China, or the post-Plaza Accord expansion of business and production networks that led to the de facto economic integration of "East Asia," the regional system at a specific time and place and the networks and pathways it creates have been as important as locally, nationally, and globally produced ones in shaping the everyday lives of the people in what is now called the Philippines.

Region also matters in other ways. The territories in the South China Sea that constituted what the Chinese called Nanyang were the site of immigration from the mainland as far back as the seventeenth century (notwithstanding bans on migration by the Ming and Qing states), if not earlier, a trend that intensified in the late nineteenth to mid-twentieth centuries. In terms of trade, a regional network has helped knit, over the centuries, various communities in what is now called East Asia (encompassing China, Japan, Korea, and Southeast Asia), with people whom we now call "Chinese," along with many other groups (including what we now call "Malays"), playing a role in both precolonial and colonial economic development in the East.

The presence of a neighboring, powerful mainland dynastic state (or states) under Ming and Qing governance was an important factor in the shaping of Southeast Asian polities in the context of what is now called a "tributary trade" regional system,[46] into which European traders and states such as the Dutch and the Spaniards had sought to insert themselves by creating port cities in their colonies in Southeast Asia in the sixteenth and seventeenth centuries. Anxiety about the shadow cast by the mainland-Chinese dynastic state over the region had unfortunate consequences: Spanish paranoia about invasion periodically tipped into violence, resulting in the massacres of the Chinese migrant population in early colonial Philippines. Moreover, incursions by "pirates" such as Limahong and Koxinga (Zheng Chenggong)—the last one a "pirate" in Spanish/Philippine eyes, later reclaimed as a patriot in colonial-period and modern Chinese eyes, and a "hero" to the Japanese to boot—had made the Spanish sensitive to the issue of the proximity of the mainland's Ming and later Qing dynastic states. The mainland would eventually be enmeshed in a nineteenth-century regional order in which Europeans, Americans, and Japanese competed for power and access to markets and resources. Penetrating China's fabled market was an important factor behind the decision by the British (albeit briefly) in the seventeenth century and Americans in the late nineteenth and early twentieth centuries to colonize the Philippines.

In the twentieth century, the looming presence of neighboring Communist China—and the regional and global network of revolutionary cooperation and aid extended by the Chinese Communist Party to communist parties in Southeast Asia (discussed in chap. 4)—became a policy issue and concern in the postwar period, when the Philippines was integrated into "America's Asia" (to use Friedman and Selden's [1971] term), which was built on a hub-and-spokes system of bilateral security treaties with the U.S. as hub, as well as a triangular trade system involving the U.S., anti-Communist Southeast Asia, and Japan (Shiraishi 1997; 2012). Among newly minted nation-states, the question of how to deal with the foreign Chinese was framed and couched in the concepts and language of American sociology, which circulated regionally through America's Asia among their political and intellectual elites (discussed in chap. 2). In recent decades, the regional and global circulation of Anglophone discourses of transnationalism (see the now-classic Ong and Nonini 1997a) and comparative thinking on the Southeast Asian "Overseas Chinese Question" would (re)shape the terms, frameworks, and agenda of scholarship on the "Chinese" from one concerned with Chinese "integration" into the national polity to one that stresses "flexible citizenship" (Ong 1999) and strategies of accumulation in a globalizing, capitalist world.

Ethnic Chinese in Southeast Asia and (mainly Anglophone) Asia-Pacific (the U.S., Canada, Australia) were, indeed, well aware of each other's situations in different domiciles across the region and the world. Southeast Asian "Chinese" thinking about the "Chinese Question" was also partly informed by regional comparisons and the circulation of (largely American-mediated) discourses of race and ethnicity, most notably the concepts of assimilation and integration. Events like the 1965 coup and 1997–1998 anti-Chinese riots in Indonesia, the Emergency in Malaya, and the Tiananmen Incident in China reverberated across Chinese communities in Southeast Asia and the world. A regional discourse for enframing the Chinese Question and a regional consciousness arising out of the dense flows, movements, linkages, and interactions among people—not just Chinese—are historically rooted in the geopolitical systems that evolved from the colonial to postcolonial and post-Cold War periods. A key point made in this book is that the impact of the so-called West was not simply a result of extensive and intimate contact between the Euro-American metropoles and "peripheral" Asia; this contact itself was coursed through, and mediated by, the pathways and connections opened up within Asia itself.

The current regional system is one in which the U.S. and Southeast Asian countries have established diplomatic relations with mainland China from the 1970s onwards, but while mainland China is already well-integrated into the post-Cold War regional and global economy, it remains outside the U.S.-led hub-and-spokes security system. This disjuncture between security and economy has generated tension on issues pertaining to territorial claims (notably between China and Vietnam as well as the

Philippines). The transformation of the Japan-U.S.-Southeast Asia triangular
trade system of the postwar period into the China-U.S.-"rest of Asia" system
of contemporary times underscores the increasing importance of China
as the biggest market in the region. Regional designations such as "East
Asia"/"Asia-Pacific" aimed at connecting the China market to the regional
system, with or without the U.S., have different ideological uses, conceptual
boundaries, and member nations. Taken together, these designations point
to specific patterns and densities of trade, investment, and movements of
people and labor in this "growth region" (discussed in chap. 5).

Of crucial importance to *Chinese Question* is Aihwa Ong's (1999, 7)
observation that "[g]lobal capitalism in Asia is linked to new cultural
representations of Chineseness (rather than 'Japaneseness') in relation to
transnational Asian capitalism." The fact that capitalism in the region is
associated if not conflated with ethnic Chinese (family) business has had
enormous implications for changing public perception of the Chinese in
Southeast Asia from pariahs to entrepreneurs, from villains to heroes of
the nation (see chaps. 5 and 6). But as Wang Gungwu has forcefully argued
(2003e, 154), in the modern history of Southeast Asia, "the Chinese played
a role in stimulating some kinds of nationalism, some kinds of capitalism,
and also some kinds of socialism and communism in several countries."
Current writings on Chinese transnationalism sometimes install a
dichotomy between nationalism and transnationalism, in effect privileging
transnationality over nationalism. This dichotomy, as Wang shows, is
problematical because the dichotomy between cosmopolitanism and
nationalism is a spurious one, particularly in the case of the Chinese, who
contributed to the development of capitalism, nationalism, and socialism/
communism in Southeast Asia. Moreover, a country like the Philippines,
whose national self-definition is constitutively as well as strategically
hybrid in its propensity to mediate different cultures, communities, and
worlds, depending on the needs and exigencies of the moment, and whose
people are now globally (as well as regionally) deterritorialized, does not
readily fit in any one side of the opposition between cosmopolitanism and
nationalism. A more critical perspective is, therefore, needed, one that
looks closely at earlier forms of "transnational" activities, both of Chinese
merchants, as has been done by Richard Chu (2010) and Andrew Wilson
(2004) in their studies of Chinese and Chinese mestizo merchants at
the turn of the century, as well as Chinese laborers and also activists who
interacted closely with Filipino and other Southeast Asian counterparts as
part of a "socialist ecumene" (to use the term coined by Bayly [2008; 2007]).
This book offers a modest contribution to the burgeoning scholarship on
ethnic Chinese in Southeast Asia, and the Philippines especially, by looking

at the transnationalism of Chinese labor and communist internationalism (see chap. 4) in order to elucidate the complex interrelationship between nation and transnationality, one that is not reducible to the dichotomy of repressive nationalism versus liberatory transnationalism (Appiah 1998; Cheah 1998; Jurriëns and De Kloet 2007; Benton 2007).

The ethnic Chinese have become exemplary taipans (tycoons) in an age of de facto regional and global economic integration, a development that simultaneously recalls the nineteenth-century high noon of globalization while exceeding its historical roots in terms of scale and scope. In her study of the cultural logic of transnationality at work in the figure of the elite "Chinese" as exemplary capitalist and flexible citizen, Aihwa Ong (1999, 2–3) argues that, in the age of global capitalism, "[t]he realignment of political, ethnic, and personal identities is not necessarily a process of 'win or lose,' whereby political borders become 'insignificant' and the nation-state 'loses' to global trade in terms of its control over the affiliations and behavior of its subjects." Ong shows how the very "flexibility" of the taipan "is itself an effect of novel articulations bet regimes of the family, state, capital, the kinds of practical-technical adjustments that have implications for our understanding of the late modern subject" (3). These novel articulations and their myriad effects and consequences in local, national, regional, and global contexts are the subject of this book.

Chapter 1 looks at the history and discourse of citizenship ideas and practices in the Philippines, and analyzes the ways in which the inclusion and exclusion of the "Chinese" are effected through highly contingent acts of judicial interpretation. The chapter discusses Jose Angliongto's *The Sultanate* (1969), the first Chinese-Philippine novel, which focuses on the politically contentious, economically overdetermined, and ideologically riven discourse and practice of citizenship during the first two and a half decades of the postindependence period, in the context of Cold-War anticommunism and Filipino nation-building. Over the centuries, representational practices of excluding and including the "Chinese" and "Chinese" mestizo were based on differing interpretations and valuations of blood, land, and conversion as conditions of settlement and, later, citizenship. The novel concerns itself with the ritual expression of patriotism on which citizenship is predicated. Naturalization is founded on the idea of "conversion" as an inner transformation of the individual, but there is a structural indeterminacy in the idea that acquiring citizenship means proving oneself deserving of being called "Filipino" by being a "good citizen." This indeterminacy, which consists of the lack of transparency between a person's "inner" thoughts and "external" expressions, fuels the obsessive search for the "true meaning" of that person's decision to acquire citizenship, and creates a dichotomy between "good Chinese" and "bad Chinese" that remains unresolved, even when a Chinese chooses to identify *with* the Philippine nation-state and its interests, particularly in a time of political turmoil, when the legitimacy of the state itself comes under question, as it did toward the end of the 1960s and beginning of the 1970s, with the activism that created the First Quarter Storm.

Chapter 2 recounts the celebrated case of the deportation of the Yuyitung brothers (who edited and published *Shang Bao/Chinese Commercial News*, the Chinese-language periodical with the highest circulation in the country), as a test case for the problem of "integration" of the ethnic Chinese in the postwar Philippines. Popular challenges against the Marcos state and the redrawing of the parameters of citizenship by the state itself during and after martial law in light of domestic imperatives and regional economic and geopoliticial developments would lead to the state-led mass naturalization of the Chinese. But this chapter also shows how debates on assimilation and integration were themselves shaped by a wider regional and global context of activism in the U.S. (in the form of the civil rights movement) and in Southeast Asia (through the actions of a group of second-generation Chinese Filipinos), as well as the regional circulation, mediated by area studies scholarship and scholars, of—and debate over—the sociological terms "assimilation" and "integration." This chapter shows how integration of the Chinese into the national community was achieved in the realm of popular imagination by two landmark films, *Dragnet* and *Ganito Kami Noon, Paano Kayo Ngayon?* even as racist depictions of the Chinese continue to have currency in both popular and nationalist discourses, as exemplified by the Chinese character in the classic film *Maynila: Sa Mga Kuko ng Liwanag* (Manila: In the Talons of Light).

Chapter 3 discusses the persistence of anti-Chinese sentiments and their reformulation by the phenomenon of kidnapping, which targeted rich and middle-class Chinese during the late 1980s and 1990s. Not only does kidnapping reinforce the historical identification of the Chinese with capital and money. In coercively turning the Chinese capitalist into a commodity that can be "ransomed" for cash, it mimics the extractive logic and practices of the Philippine state, whose representative agents and policies routinely treat the "Chinese" population as cash cows. Public responses to kidnapping are also revealing of the contradictions of the discourse of citizenship, which assumes the formal equality of citizens while repeatedly coming up against the reality of economic inequalities. Kidnapping exposes the everyday violence engendered by the social tensions resulting from these inequalities, and the blurring of boundaries between state and criminality that is an important feature of postwar Philippine politics and culture.

Chapter 4 looks at a different tradition of incorporating the Chinese into Philippine nationalist discourse by focusing on the multiple identifications and belongings evinced by a form of revolutionary cosmopolitanism, and its role in the formation of nationalism, Chinese and Philippine, as practiced by overseas Chinese guerrillas. Working together with their local Hukbalahap comrades and various ethnic and tribal communities in Japanese-occupied Philippines, these guerrillas were part of a transnational political network that took shape under the historically unique circumstances of interimperialist rivalry and war and international communist movement from the early twentieth century to World War II. The chapter investigates the biographical, organizational, and fictional embodiments of revolutionary cosmopolitanism in the life stories of the authors Du Ai (1914–1993) and his wife Lin Bin (1922–2008), the history of the Wha Chi guerrilla forces, and their cowritten novel *Fengyu Taipingyang* (Storm over the Pacific), which show the deep and intimate connections between anticolonial Chinese nationalism and Philippine radical nationalism, framed by the reach and limits of translation and forged in the community of fate without guarantees, through love and suspicion, friendship and betrayal, kinship and rejection in the difficult and uncertain wartime conditions. The chapter sketches the afterlife of revolutionary cosmopolitanism and dual nationalism in the ideologically hostile and racially exclusivist Philippines after the War under anticommunism, postcommunism and national chauvinism, and their recent partial recuperation by the government and by the polycentric left in a more inclusive, pluralist, and integrationist manner in the 1990s and thereafter.

Chapter 5 discusses how "Chineseness," historically identified with commerce, capital, and communism, and long defined by its problematic relationship with Philippine nationalism, has been reconfigured over the last three decades in line with the geopolitical, demographic, economic, social, and cultural transformations of the Philippine nation-state and society. This chapter analyzes the potentials and limits of "Chineseness" in such films as *Mano Po* and *Crying Ladies*, which draw on the discourse of national integration to situate the "Chinese Filipino" within the territorial boundaries and conceptual parameters of the Filipino nation-state. The films also point, however, to the ways in which "Chineseness" and "Chinese identity" have come to epitomize regional and global, rather than strictly national, capitalist, and cultural flows that the nation-state seeks to capture and appropriate, but always at the risk of being transformed by these flows. Where *Mano Po* attempts to reterritorialize "Chineseness" by embedding the

"Chinese Filipino" within the Philippine nation, *Crying Ladies* seeks to defuse the class tensions and nationalist resentment ignited by deterritorialized "Chineseness" by turning "Chinese" flows and connections into new sources of social power and capital.

Chapter 6 looks at attempts on the part of mestizos—among whom are the Zobel de Ayalas, the most socially prestigious and admired "Spanish-Filipino" family in the Philippines—to reclaim their "Chinese" heritage. The most important consequence of the economic rise of East Asia and mainland China has been the increasing prestige of the "Chinese" and its cognate, "the Chinese family," and their incorporation not only into the Filipino national imaginary, but also into the ranks of the Philippine elite, whose legitimacy has come under attack while the once-despised "Chinese" are hailed as "heroic" entrepreneurs. This inclusion of the Chinese among the ranks of the Philippine elite signifies not only the crisis of elite legitimacy and subsequent attempts at elite consolidation, but also the expansion of a regional network of politico-business alliances with mainland Chinese as increasingly visible and weighty players in various countries in East Asia. Despite the growing visibility and desirability of "Chinese" entrepreneurial and social power as embodied by the hybrid "Chinese," "Chineseness" itself remains deeply entangled with the issue of class and capital, which define its fraught relationship with the Filipino nation and which can potentially reactivate deep-seated ambivalence about, if not resentment of and violence against, "alien capital/ists." Moreover, the behavior of an increasingly assertive mainland China on the regional and global stage is bound to provoke resentment among its less powerful neighbors, in ways that may negatively affect public attitudes toward the ethnic Chinese population in their midst.

With Mainland China itself becoming integrated economically in the region and world, while remaining outside of American-mediated security system of East Asia, the question of China's "soft power" (Nye 2004; the term was first coined in 1990)—its ability to "seduce" (x) or "attract" others into wanting and doing what it wants—has become a fashionable topic (Ding 2008; Li 2008; 2009; Kurlantzick 2008, among many such books). But relatively little has been written about the cultural and social dimensions and implications of China's rise for Southeast Asia.

Chapter 7 examines the "Chinese renaissance" in Southeast Asia—the increasing visibility, acceptability, and assertiveness of ethnic Chinese in this region—by illuminating the historical and contemporary processes of "becoming-Chinese" in both China and Southeast Asia. Going against conventional expectations of a Sinocentric regional order in the making, this chapter argues that distinctly regional circulations and flows of people and ideas helped create a specific pattern of hybridization—enabled by Sino-Japanese-English translingual practices (to use Lydia Liu's [1995] term) and the creation of an Anglophone-elite and middle-class Asia embedded in a larger Anglophone world—that was crucial to the making of modern China and modern Chinese, a making in which Southeast Asia and its "Chinese" populations played an important role. By looking at the processes of identification and self-invention among "Chinese" from Southeast Asia, the chapter argues that, far from Southeast Asian Chinese becoming more like mainland Chinese, certain sections and classes of the mainland Chinese population are becoming more like the Southeast Asian "Anglo-Chinese" who have historically played an important role in the modernization of China.

Who is a citizen, who can become one, who cannot, and who doesn't need to are questions that are deeply implicated in the self-understanding (Brubaker 1992, 1) and making of a nation-state. The idea of a "bounded citizenry" (ix) is based on the distinction between citizen and foreigner, and this boundary can be a conceptual, ideological, and legal one. But, as Rogers Brubaker has shown in his comparative study of citizenship regimes in France and Germany, "the manner in which it [citizenship] is bounded varies from state to state" (x). In France, the Revolutionary and Republic traditions helped forge a state-centered and assimilationist notion of citizenship that promoted political inclusion of foreigners, but this inclusion is conditional on cultural assimilation. Germany's politically fragmented history, on the other hand, nurtured a Volk-centered and differentialist notion of citizenship based on the ethnocultural unity of the nation (1–2).

The Philippine case shows that ideas and practices of citizenship can be—and have been—highly contingent, mutable, and internally contested, as state and society respond to geopolitical and economic developments in the region and the world. These citizenship regimes were themselves crafted out of domestic exigencies, needs, and concerns, even as the state(s) that presided over the making of these regimes continually came under question in the face of opposition and challenges from various social forces and movements. What this reveals is a country in which different kinds of citizenship regimes have been put in place over a period of just a century, each regime responding to a different set of imperatives and creating different models of nationhood and national self-understanding. These models range from a revolutionary-republican one that was in many senses quite radical in its political and cultural inclusiveness to a colonial one that drew on a liberal, activist strain in American legal thought to selectively uphold jus soli (citizenship by place of birth) to a Commonwealth and postindependence one that redefined "Filipinoness" in absolutist, ethnocultural terms of blood and descent to a statist one that embarked on mass naturalization by administrative fiat to a postdictatorship one in which the very notion of a "bounded citizenry" (ix) itself has undergone profound changes in light of the deterritorialization of Filipino labor and the pressures brought to bear on nation-states by global capitalism.

These models are not simply products of state formulation and initiatives. The Philippine state is notoriously prone to penetration and manipulation by its political and economic elite, and its legitimacy has continually been challenged by social forces, including armed resistance by people whom the state had considered "Filipinos" and who are active in Communist, Moro, and indigenous people's movements. Posing the "Chinese Question" as an issue that focuses exclusively on the "Chinese" runs the risk of valorizing Chinese "oppression" at the cost of ignoring the enormity of the suffering and tribulations experienced by other minorities in the Philippines, as well as the majority of the Filipino population living in poverty. A consequence of this narrowness of focus on the Chinese is a distorted view of history, whether national or regional. An example of this blindness is the portrayal by Chinese-language popular media and even some academic writings of the 1965–1966 massacres in Indonesia as an "anti-Chinese genocide," a reductionist account that downplays the death of hundreds and thousands of non-Chinese Indonesians.[47]

In fact, the integration by administrative fiat of the Philippine Chinese in the 1970s coincided with the breakdown of postwar integration of the Muslims into the Philippine polity, as large-scale Christian migration to the southern Philippines and encroachment on ancestral land and economic disparities between Muslims and Christians sharpened religious and social differences and sparked a separatist war waged by the Moro National Liberation Front against the national government, a war that claimed 120,000 lives, turned 1 million people into internally displaced persons, and forced 100,000 Muslims to take refuge in Malaysia (Eder and MacKenna 2004, 72). Gestures toward political inclusion and cultural pluralism on the part of the Philippine state have in no small measure been a product of individual and communal activisms on the part of various ethnic groups, including but not limited to the Chinese, across the spectrum of the Philippine population.

The challenge for this book is to understand how the boundary between "Filipino" and "Chinese" was constructed as a basis for imagining the Philippine national community, and how it is historically negotiated, accommodated, at times evaded, and under certain circumstances, even breached or repudiated within Philippine society itself. If the "Chinese" constituted a foreign Other against whom the "Filipino" (including the mestizo) was defined and understood, a look at how these terms themselves have undergone substantive changes affords some understanding not only of the changing definitions of Filipino nationness, but more important, the social and political struggles and stakes entailed therein.

The chapters in this book offer a series of vignettes of a postcolonial Philippines, with some comparisons with other Southeast Asian countries, in the throes of national, regional, and global transformation, transformation that has been felt and experienced in economic, political, social, and cultural terms, in ways that have transformed the "Chinese Question" itself from problem to opportunity, however fraught with unresolved issues. For in the act of erasing certain social boundaries, old ones may be reinforced even as new ones are created. Looking at the situation of the "Chinese" forces us to question when the boundaries that included and excluded the Chinese were constructed, who were included and excluded, and in which realms of economy, politics, society, and culture new boundaries have sprung up after old ones were dismantled. Finally, *Chinese Question* addresses the question of "Chinese" itself—what it means, who has claimed it, for what purpose has it been invoked as a term, and what the future of this region we call East Asia/Asia-Pacific will be in the wake of the rise of East Asia, and China more particularly.

In what ways have young generations of "Chinese Filipinos," particularly the cultural workers and intelligentsia among them, responded to the "Chinese Question" and to the debates and imperatives of their time? How have they dealt with, as well as remade, the terms by which "Chinese" claim membership in a Filipino national community that they can neither uncritically embrace nor completely repudiate? How have they actively intervened to reshape the image and position of the "Chinese" in the national imaginary? To what extent have the geopolitical, economic, and political transformation of the Philippines, China, the region, and the world enabled new articulations, but also disjunctions, between Chineseness and Filipinoness, and what are their potentials and limits? What contradictions and impasses arise from discourses and practices of citizenship and ethnic (self-)identification and ascription, and how do literary and cinematic works help us make sense of them, while enabling us to imagine the unimaginable?

The films under discussion—*Mano Po*, *Crying Ladies*, *Dragnet*, and *Ganito Kami Noon, Paano Kayo Ngayon?*—vary greatly in terms of artistic merit, but they do have one thing in common: they have achieved "mainstream" status as Filipino films, and are accessible to Filipinos who cannot read or understand Hokkien and Mandarin Chinese. Charlson Ong, without doubt the most gifted and prolific of all Chinese Filipino writers active today, is a major voice in Philippine arts and letters, and two of his works—a short story and his first novel—are discussed in this book. *Chinese Question* also deals with two other novels of widely divergent quality— an obscure one by an amateur and written in English, and a classic work of regional literature in two senses of "region" (Huanan, or South China region within China and "regions" within the Philippines, on the one hand, and the Nanyang/Southeast Asia and Asia-Pacific/East Asia regions, on the other hand). Davao native Jose Angliongto's *The Sultanate* was addressed to an Anglophone "overseas Chinese" audience. Its abiding preoccupation with the need to differentiate one "type" of Chinese from another, and the need for Chinese to show that they are "good citizens" of the nation- state that they settle in, offers a good opportunity to examine more critically the idea and practices of citizenship that also haunt a number of literary and cinematic works produced by the postwar generation of ethnic Chinese, including *Dragnet* and *Mano Po*. China-based Du Ai's novel *Fengyu Taipingyang*, first published in China, deals with Chinese guerrilla interactions with Filipinos during World War II, and stands out among Chinese-language literary works produced in the Nanyang (Southern Ocean) because it is, apart from Kun Luo's *Nanyang Lei* (whose author did not live in the Philippines) and overseas Chinese returnee Bai Ren's *Nanyang Piaoliuji*, the only other—and the longest—novel on the Chinese in the Philippines published so far. Its target audience is "Chinese," but Du Ai himself also speaks at the interfaces of "Chinese" communities within China (from a Huanan, or South China, perspective), the Philippines (as a "Chinese"), and the Nanyang region and the world (as a huaqiao, or "overseas Chinese"). His novel's evocation of the "foreign" Chinese involvement in the Philippine anticolonial nationalist struggle against the Japanese during World War II exposes the limits of conventional ideas of citizenship based on territory and "blood" that would simultaneously posit a unitary entity called "China" while delimiting this "China" from its Southeast Asian neighbors.

Each of these writings and films addresses head-on issues and concerns that are central to thinking through, if not rethinking, the basic tenets of nationalism and identity in both the Philippines and China, and the region and the world more generally. Each explores the potentials and limits of citizenship in delineating the terms of belonging and membership in a given community, whether "Chinese," "Filipino," or others. Each grapples with the aporia of citizenship, with the irresoluble contradiction between formal political equality and actual economic inequality, and with the historical mutability of the concepts of nation, state, and people that shape the citizenship policies and practices. Each is a record of its own time and place(s), bound by the concerns and exigencies specific to the period and place(s) in which the work was produced. But each also bears witness to forgotten stories and histories that may offer possibilities for intellectually and politically interrogating, and moving the public debate beyond, the Chinese Question.

Notes

1   Philippine equivalent of the Latin American telenovela.
2   Kim Chiu has played a half-Japanese, quarter-Chinese character named Kim Chan Sukimura in the TV series *Aalog-alog* (Shaking 2006), and a Chinese-surnamed Cebuana named Melody Go in the sitcom *Gokada Go!* (2007). But she is best known for being the winner of the *Pinoy Big Brother: Teen Edition* reality show, and for being paired with the Filipino-American actor, Gerald Anderson, in a number of commercially successful movies.
3   "Mano po" is a form of greeting in which one brings an elder's hand to one's forehead in a traditional Filipino gesture of expressing filial piety or honoring one's elders.
4   Lily Monterverde is a Chinese mestiza; her brother was a principal of Uno High School, which offers a Chinese-language curriculum. See chapter 5.
5   Mestiza Heart Evangelista, who is also publicly billed as a "Filipino-Chinese actress" (Viva.com 2011), was cast in *Mano Po 6: A Mother's Love* (2009), for which she won a Best Supporting Actress award at the Metro Manila Film Festival.
6   In this book, the word "Chinese" is used with quotation marks to signify that it is a problematical term and bears traces not only of local and national, but regional and global histories and circulations of ideas, peoples, and political and social technologies.
7   Grace Christian High School is not located in Binondo, the proverbial "Chinatown" of Manila, but in Grace Village, Quezon City. By "Chinese," Lo presumably means Hokkien, not Mandarin.
8   Rogers Smith (2003) has argued in favor of the important role of "ethically constitutive stories" of peoplehood in the construction of collective identity.
9   I am using the word "identification" rather than "identity" to stress the unsettled nature, contingency, and provisionality of such claims to "Chineseness" by both "Chinese" and Chinese mestizos alike. Judith Butler (1993, 105) argues that "Identification is constantly figured as desired event, but one which finally is never achieved; identification is the phantasmatic staging of the event. In this sense, identifications belong to the imaginary; they are phantasmatic efforts of alignment, loyalty, ambiguous and crosscorporeal cohabitation; they unsettle the 'I'; they are the sedimentation of the 'we' in the constitution of any 'I,' the structuring presence of alterity in the very formulation of the 'I.' Identifications are never fully and finally made; they are incessantly reconstituted and, as such, are subject to the logic of iterability. They are that which is constantly marshaled, consolidated, retrenched, contested and, on occasion, compelled to give away."
10   The use of the word "hybridization" (and related terms like "hybrid") in this chapter is not meant to imply that there is a preexisting purity that is then subject to cultural mixture.

11   Although there are different ways to theorize "Southeast Asia" as a geographical, cultural, and intellectual "area" (see, for example, the reflections by Reynolds 1995; Wolters 1999; and Reid 1988, 1–10), I am using "Southeast Asia" here in the more contemporaneous sense of an American-mediated Cold War discursive and institutional construct (see Emmerson 1984; Koizumi 2006).

12   It is important to note that there were Southeast Asian countries that opted for political nonalignment at certain periods in the postwar era; these included Cambodia and Laos, before they went Communist; Burma, and Indonesia under Sukarno. The Bandung Conference of 1955 promoted the concept of nonintervention while eschewing superpower-led collective defense. These concepts would in turn shape the future Association of Southeast Asian Nation's institutional design, which is based on the rejection of superpower-led regionalism (Acharya 2009, 69). But it is also important to note that nonaligned, Guided Democracy Indonesia had close economic ties with countries such as Japan that were part of the Free Asia regional system.

13   Cense thinks that this shared vocabulary was the result of the migration of sangley from Filipinas to South Celebes.

14   Citing contemporary sources does not settle the issue of etymology, since the sangley artist who drew the Boxer Codex as well as the sangley residents in the colony would no doubt have found it strange for lanlang to be literally called "trade" by Spaniards, and might have used instead the most relevant and meaningful phonetic transcription of sangley: sionglai (frequently coming).

15   Hokkien, known as Minnanhua (闽南话 Southern Min topolect) in China and Hoklo in Taiwan, is spoken in parts of southeastern China and Taiwan. It is the lingua franca of the Philippine Chinese, and is spoken by sections of the ethnic Chinese communities in Singapore, parts of Indonesia (for example, Medan), Malaysia (Penang), and elsewhere in the world. See Klöter 2011 for an analysis of the "early Manila Hokkien" spoken by the sangleyes.

16   Some Chinese-Filipinos, for example, protested against the use of the word "intsik" to refer to Mandarin-language courses offered by the University of the Philippines (Tan 2011).

17   The Javanese "tjino" did not have negative connotations, but with the rise of Chinese nationalism in the early twentieth century, nationalists began using the Hokkien "Tionghoa" 中华. Orang cina acquired a negative connotation, and young Indonesians sometimes referred to themselves as orang Chinese (note the preference for the English word) to distance themselves from the Suharto regime's transformation of cina into "China." I thank Ben Anderson for this information.

18   This should not be read as an attempt to excuse the racism and Han chauvinism of the ethnic Chinese, of which there are, as with any group of people anywhere in the world, plenty of examples and counterexamples. Lydia Liu (2004, 31–69) complicates the picture in her study of the making of another loaded term,夷 /yi/barbarian, into an "hetero-linguistic" supersign, one that "gathers into itself the Chinese and English etymologies and binds their commensurability to a fantastic semantic whole" (33). In the mid-nineteenth century, the British took offense at the translation of "yi" in their international treatises with China because of their insistence on translating the term into English as the pejorative "barbarian" and proof of unregenerate sinocentrism (notwithstanding the fact that yi was neither exclusively applied to foreigners, nor necessarily negative in connotation), and then sought to ban the term

from being used in the Anglo-Chinese Treaty of 1858. The vision of sovereignty that this supersign propounded was one that had political effects, not least of which was war. Critical of the "glib evocation of the word 'barbarian' by academic and popular writings of the past hundred and fifty-odd years in the West and elsewhere," Liu asks: "In what sense does the Chinese character *yi* provide hard linguistic evidence for the theory of Chinese xenophobia that has prevailed for so long in modern historiography? Is the theory itself not already indebted to the ban on the supersign *yi*/barbarian at one time or another?" (39).

19 I thank Junko Koizumi for this information, citing the index to 清代籌辦夷務始末 (Qingdai Chou Bian Yi Wu Shimo).

20 A more neutral way of describing these "corsairs," or "pirates," is that they were basically armed traders whose activities fell outside the purview of the state. Zheng is a "pirate" in the eyes of both the Spanish and Qing authorities.

21 A good discussion of Tang ethnic identity can be found in Abramson 2008.

22 The Republican government under Chiang Kai-shek enacted a new Citizenship Act in 1929 that basically affirmed jus sanguinis and furthermore stated that a Chinese who applies to become a citizen or national of another country may only lose his or her Chinese citizenship upon the permission of the Chinese Ministry of the Interior.

23 Interestingly, in Japanese, a language that shares certain vocabulary and pronunciation with Minnanhua/Hokkien, 出世 has a positive connotation of achievement, of having attained some status in the world or making a name for oneself in the world. For sangley to have converted to Catholicism meant that they were either true believers or settlers with enough of a stake in the Philippine colony to want to embrace the religion for the benefits and incentives (marriage, travel, and business) it offered, or both.

24 Even the pejorative *chekwa* (*tsekwa*), a slang word derived from *intsik*, has been reclaimed by Chinese Filipinos. Kitty Go, former editor in chief of *Preview* magazine and publisher of *Cosmopolitan*, *FHM*, and *Yes!* magazines, has a blog in which she regularly refers to herself as "chekwa" and to the Philippine Chinese community as "Chekwa Federation." The cosmopolitan Go, who was educated in the Ateneo and the U.S., has lived in New York, Los Angeles, Manila, Taipei, Tokyo, London, and Megève. In 2005, she published a novella, *When Chic Hits the Fan* (2005a), that created controversy because of its thinly veiled expose of the foibles, peccadillos, and pretensions of "high society" in the Philippines. Another book, *Chic Happens* (2005b), quickly followed in the same year. The book affords some insights into the social hierarchy that obtains within elite ranks. Whereas Go herself has been able to mix in some of the most rarefied social circles, she nevertheless notes that "high society" remains striated by divisions across racial lines: the "Holy Grail" (2005a, 16) consists of the Spanish-Filipinos, while Chinese-Filipinos (here "Chunkua Federation") are considered too nouveaux-riches and "too unchic to be in society pages" (ibid.). Much of the *Chic* books would appear to be devoted to satirizing "social climbers" whose socioeconomic backgrounds, education, and demeanor are considered déclassé by established elites.

25 Among the most noteworthy are the anthologies by Arriola and Pe 1989; Shi Yingzhou 施颖洲1992; Yun He 云鹤2000; and *Shang Bao* 2001; as well as Joaquin Sy's (施华谨) translations into Filipino of Chinese-language poetry and prose written by Philippine Chinese (see, for example, Sze 2011; and the National Book

Award-winning translation of Bai Ren 2007). Aside from Charlson Ong's novels and short stories, notable single-authored English-language collections of short fiction include R. Kwan Laurel's *Ongpin Stories* (2008) and Xin Mei's (pseud.) *Afraid to be Chinese* (2006). Yun He's multivolume anthology collects the writings of Philippine Chinese literary notables such as Lin Quan 林泉, Shi Yuehan 施约翰, Ming Che 明澈, He Quan 和权, Ruo Ai若艾, Shi Liuying 施柳莺, Qiu Di 秋笛, Suo Shi 莎士, Chen Mengzi 晨梦子, and Chen Qionghua 陈琼华. Key studies of Chinese Filipino writings include Yap 1970; Sy 1979; Susie Tan 1993, 1994a, 1994b; Fang 1988; Tope 1993; 2000; Cruz 1996; and Lua 2001. Distinguished critic and creative writer Isagani Cruz published the first Philippine textbook, *Ang Ating Panitikan* (1984, coedited with Soledad Reyes), to include literary translations from Chinese.

26   See Gayatri Spivak's discussion (1988, 276–79) of the conceptual slippages between the two senses of representation embodied by the German terms *darstellen* (artistic portrait) and *vertreten* (political proxy).

27   See also the biography of Joseph Estrada by Zeus Salazar (2005), who explores the upper-middle-class mestizo Estrada's embodiment—through his identification with (and use of) Filipino vis-á-vis English and his popular screen persona—of the role of defender of the oppressed and man of the masses. Estrada's supposed lack of education (he graduated from the elite Ateneo High School, but became a college dropout) and his profession as actor made him the target of elite criticism, even though in many respects he came from their ranks. Jokes surrounding Erap's English (called ERAPtions) serve as indices of elite disapproval of Erap as well as Erap's populist appeal.

28   An important exception is Filósofo Tasio, who explicitly refers to his Chinese mother with some affection (Anderson 2008, 45).

29   See John Blanco's (2009, 209–26) analysis of the fiction written by *peninsulares* (Spaniards born in Spain) such as Francisco Paula de Entrala's *Sin título* (1881).

30   On the formation in Cebu of a multiethnic "urban aristocracy" that included Chinese mestizos, see Cullinane 1982. On the Filipino *principalia, ilustrado*, and "elite," see also the thoughtful discussions by Owen 1974; Guerrero 1977; 1982; Majul 1977; Schumacher 1991; Simbulan 2005; Cullinane 2003; and Coronel, Chua, et al. 2007.

31   Hedman and Sidel's argument about the "longer lineages and deeper roots" of "'Chinese capital'" (2000, 67), on the basis of which they identify "another kind of oligarchy" consisting of "Chinese" business dynasties (79) rightly highlights the ability of a small class of wealthy Chinese to gain economic clout despite anti-Chinese legislation of the Commonwealth and early postwar years. But the idea of business "dynasties" runs the risk of glossing over crucial questions of scale as well as vicissitudes of changing fortunes (often caused by the death of the patriarch and the division of inheritance and business among the children) even within a clan as prominent as the descendants of Pedro Gotiaoco, the Gotianuys, Gokongweis, Sy-Gaisanos, and Gotianuns, whom the authors hold up as a typecase. It is true, for example, that the Gotianuys and Gotianuns have had a measure of staying power in being able to translate their great-grandfather's wealth into economic and social prominence over decades (on the issue of Sergio Osmeña's links with Pedro Gotiaoco, see Flores 2010). Others in the clan, however, have seen reversals in their own lifetimes. John Gokongwei Jr.'s case is perhaps the most dramatic: he grew up in affluence, but the untimely death of his father (who owned a chain of movie houses) plunged the family into financial crisis, and Gokongwei struggled for years to build

his own buy-and-sell business. His subsequent personal fortune would dwarf that of his ancestors and his contemporaries. While he socializes with the likes of the politically influential and socially ascendant Lopezes, he and his children have not married into the ranks of the Filipino elite. Is it possible to speak of an "oligarchy" of "Chinese-business dynasties" in terms of the classic definition of "rule by the few" when ethnic Chinese, unlike their mestizo counterparts, did not traditionally exercise direct political power nor enjoy social and cultural prestige and the so-called business dynasties are not always stable nor enduring? Among wealthy Chinese, there is a clear sense of the scale and limits of their wealth in comparison to that of their peers, and it is quite clear that the taipans who made their fortune in the postwar years are a different group of people from their counterparts in the prewar years. Moreover, it is not unusual for newly minted Chinese millionaires to rewrite their family histories by endowing their own parents and ancestors of rather more humble origins and limited means with the prestige-titles of "Don" and "Doña."

32   A Chinese mestiza and a German, as well as Filipinos, are among its ancestors.

33   Victor Purcell (1965, 522–23), drawing on the index of Blair and Robertson (1903–1909, 55: 195–96), cites the following Spanish opinions of the Chinese during the nearly four centuries of Spanish colonial rule: under negative, "barbarous, mean, impudent, importunate, deceitful, unwarlike, cowardly, avaricious and greedy, addicted to sodomy and secret sins, tyrannical, ignorant, superstitious, vicious, intemperate, lustful and sensuous, polygamous, disloyal and faithless, evil-minded and wicked, mercenary, covetous, timorous, suspicious, cautious, cunning, unchaste, treacherous, shameless, vile, addicted to gambling, addicted to bribery, unscrupulous, rascally cruel (in tortures, penalties, etc.), conscienceless, nomadic, fond of litigation, commit perjury, have tendency to revolt, inconstant, proud, talkative, extortionate, not spiritually minded, inclined to sorcery" (the index additionally lists "talkative," "lazy," "unwarlike"); under positive, "civilized, humble, polite, ingenious, intelligent, imitative, careful of women, industrious, valiant and spirited, shrewd (generally in trade), generous, able and discreet, kind, honorable, tractable and docile, simple and unsophisticated, clever, possesses good memories, not hostile to foreigners, grateful, religious, respect old age, legally minded, sensible and prudent, energetic, enterprising, fond of learning, cultured, respectful, sober, patient, peaceable" (the index also includes "warlike").

34   During the 1638 rebellion organized by the sangleyes, in protest against Governor Hortado de Cuerva's attempt to force them to work in rice plantations around Manila, the Dominican parish priest Francisco de Herrera blockaded himself along with 160 mestizos de sangleyes inside the Binondo Church, but the governor ordered the mestizos to be removed from the church "because they [the mestizos] were continually making signs and passing notes [to the sangley rebels]"! (Blair and Robertson 1903–1909, 29: 228).

35   Investigation into the genetic makeup and history of the Philippine population is still in its infancy, but a study conducted by a biologist, Antonio Gonzalez-Martin, in Spain (reported by Santamaria [2012]), based on a limited sampling, suggested that "an important part of the maternal lineage [of Filipinos] is connected to groups that migrated from China and Taiwan between 4,000 and 6,000 years ago."

36   In terms of numbers, in the late 1990s, Indonesia (5,460,000) has the largest population of Chinese, followed by Malaysia (5,261,000), Thailand (4,813,000), and the Philippines (850,000). The percentage of ethnic Chinese in relation to total

population is 29.6 percent for Malaysia, 8.6 percent for Thailand, and 3 percent for Indonesia. Singapore is 77 percent ethnic Chinese and Brunei 16 percent (estimates provided by Suryadinata 1997, 21). It must be noted, however, that these statistics, compiled from different sources, are problematical in the sense that they are often rough estimates based on citizenship and other criteria. In the case of Chinese in the Philippines, it is difficult to count ethnic Chinese once they have acquired Filipino citizenship. Calculations of ethnic Chinese participation in the economy, for example, extrapolate the ethnicity of the company stockholders from their surnames, but it is well-known that surnames alone do not tell us anything about the self-identification of the person, and this form of counting overlooks the fact that ethnic Chinese may have acquired non-Chinese surnames through baptism and other means.

37 The term "hybridity," popularized by Bhabha (1994), Garcia Canclini (1990), Hall (1996), and Robert Young (1995), has been a subject of heated debate among exponents and detractors alike. Most prominent among the latter are Ahmad (1994; 1995), Parry (2004), and Kraidy (2005). The Philippine case provides a cautionary tale against naïve celebrations of hybridity as "critique" and "resistance," since the issue at stake is not simply one of challenging the "essentialism" and exclusivism of Filipino nationalism, but dealing as well with the fact that strategic hybridity has been an important means by which the Filipino elite has cemented its wealth, social status, and power *as elite* through its claims and capacities to mediate different cultures and worlds beyond Philippine territory. Strategic hybridity is not, moreover, the exclusive privilege of the elite. See, for example, Fenella Cannell's (1999, 203–26) important discussion of indigent Bicolanos and particularly the male-transvestite *bakla*'s mediation, appropriation, and domestication of the cultural products, repertoire, and codes of behavior associated with the elite and the "foreign" (especially American). The "Manila men," historical precursors of today's globalized Filipino seafarers, as well as Filipino musicians working in Asia and the world (Aguilar 2011b); networks of nationalist and communist activists (Onimaru 2011); and overseas Filipino workers are also among the most important traveling mediators and agents of Philippine modernity.

38 Ironically, the fact that ethnicity loses its salience for the state once a Chinese "becomes" a Filipino is a source of frustration to scholars of overseas Chinese, who are unable to come up with accurate statistics on the actual number of "Chinese," both Chinese citizens and Filipino citizens, in the Philippines. Instead, they have depended on extrapolation from statistics provided during the Spanish and American periods.

39 See, for example, Khoo Boo Teik's fine intellectual biography (1995) of Mahathir Mohamad.

40 I thank Jafar Suryomenggolo for the information on the "web of certification" by which the Indonesian state identifies Indonesians as Chinese.

41 In *Chinese in the Philippines: A Bibliography* (See and Ang-See 1990, 90–100), the majority of the articles listed under the heading "Economic Nationalism and Filipinization" deal with the retail trade nationalization law rather than the "Filipino First" Policy.

42 For a summary of the provisions of Republic Acts 1180 and 3018, see Azcuna 1969, 89–91.

43 For excerpts of the Bell Trade Act and the Military Bases Agreement, see chapter 4 of Schirmer and Shalom 1987, 87–103.

44 An important difference is that unlike the Chinese, whose ethnicity is often conflated with (middle or upper-)class status, the majority of overseas Filipino workers perform work that is not considered "middle class" (i.e., entrepreneurs or professionals), even though their earnings abroad make them technically "middle class," at least in terms of income, in the Philippines.

45 On the complex responses of Southeast Asian states to China's territorial claims, see Shiraishi 2012.

46 See Hamashita 2008; and Arrighi, Hamashita, and Selden 2006. Hamashita's influential notion of tribute-trade, in which politics and economy are assumed to be closely intertwined, is not without its critics (see Wang Hui 2011, 45–59; Hau and Shiraishi 2012). A nuanced study that looks at the tributary system from the perspectives of both the mainland "Chinese" dynastic states and polities in what is now Southeast Asia is Oliver Wolters's classic study (1970) of the fall of Srivijaya.

47 A clarification is needed here: the massacres of 1965–1966 in Indonesia were not pogroms of Chinese in the sense of Chinese being targeted for their ethnicity, but rather, mass killings of hundreds and thousands of native Indonesians as well as a sizeable number of Chinese who were regarded as, or accused of being, "communist." Charles Coppel (2008, 117–18) is rightly critical of the characterization of the Indonesian massacres by popular media as well as academic writings as an "anti-Chinese genocide." The massacres claimed far more non-Chinese Indonesian lives (particularly in the rural areas) and are better understood as "politicide" (118). Coppel's estimate (1983, 58–61) of two thousand Chinese Indonesians killed during this time leads him to argue that the numbers are "disproportionately low," given the percentage of Chinese Indonesians relative to the population.

1

CITIZEN

Of the six novels on the Philippine Chinese that have been published in and outside the Philippines over the years, Jose L. Angliongto's *The Sultanate* (1969) is the first, but by far the least read and appreciated. It lacks the luminous prose, narrative drive, and rich characterization of Charlson Ong's prizewinning *An Embarrassment of Riches* (2000b) (discussed in chap. 6) and highly touted *Banyaga: A Song of War* (2006). Although well-known as a businessman, newspaper columnist, and civic pillar of the community in his native Davao City, Jose Angliongto has not achieved the literary and (inter)national recognition accorded *guiqiao* (overseas Chinese returnee) writers Bai Ren and Du Ai (whose novel is discussed in chap. 4) in China.[1] Nor has *The Sultanate* matched the commercial success of Burma-raised Kun Luo's (Zeng Kunluo 曾昆洛) multigenerational Philippine-Chinese saga, *Nanyang Lei* (南洋泪 Nanyang Tears, 3 vols., 2003, 2005, 2009), the first volume of which had gone into three printings and was turned into a twenty-five-part television mini-series in China ("Dian shi lianxu ju *Nanyang lei* ershi ri zai Jinjiang kaiji" 2005).

For all that *The Sultanate* has been overshadowed by the five other succeeding (and successful) novels, there is little in Angliongto's book to suggest an overriding preoccupation with the question of literary merit and reputation (of which, admittedly, the novel possesses little). The fact that the book jacket, normally written by or with the cooperation of the author, places *The Sultanate* in the "best tradition of the *roman ancien*" indicates that Angliongto is concerned less with aesthetic innovation than with modeling his work on the ancient novel's groundedness in contemporaneous everyday life. This is borne out by the book cover blurb's insistence on the timeliness of the novel, its ability to refer, and direct the reader, to the "here and now" of Philippines circa 1969: "Intended primarily for the Overseas Chinese, it [*The Sultanate*] is a serious attempt at portraying our times.... [The author] has been able to invest this, his first book, with urgency, immediacy and relevance. The reader of this novel will not fail to see the cogency of its material; he [*sic*] will not miss the compellingness of its contemporaneity. It is as up-to-date as this morning's newspaper headlines." Just as important, and in line with the aim of ancient novels (Holzberg 1995, 26–27), *The Sultanate* sets out to depict certain ideals through a narrative account of the providential experiences

Jose Angliongto's *The Sultanate*

of a given character. Just what these ideals are is suggested by the novel's focus on the travels, adventures, and romances of a patriotic young overseas Chinese in the Philippines, whose "search for identity also becomes a struggle for national identification" (Angliongto 1969, book jacket).[2]

Why was such a novel addressed to such an audience about such a topic written at such a time by such a writer? And what accounts for the novel's relative obscurity?

This chapter proposes to read *The Sultanate* as an historically embedded, culturally specific act of writing (and reading) (Miller 2001, 63, 64). The novel's value lies in its revelation of the politically contentious, economically overdetermined, and ideologically riven discourse and practice of citizenship during the first two decades of the post-independence period. Over the centuries, various "regimes of truth" (Foucault 1980, 131) created by Spanish and American colonial states and the Philippine nation-state produced facts, beliefs, values and mores centering on the problematic position of the sangley/chino/intsik/"Chinese"[3] *vis-a-vis* the Philippine colonial society and national community. These regimes of truth underpinned the representational practices of exclusions as well as inclusions based on differing interpretations and valuations of blood, land and conversion as conditions of settlement and, later, citizenship.

The Sultanate lends itself to being analyzed as an historical, social and autobiographical document of its time. The ritual expression of patriotism

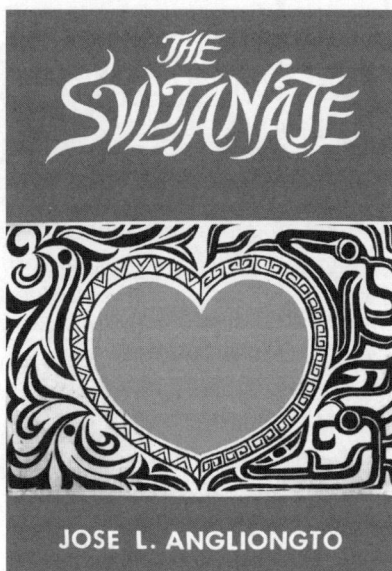

on which citizenship is predicated is at the heart of *The Sultanate*. The novel speaks to the concerns of the postwar generation of ethnic Chinese in the Philippines, increasing numbers of whom were receiving tertiary education and interacting more and more with Filipinos outside the traditional ethnic enclaves. A number of these second- and third-generation ethnic Chinese found themselves grappling with the challenges and conundrums of citizenship. How does one prove oneself a "good Filipino" in a context in which being Chinese and even Chinese mestizo is considered a liability and Filipino citizenship offers no immunity against racial prejudice? Here, the idea of citizenship is not limited to the question of discharging one's civic responsibilities as required by the state and society, but more fundamental issues of personal intention, conviction, choice, and action. The acquisition of citizenship is founded on no less than the idea of "conversion" as an inner transformation of the individual as well as the condition of membership in a community.

The Sultanate, however, unwittingly exposes the structural indeterminacy that lies at the heart of the idea that acquiring citizenship means proving oneself deserving of being called "Filipino." This indeterminacy, which consists of the lack of transparency between a person's "inner" thoughts and "external" expressions, fuels the obsessive search for the "true meaning" of that person's decision to acquire citizenship. Moreover, popular challenges against the Marcos state and the subsequent redrawing of the parameters of citizenship by the state itself following the imposition of martial law further vitiated the social impact of the novel as some of the ideas it espoused achieved orthodoxy while others were quickly rendered obsolete.

Deglamorizing the Chinese Mestizo

The main events in *The Sultanate* unfold in the immediate aftermath of World War II. Recently widowed, fifty-year-old Generoso Dy Angco, a successful businessman, leader of the Chinese community in Davao, and son of a Chinese trader who married a Tausug princess, is assassinated allegedly at the instigation of his business rivals. His three Philippine-born, grieving sons deal with the tragedy in their own ways. Rolando, the youngest, finds himself adrift, rudderless, as he strives to carve out his own niche and establish his own identity without being overshadowed by his two highly accomplished brothers. Mariano, the eldest, concentrates on business, eventually becoming a tycoon. Grieving is more protracted for middle son Ricardo, whose father's death triggers an identity crisis. Frustrated by the inability of his relatives and the factionalized Chinese community to bring his father's killers to justice, Ric embarks on a study trip to China. He writes to his brother Mariano with his observations of a China in political and social crisis and returns to the Philippines determined to build "his own sultanate out of sweat and brawn" (Angliongto 1969, 14) and "in the hearts of people" (149). Convinced that the communist takeover of China means that the security of the Philippines is at stake (130) and setting out to prove "to the Filipino people that those who came from Chinese stock are as good citizens if not better than those of Malayan, Indonesian, Spanish or even American extraction" (120), Ric becomes a counter-espionage agent for the Philippine state, and spends ten years working undercover within the Chinese community to identify the "red infiltrators." In his conversations with his Filipino contacts, he discourses at length on the Chinese Question and proposes easier access to citizenship and assimilation as the solutions. Ric falls in love with Lileng; the lovers are cleaved—in its double senses of clinging together and splitting apart—by their respective patriotic commitments to the Philippines and Taiwan. The relationship ends when Lileng elects to move to Taipei to look for a job there. Another woman who makes a deep impression on Ric is Chin Fong, an ardent communist sympathizer whom "Ric almost married," and with whom Ric "tangled in history and Chin Fong tore him to shreds" (215). Tragically, Chin Fong commits suicide after she returns to communist China. Ric buys an islet south of the Mindanao Sea to serve as the "seat of his sultanate" and transplants the molave saplings planted by their father in the old family property. The book ends with Ric holding the hands of his Filipina lover, Esperanza.

The Sultanate addresses the issue of national community and belonging through its evocation of protagonist Ricardo's life and career as a "good citizen." If the concept of citizenship is a way of specifying the relationship between the state and individual as well as a way of formulating the conditions of membership in a community, then what does The Sultanate tell us about the terms and limits of "Chinese" membership in the Filipino national community?

The question of citizenship loomed large in postwar public, scholarly, and policy debates about the "Chinese Question." As mentioned in the Introduction, Chinese were variously identified with capitalism, communism, and cultural chauvinism, and viewed as economically dominant, politically disloyal and culturally different. They were the specific targets of economic nationalism in the form of retail and other nationalization laws in the 1950s to 1960s. Periodic raids by the Philippine military (with the help of the Guomindang/Kuomintang [hereinafter KMT] branch in the Philippines)—often tantamount to extortion—were conducted in the name of weeding out the "communist" elements of the Chinese community, the most notorious being the one in December 27, 1952, which rounded up more than three hundred Chinese.[4] "Overstaying Chinese" was another issue, accompanied by public clamor for mass deportation. "Once a Chinese, always a Chinese" was a recurring refrain (Immigration Commissioner Emilio Galang, quoted in Ople 1958, 18), as journalists and pundits publicly called for the assimilation of the Chinese.

In the wake of China going Communist in 1949 and the Hukbalahap rebellion (1946–1954) mounted by the Partido Komunista ng Pilipinas (PKP Communist Party of the Philippines) against the Philippine state, the term "Chinese" and its anthropological-sociological variant, "Overseas Chinese," became a domestic as well as international issue and policy concern in the Philippines and in the "Free Asia" ("free" here meant Communist-free) regional system wherein the U.S. served as hegemon, patron, and Big-Brother security hub. More than just a security matter, the "Chinese question" or "Chinese problem" was intimately linked to the issue of national belonging and culture. The blurb on the book jacket proclaims that *The Sultanate* is "intended primarily for the Overseas Chinese," although the book's regional scope has been largely circumscribed by the localized nature of its production, distribution and circulation as a book, which has limited the readership to a small, English-reading public in the Philippines. Nevertheless, the fact that Angliongto intended his novel to be read not only by the Philippine Chinese, but by "Overseas Chinese" more generally (the majority of whom were based in Southeast Asia and North America at the time the novel was published), shows the extent to which Philippine Chinese like him were aware that the issues they faced were not specific to the Philippines, but had application and implication elsewhere, not least in parts of Southeast Asia, the U.S., and the world. This (mainly Anglophone) regional/global perspective adopted by Angliongto in *The Sultanate* is also revealing of the extent to which American-mediated sociological discourses provided the language and conceptual framework through which the "Overseas Chinese" was constructed as an object of inquiry and policy—a point that will be taken up in the next chapter.

Given the political, economic and cultural construction of the Chinese as "aliens," acquiring citizenship was a protracted, difficult, and expensive process. Charles Coppel has argued that the post-colonial Philippines differs from other Southeast Asian countries in the role played by judicial interpretation—an American legacy—in granting as well as restricting Chinese access to citizenship (Coppel 1974, 79; Aguilar 2011) through the application since 1935 of the principle of *jus sanguinis* ("law of blood") in determining Chinese membership in the Philippine national community. The terms, laid down by the Commonwealth and post-colonial state, by which "Chinese" inhabited (or were allowed to occupy) the political space of the Philippine nation, depended on juridical legislation and the value it assigned to land (the question of place-origins), blood (the question of racial difference), and conversion (the ability to undergo fundamental change through personal transformation) in determining "Chinese" acquisition of citizenship. Given this juridico-legal context, litigation became the principal means by which the Chinese spoke to, and negotiated with, the state.

What makes Angliongto's novel noteworthy is his choice of the "Chinese mestizo" as patriarch. Generoso Dy Angco is the son of a Chinese trader made good who converted to Islam and fell in love with a princess of the Sulu sultanate. As part of the dowry, the sultan awarded the Chinese trader the island of Siasi near Jolo in western Mindanao. The princess, however, died in childbirth, and her grief-stricken husband asked the sultan for permission to bring his son back to China to be raised by his Chinese first wife. Raised as "Chinese" but proud of his mixed-blood royal heritage and property claim, Generoso undertakes the process of naturalization and obtains Filipino citizenship, which he then passes on to his sons, who are now considered "native-born" and who, unlike their Muslim grandmother, are "devout Catholics" (Angliongto 1969, 7).

No doubt the choice of a mestizo protagonist over a "pure Chinese" may have been dictated by hopes of attracting a wider readership and facilitating readerly identification with the main characters among the Filipino public. But this genealogical detail is not a mere function of literary convention. The "prehistory" of the novel embroiders on a common motif in textual renderings of Philippines-China relations—reading the nation form back in time, it points to evidence of centuries-long historical, bilateral linkages between "Chinese" and "Filipinos" in the form of trade, tributary, migrant, and personal connections in order to advance the notion of "close" relations between the two peoples. The reality, however, is more complex: various polities in Mindanao had been maritime trading centers independent of Spanish Philippines, and Mindanao itself had been administered separately by the Americans (Abinales 2000b). Chinese traders did convert to Islam and marry into royalty, accounting for surnames like Tan and Kong among the ranks of the present-day Muslim elite (S. Tan 1994). The career of Maguindanao strongman Datu Piang—son of an Amoy trader, "minister of lands" and economic advisor to the powerful Datu Uto, and married to the daughter of Datu Uto's ally[5]—has been held up as a typecase of the longstanding "harmonious" relations between Chinese and Muslims (Ang See 2004b, 48).

Moreover, intermarriage is commonly taken in sociological literature as a key index of incorporation if not assimilation (Marcson 1951, 75; for the Asian American case, see the excellent discussion by Yu 2001, 56–63). Living proof of the fact that racial boundaries are constantly being breached, the mestizo physically embodies the fusion or amalgamation of ethnic or racial groups, thus making hybridity a genetic fact rather than a mere metaphor of cultural exchange and border-crossing. Far more important, mestizoness, rather than "pure" nativeness, is the dominant feature of Philippine elite self-representation and popular identification, with fairness being prized over *kayumanggi* (brown) skin as the standard of beauty. Given the extent of intermixing among the Philippine population, particularly among its elite, the resulting line between "Chinese" and "Malay" is not easily drawn.

"Malay" as a term was used in reference to the Jambi region of Sumatra (Milner 2008, 85). It was associated with claims of descent from the kingship of Srivijaya and Malacca, with the commercial diaspora and urban culture that developed in the port cities of the region, and with the Islamic *umma* or community of believers (Reid 2004, 1–24). Tony Milner (2008, 89) cautions against taking this term of abstraction for granted, noting the important role played by European colonialism and its classificatory systems and knowledge production in the "concept-building" of a word that would go on to generate racial and national consciousness by and among self-identified "Malays."[6] Attempts at fixing Malayness as a racial identity are fraught because the term historically encompassed an ethnically mixed, heterogeneous population that included people who would come to be known as "Chinese." Milner (2008, 10) argues that "The category 'Malay' brings together many peoples, many histories." Commenting on the call for mass deportation of the Chinese in 1952, for example, journalist Teodoro Locsin argued that the average Filipino could not claim "previous occupation" of Philippine territory owing to the then-popular theory that the Philippines was an empty land subsequently populated through "waves of migration" by "Negritos," "Indonesians," and "Malays." To compound matters, judging who is liable for deportation creates the further problem of "Who goes? Full Chinese? Half? Quarter?" (Locsin 1952). *The Sultanate* highlights prominent Filipinos like Jose Rizal's Chinese ancestry (1969, 23) and, in another passage, has Ric repeating the truism, popularized by elementary and high school textbooks, that the Filipino "race" is "produced by the comingling [*sic*] of Malayan, Arab, Chinese, Spanish, English, American, Japanese, Hindu and Indonesian blood" (120).

If the fusion of ethnic groups through intermarriage is a universally human condition, and if the Filipino "race" is generically "mestizo" and many of the country's national heroes and leaders—including presidents

Jose Laurel, Elpidio Quirino, Ramon Magsaysay, Ferdinand Marcos, and Corazon Aquino—are technically "Chinese mestizos" (A. Tan 1987, 1), then what accounts for Angliongto's contention that Chinese mestizos were "treated as second-class citizens" in the postwar period? The "deglamoriz[ing]" (Angliongto 1969, 120) of the Chinese mestizo is intimately tied to the construction of the "Chinese" as politically and culturally "alien" in the post-independence period. The debased status of the Chinese mestizos, however, can only be understood within the context of a larger and longer history of changing ideas about blood, birth, domicile, and conversion that are crucial in defining the terms of membership in the Spanish and American colonial society and Philippine national community.

Blood, Land, and Conversion

Mestizo and its linguistic variants like *métis* were used in census classifications in the colonial Philippines and Indochina. The British also used terms like Anglo-Burmese to classify and count children of mixed parentage or ancestry. Although the Spanish did not install a "rationalized" census until the last few decades of their colonial rule,[7] they were the only European power in Southeast Asia to have created a separate legal category for people of mixed-blood ancestry (Wickberg 1964). Because few Spaniards settled in the Philippines, Philippine colonial society was not characterized by the highly ramified social distinctions based on fine gradations of skin color that once obtained in parts of Spanish America (which also had a sizeable population of descendants of African slaves), and the category of mestizo mainly referred to the far more numerous numbers of people of mixed Chinese ancestry.

In his classic study, Edgar Wickberg stated that Chinese-mestizo "membership is strictly defined by genealogical considerations rather than place of birth" and by the fact that the Chinese mestizo's "cultural characteristics could be distinguished" from Chinese and natives' (62). Wickberg also argued that although legal distinctions helped create social distinctions among the population, Philippine colonial society was not a rigidly bounded plural society because social mobility was facilitated by intermarriage based on conversion to Catholicism (66). Deploying sociological jargon, Wickberg argued that religious conversion was a "method of taming and perhaps assimilating the Chinese," and Binondo (the heart of what would, centuries later, eventually be called "Chinatown") an "acculturation laboratory for Catholic Chinese and Chinese mestizo community" (70).

Wickberg's useful analysis needs some unpacking and qualification if we are to obtain insights into the specific valuation that the Spanish accorded blood, territorial nativity and conversion in defining the Chinese mestizo vis-à-vis the *sangley*. As discussed in the Introduction, the *sangley* was intimately associated with the economic activity of trade: even though there were sangleyes who worked as artisans (and in some cases farmers and fishermen), sangley involvement in the China-Manila-Mexico galleon trade was a key element of the early Spanish colonial economy. The sangley was also characterized by his high level of mobility, that is, his "frequent coming" from somewhere not here but near. Furthermore, geopolitics had an important bearing on Spanish attitudes toward the sangley. Attacks led by "corsairs" Limahong and Koxinga as well as visits by emissaries from the Ming and Qing courts were important reminders of the looming presence of the nearby "celestial empire." Such an awareness on the part of the Spaniards stoked paranoia about invasion and led to massacres and expulsions of the sangleyes.[8]

Conversion, however, was the principal condition of sangley settlement in Spanish colonial society. Conversion to Catholicism allowed the sangley to establish permanent residence and move around within the bounds of the colonial territory. But Catholic sangley mobility was limited to the territorial bounds of Spanish soil; in principle, the sangley could no longer go back to his place of birth in Fujian or elsewhere in China. The sangley infidel (*infiel*), on the other hand, was by definition a "transient" who could move only between the Parian ghetto (and occasionally, nearby areas) and his place of "origin" in Fujian, but not elsewhere *within* Filipinas.[9]

Wickberg (1965, 16) stated that "acceptance of baptism was a shrewd business move for a Chinese. Besides reduced taxes, land grants, and freedom to reside almost anywhere, one acquired a Spanish godparent, who could be counted upon as a bondsman, creditor, patron and protector in legal matters." Far more crucially, conversion allowed the sangley—by definition male—to marry native women (in the absence of immigration by sangley women). Their offspring would automatically be classified as mestizo. The creation of the mestizo de sangley as a legal category meant that while the children that a native woman bore her sangley husband would be marked as having sangley blood, they could not be considered as "pure" sangley, even if they had been raised to identify themselves as such. In other words, at least until the 1880s, while sangleyes mestizos could choose to be reclassified as "natural," the one thing that these mestizos were discouraged from becoming was sangley just like their father. The father's sangley status was something that he, and only he, embodied. Self-identification as sangley was not fully inheritable because the *sangley*'s physical origin in someplace not here-but-near was indivisible from his physical body, and in its "pure" form passed out of colonial society with the extinction of that body. Moreover, the fact that the sangley infidel was not allowed to marry meant that there would be no such thing as a "sangley family" in the Philippines, since that family could only be established "back home" in Fujian. In this sense sangley was defined not simply by his economic activity, but by his natal origin outside but near the colonial territory. This meant that there would be no native-born (i.e., Philippine-born) sangley whereas mestizo offspring of Christianized sangley were almost certainly native-born.

In reality, however, the continuous influx of Chinese immigrants prevented Binondo—which originated as a land grant to Catholic Chinese and their mestizo descendants—from becoming an "all-mestizo" community. It is also likely that converted Chinese established dual families in Fujian and Filipinas, with their China-born sons (as well as mestizo sons who were raised in China) subsequently joining them in the Philippines as immigrant "sangley." "Sangley" was basically coded as a first-generation phenomenon, one that theoretically speaking could not be perpetuated in its "pure" form across generations within Spanish Philippine territory.

Unlike men, women migrated to different categories through marriage (Wickberg 1965, 33; Chu 2002b, 47; Chu 2010, 172–73): a mestiza who married an indio (native) or Spaniard changed her status to that of her husband's. But the limits of that categorical migration were set by the sangley: an india who married a sangley remained an india, and was allowed to change her status to mestiza *only upon his death*.[10] Thus, like her offspring, she did not or could not, by marrying a sangley, be considered sangley herself, although she could claim the social status that mestizoness conferred as her inheritance upon his death.

The creation of mestizo as a mediating category illuminates Spanish conceptions of the link between "biology and economics" and Spanish beliefs that different cultures should be kept apart rather than mixed together (Wickberg 1964, 64). The mestizo's blood link to the sangley allowed mestizos—who were thought to inherit not only their fathers' capital but also their "financial aptitude" (86)—to engage in trade. Indeed, mestizos flourished in that occupation and became ascendant as a social group during the near-century-long period between the time when the Chinese were expelled from the colony following the British occupation of Manila in 1762–1764[11] to the time when Chinese immigration was once again tolerated in the 1850s. Chinese mestizos by the mid-nineteenth century were sufficiently differentiated from their increasingly distant Chinese forefathers to have created a distinctly hybrid mestizo culture that combined elements of both Chinese and native cultures. The more prosperous of their kind were able to have their children educated in Manila and in Spain (and to a lesser extent other places in Europe) at a time of substantial institutional and economic reform in both the Philippine colony and the Spanish metropole. Just as important, their blood ties to their native mothers and their territorial nativity in the Philippines meant that they were usually raised as Catholics by their (no less entrepreneurial mestizo or india) mothers and, unlike their fathers, could claim to be born *of* the land and therefore able to acquire land, which is what they did when they faced stiff competition in trade from the Chinese after the 1850s ban on Chinese immigration was lifted.

By the mid-nineteenth century, however, the terms regarding membership in legally defined groupings were also undergoing change in line with the economic transformation of the colony and its deepening integration into the global economy. Conversion was no longer the sine qua non of permanent settlement. The mestizo category was legally abolished in the late 1880s. The term sangley, though still used in public discourse as late as Rizal's *Noli me tangere* (1887), was gradually replaced by the nationality-inflected term *chino* in bureaucratic usage. A few mestizos, such as Ildefonso Tambunting, chose to identify themselves as "Chinese" (Wickberg 1964, 95).

Beginning in 1849, Chinese immigrants were categorized as either transient or permanent. Mobility and settlement, however, continued to be disentangled by the contingencies of colonial policy, as when Spaniards passed a law in 1886 prohibiting Chinese from living permanently in the provinces, and attempted without much success to prohibit them from trading with the Moros (Muslims) in 1888. Regulations concerning nationality in Spanish Philippines considered "persons born in Spanish territory" or persons whose fathers or mothers were Spaniards to be Spaniards. In cases in which a child's parents were foreigners, the parents had to be naturalized or else have "acquired a residence in any town in the monarchy." These applicants had to "declare" before officials that they chose Spanish nationality "in the name of their children." Upon reaching majority, the children had to express their "desire to enjoy the citizenship of Spaniards" (*Official Gazette*, vol. 1, 1903, 189, cited in Jensen 1956, 289). In practice, the Spanish regulations for determining subjecthood were so confusing that they subsequently created problems for the American colonial state.[12]

Their growing affluence as a group enabled mestizos to send their children to school in Manila and abroad, particularly Spain. Mestizos were, along with their native counterparts, some of the most Hispanized among the Philippine population, and because they found their room for political advancement and recognition in the Philippines blocked by Spanish racial prejudice, also among the most politically articulate. Not surprisingly, these mestizos' nascent national consciousness was compounded of varying emphases on claims to belonging by "race," migration to and birth on Spanish/Philippine soil, domicile, and blood ties to the naturales/indios. Filomeno Aguilar's (2005) incisive analysis of *ilustrado* (lit. "enlightened") nationalism reveals the extent to which nineteenth-century racial and wave-migration theories informed these ilustrados' ideas of national origins and boundaries, ideas that occluded the Chinese mestizoness of many of these ilustrados while excluding the "mountain tribes" and the "Chinese."[13] This nationalism created a space for the articulation of Chinese-mestizo interests with those of the *naturales* (natives) (and, less frequently, Chinese-mestizo interests with those of the *chinos*), but *not* the articulation of Chinese interests with those of the naturales, as "Chinese" came to be defined as alien to the national community (Hau 2000b, 140–52). The Chinese and their mestizo offspring in Mindanao had a slightly different trajectory in the nineteenth and early twentieth centuries mainly because they were (an indispensable) part of a "ports and polities" regional maritime network (Abinales 2000a, 196) that only later became increasingly circumscribed by the Philippine nation-state (Abinales 2000b).

Although "mestizo" still appeared in the census of the late nineteenth century, Daniel Doeppers' study (1994, 84) reveals a noticeable decline in the percentage of population classified as mestizos chinos, from 15 percent during 1868–1870 to 13 percent in 1882 to 6.5 percent in 1892 to, most dramatically, a mere 1 percent (among living adult males) in 1903. This decline in relative size of the Chinese mestizo population owed a great deal more to the bureaucratic, and often arbitrary, reclassification of adult males and the decision to baptize infants as "naturales" than to any substantive decline in actual population of people who in earlier times would have been categorized as "mestizos." Doeppers argues that it was the "natural" category that gained the upperhand over "mestizo," as Chinese mestizos officially became non-mestizo "natives" "in order to pay less head tax, secure greater opportunities, and legally assume leadership roles in the civic institutions of the expanded majority population" (86). It should be noted, however, that these reclassifications occurred in some places (notably urban Manila and Cebu) but not in others (Bikol), underscoring the diversity of Philippine society (ibid.).

Richard Chu's study of first-generation Chinese mestizos *Chinese and Chinese Mestizos*, although not in fundamental disagreement with Wickberg's and Doeppers' main thesis, offers nuanced case studies that shed light on the "variegated and constantly changing meanings of identities" (Chu 2010, 10) among the Chinese and Chinese mestizo elite, and complicate the big picture Wickberg paints of the rising antagonism between Chinese mestizos and Chinese, the deepening identification of the Chinese mestizos with the interests of the "naturales," and the eventual disappearance of Chinese mestizos into the new political identity, "Filipino," that they helped define.

Chu argues that the social and political divide between Chinese mestizos and naturales on one side and *sangley/chinos/intsik* on the other side was by no means solely a creation of Spanish colonialism. Equally important, he argues, twentieth-century American and Commonwealth codification and application of citizenship laws, coupled with rising Chinese and Filipino nationalisms and the push-pull factors of large-scale Chinese immigration to the Philippines, were instrumental in crystalizing ethnic divisions as Chinese and Chinese mestizos found their multiple claims, identifications, options and practices—among them bigamy/polygamy, dual families, interracial marriages, contacts with non-Filipinos, sojourn and education in China, having mestizo offspring instead of "pure" Chinese children— increasingly narrowed if not curtailed by the dichotomous, either-or, logic of Chinese, Philippine, and American nation-state-oriented and nationalist discourses and practices.

Thus, while Wickberg's arguments about the "disappearance" of the Chinese mestizos and the rift between mestizos and Chinese generally holds true, as a *longue durée* argument, of Chinese mestizos who were several generations removed from their Chinese forefathers and who lived in the provinces, the life stories of a number of prominent Manila-based first-generation Chinese mestizos, men like Mariano Limjap and Ildefonso Tambunting, illuminate the fact that "ethnic categories are better understood as flowing along a shifting and problematic continuum" (Chu 2010, 14), particularly toward the end of the nineteenth centuries. Like their Chinese merchant fathers (among the most prominent were Joaquin Limjap and Ignacio Sy Jao Boncan), these mestizos could speak or understand not only Spanish and the local Philippine languages, but Hokkien as well; built extensive social and commercial networks with Chinese, natives, and foreigners; traveled constantly and widely; acquired their knowhow in business as much from their China-born fathers as from their locally-born mothers (whether mestiza or india); and educated their children in China, Hong Kong, Spain, and later America.

Although Mariano Limjap identified himself as a "Spanish mestizo" just like Rizal's Capitan Tiago, he represented his Chinese father, a Spanish subject, in business deals and traveled to China and Hong Kong; maintained links with relatives in China; served as a member of the Malolos Congress under the Philippine revolutionary government; and entertained high officials from both China and America. A more unusual case was that of Bonifacio Limtuaco, who spent his childhood in China and later requested a change of legal status from mestizo to *sangley*, appearing in public dressed in "Chinese" clothes.

Chu's account of Mariano Limjap's career as an "ilustrado" offers vital clues to understanding the seemingly contradictory argument made by Michael Cullinane (2003, 363 n. 56) who, in his study of ilustrado politics, noted that Chinese mestizos such as Telesforo Chuidian and Mariano Limjap, although well-educated and socially prominent, were not actually considered "ilustrado," a term that meant "educated" or "enlightened" (Hau 2011). These first-generation Chinese mestizos, precisely because of their continuing connections with the Chinese, may have been perceived as "like us" but also simultaneously "not like us" by the larger society and by other mestizos with roots in the mid-eighteenth to mid-nineteenth century historical phase of Chinese expulsion and mestizo ascendancy (Aguilar 2012a), mestizos, in other words, who were already at a remove from their Chinese ancestry.

While Chinese mestizos like national hero Jose Rizal—technically a fifth-generation mestizo, although his father changed their legal status to "natural"—downplayed, if not rejected, their "Chinese" origins, a cursory look at the Philippine press in the early decades of the twentieth century also bears out the fact that negative attitudes were not necessarily nor universally shared. Pro-Chinese attitudes were evident in the first decade of the American occupation. Articles in *El Renacimiento Filipino* (1911a, 1911b), for example, show that, around the time China became a republic, Filipino nationalists, well-aware of Sun Yat-sen's connections with the Philippine Revolution, were sympathetic to the Chinese and to Chinese nationalism. One article (1911a) praised the Perak-born anarchist Chang King Ngok, who tried to assassinate Admiral Li Chun in China, and was executed by the Qing state, while another (1911b) criticized the racial prejudice (*prejuicio de raza*) that led to the impugning of *insik* "rebel" Juan de Veyra (Eng Kang)'s posthumous reputation.[14]

What these apparently divergent attitudes toward the Chinese suggest is that "Chinese" and "Filipinos" lived in a country in a transitional era where social distinctions among them—lodged in the intangible realm of perception and discourse—existed but were in flux, and Chinese and Filipino nationalisms were not always mutually exclusive. Positive and negative mutual images were part of an existing "pool" of discourses that could be used as circumstances and political agenda required.

The political projects that espoused revolution against Spain and America in fact exceeded the racial categories established by the colonizers and the jus soli and jus sanguinis principles established by international law. This malleability of "race" can be gleaned from Rizal's *El Filibusterismo* (1990, Chapter 33, 248–49), in a chapter where Simoun urges Basilio to join his uprising:

> Cabesang Tales y yo nos reuniremos en la ciudad y nos apoderemos de ella, y usted en los arrabales ocupará los puentes se hará fuerte, estará dispuesto á venir en nuestra ayuda y pasará á cuchillo no solo á la contrarevolucion, sino á todos los varones que se nieguen á seguir con las armas!
>
> —A todos? Balbuceó Basilio con voz sorda.
>
> —A todos! Repitió con voz siniestra Simoun, á todos, indios, mestizos, chinos, españoles, á todos los que se encuentren sin valor, sin energía...Es menester renovar la raza! Padres cobardes solo engendrarán hijos esclavos y no vale la pena destruir para volver á edificar con podridos materiales.

> ..."Cabesang Tales and I will meet in the city and take over it, and you in the suburbs will occupy the bridges and fortify them, and be ready to come to our aid and put to the sword not only the counterrevolution, but all who refuse to join in taking up arms."
>
> "All?" stammered Basilio in a muffled voice.
>
> "All!" repeated Simoun in a sinister voice. "All—indios, mestizos, Chinese, Spaniards, all who are without valor, without vigor. It is necessary to renew the race! Cowardly fathers will only beget slavish sons, and it is not worth destroying, only to rebuild with rotten materials..."

As the above passage shows, the community created by revolution does not limit itself to the terms set by Spanish colonial policy and practice.[15] It is not identity by blood or place of birth or permanent residency that determines who will or will not be spared, but rather, revolutionary action, the individual decision to "join in taking up arms."[16] Indeed, the presence of a "fullblooded" Chinese, Ignacio Paua, in Emilio Aguinaldo's revolutionary army does point to an expanded definition of political membership based on the common endeavor of revolutionary activism beyond the dichotomy between jus soli and jus sanguinis established by international law (Kaisa para sa Kaunlaran 1989).[17] Other than Paua, non-Filipinos—Japanese, Spaniards, Americans (including Black Americans), Cubans, French, Italians, among others—took part in the war against Spain and later America as combatants on the side of Filipino insurgents (Dery 2005).

The idea of membership in a community forged by revolutionary endeavor can be found as well in the constitution of Macario Sakay's Tagalog Republic (Republika ng Katagalugan) (1902; quoted in Ileto 1989, 177), which nationalized the ethnolinguistic category of "Tagalog" by expanding its coverage to encompass all *anak* (children)—a term ambiguous enough to suggest more than the fact of simply being born—of the Kapuluang Katagalugan ("Tagalog archipelago"):

> maputi, maitim, mayaman, dukha, marunong, at mangmang lahat
> ay magkakapantay na walang higit at kulang, dapat magkaisang
> loób, maaring humigit sa dunong, sa yaman, sa ganda, dapwa't hindi
> mahihigitan sa pagkatao ng sino man, at sa paglilingkod nang kahit
> alin.

> Fair, dark, rich, poor, learned, and unlettered, all are equal, no more, no
> less. All must be united [lit., must be of one *loob*]. Some may have more
> wisdom, wealth, beauty, but not in any way that exceeds the humanity
> [pagkatao] of any one, and all in the service of whatever cause.

This inclusiveness extended to the provisions of the 1899 Malolos Constitution of the Philippine revolutionary government, which was quite radical in its use of the principle of residency rather than "blood" and place of birth as the basis for citizenship, as shown by Filomeno V. Aguilar's pioneering study (2011a). Drawing inspiration from the Spanish Civil Code and forged out of the exigencies of revolution, the Malolos Constitution made the principle of jus soli or citizenship by place of birth the basis for extending citizenship to foreigners (see Aguilar 2011a, 88–90). Persons born on Philippine territory were considered Filipinos. Even more interesting is the Constitution's residency requirement for citizenship. Persons who had resided continuously for two years in any place in the Philippines and who undertook the duties of citizenship such as paying taxes were also eligible for Philippine citizenship. Invoking the principle of domicile—here, domicile is not defined in terms of the now-common idea of permanent residency, but rather, the minimal requirement of two years of residence—made the Malolos Constitution the most politically inclusive of all Philippine constitutions (ibid.). The Malolos Constitution is also remarkable in another respect: it did not stipulate that naturalized Filipinos citizens had to renounce their former nationality and swear allegiance to the Philippine state.

Written in the context of national consolidation, the Constitution sought to encompass all inhabitants within Philippine territory under a single government (ibid.). The pragmatics of establishing and running a state, in effect, nurtured a cosmopolitan vision of citizenship that did not think or seek to colonize and channel all forms of sentiments and attachments to place into political loyalty to only one territorially bounded nation-state. Instead, it sought to draw on all available resources and humanpower to help create the new nation-state. The Philippine revolution may not have necessarily spared the "Chinese" from being the targets of violence, but its novelty lay in its pragmatic view of what a Filipino community could be, one in which anybody who resided for a time in the Philippines was to be treated as de facto part of the Republic. Aguilar (ibid.) argues that this kind of thinking was well ahead of its time, not least in the fact that it did not problematize its citizens' sense of belonging and attachments, which could (and were allowed to) be multiple. Residency already constituted proof of a person's involvement in, and contribution to, the affairs of the nation. But, alas, the Malolos Constitution's radically inclusive vision of citizenship was cut short by the American occupation and remains unrealized even now, in the era of so-called globalization.

Americans allowed Chinese free rein to travel all over the Philippines, but applied the Chinese Exclusion Act to the Philippines in an effort to prevent Chinese labor immigration and "to preserve the Islands for the natives thereof" (*Congressional Record* vol. 35, 3801, cited in Jensen 1956, 110). A citizenship bill debated in the Philippine Assembly in 1916 sought to bar "Asiatics" from acquiring citizenship (for a nuanced account of the debate and the uncertain fate of the bill, see Aguilar 2011a). The application of the Chinese Exclusion Act created some confusion and controversy over what "Chinese," "Chinese persons," "Chinese race" and "a person of Chinese descent" meant (123). Americans applied the principle of jus soli to "Spanish subjects," but drew on the principle of bloodline to define who counted as Chinese. Thus, a Chinese was anyone whose parents were both Chinese and those whose fathers *or* mothers were "pure Chinese." One who had "predominantly" Chinese blood, even when this was mixed with white blood, was counted as Chinese. By the terms of the exclusion law, the "Chinese" could not be naturalized because they were not eligible for citizenship (Jensen 1956, 290), and only merchants (along with travelers, diplomats, and students) and their families were allowed re-entry into the Philippines. The net effect was to reinforce, like the Spaniards, the conflation of "Chineseness" with mercantile capitalism; but unlike the early Spanish treatment of the "Chinese" as an essentially first-generation attribute, American regulations cemented the link between "Chinese" and "merchant," and made this identification something that was to be inherited across generations.

But again, reality eluded the strictures of theory. Chinese exclusion helped institutionalize the split-family system whereby Chinese men married women in China, and had their eldest son brought to the Philippines at a young age. The eldest son, now a migrant, would go back to China to get married and in turn had his eldest son brought over. Furthermore, the exclusion law did not prevent new Chinese immigration because "paper sons" claiming fictive kinship to "Chinese merchants" could circumvent the restrictions, and some Chinese opted to smuggle themselves in through Sulu (with the help of enterprising Moros).

Far more crucially, American-era judicial interpretation read the law in different ways under different contexts. Filomeno Aguilar's close reading (2011a) of American-era Philippine court records reveals that, apart from ethnic self-identification, place of birth and domicile, especially in the case of those who resided abroad (China) before reaching the age of majority, were important factors that informed Supreme Court decisions that upheld jus soli citizenship. Aguilar traces the history of jus soli citizenship to the landmark rulings in the case of Go Siaco and Benito Muñoz in 1911. Go Siaco had been born in the Philippines, and had lived for more than thirty-five years in the country with his native mother, while Muñoz, whose Chinese father resided in the Philippines, was himself raised in China but had expressed "honest" intention to return to the Philippines (98–99). Selection of country of residence by adults, along with familial ties and personal sentiments, also figured in Supreme Court rulings in favor of Chinese mestizos. Equally interesting is the landmark 1917 Supreme Court ruling that a child born of Chinese parents in the Philippines was a Filipino citizen (Jensen 1956, 290; see the discussion in Aguilar 2011a, 103–4). Thus, while the exclusion law remained in effect until 1940, judicial interpretation selectively applied jus soli to extend citizenship to the Chinese and Chinese mestizo.

The Philippine Commonwealth, however, chose to uphold Chinese exclusion and made jus sanguinis the basis of Philippine citizenship, barring Chinese from owning land, exploiting Philippine natural resources and operating public utilities.[18] Postwar Philippine judicial interpretations of citizenship claims, backed by the disciplinary mechanisms and punitive force of the state, were crucial in constructing and cementing ethnic boundaries based on a dichotomous logic. From the late 1930s to the early postwar period, nationalist attempts to (re)shape bodies of "Filipinos" and "Chinese" especially through families, schools, work, and legislation would have crucial incremental effects in defining and solidifying ethnic differences between Filipinos and Chinese.

In the postwar period, various incentives that gave Filipinos special preference and priority in obtaining business license also worked to curb

Chinese economic activities (Appleton 1960, 155). The difference is that while mestizos used to be exempted from the restrictions imposed on their Chinese fathers, the principle of bloodline could be used against the mestizos as their "Chineseness" (and all the negative economic, political and cultural associations surrounding it) came to overshadow their Filipino ties. Mestizos could, in the past, elect Filipino citizenship upon maturity, but in 1947 the Supreme Court, citing the 1909 Chinese Nationality Act, held that a Filipino woman who married a Chinese citizen took her husband's nationality, and for that reason, her mestizo progeny were considered Chinese. But since the gate to citizenship was policed by judicial interpretation, decisions were made on a case-to-case basis. While there were judges who applied the 1947 Supreme Court decision to bar mestizos from Philippine citizenship, some mestizos continued to acquire citizenship upon reaching twenty-one-years-old (a discrepancy noted by Weightman 1959, 215).

In sum, despite the reduction of legal categories to Spanish, Filipinos and Chinese in the late nineteenth century, Chinese-mestizo identity in everyday life was "multiple," "ambiguous" and "flexible" (Chu 2002b, 46; 2010, 13–14, 114–15, 258–59, 265–66). Renewed large-scale immigration after 1850, coupled with innovations in steamboat technology, the lifting of travel bans that had hitherto restricted Chinese mobility within the colony and between the colony and China, and the Qing state's efforts to mobilize "overseas Chinese" and their money for its agenda, ensured that mestizos, especially first-generation and second-generation ones and depending on where they lived, how they were educated, how involved their fathers were in their upbringing, and what social and business opportunities they had to mix with "Chinese" and "Filipinos," did not necessarily "disappear" (a trajectory taken by many of the earlier mestizo generation of 1740–1850), but could maintain links with both Filipinos and Chinese across generations and territories, and claim Chineseness or Filipinoness (or both) as circumstances allowed or required.

Various Chinese nationality laws based on jus sanguinis since 1909; the establishment of Chinese institutions such as schools, churches, chambers of commerce, and clan and other organizations; and the nationalist Kuomintang's (followed, in the 1930s, the Chinese Communist Party's) active interest in "overseas Chinese" (regardless of their citizenship) laid the groundwork for attempts to (re)sinicize the "Chinese" and their mestizo offspring. The first four decades of the twentieth century had witnessed a substantial increase in the immigration of women and children from China as immediate relatives of Chinese merchants who were already based in Manila, and, after the Sino-Japanese war broke out, as war refugees. It was during these decades that stable communities of "Chinese families"—made up of "Chinese" fathers and mothers and their offspring—first became a sociological fact.

Chu traces the usage of the Hokkien term for mestizo, *tsut-si-a*, to Chinese nationalist efforts to reclaim the mestizo in the politically tumultuous 1920s and 1930s (Chu 2002a, 61). *Tsut-si-a* functioned as a term of selective inclusion and exclusion that drew on the discourse of blood descent and intermarriage, but the boundaries were laid down not simply by racial distinctions, but also by shifting cultural, political, and circumstantial definitions of Chineseness in terms of family names, language, ancestral links to *Tengsua* (Tangshan, "Tang mountains"), residential space, school ties, religious affiliations, business networks, knowledge and practice of "Chinese culture" (however variably this was defined), relations with "Chinese" and "non-Chinese," and responses to political events taking place in China and the Philippines. A *tsut-si-a* who speaks Hokkien, lives among *lanlang* ("our people"), marries a *lanlang* or another *tsut-si-a*[19] (for example in Cebu City), is educated in a Chinese school, does business or worships with *lanlang*, and follows the events in China or Chinatown, is considered one of "our people," just as a Filipino raised as "Chinese" is considered *lanlang*. *Tsut-si-a* may be invoked in an inclusionary way in instances where a mestizo is part of one's business and social network. A mestizo whose Filipino connections are a business asset may also be considered *lanlang*. In Vigan, the capital of the northern province of Ilocos Sur, for example, some of those who are considered "Chinese" by Filipinos actually call themselves mestizo (Miyahara 2008b).

Blood or race assumes explanatory force mainly in discussions of a mestizo's upbringing and life choices, especially as these bear on the mestizo's ability (or inability) to speak Hokkien and socially interact with *lanlang*. Being accepted socially as Chinese does not preclude the fact that what or who counts as "Chinese" and what "Chineseness" means may change over the years and according to circumstances. Rather than signaling a fixed conception of primordial attachment, multifarious ideas of *lanlang* and *tsut-si-a* take shape within the context of citizenship regimes in both Philippines and China, geopolitics, homeland (in the plural) influences, and the contingencies of everyday life and social interactions across the seas and generations.

By the postwar period, on the one hand, Philippine laws and regulations (passed by both central and local governments) aimed at preventing Chinese from practicing professions and owning land further drove the Chinese deeper into their economic niche even as retail and other nationalization laws forced some Chinese into unregulated areas like light industries or complicity in the netherworld of corruption and extortion that turned the alienness of the "Chinese" into a profitable informal business for government officials, military personnel, and professional criminals alike. On the other hand, Cold War geopolitical and strategic considerations as they affected the Chinese assumed institutional form in the Treaty of Amity between the Philippines and Republic of China within the context of America's "Free Asia" containment policy (Wickberg 2006, 22).[20] This 1947 treaty guaranteed the property rights of Chinese citizens and gave Taipei the right of supervision of Chinese schools. The Kuomintang and the embassy of the Republic of China, and the umbrella community organizations created under their guidance, played a visible and preeminent role in politically and culturally policing the Chinese community, with the active backing and cooperation of the Philippine government and military, which relied on the KMT for information about the political activities of the Philippine Chinese.

The Kuomintang saw itself as a government in exile and the "true" legatee of the Chinese Republic. Its attempts at sinicizing the Chinese community in the Philippines took place alongside its efforts to "nationalize" the Taiwanese and other "overseas Chinese." In the 1950s to early 1960s, the government's promotion of Chinese culture functioned mainly to reinforce the myth of cultural continuity and shared origin among Chinese and overseas Chinese. Later, reacting to the Cultural Revolution and the political turmoil in Hong Kong, the KMT began promoting an increasingly conservative version of "traditional Chinese culture" through the disciplinary mechanisms of school, media, family and workplace (Chun 1995, 30).

The first two decades of the post-independence period thus saw mestizo identity becoming far more circumscribed by the either-or logic that distinguished Filipino from Chinese. By that time, the descendants of Chinese mestizos who had become Hispanized in the nineteenth century had become Americanized in the twentieth, and formed the social base of a national oligarchy whose wealth was based on its acquisition of friar lands during the American period and whose power came from its participation in American-introduced electoral politics (Anderson 1998). Having effectively distanced themselves from their "Chinese" origins, these erstwhile mestizos could be distinguished from other members of the elite only by the Hokkien suffix "Co" in their surnames (e.g. Cojuangco) and the occasional appearance of *chinito* features in their descendants. Newspapers of the time routinely used words like "Sinos" as a blanket term to refer to naturalized and alien Chinese, and to Chinese as well as Chinese mestizos (Miyahara 1997, 75). While some mestizos came to be seen as and lumped together with the "Chinese," the term *mestizo* itself in popular usage was stripped of its sociological and historical reference to the now alien and devalued "Chinese" and came to be increasingly ascribed to Filipinos of mainly white (American or European) ancestry whose hybridity indexed the hegemonic power and prestige of "white" America/Europe.

The Logic and Limits of Civic Conversion

The long-term historical shift in the status of the Chinese mestizo is encapsulated in the following exchange from *The Sultanate* between Ric and his cousin Maning (Angliongto 1969, 120):

> Maning told Ric, "If you want to be a Filipino, try hard to prepare yourself to be a good one. Show to the Filipino people that those who come from Chinese stock are as good citizens if not better than those of Malayan, Indonesian, Spanish, or even American extraction."
>
> "Yes, Maning," said Ric. "I'll try hard to do as you say. But what is a Filipino, a good Filipino?"
>
> Maning was silent for a good while. Finally, he answered, reflectively. "The measure of a good Filipino is not the color of his skin or his eyes or his hair or the type of blood that flows in his veins. The accident of birth is minor. The true measure is the heart that feels, the mental attitude and, most important of all, the way he behaves."
>
> "I believe deep in my heart that the Filipino race is one of the finest in Asia," said Ric with feeling. "I wish to belong to this race which was produced by the comingling [sic] of Malayan, Arab, Chinese, Spanish, English, American, Japanese, Hindu and Indonesian blood. But why are the Chinese mestizos discriminated against? They are treated as second class citizens. Look at the handsome Spanish mestizo or the American mestiza. The Chinese mestizo or mestiza is deglamorized. They [Spanish or American mestizos] are glamorized. Is it the manner of speaking or the shape of the eyes or the texture and color of the skin?"
>
> "The texture or the color of the skin of the Chinese mestizo or mestiza," said Maning, "is the finest in the world—whatever the blend. It is smooth and devoid of blemish."[21]

The above passage shows how, as the word *mestizo* was becoming selectively desinicized and resinicized, Chinese mestizos found themselves living with competing public discourses and disciplinary mechanisms of

Filipinization and Sinicization and their either-or logic. The flexibility which had once enabled the mestizo to flourish in the colonial Philippines had become problematic.

But the passage above also shows how defensiveness on the part of the Chinese mestizo can quickly shade off into racism: thank God for the smooth, unblemished skin of the fair-skinned mestizo/a! Unable to identify with their "Chinese" parent or ancestor yet also despising their darker-skinned compatriots, these mestizos position themselves on the upper rungs of Philippine society by identifying with the values and standards of their "white" and Spanish and American colonizers. In its virulent form, this white identification enables the mestizos to look down on both Chinese and Filipinos. The irony, of course, is that in the eyes of racist Spaniards and Americans, these mestizos are not white enough, and never will be.

In *The Sultanate*, mestizoness is thematically rendered, in terms borrowed from sociological discourse, as experientially fraught in-betweenness, in other words, an "identity crisis." Middle son Ricardo feels himself caught in the middle of two cultures: he "sometimes felt that his person was rooted in China" even though he was "loyal to the land of his birth" (Angliongto 1969, 6). Ricardo's trip to China is illuminating, but it also quickly disabuses him of any illusion he may have had in considering himself "rooted" in China: "Home to me, I realized, was not here in Mother China but there in the Philippines" (83). His acquaintance Commodore Chan's exhortation that a "Chinese is always Chinese anywhere in the globe" notwithstanding, Ric finds that his Mandarin is not understood in Shanghai. He deplores arranged marriages that turn Chinese women into "victims of petrified customs and traditions" (110). Ric's journey to "Mother China" is basically a rite of exorcism aimed at expelling the personal demon of double consciousness that keeps him tethered to "Mother China" even as he calls Philippines "home."

Bidding "farewell to Mother China," Ric is determined to prove himself a natural-born Filipino who inherits his Filipinoness from his naturalized mestizo father. To some extent, Ric's "assimilation" is a function of his physical distance from Manila, where the majority of Chinese are concentrated; provincial Chinese are considered by scholars to be more readily assimilable than the Manila Chinese (see, for example, the arguments by A. Tan 1988, 182 and C. See 1989, 326–27). Davao, where *The Sultanate* is set, was a frontier zone where Chinese lived alongside Filipino Christian settlers and the numerous and economically competitive Japanese migrants in the prewar era, and was thus a land where the foreignness of the "Chinese" was not as visibly marked as elsewhere.

For *The Sultanate*, assimilation is a sociological process, but far more important, it is an individual decision.[22] Ric recalls that by blood and place of birth, his father Generoso could have claimed the land of Siasi and, by extension, the Sulu sultanate, through his Tausug mother. But rather than assert his Filipinoness on the basis of either blood or territorial nativity, Ric opts to build a "sultanate in the hearts of the people of his adopted land":

> It was a sultanate of a different kind, unlike the principalities and
> kingdoms of the old days. There was neither scepter nor crown nor
> throne. There were subjects, the people, co-workers and friends
> and wards over whom the ruler had no power of life and death. His
> privilege to rule was premised on the love of the people for him and
> his concern for their welfare. (149)

The Sultanate argues that the true meaning of citizenship does not lie in the standard definitions of citizenship by either "blood" or the "accident of birth"; these definitions merely enforce the idea of citizenship as something ascribed, something involuntary. Nor is it a question of attaining the right social status. The "true measure" is the "heart, mental attitude and action" (120) of a "good citizen." Citizenship is matter of choice, of *earning* the right to be considered Filipino. The biographical note on the book cover presents the author, Angliongto, as an exemplar of assimilation: born in Davao and married to a Filipina doctor, he served in the Philippine Army as a lieutenant, was president of the Davao Jaycees and Davao Citrus, Cacao and Coffee Planters' Association and member of various civic and business organizations.

Ric differs from his brother Mariano in the career paths they choose to assert their claim of belonging. In Mariano's case, this has meant achieving the kind of large-scale economic success that allows him to breach the social boundaries that separate Chinese from Filipinos. Money—lots of it—allows him to lift himself into the ranks of the Filipino elite, much as money had once enabled the mestizos to challenge the social-status hierarchy based on lineage considerations in Spanish Philippines (Wickberg 1964, 87). Secure in his standing as a tycoon, with businesses spread across "Manila, Tokyo, Luzon, Visayas and Mindanao" (241) providing employment for Filipinos, Mariano offers himself as an example of successful assimilation by virtue of his faithful execution of his civic obligations as a Filipino citizen:

> "We have been assimilated in Philippine society. I married a *Tagala*.
> I have sent all my children to the best Philippine schools. Most of
> my friends are Filipinos. I'm a commissioned officer in the armed

forces, a reserved officer. I belong to most of the Filipino civic clubs. I have contributed generously to charitable causes. I have paid taxes religiously. I have contributed in a modest measure to the progress of this country by establishing industries and furnishing employment to a number of Filipinos. Are these not proof enough that I'm a good Filipino?" (155)

Mariano in effect illustrates that being rich and successful—in other words, becoming the living embodiment of the proverbial "rich Chinese"—is one way of being a good citizen. While Mariano is enthusiastic in discharging his responsibilities as a "good Filipino," he remains aware that his actions "will not erase the prejudice against the Chinese mestizo" (ibid.):

"Walk down the street—the policeman will treat you as a Chinese. You go to the government offices: Customs, Internal Revenue, Labor Office, even the judicial offices—they will either consider you a Chinese or a Filipino second class citizen." (Ibid.)

Mariano's cynical solution is to get rich because "[i]t's your money they [Filipinos] respect" (ibid.). The best that can be done is not to "change the world" (154) but live up to the popular association of Chineseness with business sagacity and industry.

But the idea that money can "buy" respectability cannot completely purge money of its other, negative associations with exploitation and inequality, and serves only to further reinforce popular assumptions about the stereotypical "Chinese" big capitalist. Partly motivated by sibling rivalry, Ric opts for "personal recognition" rather than "subordinating [the] self to the one running the business for purposes of cooperation" (158).[23] He sets out to prove that he is a "good Filipino" who loves his country and professes absolute loyalty to it by pursuing a different set of goals and actions. The arena he works in is not the economy, but ideology. Having witnessed China turn Communist, Ric undertakes to prevent the same thing from happening in the Philippines. In this regard, and despite his misgivings about having to "masquerade" as "Chinese" so soon after he has mentally renounced his allegiance, he works as a counter-espionage agent, spying among the Chinese community to identify the Chinese communists who smuggle themselves into the Philippines through Mindanao, and who "mix with Chinese residents" and "infiltrate schools" (177).

Ric sees his service as a way of "earning" his citizenship by acting like a "true Filipino."[24] This entails working to advance the Cold War anti-communist agenda of the state. As an "insider," Ric utilizes his linguistic skills and kinship and social connections with the *lanlang* to ferret out subversives. Being a "good Filipino" means weeding out the "bad Chinese," while simultaneously advocating the integration of the "good Chinese" into the Philippine mainstream. Expressing dissatisfaction with the KMT branch for having been "infiltrated by our enemies" and for being captive to the factionalism of the Philippine Chinese community, Ric opts to work directly with the Philippine state, acting almost literally as its eyes and ears among the Chinese community. This identification with the Philippine state means embracing its cold war logic and practices without recourse to the (self-interested) mediation of the "foreign" KMT and Chinese embassy.

Even Ric's romantic life is shaped by the lines drawn by geopolitics. Ric falls in love with Lileng, who is as patriotically attached to the Republic of China as he is to the Philippines. Their love of country brings them together and sunders them. Ric finds stimulation in his debates with the intellectually formidable leftist Chin Fong, but he is not (or perhaps cannot bring himself to be) sexually attracted to her. Romantic passion is ignited by, and in turn stokes, nationalist passion, and plays itself out within the scope and limits of the Philippines-Taiwan Cold War partnership.

The irony, of course, is that the success of Ric's mission depends on his ability to appear Chinese and be considered Chinese by the Chinese. It is his "Chineseness" that makes him an asset to the state. As an agent of the state, he must speak Hokkien and live as "Chinese" so as to be taken as Chinese not just by the Chinese but also by Filipinos. Since nobody, not even agents of the state other than his direct Filipino superiors, knows that he is working for the state, his public service is kept secret from the public. Not surprisingly, he is (mis)taken for Chinese by other agents of the Philippine state, and finds himself prey to extortion and harassment by certain Filipino agents of the state. At the same time, his return "to the fold" of the Chinese community puts him at risk of being branded as a "traitor" and embroiled in the internecine conflicts that belie the myth of homogeneity and clannishness of that community. His father, accused of being both a Japanese collaborator and pro-Chiang Kai-shek, had been a casualty of enemies unknown: Ric has not been able to determine whether the assassination was undertaken by communists, tong (secret society) members, blackmarketeers or rival businessmen.

The demands of secrecy ensure that Ric's motives and actions are understood and appreciated only by himself and by a few people. In this sense, while misunderstandings by others put his life at risk, Ric may still rely on one or two people other than himself to provide verification and recognition of his good citizenship. But even though *The Sultanate* grants

Ric this lifeline of external verification and recognition by the Philippine authorities, his primary source of verification is, apart from Ric himself, the reader of the novel. The reader's access to Ric's thoughts and actions enables the reader to bear witness to the sincerity of Ric's motives and intentions. The novel puts the reader on a par with Ric as the principal sources of authority on the subject of Ric the good citizen (or on Ric as the citizen subject par excellence), for not even Ric's bosses can see into Ric's heart and read his mind.

In effect, the reader is the one who reads Ric "like a book." The novel's main function is to verify Ric's motives and actions as "good citizen." The fact that it goes through such lengths to do so points to an irresoluble structural indeterminacy at the heart of citizenship. The patriotism that informs the concept and practice of citizenship is institutionally and ritually promoted by schools, government offices, and business settings. Citizenship is thus a representational practice, something that is embodied and enacted by persons in their relationships with other persons. For this reason, it is deeply implicated in power relations, identifications, and sources of authority beyond the concrete "here and now" of a given encounter, even as its meaning and practice are bound to specific contexts of speaking and acting.

One claims and exercises citizenship by what one says and does under specific circumstances. Yet the meaning and practice of citizenship also exceed these contexts of saying and doing because citizenship is structured by affect, and by the attendant questions of sincerity and intentionality, which are neither transparently accessible nor readily verifiable by speech or action. Acquiring citizenship in the Philippines is loosely modeled on religious conversion in that it entails a break with the past through the adoption of a new political identity, and renunciation of allegiance to one political entity in favor of the transfer of loyalty to another.[25] Since this political conversion is constitutively personal and assumes a transformation that takes place within a person, it is primarily certified by the feelings and motives of the convert himself or herself. The convert is the ultimate source of authority on herself.

Sincerity is publicly proclaimed by the applicant, who formally signifies his or her desire or willingness to acquire citizenship through a statement before the authorities. The applicant is also required by law to pay newspapers to publish his or her petition for citizenship, and is backed by the sworn statements of witnesses. In the public petition, the prospective candidate offers his or her life as a story, an orderly arrangement of biographical details, complete with physical description and family history. This life story follows the testimonial format[26] of a confessional narrative of acculturation and conversion based on the evidence of the candidate's duration of residency, occupation, linguistic proficiency in English and at least one Philippine language, upbringing of children and "social mingling" with Filipinos, adherence to the Constitution,[27] and declared intention to "become a citizen of the Philippines" and "renounce absolutely and forever all allegiance and fidelity to any foreign prince, potentate, state or sovereignty and particularly to Nationalist China." Also included is the applicant's income tax return.[28] To become a citizen, one must lay out one's life like an open book for all to read as a condition of admittance to a political and cultural community.

But if, as Webb Keane has argued (2006, 317), "in being sincere, I am not only producing words that are transparent to my interior states but am producing them for you; I am making myself—as a private and inner self—available for you in the form of public, external expressions," this public accountability of the self can only be externally manifested through the materiality of the political convert's words and deeds, not just what is said or done, but how, where, before whom, in what language and behavioral context. In a circumscribed religious community, the sincerity of words and deeds is not a deeply problematic issue because the authority to decide on the question of authenticity rests not simply on one's neighbors and the earthbound religious authorities, but on one's personal relationship with an omniscient God. In a secular context, however, the authority rests primarily on an all-too-fallible state and its representatives. Another difference is that the religious convert is conceived as a porous self, susceptible to as well as receptive of outside (for example supernatural) influences, whereas the secular era valorizes a fortress-like autonomous individual whose thoughts and motivations, at least since Darwin and Freud, are not so readily fathomable.

The idea that no one, not the public witnesses, not even the political convert herself, has unmediated access to the convert's "intentions" means that words and deeds cannot always be taken as direct expression of the sincerity of one's "change of heart." Even if people acted as if they felt attached to the community, how is one to know for sure? The "true measure" of political conversion is tested at its very limits—that is, by the martyrdom of the citizen. A citizen signifies her sincerity through her actual sacrifice of her life and all that she values. This logic accounts for why life-and-death situations such as those of the Philippine revolution and the Pacific war have been held up as examples of how "good Chinese" can ally themselves with Filipino patriots (Cristobal 1965, 12; Taruc 1953, 76).

But in the absence of such life-and-death situations, and because real people do not always lend themselves to being "read like a book" (and even if they did, the problem of reading them "correctly" remains), the structural indeterminacy of conversion means that conversion itself resists closure: without the guarantee of an all-knowing final authority, civic conversion is inherently ambiguous and always incomplete, because the convert's faith or loyalty must be determined and affirmed and tested again and again. Not even religious discourse is completely free of this ambivalence.[29] Spaniards energetically converted the infidel sangley to Catholicism while in the same breath bemoaning the "insincerity" of the converts. Colonial texts abound with Spanish criticism of the base, instrumental motives of the Chinese for converting, motives rooted in Chinese desire to avail themselves of the privileges accruing to converts, such as marriage, permanent settlement, mobility, and economic advancement, while continuing to practice ancestor worship (see, for example, the sources cited in Jensen 1956, 30–31; Weightman 1959, 372). The Spaniards offered material incentives for conversion but worried that these rewards would overshadow the spiritual goal of salvation. Spanish ambivalence cannot be explained away by retailing empirical instances of Chinese "insincerity" because indeterminacy is intrinsic to the discourse of conversion. Similarly, charges of "citizenship by convenience" have been leveled at the Chinese when they apply for citizenship, even as the Chinese are enjoined to "assimilate" themselves into the Filipino national community. In a secular context, the foundation of "truth" about oneself rests on the very individual whose thoughts and actions are not always transparent even to herself.

The structural indeterminacy of civic conversion creates the perennial public problem of how to tell "good Chinese" apart from "bad Chinese." In religious conversion, sincerity, while reflective of the "inner state" of the convert, is not necessarily linked to the question of a convert's virtue, since it only requires that the person *desire* to be virtuous. Religious conversion is only the first step to virtue. But in political conversion, the question of authenticity is conflated with the question of virtue, since civic conversion hinges on a person's prior qualifications for being granted citizenship. The transfer of personal political loyalty requires official recognition of a person's irreproachable conduct. Therefore, from the viewpoint of the state, accepting a "good Chinese" as Filipino simultaneously entails justifying the rejection of "bad Chinese." But who has the authority to decide?

In post-independence Philippines, the authority accorded to judicial interpretation puts the power of decision in the hands of individual judges. Given that decision is made on a case-to-case basis, judges routinely assess individual character and qualification on the basis of an examination (in effect, a close reading) of the individual's life and career. And because intentions and allegiance are not self-evident even from words and deeds, judges find themselves looking "beyond" the external appearance and acts of the individual to discover the "true meaning" and proof of integration. A naturalized citizen could be deprived of citizenship because of a legal technicality or proof of bad conduct. Moreover, in line with the practice elsewhere in the world, naturalized citizens remained on "probation" for the duration of their lifetimes; only upon their deaths can their descendants acquire the rights of "natives" (Jiang 1974, 95). Such attempts to construct, imagine, and police the intentions of the Chinese highlight the very fine line between judging an individual by her merit alone and judging an individual on the basis of her group membership, a line that, it so happens, is frequently breached. Civic conversion rests on individual decision alone, and precisely because this decision is not transparently readable, it can be used to justify exclusion based on that individual's membership in an alien group.

Some judges, in fact, having prejudged the Chinese Question, "prided themselves in not having approved a single case of naturalization" by routinely invoking technicalities such as Chinese petitioner's failure "to show that the laws of his country permit Filipinos to be naturalized therein as citizens" and the fact that "no evidence had been adduced to prove that the petition and notice of hearing had been posted in a public and conspicuous place in the office of the clerk of the court or in the building where said office is located" (quoted in Yuyitung 1966, 36).

The community defined by citizenship emerges out of the distinctions between "good" and "bad" Chinese. These distinctions are not mere descriptions or explanations of reality, but are rooted in the structural indeterminacy of civic conversion on which citizenship is founded. Scholars on the Philippine Chinese have noted this preoccupation with distinguishing "good" from "bad" Chinese in their analysis of historical discourses on the Chinese without accounting for the underlying logic of this obsession (for example, Weightman 1959, 372). *The Sultanate* replicates the logic by contrasting its protagonists, the Dy Angcos, to unscrupulous businessmen and criminal hoarders and profiteers like Taba "Fatty" Uy. Ric proves that he is a good Filipino by turning over the "bad Chinese" to the police while urging the integration of the "good Chinese." This Manichean bifurcation of Chinese into good and bad "humanizes" individual Chinese (Cristobal 1965, 12) while also reinforcing negative images of the Chinese as a group, thereby aggravating the public demonizing of the Chinese (cf. Yu 2001, 191). For on the one hand, there are always good and bad people, and to say so would be stating something so obvious and commonplace as to be meaningless. On the other hand, because of the abiding concern with intention and the lack of direct, unmediated access to such intention, the Chinese are routinely judged not only by their words and actions as individuals, but also according to their perceived membership in a group, the "Chinese," with all the patterned behavior and positive and negative assumptions ascribed to this group.

In his effort to show the complexity of the "Chinese," for example, Ric's disquisition on the question of Chinese assimilation results in conceptual hairsplitting of the most elaborate sort: metropolitan or "Ongpin" Chinese and the provincial or rural Chinese, among whom are Chinese educated in Chinese schools and those in public schools, the native-born and the immigrants; "those who came to the Philippines before the Commonwealth but before the outbreak of the Second World War, [and] those who came after the communists took over the mainland China," the latter being the "overstaying Chinese"; "based on attitudes and feelings toward their adopted country, we have the prewar and the postwar Chinese"; and the "sort of" new generation created after the war (Angliongto 1969, 182–84).

What this shows is that the act of accepting an individual as "stranger" or "one of us" depends on the past history, power, and standing of the one who is judged and the ones who judge, as well as their relations to each other. These relations are not just between individuals, but are shaped as well by institutions and categories, including discourses of "Chineseness" and the representational practices of inclusion and exclusion. A (Chinese-) mestizo congressman may well count Chinese among his friends and neighbors and be on good terms with them while voting in Congress for economic legislation against the "Chinese" as a group. Or a Chinese-hating Filipino may nevertheless love Chinese food or find Chinese women sexually desirable. How "freely" felt is love of country (whether "China"—claimed by which government, the Republic of China or the People's Republic of China?—or the Philippines), given the discrimination and disincentives of the state and public against Chinese? And is one to be blamed for choosing to remain Chinese given the government's complicity with KMT efforts to "resinicize" the Chinese community?

There is in fact no single authority to decide what counts as good and bad Chinese. For this reason, "good" and "bad" depend as much, if not more so, on circumstances and the people and institutions that arrogate to themselves the right to define who is a "good" or "bad" Chinese as on the apparent "sincerity" and "intentions" of the Chinese.

The Sultanate seeks to define citizenship in ways that go beyond the ascriptive, involuntary aspects of membership in a national community by birth or blood. However, its affirmation of a voluntarist idea of citizenship based on contract and consent comes up against a number of irresoluble issues, not least of which is the nature of the state to whom the "good citizen" fulfills his duties and obligations. What happens when the state itself lacks legitimacy, or its claim to represent the Filipino national community is challenged by elements of the society on whose behalf the state claims to speak and act?

As it turned out, unfolding events in the late 1960s and early 1970s were to overtake *The Sultanate* and its logic of civic conversion.

Filipino readers in 1969 and the early seventies will find in *Sultanate* protagonist Ric's letters from China much to remind them of the political turmoil in pre-martial law Philippines—the "nepotism, partisan politics, cliques, graft and corruption" (Angliongto 1969, 91), the low morale of people, the "loss of faith in government" (119). The backcover of *The Sultanate* explicitly establishes this parallel: "The letters reproduced in the chapter, 'Farewell to Mother China'...will constitute, for the alert reader, a recall, not partial but total, of student demos today, a constant feature of our national life and the national scene." In his letters from China, Ric is critical of the Chinese Nationalist government's crackdown on demonstrations (104), and observes the loss of confidence in the government and the breakdown of law and order across China (103–7).

By directing the reader to link the events in China to those in the Philippines, *The Sultanate* uses China to serve as a warning of what may happen if things are allowed to run their course. But while Ric proves himself worthy of being "Filipino" by embracing the state's anti-communist agenda, his sympathy for the plight of the Chinese people, and his intellectual attraction to the impassioned leftist Chin Fong would have provided enough ammunition for agents of the state to make a case about "subversion."[30] In the novel, Ric's status as a counter-espionage agent does not grant him immunity from harassment by venal government officials, and the secrecy of his mission precludes his being able to defend himself against accusations of subversion (205). Appearing as a "genuine" *intsik*, he is taken as such, and lives in fear of Chinese reprisals, since his job of spying on the Chinese community and denouncing Chinese subversives to the state makes him a "traitor" in the eyes of the Chinese. In a conversation with his superior Frank, Ric expresses his frustration by pointing to the possibility of "the majority of the Chinese in the Philippines, including the naturalized Filipinos, becom[ing] sympathizers of Red China because they are driven to it" by Filipino extortionists (208).

The irony of Ric's (and Angliongto's) identification with the anti-communist state is that the legitimacy of that state was increasingly challenged by the radicalization of the Philippine youth and Philippine politics in general in the late 1960s. Given the critique of state legitimacy by activists, *The Sultanate* resolves the danger of Ric's (misplaced) loyalty by having Ric withdraw from politics altogether and retire to his enchanted island. If establishing a sultanate in one's heart is too complicated, then buying land appears to be the next best thing: one can at least be a sultan (albeit Christian) of one's own latifundium! Questions of intention and feelings—all intangible—give way to tangible land and property, a fact already prefigured by the novel's recurring comparison of the Dy Angco brothers to trees and the attendant metaphors of "rootedness." The novel alludes to the political turmoil in the Philippines while sparing its main character from having to explicitly comment and take a stand on current events. By doing so, the novel seals itself off from uncomfortable questions raised by anti-Marcos forces about the ideological foundations of the state for which Ric has worked. The price *The Sultanate* pays for refusing to engage this critical interrogation of state legitimacy is its own (and Ric's) increasing social irrelevance.

It would take an act of state—a state that, by the early 1970s, had come under heavy pressure from economic, political, social, and ideological challenges—to resolve the thorny issue of Philippine citizenship for the "Chinese." But the state would do so in ways that would simultaneously affirm and question the very premise of "good citizenship" on which *The Sultanate* builds its case for Chinese "assimilation" into Philippine society. By then, the language for making sense of the "Chinese in the Philippines" would also change.

Notes

1   Bai Ren, author of *Nanyang piaoliuji* (Adrift in the Southern Ocean, 1983), counted Zhou Enlai among his admirers and was, for that reason, targeted for criticism by Jiang Qing and Lin Biao during the Cultural Revolution (Hau 2004, 17–18). Du Ai is discussed in Chapter 4.

2   *The Sultanate* can also be read as a form of autobiographical fiction. The assassination of Generoso Dy Angco is based on the real-life murder of prominent businessman Ang Liongto just after World War II. I thank Jojo Abinales for his help in locating the newspaper accounts of this case.

3   See Chu 2010, 69–70 for a discussion of the usages of the terms.

4   When the cases were finally settled, only one was convicted of subversion (Miyahara 1997, 76; Research Staff of Pagkakaisa sa Pag-unlad 1973, 228).

5   For biographical details and a nuanced analysis that historicizes the Maguindanao relationship with the Philippine colonial and national state, see Abinales 2000a.

6   An excellent study of the changing meanings of "Malay" in the context of political debates in colonial Malaya is Milner 2002.

7   On the "power of the grid" of the census to shape the historical imagination and discourse, see Anderson 1991, chapter 10.

8   Charles Coppel (1974, 75) has argued in favor of the salience of "China" in the construction of the Southeast Asian "Chinese" as disloyal other in the post-colonial context: "The Chinese are suspect not merely because they seem 'foreign,' but also because their country of origin is situated nearby and is larger and more powerful than the Southeast Asian states."

9   A good overview of the role played by conversion in the "de-sinicization" and "becoming-subject" of the sangley migrants is Sugaya 2011.

10   Wickberg (1965, 33) here notes only that the india was classified as mestiza, along with her children.

11   Manila's Catholic Chinese had supported the British and their liberalization of the colonial economy, particularly in exports (Wickberg 1965, 17; Wilson 2004, 49).

12   I thank Jun Aguilar for this information.

13   See also Benedict Anderson's quantitative analysis of the political and social vocabulary of Rizal's novels in Anderson 2008, 30–33, and Megan Thomas' discussion (2012, especially Chapter 2) of ilustrado ethnology, which "reproduced Catholicism's borders, marking highland peoples as outside of this people in the present but potential members in the future, and excluding contemporary Muslims entirely" (202).

14   Juan Bautista de Veyra (Vera) was governor of the sangleyes at the time of the 1603 sangley "uprising," and was imprisoned by the Spaniards on suspicion of organizing the revolt. The 1603 uprising resulted in the massacre of more than twenty thousand sangleyes.

15   This does not mean that the "Chinese" were spared discrimination and violence during the Philippine revolution. Some Chinese stores were looted, and Chinese were subject to higher taxes and "donations" (not all of it voluntary) by the revolutionary government (see Apilado 2001).

16   An important exploration of the question of "race" as worked out through "revolutionary praxis" is Blanco 2011.

17   "Insik Pawa's" role in the arrest of the Bonifacio brothers, however, embroiled him in the partisan politics among Filipino revolutionaries (see, for example, the account by Alvarez 1992, Chapter 38, 98, 334–35).

18   The 1940 Immigration Law imposed a quota on the entry of new Chinese immigrants. First set at 500 new immigrants, the quota was drastically reduced to 50 following Philippine independence, but has been suspended since 1949. Congressmen who were apportioned immigration quotas from 1945 to 1952 charged three-thousand- to five-thousand-peso "fees" for their sponsorship of Chinese new immigrants (see Jiang 1974, 100).

19   See Miyahara 2008a for a nuanced discussion of the biopolitics of "Chineseness" and the distinctions—based on intermarriage—that it draws between *lanlang* and *tsut-si-a* in Cebu.

20   The Philippines was the only Southeast Asian country that Chiang Kai-shek visited (albeit in an unofficial capacity) in 1949, just three months before the Communists took over China. See Hsiao 1998, 42–46.

21   This remarkable passage illustrates the pitfalls of racializing the Chinese mestizo: the characters are at pains to argue that a "good Filipino" cannot be judged by the

color of her skin, but then go on to rhapsodize about the "texture" and "color of the skin" of the Chinese mestizo!

22 In his pathbreaking study, Henry Yu (2001) has argued persuasively in favor of the intimate connection between American sociology as an academic discipline and ethnicity and racial identity as modes of self-understanding and identification. Not only did sociological terms like "Oriental" and "assimilation" provide both the language and the intellectual framework by which "Asian Americans" were defined as a group category. Just as important, American sociology (and its sister discipline of anthropology) provided the conceptual tools through which Asian Americans understood themselves (8, 9). It is not an accident that missionaries were key agents in the production of knowledge about "Orientals" and the "Orient." Conversion was a powerful incentive for missionary work in the Orient, but it also crucially underpinned ideas of cultural consciousness and social change brought about by migration from the Orient to America. Religious conversion and cultural assimilation—or sometimes, both at once—were associated processes (56) in the sense that sociologists modeled their ideas about cultural assimilation on spiritual conversion, the validity of which they took for granted (65–66). Cultural assimilation would, in turn, as argued in this chapter, provide the blueprint for citizenship and naturalization. In the *Sultanate*, religious conversion and cultural assimilation are intertwined in the fact that the native-born Dy Angcos are raised as devout Catholics. On the fraught career and signification of the term "Moro" in Philippine colonial and post-colonial discussions of citizenship, see Blanchetti-Revelli 2003).

23 The third brother, Rolando, whose story is treated rather perfunctorily in the novel, manages his own string of businesses, which are nowhere near as large as elder brother Mariano's empire, but afford him a great deal of personal satisfaction.

24 Cf. President Gloria Macapagal Arroyo's speech before a group of Chinese applicants for Filipino citizenship in 2001, just after she signed into law Republic Act no. 9138 (Administrative Naturalization Law): "Citizenship must be earned.... Citizenship is not hanging up your residence papers on the wall but by living day-today as a true Filipino. It is earned by fulfilling the obligations of citizenship, like voting, paying taxes, obeying the laws, and if necessary, bearing arms and fighting for your country" (quoted in De Quiros 2001, who then goes on to remind his Filipino readers of their citizenship obligations).

25 Webb Keane (2006, 309) has argued that academic assumptions about "human identity, rights, liberation, individuals and society"—rooted in "Western culture's" "core concerns with and ways of conceptualizing the self, objectification, agency, authority, power and materialism"—are deeply (and often unwittingly) indebted to Judeo-Christian thought and practice. See also Cannell 2006's illuminating discussion of modernity being modeled on the idea of conversion (30–39).

26 I thank Jun Aguilar for pointing out that the historical parallel to the above public confessional text is the testimonial associated with evangelical Protestantism, particularly the so-called American "Great Awakenings" or religious revivals that took place between the eighteenth and nineteenth centuries. The testimonial is similarly concerned with the authenticity of conversion through individual self-examination and transformation. On the historical origins of the evangelical conversion narrative, see Caldwell 1983 and Hindmarsh 2005.

27 This adherence evidently entails renouncing, among other things, polygamy (at least by non-Muslims) and assassination (see Chapter 2).

28 See, for example, Nat. Case no. C-31, "In the Matter of the Petititon of Ng See Kui also known as Flaviano Uy Suy Cui alias Flavy to be Admitted a Citizen of the Philippines" (*Daily Mirror* 1970).

29 See Vicente Rafael's excellent discussion of confession and the logic of conversion in *Contracting* Colonialism (1988, Chapter 3).

30 Not even local KMT officials were exempt from the anti-communist drives of the military (Miyahara 1997).

2

CHINESE FILIPINO

A year after *The Sultanate* appeared in print, a deportation case involving two "Chinese" brothers became a cause célèbre in the Philippines. On March 21, 1970, Quintin Yuyitung and his brother Rizal, publisher and editor respectively of the leading Chinese-language daily *Chinese Commercial News* (商报 *Shang Bao*, hereinafter *CCN*), were abducted at the Manila Press Club by Philippine authorities and flown to Taipei to stand trial on the charge of spreading Communist propaganda through print (for details on the case, see the articles collected in Yuyitung 2000). The evidence marshaled to argue the case against the brothers consisted of articles and news items deemed "favorable to the Communist cause and derogatory to the Philippine government" (xxiv) from the *Chinese Commercial News*, published between 1949 and 1962. The brothers also faced additional charges of currency blackmarketing (remitting Philippine pesos to China without license).

At the hearing, reporters learned that forty-seven out of the sixty-eight articles were actually translations of news dispatches by Associated Press, Agence-France Press, Reuters and UPI (xvi). The local news items that were singled out were mostly reports on the student demonstrations then taking place in Manila that would later be known as the First Quarter Storm (see Lacaba 1970).

At the time, the Yuyitung case was widely interpreted as Ferdinand Marcos's way of "testing the waters for imposing martial law" by attacking the "weakest link": the Chinese press (xvi). Denounced by the Philippine media as *palabas* (show) (Locsin 1970 [2000], 182) and *lutong macao* (lit., "macao cooking," or fixing, Rama 1970 [2000], 174), the case against the brothers rested on selective, decontextualized, and politicized interpretations of texts. An "expert witness" from a rival press who testified for the persecution argued that the *CCN* was communist because

The Yuyitung brothers

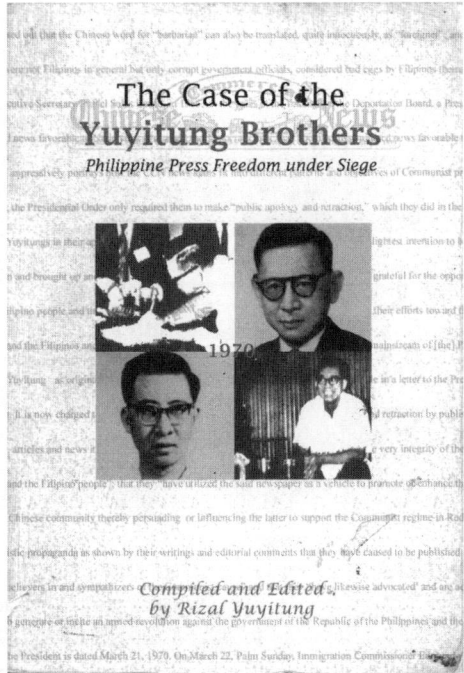

it printed words like "imperialism," "feudalism," "fascism," "protracted struggle," and "serve the people," and because the newspaper used the term "Peking" instead of the Taipei-designated "Peiping" to refer to mainland Chinese capital (Lacaba 1970 [2000], 30). A poem, "To Those Suffering Compatriots Who Entered Illegally," and a CCN article that used the word "stinking barbarians"[1] (臭番 choufan; in Hokkien, tsaohuan) to refer to corrupt government officials were read as derogatory of Filipinos (24). The Yuyitungs were also accused of funding leftist organizations based in the University of the Philippines (UP) and spreading "Maoist propaganda" in the UP Asian Center—charges that were in turn refuted by the defense (33). CCN was faulted for publishing news about China, including the exploding of the hydrogen bomb, writer Han Suyin's visit, and the first Chinese satellite (37).

Filipino journalists criticized the government's reliance on information provided and translated by the Kuomintang branch and Republic of China Embassy in the Philippines, pointing to the dangers "posed by the activity of a foreign political party in this country [Philippines]" (Granada 1970 [2000], 104), and the lack of due process on the part of the Philippine government. Others, however, defended Marcos by saying that the president's decision to sign the deportation orders was an "act of state" (De Leon 1970 [2000], 125) and could therefore bypass the due process of deportation hearings.

It quickly became known that the Yuyitungs had run afoul of certain Chinese community leaders and the KMT and the Embassy of the Republic of China for refusing to toe the Taipei line (which apparently included prescriptions on what to print and the size of the headline font and amount of space devoted to the article). The wide readership enjoyed by the *CCN* had to do with the newspaper's "independent stance and crusading zeal" (Guerrero 1970 [2000], 93), its criticism of Chinese wrongdoings, and its advocacy of integration and assimilation. The reality was that, for all of Taipei's attempts to establish itself as a "cultural substitute" for the mainland (Chun 1995; Wickberg 2006, 23), attempts that did succeed in creating multiple linkages between Taiwan and the Philippine Chinese, Hokkien family ties to the ancestral land in China were not easily replaceable (25) by a transfer of loyalty to Taipei, nor, given the disconnection between the Taiwan state and the mainland territory of "China" to which the Philippine Chinese traced their origins, could interest in developments in mainland China and pride in China's achievements be fully rechanneled to Taiwan. Moreover, as some young Philippine Chinese, born and raised and educated in the Philippines and interacting more and more with Filipinos, became politicized (if not radicalized) during the late sixties, they sought autonomy from, and became increasingly critical of, the conservative Chinese establishment (26).

The Yuyitungs were known for their advocacy of citizenship by jus soli and mass naturalization by administrative process. Rizal Yuyitung received an award from the National Press Club for his article "It's Time for Change" (adapted from his 1961 Chinese-language article "Shi tuibian de shihou le" 是蜕变的时候了), which argued for the "integration" of the Chinese resident minority into the national community through "reorientation and reeducation processes" (Yuyitung 2000, 24; for the Chinese version, see Yu 1961b).

Originally written in the context of the Filipino-First policy under President Carlos P. Garcia (1953–1957), who sought to Filipinize the economy (particularly in import trade and labor employment) by nurturing domestic industries and encouraging Filipino investments in the late 1950s,[2] Yuyitung's Chinese-language essay argued that the only way (*weiyi de chulu* 唯一的出路) to solve the Overseas Chinese Question/Problem (*huaqiao wenti* 华侨问题) is by means of the struggle for equality (*zhengqu pingdeng* 争取平等) through political integration, that is, by extending citizenship (公民权 *gongmin quan*) to the Chinese (1961b, 34, 38). For citizenship to be a normal process (*putong de gongli* 普通的公理) rather than a favor (*enci* 恩赐) granted to the Chinese, the Chinese themselves must seize the initiative to show that they are an asset (*zichan* 资产), rather than a liability (*fuzhai* 负债), to the Philippines.

Yuyitung cited the changing demographic profile of the Chinese in the postwar, Cold War era—the fact that the majority were now Philippine-born and Philippine-grown (37), the fact that most were not willing or able to go back to Communist China (36) and would not be able to bring their earnings back to China (38)—to argue in favor of Chinese acquisition of Philippine citizenship. Yuyitung used the classic phrase 落地生根 (*luodi sheng gen*), putting down roots in the country (37), and called on the Philippine Chinese to undergo a process of "molting" (*tuibian*), to shed the "bad" features—among them, Han-Chinese chauvinism (大汉族主义, *dahanzu zhuyi*, 40–41)—of their Chinese identities and, in acquiring Filipino citizenship, become "good Filipino citizens" (34), proclaim their loyalty to the Philippine state, and actively cultivate the "best" features of their Chineseness (in the form of Chinese culture and enterprise) in order to contribute to the development of the Philippine nation and culture (39).

For Yuyitung, "assimilation" (*tonghua*, 同化) was a long-term process（相当长的期间）(41) that should not be coerced. Rather, it resulted from the "integration" (*ronghua*, 融化) (35, 36) of the Chinese amongst the Filipino people. Yuyitung invoked the historical example of cultural "mixing" exemplified by Chinese mestizos like Jose Rizal (40), while also stating that the Chinese culture of the overseas Chinese community (*qiaoshe* 侨社) would and should not be completely erased (41). While calling on the Chinese to study the Philippine language, culture and history, Yuyitung nevertheless believed that they could retain their own language (ibid.), because—like many Filipino intellectuals of the time—he assumed that Philippine culture itself was not an end result, but rather an ongoing process of formation (ibid.). Since state regulations against migration prevented substantial inflows of new migrants into the Chinese community, the Philippine Chinese should themselves serve as the "new blood" (*xin xue* 新血) and "new cells" (*xin xibao* 新 细胞) (35, 39) of the Philippine nation by actively participating in, and contributing to, the creation of its culture (41).[3] Although built on the bifurcation between "good" and "bad" Chinese (as discussed in chap. 1), Yuyitung's advocacy of *tonghua* encompassed voluntarist ideas of cultural preservation as well as amalgamation, political integration as well as Filipinization. Following the deportation of the Yuyitungs, articles in the *Chinese Commercial News* began to highlight Yuyitung's advocacy of *tonghua*, "assimilation" [Xü 1972] as part of their defense of his "Filipinoness."

Ironically, the Yuyitungs' campaign for citizenship by jus soli and mass naturalization by administrative process was viewed as a threat to the Kuomintang-dominated Chinese community establishment. Long-running internecine conflicts had seen the Yuyitungs' father and *CCN* founding publisher—later executed by the Japanese—accused of being a loyalist to the Beijing "warlord government" in the 1920s, and then criticized for reporting KMT losses during the Sino-Japanese war. The Yuyitungs themselves were Philippine-born, and had never been to Taiwan—the embassy having refused to issue them passports and the Yuyitungs having renounced their Chinese citizenship. As one journalist put it: "The transgression that the Yuyitungs committed, if at all, was to have run their paper as if they were Filipinos" (Valencia 1970 [2000], 134). The brothers were eventually sentenced to two- and three-year confinement in a Taiwan reformatory school (x, xi).

The deportation was widely criticized by the Philippine media as a violation of press freedom and provoked international condemnation. Far more instructive, the Yuyitung case exposed the limits of civic conversion and citizenship for the Philippine Chinese. Quintin and Rizal Yuyitung had bolstered their call for easing Filipino restrictions against the naturalization of Chinese by trying to live as they preached: they resided among Filipinos (in Sierra Madre, Quezon City) instead of the so-called Chinatowns and sent their children not to Chinese schools but to Philippine schools (their children did not study Chinese). The Yuyitungs claimed descent not only from Manchus, but also from no less than Kumalalang chieftain Ganlai Yibendum, who died on a tributary mission to the Ming state in 1420 (Yu 1997, 25–32).[4]

Despite all the talk of assimilation based on the bifurcation of the Chinese into good and bad, an act of state, founded on highly politicized (mis)readings of the Yuyitungs' words and deeds, was all it took to put and keep these two "Chinese" in their place. The Yuyitungs' plight would in turn reignite public debates on the citizenship status of the Philippine Chinese and prepare the ground for an eventual shift in public and official opinion in favor of the political integration of the Chinese into the Filipino "mainstream."

Unfolding in the wake of the radicalization of Philippine politics in the early 1970s, the Yuyitung case provided critics of Marcos with the opportunity to criticize if not question the very legitimacy of the government itself. In fact, leftist student organizations were vocal about their support for the Yuyitungs, criticizing the government in language—"KMT bandit gang," "Marcos fascist puppet regime," and "U.S. imperialism"—far more incendiary and "leftist" than the words that were lifted out of the CCN articles (45, 46, 51, 52). For these activists, the government itself was "bad," its legitimacy undercut by its corruption, its penetration by elite interests, and its brutal suppression of the "millenarian" Lapiang Malaya (lit., "Freedom Party," led by Valentin de los Santos, whose armed followers marched to Malacañang Palace and were repulsed by the police in 1967) and, most notably, the Mindanao conflict from the 1970s onwards.

How could one be a "good Filipino" when one worked to shore up a corrupt and brutal regime? The authority that decided which Chinese was "good" or "bad" was now judged and found wanting. Citizenship in the abstract posits the formal political equality of all members of the Filipino national community, but the assertion of formal equality belies the reality of economic inequality, social divisions, religious prejudice, and ethnic differentiation that have fueled secessionist challenges against the Philippine state, notably from the Communist, Muslim-nationalist (Moro National Liberation Front), and Islamic movements.

Integrating the "Chinese" by Administrative Fiat

There is some irony in the fact that it was the authoritarian regime under Ferdinand Marcos that took the crucial step toward the national integration of the Chinese. In 1975, less than five years after *The Sultanate* was published and the Yuyitungs were deported, Marcos signed Letter of Instructions (LOI) 270, "Naturalization of Deserving Aliens by Decree," which implemented the mass naturalization of the Chinese and other foreigners. Its stated aim was to "integrate" into the "national fabric" "permanently residing aliens" who have "developed and demonstrated love for and loyalty to the Philippines and affinity to the customs, traditions and ideals of the Filipino people, as well as contributed to the economic, social and cultural development of our country" (LOI 270, 1975). As of 1985, about 50,000 Chinese had submitted applications under this LOI (Tan 1988, 200).

The LOI 270 signaled a decisive shift in Philippine domestic and foreign policy toward mainland China and the "Chinese Question." In signing the LOI, then-President Ferdinand Marcos was not merely following American President Richard Nixon's lead in forging entente with communist China. Facing Muslim rebellion in the south (which had threatened to disrupt Philippine access to oil provided through the Organization of Petroleum Exporting Countries) and the possibility of American withdrawal from Vietnam (Aguilar 2012b, 392–93), Marcos formulated his new Asia policy in the late 1960s in light of the imminent expiration of the Laurel-Langley trade agreement, which had effectively tied the Philippine economy to the United States, and the decline of Philippine trade with its erstwhile primary trading partner (Lim 2001). The new Asia policy sought to strengthen Philippine trade links with Asian and socialist countries, particularly with China (278). In addition, the Marcos government needed to secure oil supplies from China to deal with the 1973 oil crisis, and to undermine the Communist movement in the Philippines by asking China to adopt a "hands-off policy" toward Philippine internal affairs (Lim 2001, 281; Tiglao 1990c, 71; Aguilar 2012b).

Drawing inspiration from similar efforts by neighboring countries to address the citizenship status of ethnic Chinese in Southeast Asia, particularly Malaysia and Indonesia (Aguilar 2012b, 399), mass naturalization of the Philippine Chinese led to the acquisition of Filipino citizenship by a substantial portion of the Chinese population, whose changing demographic profile, as exemplified by Jose Angliongto and the Yuyitung brothers, during the postwar era made "integration" an attractive option (Wickberg 1997, 170–71). The Chinese who came of age in the 1960s constituted the largest group of Chinese, a majority of them Philippine-born, but also the first group to lack direct and substantial contact with a China that had gone Communist and was therefore closed off to America's "Free Asia," and the first to receive university education and have wide social contacts with non-Chinese (ibid.).

Mass naturalization legally incorporated the Chinese "alien" into the Filipino nation; by relying on administrative fiat, it relaxed the conditions for acquiring citizenship, which had been expensive (given a postwar exchange rate of between P2 to P3.90 per American dollar), with total legal and extralegal expenses ranging from PhP30,000 to 50,000 (McCarthy 1974, 25), effectively barring indigent Chinese from applying for citizenship. Citizenship enabled a number of Chinese to move out of the commercial niche and join the professional class (as lawyers, doctors, architects, engineers), even producing a number of Chinese-Filipino cultural workers (writers, visual artists, filmmakers).

But martial law exacted a stiff price from Philippine Chinese literature: no literary works or columns were allowed publication in the sole, officially sanctioned Chinese newspaper, *United Daily News* (*Lianhe Ribao*). No doubt the Yuyitung case, in which a poem published in *Chinese Commercial News* was entered as evidence of the Yuyitung's alleged attempt to smear the integrity of Filipino government officials, provided ample evidence of the fact that literary works, in lending themselves to multiple interpretations, can be read in ways that may prove detrimental to their authors. Marcos and the KMT were not the only ones guilty of over-"interpreting" literary texts: in Communist China, Wu Han's 1959 historical drama *Hai Rui Dismissed from Office* (*Hai Rui Ba Guan*海瑞罢官), initially praised by Mao Zedong and later condemned by Jiang Qing and Yao Wenyuan (a member of the Gang of Four) as a thinly veiled allegory of Mao's dismissal of his minister of defense Peng Dehuai, sparked a "literary battle" that raged within the upper echelons of the Communist Party and resulted in the consolidation of Mao's faction at the helm of the Cultural Revolution.

Marcos's act of state bypassed judicial interpretation, legislative deliberation, and to some extent public debate (by then subject to censorship under martial law) in favor of an executive decision to politically integrate the Chinese. Where an act of state had targeted the Yuyitungs for persecution, it would also function to resolve the problem of citizenship for the Philippine Chinese. The authority and arbitrariness of state power were arrogated by the president instead of being left in the hands of judges, lawmakers, bureaucrats, and a divided public.

Given the suddenness of the decision, Marcos's "act of state" fueled the "rumor"—believed and repeated by many Chinese and even some of Marcos's own officials—that Marcos, who was known to refer to himself as a descendant of the sixteenth-century "Chinese pirate" Limahong, was the illegitimate son of a scion of the affluent Chua family which regularly provided Chinese community elite leadership and enjoyed strong links with the KMT. This proclivity for attributing Marcos's solution of the Chinese problem to his Chinese blood downplays the fact that Marcos in his long career had made milking cows of the Chinese, and had allegedly received a substantial "commission" for this particular act of state (Tiglao 1990c). Interestingly, Rizal Yuyitung is related by marriage to the Chuas of Batac, Ilocos Norte. His mestiza wife Veronica's uncle, Felipe Chua, was with Marcos in Palawan when the Yuyitungs were arrested. Her other uncle Julian, if rumors about Marcos' being a Chinese mestizo are true, would have been Marcos' half-brother![5] Blood connections certainly did not save the Yuyitungs, who were known to be critical of the KMT-dominated Chinese community leadership. Ironically, the persecution of the Yuyitungs turned out to be one of the last public displays of KMT influence in the Philippines.

Mass naturalization had enormous implications—both material and intellectual—for the "Chinese question." It entailed no less than a shift in the discourse of Philippine nationalism away from monoculturalist and melting-pot claims of assimilation, routinely associated with ideas of absorption and amalgamation, toward a political definition of national belonging, which held that ethnic or minority groups could be "integrated" into Philippine society while preserving their cultural identities (Cariño 1988, 47).

The ascendancy of the integration discourse over assimilation was a product not only of domestic policy and social change but also of international developments, scholarly debates, and political struggles as well. The aftermath of the two world wars and decolonization saw important changes in the discourses, technologies, and models of race management (Goldberg 2002, 211). Race, which was delegitimized as science and policy in the wake of the Holocaust in Europe, came to be recoded in "colorblind" terms as problems of illegal migration and criminality (212–13), on the one hand, and replaced by the de-essentialized but amorphous category of culture, on which the emergent discourse of ethnicity was based, on the other hand.

Assimilation, which originated as a term in the late nineteenth century and was popularized during the first three decades of the twentieth century, is most commonly used in American sociology, particularly the influential theories propounded by Robert Park and other scholars affiliated with the University of Chicago (Yu 2001, 8). Moving race away from discussions of biology and toward discussions of culture (as Franz Boas had done for the field of anthropology) at a time when Asian immigration was perceived as an economic threat and Asians were racialized as perpetual foreigners in America, Park instead posited "race" as a matter of consciousness, one whose migratory path led it through a "cycle" of competition, conflict, accommodation and, through increased social contact with the mainstream society, eventually assimilation or Americanization (40–41). Cultural consciousness became the focus and agenda of sociological studies of race relations and immigrant adjustment to American life. Timing is crucial to the popularization of the term: Asian immigration to America had slowed to a trickle in the interwar and immediate postwar periods owing to draconian anti-immigration laws (Waldinger 2001, 16), a trend that would be reversed only in 1965.

Shaped by modernization theory (ibid.), the concept of assimilation assumed that ethnicity, along with similar older forms of social organization, was bound to disappear as immigrants "acculturated" to mainstream society, whose values, norms, expectations, and aspirations these immigrants would embrace and substitute for their own personal, familial, and group perspectives and loyalties. While assimilation originated as a description of acculturation, offering as it turns out a none-too-precise nor accurate account of race relations in America, it also came to articulate a normative stance, one that carried a specific vision of the American nation along with prescriptions for communal bonding and national life (11). Both vision and prescription operated on the basis of a dichotomy between a homogeneous, often imprecisely defined "mainstream" self and its foreign-originating, radically different, and "immigrant" other. A description of acculturation, of the way the culture and perspective of immigrants change over time in a given place (as reflected in their choice of residence, language, and marriage partners), could be, and was used, to bolster the belief that this unilinear course of development was what *ought to be*, a rite de passage that every immigrant *should* undergo.

Such a concept of assimilation came under attack for its ethnocentric one-sidedness, which privileged the White Anglo-Saxon Protestant middle-class as the normative standard (Alba and Nee 2003, 2), and glossed over crucial issues of conflicts, differences, and contestations within the so-called mainstream itself in the wake of the American civil rights movement and the rise of identity politics. Assimilation was criticized for its inability to account for the reproduction and perpetuation of inequalities and exclusions that kept certain immigrant groups poor or disadvantaged across time. Neither could it account for the fact that the success of other immigrant groups in specific economic niches could help secure better socioeconomic opportunities for some members of these minority groups. More, the concept, by assuming the unidirectionality of cultural change in favor of a minority group adapting to the mainstream culture, offered no means for understanding the extent to which dominant societies could themselves be shaped or transformed by their interactions with these so-called others (see the critiques in Alba and Nee 2003, 1–66; Waldinger 2001, 11–21).

The term integration was sometimes used interchangeably with "assimilation." In the field of urban sociology, for example, Chicago-trained Rose Hum Lee's *The Chinese in the United States* (1960) made the term "integration" synonymous with "assimilation" and held up the integration of the "Overseas Chinese"—to the extent of becoming indistinguishable from the local population—as the ideal to which Chinese in America should aspire (Yu 2001, 128). Integration was used in discussions of apartheid in South Africa in 1940, before gaining ground through the African-American civil rights activism in the segregated American South in the 1950s and 1960s. In more recent decades, it has been deployed in European debates on immigration and settlement (Favell 2005; 1998, 3). Elsewhere, racial democracy in Brazil, ethnic pluralism in Europe, and official multiculturalism—a policy first implemented in Switzerland before gaining some traction in Canada and Australia in the late 1960s and early 1970s, and Great Britain in the 1990s (even though its implementation in different countries has been uneven and inconsistent)—sought to allay fears of the viability of national identity in countries where postwar large-scale international migration had created sizeable and distinct cultural communities, especially within the First World countries.

The call for integration shaped the scholarship on the Chinese in Southeast Asia, even as scholarly works provided ammunition for the reformulation of state policies on the "Chinese." In the first few decades of the postwar period, Southeast Asian states were concerned with stabilizing their regimes and viewed the presence of neighboring Communist China and the political activism of ethnic Chinese populations in their territories as external and internal threats to be addressed through a combination of repression, containment, and control. Philippine state policies and practices formulated the "Chinese Question" by constructing the "Chinese" as the "other" of the national community. But the state was also engaged in modernization projects that required the selective inclusion and exclusion of Chinese minorities who played an important role in its economy (cf. Ong and Nonini 1997a, 7).

Scholarly debates reflected, if not effected, the evolution of state policies and practices. In his survey of the field, Wang Gungwu (2003f) notes that scholarship on Chineseness before the 1950s worked within the parameters defined by what he calls nationalist and historical identity, before giving way to the preoccupation with understanding Chineseness through the study of local, communal, and cultural identities in the 1950s and 1960s, and the reconfiguring of cultural identity into "ethnic identity" as well as the popularity of class analysis in the 1970s. By the 1980s and 1990s, diasporic transnationalism, globalization, and flexible citizenship had become the catchphrases of the burgeoning overseas Chinese studies.

Because Southeast Asian postcolonial states had perforce to deal with the challenge of governing heterogeneous populations, terms like assimilation and integration—with their often variable, shifting definitions—provided a "scientific" idiom for framing public and policy debates on the issue of Chinese long-term settlement in Southeast Asia. In the 1950s, these terms competed to provide intellectual ammunition for those who had clear ideas about the desirable form that the relationship of the "Chinese" with their respective Southeast Asian countries ought to take. The intellectual ammunition—the very language in which the Chinese Question was posed and its assumptions and implications worked out in policy and practice—would be provided by, and legitimized through, the academic network and community of students and scholars, many of them American-trained and working on the "overseas Chinese" in America and Southeast Asia.

Comparing "Overseas Chinese" in Southeast Asia

Scholarly research and reflection on the "overseas Chinese" question were informed by comparative thinking about the situation of the ethnic Chinese, particularly in Southeast Asia, the key region of immigration from the mid-nineteenth century to the first half of the twentieth century. For the fledgling nation-states in anticommunist "Free Asia," the close presence of Communist China was not just a major policy issue and concern. This proximity had important implications because of Chinese Communist Party aid to local communist parties in the region (see chap. 4), as well as the fact that the "overseas Chinese" not only constituted the largest group of foreign minority in these Southeast Asian countries, but were disproportionately represented in their national economies. Dealing with an undesirable, if not dangerous, foreign minority entailed the adoption of a sociological discourse that propounded concepts of "assimilation" and "integration" and provided policymakers and politicians with a theoretical language for constructing a schema of society that, by definition, could be remade according to specific programs and policies. In positing the level and depth of cultural interaction between and among immigrant groups and their "home" as well as "host" societies, this schema assumed that immigrants and the "mainstream" societies were discretely bounded entities. Concerned less with the intellectual challenge of tracking human movements across space and time and their impact on the physical, social, and intellectual terrains they traverse than with issues of border control, social regulation, and nation-building, these bureaucrats, policymakers, and intellectuals drew on sociological discourse to uphold their respective political and social projects. Far from being merely descriptive, these sociological terms had normative implications because they provided the conceptual tools and the language for sketching the contours of the ideal (almost always national) community, thus setting the parameters by which government policies aimed at "social engineering" (to borrow Glenn May's contextualization [1980] of an earlier American colonial context) of the national community could be formulated and prescribed. The line between description and prescription was not only a thin one, but one that was frequently crossed by scholars and policymakers alike who were not immune to playing preacher and prophet.

Studies of the Chinese in Thailand, for example, have been shaped by the highly influential assimilation paradigm advanced by the American expert on China, G. William Skinner (Cushman 1989, 222), whose pioneering *Chinese Society in Thailand: An Analytical History* (1957) and *Leadership and Power in the Chinese Community in Thailand* (1958b) took as their central concern the question of Chinese "assimilation" into Thai society (Koizumi 2008; 2006).[6] His identification of generation, education, language, and membership in organizations as key variables in determining the extent of Thai Chinese elite assimilation led him to predict that "the entire Chinese community will inevitably move more rapidly toward complete assimilation to Thai society" (Skinner 1958b, 319; cited and discussed in Koizumi 2008, 200).[7]

Skinner's fieldwork[8] on the Thai Chinese would in turn lead him to a comparative study of ethnic Chinese in Thailand and Java (1960). Shaped as much by the American Cold War imperative of containing communism as by Southeast Asian nationalist concerns with containing Chinese economic "dominance" (Koizumi 2008, 209–10), his comparative work and his thesis on the successful assimilation of the Chinese into Thai society would inform the thinking and writings of other scholars on other Southeast Asian countries (for example, Lea Williams 1966, 81–89; cited in Koizumi 2008, 215).

Edgar Wickberg's classic study of the Philippine Chinese in the mid- to late nineteenth century, *The Chinese in Philippine Life, 1850–1898* (1965), cited a number of Skinner's writings (1958a; 1957; 1961) on Thailand and Java. From a comparative perspective, Wickberg placed "the historical experience of the Chinese mestizos in the Philippines" (1965, 240) "somewhere between the two extremes" exemplified by Thailand, on the one hand, where rapid assimilation of the Chinese took place before the twentieth century, and Indonesia, on the other hand, in which an "assimilation trap" (here Wickberg used Skinner's phrase from his comparative study of Chinese in Thailand and Java [1960]) had led to a "prolonged delay in the assimilation of Chinese descendants in Java" (Wickberg 1965, 239):

> The mestizos, like the peranakans, formed a distinct group with a culture of its own, a mixture of Chinese and indigenous elements. Where there were enough mestizos to form gremios, assimilation was retarded. Like the peranakans, the mestizos had a recognized legal status, established by the colonial government.
>
> Nevertheless, the mestizos were assimilated to indio society (or perhaps it is better to say Filipino society) more rapidly than the peranakans were to Javanese society. Indeed, where mestizos were not numerous they may have been assimilated as rapidly as Chinese descendants were in Thailand. The most important reason for the pattern of mestizo assimilation in the Philippines was the nature of Spanish cultural influence and the native response to it. In Indonesia the Dutch, prior to 1900, sought to maintain indigenous society as it was, influenced as little as possible by Dutch culture. The Spanish, by contrast, sought to hispanize the Philippines. Thus, although indio culture lost prestige as the result of conquest, the Chinese could still be assimilated to the indios because both of them were heading in the same direction—toward the acquisition of Spanish culture, which was equally available to both. The indios were almost all Catholics. The india mother of the mestizos were, therefore, almost inevitably Catholic and raised their children in that faith. Hence there was no religious barrier to continuous intermarriage of mestizos and indios. Moreover, the mestizo was regarded from the start as a special kind of Filipino, not a local Chinese. And he could rather easily switch legal status to that of indio.

Finally, Philippine society was not a classic plural society. Ethnic
and class lines were not congruent. And, like Thai society, it was
open and accepting toward those who regarded themselves as (in the
Philippine case) Filipinos. Mestizos could adopt Spanish surnames
and personal names and be accepted as Filipinos. Why not? Indios
were doing it too in the nineteenth century. Or they could even retain
Chinese surnames (which they combined with Spanish personal
names) and be accepted as Filipinos, once they adopted Filipino dress
and attitudes. Indeed, the very question of what was "Filipino" in
dress and attitude was, to an important degree, decided by mestizos.[9]
(240–41)

Wickberg's seminal work on the Chinese mestizos revealed the
extent to which the Chinese mestizos constituted an important subgroup
of the modern-day Filipino "elite." Skinner would, in turn, draw on
Wickberg's writings in his 1996 essay on "creolized Chinese societies" in
the Philippines, Java, and the Straits Settlements of Malaya. Skinner drew
out the implications of Wickberg's major argument by pointing out how,
in the context of substantive changes in late nineteenth-century colonial
Philippines, intense economic competition between the chinos and Chinese
mestizos fueled the "increasing antagonism between China-born Chinese,
on the one hand, and Mestizos and *Indios* together, on the other. Indeed,
anti-Chinese sentiment was part of what brought Mestizos and Indios
together as the century drew to a close" (1996, 85). He linked the failure of
Sinicization of the mestizos to the "attraction" of Hispanization, and the fact
that the indigenous elite embarked on the same path toward Hispanization
as their mestizo counterparts did. In effect, the kind of "Filipino" culture
that the elite contributed to shaping was a product of both indigenous and
mestizo efforts.

> The pan-Chinese movement, with its promise of cultural purity
> through resinification, never had a chance in the Philippines. It was
> a lost cause there because by the late nineteenth century a perverse
> kind of Westernization had taken Mestizos beyond the point of no
> return. I have already mentioned the attraction that the culture of
> colonial powerholders held for creolized societies. In the Philippines
> Spanish authorities from the early centuries positively encouraged
> Hispanicization, and in this regard they were quite evenhanded
> between Mestizos and Indios. Wickberg's authoritative accounts
> of Chinese life in the last decades of the Spanish period convey the
> impression that Mestizo elites were then in hot pursuit of Spanish

culture—but also, alas, it appears, were indigenous elites. This
convergence has its irony. One reason the descendants of Chinese
spurned indigenous society during the formative years was that,
lacking a literate tradition or a ruling class, it was seen as culturally
inferior. Yet for that very reason Indio elites had no specifically
indigenous high culture to aspire to, and the Filipino civilization that
was evolving in the nineteenth century was necessarily informed by
Spanish culture and Roman Catholicism. Mestizo culture was by the
1880s no less Spanish and no less Catholic than was Indio culture.
Thus, paradoxically enough, when the legal distinctions between
Mestizos and Indios were abolished in the 1880s, the very economic
superiority that had made individual Mestizos reluctant to assimilate
facilitated the integration of upper-class Mestizos *en bloc* into the
emerging national society as the *dominant* element of the Filipino
elite. In a very real sense, Filipino culture was formed by the Mestizo
and *Indio* elites acting in concert. Thus the Chinese Mestizos were
not really absorbed into indigenous society; rather, they merged with
it to form modern Filipino society. To this day, Mestizo elements are
apparent in the culture of the Filipino elite. (89–90)

Skinner echoed Wickberg in contending that "[t]he descendants of
nineteenth-century Mestizos are Filipinos, rather more prominent and
better off than most, but no less likely than others to engage in antisinitic
politics" (93), and ended his essay by pointing out the contrasting case of
the Indonesian *peranakan* (local-born "Chinese," including mestizos),
whose culture had survived "reasonably intact" but who were "settling
rather uncomfortably into the role of yet another *sukubangsa* [ethnic group]
within the ethnic diversity that is modern Indonesia" (ibid.). Here, the
Chinese mestizos' success in merging with *indios* to form the Filipino upper
class was contrasted with the postcolonial fate of the Indonesian "Chinese,"
whose position within the Indonesian national community would remain
problematic for most of the twentieth century.

This comparative perspective not only provided scholars with a
regional "field" for formulating the Chinese Question. More crucially, it
helped shape the thinking of their "subjects" of study—no less than the
Southeast Asian "Chinese" themselves, who appropriated the sociological
language embedded in these scholarly studies of the Chinese. Indonesian
"Chinese," for example, have grappled with their own identities vis-à-vis
Indonesian society by deploying the same sociological language employed
in scholarly studies of the Chinese in Southeast Asia. Leo Suryadinata's
translation of Indonesian-Chinese primary sources (1979) points to

the liveliness of the debate between what he categorizes as "pluralists" who identified themselves politically with Indonesia while desiring to remain culturally Indonesian Chinese, and "assimilationists," who favored "complete assimilation" and the establishment of multiracial organizations (including political parties).

"Assimilation" entered Indonesian public discourse in the 1950s. The movement in its favor is said to have reached a peak in 1960–1961, with the public pronouncements of ten prominent peranakan leaders favoring "complete assimilation" and the formulation of an "Assimilation Charter" in 1961 (Suryadinata 1979, 141). Among its foremost exponents was Ong Hok Ham (or Onghokham, his preferred byline), whose thinking on the Indonesian Chinese situation was informed by his field research on Chinese mestizos in the Philippines, as evident in two 1959 essays, "Warganegara Filipina yang mempunyai darah Tionghoa" (Philippine citizens who have Chinese blood) and "Proses asimilasi keturunan Tionghoa di Filipina" (The assimilation process of descendants of the Chinese in the Philippines), which were eventually collected in his *Riwayat Tionghoa peranakan di Jawa* (2005, 153–73). Onghokham had visited the Philippines in the late 1950s as a young journalist, and had even worked as a research assistant for G. William Skinner, before commencing graduate studies at Yale University in America.[10]

Onghokham was interested in the Chinese mestizo (warganegara Filipina yang mempunyai darah Tionghoa), whom he held up as a typecase of successful assimilation. Onghokham noted a fundamental bifurcation in the Philippine concept and practice of citizenship, and compared it with the tripartite structure of citizenship in Indonesia: "In the Philippines, one is either a Filipino citizen or a foreign citizen. There is no sense of a 'third citizenship' located in between the two kinds of citizenship" (*Di Filipina seorang adalah warganegara Filipina atau warganegara asing. Tak ada pengertian satu 'kewarganegaraan yang ketiga' yang terletak antara pengertian dua macam kewarganegaraan di atas itu*) (Ong 1959 [2005], 153). For Onghokham, the "Chinese problem" (*soal Tionghoa*) in the Philippines was a problem that concerned only those Chinese who did not hold Philippine citizenship, while in Indonesia there were basically two "Chinese problems": one concerning Chinese citizens, and the other Indonesian citizens of Chinese ancestry (154).

This "third citizenship" reserved exclusively for Indonesian Chinese simultaneously integrated and segregated the *totok* ("pure Chinese") as well as the peranakan (mestizo), including peranakan who had lived in what is now Indonesia for many generations and who no longer spoke any Chinese topolect. Third citizenship was a legacy of Dutch colonial state policies toward the "Chinese." Whereas Christian conversion was an important tool

for integrating the sangley and their offspring into the Philippine colony
and the early Spanish colonial state created a separate legal category for the
mestizo offspring of Catholic sangley, the Calvinist Dutch harbored no such
missionizing zeal until quite late,[11] and, contra Wickberg's assertion, did not
create a separate legal category for mestizos (whether Chinese or Dutch).
Instead, they chose to lump totok and peranakan together as "foreign
orientals" (*Vreemde Osterlingen*), a category instituted in 1907 for Chinese,
Arabs, and Indians, and others who were born in the Indies and had resided
in the colony for at least ten years (Leo Suryadinata 1993, 83–84).

The Citizenship Act of 1946 granted citizenship to all Chinese born and
residing in Indonesia by jus soli, while applying jus sanguinis to people of
Indonesian descent (Wilmott 1961, 25–26). A new citizenship agreement
in the early 1950s gave the Indies Chinese a two-year period in which to
repudiate Indonesian citizenship if they desired to be considered nationals
of China (29). A Dual Citizenship treaty between Indonesia and China was
signed in 1955, but the 1958 Citizenship Act, which set a two-generation
requirement that allowed a foreigner to take Indonesian citizenship if his
or her father was born in Indonesia and if s/he repudiated his or her former
citizenship, effectively foreclosed the possibility of dual citizenship for the
Chinese, while also ensuring that Chinese aliens and their descents who did
not opt to adopt Indonesian citizenship at the time would have difficulty
acquiring Indonesian citizenship in the future (41).[12]

While the fraught issue of postcolonial citizenship formed the backdrop
of Onghokham's reflections on the Indonesian Chinese, his thinking on the
situation in Indonesia, like the Yuyitungs' and historian Edgar Wickberg's
on the Chinese in the Philippines, owed something to the language and
concepts of American sociology. His essay, "Proses Asimilasi Keturunan
Tionghoa di Filipina" (163–73), argued that assimilation as social process
was more important than assimilation by fiat, and pinpointed the crucial
role of religious conversion (whether out of conviction or opportunism),
intermarriage, and the compadrazgo (co-godparenthood) system in
facilitating assimilation: "We can see from the assimilation of Chinese in the
Philippines that those of Chinese descent could be merged into one non-
Chinese society and the myth that they always cling to their racial qualities
and traditions is, over time, destroyed" (*Dari asimilasi keturunan Tionghoa
di Filipina kita melihat bahwa keturunan Tionghoa juga dapat dileburkan
ke dalam satu masyarakat bukan Tionghoa dan mitos bahwa mereka selalu
berpegang teguh pada sifat-sifat dan tradisi-tradisi rasial makin lama makin
dihancurkan*) (173).

So far, so sociological. But Onghokham's anecdotes, based on his travels
through the Philippines, were equally if not far more revealing because they

offered Indonesian readers the author's trademark, sharply observed vignettes of the social antagonisms seething within Philippine society, tensions that belied the happy history of "Chinese" smooth assimilation into Philippine society. The first anecdote concerned de facto anti-Chinese prejudice:

> In Manila, I visited one of the nationalist organizations that were very anti-Chinese. The head of that organization pointed out to me a number of leaders who had Chinese blood, saying, "Yes, there are many among our nation who have foreign blood. But we are all Filipino patriots."

> Saya di Manila pernah mengunjungi salah satu organisasi nasionalistis yang sangat anti Tionghoa. Ketua organisasi itu lalu meunjukkan kepada saya beberapa pemimpin yang mempunyai darah Tionghoa sambil mengatakan "Ya, di antara bangsa kita banyak yang mempunyai darah asing. Tetapi kita semuanya adalah patriot-patriot Filipina."
> ("Warganegara Filipina," 157)

Here, hybridity itself was an acknowledged, stated fact among the Filipino political elite, but tracing one's ancestry to a Chinese did not inhibit a (Chinese-mestizo) Filipino nationalist from being vociferously anti-Chinese. In fact, the Filipino nationalism that took root among the elite was one that was well-aware of its mestizo hybridity but, in defining its hybridity as territoriality rooted and local (meaning "not foreign"), it succeeded in resignifying the term "Filipino"—which had hitherto exclusively referred to Philippine-born Spaniards and their creole descendants—while simultaneously defining the "Chinese" as alien.[13] This fraught history of entanglement and estrangement between Chinese mestizos/Filipinos and Chinese would have an important impact on late twentieth-century efforts to reclaim "Chinese" mestizoness for the purpose of regional identification with rising East Asia and China more specifically[14] (see chap. 5).

And what of the "Chinese" themselves? Some were better off than others when it came to experiencing racism. Not one to shy away from calling a spade a spade, Onghokham provided another revealing anecdote in "Proses Asimilasi" about the rich Chinese, who had the money and power to insulate themselves against the anti-Chinese policies of the state through assiduous cultivation of—and fraternization with—its Filipino leaders. Onghokham recounted an incident where he attended a baptismal party thrown by a prominent Protestant Chinese businessman for his son. Among the godparents of the son were Vice-President Diosdado Macapagal and Senator Eulogio Balao (whom Ong called "General Balao"). Not only were the godparents from rival political parties, but Senator Balao happened to be one of the leaders of the anti-Chinese movement in the Senate (167). Onghokham mused: "the funny thing is that" (*lucunya ialah bahwa*), by the Filipino ethics (*etika* Filipina) of the compadrazgo system, the senator who denounces the Chinese on the Senate floor has to make exceptions (*harus mengadakan perkecualian-perkecualian*) for his Chinese co-godparent for the sake of his godson. Conversely, the "totok" (China-born) Chinese, come election time, has to help the senator retain a seat in the senate, where the latter will continue to sponsor anti-Chinese laws, from which the rich Chinese can at least exempt himself![15]

A third, no less revealing, anecdote (172) concerned a trip that Onghokham made to Bicol on the southeastern end of Luzon, where he met a "totok" Chinese who, at first glance, might have been the living and breathing model of successful assimilation: married to a Filipina, he sent his children to university in Manila, and his children and grandchildren were accepted by the Filipino villagers as one of themselves. There were problems, however, on the way to becoming-Filipino. One was his regrettable tendency, when drunk, to bluntly criticize Filipinos whom he didn't consider "useful" (*Orang Tionghoa itu dengan terus-terang mengecam orang-orang Filipina yang dia anggap tak berfaedah, terutama kalau dia sudah mabuk karena terlalu banyak minum*). The other was his strained relationship with his children: he had been angered by his daughter's marriage to a Filipino and did not want to get to know her child/ren. He was also incensed at a son of his, but for a different reason: the son had become an activist, and had recently been sent to India as part of a delegation of students from the nationalist Manuel L. Quezon University (in Manila).[16]

While Onghokham used the case of the Chinese mestizo to argue in favor of assimilation and acculturation for Indonesia, the vignettes he presented from his travels across the Philippines tell a more messy and complicated story, one of racial prejudice but also pragmatic (if cynical) accommodation on both Chinese and Filipino sides. These anecdotes bear out the multivalent nature of nationalism itself, its exclusionary and inclusionary impulses and capacities, and the realities and exigencies of different kinds and classes of people being thrown together and having to live with each other in a given place and time.

In a sense, as the situation in martial-law Philippines confirmed, the normative implications of assimilation and integration would take a backseat to the actions, concerns, imperatives, and "will" of the state. Nobuhiro Aizawa's (2010) study of the Indonesian government policy toward the ethnic Chinese under the New Order regime reveals that it was not necessarily anti-Chinese racism, but rather anticommunist security concerns about

Indonesian Chinese's (especially Baperki leaders'[17]) links with mainland China that were instrumental in defining the state's anti-Chinese policies. Addressing the security "threat" had to be grounded in the Indonesian state's ability to distinguish between ethnic Chinese and non-Chinese Indonesians, on the one hand, and between "alien Chinese" and "Indonesian Chinese" (i.e., Indonesian citizens of Chinese descent), on the other hand. The question of assimilation and integration in a sociocultural sense was intimately linked with the state's immediate security concerns in the wake of the large-scale massacre that killed hundreds of thousands of Indonesians (not just Chinese) and catapulted Suharto into power. The result was a legalistic approach, backed by New Order surveillance and repression, to the question of national security. Assimilationist measures included the banning of Chinese-language education, border-crossings between China and Indonesia, and visible displays of Chineseness (including shop signs). Requiring the entire Indonesian population and its foreign residents to register themselves, and requiring "Chinese" to register as "Chinese," became the principal means by which the state could keep track of its "people" in the name of national security. This differentiation between "Chinese" and "Indonesian," as well as between "alien Chinese" and "Indonesian Chinese," would remain in place for the duration of the New Order.

The Triumph of "Integration" Discourse in the Philippines

A symptom of the social fissures occluded by the unilinear and unidirectional account of cultural change in assimilation discourse as well as an expression of the changing realities of ground-level political, economic, and cultural practices is the growing popularity of the resignified term "integration" as an alternative to "assimilation," not just in Indonesia, where Unity in Diversity (*Bhinneka Tunggal Ika*, a national motto adopted in 1950) is an integral component of national self-fashioning, but also in the Philippines.

As shown in the above discussion of Yuyitung's essay on the overseas Chinese Question, integration and assimilation had hitherto been used loosely, sometimes interchangeably (see, for example, Ople 1958), in the 1950s. But by the 1960s and early 1970s, "integration" had begun acquiring its current denotation of cultural differentiation and preservation. By the 1980s, in the Philippines, the difference between assimilation and integration would crystallize in the discourse propounded by Kaisa para sa Kaunlaran (discussed in the next chap.), whose pioneering precursor was Pagkakaisa sa Pag-Unlad (Unity for Progress), Inc.

A civic organization formed by Chinese-Filipino students from the Ateneo de Manila University, University of the Philippines, Maryknoll College, the University of Mindanao, and other reputable academic institutions with the aim of promoting racial tolerance and better understanding between Chinese and Filipinos, Pagkakaisa was established by two young Chinese Filipinos, Bernard Go and Chinben See, to lobby for jus soli citizenship at the 1972 Constitutional Convention (Ang-See 2011). Pagkakaisa's vice president, Bernard C. Go, was a graduate of the Jesuit-run Ateneo de Manila University, held Chinese citizenship, and would later be instrumental in bringing together a group of young and talented writers, Herman Tiu Laurel, Henry Lim, and Ricardo Lee, to work on the screenplay for the Joseph Estrada vehicle, *Dragnet* (discussed in the next section).

In 1974, Pagkakaisa sa Pag-Unlad published a landmark volume, *Philippine-Chinese Profile: Essays and Studies* (McCarthy 1974), which brought together some of the leading scholars of Philippine and Overseas Chinese studies (including the economic anthropologist John Omohundro and Indonesianist Charles Coppel), civic leaders, academics, and young civic-minded Chinese Filipinos, most notably Teresita-Ang See,[18] who served as executive secretary of Pagkakaisa and would go on to be a founding member of Kaisa para sa Kaunlaran (see chap. 3). In his lead essay, "The Chinese in the Philippines" (1974, 2), editor Charles McCarthy, author of *Philippine-Chinese Integration: The Case for Qualified Jus Soli* (1970), defined integration in the following terms:

> Integration is a process of making whole or entire; it makes a social system, one well-knit whole. Communication, considerable consensus, and cooperation are basic elements of this process.

> A society is integrated when its members, regardless of their race, creed, or place of origins, move freely among one another, sharing the same opportunities and privileges, bearing equal concern for one another's needs, and assuming equal duties in promoting the common good. This requires a wearing down of the distinctions, a pulling down of the walls, between group and group. Unless it is pushed to the extreme point of *absorption*, in which the identifying traits of the minority are all replaced by corresponding characteristics of the majority, or to *total* assimilation through a "melting pot" process in which both groups lose their distinct identities and end up with a new common one, integration respects accidental features and different individual qualities in the people concerned. Unity is possible without complete conformity.

Here, integration was based on the assumption that ethnic markers are "accidental" features that do not have a fundamental bearing on social interaction, economic opportunities, and working toward the "common good." McCarthy himself did not discount the fact of either absorption or assimilation, but noted that there is a class dimension to this issue: "The very rich and the very poor can cross the lines between Filipino and Chinese easily enough, but the larger middle-class group is sluggish" (15).[19] McCarthy did not address the ironic fact that the "mainstream" Philippine society into which the Chinese Filipino was supposed to be integrated was also likely to be defined as middle-class in its values, orientation, and aspirations. The crux of the issue, however, centered on the question of citizenship, with the edited book carrying articles that weighed in on the pros and cons of jus soli,[20] which the legally trained Australian expert on the Indonesian Chinese, Charles A. Coppel, considered as having merit in "its ability to ensure that within a generation the alien minority will have disappeared" (1974, 87).

The integrationist discourse argued that the "uniqueness" of cultural groups did not detract from peaceful coexistence and meaningful exchanges among these groups within a single polity, and the "cultures" of these groups enriched the national culture rather than impeded its development. The discourse of integration, however, continued to affirm a set of assumptions about the relationship between the individual and the nation-state. LOI 270 laid down a number of important prerequisites for citizenship. First, applicants for naturalization had to "develop" and "demonstrate" "love for and loyalty to the Philippines." The conjoining of affective ties and political loyalty in one phrase made it appear that love and loyalty each followed naturally from the other. Furthermore, "loyalty to the Philippines" was conflated with loyalty to the Philippine state. One basic precondition for acquiring citizenship was that the applicant should not have been engaged in "assassination" and other subversive activities. But opposition to the state did not automatically mean disloyalty to the nation: leftist organizations in the 1960s and early 1970s routinely invoked the good of the nation in challenging the state. Second, applicants had to demonstrate "affinity to the customs, traditions and ideals of the Filipino people." Given the ethnic heterogeneity of the "Filipino people," what these specific "customs, traditions, and ideals" remained largely unspecified. In fact, longstanding negative perceptions of, and attitudes toward, Muslim and indigenous minorities would suggest that these customs, traditions, and ideals tended to be defined in Christian, urban, and middle-class terms. Moreover, how could the "customs, traditions, and ideals" specific to the "Filipino people" be definitively identified when the history of the country (and that of other countries) showed that commonality of identity based on shared history, language, and religion could not be readily assumed to bind people into a single community? This incapacity to define certain values as specifically national is by no means unique to the Philippines, since countries like Australia are similarly bedeviled by assumptions of "national" values that turn out, upon close examination, to be quite universal and indistinguishable from the "cultural values" of other countries (Joppke 2010, 126).

Such conundrums underlie and beset the discourse of integration, but in the Philippine context, they were largely glossed over by the actual pragmatics of naturalization by fiat, a fact that owed more to the shifting priorities and strategies of the Philippine state from the 1970s onwards than to the achievement of a national consensus on Filipino national culture and identity (Aguilar 1999, 315–20). This can be seen in the changes in the Philippine Constitution's articles on citizenship that pertained to mestizos. Reversing the Supreme Court decision of 1946, the 1973 Constitution allowed a Filipina married to a Chinese to keep her citizenship; although there was some ambiguity concerning the status of the mestizo owing to the constitutional definition of a Filipino as a person "whose father and mothers are [Filipino] citizens," the offspring of a Chinese-Filipino marriage was allowed once more to elect Philippine citizenship. The 1987 Constitution would further clarify the legal ambiguity of mestizos by extending citizenship automatically to children with at least one parent holding Filipino citizenship. The significance of these two Constitutions lay in their loosening of the restrictions surrounding the citizenship status of the Chinese mestizo.

Adopting an integrationist stance would enable the Philippine state to pursue its policy of attracting capital and technical flows, especially from America and the emergent East Asian region (see chap. 5). In hopes of generating much-needed income, the state has resorted to commodifying citizenship by granting permanent residency to moneyed foreigners in hopes of attracting investment (see chap. 3). Over the past four decades, it has also sought to tap the skills, talent, and capital of Filipino migrant workers and settlers abroad by deploying the term "balikbayan" (lit., "return to one's town/country") to refer to Filipino immigrants and their descendants (Szanton Blanc 1996), as a way of stressing their continued connections with their "home" country.

This re-nationalization of Filipino communities abroad culminated in the 2003 Dual Citizenship bill (Republic Act 9225, enacted in 2004) which enabled natural-born Filipino migrants who had acquired foreign citizenship while abroad to re-acquire Philippine citizenship. Note, however, that only *natural-born* Filipinos (and their unmarried legitimate or illegitimate children below eighteen years of age) who have given up their Philippine citizenship when taking another country's citizenship through naturalization are eligible to reacquire Philippine citizenship. Naturalized Filipino citizens as well as dual citizens (i.e., those who have both Philippine citizenship and foreign citizenship not acquired through naturalization) are not covered by this law (Bureau of Immigration, Philippines 2012). Neither Chinese who became Philippine citizens by naturalization nor Chinese who were born in the Philippines but who hold a mainland or Taiwanese passport and who want to acquire Philippine citizenship are eligible to apply under this law. Given such restrictions, the dual citizenship law arguably had far less impact on the Philippine Chinese than Marcos's LOI 270.

Writing before the mass naturalization of the Chinese by LOI 270, the scholar Gerald McBeath had in mind the Yuyitung case when he noted that Philippine Chinese youths, "in approaching political integration, present[ed] an optimistic picture for the future of the Chinese community," but that— short of measures being "externally imposed"—the conservative Chinese community leadership and the "disinterest of most Philippine Chinese" in integration presented obstacles to the full achievement of political integration (1973, 240). Events since then have shown that external imposition by acts of state matter as much as, if not more than, proclamations among Chinese of "good" citizenship and scholarly descriptions of assimilation and integration in terms of individual choices and actions over generations. In a less hostile political environment, Chineseness is no longer a defensive form of self-identification and strategy of survival, but can be finally reinvented as a "special kind of Filipino" (Hedman and Sidel 2000, 84), just like the Chinese mestizos in the Spanish Philippines (Wickberg 1965, 31).

Nevertheless, assumptions of good citizenship still constituted the basis of the state rationale of "integration." LOI 270 (1975) explicitly stated that "Chinese permanently residing in the country who, having developed and demonstrated love for and loyalty to the Philippines and affinity to the customs, traditions and ideals of the Filipino people, as well as contributed to the economic, social and cultural development of our country, may be integrated into the national fabric by grant of Philippine citizenship." The integrative stance of LOI 270 would be repeated in the Republic Act no. 9139 (The Administrative Naturalization Law of 2000) signed by President Gloria Macapagal-Arroyo in 2000: applicants "must be born in the Philippines and residing therein since birth" and must have received primary and secondary education in accredited schools where "Philippine history, government and civics are taught and prescribed as part of the school curriculum" and have children enrolled in "similar schools." Applicants are required to be literate in Filipino "or any of the dialects of the Philippines," "must have mingled with the Filipinos and evinced a sincere desire to learn and embrace the customs, traditions and ideals of the Filipino people" (*Shijie Ribao,* 2001).

But these assumptions gloss over the fact that it is not only Chineseness but Filipinoness itself that has undergone important redefinition in light of the Filipino diaspora from the mid-1970s onwards (see chap. 5). The ritual expressions of patriotism have also been transformed as well, as the idea of a national community built on shared identity, principles, and values (whether political, moral, or ethical) has come under pressure from globalization. It should be noted, however, that although the so-called procedural state that took shape in Europe after the 1960s has adopted a stance of "principled neutrality" on issues of identity and morality (Joppke 2010, 112), the question of political and cultural integration continues to haunt even the most liberal versions of state policy and practice on immigration and immigrants, particularly in the wake of the September 11, 2001 "terrorist" attacks in the United States and succeeding events in Europe. "Citizenship tests" of varying degrees of "difficulty" have been used in countries like the United States, the United Kingdom, Australia, Germany, and Holland to gauge the sufficiency of integration of immigrants who apply to become full-fledged members of their national communities.

In the United States, for example, literacy tests once served as an instrument for controlling immigration from Eastern and Southern Europe and civics tests were later introduced to limit immigration from non-Western Europe and Asia (Etzioni 2007, 354). The 1952 Immigration Act that required both tests was informed by sociological theories of cultural assimilation and designed to weed out communists and their sympathizers, while the 1985 Immigration Reform and Control Act was targeted at illegal migrants from Latin America (ibid.). In Germany and Holland, citizenship tests are specifically aimed at "integrating" Muslim immigrants and their children.

But the vicissitudes of international migration in the postwar era have also reconfigured the terms of membership in the nation-state. Because loyalty and love are held to underpin integration into Philippine society, contributions to the "economic, social and cultural development of our country" by overseas Filipino workers (OFWs) can be made even without being physically "rooted" in the Philippines. Moreover, demonstrating one's love of country no longer precludes declaring one's political loyalty to another country and taking up citizenship and residency elsewhere. Affinity to the "customs, traditions and ideals of the Filipino people" has been redefined flexibly enough to encompass non-Filipino nationals who may not necessarily speak any Philippine language, or send their children to Philippine schools, or even "mingle" socially with Filipinos. More

Chiquito as *Mr. Wong* (Sotang Bastos Productions, movie poster courtesy of Video 48)

important, money talks, as foreigners with enough capital to invest in the Philippines can now be entitled to permanent residency with the option of either applying for naturalization, or remaining a permanent resident, able to enjoy the rights and privileges thereof.

The "Chinese" in Philippine Popular Culture

The shift in state attitude and policy toward the Chinese found expression in popular culture through two films released in the 1970s. In the early 1970s, three Chinese-Filipinos, Herman Tiu Laurel, Henry Lim, and Ricardo Lee, using the collective pseudonym R. H. Laurel,[21] wrote the screenplay for *Dragnet* (Manila Dragnet, 1973), a crime action movie starring the enormously popular film star, Joseph Estrada. *Dragnet's* sympathetic portrait of the "Chinese" was a first in Philippine cinematic history, and marked the first effort by a major mainstream film to present a positive picture of a "younger generation" of "Chinese" to a wider Philippine audience. Its strong integrationist message heralded the mass naturalization by administrative fiat two years later.

Prior to *Dragnet*, comedians like Dolphy (born Rodolfo Vera Quizon) and Chiquito (Augusto Valdez Pangan) had played Chinese characters on stage and screen with great success. Dolphy—himself of Chinese-mestizo descent—achieved popularity early in his stage career with his comic alter ego, Go Lay (also spelled Golay), a Chinese vendor turned court witness, who convulsed audiences with his heavily accented, broken Tagalog. But Dolphy stopped playing Go Lay on stage when he moved to radio because he had been advised that his comic caricature of the Chinese would not help his career, since many of the radio sponsors were Chinese and might be offended by his portrayal of the Chinese (Ancheta 2006, 82). Nevertheless, Dolphy considered Go Lay an important breakthrough in his career as a comedian: Go Lay was, in his words, "a riot, *naging kwela*. That's the start of show business for me, *nung naging* comedian *na ako* [It was a riot, a hit. That's the start of show business for me, when I became a comedian]" (ibid.).

Chiquito's crime-fighting Mister Wong appeared in a series of hit movies from 1963 to 1982: the eponymous title film (1963), *Mr. Wong vs Mistico* (1964), *Wild, Wild Wong* (1967), *Mr. Wong Strikes Again* (1969), *James Wong* (1973), *Dynamite Wong and TNT Jackson* (1974), *Mr. Wong and the Bionic Girls* (1977), and *Mr. Wong Meets Jesse & James* (1982). Sporting a Qing-style coronet-shaped hat, Fu Manchu moustache, queue, and buckteeth, Mr. Wong triumphed over a series of opponents by virtue of his diligence, resourcefulness, and intelligence. Although Chiquito adopted the trademark Fu Manchu features for his comic portrayal of Mr. Wong, he also based his character on Chinese-American fictional detective Charlie Chan in an effort to showcase Mr. Wong's sagacity and resilience. Chiquito's daughter Eliza Pangan had this to say about her father's "love affair" with his Chinese character and Chinese reaction to Mr. Wong ("Chiquito, SLN" 2007):

> *Sabi n'ya, lagi-lagi ang mga* Chinese *daw noon were portrayed as tindero ng taho* [He said that in the past, the Chinese were always portrayed as beancurd vendors]. He made something out of that, but instead of mocking the Chinese, he uplifted them and celebrated their virtues when he was already doing films. *Kaya, gusto s'ya ng mga* Chinese *noon* [So, in those days, the Chinese liked him].

Dolphy and Chiquito's portrayals, though not unsympathetic, for the most part relied on caricatures of the Chinese in looks and in speech for high comic relief. In contrast, *Dragnet* drew on a different set of cultural references for its portrait of the Chinese. Instead of vendor or mandarin, it opted for the martial arts hero, a staple of *wuxia* films from Hong Kong in the postwar period. Shown in movie theaters across Chinatowns in Manila,

Southeast Asia, and America after World War II, Hong Kong cinema had gone global in the early 1970s with the success of American-born and Hong Kong-raised Bruce Lee, who introduced his particular brand of muscular-heroic "Chinese" in films such as *Big Boss* (1971), *Fist of Fury* (1972), and *Way of the Dragon* (1973).[22]

But there is an important difference between the persona represented by Bruce Lee and the martial arts expert in *Dragnet*. Bruce Lee's films have been read as projections of a kind of self-assertive, confident, and masculine Chinese nationalism (Teo 1997, 110–11). Indeed, in a succession of commercially successful films that appealed to an international (and in particular, overseas Chinese, Asian, and African-American) audiences, Bruce Lee enacted a form of Chinese "revenge" on a series of racialized opponents—white, black, Japanese—who allegorically stood in for the agents of the century-long history of Chinese oppression and humiliation. This muscular-Chinese nationalism provided an antidote to the archetypal effete (and evil) "Fu Manchu" or asexual-sage Charlie Chan of Hollywood movies. Lee's appeal to "overseas Chinese" audiences[23] lay in the kind of Chinese nationalism he embodied:

> The nationalism of Lee's films is better understood as an abstract
> kind of cultural nationalism, manifesting itself as an emotional wish
> among Chinese people living outside China to identify with China and
> things Chinese, even though they may not have been born there or
> speak its national language or dialects. They wish to affirm themselves
> and fulfill their aspirations by identifying with the "mother culture,"
> producing an abstract and apolitical type of nationalism. (111)

Dragnet, however, is not interested in celebrating pride-evoking Chinese nationalism based on emotional ties to the "mother culture." Its concern, rather, is to show Chinese solidarity with the Filipino. Martial arts expert Tsing Tong Tsai[24] plays Tiong Chan, a young, Philippine-born, working-class Chinese karate instructor who witnesses the murder of a Chinese friend and *kumpadre* (ritual kin) of police Sgt. Joe Guerrero (Joseph Estrada). Tiong Chan's status as a working-class foreign national, his filial piety, and his family history—his father once got involved with the police and thereby suffered persecution, resulting in the loss of his store and his inability to find a job to provide for his family—militate against his involvement in the police affair. But when his little brother is killed by a bomb trap planted in the karate instructor's locker, Tiong decides to follow his sister Susana's (Grace Chua) advice to do "his duty as a good citizen" (as she puts it) and help Sgt. Joe Guerrero bring the killers—members of a crime syndicate that extorts from Chinese businessmen—to justice. By choosing to get involved, he ends up realizing that the fate of the Filipinos is also intertwined with his own (R. Lee 2011).

Early in the film, Sergeant Guerrero, frustrated at the lack of cooperation from the Chinese victims of the syndicate—aggravated by the fact that most of the conversations are conducted by the Chinese in Hokkien, which he cannot follow ("malay ko ba kung pinagbibili na ninyo ako rito" [how do I know you're not selling me off already])[25]—testily informs the group of Chinese businessmen:

> Anong gusto ninyong mangyari? Magtayo kayo ng sariling republika dito sa Pilipinas? Di maaari yan. Dito kayo nag-hanap-buhay, dito ninyo pinalaki ang inyong mga anak, at maaaring dito na rin kayo mamamatay. Kaya kailangan ninyong makipagtulungan sa amin, at kung ayaw ninyo, umuwi na kayo sa Tsina.

> What do you want to happen? Establish your own republic here in the Philippines? Not possible. You earned your living here, raised your kids here, and it's possible that you may die here as well. So you should cooperate with us, and if you don't, then you should just go back to China.

Joseph Estrada in *Dragnet* (JE Productions, movie poster courtesy of Video 48)

The irony is that Joe Guerrero eventually discovers that the very people who appear to be championing the Chinese—the articulate lawyer Atty. Lim (by implication a Chinese mestizo, played by Ruben Rustia), who negotiates on their behalf, and the millionaire doctor-philanthropist (Vic Silayan), whose daughter Eva (Eva Reyes) falls in love with Guerrero—are involved in the syndicate that preys on, and terrorizes, the Chinese. The doctor-philanthropist, Vicente Cardenas, a self-declared "friend" of the Chinese, speaks eloquently of the desire of the "younger generation of Chinese" to "be integrated into Filipino society, to be accepted as equals, as citizens, like you and me, not second-class human beings." He goes on to say: "*Anong ginagawa nating mga Pilipino, mababa na ang tingin natin, parang pinandidirihan, tawagin natin ng beho, e kung tutuusin mo*, their civilization and culture is [*sic*] older than ours" (What do we Filipinos do? We look down on them, are repulsed by them, call them *beho* [*intsik Viejo, tulo laway*: old drooling chink], but if we think about it, their civilization and culture are older than ours.) This same defender of the Chinese is later revealed to be the true mastermind of the crime syndicate.

Dragnet's strong integrationist stance builds on generational differences in attitudes and perspectives between the "conservative" parents, on the one hand, whose bad experiences cause them to shy away from any involvement with the police, and the "younger generation," on the other hand, who, in the words of sister Susan, have "different values" and "believe in better cooperation between Filipinos and Chinese." Tiong Chan chafes against his parents' injunction to keep silent to protect the family from being victimized further; he experiences his inaction as a form of impotence, a slur on his masculinity: "*Anong klaseng lalaki ako, natatakot humarap sa katotohanan?*" Macho Sergeant Guerrero later exploits this when, talking to Tiong's sister, he makes fun of Tiong: "*Bakit? 'Di ba siya lalaki?*" (Why? Isn't he a man?) Cornering Tiong at the karate gym, Guerrero taunts him by asking if he is "sioke" (gay). The two engage in a mano-à-mano fight, neither one besting the other, forcing Guerrero to admit grudgingly that Tiong is good at karate. Guerrero then makes a final appeal to Tiong: "*Ako'y isang Pilipinong nagmamalasakit sa kapwa mong intsik, nguni't ikaw, anong ginagawa mo? 'Sasawalang kibo ka. Kapag pinagpatuloy mo iyan, habang panahon na lamang pagsasamantalahan kayo, at maaaring sumunod na biktima ay ikaw at iyong pamilya*" (I'm a Filipino who empathizes with your fellow Chinese, but you, what are you doing about it? You stay silent. If you continue doing this, you will always be exploited, and the next victims might be you and your family).

Just as Sergeant Guerrero, out of sympathy to the Chinese, flouts the advice of his superior to "just forget about the Chinese" ("*Kalimutan mo na ang mga Intsik*"), Tiong Chan flouts his parents' wishes that he not get involved. Both Tiong and Guerrero subject themselves to danger, violent reprisal, and possible death, Tiong in order to avenge his younger brother's death and Guerrero his Chinese kumpadre's (and also do his duty as an "incorruptible, most capable" cop, in the words of Dr. Cardenas). As witness, Tiong holds the key to solving the case. But in weaving the plot around Tiong's decision to help out in the face of danger to his own safety, his own life and his family's, *Dragnet* makes the regional/global figure of the martial arts hero a stand-in, not of an assertive Chinese nationalism against a century of humiliation by western (and Japanese) colonial powers, but rather, a masculinist version of Philippine civic nationalism based on interethnic solidarity and mutual aid. In the film, the "Chinese" is not a passive "weakling" who is easily exploited or victimized. Moreover, the hitherto alien-Chinese and the Filipino find a way to work together for the common good of "their" country, the Philippines. In this way, the film makes a case for the "integration" of the Chinese into the Filipino popular imagination on the basis of the desire and willingness of "Filipinized Chinese"—now calling themselves *pinsinos* (an abbreviation of Pilipino and Sino, and meaning "Pinoy na intsik," as Bernard Go [1974, 234–35] explains it), *sinpinos*, and later, Chinese Filipinos and Tsinoys—to be "good citizens" and perform their civic duties and obligations as Filipinos.

There is a certain irony in the fact that *Dragnet*, a film about a crime-fighting cop working to uphold the law, was co-written by an activist, Ricky Lee, who had gone "underground" when martial law was declared and collaborated on the film script while he was in hiding from the Marcos government. Pagkakaisa founder Bernard Go was the one who obtained funding from ten other ethnic Chinese businessmen for the film project (Ang-See 2011).[26] He had initially contacted Henry Lim[27] about writing the script for *Dragnet*, and Lim in turn brought in Herman Tiu Laurel and Ricardo Lee (Laurel 2011). Herman Tiu Laurel (2011) recalls that "Henry got a room in Tropicana Hotel where we could work on the script." Laurel states that "one of the motivations of Bernie Go was to bring the Tsinoy and Filipinos' sense of community closer together; it was a time that kidnappings of Chinese were on the rise and there were undertones of anti-Chinese sentiment being stirred in activist rhetoric while [President] Marcos was being more open with the naturalization of thousands of Chinese. It was also only a few years after the Indonesian pogrom against Chinese-Indonesians; though I never heard this raised in any discussion, I do know that the incidents in Indonesia reverberated in the Philippines (and again during the fall of Suharto as Chinese businesses were being burned there)."

These young writers were working in a time of intense political ferment that led up to the declaration of martial law in 1972. With mainland China going Communist, direct travel between China and the Philippines had become difficult, and Hong Kong and Taiwan emerged as the hubs of overseas Chinese organizations and activities, including the production of popular culture.[28] As mentioned before, the postwar years also witnessed a demographic shift in the Philippines as second- and third-generation Chinese Filipinos came of age. Herman Tiu Laurel, Henry Lim, and Ricardo Lee were part of the activist movement (Laurel 2011). The idea of activist Chinese had precedents in World War II (see chap. 4), but a crucial difference was the terrain in which they operated. While Chinese guerrillas for the most part remained oriented toward the national salvation of "China," these second-generation activists explicitly identified themselves as Filipinos. These postwar *pinsinos/sinpinos* were among the first Philippine Chinese to go to university in large numbers, and there became involved in organizational activities that included outreach and charity work in depressed areas like Sapang Palay (located in Bulacan). Some of them joined progressive social movements, a number of which were instrumental in challenging the state's claim to be the legitimate representative of the Filipino national community and arbiter of Filipino national culture (see the next chapter).[29]

Herman Tiu Laurel's (2011) personal background—family, friends, education, and political orientation—did indeed play a role in defining his sense of himself as a "Chinese Filipino":

What I recall from my upbringing and childhood experiences that
I consider crucial to my attitudinal direction, i.e., the non-business
direction, "nationalist" and pro-Filipino commitment in Life, very
political-ized outlook are the following very specific instances:

a) My mother's frequent admonition to "return something to this
country (Philippines) that the family has benefitted from," which I
heard from her from very early childhood to my teens;

b) The early education in Filipino schools enforced by
the citizenship "naturalization law" requirement. I started my
kindergarten in San Beda while enrolled in kindergarten in Hope
Christian High School, and though I quit San Beda after grade one, I
was also made to quit Hope Christian and moved to St. Stephen's High
School, which had had a reputation (I learned in later years) for being
less Chinese than Hope;

c) On the political aspect, this is what I often recall: my "Eagle
Club" in the elementary where I organized classmates who cared to

join and engage in "wars" every afternoon with other groups. I'd draw
symbols to represent our "Eagle's Club," we'd pick (or organize) fights
(sword fights) in the school quadrangle, and fight until we were late
for class and get an earful from the teachers. In essence, I think as
an adult today I am still doing the same, but for more sophisticated
purposes—is the political mindset innate?

d) I had then quit the Chinese classes after grade six, just as my
elder brothers had (though two sister also in St. Stephen's continued
on to finish Chinese High School); in the elementary I had a Filipino-
Chinese classmate who became very close to me; and another Filipino-
Chinese "crush" at maybe fourth grade named Susan who impressed
me a great deal by her industry—I visited her at home once and saw
her sweeping and scrubbing their sala, a scene which humanized my
view of the "katulong" who did that in my parents' huge house and my
"friend"['s] and blurred the distinction between Filipino "katulong"
and "Filipino friend";

e) High school in a very Anglicized school made a great deal
of difference as an American drama coach spent time with us in
the drama guild, and I won English speaking awards (though I
won a Chinese speaking award in the elementary [school]). Having
quit Chinese class by then, I drifted farther and farther away from
Chinese culture. Music, dance, the Anglicized barkada, movies, books,
inundated my cranium. A female classmate who could still act out
Chinese Peking Opera was asked to perform a short sample started
looking weird to me—that's when, on hindsight, I saw Chinese culture
as alien to me already. High school politics was a major factor, I ran
campaigns and won, and it proved absorbing and exciting, certainly
much more engaging than my studies;

f) College, activism: this was probably the defining period
in my politicization, having observed through media and only
vicariously the various politics and issues of the 1960s—from the
Kennedy assassination in the U.S. to the anti-U.S. demonstrations of
the [leftist youth organization] Kabataang Makabayan in Manila—
and wondering what it was all about. It was also a period of
adolescent searching for that "purpose" in life, reading [Christian
theologian Dietrich] Boenhoeffer, [*True Believer* author Eric]
Hoffer, Bertrand Russell, etc. at De La Salle [University] in my
first year and yearning for involvement, I registered my interest
in Student Council activities immediately.... [F]rom there I was
recruited into the See Haus of Jesuit Jose C. Blanco then Kasapi
[the "social-democratic" Kapulungan ng mga Sandigang Pilipino,

Assembly of Philippine Organizations] in 1970, and chairman of
Kasapi in 1986;

g) Kasapi politics intersected with higher levels of politics of
the traditional political parties as well as the ideological politics of
the Philippine Left. In 1971, I was seconded by Kasapi to the office of
Delegate Raul Manglapus at the Concon [Constitutional Convention].
In 1980, I was seconded to the office of Senator Roxas by Kasapi
and served as aide and secretary to the UNIDO [United Nations
Industrial Development Organization]. In between I had helped
organize as a founding member of the founding congress of the PDP
[Partido Demokratiko ng Pilipinas], identified with Nene Pimentel,
and later the SDP [Social Democratic Party] of Kit Tatad. Edsa I, I
belatedly joined and only due to the murder of Evelio Javier who was
a "compadre" (though a generation older than me). I was drafted by
Kasapi and I volunteered too, at the Philippine Refugee Processing
Center administratorship.[30]

Born in Bicol to a Chinese father and Filipino mother, Ricardo Lee
studied in a Chinese school in Bikol from elementary until high school.
"I was adopted by my relatives when I was five after my mother's death. I
ran away from them, and from Bikol, after high school. I went to Manila,
went solo from then on. A working student, I took up A.B. English at UP
[University of the Philippines] Diliman. I got involved in activism during
the martial law years, dropped out of fourth-year college to go full time
underground. I was in prison the whole of 1974" (Lee 2011b). A gifted
writer, Lee achieved literary fame with his Palanca prize-winning short
story, "Huwag! Huwag mong Kukuwentuhan ang Batang si Wei-fung"
(1968), a seminal work of fiction that dealt with the experiences of the
"Chinese"—their "identification with China and things Chinese" (Teo
1997, 111), their fraught relationship with Chinese mestizos, the Chinese
mestizos' deep-seated ambiguity about their "Chineseness," and the
ideological and political divisions within the supposedly homogeneous
Chinese community—from the points of view of both Chinese and Chinese
mestizos (see Hau 2000b, 169–75, for an analysis). Lee (2011a) states that
"I got into writing while I was living underground, and worked on *Dragnet*
for Joseph Estrada, but used a pseudonym. My second uncredited script
was *Itim* [Rites of May, 1976, directed by Mike de Leon]. My first officially
credited script was *Jaguar* [1979, directed by Lino Brocka], which I co-
wrote with Pete Lacaba" (Lee 2011b). Lee would go on to become one of
the most important and popular screenwriters/playwrights in Philippine
cinema, recently publishing two bestselling novels, *Para kay B* (For B, 2008)

and *Si Amapola sa 65 na Kabanata* (Amapola in 65 Chapters, 2011c)—the latter "a satire on a gay *manananggal* [viscera-sucker] revolutionary"—and working on "a political saga spanning the 1970s through the 1990s" (San Diego 2008).

As for the star of *Dragnet*, Joseph Estrada would go on to pursue a different, and no less successful, career as a politician, reaching as high as the vice presidency (1992–1998) and eventually the presidency of the Philippines. In a strange, negative twist to the plot of *Dragnet*, Estrada's fate became deeply intertwined with that of the "Chinese" kumpadres with whom he fraternized. As mayor of San Juan for seventeen years (from 1969 until the EDSA revolution), he governed an area that included a substantial number of upper-class Chinese, who had moved out of Binondo/Chinatown into affluent "villages" in the suburbs outside Manila proper.[31] Among these residential pockets, Greenhills in the mayoralty of San Juan was known as the "second Chinatown" (Chua 2000). Estrada counted a number of Chinese among his closest friends: one of them, a high-stakes gambler named Charlie "Atong" Ang, would achieve notoriety in the *jueteng* (illegal lottery) scandal that led to President Estrada's impeachment on charges of bribery, corruption, betrayal of public trust, and culpable violation of the Constitution. Others formed part of his "midnight cabinet" that advised him on affairs of government, and fronted for him on real-estate deals (ibid.).[32] But Estrada's stint as head of the Presidential Anti-Crime Commission under the Ramos administration in the late 1990s also earned him good credit among ethnic Chinese after a series of highly publicized and successful operations against kidnappers (Grafilo 1998; *Malaya* 1998), even as kidnappings continued to happen under his watch (see the next chapter). Herman Tiu Laurel (2011) pointedly observes that "Erap [Estrada] is a major factor in Tsinoy and Filipino's warm attitudes, a fact that the Makati *tisoys* [mestizos] have used against Estrada in their demonizations of Estrada, especially during the runup to the Edsa Dos coup—stirring up anti-Chinese feelings around Dante Tan, Atong Ang."

Three years after *Dragnet* was released, Eddie Romero's masterpiece *Ganito Kami Noon, Paano Kayo Ngayon?* (1976) went even further by reaching back to the past and literally making a place for the "Chinese" in Philippine history through its portrayal of the heroic Intsik Liu, played by *Dragnet*'s Tsing Tong Tsai, a nineteenth-century Bruce Lee who befriends and sacrifices his life for protagonist Kulas Ocampo.

Ganito Kami Noon, Paano Kayo Ngayon? is the first critically acclaimed film to articulate the integrationist stance broached by academics (McCarthy 1974, 22) and later taken up so prominently in later decades by organizations such as Kaisa para sa Kaunlaran and by *Mano Po* (discussed in

Ganito Kami Noon, Paano Kayo Ngayon? (Hemisphere
Pictures, movie poster courtesy of Video 48)

chaps. 3 and 5 respectively). Its timing was, like that of *Dragnet*, fortuitous: Romero's film was released one year after LOI 270 implemented the mass naturalization of the Chinese.

Ganito Kami Noon, Paano Kayo Ngayon, like *Dragnet*, is notable for its sympathetic treatment of the Chinese.[33] Its contribution lies in its (re)vision of Philippine history as an inclusive rather than exclusionary process of becoming-Filipino, one that makes a place for the Chinese in the Filipino national community. Set in turn-of-the-century Philippines and covering the last years of the Spanish regime and ending with the arrival of the Americans, *Ganito* highlights the changing meanings of Filipinoness by following, in *Bildungsroman* fashion, a naive young Tagalog named Nicolas Ocampo, who journeys to the capital in the midst of the Philippine revolution. The movie is concerned primarily with Kulas's growing consciousness of what it means to be "Filipino." The first use of the term occurs in Kulas's encounter with a Spanish priest, who prevails upon Kulas to escort his illegitimate child to the capital. Padre Gil tells Kulas that the child will not be difficult to find, since he is "the only Filipino in the village." Kulas next encounters the word in a different context when native rebels declare that they, Kulas included, are all Filipinos. Kulas deduces that one becomes a Filipino by being born and by growing up in this country.

Kulas's consciousness of the shifting meanings of "Filipino" further develops when he meets the *Intsik* Liu, who ferries him and little Bindoy to Manila. Liu is initially reluctant to help Kulas, but something in Kulas's naiveté—Kulas continues to smile broadly even after Liu refuses to help—makes Liu change his mind. On the boat to Manila, Kulas shares his newly acquired idea of Filipinoness with Liu. To be Filipino, as the rebels defined it, meant being born and growing up here.

"*E, di Pilipino din ako* (Then I am also Filipino)," says Liu.

Kulas laughs. "*E, maliwanag na Intsik ka*" (But it's clear that you're Chinese).

To which Liu answers, "*E, ikaw, Tagalog, taga-bundok, paano ka naging Pilipino?*" (And you, a Tagalog from the mountains, how did you become Filipino?)

When Kulas admits his confusion, Liu tells him: "*Walang diperensya 'yan, isa ang buhay, parehong miserya*" (There is no difference. Each has his own life, but all of us share the same misery).

Liu helps Kulas escape with the wounded rebel Kidlat and pays for this good deed with his life. Liu's "Chineseness," however, often spurs the distrust of those who are less "naive" than Kulas. While hiding out at Liu's house, Kidlat overhears Liu conferring with other Chinese in Hokkien and, mistakenly assuming that Liu intends to turn them over, threatens to harm Liu's wife. Liu suddenly turns into Jackie Chan and quickly disarms Kidlat. A retreating but still mistrustful Kidlat snarls: *"Tandaan mo, magtata-gumpay ang rebolusyon!"* (Mark this: the revolution will triumph!)

Romero's sympathetic treatment of the Chinese can be seen in the fact that he takes the viewer, through Kulas's viewpoint, into Liu's home.[34] In *Ganito*, as in *Dragnet*, we see the humanized Chinese in their homes. Liu welcomes Kulas to his home, and is seen with his family, eating, teaching the children abacus, working, and being teased by his wife. Liu even teases Kulas by telling him, straight-faced, that the delicious food he is eating in Liu's house is cooked lizard. In one short scene, Kulas laughs while Liu recounts answering a surprised Spaniard in Spanish. The other Chinese, who are also at the table, make their comments about Liu's Spanish in Hokkien. Liu's friendship with Kulas, which is based in part on Liu's ability to communicate in both Tagalog and Hokkien (plus Spanish), is strengthened by Liu's implicit trust in Kulas, his unstinting succor, and his eventual sacrifice to save his friend. A tearful Kulas later tells Liu's widow: *"Siya [Liu] ang nagbigay-halaga sa aking pagkatao. Kung hindi dahil doon ay sana buhay pa siya"* (He valued me as a human being. If it hadn't been for this, he would still be alive). Kulas's journey therefore parallels his own growing consciousness of the inclusiveness of "Filipino." At the end of the movie, a more mature Kulas feels that he at last understands that he is a "Filipino."

Part of what it means to be Filipino, as Romero's film makes clear, can be understood not only as a sense of shared history, but also as a sense of obligation and trust forged in the process of being thrown together. But while *Ganito Kami Noon* and *Dragnet* were instrumental in presenting and disseminating positive images of the "Chinese," the image of the "Chinese" as alien and capitalist persisted and continued to exercise a hold on the Filipino nationalist imagination.

The Yuyitung case highlighted the political vulnerability of even the most passionate advocates of the Filipinization of the Chinese. As the court case against the Yuyitungs dragged on, a wave of kidnappings in late 1971, in turn, spotlighted the vulnerability of the "Chinese community," particularly its business people (*Manila Bulletin*, 1971). (The revival of the kidnapping phenomenon in the late 1980s will be discussed in the next chapter.) An equally strong impression was created by the execution by firing squad of Chinese drug dealer and heroin manufacturer, Lim Seng,[35] in December 1972. What distinguished this event from other cases of capital punishment was that it was broadcast live over national television, enabling Marcos to make a public example of Lim as a deterrent against drug trafficking and to showcase the reach and might of the state under martial law. Beyond the national penitentiary, the state's power over the life and death of its "people" would be most keenly felt by the far larger number of people who suffered its extrajudicial torture and killings, and by the war in Mindanao. The latter alone would claim more than a hundred thousand lives and lead to the displacement of more than a million Filipinos.

Under martial law, the state had provided an administrative solution to the problem of citizenship for the ethnic Chinese, but also made sure that the legal solution would be backed up by the Filipinization of Chinese schools, which cut the number of hours of Chinese instruction and ensured that future generations of Philippine-born Chinese would be barely literate in Chinese (though many second-generation people can still speak some Hokkien).

Just as significant, negative images of the Chinese persisted in the popular media and among certain segments of the nationalist intelligentsia. Perhaps the most exemplary articulation of the Chinese as Other to the Filipino national community is Lino Brocka's widely touted masterpiece, *Maynila: Sa Mga Kuko ng Liwanag* (1975), based on the classic novel by Edgardo Reyes (1986 [1967–1968]) and scripted by noted writer Clodualdo del Mundo. The Brocka film came out in the same year as LOI 270. The film contains a memorable line that encapsulates the most persistent idea about the Chinese: *"Pero, pare, Intsik 'yan. Tiyak na makuwarta 'yan"* (But that one is Chinese, man. He must certainly be rich).

This line, uttered by one of protagonist Julio Madiaga's friends, sums up the general tone of resignation and forbearance with which most of the movie's characters accept the oppressive status quo even as it singles out the "rich Chinese" as the embodiment of that status quo. Up to this point, Madiaga (Bembol Roco) has not yet seen Ligaya (Hilda Koronel), his sweetheart, whom he has been trying to locate in Manila. The clues he has been following lead him to a Chinese store at the corner of Ongpin and Misericordia Streets. Right in the heart of Manila's Chinatown, he is turned away with rude abruptness by Ah Tek (Tommy Yap), the owner of the Chinese store. Madiaga believes that his beloved Ligaya is being kept prisoner by the Chinese. Madiaga has just asked his friend Maximo (Pio de Castro) for advice on rescuing Ligaya. Maximo's answer is that Madiaga would need money to get anything done in Manila, and the fact that Madiaga's antagonist is Chinese (and therefore rich) gives the lie to Madiaga's illusions of freeing Ligaya by righful means.

A thin figure of a man, with crooked posture and an accent only slightly less pronounced than that of the Chinese restaurant owner across the street who slaps a serving girl in front of Julio, Ah Tek embodies the deforming and dehumanizing violence, the rapacity and alienation that characterize the city itself. The picture of Ah Tek that the viewer gets is painted mostly from Ligaya's tortured account. From her story, we gather that Ligaya had gone to Manila, ostensibly to work in a factory and to study. But Mrs. Cruz, her "recruiter," promptly sold her into white slavery. The Chinese Ah Tek, a customer, apparently fell in love with her, monopolized her services, and set her up in his house. Eventually, she bears him a child, but her attempts to escape and to take her child with her are met with threats, beatings, and, finally, murder.

In contrast to Madiaga and his friends, whose personalities and idiosyncrasies are treated in some detail, Ah Tek is an insubstantive, shadowy figure glimpsed only sporadically and in brief, obstructed shots throughout the film. Madiaga glimpses Ah Tek for the first time when the Chinese appears behind the accordion gate of his house and, after a one-line query, shuts the door on the inquiring Julio. At Ligaya's funeral, Ah Tek is seen from a distance among foliage and tombstones, his expression hidden behind sunglasses. Even the last confrontation, during which a vengeful Julio repeatedly stabs Ah Tek, gives us mostly shots of Ah Tek's blood-stained back and upraised hands.

This filmic strategy of keeping the Chinese at a distance predisposes the movie to being read in allegorical terms. The names of the characters—Madiaga (a near-homophone of *tiyaga,* or industry) and Ligaya Paraiso (happiness and paradise) and Mr. Nigad (from *ganid,* or greed), for example—stand in for virtues and vices writ large. Ah Tek's name is a homophone of *atik,* the Tagalog slang for money, never mind the fact that Ah Tek is actually not a Chinese name.[36] The city also becomes a central trope for the Fall, the End of Innocence, and is principally evoked by images of constriction and closure. Although Ah Tek does not maltreat Ligaya, he insists on keeping her caged in his store-cum-house. Ligaya speaks of feeling as though her life were a matchbox; she ends up, quite literally, in a box. A grieving Julio then murders Ah Tek.

In the final scene, a mob chases Julio down an alley, with the camera zooming in for a final close-up of a terrified Julio's open mouth. The claustrophobic feel of the movie is enhanced by the contrast that the film establishes between, on the one hand, the tender and almost idyllic shots of Ligaya and Julio in the expansive countryside (the beach, for instance), and, on the other hand, shots that confine the main action in Manila to specific areas. There are evocations of the cacophonic and claustrophobic melée of the market, the squatter areas, and Julio's workplaces (notably the construction sites and the gay bordello). But in this film, Chinatown, the city within the city, with its garbage-paved streets, dirt-smudged stores, Mandarin songs, car horns, and Hokkien-Tagalog chatter, becomes a synecdoche of urban, corrupt(ing) and alien Manila itself.

Real life, however, would prove to be far more recalcitrant than the black-and-white picture painted by *Kuko*. Finding itself under pressure to literally "clean up" the capital, the Manila city government under martial law came up with an ingenious solution: why not turn Chinatown itself into an income-generating tourist attraction? Aimed at showcasing "Chinese influence in [*sic*] the origin of the modern Filipino," the plans included the construction of Chinese pagoda gates at Rosario, Ongpin, and San Fernando Streets; restoration of Spanish-era buildings, building façades with Chinese motifs and "injection of Chinese atmospheres [*sic*] in the form of lamps, lanterns and hangings"; and building of monuments and cleaning of the esteros (canals) (*United Daily News*, 1973). The plans to turn Chinatown into a showcase of the Chinese-mestizo hybridity of Filipino culture extended to the docking of "sampans" (wooden boats) and celebrations of Chinese New Year and other festivals (*Bulletin Today*, 1973a, 1, 5; 1973b, 1, 5).

Not all the plans were or could be realized: The mayor of Manila expressed disappointment that "Chinatown" Binondo had "lost the quality that sets it apart from the rest of the sections in the city" (Genovea 1972, 3), and found it expedient to set up pagoda gates and order the business establishments to put up "Chinese signs" to mark the area's "Chineseness," just as Philippine newspapers began searching for the "vanishing breed" of "Chinatown Chinese" (*Times Journal*, 1973, 20).

In a final twist of the national narrative, the integration discourse of the state would make much of the "foreign" Chinese becoming more Filipino in the postwar years while failing to anticipate the fact that Filipinos were gradually becoming, in a sense, more "foreign" in the wake of large-scale labor migration and long-term residency abroad—a trend that originated in the 1960s and 1970s and accelerated over the next three to four decades. In the novel version of *Sa Mga Kuko ng Liwanag* (1986 [1967–68], 144–45), author Edgardo Reyes compared Chinese migrant men to the pirate Limahong rather than to Comrade Mao, an analogy that resonated with the sixteenth-century Tagalog definition of the Hokkien term *langlang* as "pirate, or corsair" (Scott 1994, 190; see Introduction): "Sapagkat ang paglisan sa sariling Ina upang sumuso sa bukal na buhay ng ibang dibdib ay isang pailalim na pamimirata" (Because leaving one's Mother[land] in order to suckle on the fountainhead of life from another breast is an underhanded form of piracy). Extending Reyes's comparison to present-day Philippines now ran the risk of making Limahongs of all Filipino migrant workers abroad.

The datedness of *Sa Mga Kuko ng Liwanag* underscores how quickly some of the ideas of the novel and film achieved orthodoxy even as subsequent events rendered the other ideas problematical within just a few years after the release of film and novel. Assumptions about state and citizenship that obtained in the 1960s and early 1970s now seem at once orthodox and obsolete in a world and region where China has reinvented itself as a socialist market state, where pluralism is now a global ideal[37] (though not always successfully implemented in practice), and permanent residency and citizenship need not be earned, but can be acquired—and is actively courted by the state—for a price.

Notes

1   On the translation of fan as "barbarian," see the Introduction, footnote 18. Chinese call other Chinese *tsaohuan* to signal their disapproval of the latter's uncouth or unseemly behavior, bad manners, and questionable lifestyles.

2   In 1960, Immigration statistics provided by Zheng Yingda, secretary-general of the Federation of Filipino-Chinese Chambers of Commerce and Industry showed a total Chinese (i.e., Chinese citizens) population of 117,216. The social composition of the ethnic-Chinese population can be ascertained by the following breakdown by occupation (*Shangzong mishuchang Zheng Yingda shumian tanhua*, 1961, 7–8): store owners, 11.65 percent; managers, 4.75 percent; store employees, 16.1 percent; professionals, 4.5 percent; laborers, 3.3 percent; house employees and housewives, 9.4 percent; students ten years and older, 17.2 percent; children below ten years of age, 21.5 percent; unemployed or retired, 6.4 percent; undocumented workers, 5.2 percent.

3   For an analysis of Yuyitung's position on assimilation, see Xü 1972; and especially McBeath 1973, 237–40.

4   In effect, the Yuyitungs were real-life counterparts to "the Lost Prince of Siasi" (the working title of *The Sultanate*; see chap. 1)! William Henry Scott (1989, 9–11) notes that during the fifteenth century, the "Eastern King" Paduka Batara died on Ming territory while on his mission, as did Ganlai Yibendum of Kumalalang on a subsequent mission, and some of their progeny remained behind and intermarried with the native population.

5   On Marcos's alleged Chinese father, see Seagrave 1988, 22–24; on Veronica Yuyitung's connection to the Chuas of Ilocos Norte, see Maximo Soliven's article in Yuyitung 2000, 151.

6   The following discussion on Skinner is based on Junko Koizumi's (2008; 2006) excellent analysis.

7   See Koizumi's analysis (2008, 212–14) of the difference in opinions on methodology between the American Skinner and the British Victor Purcell, long-time colonial official in Malaya and author of another classic in overseas Chinese studies, *The Chinese in Southeast Asia* (1951).

8   Skinner and Wickberg's generation of experts, China scholars by training, were unable to do fieldwork in the communist mainland, and therefore turned their attention to Chinese communities in Southeast Asia.

9   John Furnivall's concept (1991) of "plural society" does not address the question of class but, rather, focuses on occupation. I thank Benedict Anderson for his comments on Wickberg's text.

10   I thank Jafar Suryomenggolo for this information.

11   My thanks to Ben Anderson for pointing out the difference in the role of religion in Dutch and Spanish colonial policies.

12   On the idea of citizenship as inheritance in Indonesia, see the insightful work of Filomeno Aguilar (2001). The Citizenship Law of 2006 applied jus sanguinis (and selective jus soli in cases where the citizenship of a child's parents are uncertain) to the population.

13   Nor are Spanish mestizos immune to public resentment, however much they are also admired for their fair skin and Caucasian features. Ong names the "national hero" (*pahlawan nasional*) Manuel Quezon as a "peranakan Spanyol," and Senator Emmanuel Pelaez as having mixed Spanish and Chinese blood (*darah*), but observes that there are newspaper articles that are critical of the Spanish *peranakan*, citing as example the criticism that Andres Soriano y Roxas of San Miguel Brewery prefers to hire fellow Spanish to work in his company. Ong claims that while Spanish or American *peranakan* are not yet 100 percent accepted (*belum diterima seratus persen*) by the Filipino community, Chinese mestizos are (2005, 161).

14   There is a debate both within the Chinese community and on the Internet over efforts on the part of some Chinese organizations (notably the organizers of the *Manila Times*-sponsored Jose Rizal awards honoring Chinese contributions to the Philippines) to reclaim Jose Rizal by highlighting his Chinese ancestry. Alfonso O. Ang (Tu Yiban) has written an important critique of Chinese-language scholarship on Rizal, "Rizal's Chinese Overcoat" (Li Cha de Zhongguo wai yi) (2005), that offers an appraisal of the extent of Rizal's anti-Sinicism.

15   Saya umpamanya pernah dating ke satu pesta, untuk merayakan dipermandikannya anak seorang Tionghoa (asing) yang beragama Protestan. Dia adalah seorang pedagang besar dan dalam perayaan itu yang menjadi ayah rohani anak yang berwarganegara Tiongkok itu adalah wakil presiden Filipina Macapagal (partai liberal) dan Jenderal Balao, yang bukan saja berpartai Nacionalista (lawan partai liberal), tetapi beliau juga adalah salah satu pemimpin di senat dari gerakan anti Tionghoa. Lucunya ialah bahwa, menurut etika Filipina, Senator Balao yang mengecam habis-habisan golongan Tionghoa asing di senat, harus mengadakan perkecualian-perkecualian untuk anak dan kawan rohani Tionghoa totok itu. Di lain pihak orang Tionghoa totok itu harus membantu senator Balao dalam pemilihan umum dan membantu supaya beliau dapat duduk dalam senat dan membuat undang-undang anti Tionghoa dari mana dia tentu diperkecualian. (Ong 2005, 167)

16   Proses asimilasi di Filipina sampai sekarang masih berjalan. Saya dapat menyaksikan sendiri di suatu dusun di daerah Bicol (Luzon Selatan), di mana tinggal seorang Tionghoa totok tetapi menikah dengan wanita Filipina. Orang Tionghoa itu dengan terus-terang mengecam orang-orang Filipina yang dia anggap tak berfaedah, terutama kalau dia sudah mabuk karena terlalu banyak minum. Anak-anak orang Tionghoa itu dikirim ke universitas-universitas di Manila, anak perumpuannya menikah dengan seorang Filipina. Tentu ayahnya marah dan sampai sekarang tak mau kenal dengan anak perempuan ini, tetapi juga dengan anak laki-lakinya yang sekarang berwarganegara Filipina. Anak laki-laki ini, umpamanya, dikirim ke India untuk mewakili satu golongan mahasiswa di Filipina yang nasionalistis dan dari

universitas Manila yang paling nasionalistis, yaitu Manuel el [sic] Quezon University. Oleh penduduk desa maka anak-anak dari orang Tionghoa itu diterima sebagai warganegara Filipina biasa, seperti penduduk desa lainnya. (Ong 2005, 172)

17   Badan Permusjawaratan Kewarganegaraan Indonesia (Consultative Body for Indonesian Citizenship) was an organization founded in 1954 by a group of *peranakan* to work for equal treatment of the Indonesian Chinese. I thank Ben Anderson for explaining the rationale behind the New Order treatment of the Chinese.

18   Teresita Ang-See was born to a Filipina-American mestiza mother (middle name Davenport, from Virginia) who, after her marriage, was brought to China by her Chinese husband, and learned to speak and write Chinese. Tessy Ang-See [2011] writes of her mother's sojourn in China that, "to stop the discrimination and harassment, when asked if she can do witchcraft, *mangkukulam*, she said yes." Ang-See was educated in the Anglo-Chinese School, Chiang Kai-Shek High School, and the University of the Philippines (where she obtained a degree in Political Science and, as the only ethnic Chinese student in her class, was able to interact closely with her Filipino classmates). She contributed the article "Citizenship Discussion in the Convention—The Case for Qualified Jus Soli" to the McCarthy volume (1974). She was married to the anthropologist Chinben See, founding member of Pagkakaisa and a leading expert on the Philippine Chinese whose extensive collection of source materials on the Chinese in Southeast Asia forms the core library holdings now housed in the Kaisa-Angelo King Heritage Center in Intramuros, Manila. Among her best-known scholarly works are the essays collected in the three-volume *Chinese in the Philippines: Problems and Perspectives* (1997a; 1997b; 2004a). Her exemplary activism on behalf of victims of kidnapping and Kaisa para sa Kaunlaran has made her one of the most well-known Chinese Filipinos in contemporary Philippines as well as abroad (see chap. 3).

19   An essay by historian Horacio de la Costa (1974, 58) argued that "[T]here must be a recognition on our part, on the part of us Filipinos, the national community, a recognition that you do not have to be made un-Chinese, ceasing to be Chinese in culture by becoming a Filipino citizen."

20   The articles were written at a time when the citizenship issue was being debated at the 1971–1972 Constitutional Convention. McCarthy was himself an advocate of citizenship by qualified jus soli.

21   "R" stood for Ricardo, "H" for Henry, "Laurel" for Herman Tiu Laurel. I thank R. Kwan Laurel for directing me to *Dragnet*. Information on the film is based on e-mail communication with Herman Tiu Laurel, Ricardo Lee, and Teresita Ang-See.

22   On Hong Kong cinema as "regional cinema par excellence," see chapter 7.

23   Lee's films, popular among Asian as well as African-American audiences (on the African-American case, see Spady, Dupree, and Lee 1995, 40–46), they helped create the kung fu genre in the Philippines and launched the careers of actors like Rey Malonzo, Ramon Zamora, and Roland Dantes.

24   Tsai would go on to appear in a number of action films, and become head coach of the Wushu Federation of the Philippines. He is now based in Baguio.

25   The film is an interesting study in code switching. In front of Guerrero, the Chinese speak among themselves in Hokkien, even when they can speak Tagalog. Tiong mixes Hokkien and Tagalog when he speaks to his siblings. Susana converses with Guerrero almost exclusively in English, while Guerrero's superiors bark their

order in English. With the English-speaking philanthropist Dr. Cardenas, Guerrero answers in English and Tagalog, but takes great pains to put down the "sosyal" daughter Eva by calling her "Aling Eba," to which Eva responds with an ironic "Mang Joe." Tiong's parents speak almost exclusively in Hokkien, but in the final scene, the father addresses Guerrero directly in Tagalog.

26 According to Teresita Ang-See (2011), Bernard Go and Herman Tiu Laurel "examined most of the movies produced [at the time] and found [Joseph] Erap Estrada's movies to be consistently with social themes and chose him" for the film project. "There were two premier[e] showings of *Dragnet*, one by Siong Chong [Federation of Filipino-Chinese Chambers of Commerce] and one by Pagkakaisa... [T]he Pagkakaisa *siyempre* [of course] has cheaper tickets and allowed most of the media to get in... [T]he Siong Chong is upscale...[T]he two premier[e]s in fact elicited negative comments on social class."

27 Lim died in Cebu a few years ago (Laurel 2011).

28 The Philippines was itself a market for overseas Chinese cultural products, and Philippine producers were active in the Hokkien-language film industry in Cold War Asia. Films were produced in Hong Kong and then exported to Manila, southern Taiwan, and Singapore. See the illuminating research by Jeremy Taylor (2011).

29 On Kasapi politics, Laurel (2011) remarks that the "Chinese question" "does become an issue occasionally, as in the case of my early Kasapi years, where one particular sector leader working with the small retailers (*magtitingi*, i.e., cigarette vendors, market vendors, etc.) raised the issue during a 'criticism-self-criticism' session, though it never became a problem. The anthem of Kasapi had this line: '*Tayo ang Sambayanan ng tunay ng Sandigan ng Pilipinas... Walang singkit, walang puti ...*' [We are the People/Citizens of the true Pillar of the Philippines...No slit-eyes, no whites...], but that would be occasion to grin while singing and pointing to me and Linggoy Alcuaz (*puti*). Being 'Chinese' really has never been a major issue, and that may be unique to Filipino political culture." The pattern of Anglo-hybridization described by Laurel has a regional history and basis (see chap. 7).

30 Laurel (2011) also identifies two formative events that shaped his life: "h) Edsa II was more significant in my evolution as by this time I had rejected Edsa I's premises and saw through the sham of Western-led democracies and liberal economics, though the beginnings of this change goes back to the mid-1990s and particularly the Asian Financial Crisis which revealed the anti-Asian financial manipulation and attack by Western financial institutions. In this period I formed the conviction that the Western power elites (say, Brzezinski as the ideological epitome) are out to restore Western hegemony and demolish the emerging multi-polar global power structure, and reinforced my commitment and energy to help the rest of the World fight back through the "information war" that I am engaged in today'; i) I have stayed the course and still shun full-time business engagement as I can find no global relevance in just focusing on one financial or economic project while global, historical evolution is being fought over; and on a very practical, personal level, the pinnacle of business success has been achieved by other siblings and there is no room to leave a mark there."

31 See the interesting study by Guéguen (2010) of the mushrooming of "Chinese villages" in Quezon City.

32 Among the claims made about the influence exercised by Estrada's "Chinese" friends on the president were Philippine Constitution Association chair Exequiel

Garcia's allegations that Estrada's "Chinese friends" were behind the president's proposal to amend the Constitution to allow foreigners to own land (Cueto 1999, 2). In his newspaper column, journalist Ramon Tulfo (1998) criticized former senator Ernesto Maceda for the latter's anti-Chinese "racism": "He [Maceda] said that the biggest winners in the election of President Erap are the *Chinoys,* or Chinese Pinoys, who have been appointed by Mr. Estrada as his consultants and advisers. What's wrong with appointing Chinoys to government posts? They are as Filipino as Maceda. The former senator should remember that the national hero, Dr. Jose Rizal, was part Chinese." Tulfo goes on to say that "what was uncalled for in Maceda's column...was [*sic*] the lines that read, 'In Indonesia, the ongoing revolt has been principally sparked by the natives' resentment of the rich Chinese and their control of the country's economic life. At least in this country, we don't kill them or rape their women. We either kidnap them or make them presidential advisers.' Now, that's racism." See footnote 6 of chapter 6.

33   The screenplay was co-written by Eddie Romero with Roy Iglesias, who would go on to write the screenplays for the *Mano Po* franchise, discussed in chapter 5. Chapter 4 will argue as well that a shift in the nationalist attitude toward the Chinese derives its main impetus from the influence and cachet of Maoism during the late 1960s.

34   Brocka's film, *Maynila...Sa Mga Kuko ng Liwanag* (discussed in this chapter), in contrast, keeps the viewer, following Julio, outside Ah Tek's house. Even the climactic scene has Julio entering the house, only to chase Ah Tek out of the house and into the darkened hall and down the steps.

35   In the Chinese community, it was whispered that Lim Seng was just a "small fry"; his Chinese boss, a notorious big-time syndicate druglord, was able to safely flee the country.

36   Apolonio Chua's (1976/1977, 111–14) reading of Edgardo Reyes's classic novel, a reading that was strongly influenced by the critical reception accorded Lino Brocka's filmic adaptation of *Maynila*, has rightly pointed out that the name Ah Tek does not exist in Mandarin or Hokkien. Ah Tek functions as the personification of capital in the novel, a personification that would be translated into reality in the 1990s by the kidnappings of ethnic Chinese (discussed in the next chapter).

37   Part of the differentialist turn in sociology entails the rethinking (and recuperation) of the concept of assimilation for the reality of ethnic pluralism in the globalizing world (see Alba and Nee 2003).

3

·······

C
A
P
I
T
A
L

·······

Postwar Philippine nationalism has relied on the popular association of "Chinese" with money for its critique of Philippine social problems and realities. Among the literary texts that make this connection between the Chinese, on the one hand, and commerce and capital, on the other hand, is Amado Hernandez's classic novel *Mga Ibong Mandaragit* (Birds of Prey, 1969), which features a character named Son Tua, a millionaire Chinese who begins with nothing but goes on to build an empire based on gambling and opium. Son Tua then colludes with the landowner Segundo Montero to set up a corporation for smuggling and selling contraband jewelry and arms.[1] Hernandez's treatment of the Chinese is distinguished, in hindsight, by its prescient handling of Son Tua's fate: the Chinese is kidnapped by "outlaws" (*taong labas*) and the novel ends without the reader ever knowing if Son Tua was ransomed or killed by his kidnappers.[2]

In spite of mass naturalization and the rise of integration discourse, such images of the Chinese as alien criminal-capitalist continued to enjoy a certain currency in the domain of artistic and literary production in the 1970s and 1980s. The phenomenon of kidnappings from the late 1980s onwards did not merely highlight the conflictive relationship between Philippine nationalism and the Chinese question, one that hinged on the problematical issue of economic inequality within the discourse of citizenship, as well as the nature of the Philippine state itself. The kidnappings also served to flesh out this conflictive relationship in a spectacular and material way.

Incidents of kidnapping reached a record high in 1997 (*Philippine Star*, 1998a) (Table 1). In his *Ulat sa Bayan* (State of the Nation Report), then-president Fidel Ramos admitted to his administration's failure to curb the rampant criminality that has "lacerated Philippine civil society," and pledged to devote the last eighteen months of his incumbency to solving the problem (Pablo 1997).[3] Two civic organizations formed in the wake of the early wave of kidnapping in the 1990s, the Citizens Action Against Crime and the Movement for the Restoration of Peace and Order, have kept track of the cases, whether reported or not, involving kidnap-for-ransom (table 1).[4] At its peak in 1996 and 1997, the Philippines ranked fourth behind Colombia, Mexico, and Brazil in terms of number of kidnap victims (*Philippine Star,* 1998b), and was branded by *Forbes Magazine* as the "kidnap capital of the world" (Zulueta 1998). Between 1993 and 1998, kidnap gangs were estimated to have taken in more than P600 million worth of ransom (Zulueta 1998; see also Dalangin 1995).[5] These cases generally involved either the abduction of businesspeople or that of their immediate family members. Over a period of a decade, from the mid-1990s to mid-2000s, over two thousand three hundred people had been kidnapped, at an average of two victims every three days (Ang-See 2004c). In the 1990s, more than eighty-six kidnap victims were killed either directly by captors or accidentally in crossfires between kidnappers and government forces.

The conflictive relation between nationalism and the Chinese question comes out in the most unguarded and commonsensical responses of ordinary people to the kidnappings. In the December 1995 issue of the Chinese Filipino news digest *Tulay* (lit., "bridge"), Jacqueline Co (1995) related the following anecdote: "Two years ago [i.e., in 1993]," she wrote, "I asked a University of the Philippines [UP] graduate student if she was bothered by the spate of

Table 1. Kidnapping Statistics

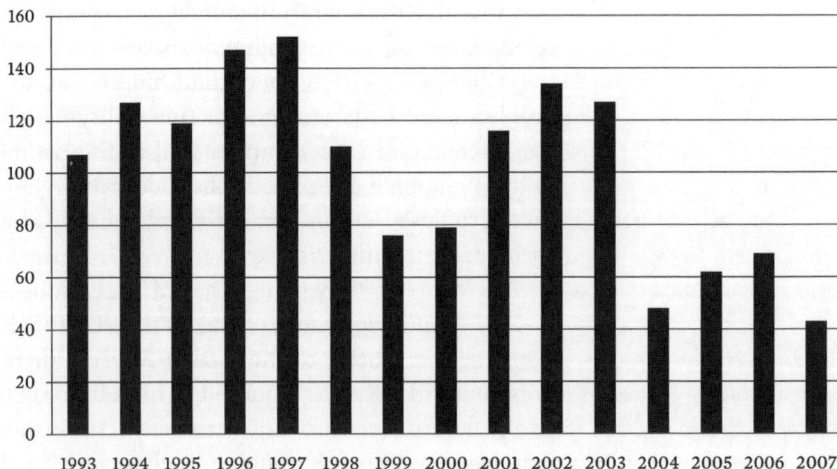

Sources: Tulay 2007 and 2008

kidnapping in the country. Her response was, 'No, because I am not Chinese and I am not rich.'"

The UP student's statement affirms the commonsensical understanding that the rich Chinese were the main victims of kidnapping. These kidnappings unfold around a narrative that features such well-worn storyline conventions as the exchange of huge sums of ransom money, a rogue's gallery of cops and military personnel, shootouts between government forces and kidnap gangs, and the accidental or deliberate killing of kidnap victims. Although the Chinese "community" is often understood and depicted as a cohesive social body, a state within the state,[6] this "enclave" has seemingly broken out of its internal borders (to use Fichte 1922, 223–24) and taken over the *fin de siècle* urbanscape. A report in the *New York Times* explains the connection between space, economic prominence, and extortion: "[t]he highly visible role of the Chinese in Philippine economic growth—the Chinese-owned shopping malls and high rises that are transforming Manila—have made them obvious targets of extraction" (Mydans 1996).

The tenacity of deeply held beliefs about "Chinese capital" largely determines the kind of responses available to ethnic Chinese, like Co, when they deal publicly with the kidnapping issue. One strategy has been to emphasize the fact that the Chinese are not the only victims of kidnap-for-ransom, the idea being to disentangle the identification of "Chinese" ethnicity with the capitalist class. Co goes on in the rest of her article, for example, to argue that the kidnappers, instead of preying exclusively on the members of the ethnic Chinese community, *as is universally believed*, are now more "democratic" in their choice of victims as recent demographics of kidnap victims appear to have cut across class, racial, and geographic lines. Co's argument implicitly stresses that kidnapping is no longer a "Chinese" problem because it has become, indeed *should* be considered, "everybody's problem."[7]

Co's arguments notwithstanding, a large number of the most success-ful and spectacular cases of kidnapping, both in terms of the amount of ransom paid and the circumstances surrounding the death of the victims, have involved and continue to involve the ethnic Chinese.[8] Kidnapping bears out the conflation of ethnicity and class that casts the Chinese as obvious and proper targets of extraction. This conflation, which turns the Chinese into "perfect victims" because of the (by definition) criminal nature of their capitalist activities, calls into question a number of assumptions that underpin the notion of citizenship: first is the idea of formal political equality of all citizens in the eyes of the state; and the second is the idea that citizenship entails membership in a state whose raison d'être is to maintain "peace and order" and protect its citizens from violence.

Claiming Citizenship

Co's article reveals something more than the mere fact that kidnappers are now indiscriminate in their choice of victims. Co's argument that kidnapping is no longer a Chinese community problem has two intended recipients: the Filipino public and the Philippine state. Her message tries to engage the public and the state in an interlocutory relation. The content of this dialogue between the Chinese and the Filipino public and state draws substantially, at least on the part of the Chinese, on the discourse of citizenship and rights. If kidnapping constitutes a kind of resistance to the juridically defined notion that citizens are equally subject to the same law,[9] it does not come as a surprise that attempts on the part of the Chinese to formulate a position against kidnapping have anchored their argument in the invocation of citizenship and rights which kidnapping abrogates—the right to freedom, equality, security, and property, for example. Co's argument that kidnapping is and should be treated as "everybody's problem," for instance, imagines the possibility that every Filipino, and not just every Chinese, is a potential victim of the kidnap-for-ransom crimes; the argument urges all Filipinos to seek a solution to the problem and ultimately expects the proper response from the state.

This kind of generalization widens the political scope of responsibility to include all Filipinos and thereby "depoliticizes" the issue by unraveling the identification of kidnapping with the Chinese. But such a depoliticizing generalization also creates, paradoxically, a venue for politicizing specific rights-claims, in this case, the rights-claims of Chinese Filipinos. In other words, the point at which kidnapping becomes everybody's problem serves at one and the same time to call attention to the way in which kidnapping has abrogated the specific rights to freedom and equality of the Chinese Filipinos. This paradox also informs most public responses to kidnapping, responses that have tended to oscillate between claiming that kidnapping is an "equal-opportunity menace" (Saspa 1995) and noting "a form of nationalism" at work in the kidnapping of the Chinese (*Philippines Free Press,* 1992b).

Timing is a crucial element in accounting for Chinese responses to the kidnappings. It is no coincidence that the Chinese Filipinos began "speaking out" as individuals and, more importantly, as a group on the issue of kidnapping at about the same time that the media began carrying reports about the entry of the ethnic Chinese into politics (Sy 1995).[10] To be sure, this was not the first time that the Chinese have involved themselves in politics, as the Yuyitung case discussed in chapter 2 shows. More than sixty years ago, just after the end of World War II, nearly one thousand Chinese led by

Huang Jie and Li Yongxiao, noted leftist resistance leaders, participated in a mass demonstration on September 23, 1945, against Manuel Roxas, whom they denounced as a collaborator. (More about Li Yongxiao in the next chapter.)

The political action of the Chinese, however, was regarded by some Filipino politicians as "unwarranted interference in the internal affairs of the Philippines" (Tan 1981, 113–14). As the editorial of *The Manila Post* put it: "The Chinese can advance no justification for butting into the Philippine collaborationism question, or into any of our domestic affairs, for that matter. In passing judgment on our congress, the Chinese have stepped over the heads of the Filipino people who had elected their people to congress, the Filipino people who are the only legitimate critics of the officials they have willed into office" (quoted in Yung Li 1996, 170).

What makes the situation of the Chinese of 1995 different from that of the leftists in 1945 is that the Chinese criticism of the Philippine government today can no longer be seen to warrant the same kind of dismissive response from Filipino politicians. In claiming citizenship,[11] Chinese Filipinos are saying that they are no longer speaking to the state as Chinese, but as "Chinese Filipinos." For these second-, third-, and fourth-generation "Tsinoys," speaking out, sometimes critically, is part of the universal right to politics to which they are entitled as citizens of the Philippines.

The terminological shift from Chinese to Chinese Filipino, however, is telling in another sense, since it indicates an attempt on the part of self-identified Chinese Filipinos to distance themselves both temporally and conceptually from the politics of the 1945 Chinese. The claim to citizenship is a claim *against* a certain kind of "Chinese," an "alien" Chinese who may or may not identify with the Filipinos and may or may not stand outside the bounds of the Filipino imagined community. Chineseness here involves multiple forms of identification that are not so easily contained within either Philippine or Chinese borders, nor fully recuperable in the name of either nationalism or internationalism (as will be discussed in the next chapter).[12] This Chinese exceeds the juridical bounds of both jus soli and jus sanguinis citizenship that tries to neutralize or domesticate the (often secret) immigrant, either by criminalizing him or her as an illegal alien or—and this perhaps amounts to the same thing—by "naturalizing" him or her as a citizen. This "Chinese" exposes the fact that the extremes of rejection and absorption both imply a refusal of difference as well as a denial of the violence of institutional inclusion and exclusion that founds any political community.

In claiming membership in the body of citizens, the Chinese Filipinos repudiate the concept of "aliens without rights" imputed upon Chinese leftists during the latter's participation in the mass protest against the collaborators. Chinese speaking as Filipinos put pressure on the state to act on the kidnappings. Moreover, their active participation in the political arena as concerned citizens makes them members of a resurgent Philippine civil society in the post-Marcos era.

It is no coincidence that terms like civic consciousness and duty, social justice and moral recovery were being bandied about in public and official forums at the height of the kidnapping,[13] with the post-EDSA period witnessing the proliferation of nongovernment organizations (NGOs) and the "rise of civil society" debates.[14] This appears to be a time when the state itself has explicitly organized its separation from society (Ramos 1992; 1993), even as the state increasingly relies on civil society to take on part of the state's responsibilities and obligations of ensuring the welfare of the people. In the meantime, public criticism of government economic policies has tended to focus on the government's overemphasis on showcasing the "democratic" features of the Philippine political system—a defensive posture against its authoritarian but better performing neighbor states in Southeast and Northeast Asia—while failing to adequately intervene in the economy through the reorganization of the private sector (Saspa 1996, 6). Aggressively pursuing the policy of attracting foreign investments, President Ramos had logged more mileage points than any other Filipino president in history, taking thirty-two trips abroad as of November 1997 (Soliven 1997). At the same time, however, state efforts to secure investment by showcasing the attractions of the Philippine democratic system are undermined by the state's failure to maintain peace and order, and, more than this, by the often empirically violent flouting of the law by the very people who are assigned to enforce it.[15]

The kidnappings point to a far more fundamental failure of the concept of the political (community?) that forms the raison d'être of the state as human association. If a state is characterized by its ability to create a zone of "peace, security and order" within the bounds of its territory while claiming the right to declare war on other states (Schmitt 1996 [1922, 1963], 10, cited and discussed in Joppke 2010, 3), then the Philippine state's failure to provide even the most basic measures of security and protection for its citizens, as well as for foreigners residing in the country, calls into question the very status of the state as the "paramount" human association for the Philippine political community.[16]

Max Weber's classic idea (1947 [1913], 154) of the state as "a compulsory political association with continuous organization" that possesses an "administrative staff [that] successfully upholds a claim to the *monopoly* of the *legitimate* use of physical force in the enforcement of its order" takes on sinister meanings when the legitimacy of the state is in question, when the "administrative staff" (particularly the agents of state-sanctioned violence) themselves are routinely portrayed in the media as criminals who violate the rule of law and victimize the people they are supposed to protect. Charles Tilly's (1985, 169–86) counterintuitive notion of "state-making as organized crime," with "racketeer governments" that offer "protection as business," while principally based on the historical experience of early Western Europe, assumes an almost literal meaning, albeit in a very different historical time and context, in the Philippines: the state is routinely perceived by its own "people" as an alien, predatory entity, some of whose representatives are known to act in ways that make them no different from the common criminals preying on the people whom these agents of the state are supposed to protect.

Moreover, formal recognition of equality in law, the very condition of property and rights that citizenship is supposed to uphold, appears almost illusory because of the real (and often visible) discrepancy between political equality and economic *in*equality. The problem is complicated by the fact that the resulting social, economic, and political tensions and antagonisms cannot be explained away as something that comes from outside and is then "inflicted" upon society. The antagonist here is not another state (albeit the Philippines' dispute with China over the Spratly Islands and Scarborough Shoal has generated some military saber-rattling on both sides); this violence comes from within the nation-state itself and is directed mainly at Filipinos. The anxiety which attends the everyday threat of violence or every rumor of martial law, constitutional change, and overstaying presidents underscores the fragility (but also resilience) of civil society while showing the extent to which state and society are intimately linked.

Co's article and the Chinese Filipinos' entry into politics attest to the fact that the ethnic Chinese began using the discourse of citizenship, the affirmation of the universal right to politics extended to all Chinese, in order to address the stereotypical conflation of ethnicity and class that the phenomenon of kidnapping reinforces. The Tsinoys' invocation of citizenship and the discourse of equality and liberty (Balibar 1994) sought to disentangle the conflation of ethnicity and class by kidnapping. But the discourse of citizenship remains haunted by the question of class, that is, the question of political equality in the face of economic inequality. The unresolved issue of economic inequality is complicated by the Chinese's problematical relationship with the Philippine state and nation. This chapter explores this conundrum by looking at the specific response of Kaisa para sa

Kaunlaran, a civic organization of young Chinese Filipinos that had emerged as the unofficial spokesperson organization of the Chinese community in light of the rampant kidnapping incidents in the early 1990s.

The "Booming Business" of Kidnapping

The first incidents of kidnapping during the Aquino regime were not reported in Manila, where more than 50 percent of the Chinese in the Philippines reside (Ang-See 1995), but in Central Mindanao, specifically Cotabato City (see also Fuller 2000). The kidnapping-for-ransom of Chinese Filipino businessmen broke into the headlines in late 1989.[17] By late April 1991, the Chinese Filipino news digest *Tulay* reported seventeen "rumored" cases of kidnapping in Manila, none of which had been officially reported to the police (Co 1991). Kidnapping cases would continue to be documented well into the twenty-first century, despite President Gloria Macapagal-Arroyo's confident assertion in her 2005 State of the Nation Address that kidnapping-for-ransom was a "thing of the past" (Del Puerto 2005).[18] Since 2010, kidnapping incidents have been on the rise again in Mindanao (in places like Cotabato and Basilan), with going rates of P5 million to P15 million for locals and U.S. $1 million to U.S. $5 million for foreigners (*Philippine Star*, 2011), rates that are higher than the average rates of between P800,000 and P1,000,200,000 paid out in the national capital (Dizon 2011). An annual kidnapping report prepared by Pacific Strategies and Assessments (PSA 2012, 2) indicated that there were 122 cases involving 185 victims in 2011, representing a slight increase over the 119 cases recorded in 2010, but below the figures for 2008 and 2009 (135 and 138 respectively). The PSA reported a 79 percent increase in kidnapping cases between 2002 and 2011, with over 100 cases being recorded each year since 2006.[19]

Several theories have been advanced to account for the upsurge of kidnapping cases in Cotabato: kidnapping-for-ransom was quick and easy money for common criminals; the Corazon C. Aquino government had failed to pay rebel returnees to the government fold their regular monthly stipend of P1,500; kidnapping helped to fill the coffers of the Moro National Liberation Front and the New People's Army; the tolerance of the kidnapping by government officials was part of a secret agenda on the part of the state involving the creation of armed civilian groups like the Citizens' Armed Forces Geographical Units, the undermining of the leadership credibility of the Autonomous Region of Moslem Mindanao, and the much-rumored reimposition of martial law (Co 1991; Mydans 1996). Part of the blame has been laid at the doors of the Philippine National Police (PNP): the politicization of promotions in the PNP has resulted in the loss of morale among the competent and honest members of the police force (Teresita Ang-See, cited in *Philippine Star*, 2011). Transnationalized Chinese drug and kidnapping syndicates from mainland China, Hong Kong, and Taiwan have also been identified as culprits behind the kidnapping of Chinese nationals (*Tulay*, 2000; Villanueva 2007). A suggestive link has been made between kidnapping and electoral politics based on kidnapping incidents from 1993 to 2006: *Tulay* (2007) noted a "marked increase in KFR [kidnapping-for ransom] incidents in 1994, 1997, 2003, one year before elections." The veracity of the above theories can only be tested against the indubitable evidence of the membership of rogue police and military officers and personnel in the kidnap gangs (*Tulay*, 1992; *Philippines Free Press*, 1992a).[20]

Kidnapping has been called a "growth industry" and a "booming business,"[21] and to a certain extent, it does employ the kind of systematic labor, large personnel, and capital outlays in the form of weapons and vehicles, that characterize an industry explicitly geared to profit-making. The difference, however, is that kidnapping foregrounds aspects of commodity relations specific to capitalism in a spectacular way. Like any industry, kidnapping is premised on the power of a commodity to command other commodities in exchange, a power of exchangeability that Karl Marx calls "value" (Marx 1977, chap. 1, 3C, 1). In this case, the commodity happens to be a human being, the capitalist or someone related to the capitalist. The act of kidnapping transforms the body of the victim into an object of exchange, thereby replicating the logic of commodification that treats the commodity, whether capitalist or kindred, as qualitatively equal but quantitatively differential: all kidnap victims are alike except in terms of the amount of value that they "contain." Value here is determined by the victim's net worth, that is, by the victim's access to accumulated capital in the form of money. Kidnapping transforms the body of the capitalist into a commodity, the value of which is based on the capitalist's possession of money, which, in turn, comprises the accumulation of unpaid surplus labor of the past that is appropriated by the capitalist in the present. The capitalist's body is thus a commodity the value of which is a calibration of the capitalist's accumulation of unpaid surplus labor. An editorial in the *Philippine Daily Inquirer* (2001) sums it up this way: "If the Chinese can build malls and dominate retail [sic], heck these gangs can kidnap mall magnates and make them items for retail exchange."[22]

There is a certain irony, then, in the fact that kidnapping does to the capitalist what capitalism does to the laborer.[23] If capitalism institutes a circuit in which the capitalist buys the labor power that the laborer sells for a price, the wage, kidnapping institutes a circuit in which the capitalist buys himself back for a price, a fraction of his total net worth. Kidnapping makes the capitalist an almost *literal* personification of capital, in the same sense that capitalism makes the laborer the personification of his own labor power. Perhaps the real irony lies in the fact that, by making the capitalist its primary source of extraction, kidnapping trains the lens of inequality inherent in the capitalist relation onto those who are seen as playing a role in perpetuating this inequality.

The peculiarity of the kidnap-for-ransom phenomenon in the Philippines, however, consists of its victimization of ethnic Chinese in public spaces.[24] By publicly subjecting the capitalists and their relatives to the forces of capital, kidnapping seemingly erases the subjective and human qualities of the victim, and regards the victim as no more than an instrument of capital. Kidnapping, therefore, is often experienced as a loss of subjectivity.[25] What further distinguishes the kidnappings of this decade from those of the past is the degree to which these kidnappings have become highly "professional" operations. That is, their success depends on the speed of communication, negotiation, and exchange, which are made possible to a great extent by mobile phones, ATM machines, and computerized banking. In targeting the Chinese as obvious sources of extraction, kidnapping frames the issue not in terms of the fact that many of the businessmen (and women and their children) who were kidnapped happened to be Chinese, but that those who were kidnapped *were* Chinese businessmen. Kidnapping seems to give a new twist to Marx's observation that "commodities cannot go to market by themselves and perform exchanges in their own right," and that the possessors of these commodities need to "place themselves in relation to one another as persons whose will [*Willen*] resides [*haust*] in these objects and must behave in such a way that each does not appropriate the commodity of the other, and alienate his own, except through an act in which both parties consent" (Marx 1977, 1: chap. 1, 4, 178). Although Marx's observation pertains to the juridical form of the contract, his observation also makes a compelling point about how the absolute abstraction of the individual as "legal" personality is posited alongside the abstraction of possession into property.

But in a situation where the kidnap victim's will inhabits the commodity that is the kidnap victim himself or herself, how does one draw the line between commodification of the kidnap victim and the personification of capital by the Chinese?[26] Kidnapping highlights the process through which an "idea or spiritual form is incarnated or given a prosthetic body, which is then (mis)taken by the subject as his or her own corporeal body. The subject's real body thus becomes spectral when it incorporates this prosthetic body."[27] Kidnapping creates a situation wherein the Chinese victim, in order to survive, actively/passively takes on the stereotype of Chinese-as-capital as a "second nature." The lives of these victims are prolonged only insofar as they are commodities that are "worth" something, even if this commodification renders them equally vulnerable to racist slurs, torture, and rape. In the moment of kidnapping, the victims actively/passively take on the stereotypes of Chineseness, in fact *live* these stereotypes as though they were coextensive with their own bodies and consciousness. More than just a signifier, the term Chinese, with all its attendant associations, assumes the character of a referent, a something *there*, something finite that "takes on and is trapped by specters of what it is not."[28] In its distinctive way, kidnapping highlights the persistence—even in the face of critiques that expose the contingent and nonnatural character— of the truism about the Chinese as "material men" (to use James Rush's [1991] term) whose virtual nationality within the Philippine neo/colonial state remains a politically charged and contested issue.

Ethnicity=Class: The Chinese Merchant and Capitalist

Kidnapping is as much a signifying act as it is a social relation because it invites and fulfills a certain public demand for knowledge of social relations. At least two main narratives about "the Chinese" are at work in the responses to the linking by kidnapping of ethnicity and class. The Chinese are objects of class resentment because, "rich" people who benefited economically from the status quo, they come to stand in for the evils and abuses of the present social system. On the other hand, the Chinese are objects of nationalist distrust because the Chinese represent, by virtue of the history of their seemingly symbiotic relationship with the colonial and neocolonial state (born of their dependency on state policies and priorities), the living, foreign trace of the colonial history—itself seen as foreign and external—of the Philippine state and nation.[29]

While the language used to describe the "Chinese" has undergone revision from the Marxist "pariah capitalist" or "bourgeoisie without political power" within the colonial and nation-state to liberal "middle-classes" and "entrepreneur" who mediate regional capitalist and cultural flows (see chaps. 5 and 6), what has remained constant is the identification of "Chineseness" with commerce and capital. What has changed, then, is not this identification, but rather the nature and scope of "Chinese" economic activity, and the meanings that accrue to these activities. A crucial difference between the negative images of the Chinese in the twentieth century and the positive ones in the twenty-first century lies in a relatively new phenomenon: the rise of the Dragon Economies of Taiwan, Hong Kong, and Singapore, in the 1980s and 1990s, and the creation of a "socialist market

economy" mainland Chinese state, whose presence would be strongly felt in
the economies of the region and the world from the 1990s onwards.

A look back at history is needed to understand how changes in the
economic activities of the Chinese informed the changing positions of the
Chinese in Philippine society.

Large-scale Chinese immigration to the Philippines had been a direct
consequence of colonialism and had been subject to colonial regulation.
Spanish colonizers encouraged Chinese immigration in their effort to
establish a colonial outpost by which they sought to insert themselves into
the lucrative regional maritime trade network centered on China. Edgar
Wickberg notes (1965, 24) that patterns of immigration (by mostly Hokkiens)
had "established certain occupations as 'Chinese' and made gravitation
to them the line of least resistance." This cementing of occupation and
ethnicity was characteristic of the division of labor specific to three distinct
economic systems in the colony—a "Western" one relying on the galleon
commodity trade; a "native" one based on subsistence, provisioning, and the
import of Chinese cloth and silver; and a "Chinese" one that mediated the
maritime trade between China and the Philippines, but was also involved
in artisanry and provisioning within the Philippines. Wickberg argues that
the "Chinese economy" acted as a link between the other two systems. The
"Chinese" during this time was less a community than a group "with as
much ties to non-Chinese as to Chinese" (41).

The transformation of colonial Philippines into an exporter of raw
materials and importer of foreign manufactures in the shadow of growing
British presence in the region from the late eighteenth century onwards
forced the Spanish to ease some of their restrictions on Chinese residence
and mobility. No longer confined to Manila, the Chinese scattered
throughout the colony as part of a newly integrated, single economic system
under which they functioned as wholesalers of imported goods, processors
of Philippine produce, monopoly contractors and coolie brokers, laborers,
provisioners, and direct importers and exporters (63). Chinese middlemen
came to play a crucial role in connecting the Philippine economy to the
global and regional economy.

For most of the Spanish colonial period, Chinese traders could not be
called "compradors" in the strict sense of the word because they operated
on personal credit in their dealings with westerners, Spanish, and Filipinos,
and were advanced cash or credit without security by Western business
firms (80). As late as the 1850s, the scarcity of money forced abaca traders
to rely on the barter system to exchange goods (97). Moreover, the capital
base of the Chinese was smaller than that of Americans and Europeans in
the Philippines (Cariño 2001, 104). Although Chinese dominated the retail

trade, opposition to their "control" (notwithstanding the fact that there is no reliable measure of the size of the Chinese share in the colonial economy, nor in contemporary economy) became a colony-wide issue only in the last fifty years of the Spanish rule. It was largely in reaction to this rising tide of anti-Sinicism, fanned by the Spanish to channel popular dissatisfaction away from Spanish rule onto a more pliable scapegoat, that made the Chinese conscious of themselves as a "foreign" community and as "national minority" (Wickberg 1965, 148–52).

American application of the Chinese Exclusion Act to the Philippines drove the Chinese even more deeply into the mercantile niche (in 1930, Chinese controlled 90% of the retail trade) while creating the legal fiction that "all" Chinese immigrants were merchants. Operating mainly in the domestic market at a time when the Philippine economy was becoming increasingly tied to the U.S. market on a preferential basis (Wong 1999, 36, 53), Chinese merchants with their limited capital outlay, intensive labor input, small employment, and high liquidity faced rising competition from foreign (especially Japanese) and Filipino entrepreneurs and became visible targets of nationalist legislation. Far more crucially, their visibility as merchants made these merchants the targets of popular nationalist criticism and action.

What accounts for the visibility of the merchant? (The following discussion is indebted to Marx 1981, 382–451.)

The merchant represents the point at which money appears and disappears in the presence of ordinary people. He mediates between the process of transforming money into commodities and vice versa and thus fulfills one specific function within the division of labor of the capitalist system. But because the merchant operates exclusively within the sphere of circulation, which is the most visibly public and accessible field for the majority of the population, the most obvious form in which capital makes its appearance is in the money and wealth of the merchant. The quotidian character of the relationship between the merchant and his customers— the daily exchange (in the market, the *sari-sari* store, the grocery, and the supermarket) that is crucial for meeting individual needs—may account for why, to most people, the everyday interaction with the merchant is likely to be the "pure" form taken by capitalist relations. As Marx has stated, "[c]ommercial capital, therefore, is absolutely nothing more than the commodity capital of the producer which has to go through the process of transformation into money, to perform its function as commodity capital on the market; only instead of being an incidental operation carried out by the producer himself, this function now appears as the exclusive operation of a particular species of capitalist, the merchant, and acquires independence as a business of a particular capital investment" (382).

The visibility of the merchant and his exclusive confinement to the equally visible public sphere of circulation means that even though the merchant performs only one among many functions in the capitalist system, capital itself appears prima facie in "his" sphere and comes to be associated with—and is taken at face value as the exclusive function of—the merchant as a specific agent of circulation distinct from the producer. This may explain why the merchant and his shop are often the first and favorite targets of mass action during moments of crisis. The "alienness" of the Chinese cements, and is cemented by, this association of the "alien" merchant with alienating capital, so that the merchant appears in the public imagination as *the* personification of capital with a consciousness and will.[30]

The conflation of ethnicity and class therefore owes something not just to colonial policy and practice, but to the nature of mercantile operation, or more specifically to the racialized segmentation of labor that mercantile capitalism allows. The historical association of the Chinese as an ethnic minority playing the economic role of merchant capitalists within the colonial economy may have been cemented by the "elastic" nature of the space of mercantile trade: its potentially limitless capacity for expansion can accommodate people from the "outside," foreigners, so to speak, who need not necessarily belong to the group which controls the means of production.[31]

The displacement of the producer by the merchants is crucial to the operation of racial discourse. While the position of the middlemen opens up new relations that confer upon the merchant a degree of influence and leverage vis-á-vis both labor and capital, it also renders the merchants particularly vulnerable not just because the tension between labor and capital is deflected onto them, so that antagonism is directed against the middlemen by the frustrated worker, but because the middlemen work within a force field of relations that they do not dominate, whose preconditions they do not create.

Moreover, it is not just that merchants signify money, but what the merchants sell, that is, commodities, which renders them vulnerable to public hostility and protest. As a crucial liaison between commodities and money, the merchant, whether or not he is actually guilty of it, becomes the object of public paranoia about hoarding. This paranoia about hoarding—the public fear that the merchant is withdrawing money or goods from circulation or delaying it, and making a profit out of the delaying of the circulation—exists side by side with public hostility to the merchant's act of consumption—the anger directed at the merchant's "conspicuous" consumption of goods that are produced by means of exploiting the labor of the worker.

The contradictions and tensions inherent in social relations are thus evident in the character of money relations, since money, too, mediates between production and consumption and, as an object of exchange as well as an object of desire, it is the tangible form through which social relations between individuals are realized and, just as important, rendered visible. But how rich does a merchant have to be to count as a merchant? Marx has noted that if "his business and his capital are small, he may himself be the only worker employed" (403) and "if the capital advanced by the merchant is small, the profit he realizes may not be any greater than the wage of a better-paid skilled worker; it may even be less than this" (404). The merchant-owned, family-operated, intensive-labor and low-capital-input small business typically involves the merchant's self-exploitation as well as exploitation of family members (especially women and children).

Yet what distinguishes the merchant from the worker is that, for Marx, the labor of the merchant "is not value-creating labor" (408). Since merchants themselves are not seen as taking part in the making of value—an important feature of the production process involving laborer and producer—they are viewed as "parasites" who insert themselves within the process of exchange and initiate a perpetual process of buying and selling, or reselling at a more expensive price. They are held to derive their livelihood from the prolongation of class exploitation but are themselves not considered producers of value. Because they deal in commodities—the product of labor—they are blamed for the exploitation of the laborer, the alienation of the laborer from his or her labor. To be a merchant or a capitalist is in some ways to be a "criminal."

Marx did not consider the fact that surplus value can be extracted not only from price differences, but from differences in space and time of circulation, that is, the time it takes to transport commodities over distances and the speed with which goods can be moved from place to place. There is also some debate within Marxist theory on what kind of labor is value-producing, and whether labor that produces commodities is the only labor that counts as productive. If labor is defined this narrowly, then state employees and clerical workers, and not just those in distribution (such as merchants), would in effect be considered "parasites" as well (Worsley 2002, 35). Marx himself left answering this question for another time; he simply noted that more investigation was needed to determine the law of necessary labor in the circulation sphere, how the work of the merchant maintains the value of constant capital, and the role of commercial capital in the overall reproduction process (1981, 408).

Marx's discussion of the merchant also assumes the relative downplaying of mercantile capital in favor of industrial capital. The "old" form of mercantile capital is spotlighted in the European colonies precisely because the colony is thought of in terms of an old-fashioned notion of the market rather than a sophisticated distribution system where the middleman may eventually be eliminated or minimized. Colonialism had been crucial to the development of capitalism in Europe: the colonies were constructed and treated either as sources of raw materials and unskilled labor power or as markets for European manufacturing. This comprador condition of the colony/neocolony was displaced onto the Chinese in Southeast Asia, including the Philippines, a displacement that has persisted to this day even though changes in the economic conditions of the country in the mid- to late twentieth century have permutated the concept of "Chineseness" to accommodate the idea of the Chinese as consummate professionals, as lawyers, doctors, business managers, artists; as manufacturers and real-estate developers; and as agents of finance capital by the end of the twentieth century.[32]

Changes in state policies and prevailing economic conditions would be instrumental in determining the specific nature of Chinese economic activities at a given period in Philippine history (Cariño 2001, 101). It was, for example, the Retail Nationalization Act of 1954 that forced Chinese merchants out of the retail trade and into light manufacturing, where some of them flourished.

John Omohundro has used the term "merchant society" in his study of Chinese business families in Iloilo to describe the way in which Chinese have historically defended their position in Philippine life by being "successful merchants" even as "their mercantile success is maintained by being ethnically Chinese. So the occupation and the ethnic group have become nearly one" (1981, 84). If Chinese cultural features which are conducive for business are preserved, while others are dropped, then "Chineseness" itself is not an artifact that is simply "transported" to and replicated in the Philippines, but is rather reworked and reinvented according to the demands and conditions of Philippine life. Contingent cultural reinvention explains the fact that "pure Chinese who marry each other resemble their ancestors less each decade and Filipinos more" (132).

Omohundro states that "Chinese ethnicity owes much to the fact that all Chinese are merchants. Until recently, to cease to be a merchant is to leave the ethnic group" (187). This argument, however, needs to be qualified in the wake of major changes in the Philippine economy in the postwar period. The protectionist era of exchange controls and import-substitution of the 1950s and early 1960s had seen an initial increase in manufacturing activities, but this surge was followed by stagnation. Temario Rivera (1995, 1) notes that between 1961 and 1987, the share of total employment of manufacturing fell from 12 to 10 percent, and between 1972 and 1988, its share in the gross domestic product (GDP) remained relatively unchanged.

The liberalization, deregulation, and privatization of the Philippine economy that occurred under the Aquino administration after the fall of Marcos in 1986 were continued by the Ramos administration into the 1990s. A number of Chinese Filipinos were able to make huge fortunes in the service sector. Their stories of making it to the ranks of the superrich corresponded in large part to the major restructuring of the Philippine economy after the Marcos era: while the service sector expanded, manufacturing did not manage to regain either the share of GDP nor the share of total employment that it had had in 1981 (Krinks 2002, 145). The lion's share of domestic investment, in fact, went into the service sector rather than manufacturing (146). Not only has the service sector's share of the national income increased; it has also become "the major center of accumulation, particularly through the financial services industry, real estate and the industries involved in information technology" (188). Moreover, trade liberalization under the Ramos administration had spurred the creation of regional alliances and networks that linked Filipino (and Chinese Filipino) with Japanese, Taiwanese, Hong Kong, Malaysian, and Singaporean companies (147), thereby integrating the Philippines into an East (both Northeast and Southeast) Asian "regional network of investment, production and trade" (ibid.). This regional integration of the Philippines would have cultural ramifications, as discussed in chaps. 5 and 6.

A good number of taipan fortunes were consolidated in the postwar period, as Chinese-Filipino big business expanded from import-substitution manufacturing (where big merchants had shifted following the retail trade nationalization act in the 1950s) into real estate, finance, and other economic activities. Yoshihara Kunio (1985) estimated that 32 percent of the top manufacturing firms in 1965 were owned by Chinese Filipinos, who were mainly involved in tobacco, paper and paper products, metal fabrication, soap and cosmetics, and rubber, while Temario Rivera (1995) found that, a little over thirty years later in 1986, Chinese Filipino firms dominated three manufacturing sectors—tobacco and cigarettes, textiles, and rubber footwear.

Nevertheless, Ellen Palanca's study of the top corporations in the Philippines in 1990 revealed that while 36 percent of the top 1,000 corporations were predominantly owned by Chinese-Filipinos (1995, 552), the ethnic composition of the very top thirty corporations was predominantly Filipino (ibid.). Filipino-Chinese corporations lagged behind their Filipino counterparts in terms of total sales, net income, total assets, liabilities, and equity. Ethnic-Chinese-owned corporations have tended to be family-based; clustered in manufacturing, trade and finance, insurance and real estate; and relatively small in size, owing to Chinese propensity to establish conglomerates rather then concentrate on building one business (Palanca 1995, 557–59; Rivera 1995, 9–10). While ethnic Chinese are disproportionately represented in the commercial sector (with a 51.2% share in total number of firms and 60% share in total sectoral shares in 1990) (Palanca 1995, 563), their small and medium-size enterprises have had to contend with the challenges of fierce competition among themselves (as well as retail giants like SM and Robinsons) and from non-Chinese Filipinos and foreigners, with the threat of "trade concentrization" (Dannhaeuser 2004, 2) in the retail trade sector. Thus, although scholars like Omohundro (1981, 85) do not believe that the Chinese are divided into classes, they nevertheless note imbalances in power and prestige relationships among the ethnic Chinese that "bear similarity to class relationships."

In a context where citizenship and nationalism have undergone changes in light of regional and global economic development from the 1960s onwards, truisms regarding Chinese business acuity and resilience would establish the Chinese as exemplary citizens of an era of economic liberalization in the so-called Asia-Pacific Century, to which ideal the post-Marcos governments have aspired (to be discussed in chaps. 5 and 6).[33] A "developing" country like the Philippines places an official premium on its citizens' entrepreneurial skills and activities. To some extent now safely Filipinized, Chineseness can be associated with modernity (the idea of national "development") and with the consumption of goods (the idea of an expanding "middle class"). Chinese-Filipino entrepreneurship need no longer be seen as a criminal act of expropriating the national patrimony, since it can now be coded as a good Filipino citizen's "patriotic" contribution to the nation-state. The identification of the Chinese with money may render the Chinese vulnerable to accusation of capital flight, but a number of Chinese have argued against this by insisting that Chinese Filipinos continued to invest in the Philippines during its most troubled times (that is, during the economic and political meltdown of the mid-1980s) instead of funneling their money abroad (Tiglao 1990b, 68). This kind of argument sets up a contrast between the "old money" Spanish mestizo families and the "new money" Chinese.[34]

But given that the fruits of economic development are unevenly distributed among the Philippine population, it is not surprising that nationalist resentment has focused on the "Chinese," whose "foreignness" (despite the fact that the most successful Chinese businesses are headed and run by Filipino citizens) continues to stand for all that is "alien" and alienating within the body politic. That the issue of the "alien" Chinese often shades into the issue of "alienating" capital is no doubt a consequence of the ambivalent relationship among the nation, the state, and capitalism. The advent of globalization has reformulated this relationship between the nation, state, and capitalism, but without quite overcoming this ambivalence about predatory capitalism nor muffling the call for redistributive justice.

It seems doubly ironic to note the fact that—if there is indeed a connection between kidnapping and electoral campaigns—it is "kidnapped" Chinese money that has helped underwrite the cost of carrying out the political programs of groups or factions that work within (as well as those that work against) the state.[35] As a form of social relation, kidnapping owes its historical provenance and success to the long and often troubled relationship between the Chinese and the state, to the Chinese's economic role as middlemen and bourgeoisie in the colonial and early postcolonial era, an economic visibility that has been heightened by the Chinese's perceived cultural difference and alienation from the body politic.[36] The most immediate and visible effect of this relationship has been the creation of the Chinese as a perfect victim, seen in the perennial uneasiness and distrust with which the Chinese have dealings with government officials, their reliance on forging symbiotic alliances with government officials, and their relative readiness to pay the ransom.

This kind of behavior on the part of the Chinese has often been criticized by the media and by the law enforcers themselves, but rather than simply blaming the victims, one way to understand the way in which the Chinese have chosen to respond to the state is to look into the way in which the state has chosen to speak to the Chinese. Kidnapping lays bare the tense relationship between the Chinese and the state. The postcolonial nation-state necessarily constitutes itself in terms of a formal repudiation of economic and political inequality, and of the colonial past. These two strains, in fact, come together in the state's periodic attempts to deal with the problem of the legal status of the Chinese and in its attempts to safeguard the economic and political interests of the Filipinos against the "virtual nationality" of the Chinese. The uniqueness of the present state policies on the Chinese, however, consists of their similarity to kidnapping-for-ransom: even though they continue to operate on an extractive logic vis-á-vis the Chinese as they had done during the colonial and postwar periods,[37] the main difference is that they operate in a terrain wherein the overlapping of membership in kidnap gangs and state apparatuses has rendered the legal/criminal distinction inoperative. It becomes very difficult to determine whether the state is acting like a criminal, or if the criminals act like the state. (For motorists in Manila who routinely fall prey to traffic-cop extortionists or Filipinos who have had to pay to "expedite" the processing of their documents by the state bureaucrats, this is hardly a new insight.)

The enactment of the Alien Social Integration Act (ASIA) of 1995 further underscored the blurring of the legal/criminal distinction in the Aquino and Ramos administrations' policies toward the Chinese. Immigration Commissioner Leandro Verceles explained that the Act was necessitated by the state's intention of bringing "illegal aliens into the mainstream, and [thus] mak[ing] them active participants in [the country's] development" (*Manila Chronicle*, 1995). Active participation here was, however, interpreted in strictly monetary terms in the form of fees—P200,000 per Chinese male adult, P50,000 for spouses, and P25,000 for dependents. The government expected to earn P40 billion from the Chinese, and had strengthened its persecution of illegal aliens in order to drum up more participants (ibid.).[38] Lest it be thought that this Act only affected illegal aliens, it bears noting that Chinese with Filipino citizenship have not been safe from the state harassment and official inquiry into the history of their immigration and naturalization (the investigation of prominent businessman William Gatchalian being the most celebrated case).[39] In light of the instrumentalization of citizenship (Aguilar 1999), the state has made it easy for Taiwanese and other foreign investors to secure their permanent residency in the Philippines, while rendering the situation of Philippine-born Chinese problematical by virtue of the threat of jus sanguinis illegality which continues to shadow their citizenship status as well as that of their progeny.

If there is one thing that kidnapping illuminates, it is that the extractive logic that used to be identified with the colonial and postcolonial state vis-á-vis the Chinese has become generalized and diffused throughout society. This generalization of criminality highlights the violence of everyday life in the Philippines and the incapacity of the state to enforce security. But it is in part also a consequence of unequal development, not only within the nation-state, but between nation-states. Unequal development translates into active pursuit of transnational capital, in the name of "global competitiveness," which has involved the exploitation and outward movement of the Filipino labor force.[40] The Philippine state, like most Third World countries, attempts to apply the seemingly universal economic laws of capitalist development to its territories, but is forced to rationalize its repeated failure to follow the path of the industrialized countries. Not surprisingly, criminals like the kidnappers have been routinely blamed for undermining the political stability of the country, and thereby driving away foreign investment. At the same time, the state is regularly criticized for its inability to guarantee its citizen's rights to freedom, security, and equality both within and beyond its borders. Indeed, Filipino domestic worker Flor Contemplacion's hanging in Singapore in 1995 provoked a veritable outpouring of national(ist) grief and anger directed as much against the "ineffectual" Philippine state as against the "punitive" Singaporean state.

Kidnapping also shows the instability—a perennial flickering—of the hyphen between nation and state. In the kidnappings, the Chinese find themselves in a position whereby their lives and safety are actually in the hands of a state that can only be spoken to and made to listen if the Chinese speak *as* Chinese. The Chinese's relationship with the state is a deeply conflictive one of dependence and distrust, yet the Chinese have been historically dependent on the state's ability to secure their continued existence within the Philippines and must perforce deal with the consequences of this dependency.[41] The concepts of home and nation that take shape in the language and practice of "Chineseness" are thus haunted by the memory of— or anxiety about—displacement (Derrida 1994, 83).

In similar terms, the political efficacy and contradictions of both Chinese and Filipino responses to kidnapping are forged within the very flicker of the hyphen between nation, state, and capitalism. Kidnapping appears to provide the public with a handy account of both the political and economic alienation of society in general and, at the same time, the state's mediation of inequality in both national and global terms.[42] Put another way, kidnapping highlights in the most visible and audible way the primary mode in which the state *speaks*. The language that kidnapping and the state speak is that of inequality, and the term "Chinese" is a signifier of the givenness of this practical inequality, an inequality that the state can neither master nor abjure, anymore than the Chinese can repudiate or accept the state.

Who/What is a Citizen?

How has Kaisa para sa Kaunlaran intervened in debates on the "Chinese" in order to question the necessary link between ethnicity and class? It has done so by invoking the discourse of citizenship and of rights to equality and liberty as an antidote to the state's identification of the Chinese with capital. The kidnapping crisis has been central to its attempts to (re)define the Chinese within the parameters of citizenship, since kidnapping brought things to a head, so to speak, by serving as the latest manifestation and practical realization of the conflation, but more important, as the site of debate and contestation over this conflation.

For Kaisa, the kidnapping crisis had the unforeseen effect of providing the crucial impetus that allowed the organization to take on the spokesman function, establishing itself as a rival of the erstwhile spokesperson organization of the Chinese community, the Federation of Filipino Chinese Chambers of Commerce. Kaisa intervenes in the representation of the Chinese as a collective subject by attempting to reorient the stereotypical identification of the Chinese with capital. In the early 1990s, it became one of the most visible Chinese organizations in the country. The existence and visibility of Kaisa owe something to its avowed difference from the conservative official spokesperson organization of the Chinese community, the Shangzong (Siong Chong, an abbreviation for the Federation of Filipino-Chinese Chambers of Commerce and Industry).[43] Members of Kaisa are mostly young business-men and professionals, and the organization has declared itself to have civic rather than economic goals. To wit, Kaisa has concentrated on research and publications, including the monthly and now biweekly English and Tagalog-language news digest *Tulay*, the first issue of which, not incidentally, appeared on June 12, 1987, and the monthly Chinese-language column *Ronghe* (lit., "fuse" or "merge")[44] which appears in *Shijie Ribao* (*World News*), the Chinese daily with the largest circulation in the Philippines; public relations—making several representations with the Office of the President, with Congress, the Department of Justice, among others, on issues affecting the Philippine Chinese; and social work.[45]

Heir to the integration advocacy of Pagkakaisa sa Pag-Unland (see previous chapter), Kaisa's credo establishes its integrationist stance quite clearly: "The Philippines is our country,/it is the land of our birth,/the home of our people./Our blood may be Chinese,/but our roots grow deep in Filipino soil,/our bonds are with the Filipino people./We are proud of the many cultures,/which have made us what we are,/it is our desire, our hope and aspiration—/that with the rest of our people,/we shall find our rightful place/in the Philippine sun" (*Tulay*, June 12, 1987, 1). The fact that this credo is written in English points to an important difference between Kaisa and the much older and rival spokesperson organization, the Federation of Filipino-Chinese Chambers of Commerce and Industry. Kaisa's use of English and Tagalog in both its internal and external communications represents the first break within this century between the spokesperson function and its "native" medium of communication. If Chineseness used to be tied to linguis-tic nationalism (here, Chinese encompassed Hokkien and *putonghua*), Kaisa represents a new appropriation of Chineseness, one that veers away from a Sinophone definition of Chineseness toward a pluralistic definition of the Philippine nation that acknowledges and tolerates, if not celebrates and capitalizes on, cultural differences.

This pluralistic notion of Filipinoness is based on the political integration of the Chinese: by acquiring Philippine citizenship, the "Chinese" are now members of the Philippine nation, and therefore entitled to speak to the state as "Filipinos," without being dismissed or ignored by other Filipinos.

Compared to the Federation, Kaisa has been vocal in its criticism of the government, focusing on the government's failure to "maintain law and order" in the face of rampant kidnapping, and its exploitation of the Chinese community, its treatment of the Chinese primarily as "sources of relief funds and campaign contributions" and a "convenient scapegoat for economic ills."[46] When asked about Kaisa's criticism of the government, Teresita Ang-See, one of the founders of Kaisa (see chap. 2) and the most publicly well-known critic of kidnapping, has stated in an interview: "When I started to speak up about the peace and order situation, I did so conscious of the fact that as a Filipino, it is not just my right to do so, it is my responsibility, too" (Ang-See 1995). This statement not only recasts the so-called Chinese as Filipino, but affirms the Chinese-as-Filipino's right to politics. The claim that the Chinese are Filipinos is both a cultural and a political claim, because it not only reiterates the demand for citizenship, but also for what Etienne Balibar has called the "*public* inscription of freedom and equality" (1994, 49). The credo of Kaisa suggests that accession to full political rights redefines the Chinese in terms of their historical belonging to the Philippine nation-state.

Kaisa's credo also explains the provenance as well as function of a news digest like *Tulay*. The demand for public recognition, *in writing*, of the Tsinoy's right to freedom and equality antes up the stakes in talking successfully to the state. Kaisa has criticized the government for its inability to forge a comprehensive, cohesive, and responsive policy on the Chinese in the Philippines (*Tulay*, 1994b). Kaisa constructs a referent for the term "Chinese" by adopting an integrationist stance. Kaisa's credo is oriented toward the transformation of the idea of citizenship as inclusive of *all* people, including the Chinese by its insistence that the Chinese have a "rightful place in the Philippine sun" and are among the many peoples who are also finding *their* rightful places in the Philippine sun.

At the same time, Kaisa sees its integrationist agenda as distinct from the state's domestication of cultural difference as a "foreign," "alien" source of revenue. While Kaisa insists on the inclusiveness of the idea of citizenship and its ability to accommodate cultural difference (the "Chinese heritage"), it denies with equal fervor the idea that rogue state officials have about the Chinese as milking cows and scapegoats. In so doing, Kaisa finds itself dealing simultaneously with the state and with the problem of cultural difference. The challenge for Kaisa lies in constructing a practical conduct on both these levels—how to talk to the Chinese and how to talk to the state—without synthesizing or collapsing them both into a monolithic assumption of "Chinese interests." For previous spokesman organizations, like the Philippine Chinese General Chamber of Commerce and the Federation of Filipino-Chinese Chambers of Commerce and Industry, collapsing the state's naturalization of Chineseness as foreign, on the one hand, and the idea of Chinese cultural difference, on the other hand, had not been a problem, since it was precisely this conflation that allowed them to represent, and speak on behalf of, "alien" Chinese interests to the state.[47]

Who/What is Chinese?

Who are the constituents on whose behalf Kaisa speaks? Kaisa commits itself to an idea of nation that is not a mere set of all citizens; as the first stanza of its credo makes clear, it is the claim to historical belonging that guarantees the citizenship rights of the Chinese. This idea of the nation, however, remains dependent on a state whose legitimacy has been continually under challenge during the Commonwealth and postwar era from various social movements and militant organizations.

On the occasion of the Chinese New Year in 1995, the Alex Boncayao Brigade (ABB), a breakaway faction of the Communist New People's Army, faxed a letter to the media, a letter addressed specifically to the Chinese Filipinos, urging them never again to allow themselves to be "milking cows" of corrupt government officials. The ABB also threatened to execute more "corrupt police officers involved in kidnapping," and vowed to "hunt down ...officials and other notorious elements in the bureaucracy who victimize the Chinese community." The ABB said that it was not against economic development as long as it "benefits our country and people." As long as the workers' welfare is assured, the ABB promised to "foster industrial peace." Finally, the ABB stated that the Chinese Filipinos were "integral parts of the nation who should not be treated as second-class citizens," and declared that "there can be unity of purpose despite the cultural diversity."[48]

When Teresita Ang-See was asked to comment on the ABB statement, she gave a very interesting response. She expressed surprise and comfort in the fact that "the leftist group seem[ed] to be stretching out its hand to the Chinese Filipino community." At the same time, however, she noted that it was a big shame that such statements had to come from the ABB. "It would have been better, and we would have been happier," she said, "had such statements come from the government itself" (Kiunisala 1993).

The ABB's assertion of the discourse of rights and citizenship would seem to echo the position taken by Kaisa—its insistence that the Chinese should not be treated as second-class citizens, for example, as well as its emphasis on the coexistence of unity of purpose and cultural diversity. Ang-See's statement reveals the fact that Chinese Filipino kidnap victims have had to rely on the state to redress their grievances. But as the state persists in employing an extractive logic in its dealings with the Chinese, Chinese Filipinos find themselves in the difficult position of having to cooperate with a state that kidnap victims may not necessarily trust. This forced reliance on the state sometimes means supporting state programs that may turn out to be deeply flawed: an example is Kaisa's support for Miriam Defensor Santiago's Alien Legalization Program (ALP). On March 27, 1996, Immigration Commissioner Leandro Verceles announced that aliens who had applied for permanent residency under the ALP had to re-apply under the ASIA and pay the new and increased fees of P200,000, up from the original P50,000. Although this statement was later rescinded when Fidel Ramos signed the ASIA into law, it remains a fitting example of the cupidity characteristic of state policies toward the Chinese.

Because Kaisa, out of necessity, pins its main hopes on addressing the state and getting the state to act, its notion of the Chinese is necessarily circumscribed by the terms of the referent that the state "sees." Kaisa has always highlighted the existence of indigent Chinese. But, as noted in the Introduction, Philippine census statistics make it difficult, if not impossible, to gauge the extent to which ethnic Chinese live below the poverty line. Historian Edgar Wickberg's estimate in the early 1990s that more than 20 percent of the Chinese lived below the poverty line seems necessarily speculative, given the lack of available statistics (1992, 52–64). Where the middle and upper-class Chinese can integrate into the so-called mainstream of society *as Chinese* Filipinos, the rest of the Chinese, that is, the poor Chinese, are assumed to disappear into the masses. The point at which one becomes or does not become Chinese, the point at which one *appears* as Chinese on the social map, turns out to be a question of property. Kaisa's production of a collective referent called the "Chinese community" appears to be tied closely to the interests of its largely middle-class Tsinoy members, even as it has made admirable efforts to reach out to the poor, whether Filipino or Chinese, through its extensive outreach projects, such as blood donation drives, building of schools, and other activities. Kaisa has also been vocal in calling public attention to the plight of new Chinese migrants who are not Filipino citizens, as these new migrants find themselves being subject to extortion and arbitrary arrest (see chap. 6).

The idea of fraternity, of a Chinese "community" whose interests can be defended, is thus not self-evident. Kaisa's revaluing of "Chinese culture" and its contribution to Philippine society comes at a time when public space itself has been emptied of the "Chinese." Chineseness is marked visibly in temples, cemeteries, and TV programs, but these "Chinese" spaces do not bear the imprint of the lived experience of Chineseness, particularly among younger generations of Chinese Filipinos,[49] who distinguish themselves from the "Genuine Intsik" new migrants who are now the bearers of "traditional" Chinese culture and the main force behind the survival of the Chinese language and community organizations. The traditional day-long Chinese celebration of All Soul's Day disappeared after Chinese community officials banned parking inside the cemeteries because of traffic jams. TV programs run Hong Kong and Taiwanese soap operas that the younger generation can no longer understand, thanks to the decrepit Chinese-language curriculum of "Chinese" schools. Opera troupes are manned by Chinese-mestizo actors who learn their lines phonetically, and attendance is feeble. Tellingly, the much-touted Chinese "traditional rituals" that attend engagement and wedding ceremonies are often remembered only by the Filipino cameramen who videotape and, in fact, orchestrate the ceremonies. Further, as Chinese Filipinos are increasingly being integrated into Philippine society, it is the new migrant who is marked as "alien," the genuine intsik.

Most ironic of all, becoming-Filipino is not enough to shield one from "criminals" working inside and outside the state. The violence of everyday life in the Philippines (for homicide rates, which showed a dip between 2007 and 2009 down to 5.4 per 100,000 people, but with high estimates of between 14.7 and 18.2 from 1999 to 2003 [United Nations Office on Drugs and Crime 2011, 109]), has targeted ordinary citizens, regardless of their ethnicity. Kidnappings in the form of arbitrary arrest and detention, and forced disappearances (extrajudicial killings) were commonplace during the Marcos era, and continue to occur well into the present. In the past decade alone, ninety-six journalists have been killed, making the Philippines the second deadliest country in the world for journalists (*Philippine Daily Inquirer,* 2011a). Fifty-eight people, including thirty-four journalists, were kidnapped and murdered in Maguindanao, Southern Philippines, in a single, bloody episode of election-related violence that implicated the governor of Maguindanao, Andal Ampatuan Sr., an ally of President Gloria Macapagal-Arroyo, as well as his two sons, both also elected officials.

"Mismanagement of Grief"

At the height of the kidnapping phenomenon, Charlson Ong, one of the most prolific and respected writers of his generation, published a short story that dealt with the human cost and consequences of kidnapping from the perspective of the Chinese victims and their families. Entitled "Mismanagement of Grief" (1996), the story focuses on the efforts of one grieving family to comprehend and live through the terrible accident that had claimed the life of their beloved Sophie Tanpoco Lim, a young kidnap victim killed in the crossfire between government forces and the kidnappers. "Mismanagement of Grief" is based on a similar but real-life incident that had occurred in early 1993, when bungled government rescue operations resulted in the death of high school student Charlene Mayne Sy and provoked a tremendous outpouring of grief and protest from the Chinese community in Manila.

Ong's short story was the first fictional treatment of the kidnapping phenomenon by a Chinese Filipino writer to appear in a major Philippine publication (*Philippine Graphic*). This in itself is noteworthy, but it also highlights the fact that a writer of Ong's stature[50] may choose to draw on the experiences of the Chinese in the Philippines and write almost exclusively from a "Chinese" perspective without his writing being in any way considered "limited" or "narrow" in range. It is not inconceivable that Ong's sterling literary reputation may have even been secured precisely through—not despite—his creation, and his consistent deployment, of a specifically Chinese imaginary.[51] In populating his fiction with Chinese characters, he appears to have mapped a literary terrain with a rich lode of experience, memory, and history.

To be sure, Ong is not the first to write in English about the Philippine Chinese—Alexander Sycip did so during the prewar period; Benito Lim (1958; Hau 2000a) did it in the late 1950s and early 1960s, while Paul Stephen Lim (1982) published a collection of stories, the most well-known of which may be considered examples of autobiographical fiction, in the early 1980s. But it is a sign of those times that Benito Lim wrote sporadically and has yet to publish his collected fiction, while Paul Stephen Lim felt compelled to explain, in the preface to his book, his decision to write about the experiences of the Philippine Chinese by denying the specificity of this experience and by invoking, instead, his desire to be considered, not as an ethnic writer, but as a writer, period. It does not help that Lim's legitimate fear of being ghettoized as a writer, of being pigeonholed as a purveyor of fiction with an ethnic flavor, is exacerbated by critics who feel that they must constantly underscore the "transcendent" or "universal" appeal of literary texts produced by nonwhite writers while assuming that the works of white writers are necessarily already universal (Lim 1982, Author's Preface).

There is some irony in the fact that the kidnapping phenomenon, and all the attention that it commands in the public sphere, may have actually helped to clear a space for the articulation and interrogation, not just by writers like Charlson Ong but by activists as well, of the ambivalent status of the Chinese in the Philippines. International developments such as the growth and institutionalization of ethnic studies and cultural studies programs in American universities, and the growing interest in ethnic

Chinese in East Asia and their role in regional capitalism, and the new cosmopolitan forms of subjectivity that their current activities embody, are but two of the conditions of possibility that are crucial for understanding the provenance of Philippine Chinese fiction in English.

But Ong's story poses questions that ultimately force a rethinking of commonsensical ideas about "Chinese culture" and about Chineseness (that is, what makes a Chinese "Chinese"). Ong's story exposes the fact that the word "Chinese" is implicated in public discourses that are intimately connected to politics and economy, specifically to the concept of money and to the concept of citizenship.

When Richard, the narrator of the story, attends the wake for his cousin Sophie, he is drawn into an argument with his father over the family's decision to emigrate to Canada in the aftermath of the tragedy. Richard's father tells him: "What do you want to stay in this godforsaken country for? Hasn't it hurt us enough? We're not wanted anymore." Richard, however, has decided not to follow his family to Canada, and tells his father that he intends to remain in the Philippines. In addition, he reproves his father for trying to force his reluctant grandmother to relocate to Hong Kong.

When asked by the enraged father why he insists on staying, Richard blurts out: "This is the only place in the world where I can become president." The text tells us that when Richard makes this statement, he suddenly feels himself "imbued with new power." Richard tells his father that he wants to stay behind with his grandmother to take care of the ancestral artifacts in the house. The father promptly bars Richard from attending Sophie's funeral, and then proceeds to disinherit him with a one-time gift of P200,000, and refuses to let him enter the house to take care of their house icons. Richard, however, understands that his father's draconian measures are a kind of concession, after all, a grudging acknowledgment of Richard's right to live as he pleases and where he chooses.

Although the story was written before the passage of the Alien Social Integration Act (ASIA) of 1995, Ong would have appreciated the prescient irony of his main character's father leaving him P200,000, the exact sum specified by ASIA to "integrate" Chinese of dubious legal status into Philippine society. This is, in other words, the exact amount that would have enabled Richard, in real life, to "buy" his permanent residency and take the first step toward acquiring the Filipino citizenship that would allow, if not him, then his children, to run for president of the country.

Richard's statement that the Philippines is the only place in the world where he can be president must be read not merely as an assertion of the Chinese's claim to historical belonging in the Philippines. It is also an assertion of, or better yet an insistence on, the Chinese's right *to* the

Philippines, a right that is supposed to be guaranteed theoretically by the juridical concept of citizenship but is actually denied in practice by the state, which had historically deprived most Chinese, even those who had been born and had grown up in the Philippines, of the opportunity to exercise this right, either through outright discrimination or through repeated extortion and intimidation. A law like ASIA, which was originally conceived to redress the grievances of Philippine Chinese residents who have been shortchanged by the Philippine state's long history of overly restrictive immigration and naturalization policies, ultimately ends up discriminating against a sizable number of Chinese who cannot afford to pay the exorbitant fees charged by the government. In fact, ASIA serves to reinforce the racist idea that all Chinese are rich and to make the Chinese the convenient milking cows of a government in serious need of replenishing its empty coffers. And in commodifying the terms of membership in the Filipino national community, it also reflects the state's increasing instrumentalization of citizenship (Aguilar 1999).

Moreover, this cultural-political assertion of belonging must also exist alongside, if it is not shaped by, the Filipino public's perception that associates the Chinese with money. Kidnapping seems to affirm most Filipinos' belief that all Chinese are rich and ostentatious, but takes this popular stereotype to its logical conclusion by treating the Chinese as an object of exchange, a literal commodity. Sophie Lim is described by Richard as a spendthrift, whose carelessness with money is tied to her active consumption of goods, but she in turn becomes, quite literally, a commodity to be exchanged for ransom money.

Furthermore, the conflict-ridden relationship between nation, state, and capitalism has material effects on the bodies of the Chinese. Truisms regarding Chinese business acuity and resilience establish the Chinese as exemplary citizens of a new regime of economic liberalization, an ideal to which the post-Marcos governments aspire. The identification of the Chinese with money is therefore inflected by the double-edged association of the Chinese not only with modernity, especially with the idea of national economic growth and development to which the Chinese are supposed to contribute, but also with the consumption of goods, with the idea of a stable middle class that is perceived to be a necessary component of the nation-state.

Ong's story shows the extent to which the discourse of citizenship is conflictual and contradictory. Given the contradictions that haunt modern politics, as Etienne Balibar (1994, 55) has argued, what remains central to any invocation of rights is not only the history of naming and the creation of individual and collective referents that seek to grant the discourse a degree of enunciative and practical stability. What remains central to any invocation of citizenship and rights, as Balibar has noted, is the question of power relations, the issue of inequalities, and of "the foundations (equality, liberty, property, fraternity) that are constantly invoked in order to institute inequalities and thereby limit or annul the freedom of an entire 'class' of humanity." As Balibar writes: "[B]ehind these inequalities, there is a kind of difference that cannot be overcome by the institution of equality. This does not mean that equality is not the formal condition of liberation. It only means that it remains purely external, that is, there can be no 'political solution' purely in terms of equaliberty" (ibid.)

"Chinese" must be seen as a term, following Balibar, that is inscribed in a relation of collective inequality which is "reproduced, exercised and verified as a personal relation, which is to say that instituted state power does not subject the same individuals, nor the same class of individuals, by the same means, even though it does not stop adding to itself in the process" (ibid.). In resisting the juridically defined notion of citizenship that subjects everybody equally to the law, kidnapping is only the generalized form of the way that the state has chosen to speak to the Chinese.

But while it is necessary to challenge the ways in which the state has constrained the discourse of citizenship, the kidnapping phenomenon reveals that the discourse of citizenship presupposes the existence of a state and therefore citizenship cannot be thought outside of state inter-pellation. The Chinese recourse to citizenship as a matter of strategy is determined by the specific characteristics of the Philippine colonial and postcolonial state, even as it is indicative of the historical negotiations in which the Chinese have engaged in order to secure a space for themselves within the bounds, perhaps even the teleology, of the nation. Given the contradictory articulations of Chinese belonging to the Philippine nation-state, Chinese attempts since the post-EDSA period to counterpose themselves as a body of citizens against the state have been instrumental in putting pressure on the state to address the law and order situation. But a political solution to the kidnapping crisis, while necessary, may prove to be ineffective if this solution fails to curb the extractive capacities of the state toward the Chinese or curtail the violence that state officials (and especially their criminal cohort) are capable of bringing to bear not only on the Chinese Filipinos, but on the Filipino population more generally. Chinese reliance on a traditional discourse of citizenship to deal with the problems posed by social antagonisms in the Philippines may run the risk of treating antiracism as just one issue requiring a single voice, rather than as part of a polyphony of critical voices (Mouffe and Laclau 1985, 191) bearing testimony to the plurality of social struggles, which have the potential to extend the field and practice of "democracy" (173) to the larger Philippine society.

Kaisa deserves credit for directing public attention to the kidnapping phenomenon, and for putting pressure on the government to address this problem, even at risk of life and limb of its most articulate member, Teresita Ang-See. At stake is the very concept of citizenship and its capacity for inclusiveness and exclusiveness. In what way can the state be transformed, partly through a rearticulation of the meaning of citizenship in a way that opens up the possibility of justice, a justice that is not a simple matter of calculable distribution or restitution, but a justice open to the call for emancipation? For the Chinese Filipinos, heeding the call for justice entails listening to the call of other voices, the plight of other people across time, and undoing the fifty years of neocolonial amnesia. Kidnapping exposes the fact that a political community is formed through selective inclusion and exclusion not only of the "Chinese," but those who would consider themselves—and are considered by others as—Filipinos.

Notes

1   For a study of the images of the Chinese in Philippine literature in English, see Sy 1979 and Yap 1970.

2   Kidnapping is not unknown in nineteenth- and twentieth-century Philippines. In Rizal's *Fili* (1891, chap. 10), Cabesang Tales joins a band of *tulisanes* (bandits) who are known to kidnap wealthy people for ransom. Although categorized as criminals by the state, banditry is also depicted in the novel as having revolutionary potential, as Simoun relies on Tales's help to organize a rebellion. Yung Li Yuk-wai (1996, 156, 158) notes that kidnappings were commonplace in Chinatown in the early postwar years as armed criminals preyed on wealthy individuals and families. This category of "extortionists and kidnappers" allegedly included Chinese leftist guerrillas (Yung Li 1996, 158; citing Tan 1981,106–7).

3   The report also noted that 29 people were kidnapped (about one victim a day) in November, the same month that the Philippines hosted the Asia-Pacific Economic Cooperation summit in Subic. The figures are based on reports by two civic groups, the Movement for the Restoration of Peace and Order and Citizens Action Against Crime. The total amount of ransom money paid in 1995 has been conservatively pegged at P99 million. This estimate only covers known payments; in many cases, the exact sum of ransom money remained unknown. The statistics were provided by the Movement for the Restoration of Peace and Order and the Citizens Action Against Crime in their joint press conference on October 31, 1996. For statistics in 1998, see *Tulay,* 1998a.

4.   Official statistics provide lower figures (*Malaya,* 2005): The Philippine National Police (PNP) records give the following figures: 51 cases in 1995; 56 in 1996; 97 in

1997; 113 in 1998; 50 in 1999; 48 in 2000; 99 in 2001; 66 in 2002; and 87 in 2003. The Citizens Action Against Crime reported 71 Tsinoy abductions in 2006 (Diaz 2006).

5   The figures for 1994 include Fr. Cirilo Nacorda and the 78 teachers abducted by the Abu Sayyaf in Mindanao, on June 8, 1994.

6   The metaphor of a Chinese state within the state can clearly be seen in a series of articles on the internal politics of the Federation of Filipino-Chinese Chambers of Commerce and Industry, Inc., written by Robert C. Villanueva (1993a, 1993b, 1994) at the height of the kidnapping crisis.

7   "The exclusive club the kidnap and other crime victims belong to has been democratized by sheer numbers. Few people will still think that kidnapping is a Chinese community problem if they read the latest statistics" (Co 1995).

8   The most well-known cases include high school student Charlene Mayne Sy, who died in a shootout between her abductors and government forces at the EDSA-Quezon Boulevard junction in January 1993; and college students Kenneth Go and Myron Uy Ramos, who were tortured and killed by their captors in September 1992. From 1991 to 1996, more than 58 people have died at the hands of their abductors, or in shootouts between the kidnap gangs and government forces. The funeral of Willyson Ong, a garments trader who was executed by his kidnappers after his family failed to pay the P50 million ransom, was attended by 3,000 people (*Tulay*, 1998b). In 2003 alone, six kidnap victims died (Ang-See 2004c).

9   The link between kidnapping and citizenship was first suggested to me by Vicente Rafael when he discussed a paper about political representation and the formation of the Chinese community in the Philippines that I had read at the Association for Asian Studies Conference in Honolulu, Hawaii, in April 1996.

10   See also Evelyn Cullamar's (1995) discussion of Ephraim Areno's paper on ethnic Chinese political participation in Iloilo.

11   This claim to citizenship was made historically possible by the mass naturalization of the Chinese under the Marcos regime in 1975 (see previous chapter).

12   To push this point further, the question of the "Chinese" in the Philippines demands an examination of the affiliations between ontological and historically specific sociopolitical sites of analysis and critique. Inasmuch as the question of the Chinese within Southeast Asia is coextensive with questions of nationalism, and of colonialism, imperialism, orientalism, racism, and sexism, it is deeply implicated in the question of Occidental modernity and its planetary (uneven) scope. For a general theorizing of such affiliations, see Derrida 1994.

13   This kind of vocabulary has also been used by the Federation of Filipino-Chinese Chambers of Commerce and Industry, Inc., the official spokesman organization of the Chinese community. In celebration of *Tulay*'s eighth anniversary in 1995, the congratulatory ad of the Federation describes the Federation as "an association serving the Filipino people and committed to promote commerce and industry, foster national unity, and in every way uphold the torch of true friendship, brotherhood and understanding among all peoples of whatever race, religion or political belief, under the ideals of peace, freedom, democracy and social justice."

14   The current articulation of the discourse of citizenship owes its provenance to the events that led to the so-called People's Power Revolution at EDSA and the toppling of the Marcos administration. The general opposition to the Marcos dictatorship in the early 1980s addressed itself to two adversaries: absolutism, which represented a negation of freedom; and privileges, which represented a negation of equality. The

events of EDSA brought the two terms of equality and liberty together in public discourse. This conjoining of terms would later be appropriated by the Chinese Filipinos in their deployment of the general discourse of citizenship and rights. Since the proposition of "equaliberty" was first historically articulated during the French revolution of 1789, and since the EDSA event has often been represented as a "revolution" reminiscent of 1789, I decided to use Etienne Balibar's (1994) close reading of the *Declaration of the Rights of Man and the Citizen of 1789* as a reference for my argument.

15 This is complicated by the existence of nonreformist liberation movements such as the Communist New People's Army and the Moro Islamic Liberation Front, for which armed struggle (basically a justification of violence in the name of a social subject, "the people") is the main principle of political action. One interesting question would be: to what extent does the ontologizing of violence as the principle of political action serve to highlight the necessary relation between the law and violence?

16 On the preeminence of the question of order and violence to conceiving of citizenship, see Joppke 2010, 1–3.

17 Articles on kidnapping began appearing in *Tulay* during the last quarter of 1989.

18 A surge in the number of kidnapping cases by as much as 70 percent was reported in 2006, during her presidency (Andrade 2006).

19 PSA estimates of kidnapping incidents in the years 2006–2007 far exceed the statistics provided by *Tulay*, 2007 and 2008 in table 1.

20 A *Tulay* article (1992) lists the names and affiliations of arrested suspects. The Philippine police and military seem to be very well represented, with PNP officers in the Red Scorpion Gang, marines in the Tinsay-Espejo Gang, Philippine Army officers in the 8 "Hoodlums in Uniform" Gang, BID and NBI people in Atayde's Gang, CPD personnel in the Omar Ring, WPD in the Eddie Chang Group, the AFP (RAM) in the Morales Group, and PNP-NARCOM in the "Wang-Wang" Group. In 1995, a former police officer, Col. Reynaldo Berroya—who headed an antikidnapping task force under the Presidential Anti-Crime Commission as a replacement for two previous task force chiefs who were accused of involvement in the kidnap-for-ransom cases that they themselves were investigating (Jose Pring and Timoteo Zarcal)—was convicted of involvement in the kidnapping of a Taiwanese businessman and sentenced to life imprisonment. See also Kiunisala 1992, 10–11, 31; and Tiglao 1995b. In late 1996, the *Shijie Ribao* (World News) carried an editorial commenting on the hosting of the APEC Conference by the Philippines. The editorial voiced (in an understandably circuitous manner) the Chinese community's general belief that Fidel Ramos himself bore some responsibility for his failure as president to stem the tide of kidnappings (*Shijie Ribao* 1996, 1). At the height of the kidnappings, the Philippine National Police identified 380 organized groups that were "actively engaged in kidnapping, bank robbery, hijacking, car theft, drug trafficking, gunrunning, and other 'high-paying' crimes across the country, particularly in Metro Manila" (Javellana 1998, 1). A *Philippine Daily Inquirer* editorial (2001) lambasted the double standard that makes the government respond more promptly to kidnappings of foreign victims (in this case, Chinese-Singaporeans) than locals (Chinese Filipinos).

21 See, for example, Mydans 1996; Dueñas 1992, 34–36; and *Philippines Free Press*, 1993.

22 Robina Gokongwei, daughter of mall magnate John Gokongwei, was kidnapped in 1981, and rescued by Lt. Col. Panfilo "Ping" Lacson.

23 The seeds of this insight belong to Vicente Rafael.

24 Charlene Mayne Sy was snatched on her way to school, while Kenneth Go and Myron Uy Ramos were abducted on their way home from a party. Kidnappings have also been reported in malls and outside school compounds. In July 1997, the Chinese-language daily *Shijie Ribao* (1997, 1) began carrying readers' letters and reports concerning abductions of "Chinese-looking" people by armed motorcycle riders along Banawe Street. In reaction to these kidnappings, wealthy Chinese-Filipinos began sending their children to international schools in China, Singapore, and the U.S., although press coverage has tended to emphasize the schools in China (Nazareno 2001).

25 I am indebted to Marx's discussion in *Capital* (1977 [1867], 1:chap. 10, 1).

26 See Jacques Derrida's (1994, 158) discussion of the phantomalization of the social bond: "Persons are personified by letting themselves be haunted by the very effect of objective haunting, so to speak, that they produce by inhabiting the thing. Persons (guardians or possessors of the thing) are haunted in return, and constitutively, by the haunting they produce in the thing by lodging there their speech and their will like inhabitants."

27 See Pheng Cheah's (1996) excellent discussion of Derrida in the context of feminist theorizing of the body.

28 Rather than being a unique case, the spectralization of the Chinese points to the unavoidability of spectralization for all finite beings. For a discussion of the latter point and its implications for the analysis of historical forms of power and transformative agency, see Cheah 1996, 134.

29 The most influential twinning of these two narratives in historiographical form is Constantino and Constantino 1975.

30 The conflation of alien Chinese with alienating capital within the figure of the rapacious Chinese (male) merchant is perfectly captured by an urban legend about "Robinson," the monster-snake twin of retail magnate John Gokongwei's daughter Robina Gokongwei-Pe, after whom Robinsons is supposed to be named. According to this urban legend, which became popular in the 1990s (right around the time when "Chinese capitalism" was big news and the Chinese tycoons achieved national prominence): "The basement of Robinsons Galleria [the mall owned by the Gokongweis], a then-upscale mall located along EDSA, Ortigas, was said to be the dwelling place of Robina Gokongwei's giant half-snake, half-man twin. Some versions of the rumor say that the snake suddenly appears at dressing room mirrors, which are actually gateways to the basement. Other versions say that these mirrors serve as trapdoors which open when 'Robinson' is hungry, sending the unlucky victim down to a series of pipes and mazes to Robinson's chamber. According to the rumor, this twin likes to feed [on] unsuspecting beautiful women fitting clothes in the mall's dressing rooms." The blogger ("Urban Legend #1: Robinsons' Snake" 2007) who retells this story goes on to speculate that "Some say that the half-snake, half-man form of Robina's twin is an exaggeration of the actual condition of her twin. Robina has a twin *daw* who's deformed and this guy is the lucky charm which gave billions to the Gokongwei family."

31 Marx's *Capital*, in fact, as mentioned in the previous section, hints at the same formulation in his discussion of the mercantile operations of the Jews in Europe.

32 My thanks to Pheng Cheah for helping to draw out this point in my argument.

33 See, for example, Zulueta 1995, 1, 4. Relying heavily on the ideas of business journalist James Clad, the article blames the Marcos administration for distorting and truncating the "entrepreneurial attitude," and concludes that "Chinese-Filipinos and non-

Chinese Filipinos can best excel in a business regime where there are transparent rules consistently and fairly applied and where government paternalism is restrained" (4).

34   The fortunes of the five taipans—Henry Sy, Lucio Tan, John Gokongwei, Andrew Gotianun, and George Ty—were all made and consolidated after World War II (Zulueta 1995, 4).

35   The Federation of Filipino Chinese Chambers of Commerce established a "war chest" for campaign contributions, arguing in 1954 that channeling campaign contributions through the Federation would create a buffer between the politicians and the rich Chinese, as well as increase the political leverage of the community as a whole (see Blaker 1970, 225).

36   See Wickberg 1965; Tan 1972; Agpalo 1962; Felix 1966; Liao 1964; and, for recent materials, publications by the Philippine Association for Chinese Studies. Chinese-language histories of the Philippine Chinese include: Huang and He 1987; Liu 1969; and Huang 1957.

37   The Chinese provided one of the major sources of revenues for the colonial state during the Spanish period, mainly in the form of taxes and contract farming. James Blaker (1970) argues that American policies toward the Chinese appeared to be contradictory, laying the legal foundations for, on the one hand, depriving the Chinese of the means of political participation and, on the other hand, encouraging Chinese economic activities.

38   For Chinese reaction to ASIA, see *Tulay,* 1996. ASIA grants permanent residency status to aliens, who will then be eligible for citizenship after five years. For an account of the harassment of "illegal aliens," see *Tulay,* 1994b, 6, 13. On the revenue-generating ethos that underlies both ASIA and the Republic Act no. 9138 (the Administrative Naturalization Law), see Hau 2001. The government anticipated earnings of P6.1 billion (*Philippine Star,* 2001) from naturalizing Philippine-born aliens by charging applicants a P40,000 "processing fee" and a P100,000 "naturalization fee." Admittedly, this amount is P60,000 less than the P200,000 that illegal aliens have to pay to obtain permanent residency under the ASIA program, but it is still beyond the means of the indigent Chinese.

39   William Gatchalian was issued an identification certificate on the basis of the Commission on Immigration and Deportation's recognition that Gatchalian's grandfather was a Filipino citizen. In 1990, Gatchalian's conflict with Trade and Industry Secretary Jose Concepcion, who accused Gatchalian of nonpayment of Customs duties, led to Department of Justice, Commission on Immigration and Deportation, and National Bureau of Investigation's inquiries into Gatchalian's claim to citizenship. Although the Supreme Court ruled in Gatchalian's favor, Gatchalian's case clearly shows that business rivals (backed by government officials eager to find scapegoats for their exposed scams) can very easily use citizenship as a weapon against he Chinese. For an account of the Gatchalian case, see Hernandez 1991.

40   For an exposition of unequal development in the context of center-periphery relations within the world capitalist relation, especially as they are articulated in the Third World, see the works of Samir Amin, in particular, *Delinking: Towards a Polycentric World* (1990).

41   It is, perhaps, no accident that one of the stereotypical attributes of the Chinese in the Philippines involves their litigiousness or legal-mindedness—depending on who is praising or criticizing (Purcell 1965, 523).

42   Cf. Etienne Balibar's (1991, 206) discussion of the Jew as scapegoat in *Class Racism*. The classic text on the relationship between property and civil rights is Karl Marx's *On the Jewish Question* (1978 [1844]), discussed in the next chapter.

43   On the history of the Siong Chong as umbrella organization, see Cariño 1998.

44   It may be worth observing at this point, as a prefiguration of a later argument, that the *he* in *ronghe* is also the *he* in *hetong*, which means contract.

45   Social work includes weekly Philippine General Hospital Medicine-Assistance programs, Alay Puso feeding Center in Del Pan and Tayuman, and Tatalon Free Clinic and Immunization projects. Until funds ran out, Kaisa also coordinated with the Batibot Children's program to produce *Pin-pin*, a Batibot for Chinese Filipino kids.

46   See *Tulay*, 1994a, 13. This article was first published in the June 10, 1994, issue of *Philippine Graphic Magazine*.

47   For a history of the PCGCC, which acted as spokesman for the Chinese during the American and the Commonwealth period, see Philippine Chinese General Chamber of Commerce 1936. For a history of the Federation, organized in 1954, at the height of the anti-Communist drive with Magsaysay's blessings, see Gao 1974; Deng 1988; and Cariño 1998.

48   *Tulay*, 1995, 8. The NPA itself has disavowed kidnapping-for-ransom as a source of funds on ideological grounds. See also Kiunisala 1993, 3.

49   Instead, the Chinese have taken over "Filipino" spaces like Luneta Park for morning exercises, and they appear in "politically neutral" spaces like the malls.

50   Charlson Ong was born in Manila in 1960 and educated in the University of the Philippines. His fiction has received most of the Philippines' major literary prizes, including the Carlos Palanca Memorial Awards for Literature, the *Philippines Free Press* Annual Literary Awards, the *Philippine Graphic* Short Story Contest, and the *Asiaweek* Magazine Short Story Contest. His first collection of short stories, *Men of the East*, was given the National Book Award for fiction by the Manila Critics' Circle; his second collection, *Woman of Am-kaw*, received the University of the Philippines President's Award for Outstanding Publication. His first novel, *An Embarrassment of Riches*, which won the second prize in the Centennial Literary Contest in 1998, is discussed in chap. 6.

51   The majority of his stories deal with the Chinese in the Philippines. See, for example, the stories in *Men of the East* and *Woman of Am-kaw*. Two of the stories in *Conversion* are about the Philippine Chinese.

4

REVOLUTIONARY

Philippine stamp featuring the Wha Chi guerrillas
(Liang and Cai 1996)

I n 1992, the Philippine Bureau of Posts issued a set of stamps in honor of the guerrilla groups that were active during World War II. The stamps, labeled "Philippine guerrilla units of World War II," featured such well-known groups as Vinzon's Guerrillas, 101st Division, Anderson's Command, President Quezon's Own Guerrillas, Bulacan ·Military Area, the Luzon Guerrilla Army Forces, and the Cebu Area Command. One unit, however, stood out in the set because it was the only guerrilla group honored that was commanded by and composed almost exclusively of "foreigners," many of them noncitizens of the Philippines. The Wha Chi (华支 Hua Zhi, short for 菲律宾华侨抗日游击支队 Feilübin Huaqiao Kangri Youji Zhidui, Philippine-Chinese Anti-Japanese Guerrilla Forces)[1] is arguably the best-known organization of the Chinese guerrilla resistance movement in the Philippines.

Even though its contributions to the Filipino narrative of national liberation struggle have been recorded and corroborated by several non-Chinese—including American—sources,[2] the Wha Chi has long been identified with "national democratic," that is, leftist, activism. Its place in Philippine history has been marked out by its relationship and collaboration with the radical guerrilla Hukbalahap (Hukbo ng Bayan Laban sa Mga Hapon, People's Army Against the Japanese; the name was later changed to Hukbong Mapagpalaya ng Bayan, or People's Liberation Army), which posed a potent challenge to the Philippine state

Wha Chi guerrillas (Liang and Cai 1996)

during the first decade following the country's formal independence from the U.S. in 1946 (Kerkvliet 1979), and some members of which would go on to help found and organize the Communist Party of the Philippines-New People's Army, still active more than forty years after its establishment in 1968 (Jones 1989).[3]

"Chinese" participation in the Filipino leftist movement[4] and the contested place of Maoism and China in the development of Filipino communism are integral aspects of the Philippine revolutionary experience.

Chinese workers[5] in the Philippines were already organizing in the late 1910s and early 1920s.[6] The activities of a key Chinese labor leader—who would later appear as a character in Du Ai's novel—offer a telling microcosm of Philippine-Chinese radical history. Xu Jingcheng (1905–1971) (许敬诚 Ko Keng Seng/Co Kin Sin, original name Xu Jingbiao but also known by a number of aliases, the most important being Xu Li, or Ko Li) was born in Jinjiang, Fujian Province, China, on January 8, 1905, and at the age of twelve moved to Hong Kong, where he was taught English (he first read Marx in the English translation).[7] He made short trips to the Philippines in 1919 and 1921, before settling down in Manila in 1925. Employed as a store employee and a teacher, he led the Workers' Association (工人协会 Gongren Xiehui), which counted shopkeepers, teachers, and store clerks among its members, and was responsible for helping to set up other Chinese unions. In 1926, a Communist Youth League[8] member from China, Li Xingqiu, visited the Philippines[9] and initiated contact with Xu, who became a member and later assumed leadership of the Manila branch.[10] Xu joined the Chinese Communist Party in 1930, and served as a member of the Partido Komunista ng Pilipinas (PKP, Communist Party of the Philippines) Central Committee in 1930. Sixty out of eighty of the Philippine Young Communist League (YCL) members would join the newly established PKP (Partido Komunista ng Pilipinas 1996, 93–94). The political conflict in China extended to the Philippines as local Chinese communists clashed with Kuomintang groups. After the December 1927 uprising in China, Philippine-born Chinese Communist Party member, Li Yongxiao 李永孝 (Felipe Lee Yung Shaw [see next section], also known as Li Bingxiang李炳祥), returned to the Philippines and established contact with Ko and Li Xingqiu, and helped organize the Philippine Chinese Labor Association (华侨工会 PCLA, Huaqiao Gonghui/Hua Kiao Kong Hue, Overseas Chinese Workers' Union). These three men would be instrumental in forging ties with the Filipino communist movement.

The PCLA first forged ties with the Congreso Obrero de Filipinas (COF) workers' federation (established in 1913). But, owing to the racial politics practiced by the COF, the PCLA was kept at a "segregated distance" (93). It was founder of the Partido Komunista ng Pilipinas Crisanto Evangelista's group that actively advocated the integration of the PCLA into the Filipino labor movement and worked closely with the PCLA. The PCLA subsequently established close ties with the Partido Obrero (Workers' Party), which was organized in 1928, and led by Crisanto Evangelista and other members of the Communist Party of the Philippines. The PCLA later renamed itself the Philippine Chinese Labor Federation (PCLF, 菲律宾华侨各劳工团体 Feilubin Huaqiao Ge Laogong Tuanti) as its member unions expanded to thirty, with a total membership of 5,000 (94). The PCLF's links with Profitern (Red

Xu Jingcheng (Jinjiang Dang Shi http://www. jinjiang.gov.cn/jjds/zljc/hqfy/2005032642985. shtml, accessed 2 Sept. 2010)

International of Labor Union, established by the Communist International [Comintern] in 1921, as a form of networking between Communists and trade unions) were coursed through Crisanto Evangelista, and PCLF joined Evangelista and his group in walking out of the COF convention in 1929. Three of its members would join the board of the newly established left organization Katipunan ng Anak-Pawis ng Pilipinas on May 5, 1929 (99, 102; on the Comintern's Shanghai network, see Onimaru 2011). Close links between the Chinese and Filipino communists can be seen in the fact that three out of thirty-five members of the newly established PKP Central Committee in 1930 were Chinese: Co Sing Liat, Ko Keng Seng (Xu), and Sun Ping. One of them, code-named "Comrade C" (either Ko Keng Seng or Co Sing Liat) would be a member of the Politburo (Partido Komunista ng Pilipinas 1996, 125). A Manila Chinese left leader, a certain "Li" and an alternate, "Koo," were elected members of the Central Committee in 1938 (291); from what is known of their activities, "Li" is most probably Li Yongxiao, and "Koo" either Ko Keng Seng or Co Sing Liat.

At the beginning of World War II, Ko organized the Anti-Japanese and Chinese-Protection Committee (抗日华侨委员会 Kangri Huaqiao Weiyuan Hui) (Yung Li 1996, 79). The founding members of the Wha Chi guerrilla group were drawn from the ranks of the PCLF, renamed Philippine Chinese United Workers Union,[11] or Feilubin Huaqiao Gelaogong Tuanti Lianhehui (菲律宾华侨各劳工团体联合会 shortened name 劳联会 Lao Lian Hui in pinyin and Lo Lien Hwe in Hokkien) in 1938, after several more Chinese Philippine labor unions joined the federation. The Wha Chi was organized on May 19, 1942, as a squadron under the Hukbalahap guerrilla army.[12] A number of Wha Chi leaders were involved in training both Chinese and Filipino guerrillas (Jensen 1956, 284). Squadron 48, named in honor of China's New Fourth and Eighth Route Armies, formally adopted the name "Wha Chi" after it negotiated with the Huks to assume an independent and "neutral"[13] status as a guerrilla unit. The Wha Chi grew from fifty-two fighters to a 1944 peak of 700 members, forming five squadrons. From February 1942, to the end of the Japanese occupation in August 1945, it was active in Manila and fourteen other provinces in the Philippines, particularly in Luzon. The Wha Chi engaged in 260 battles and skirmishes, claimed to have killed more than two thousand enemy forces (mostly Filipino constabulary troops under the Japan-sponsored Philippine government), and lost seventy-seven of its own members (cf. tables 8–11 in Yung Li 1996, 84–89).[14]

Given that the Philippine state criminalized the leftist forces during most of the Cold War period, the Wha Chi not surprisingly was marginalized from official national discourse and from the largely Kuomintang-dominated and -policed local Chinese affairs of the time. Not until four years after the Philippines established diplomatic relations with the People's Republic of China, in 1975, was a monument to the Wha Chi "martyrs" (*lieshi* 烈士) finally built in the Chinese Cemetery in Manila. With formal recognition of Mainland China has come the belated re-recognition of the Wha Chi's "valuable service rendered to America and the Philippines,"[15] couched in the language of bilateral, diplomatic friendship between the Philippines and mainland China. This official recognition, however, glosses over the Wha Chi's historical connections with the global and regional socialist-cum-anticolonial network that spanned East and Southeast Asia, Russia, and America in the first half of the twentieth century.

Ironically, because of the Wha Chi's record of cooperation with Filipino and American-commanded guerrilla units during the war, Wha Chi returnees to China (officially called *guiqiao* 归侨, or "returned overseas Chinese") in the grip of the Cultural Revolution suffered the inverse of what their fellow members in the Philippines had gone through. Whereas Wha Chi veterans in the Philippines were branded and hounded as communists, Wha Chi veterans in China were stigmatized as "reactionary" and "bourgeois-capitalist" overseas Chinese (*huaqiao*) who counted among the "seven categories of sinister people" (along with landlords, rich peasants, counterrevolutionaries, bad elements, rightists, and enemy agents) (Cariño 1988, 44). Far more seriously, they were denounced as "agents of the U.S.-Chiang Kai Shek clique" (美蒋特务集团 *Mei Jiang tewu jituan*); a Gang of Four representative in Fujian Province went so far as to compare the Philippine Wha Chi returnees to a lychee tree bearing "fruits with red skin, white meat and black hearts" (菲律宾华委是棵荔枝树，结出的果是红皮白肉黑心的， *Feilübin huawei shi ke lizhi shu, jiechu de guo shi hong pi bai ruo hei xin de*) (Liang and Cai 1996, 76; 1998, 98). The fruit of this persecution was extremely bitter—more than three hundred and forty cadres in China (roughly 50 percent of the Wha Chi members) were affected, and in Fujian alone, eight (including the commanders of the Second, Third, Fourth, and Manila squadrons) died as a result (Liang and Cai 1996, 76; 1998, 99). The eight cadres were officially "rehabilitated" in November 1978, by the Fujian Committee of the Chinese Communist Party. In 1992, the same year that the Philippine government issued stamps in honor of the Wha Chi, the Office of Overseas Chinese Affairs in Mainland China sent formal greetings to commemorate the Wha Chi's fiftieth anniversary.

For members of the Wha Chi, this vindication of their role in promoting Philippine-Chinese relations underscored the Wha Chi's commitment to, and embodiment of, the "spirit of internationalism" (国际主义精神 *guoji zhuyi jingshen*) (Liang and Cai 1996, 81), or what Susan Bayly

(2007; 2008) calls the "socialist ecumene."[16] But what is notable about this internationalism—which found expression in the language of global fraternal community based on socialist and communist revolutionary solidarities, long-distance exchange, and friendship—is that it was fostered within the particular context of an anticolonial Chinese nationalism that not only was related, but also contributed, to the development of Philippine radical nationalism. While the Chinese guerrillas did not think of themselves as "dual" nationalists and their political action derived from, and promoted, a discourse of emancipation that stressed international cooperation and solidarity among leftist groups and forces all over the world, their presence in the Philippines nevertheless opened itself to the possibility of being articulated as an instance of Filipino nationalist action without necessarily precluding their loyalty and commitment to China and world revolution.

In other words, while this kind of Chinese "revolutionary cosmopolitanism" promoted political loyalty to the Chinese state and operated within the framework of China's "national salvation," it was not necessarily chauvinistic; instead, it involved forms of engagement, attachment, identification, and activism that worked both within as well as beyond the bounds of the nation-state and actively contributed to the development of indigenous nationalism as well as communism and socialism in Southeast Asia (Wang 2003e).[17] This revolutionary cosmopolitanism confirms the fact that, as historian Wang Gungwu has argued, overseas Chinese responses to nationalism not only have a place in the contemporary history of Southeast Asia (Wang 1992a, 54). They have also played a role in the making and remaking of "national" communities in both China and the Philippines. By affirming the political significance of the historic movement across borders of Chinese people who, in the name of international solidarity, aided Filipino nationalists in fighting for national liberation from the Japanese during the 1940s, this cosmopolitanism poses important questions which force a rethinking of commonsensical notions of nationness and national belonging.

This cosmopolitanism is not only historically compatible with radical popular nationalism, although this does not mean that its relationship with nationalism was tension-free.[18] The kinds of people, spaces and movements, concerted actions, emotional involvements, solidarities, and networks and connections it entailed also operated simultaneously on and across local, national, regional, and international registers. Although this cosmopolitanism was neither reducible to "nationalism" nor to "socialism," it often found itself subject to both (and sometimes either) socialist and nationalist interpellations. Such a cosmopolitanism was rendered legible and accorded recognition in noncommunist Philippines and post-Maoist

China only insofar as it could be made to fit within a nationalist narrative of liberation and/or a socialist-regional narrative of amity and cooperation. And yet these activists moved around in one country and moved across countries, meeting people and establishing local, national, regional, and international networks and connections. What makes their movements politically salient is not the fact that they travel within and across multiple borders, but the various "meanings and causes on behalf of which those crossings can be pressed into service" (Honig 2001, 80).

In a region in which nationalism retains its positive associations as a liberatory and mass-mobilizing force, cosmopolitanism can potentially reinvigorate the theory and practice of nationalism by redefining and remaking the national community, by calling into question its exclusionary borders as well as its assumed "purity" of culture and identity, and expanding the grounds and horizons for its dreams, claims, advocacies, and realizations of freedom, equality, and justice. Cosmopolitanism does so by forcefully bringing up the question of the foreigner, the alien who is supposed to remain outside the bounds of the national community, but whose selective inclusion and exclusion expose the limits and potentials of nation-making.

This chapter analyzes three different but related embodiments of revolutionary cosmopolitanism: the overseas Chinese returnee Du Ai 杜埃, his partner and artistic collaborator Lin Bin 林彬, and *guiqiao* (overseas Chinese returnees) like them; the Wha Chi organization of which Du Ai was a member; and his three-part novel (the third volume of which was written by Lin Bin) *Fengyu Taipingyang* (Storm Over the Pacific 风雨太平洋 vol. 1, 1985; vol. 2, 1988; 3 vols., 2002),[19] which memorializes the adventures of the Wha Chi during World War II. Author(s), organization, and novel map the significance, reach, scope, and—a crucial point often overlooked—limits of the cosmopolitan radical's crossings of borders and journeys across spaces. They reveal the contexts under which different peoples from different countries are thrown together, and explore the possibilities as well as constraints—worked out through the medium of kinship and language—of the friendships, solidarities, and networks that are forged in the course of their being thrown together to create a "community of fate." They expose the intellectual and organizational fault lines running through both Chinese and Philippine revolutionary movements' attempts to graft communist internationalism onto anti-imperialist nationalism. But they also point to the ways in which these crossings and connections can end up challenging received notions of national belonging and loyalty, revealing the ways in which nationalism bears the trace of what is "alien" and "other" to it and opening nationalism up for reinvention, both conceptually and practically (Hau 2004).

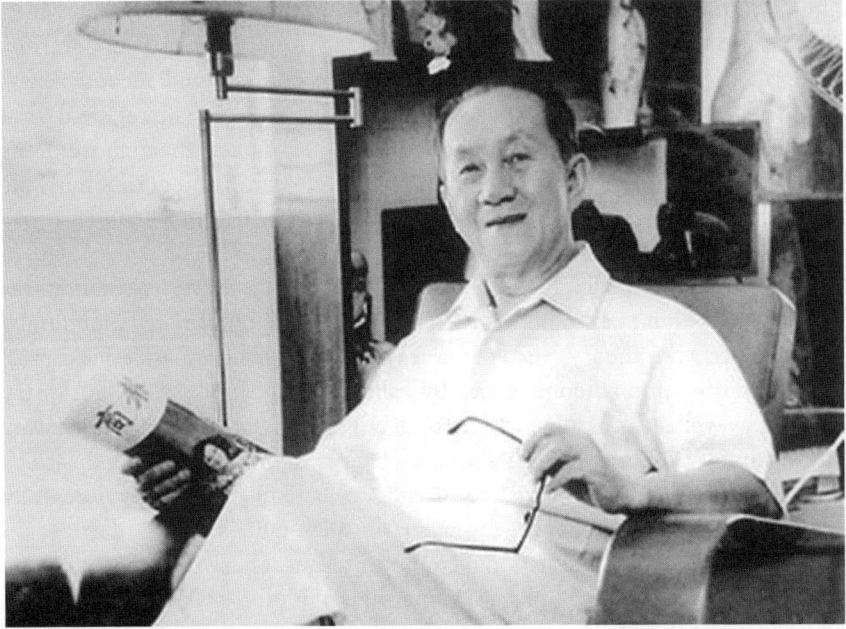

Du Ai (courtesy of Lin Bin)

Biography as Fiction

Du Ai, the pen name of the Hakka poet, fictionist, and essayist Cao Chuanmei 曹传美, was born in Dapu County, on the eastern part of Guangdong Province in 1914. Despite growing up in poverty and being forced to discontinue his studies while in junior high school, he was able to enter Guangdong Zhongshan University's literature department in 1933, graduating in 1937. Joining the leftist writers' organization, Lian Meng Guangzhou Fenhui, he edited numerous underground publications.[20]

Du Ai joined the Communist Party in 1936. He went to Hong Kong in September 1937, before landing in Manila in 1940. In the Philippines, he worked for the *Jianguo Zhoukan* and other publications, and on translations from English. Above all, he was deeply involved in the anti-Japanese resistance movement (Hu 1995), and may have been sent by the Party to the Philippines to do liaison work. In Manila, Du Ai fell in love with fellow activist Lin Bin (Lin Caiying, born in 1922, in Xiamen, Fujian Province), a third-generation Hokkien *huaqiao* who came to the Philippines when she was eight years old and studied at St. Stephen's High School and the University of Santo Tomas in Manila, and who would become his artistic collaborator. Lin Bin, a critic in her own right, has written extensively on the cultural production of the anti-Japanese movement before World War II, and on literary production by women activists.[21]

Department head of the Hua Chiao Anti-Japanese Anti-Traitor Alliance (Kang Fan) and member of the Wha Chi, Du Ai (known among the Wha Chi by the nickname Lao Cao 老曹) was one of the people who were involved in the May 1943 ten-day siege in Mount Arayat when Japanese and Filipino constabulary troops encircled the mountain to flush out guerrillas. Returning to Hong Kong in 1947, where he worked at the *Huashang Bao* and other publications, and to Guangzhou just before the Communist takeover in 1949, he served in a number of national and provincial cultural committees and writers' organizations, and was once chairman of Guangdong Province's Department of Culture. Persecuted during the Cultural Revolution, Du Ai began working on *Fengyu Taipingyang* 风雨太平洋 in the last thirteen years of his life after his retirement in 1980.[22] Only two volumes of *Fengyu* were published in his lifetime.[23] Upon Du Ai's death in 1993, Lin Bin assumed the responsibility of completing the last half of the third volume (approximately 160,000 words) by relying on extensive dictation and notes that she took on his deathbed.[24] *Fengyu* is one of the longest single works of overseas Chinese fiction in Southeast Asia.[25] *Fengyu*'s significance is enhanced by the fact that no novel-length fiction in Chinese has so far been published in the Philippines.

The Chinese writer Mao Dun, in his preface (1949, 1–2) to Du Ai's collection of fiction *Zai Lusong Pingyuan* (On the Plains of Luzon; written between 1947–1949[26] and revised in 1956 under the title *Conglin Qu* [The Forest]), noted the depth of Du Ai's immersion in the Philippines and close interaction with the Filipino people in the common battle against fascism, and commented on the artistic challenge of adequately

Lin Bin with the author in Guangzhou, China, 2001

depicting the intertwining of fates (*mingyun*).[27] Du Ai's journeys from China to Hong Kong to the Philippines back to Hong Kong and China had, at each stop, yielded poems, essays, short stories, and a long novel, but his reputation largely rests on his work for the resistance movement and his depiction of overseas Chinese and Filipino experiences in the Philippines (Yang Yi n.d.). The fact that Du Ai's Philippine sojourn provided him with the palette to paint from his imagination, observation, and experience is amply borne out by his detailed descriptions of Philippine and Chinese-Philippine everyday life.

Moreover, Du Ai hailed from the Hakka part of Guangdong Province, South China. The Hakka have a centuries-long history of migration that links them with neighboring Fujian and Jiangxi, with non-"Han" minorities in China and the borderlands, as well as Hong Kong, Southeast Asia (particularly Malaysia and Thailand), and the world. In Guangdong, such links have made the areas near and along the Pearl River Delta sites where distinctions between "Chinese" and "non-Chinese" are far from clear-cut[28]; they add an important geohistorical dimension to Du Ai's social location as a Huanan (华南 South Chinese) writer whose representative works are set in the Nanyang (Southern Ocean) territories that include the Philippines. Chinese literary critic Yang Yi explicitly connects the regional Huanan literary imagination to overseas Chinese Nanyang literature by pointing to their use of imagery rooted in a common "dream" of the big ocean (大海之梦 *dahai zhi meng*) and "love" of tropical forests (热带丛林之恋了 *redai conglin zhi lian liao*)—imagery that resonates in the theorizing of Southeast Asia as "area" (Yang Yi 2000, 3:203).[29]

Not only can Du Ai's life and career be mapped by his actual movements across national boundaries, his major work also takes journeys as its major theme and source of emplotment. *Fengyu Taipingyang* follows various members of the Wha Chi as they journey (individually or in groups) across different parts of Central and Southern Luzon. The unfolding of the novel's plot—which matches the narrative account of highlights provided by Liang Shangwan and Cai Jianhua's memoirs—is replete with place-names which serve as signposts marking Wha Chi's passage through time and space: from the early days of leaving Manila for Bataan to hunt for abandoned weaponry, to the evacuation of Chinese to Laguna and Bulacan, to the establishment of a three-month base at Mount Pasbul (called Mt. Lao Qing in the Liang and Cai memoirs) at the border between Pampanga and Bataan, to joining the Huks in attacking the town of Cabiao, in Nueva Ecija, to hiding out in Mount Arayat (known as the Yenan of the Philippines). From Nueva Ecija, Squadron Forty-eight moved to Mount Miguel at the Bulacan-Nueva Ecija border before venturing southward, marching through the Sierra Madre

Range and arriving in Laguna. In twenty-six days alone, for example, the squadron traveled 500 kilometers on foot, and marched through thirty-six towns in Bulacan, Rizal, Tayabas, and Laguna. Opting to go independent with the permission of the Huks, the squadron adopted the formal designation Wha Chi and established friendly relations with other guerrilla units, taking care not to get itself embroiled in interguerrilla rivalry and conflict by pursuing a policy of stated neutrality. Working closely with the Hua Chiao Anti-Japanese Committee (Hua Wei), an umbrella organization that included the Hua Chiao Anti-Japanese Anti-Traitor Alliance (Kang Fan) and the *Hua Chiao Guide* (the underground newspaper), the Wha Chi also fielded guerrillas in Manila, to which they returned in February 1945, in the company of Huks and the American Eleventh Airborne Division as the Japanese retreated from the capital.

The novel contains more than one hundred and eighty named characters, of which twelve are principal protagonists, and many of whom are modeled on or composites of real-life people, representing friends and foes, Filipinos (including different groups of indigenous peoples), Chinese, Americans, mestizos, and, to a lesser extent, Japanese. The two major characters of the novel, Hoster Lee[30] and his sister Li Jinfu (Miss Lee) are experienced travelers: at eighteen and fifteen years of age respectively, both left the Philippines for China to join the battle against the "warlord" Yuan Shikai. There, Hoster worked as the translator for Sun Yat-sen's Comintern adviser Mikhail Borodin while his sister, a gifted painter, served in the information unit. When the White Terror broke out in 1927, the siblings escaped to Outer Mongolia, traveled to Soviet Russia, and eventually made their way back to the Philippines via Malaysia.

The real-life people on whom some of the main characters in the novel are modeled (including Xu Jingcheng, discussed in the previous section) also traveled extensively; their itineraries provide evidence of the existence of channels of communication, and some degree of circulation, among Chinese activists from both mainland China and the Nanyang region. The careers of two leading Wha Chi leaders exemplify the geographical reach and scope of revolutionary cosmopolitanism during the high noon of Chinese anticolonial and communist nationalism. Liang Shangwan 梁上苑 was born in Kuala Lumpur, Malaya, and joined the Malaysian Communist Youth League (CYL) while attending secondary school. Captured in Singapore in 1931, and incarcerated for half a year, he went to China upon his release and then moved to Hong Kong, before arriving in Manila.[31] Even more remarkable was Felipe Lee Yung Shaw (Li Yongxiao, Li Bingxiang, 1905–1957),[32] the Wha Chi liaison officer who lent his Chinese name and some of the details of his life to Hoster Lee, one of the principal characters in Du Ai's novel. Born in Manila, Felipe Lee spoke Tagalog and studied English and Spanish, and once worked as a stove/furnace repairman. After completing his elementary education at the Anglo-Chinese School (the oldest Chinese school in the Philippines), he moved to Shanghai for high school education. He entered university in Shanghai, where he was exposed to the writings of Marx and Lenin. He was involved in the May Fourth Movement, and became a member of the CYL and the Chinese Communist Party in 1924. He moved to Beijing, but was forced to flee to South China to avoid arrest, and ended up in Guangdong, where he worked as an interpreter for Mikhail Borodin, the Comintern adviser to Sun Yat-sen during the Guomindang-Communist united front of 1924–1927.[33] In 1927, when Chiang Kai-Shek (Jiang Jieshi) turned against the Communists, Lee Yung Shaw fled to the Shanghai International Concessions, then slipped away to Manila. He became something of a legend among the Wha Chi warriors: an oft-repeated story about him concerns how, as a Wha Chi guerrilla, he was captured but managed to escape by tricking the Japanese with hours of rosary-clutching and unintelligible prayers into thinking that he was mentally unhinged and releasing him unharmed.

Du Ai's reliance on the novel form to dramatize the Wha Chi's involvement in anticolonial struggle in the Philippines sets his project apart from the memoirs, essays, biographical sketches, and historiographies produced by veteran guerrillas and their relatives, and by scholars of overseas Chinese studies. In their illumination of the concrete personal experience of international political solidarity, novels have the capacity to convey the complexity of everyday life while also capturing in prose form the epic quality of armed confrontation and its heroic (and often tragic) consequences. The omniscient narration in *Fengyu* weaves the threads of different characters' lives into a collective biography of the Wha Chi. This novel, populated by a multiplicity of characters, was coauthored with Lin Bin, whose influence is reflected in the novel's careful attention to the portrayal of its female protagonists (Li Zhiyuan n.d.).

Founding Communities of Fate

Fengyu Taipingyang poses and answers the question of what possibilities and, just as important, limits define Wha Chi's brand of revolutionary cosmopolitanism.

The novel points to a degree of interdependence and intimacy between Wha Chi guerrillas and their Filipino counterparts that is unequaled by any existing account of Chinese-Philippine relations. In fact, the novel suggests that Wha Chi's freedom of action is largely defined by the cooperation and friendship extended to the Chinese guerrillas by Filipino activists and, above all, ordinary people.[34] Following the declaration of Manila as an open city, for example, 400 Chinese, composed mainly of members of the United Workers Union (Lo Lien Hwe) and their families, evacuate Manila and head for Barrio Mandili in Cabiao, Nueva Ecija, Central Luzon, in January 1942. In this undertaking they are helped by the progressive organization Kalipunang Pambansa ng Magsasaka sa Pilipinas (National Society of Peasants in the Philippines), which mobilizes civilian population support for the Wha Chi. Wha Chi guerrillas—some of whom had helped train the Huk guerrillas—are protected and nurtured by the Filipino population in areas that are under the Huk's sphere of influence, boosting morale and providing food, shelter, medical aid, geographical guidance, intelligence information, and military support: "Once you find the people, you'll find the way" [zhao dao lao baixing jiu you chulu] (Du Ai 1988, 2:871). The support of the Chinese in the provision of basic necessities, medicines, and safehouses, as well as arrangement of transportation and communication and smuggling of documents and the *Hua Chiao Guide* is also instrumental to the Wha Chi's survival in enemy territory. In Mount Pasbul, indigenous Dumagat Aetas guide the Wha Chi through the mountain passes into safety. To quote from the novel: "We fight on Philippine soil. Our main weapon is Filipino might. We believe [xiangxin] in them, we rely [yikao] on them. This is our steadfast, unwavering principle [jianding bu ziyi de fangzhen]" (886).

Because of Wha Chi's extensive dealings with the Huks and travels through the Filipino countryside in Luzon, multilinguals and interpreters play a crucial role in mediating communication among the Chinese (for example, between Cantonese and Hokkien-speakers who do not have a command of Mandarin Chinese), between the Chinese and Filipino guerrillas, and between the Wha Chi and the civilian population. *Fengyu* records the continuous shifts in language as people speak in Hokkien, Cantonese, Mandarin, English, Spanish, Tagalog, Kapampangan, Panggalatok, and Agta, according to the demands of their interlocutors. The text of *Fengyu* is, not surprisingly, stippled with romanized and phonetic transcriptions of words, phrases, and sentences from different languages. Wha Chi guerrillas, like Paulo, who are unable to understand or speak one or more of the Philippine languages, feel their handicap most deeply. In fact, it is the relative scarcity of translators at a time when the Wha Chi are cut off from communication with the Huks and forced to march through areas outside of Huk influence that makes the Wha Chi painfully aware of the limits of their capacity to move and recruit among the native population.[35]

In the theater of war, survival depends on seeming rather than being, and destabilizes assumptions about the givenness of ethnic or cultural identities. Wha Chi survival is conditioned by the guerrillas' ability to evade or overcome the strictures of "Chineseness" and their physical appearance. In some cases, their "Chinese" features work against them, marking them apart from the townspeople. In other cases, the ambiguity of physical appearance puts them in danger as Filipinos have difficulty telling them apart from the Japanese until they open their mouths: "Are you Japanese, or are you Formosans?" (Du Ai 1985, 1:204) In yet other instances, Wha Chi guerrillas avoid capture by melting into the population, wearing civilian clothing and speaking only English, Tagalog, or other Philippine languages. In a few instances, they disguise themselves as Japanese soldiers to sabotage enemy quarters or trick collaborators.

Translation works not just to expedite communication, but also allows speakers to bring into a given language the knowledge, history, and culture encoded in other languages. There are repeated references to Filipino historical figures, such as Lapu-Lapu, Melchora Aquino, Josephine Bracken, Antonio Luna, Miguel Malvar, and Jose Rizal, to Rizal's last poem, to avocado, mangoes, coconuts, tuba, basi, and balut. Filipino folk songs are sung, dances danced alongside extended quotations from Rizal's last poem. The indigenous Baluga teach the Wha Chi to subsist on cogon grass, the Huks provide tips on how to walk with splayed toes through mud to prevent slipping. Given that the majority of the Wha Chi guerrillas are in their late teens and early to mid-twenties, the Wha Chi journeys are not simply educational (*Bildung*), but also represent rites of passage in which young Chinese acquire the "experience" that moulds them into adults.

This mixing of references is rendered early in the novel, when Li Jinfu leads her art class through a history lesson on the heroism of Philippine national hero Andres Bonifacio, founder of the revolutionary secret society Katipunan (23):

> "Children, Bonifacio's assassination is similar to what happened in China. When so-called Generalissimo Chiang Kai-shek saw that the revolution was being won in Shanghai and Nanjing, he embarked on counter-revolution and massacred many revolutionaries in order to steal the fruit of revolution. Classmates, isn't it hateful?"
>
> "Hateful!" chorused the children.
>
> "Wasn't Katipunan able to kill off the villain and get back the fruit of revolution?" [asked a student.]
>
> "Yes, the fruit of revolution has to be taken back. But the situation at the time was complicated. When the power of the Spanish

colonizers after three hundred years' rule was waning, Uncle Sam forced his way in and replaced the Spaniards."

When the children heard this, they felt that the Philippines was indeed weighed down by calamity and, with China, formed a pair of suffering brothers [*nanxiong nandi*].

A discussion of the betrayal of the Katipunan and its suppression by the Spaniards serves as a jumping board to criticism of Chiang Kai-shek's suppression of the Chinese communists, and further on, a dissection of the current situation in Soviet Russia. Analogies abound in the novel, linking and distinguishing disparate personages, events, and territories. Set during the world war, the epic sweep of the novel ranges across the entire world historical stage even as it focuses on the Chinese resistance movement in the Philippines. Comparison juxtaposes insights and analyses and serves to connect the Philippines to China, Russia, and Southeast Asian countries by narrating their histories of struggle against oppression within the framework of a particular leftist vision of international solidarity and nationalist liberation.

The limits of Wha Chi freedom of action are largely informed by the reach of translation. Because of the limited number of translators who can talk to local populations in their own languages, the Wha Chi finds itself unable to establish stable bases in areas outside the sphere of Huk influence. And, as we will see below, difficulties in communication between the Huks and Wha Chi would militate against the Wha Chi's full incorporation into the Huk battalions and necessitate the Wha Chi's adoption of a policy of logistical self-sufficiency.

The constraints within which the Wha Chi operate as a guerrilla unit are offset in the novel by stirring tales illustrating the close relationships between Chinese and Filipinos. Intimacy is dramatized by *Fengyu* in three forms: love, friendship, and kinship. The novel's narrative of struggle is interwoven with—if not, to use a different metaphor, filtered through—the narratives of at least five pairs of lovers from different class and cultural backgrounds, including two pairs that involve Chinese men and Filipino women. Unlike *huaqiao* novels that stop short of having interracial love end in consummation and marriage—a consequence of the fear that *huaqiao* patriots who fall in love with native women risk being unable to return to China—*Fengyu* painstakingly charts the separations and reunions that bring the lovers together and tear them apart, holding readers in suspense as to the final outcome of these entanglements until the very end of the book. While Marianna loses her beloved Robin Chen on the eve of liberation, Wu Qing and Maria are united in the final chapter.

Like the innumerable friendships that are forged in the exigencies of war, the book imagines people being thrown together, developing ties of friendship and romance, being separated and reunited again and again by external forces and changing circumstances. Filipino characters, such as the woman warrior Juana (modeled after the Huk heroine Dayang-Dayang), the lawyer Palucha, the Huk liaison officer Juan Talata, the mestizo Custer Silis, among others, slip in and out of the novel, appearing when least expected. An element of surprise, contingency, and incalculability marks all meetings, partings, and reunions, even as it haunts all military encounters. Even family members are separated without guarantees of eventual reunion.

The extent of this interaction not only involves the sharing of information, experiences, and lives. Friendships between Filipinos and Chinese in the novel are cemented, apart from the frequent invocation of the standard Tagalog word *kaibigan* (friend, from the root word *ibig*, "love"), by the use of two Filipino honorifics—*kasama* and *kumpadre/kumadre*. Calling each other *kasama* (lit., companion, but also comrade) puts Chinese and Filipinos in a horizontal relation of equals, while *kumpadre/kumare* draws on the Catholic ritual of baptism to form extended kinship relations by virtue of making one the godparent of the other's offspring.

This intertwining of lives cuts across state- and society-defined differences of culture and language. Where national states have tended historically to conceive of and model relations among their citizens in terms of the ideology of "the family," *Fengyu* shows that international solidarity may be modeled on ritual kinship beyond what is imagined and policed by the state.

In fact, the incapacity of the state to protect its citizens leads two lovers, Maria and Wu Qing (Puliao), to draw a parallel between the Filipinos and Chinese's experience of colonization and to couch this comparison in familial terms (Du Ai 1985, 1:264):

> Maria was moved by the fact that Chinese and Filipinos did not have control over their own lives…. "This pearl [i.e., the Philippines, "Pearl of the Orient"] is not in our hands, and the fruit in our bowl has been stolen. You have come to a place in the Pacific where orphans live."
>
> Paulo's heart leaped. "We too are orphans. It is often said that the huaqiao [overseas Chinese] are orphans abroad. Our country is a great country, but it is often oppressed by others. Because our government is corrupt, nobody takes care of us."

The Wha Chi's journeys across Luzon also provide occasions for social mapping of the local terrains, as Chinese guerrillas encounter successions of townspeoples, topographies, climates, flora and fauna, customs, and practices. Songs and stories of heroes and heroines from both countries enliven the tedium in between ambush of Japanese forces. The Wha Chi's encounter with the Baluga results in friendships that are sealed not only by the exchange of songs, poems, and gifts, but also the blasting away of Chinese prejudice against "tribal" people and Filipino prejudice against the Chinese. Reciprocity is also evident in the Wha Chi's relations with the Huks. Wha Chi guerrillas put their Chinese experiences to good use in the service of the Huks by helping to train Filipino guerrillas and organize squadrons, and serving as model units.

At the same time, Wha Chi experiences in the Philippines make it impossible for them to simply "apply" the techniques of guerrilla training and warfare that they have learned in the course of their involvement in the resistance movement in China. The Wha Chi also learn to adapt their Chinese strategies to Filipino terrain, practices, and contingencies: they modify the rules of Chinese Red Army to suit Philippine conditions and terrain, even as Mao's works provide inspiration for defensive tactics. Wha Chi's nationalism is one that is open to the world: "We Wha Chi are the people's army" (我们华支是人民的军队 women huazhi shi renmin de jundui) (Du Ai 2002, 3:1089), and "we are with every country's people in the world (我们是和全世界各国的人民在一起 women shi he quan shijie ge guo de renmin zai yiqi) (1110) are complementary rather than contradictory principles. Reciprocity also operates in the context of war: Wha Chi arrival in Southern Luzon encourages the Huks to restore their former organizational structure instead of relying on small units following Japanese clampdown on guerrillas, even as Wha Chi are aided by the Huks and other guerrilla groups when they embark on military attacks.

In sum, the Wha Chi experience memorialized by Fengyu Taipingyang affirms the necessity of rethinking the concept of communities, not as ideal collectivities that share a common origin or even common destiny, but as communities of fate "that already include difference and conflict, where heterogeneous people and groups have been 'thrown together' by history and economy, in situations where their interests or cultural ideals cannot spontaneously converge, but also cannot completely diverge without risking mutual destruction (or common elimination by external forces)" (italics original) (Balibar 2004, 132, citing Gunsteren 1998). This community of fate carries with it the hope of bonding and solidarity, but also the risks of betrayal and rejection, as Wha Chi pin their survival on Filipino hospitality while at the same time dealing with the constant threat of betrayal by some of their own and their Filipino comrades' people and confrontation with Filipino, Chinese, and Japanese "enemies." Fengyu records numerous instances of reciprocity but is all the same haunted by the pain of setbacks and failure. How ironic, then, that this community of fate without guarantees should be forged in war, a war that occasions acts of incredible courage, munificence and self-sacrifice, but also cruelty, cowardice, and self-interest.

China, the "Chinese Question," and the Polycentric Left

After the war, the paths of the Wha Chi troops diverged as some of the patriots leave for China while others decide to stay in the Philippines to help rebuild the two countries (Du Ai 2002, 3:1201). Those among the Wha Chi patriots who left did not do so without transforming Philippine life. They had made the Philippines the site of their self-realization as inter/nationalists and as the sphere of their own transformative activities. In so doing, they also helped to change Filipino perceptions of the Chinese. Luis Taruc in his book *Born of the People* (1953, 76) talks about the Wha Chi guerrillas' achievements, which help to countervail the powerful Filipino stereotype of the Chinese as exploitative capitalists:

> The presence of Squadron 48 [Hua Zhi] among the peasants shattered an old and disreputable custom, that of treating Chinese people insultingly, and in general using them as the scapegoat in the blind reaction of Filipinos to evils that lie much deeper in our society. The members of Squadron 48 became much beloved by the people of Central Luzon, who often went out of their way to give them special consideration in billeting, feeding, and assistance.

In *Fengyu*, the funeral procession in honor of the Wha Chi warrior Robin Chen in Manila, for example, draws a thousand people, including Filipinos who have heard of the "48" (Kwarenta'y Otso) and who pay their respects to the dead through cries of mourning and "Thank you, Chinese friends!" The Wha Chi are hailed as "good intsik [Chinese]" [*hao yingci*], "our own people" (*zanmen ziji de ren*) and cheered as they march through Filipino towns, stopping along the way to help townspeople capture and dispense justice to brigands and sundry collaborators (Du Ai 2002, 3: chap. 119).

Not everything about the Chinese-Philippine relations is rosy, of course, and one risks the dangers of idealizing Philippine-Chinese relations forged during the war. Taruc's second book speaks of conflicts of interest between the Wha Chi and the Huks over tactics and strategies:

When the Japanese war broke out, four of their [Chinese Communist] high-ranking officials joined us in the field. Two of them claimed to have already been given training, one in politics, the other in guerrilla warfare, on the Chinese mainland. They were attached to our Politburo as advisers and acted as liaison officers between ourselves and their own anti-Japanese resistance movement.

Their advice was often resisted by Vicente Lava, who was then our general secretary, and by myself. It seemed to us that their advice was always related to Chinese mainland activities rather than Philippine interests.

First they advised us to attack the Japanese relentlessly. Although we did so, we suspected that their motives were chauvinistic, that their main concern was with the battle then going on in China. It seemed to us that they viewed our struggle only as a diversionary action.

When our fight resulted in a fierce Japanese counter-attack, and we suffered heavy casualties, they switched to a defensive strategy, urging us to hide our guns and return to our barrios. They sent most of the members of their own organization home to China. They called this policy "retreat for defense." But the Filipinos in the field refused to put it into action. We had great respect for the Chinese comrades. But when we realized the extent of their chauvinism and self-interest, our respect quickly diminished. (Taruc 1967, 33–34)

Taruc's account, which castigates the Chinese Communists for being concerned only with China's affairs, overlooks the internal divisions and debates within the United Front—the uneasy strategic alliance of both Chinese conservative and progressive organizations in wartime Philippines—particularly on the heated and extremely divisive issue of the "Defensive Policy."[36] As recounted in the novel,[37] during the early years of the war, the Wha Chi upholds the United Front by creating a special commission headed by the United Front representative Liu Yiming. Liu advocates the retreat-for-defense policy and, when faced with opposition from Wha Chi leaders, threatens to dissolve the Wha Chi. The turning point comes when the Wha Chi decide to abolish Liu's position within their organization and carry out their own strategy, in the process forming squadrons in Central and Southern Luzon as well as Manila.

In their memoirs, Wha Chi officers Liang Shangwan and Cai Jian Hua corroborate this account by explaining that officers of the Hua Chiao Committee, a leading organization of the Chinese United Front, had used the "Retreat for Defense" policy as a pretext to curtail the activities and argue for the disbanding of the Wha Chi. Only one Wha Chi commander took the policy seriously, while the rest of the officers and members ignored the directive and continued fighting, as did the Huks. Liang and Cai also offer a detailed account of the day-to-day cooperation between Hukbalahap and Wha Chi guerrillas, an account that, despite its taking an "outsider" or "foreigner" position in its depiction of the anti-Japanese struggle in the Philippines, points to a number of important collaborative efforts among Chinese and Filipinos in engaging the enemy forces (Liang and Cai 1996, 10–13).

The controversial "Retreat for Defense" policy not only marked a crucial episode in the history of the left struggle during World War II. It would also be elevated from historical episode to element of theoretical critique that indexed the deepening divisions within the Filipino communist movement after the war. The "Retreat for Defense" policy was one of the main issues used by the breakaway Communist Party of the Philippines (CPP) to criticize PKP "errors and weaknesses."

In the document, "Brief Review of the History of the Communist Party of the Philippines: On the Occasion of the 20th Anniversary of its Reestablishment," CPP leader Amado Guerrero (Jose Maria Sison) repeats the critique thus:

> There was no clear program of anti-imperialist and antifeudal struggle going beyond the antifascist struggle against Japan and no plan to expand the revolutionary forces beyond Manila and Central Luzon. The line of the people's struggle was narrowed to armed resistance against the Japanese occupation forces and their Filipino collaborators.
>
> Even with regard to armed struggle, the leadership of the merger party with Vicente Lava as general secretary adopted the line of "retreat for defense," a policy of reducing guerrilla units into impotent teams of three to five persons and avoiding armed combat with the enemy. This line was proclaimed after the Japanese fascist troops attacked the main base of the Hukbalahap at the foot of a small vulnerable mountain, Mt. Arayat, in the middle of the Central Luzon plains.
>
> However, the people's army made significant strides in armed struggle mainly because several platoon-size and company-size units disregarded the policy and spontaneously fought the enemy; and because finally in September 1944, a Party conference declared the "retreat for defense" policy erroneous. But soon after, the U.S. military forces landed to reoccupy the Philippines and arm their puppets. (Guerrero 1988)

PKP General Secretary Jesus Lava's version (2002, 64) puts it this way: "It was only late in the 1960s, when the Maoist Chinese Communist Party decided to organize and field its own Maoist Party in the Philippines under the leadership of Joe [Jose Maria] Sison, that the matter was revived with much fanfare and venom to maliciously discredit the PKP, its leaders and its whole history of struggle and sacrifice, but conveniently without any mention of the key role in policy formulation played by the Chinese Maoists themselves." Lava alleges that conversations with those involved, especially Casto Alejandrino, revealed that, in fact, the policy had first been suggested by a Chinese comrade. Though not put into practice even after it reached lower organs, the policy was judged to be erroneous by the Central Committee in September 1944. Vicente Lava was replaced by a troika which actually included the Chinese member who had originally been involved in the formulation of the policy (ibid).

Lava's account reveals the extent to which the acrimonious nature of PKP-CPP relations was informed by the Sino-Soviet split in the mid-1960s, as other communist parties all over the world found themselves under pressure to "choose" which country they would side with. With communism now devolving into a "polycentric" movement (Worsley 2002, 4; on the pro-China orientation of the CPP, see *Ang Bayan*, 1972; 1979; 1977; 1980), internal tensions within the Philippine left resulted in the "re-establishment" of the Communist Party of the Philippines in the late 1960s. Part of the tensions and divisions within the Philippine left at the time came to be articulated with the question of China. The "growing dissidence of the pro-Chinese faction resurrected fears among the old party leadership of the Chinese Communist Party's interference in the Philippine left's internal affairs" (Malay 1984, 59).[38] This can be gleaned from a series of charges and countercharges aired in party publications, with the PKP accusing the CPP of being "local-bred parrots of Peking" (*Ang Komunista*, 1971, 1). PKP articles denounced "Maoist splittism" (*Siklab*, 1971, 2) for sowing "imperialist-inspired disunity" (*Political Review* [1971], 6) within the international socialist movement and seeking to isolate the USSR and establish "Maoist Chinese hegemony" (*Ang Komunista*, 1971).[39]

Branding "China" as an external, alien power with the capacity to intervene in Philippine politics not only provided the PKP with a potent ideological weapon for delegitimizing the Maoist faction. The PKP also raised the thorny issue of assimilation of the Chinese in the Philippines. Declaring that the great majority of the Filipino-Chinese community "belong to the working and petty-bourgeois classes, with the bulk of the assimilated Filipino-Chinese being service workers, artisans and small shopkeepers," the PKP Eighth Congress then went on to raise the specter of ascendant, unassimilated Chinese "big bourgeoisie," even after the state had embarked on its program of mass naturalization in 1975 (Partido Komunista ng Pilipinas 1980, 20–23). Charged with remitting their profits overseas (by implication to their "homeland"), these affluent Filipino-Chinese groups were seen as having "close affiliations" among themselves and an "exclusivist culture," promoted by "allegedly Filipinized Chinese schools."

In creating a schema that correlated assimilation with class belonging, so that working-class and petty-bourgeois "Chinese" were assumed to have assimilated while the rich "Chinese" were not, the PKP—like the nationalist elite and the Cold-War-era Philippine state—ended up unwittingly reaffirming a necessary link between ethnicity and class: to be Chinese *is* to be rich, and to be rich is to remain "Chinese." The language of the PKP's solution to the Chinese Question in effect mirrored that of the state's, right down to the use of the term "integration":

> The inordinate hold of the Filipino-Chinese bourgeoisie on the economy has therefore become a real problem but it is not the primary one. In the overall struggle of the Filipino people against imperialism, the Filipino-Chinese community can still play a positive role, provided they are integrated into Philippine society and recognize the primacy of national interest. Integration, however, can only result from a long process which begins with the realization that the Filipino-Chinese have a real stake in the overall progress of their country of residence and should cease cultivating feelings of loyalty to China or Taiwan. (23)

The Maoist faction's orientation to Red China, which was easily discernible in its founding documents and organizational tactics and strategies,[40] meant that the new Communist Party of the Philippines could not remain uncontaminated by its associations (in both material and ideological senses) with a "China" in the throes of the Cultural Revolution.

Reacting defensively to the specter of the "alienness" of Maoist ("Chinese") thought raised by the PKP, "nat-dems [national democrats], unlike their Maoist counterparts in Western countries have consistently refused the label 'Maoist,' arguing that it connotes allegiance to an alien, hence sinister ideology"; to be "Maoist" was to be "subservient to a foreign power" (Malay 1984, 50). Armando Malay argues that the "objective tension thus created between the desire to assuage local Sinophobic sentiments and the simultaneous necessity of establishing Marxist-Leninist legitimacy, for domestic and international consumption, was partially resolved in favor of selective de-Maoization" (ibid.). As part of the effort to Filipinize

Maoism, the 1974 party document "Specific Characteristic of Our People's War" sought to identify the specificity of the Philippine context of struggle (for instance, the formation of mobile guerrilla bases and the "centralized leadership, decentralized operations" strategy in keeping with the country's archipelagic and mountainous geography), even though the overall strategy adopted was not "substantially different from the 'protracted people's war'" formulated by Mao Zedong (51).

Despite this ambivalence toward the "foreign" Maoist ideology, the CPP had made efforts to address the issue of anti-Sinicism. Amado Guerrero's *Philippine Society and Revolution* (1979, 3, 41, 154–55), a key text of the party, provided a scathing account of "Malay racism bred by foreign and feudal exploiters of the people" and directed against "the Chinese and the Aetas" (3). He criticized the Magsaysay and Garcia administrations for resorting to "the old colonial and chauvinist trick of attacking Chinese retailers" while "mak[ing] it difficult and expensive for foreign nationals of Chinese descent to become Filipino citizens" (41, 154–55). At the same time, Guerrero pointed out how economic legislation against Chinese retailers actually was politically motivated: "Though the Garcia puppet regime was conspicuously encouraging Filipino merchants to push out merchants of Chinese nationality from the retail business, especially in the rice and corn trade, it allowed the big Kuomintang compradors to have a big share in the import-export and wholesale business and to bring their capital to Taiwan. All Chinese residents in the Philippines were coerced to manifest their allegiance to the Chiang bandit gang or else face reprisal" (44). The CPP's "Programme for a People's Democratic Revolution in the Philippines" advocated a "class approach" in dealing with naturalized Filipinos and foreign nationals in order to "do away with 'Malay' racism and chauvinism" (Communist Party of the Philippines 1990, 196–209):

> Residents or citizens of Chinese ancestry are very often the target of
> racist and chauvinist attacks launched by U.S. imperialists, modern
> revisionists, and other local reactionaries in line with their anti-China,
> anti-communist and anti-people policy. The Kuomintang comprador
> bourgeoisie should be thoroughly exposed and attacked for its class
> position and for the fact that it is an accomplice of U.S. imperialism,
> modern revisionism and all reactionaries. (203–4)

The Chinese were discussed in a separate section but in juxtaposition with "national minorities," such as the Aetas, both subject to the racism and discriminatory policies of the state. Moreover, Guerrero gestured toward the implication of the "Chinese Question" in the anti-Communist policies of the government during the 1950s and 1960s. In Guerrero's denunciation of the "big Kuomintang compradors," he was careful not to racialize the compradors as "Chinese." These compradors were, instead, *political* collaborators who benefited from the anti-Chinese legislation of the Magsaysay and Garcia administrations.

The breakaway movement's attempt in the early 1970s to disentangle Chinese ethnic identification with money and citizenship opened up the possibility of reformulating the articulation between nationalism and communism along nonracist lines. But the CPP's stance on the ethnic Chinese quickly lost its radical edge owing to the state's own changing policies on Chinese integration after 1975. As splits within the CPP in the early 1990s further reinforced the polycentrism of the Philippine left, different splinter groups sought to propound an inclusive framework for thinking the "Chinese Question," as seen in public statements released by different leftist organizations concerning the kidnapping of Philippine Chinese and the 1998 anti-Chinese riots in Indonesia. Within mainstream politics, left organizations actively courted ethnic-Chinese support for their respective political platforms and projects. The "national-democratic" organization, Bayan Muna (2001), placed an ad in the *Chinese Commercial News* during the 2001 party-list electoral campaign seeking Chinese "solidarity with us in our struggle" and citing *"kababayang Tsinoy's"* (Tsinoy compatriots') contributions to the economic development of "our country" and the great sacrifice of "Filipino-Chinese brothers who fought hand-in-hand with other patriotic Pinoys to resist Japanese invasion," in effect rehabilitating the reputation of the Chinese guerrillas who had been hailed as "good Chinese" by Filipino villagers during the war but subsequently branded as "bad" Chinese by the Philippine state during the Cold War era. Philippine left organizations, such as Bagong Alyansang Makabayan (New Patriotic Alliance, BAYAN); the General Assembly Binding Women for Reforms, Integrity, Equality, Leadership and Action (GABRIELA); and Kilusang Mayo Uno (KMU) and its partner organization Migrante, participated in a demonstration organized by the World Movement Against Racism (a Chinese-Filipino organization) to protest the Indonesian anti-Chinese riots on October 5, 1998.

Philippine Marxism's dialogue with anticolonial nationalism has involved grappling with exclusivist nationalist constructions—not all of them emanating only from the state—of the "Chinese" as aliens, as alienating capital, and as alien revolutionaries located outside the bounds of the national-popular community. Although one of the communist parties has explicitly repudiated anti-Chinese racism in its key document, the contested presence and role of "China" and the "Chinese" in the Philippine revolutionary movement nevertheless illuminate core tensions that underlie the intellectual and organizational divisions within the Philippine left.

Not surprisingly, the recuperation of the Wha Chi guerrillas by both the Philippine state and the Philippine left has meant downplaying the multiple identifications—most notably a strong China orientation[41]—claimed by the guerrillas in favor of a nation-centered narrative of "Chinese" contribution to the Filipino struggle against Japanese imperialism. The continuing vulnerability of the Philippine Chinese to criminal prosecution on charges of subversion has contributed in no small measure to the absence of explicit references to communism: the characters in the novel are avowedly nationalist while being at pains to deny that they are also communists, notwithstanding their stated sympathy for Russia and their obvious acquaintance with and citation of Mao Zedong's writings. This downplaying of popular nationalism's articulation (however fraught) with internationalist communism may also have something to do with the fact that Du Ai began working on his novel less than a year after the revolutionary regimes of China and Vietnam confronted each other over Cambodia and only two years after Deng Xiaoping initiated the reforms that put China on the path of "Socialism with Chinese Characteristics." By the time the novel was published in the mid-1980s, socialist revolution had come to be defined primarily through its excesses (i.e., the Cultural Revolution) and its "modification" along capitalist lines.

The Wha Chi's multiply-identified nationalism/revolutionary cosmopolitanism was rooted in the anticolonial and anti-imperialist struggle of World War II in which Japan was defined as an "external enemy." This inter/nationalism is not a permanent condition, nor even a stable or easily realized one, because it arises only within the context of political action enabled by a particular (and unique) confluence of historical and political contexts. Rapidly changing regional geopolitics after World War II have rendered this form of dual nationalism/revolutionary cosmopolitanism especially vulnerable to erasure by time and forgetfulness of the people on whose behalf the dual-nationalist revolutionaries undertook political action and made self-sacrifices. The Wha Chi experience highlights the importance of multilingualism and translation that enabled both Chinese and Filipino inter/nationalisms to be shaped in part by their mutual (though also fraught) coimplication,[42] and testifies to the fact that nationalism and revolutionary cosmopolitanism in this region, from their inception, were mediated by a "translated modernity" grounded not just in contacts between "Asia" and the "West," but *within* "Asia" (for instance, in Japanese mediation of "Chinese" modernity through translation of western concepts) and *between* "Asia" and the "non-West" (this point will be taken up in chap. 7). But the ways in which these political projects are remembered, or perhaps forgotten, are shaped by a highly contingent politics of memory that may endow these projects with meanings and significance beyond the stated intentions of those who undertook these projects.

Revolutionary cosmopolitanism shows that the making (and remaking) of national communities depends, in fact, on a historically situated, constitutive experience of the "outside" and of "foreignness," a potentially radical openness to the foreign other that is often ignored, if not repressed by the assertion of unnecessarily monolithic and exclusionary national identities. It highlights the fact that nationalism is not always or necessarily about boundedness, exclusivity, rivalry, and enmity, but possesses the capacity for openness, linkages, dialogue, bridges, networks, mutuality, reciprocity, complementarity, and friendship. As the *huaqiao* nationalists and their Filipino friends and comrades shared their languages and experiences, sufferings, and dreams, as well as freely and selflessly exchanged their gifts of love, life, and sacrifice, we witness their two national imaginings flow together, mixing and merging into one, and when they diverge, each one already carrying traces of the other.[43]

Notes

1   Wha Chi, the historical spelling adopted by the group in the Philippines, is also known by other spelling variants, such as Wah Chi and Hua Chi.

2   For a discussion of the difficulties faced by scholars in constructing reliable accounts of the Chinese (as well as Filipino) resistance movement during the Japanese occupation, see Yung Li 1996, 75–78, 115–16.

3   Huk veteran Cesar Lacara (also known as Tatang) in his memoirs (1988) provides a personal account of Huk cooperation with the Wha Chi when, during the last days of the war, the Chinese forces were sent to Manila to help liberate the city. Lacara's memoirs include a picture of the Wha Chi troops among the gallery of prominent freedom fighters of the left in the Philippines.

4   This chapter covers only the role played by the Chinese in the leftist revolutionary movement. For an account of Chinese contribution to the Philippine revolution of 1896, see Ang-See and Go 1996. As discussed in chapter 1, articles published in *Renacimiento Filipino,* around the time of the October uprising in China in 1911, attest to the existence of pro-Republican sentiments and support for China among Filipino intellectuals, no doubt owing to the pan-Asianist network that connected Sun Yat-sen and Japanese activists like Miyazaki Tōten to Mariano Ponce and the Philippine revolution (see Hau and Shiraishi 2009; Mojares 2011). Further research also needs to be undertaken to extend the account provided by this chapter to cover the political role of the ethnic Chinese in the anti-Marcos, EDSA (Epifanio de los Santos) "People Power," and post-EDSA social movements. A rare personal account

of Chinese participation in the so-called EDSA Revolution can be found in the oral history project that included interviews with Lyonel Ty, Jimmy Chua, and Leo Ang in Von Brevern 1986.

5 Laborers constituted 11.6 % of all Chinese in 1903, and worked in the garments, furniture, lumber, laundry, restaurant, sugar, printing, shoe, bakery, paper, construction, and other industries. Small-scale shopkeepers, teachers, clerks, and store employees were also involved in labor organizing (Wong 1999, 73).

6 The earliest labor union was the Overseas Chinese Labor Party (Huaqiao Gongdang) which counted clerks, teachers, and shopkeepers among its members and published a newspaper, the Common People's Daily (Pingmin Ribao) from 1919 to 1922, but was not known to have any connection with the Chinese Communist Party (Yung Li 1996, 60).

7 Unless otherwise indicated, the following biographical details are culled from Xu, Xu, and Xu 2001, 6–13.

8 共青团 is the youth wing of the Chinese Communist Party and was established in 1920.

9 There is no direct evidence to suggest that the central leadership of the Chinese Communist Party had a systematic program for promoting organizational work in the Philippines, but the argument that Chinese communist elements in the Philippines were basically "uncoordinated actions of individuals to seek refuge abroad" (Yung Li 1996, 65) may not strictly apply to all initiatives either.

10 The Partido Komunista ng Pilipinas' official history (1996, 93–94) records the formation, in 1926, of the Manila nucleus of the Young Communist League (YCL) of the Communist Party of China led by a Co Sing Liat, who would later be a member of the Central Committee of the PKP. The biographical account of Xu Jingcheng by his sons (see Xu, Xu, and Xu 2001, 6), however, states that Xu (Ko Keng Seng) was the head of the YCL Manila branch. Co Sing Liat was educated at the Sun Yat-Sen University in China and in the Soviet Union, and worked as editor of the The Fookien Times. I thank Ramon Guillermo for the information, based on the Comintern Archive (Crisanto Evangelista to Comrade Andreyev, "Information on the PI Situation," 1939).

11 "By March 1930, the PCLF had a membership of around 1,500 workers in 12 unions, plus 200 more in a Chinese Young Workers' Club which included calisthenics, drama, singing and other Chinese cultural groups. By March 1930 also, the Chinese YCL [Young Communist League] in the Philippines had 80 members, of whom 30 were industrial workers, 30 were handicraft workers, 10 were shopkeepers, and 10 were farmers. Of this total Chinese YCL membership, around sixty subsequently became members of the Partido Komunista ng Pilipinas [although they maintained separate all-Chinese nuclei], while 20 others remained as members of the Chinese YCL branch in the Philippines, which was directly under the YCL in mainland China" (Partido Komunista ng Pilipinas 1996, 114–5l; see also Yung-Li 1996, 79–81).

12 The Wha Chi leaders are credited with having suggested the name "Hukbo ng Bayan Laban sa Hapon." Huk leader Luis Taruc had initially favored the name "Philippine Army of Liberation" (Tan 1981, 125).

13 The principle of neutrality allowed the Wha Chi to work with other nonleftist guerrilla groups.

14 See Wha Chi 1982; Liang and Cai 1980; 1996; 1998; Tan 1981, 116–27; Yung Li 1996, 75–114; Gong 2001; 2002.

15   I quote Maximo Nocete, a Filipino major writing in 1945 about the Wha Chi, cited in Liang and Cai 1998, 105.

16   See also the important research by Gregor Benton (2007) on Chinese participation in transethnic internationalism in Russia, Germany, Cuba, Spain, and Australia.

17   This point is elaborated theoretically in Cheah 2001; see also Appiah 1998. For Chinese theorizing of the relationship between Marxism-Leninism and the national question, see Liu 1952. Liu quotes Mao Zedong as stating that patriotism is not only intimately connected with internationalism, but represents "the application of internationalism in the national revolutionary war." In her study of the *huaqiao* warriors during the world war, Yung Li (1996, 175) states that the one of the objectives of the Hua Zhi was "to unite all the Chinese in the Philippines" in the anti-Japanese struggle in the Philippines in order to "hasten the liberation of China." Yung Li, however, views the cooperation between the Chinese leftists and the Huks as an exceptional case, one that in the long run was not strong enough to overcome the anti-Communism of postwar Philippine official nationalism (173).

18   The current scholarly framing of the nationalism vs. cosmopolitanism debate is forcefully critiqued by Pheng Cheah's "Introduction" in Cheah and Robbins 1998. Huynh Kim Khanh (1982) has argued in favor of viewing Vietnamese communism as a fusion of anti-imperialist patriotism (as opposed to elite-sponsored nationalism) and internationalist communism.

19   In this chapter, I rely on the 1985 ed. of vol. 1; the 1988 ed. of vol. 2; and the 2002 ed. of vol. 3. The 2002 ed. reprinted the 1985 ed. in its entirety, but cut and spliced some parts of vol. 2 and many chapters of vol. 3.

20   The following biographical information is culled from the author's note in *Fengyu Taipingyang* (Du 2002); Du Ai 1982, 1–16; n.d., 70–71; and an interview with Du Ai's widow Lin Bin (Guangzhou, Guangdong Province, People's Republic of China, September 30, 2001). More information about Lin Bin can be found in an interview published in *Shijie Ribao*. See Hu Yaohua 1995, 11; see also "Keji xiandai zhuming zuojia Du Ai," 2008.

21   See, for example, Lin Bin 2001a, 15; 2001b, 15. For discussions of Lin Bin's place in Philippine-Chinese literature, see Jiang Hua 2001a, 11; 2001b, 7. Evidence suggests that Du Ai might have contracted a first marriage in China before he met Lin Bin.

22   In his "Preface," Du Ai 1(985) states that the idea of writing *Fengyu Taipingyang* had already occurred to him in the 1950s, but he only began working on the novel on May 1, 1980.

23   *Fengyu* was also serialized in the Philippine dailies *Shijie Ribao* (vols. 1 and 3) and *Shang Bao* (vol. 2). Lin Bin has expressed dissatisfaction with the publisher's extensive editing (and cutting) of chapters in vol. 3 of the 2002 ed. of *Fengyu* and plans to republish the novel in its entirety at some point in the future.

24   See Lin Bin's "Afterword" in Du, *Fengyu Taipingyang* (Du Ai 2002, 3:1217).

25   The 1985 (vol. 1) ed. contains 400,000 words, the 1988 (vol. 2) ed. 240,000 words. The 2002 combined ed. puts the total at 960,000 words. A Beijing ed. of vol. 2, published in 1991 by Wenhua Yishu Chubanshe, contains 251,000 words. For critical evaluation of Du Ai's place in Chinese arts and letters, see Huang Weizong n.d.; and Yang Yi 1998 OR n.d. in Biblio; 2000. For literary analyses of *Fengyu*, see Sun Ailing 1996, 267–86, 359–62; He Chuxiong n.d.; 2002a, 21; 2002b, 21. See also Li Zhiyuan n.d., 130–38.

26   For an account of Du Ai's career as a journalist, see Lin Bin, "Lao baoren Du Ai (Pt. 1)" [Du Ai the Veteran Journalist] *Shijie Ribao*, August 4, 2001, 21; and Lin Bin, "Lao

baoren Du Ai (Pt. 2)" [Du Ai the Veteran Journalist] *Shijie Ribao*, August 7, 2001, 21. Du Ai had worked under Mao Dun in Hong Kong where the latter was editor in chief of the journal *Yuanlin* (see Lin Bin 2001c).

27 Mao Dun 1949, 1; also cited in Zhuang Zhongqing 2001, 7.

28 Scholarship on South China has generally acknowledged that cultural distinctions between Han and non-Han peoples (such as the Yao) are far from simple (see Faure 1989, 4–36).

29 Yang Yi's "forest and seas" characterization of Huanan writing resonates with Anthony Reid's (1988, 1–10) theorizing of Southeast Asia in geoclimatic terms in his magisterial *Southeast Asia in the Age of Commerce*.

30 Unless rendered in pinyin, the romanized names of the characters are based on transliterations provided by Lin Bin (2005). Felipe Lee Yung Shaw also went by the name Hoster Lee (Huosite Li, as transcribed into Chinese).

31 See author's notes in Liang and Cai 1998; and Tan 1981, 121.

32 See Li Lijun 2001, 14–19; see also Antonio Tan's account (1981), excerpted in Liang and Cai 1998, 116.

33 A short article on Li (Lai 2005) claims that Li had joined the Philippine Hongmen Zhigong Dang 洪门致公党 before he went to China and that, in Guangdong, he had worked directly under Zhou Enlai, from whom he obtained permission to go back to the Philippines with his wife, Wang Yazhang 王亚璋 (an elementary school teacher turned activist who joined the Chinese Communist Party in 1925) in 1927.

34 Yung Li (1996, 66) rightly argues that the Hua Zhi's "connection with the roots of the Filipino society was the necessary criteria for the survival of a guerrilla force."

35 Liang Shangwan (in Liang and Cai 1998, 59; 1996, 47) recounts an incident (in a section subtitled "The wonders of English"/英语的奇妙作用) in which he and Xiao Lin of the Wha Chi Manila office were stopped at a checkpoint by Filipino policemen, and Xiao Lin was able to talk his way out of trouble (with the help of P200.00): "Xiao Lin later recounted that he flattered the two policemen with many kind words, but since his Tagalog was not fluent enough, he had to resort to some English that worked wonders as the two policemen's attitude softened a lot."

36 See Liang and Cai 1996, 28–29; and 1998, 37–38.

37 See chaps. 89 and 94 of Du Ai 2002, 3:907–9, 966–67.

38 Lava's memoirs recount the visit to the Huk camp in 1950 of a representative from the Chinese Bureau, and suggests that tensions between Philippine and Chinese comrades during the war may have been partly fueled by personality clashes: "Our conversation was fruitful, conducted in an atmosphere of friendship. There was no arrogance on the part of the Chinese Bureau representative. Compared to early representatives during the Japanese occupation, this one was unassuming, humble, and soft-spoken" (Lava 2002, 169–70). Owing to intense governmental repression, the Huks lost contact with the Chinese for some years. Lava also hints at the rift between the PKP and the "Maoist Chinese Party" in the early years of the Sino-Soviet split over the question of the Chinese Bureau's autonomy and right of say in Philippine affairs: "Perhaps the Maoist Chinese Party did not appreciate our position that the Chinese Bureau in the Philippines should be under the jurisdiction of the Philippine party. Perhaps the Chinese comrades also resented our decision to accept the Chinese Bureau's inclusion into the overseas Chinese committee on condition that it did not interfere with purely internal problems of Filipinos" (322).

39 See also "Issues in the Ideological Dispute between Maoism and the International
    Communist Movement," 1972, 4. Lava (2002, 322) argues that the PKP was "neither
    anti-Chinese nor pro-Soviet" and "not beholden to and certainly not under
    instructions from any foreign party." In the early years of the split, "due to meager
    knowledge of the real cause of Soviet-Chinese conflict," the PKP was "inclined to
    take more positions on various issues that coincided with Chinese side....Perhaps we
    felt some kind of kinship with the underdeveloped Chinese nation. Indeed, we were
    influenced by some Maoist perspectives on Marxism-Leninism."
40 The most obvious manifestation of this orientation was the keen demand among
    activists for "Red East" commodities, such as Mao's *Red Book* and Red Army caps. I
    thank Jojo Abinales for this information.
41 Yung Li Yuk-wai (1996, 173) gives us glimpses of the conceptual difficulties
    entailed by this multiple identification in her own discussion of the Hua Zhi.
    She cites articles written by Huang Jie and Ye Jing bearing titles like "The Sino-
    Filipino Friendship Cemented by Blood" (Zhongfei renmin xianxue ningcheng
    di youyi) and "I miss You, My Filipino Mother" (Yongyuan huainian zhou ni—
    "yineng") that appeared in the forty-fifth anniversary souvenir publication of the
    Hua Zhi, as a way of showing the depth of feeling and friendship that Chinese
    guerrillas developed for their Filipino counterparts. And then she goes on to cite
    Liang and Cai's memoirs (1980, 35), which recounts the first attack launched
    by the "inexperienced" Huks, to argue her point that there was no real sense
    of "brotherhood between Filipinos and Chinese" (Yung Li 1996, 174): "While
    friendship did develop among the Chinese and Filipinos fighting on the leftist side,
    it was too weak to influence the general attitude of the two peoples, especially in
    an anti-Communist atmosphere in the Philippines during the postwar period."
    Moreover, she attributes this lack of a sense of brotherhood to the fact that the
    Chinese resistance movement was motivated mainly by "a patriotic feeling
    towards China rather than empathy with the Filipinos," and their aim in fighting
    the Japanese in the Philippines as, to quote the Hua Zhi, "to hasten the liberation
    of China." The statements of the Hua Zhi guerrillas themselves, including the
    articles Yung Li cites, show the complexity of their emotions and attitudes toward
    the Philippines, a complexity that is not easily reducible to the kind of loyalty
    test that nationalists on either side of the borders use to separate "them" from
    "us." Ironically, it was precisely the Hua Zhi's "close" connection to the Filipino
    communist movement that made them appear "more alien in the eyes of the [local]
    Chinese [community]" (Yung Li 1996, 66), thereby "hinder[ing] their [Hua Zhi's]
    effort in taking over the [Chinese] community leadership."
42 Tellingly, the seeds for Rebecca Karl's research (2002) on revolutionary dialogue
    and international solidarity as important components of modern Chinese self-
    definition and nationalism were planted by her encounter with a group of Filipino
    communists who had escaped to China in the 1960s after being hounded by the
    Marcos government.
43 I thank Kasian Tejapira for allowing me to incorporate his astute reading of, and
    commentary on, "The Question of Foreigners: *Nanyang Piaoliuji* and the Re/Making
    of Chinese and Filipino Nationness," an analysis of Philippine *guiqiao* Bai Ren's
    novel which raises issues that are addressed and elaborated on in this present study.
    Kasian presented his comments at the Core University Program workshop at Kyoto
    University on March 25, 2002 (Hau 2004, 15–62, 273–82).

In a short span of three years, from December 2002 to December 2005, five major films that prominently featured the ethnic Chinese were released in the Philippines. Regal Entertainment's *Mano Po*[1] (2002) was the top box-office draw at the Metro Manila Film Festival (MMFF), grossing P65 million (Daza 2003; the entry on "Regal Films" in *Wikipedia* puts the figure at a little over P67 million) and garnering twelve awards (including Best Picture, Actor, Actress, Director, Screenplay, and Story). The box-office success of *Mano Po* spawned a franchise of unrelated "sequels." *Mano Po 2: My Home* (2003) was the MMFF People's Choice for Best Picture, and picked up five other prizes, while *Mano Po 3: My Love* (2004) received seven (notably Best Picture, Actress, and Actor). *Ako Legal Wife* [Me Legal Wife]: *Mano Po 4*, a comedy inspired by the plot and dialogue of *Mano Po 2*, was released in 2005 and won the Best Actress and Best Supporting Actress awards. *Mano Po 5: Gua Ai Di* (Mano Po: I Love You, 2006) and *Mano Po 6: A Mother's Story* (2009) were star vehicles for two of the country's biggest stars, Angel Locsin and Sharon Cuneta respectively. Cuneta picked up the Best Actress award at the Film Festival for her portrayal of a Chinese mestiza billionaire.[2] *Mano Po 2* lost the 2003 MMFF Best Picture Award to the highly touted *Crying Ladies*, which bagged a total of eleven local and international awards and took in P65 million at the local box office (Salterio 2004).

Regal Entertainment producer "Mother" Lily Yu-Monteverde described *Mano Po* as a "dream project" (Arcellana 2002, 10), born out of her desire to pay tribute to her parents, the copra tycoon and Fujian-born Chinese Domingo Yuchu and Sorsogon-born Filipina Profetiza Buban, by recasting their romance into an exemplary Chinese-Filipino family saga. Spanning some forty years, this "rags to riches" (ibid.) epic focuses on the three daughters of a Chinese immigrant who had married a Filipina against the wishes of his parents, chosen to settle down in the Philippines and, with his wife's help, founded a copra empire that eventually expanded into a conglomerate: self-sacrificing Vera (Maricel Soriano), who postpones her wedding and lays aside her own happiness in order to run the family's business empire; dutiful Juliet (Kris Aquino), whose sense of self is thoroughly bound up with her role as wife (to a tyrannical husband) and mother; and rebellious Richelle (Ara Mina), a party girl who scandalizes her family with her raucous behavior and drug-taking. The bonds of sisterhood are tested and strengthened following the kidnapping and rescue of two of the daughters.

Monteverde shared the credit with screenwriter Roy Iglesias—who had cowritten the script for Eddie Romero's *Ganito Kami Noon, Paano Kayo*

Mano Po

Ngayon? (discussed in chap. 2)—for crafting the stories of *Mano Po 2*, about
the three squabbling widows (a Filipina, a Chinese, and a Chinese-Filipina)
and multiple households of a murdered Chinese-Filipino tycoon; *Mano Po 3*,
about an intrepid anticrime crusader torn between her family and her long-
lost lover; and *Ako Legal Wife: Mano Po 4*, which, according to Monteverde,
was inspired by "people I know in the Chinese-Filipino community" (Red
2005).

There is more to the issue than a simple case of translating a Chinese-
Filipino producer's life experiences and observations into movies about the
"Chinese" in the Philippines. Screenwriter Roy Iglesias credited his *Mano Po*
series with "cement[ing the Filipinos'] love affair with Asia" (Cabreza 2004,
1). *Mano Po* heralded the "Asian renaissance in Philippine pop culture": a
mere five months after the release of *Mano Po*, the Taiwanese TV drama
Liu Xing Hua Yuan (Meteor Garden, originally broadcast in 2001), based on
the Japanese comic (*manga*) by Kamio Yoko, *Hanayori Dango* (Boys over
Flowers, 1992–2003), sparked a "chinovela" ("Chinese telenovela") craze
centering on the drama's four male stars, all members of the Taiwanese pop
band F4 (Flower Four). Iglesias argued that while the advent of the heavily
promoted chinovelas contributed to "Asianizing" Filipino moviegoers, this
Asianization was mediated by the global success of Asian culture industries
that churned out the Hong Kong martial arts movies and Taiwanese
romantic films of the 1970s, the gangster and action movies of the 1980s,
the Mainland Chinese epics of the 1990s, and other cultural products,
such as music, manga, *animé* (animated cartoons), magazines, and fashion.
Philippine cinema has traditionally taken its cues from industrial behemoth
Hollywood's nod of recognition and approval: *Mano Po* has been compared
to the 1993 Chinese-American film *Joy Luck Club* (Chen 2002), and Iglesias
is quoted elsewhere as saying that Viva Films' Vic del Rosario "was sure
'Mano Po' would be a hit because [Taiwanese director] Ang Lee's *Crouching
Tiger, Hidden Dragon* [2000] scored in Hollywood" (Cabreza 2004, 3). But
the growing popularity of "Chinese"[3] blockbuster films, boy bands like F4,
and Korean dramas in China, Japan, the Philippines, Vietnam, Thailand,
Singapore, Indonesia, and Malaysia throw light on the gathering weight
and force of the regional circulation and consumption of Asian cultural
products, and the regional cultural connections (Iwabuchi 2004, 2) thus
forged (on the role of popular culture in regionalization of East Asia, see
Otmazgin 2005).

Unitel Productions' blockbuster *Crying Ladies* (2003), which focuses
on Filipino professional mourners working at a Chinese wake and funeral,
similarly rode the crest of the "Asian" wave. Novice director Mark Meily
submitted the original screenplay, "Bayad Luha" (which can be translated

as "Pay for Tears," or "Pay with Tears"), to the workshop run by noted scriptwriter Armando Lao in 2000. He subsequently persuaded "megastar" Sharon Cuneta to accept the lead role in the movie by telling her that "it would be the kind of role Gong Li [the Chinese actress and former muse of internationally acclaimed Chinese director Zhang Yimou] would portray" (Cu Unjieng 2004, 9).

Chinese Filipinos, such as the Monteverdes of Regal Entertainment and Robbie Tan of Seiko Films, have been among the Philippine entertainment industry's most prominent, prolific, and powerful film distributors, producers, and star makers. (In fact, one of the characters in *Crying Ladies* dreams of being discovered by an "intsik" producer.) This remains valid as a general observation despite the fact that in the late 1990s, the Philippine film industry had been in danger of collapse as the Asian financial crisis of 1997 devalued the Philippine peso, Hollywood films dominated the Philippine box office, and film piracy, exorbitant government taxation (of up to 50% of film revenues), economic retrenchment, and falling movie attendance ate into film profits and forced many producers into bankruptcy. Big studios, such as Regal Entertainment, had had to cut back drastically on the number of films they made, and faced stiff competition from newcomers—a number of them branching out from TV production companies—such as ABS-CBN Film Productions, Inc. (later renamed Star Cinema) and GMA Productions. Talented directors, such as Marilou Diaz-Abaya, continued to work with major film studios, but it was independent filmmakers, such as Raymond Red and Brillante Mendoza, who stood to inherit the mantle of the great Lino Brocka and Ishmael Bernal, who did some of their best work under martial law.[4]

Strategies for coping with the crisis of the film industry since then have ranged from investing in big-budget, star-studded productions (of which *Mano Po* and *Crying Ladies* are examples) to entering into coproduction deals with other companies to making shoestring *pito-pito* (lit., "seven each") films. Pito-pito films made for Regal's satellite company, Good Harvest, "take their name from the studio's initial policy of completing each phase of preproduction, production, and postproduction in seven days apiece (more recently, shooting times have lengthened and production budgets have increased). Typically outfitted with a budget of P2.5 million (approximately U.S.$56,000) and no bankable stars, Good Harvest's 'pito-pitos' constitute a kind of in-house poverty-row production that the biggest film studio, Regal Films, adopted in the wake of the film industry's declining profits" (Lim 2000). Not without some irony, these "economizing efforts gave several new directors a start, and have distinguished themselves as promising innovators" (ibid.).[5] Robbie Tan of Seiko Films fared worse

207

than "Mother Lily" of Regal: he was forced to cut back on production, and also came under pressure from the Movie and Television Review and Classification Board for the adult content of his films. Tan would go on to produce digital independent films, most notably future Cannes Film Festival awardee Brillante Mendoza's *Foster Child* (2007).

The so-called crisis of Philippine cinema coincided, however, with a mini-"Chinese" renaissance in Philippine film and television. "Chinese" themes and characters were featured prominently in *Mano Po* and *Crying Ladies*. Whatever their artistic merit,[6] these blockbuster films signaled the growing presence of the "Chinese" in Philippine popular imagination and led to the mainstreaming of this subject beyond the stock character of bad-Chinese capitalist and good-Chinese martial artist. Examples include the *Mano Po* "sequels," the comedy action *Otso Otso Pamela-Mela Wan* (2004), the top-grossing *Fengshui* (2004), the independent film *Chopsuey* (2007), and the television drama *My Binondo Girl* (2011–2012).

What kind of reality do *Mano Po* and *Crying Ladies* speak of? What sort of Filipino dreams and aspirations do they articulate? What kind of identifications do they invite? In what way are these dreams, aspirations, and identifications bound up with the issue of being "Chinese in the Philippines"?

Representations of "Chineseness" in recent Philippine cinema are an index to—but also enablers of—the shifting meanings and standing of "Chinese" and "Chineseness" in the Philippines. Variously identified with commerce, capital, and communism at different points in Philippine history, and long defined by its problematic relationship with Philippine nationalism, "Chineseness" has been reconfigured over the last three decades in line with the shifting geopolitical, demographic, economic, social, and cultural terrain and class-power configuration of the Philippine nation-state. This chapter locates the cultural politics of "Chineseness" not only in "Chinese" everyday life and negotiations, but also in a Philippine nation-state in the throes of profound transformation. It situates these seemingly local, national developments within the broader global and especially region-wide (East Asian) capitalist development, and looks at how the politics of "Chinese" ethnicity and representation are implicated in emergent, market-mediated forms of national and regional identification and consciousness. Representations of the "Chinese" in such films as the *Mano Po* series and *Crying Ladies* draw on, while also popularizing, the state's adoption of a discourse of national integration that seeks to domesticate the "Chinese"—historically constructed as the "other" of the Filipino nation—in order to embed the "Chinese" more firmly within the territorial boundaries and conceptual parameters of the Filipino nation-state, or, to paraphrase the popular integrationist slogan, to help the "Chinese" find their "place under the Philippine sun."[7] These cinematic representations, however, also point to the ways in which "Chinese culture" and "Chineseness" have also come to epitomize regional, rather than strictly national, capitalist flows that the nation-state seeks to capture and appropriate, but always at the risk of being transformed by these flows. Competing "Chinese" imaginaries, which reinforce the historical conflation of "Chinese" and capital, inform the pluralist discourse of citizenship and national belonging propagated by advocates of integration as well as the Philippine state, while identifying multiple identifications and recalcitrant longings, desires, and fantasies that exceed the bounds and claims of Filipino nationness.

Class, Nation, and Region

As discussed in chapters 2 and 3, efforts of activists and organizations, such as Kaisa para sa Kaunlaran and its precursor, Pagkakaisa sa Pag-Unlad Inc., to promote integration as an alternative to assimilation, along with similar advocacies by other organizations and individuals, have contributed in no small measure to mainstreaming the integrationist stance (Cariño 1988). *Mano Po* leans heavily on the Kaisa platform in the final segment of the film, in which the young Chinese-Filipino artist Jimmy edits his documentary. Entitled *Tsinoy: A History*, the documentary employs the blanket term "Tsinoy," a label closely identified with Kaisa advocacy. The documentary features a montage of Filipino national heroes of Chinese ancestry as documented in actual Kaisa-Angelo King Heritage Center exhibits. While the Kaisa exhibits are careful to showcase these "national leaders of Chinese ancestry" as Chinese mestizos, the film-within-a-film goes one step further in reclaiming these mestizos *as* "Tsinoys."

The storyline also trumpets the integrationist message through the selfless actions of Richelle (Ara Mina), the black sheep who defies the wishes of her family and patriotically involves herself in the affairs of the nation.[8] When she is apprehended at a drug den, she agrees to work as a civilian agent to uncover the identity of a leading Filipino drug dealer. Despite pressure from her family not to testify against the drug dealer, who turns out to be a Philippine National Police director and a longtime "friend" of the family, she puts her own life (and her family's) in danger; to compound matters, she falls in love with her Filipino police handler, Rafael Bala (Richard Gomez). The integrationist message is spelled out at the end of the film, when Bala's voiceover tells the audience: *"Pinatunayan ni Richelle sa akin na hindi ka kailangang ipinanganak sa Pilipinas para maging Pinoy* [slang for Filipino]"

(Richelle proved to me that you don't have to be born in the Philippines to be a Filipino). The final words in the film also echo this point: *"Bagama't magkakaiba ang ating pinanggalingan, iisa ang ating kinabukasan"* (Even though our origins are different, we share in the same future).

Critical reception of *Mano Po* has been generally positive and has tended to situate the politics of the film's depiction of the Chinese squarely within the integrationist discourse. While criticizing the film for reinforcing the stereotype of the Chinese as wealthy, reviews (some of which were penned by Chinese Filipinos) nevertheless lauded *Mano Po* for being "another positive step in building bridges of understanding between Filipinos of Chinese heritage vis-à-vis all other Filipinos" (Flores 2002); promoting "more dialogue and understanding between Chinese and their fellow Filipinos" (Dy 2003, 15; See 2003); according "mainstream respectability" to Chinese Filipinos (Zulueta 2002); showing that the "Chinese belong among the Filipinos of whom they are inescapably a part" (David 2002); and—directly borrowing from Kaisa parlance—serving as a "testament" to the "heroic efforts" of the Chinese to find their "place in the Philippine sun" (Chen 2002). Although critical of the film's tendency to "exoticize the Chinoy community," Rina Jimenez-David (2002), a columnist of the *Philippine Daily Inquirer*, wrote that "The film is that rare creation: a commercial outing that manages, at the same time, to say something substantial and contribute to a better understanding of the society it mirrors." She called *Mano Po* a "deeply political film...[t]he film touches on the status of the Chinese-Filipinos in our society, part of the fabric of life, especially in business, and yet feeling left out and isolated. The scrutiny is even-handed. Chinese-Filipinos are in for their share of criticism, especially their indifference to the social realities around them, except when these prove to their advantage, and their penchant for buying their way out of trouble or inconvenience." Edna See (2003) expressed her hope that "next time, the story of the poor Chinoys will find its way to the big screen."

The struggle of "Chinese Filipinos" for their "place in the Philippine sun" is a legacy of economic nationalism, political disenfranchisement, and racial discrimination. Nevertheless, mass naturalization qualified Chinese Filipinos to move into the areas that had been sealed off from them. Despite the periodic political and economic crises that afflicted the Philippines, enough capitalist transformation was taking place to enable a small number of Chinese Filipinos to engage in capital accumulation on a far larger scale than had been possible, resulting in the absorption of a strata of "Chinese" into the changing Philippine class structure, increasingly characterized by a small concentration of "new rich" and the creation of new middle classes (Pinches 1996, 103–33; 1999, 275–301).

The visibility of the "Chinese" is partly conditioned by the transformative effect of "Chinese" capital not just on the economy, but on the Philippine urban landscape, with the *sari-sari* (informal retailing, literally "various kinds") and family-owned neighborhood stores giving way to malls, department stores, supermarkets, and high rises. Large-scale investments, especially by Taiwanese firms, in the Philippines in the late 1980s were instrumental in first linking the idea of regional economic development with "Chinese capitalism" and capital flows. In so doing, however, they glossed over the crucial role played by Japanese trade, aid, and foreign direct investment in promoting the economic integration of the region.[9] The emergence of mainland China in the 1990s has only served to further cement this link between regional economic development and Chinese capitalism.

While Chinese visibility had historically been conditioned by the conflation of Chineseness with commerce and money, the difference is that nowadays, "Chineseness" is no longer identified simply or necessarily with mercantile capital, but rather, associated with large-scale strategies of accumulation the scope of which extends beyond the territorial bounds of the Philippine nation-state. These accumulation strategies are notable for their unprecedented diversity, flexibility, and mobility (cf. Nonini and Ong 1997, 3–4).[10] The scale of "Chinese" capital is suggested in *Mano Po* by the way in which the founders of the family fortune, Luis and Elisa Go, are able to parlay their copra business into food manufacturing and other ventures, which are subsequently consolidated under the "Go Group of Companies" and presided over by their eldest daughter Vera (Maricel Soriano). The labor of the merchant, routinely denigrated as parasitical (chap. 3), is transmuted into the magic of large-scale and endless capitalist accumulation, the ability of capital to be fruitful and multiply and generate fabulous wealth and opportunities for display and consumption far in excess of what the wealth of the "Chinese" merchant used to command. This magical quality of Chinese capital is captured by filmic montage. In *Mano Po 2*, to take another example, Antonio Chan confidently tells his wife Sol, "*Madali pela dito Manila*" (Money easy here Manila), when they first move to Chinatown and, in the next shot, miraculously secures, presumably through his "Chinese network," a P250,000 loan from, of course, China Banking Corporation. The shot of the "Golden Dragon" sign being hoisted atop their store dissolves into a shot of the spacious warehouse in which Antonio supervises the preparation of a shipment bound for Korea.

As discussed in chapter 2, the mainstreaming of a pluralist and accommodationist stance on national identity is bound up with the shifting strategies over three decades of the Philippine state (see Aguilar 1999,

315–20). In hopes of attracting capital and technical flows, especially from the emergent East Asian region, the state has granted permanent residency to moneyed foreigners in hopes of attracting investment of as little as U.S.\$100,000. In 2008, Gloria Macapagal-Arroyo signed Executive Order 758, creating a "Special Visa for Employment Generation" that allows foreigners whose investment and business enterprises can hire at least ten Filipino employees to remain indefinitely in the Philippines, while also serving as a "pass" to permanent residency. This relaxing of state strictures against foreign business in the Philippines supplements the state's drive to reterritorialize the flows of Filipino migrant workers and settlers abroad. Deploying the term "balikbayan" (literally, "return to one's town/country") to refer to Filipino immigrants and their descendants (Szanton Blanc 1996), the reterritorialization of the Filipino "diaspora" plays up so-called Filipino values that supposedly underpin "family, communal, and national ties" in order to connect "Filipinos" (especially in the U.S. and Canada) who have become naturalized citizens of other countries as well as their second- and third-generation offspring to the Philippines. In 2003, Gloria Macapagal-Arroyo signed the Dual-Citizenship Act to "extend more economic and political opportunities to Filipinos overseas in the name of national unity, solidarity and progress" (*Philippine Daily Inquirer,* 2003).

The state endeavors to reterritorialize the flows of people, capital, and skills by relying on the discourse of national development and recoding these flows as "Filipino" so as to channel them into the bounds of the Philippine nation-state.[11] But its notion of nationness cannot avoid the contamination of money, which breeds fear and suspicion about the commodification of citizenship and the loosening of the bonds between state and nation, territory, and Filipinoness.

For instance, resentment of so-called balikbayan and professional OFWs, most often voiced by the middle classes and intelligentsia (Hau 2004, chaps. 5 and 6), fuels public debates over "brain drain" and has made a nationalist "sacrifice" (or, rather, "virtue") out of the act of staying put in the Philippines instead of seeking opportunities abroad. These anxieties are induced by the capacity of deterritorialized "Filipino" flows to create new sources of social power and social reproduction (in matters of social status, fashion, taste, and public opinion) that cannot be fully controlled or co-opted either by the state or by the Filipino elite and middle classes. After all, these flows have seen immigrants and OFWs acquire middle- or upper-class status without necessarily going through the longstanding channels of middle-class and elite socialization within Philippine society (elaborated in Hau 2011); even though they register in elite consciousness as nouveaux riches and parvenus, they effortlessly command public attention as objects of admiration and emulation, and receive official sanction as *bagong bayani* (new heroes) of the nation. That these flows come from "outside," not to mention their relative proximity to geopolitical power (especially America) that affords them unmediated access to sources of symbolic capital, endows them with a cachet that rivals that of the socially dominant and cosmopolitan Filipino elite, part of whose own prestige lies in their connections to, if not command over, the languages, signs, gestures, and objects from the "outside" (see Cannell 1999, 222).

But these anxieties are not exclusively a product of the "narcissism of small differences" (Freud 1975), of elite and middle-class self-perception and worth being challenged by those who are most like them, and the redirection of their feelings of hatred, envy, and aggression toward those who are "nearly-we." Popular sentiments are not entirely free of ambivalence, for example, in questions of language use. Elite domination had long been secured through the use of English, but the dissemination of Filipino and other Philippine languages through the mass media and the market over the past decades has unsettled the preeminence of English as the language of social power and privilege, and has marked out spaces in which the use of English—deliberately and ironically expressed as "spokening in dollars"—can be interpreted as an assertion of unwarranted superiority and provoke resentment and perhaps even outright violence. Class disparity in the Philippines is a "daily, tangible experience": class difference is "particularized in a thousand material objects," such as "canned peaches versus boiled sweet potato, plate glass versus nipa tiles, the air-conditioned chill of supermarket aisles versus the village store" (Cannell 1999, 20). In "standard" English versus *barok* (broken) English, one risks humiliation by having her grammatical errors or accent (of which she is often unaware) exposed by someone else who claims a better command of English. Difference is particularized not just by objects, but by persons on whom varying degrees of cultivation are imputed. The violence of "spokening in dollars" inheres in the act of speaking, which not only distances the speaker from those who cannot speak it well or with the right accent, but forces the latter into the uncomfortable position of risking mockery and humiliation by another. These embodied differences—of which language is but one—that divide the rich from the poor have catalyzed many of the political and social crises that periodically wrack the Philippines. Most important, celebrations of the deterritorialization of Filipino nationness run up against the enforced rootedness of the majority of Filipinos, the most indigent among whom remain confined within the boundaries of a nation-state the legitimacy of which is constantly put into question by its inability to fulfill its obligation to safeguard the "Filipino people" it claims to represent.

If the continuing conflation of "Chinese" with capital makes the "new Chinese" the visible embodiment of class difference (despite evidence of class disparities and social divisions among "the Chinese"), how can "Chineseness" be purged of its alien attributes and domesticated for Filipino consumption?

Resinifying Chinese Mestizoness

The way *Mano Po* goes about domesticating the alien "Chinese" is by foregrounding mestizoness as the defining characteristic of the "Chinese Filipino." The film, in fact, marks a kind of "resinification" of the "Chinese mestizo" in contemporary Philippine imagination. It is worth noting that the historical figures—Jose Rizal, Emilio Aguinaldo, among them—who appear at the end of *Mano Po* as "Tsinoys" do not, for example, fit the definition of "ethnic Chinese" advanced by Kaisa para sa Kaunlaran, since these Chinese mestizos did not identify themselves as "Chinese."[12] Despite the fact that Chinese mestizos constituted the large majority of the so-called mixed-blood population by the end of the Spanish period and despite the fact that a substantial number of the most prominent Filipino leaders and heroes were or are technically Chinese mestizos, the combination of Filipino official and elite nationalism and popular media production and consumption worked to redefine the term "mestizo" during the first three decades of the postindependence years to mainly signify "white" (defined as North and Latin American and European) rather than "Chinese" ancestry.

The positive revaluation of Chineseness was partly triggered by the explosion of studies of overseas Chinese business and networks in the 1980s and 1990s, and the conscription of this type of scholarship for political and ideological affirmations of "Chinese capitalism" and its role in the economic growth and dynamism of the region (Pinches 1999, 16).

Although the search for "East Asian identity" has a history of entanglement with radical nationalist and continental projects that have made "(East) Asia" a "culture area" endowed with historical reality (Dirlik 1999), the emergent "East Asian" region, with porous and shifting boundaries stretching from China, Japan, and South Korea to Taiwan, the Philippines, and Hong Kong to Vietnam, Thailand, Indonesia, Malaysia, Singapore, and Brunei, is largely the creation of market forces (Katzenstein and Shiraishi 1997) under the shadow of the American imperium (Katzenstein 2005). It is characterized by the increasing density of networks of crossborder linkages (both formal and informal), interdependence, cooperation, and collaboration in the realms of trade and investment, technology and production, financial services, transportation and communication, population flows, popular culture, and disease control (Pempel 2005, 2).

De facto economic integration, cultural exchanges and flows, and ongoing efforts at community-building underscore the growing salience of "regions" as units of analysis that add much-needed nuance (Katzenstein 2005, *ix*) to perspectives hitherto anchored in "global-local" analyses. Regional frameworks of analyses help specify globalization's uneven reach and scope across geopolitical space while calling attention to the contingent fields of forces and interactions which shape specific responses to globalization.

Regional economic integration in East Asia (or, if the United States is included, Asia-Pacific) in the wake of Japanese economic success has seen the rise of the "Four Dragons" (Hong Kong, South Korea, Taiwan, and Singapore) and, later, mainland China. Four of the economies of East Asia— China, Hong Kong, Taiwan, and Singapore—are said to be populated mainly by "Chinese" (however loosely defined); several others—Japan, Korea, Vietnam—are thought to have been influenced by Confucian thought (which stresses strong family, commitment to education, dependence on kinship, collective welfare rather than individual good, and social networks); and the visible economic role played by "overseas Chinese" communities in many Southeast Asian countries (Thailand, Malaysia, Indonesia, and the Philippines) and in China's economic growth—all of these have generated interest in "Chinese" links to regional capitalism. The term "Chinese capitalism" has been used to characterize capitalist accumulation in the Pacific Rim.

One of the popular arguments concerning the role of the "Chinese" in East Asian development is that "China" itself is not limited to Mainland China and its official state and cultural boundaries (Ang 1998, 225). In the late 1980s and early 1990s, at a time when the Dragon economies were ascendant, some scholars had advocated the use of the term "Cultural China" to encompass not just the societies populated by ethnic "Chinese" (Taiwan, Hong Kong, Singapore), but also "overseas Chinese" communities in Southeast Asia, and intellectuals or professionals working on China or the Chinese world (most prominent of these advocates was Tu Wei-ming 1991, 22). This idea of "Cultural China" had sought to direct attention away from Mainland China as the "core" toward the so-called former periphery of smaller Asian countries and the so-called Chinese diaspora in Southeast Asia that, in the 1990s (i.e., before mainland China became the economic powerhouse it now is), were viewed as engines of capitalist development. This idea assumed that even though the "Chinese" have been physically separated from "China"—the source of "Chinese culture"—nonetheless they have not lost their sense of "Chinese identity" (Wu 1991, 160). Another term, "Greater China," also gained currency as a description of the shared identity generated by interactions among Chinese-language speaking (Sinophone) populations in China, Hong Kong, Macau, and Taiwan, mainly through the circulation of popular cultural products, such as music, films, and TV shows, and through the dissemination of information and the youth culture (Chun 1996, 127).

In these past decades, "Chinese" has come to be viewed in a positive light and even as an object of desire, as evident in the current public clamor for generic "East Asian"-looking (i.e., *chinito* ["young Chinese"] features and a different shade of "white" skin) Taiwanese and Korean telenovela (television drama) actors who play rich, successful, and/or powerful men and foreground the attractions of affluent East Asia as *the* leading growth center of the global capitalist world economy.

Terms like "Cultural China" and "Greater China" are imaginable because they rely in part on cultural explanations to account for both the economic success and the cultural distinctiveness of the "Chinese."[13] "Chinese" cultural traits and factors are said to operate in the form of *mianzi* (face), *xinyong* (trust), *guanxi* (relationships, or connections), family-centered kinship structures, and ideologies that supposedly form the bulwarks of "Chinese" business and the "Confucian" or "Chinese model" of East Asian capitalism, and ethnic-based social, business, and transnational networks. These cultural explanations are actively propagated by the popular media (including journalism), scholarship, states, schools, and books, everyday "observations" at the ground level, and to some extent by the self-representation of those who call themselves "Chinese." Business management schools and their textbooks now routinely use *guanxi* (networking), *mianzi* ("face"), and *xinyong* (trust) to describe "Chinese" economic practices, arguing that these cultural traits are necessary to ensure harmonious work relations in family firms and make good management decisions (Yao 2002, 12). Culture has its political uses: In Singapore, "Confucian values" were used to explain the country's achievement of economic growth and modernization through the "Asian way" while in Taiwan, the government has sought to legitimize its claim that it is the true representative and guardian of Chinese culture (Chun 1996, 114, 116).

But there are clear limits to "culturalist" perspectives on "Chinese" identity and economic power. Many of the cultural explanations assume that Chinese is a linguistic and cultural group who evince remarkable cultural cohesion and economic power. But to speak of "Chinese culture" is to immediately raise the questions: what is Chinese and how Chinese is "Chinese" culture? The question of who is "Chinese" is a difficult and contentious issue, considering that "Chinese" is often defined as the majority "Han" population who constitute 94 percent of the Mainland Chinese population, even though the non-Han population is spread out over

60 percent of Chinese territory (Wu 1991, 167). The Bai people of Yunnan assert their difference from other Chinese, even though these differences are partly defined and promoted by the Chinese state policy on minority peoples. The *peranakan* of Indonesia call themselves Chinese, even though many of them no longer speak any Chinese language. In Papua New Guinea, poor Chinese are often not counted as Chinese, but are considered native (170–76). Mainland Chinese call themselves Hanren (referring to the Han Dynasty), but many overseas Chinese call themselves Tangren (people of the Tang Dynasty) and refer to their homeland as Tangshan (Tang Mountains), which is not China, but their local village(s). A politics of Chinese language is at work in that Mandarin is considered the official language, while other Chinese tongues are referred to as "dialects" to mark their subordination to the official language, even though many of these dialects are mutually unintelligible (Chow 1998, 10). As for "Chinese" dominance of the Southeast Asian economies, the figures cited often reveal nothing about how the amounts were arrived at (for a critique of these "statistics" purporting to show Chinese economic dominance, see Hodder 2005, 8–9, 25–26n1).

In the Philippine case, the fabled "Chinese networks"—routinely invoked in accounts of Philippine Chinese economic success—across and beyond the Asian region do not really hold conceptual and empirical water. Chinese-Filipino investments in China do not rely on preexisting ethnic-based linkages with Filipino-Chinese, other overseas Chinese, or even Mainland Chinese capital, let alone "a sense of patriotism toward China" (Cariño 2001, 117), but on the formulation by the Chinese government of policies specifically to make investment attractive for overseas Chinese (Gomes and Hsiao 2001, 15). Theresa Chong Cariño (2001, 111) shows that among Chinese big businesses, there is more evidence of competition than cooperation,[14] and joint ventures with Hong Kong or Taiwanese companies are based on considerations of expertise, technology, and capital rather than ethnic ties. She also argues that the diversification of Chinese-Filipino business is not a "method of rationalizing business, but of hedging against economic downturns or vulnerabilities in situations of high economic and political volatility" (117). Neither is there anything essentially "Chinese" about Chinese business practices, given the heterogeneity of business styles employed by the biggest Chinese companies. No research has ascertained whether small- and medium-scale "Chinese" enterprises share a "cultural style" of business management (23).

Neither are "Chinese" cultural traits, such as thrift, industry, perseverance, and sacrifice, uniquely "Chinese" nor even particular to the "merchant" as occupation (Wang 2003b, 208). Not only are they produced and reinvented in specific histories and societies and not only are their "ethnic" origins uncertain, they have also been reified so as to serve as ideological justifications *for* authoritarianism and *against* socialism. In this formulation, so-called Confucian values and practices are said to ground a historical form of capitalism, which had hitherto been constrained by socialism but which, allowed to flourish in nonsocialist "Greater China" (Singapore, Hong Kong, Taiwan, and "overseas Chinese" communities in Southeast Asia) and in a post-Maoist China, now undergoing capitalist transformation, allegedly constitutes a *superior* capitalism to that which developed in the West because of the former's communitarian (as opposed to individualist) ethos (see the thoughtful critiques of this assumption by Wang 1992d; 2003b; Dirlik 1997a; Cheah 2001). The problem with using cultural explanations to account for Chinese economic success in East Asia is that these explanations rely on simplistic, homogeneous notions of "Chinese culture" or "values" transmitted unproblematically over time. They do not explain exactly how cultural factors take shape and function (or fail to function), under conditions marked by contingency, to mediate entrepreneurship by investing the "making of business" (*zuo shengyi*) with social and existential meaning (Yao 2002, 99).

It is not possible to adopt a unified and homogeneous notion of "Chinese" culture and assume that this culture is equally shared by all ethnic Chinese. Rather, "Chineseness" is part of a politics of ethnicity by which states, communities, and individuals attempt to construct or inculcate national and ethnic identities for different purposes and projects and within contexts of often asymmetrical power relations. Culture and identity are subject to negotiation and contestation as they are selectively chosen, continually reinvented, adapted, resisted, evaded, circumscribed, or circumvented by even self-defined "Chinese" in the course of their everyday lives. Even though the myths of "Chinese" capitalism and culture do not withstand serious scrutiny and historical experience, these ideological constructions retain their political and popular appeal.

What stands out in *Mano Po* is its deployment of mestizoness as the metaphor for the strategic hybridity claimed by "Chinese Filipinos." Since most Filipinos are likely to view Sinicized mestizo and "pure" Chinese as simply "Chinese," internal distinctions between "pure" and "mixed" ancestry matter less in current Filipino ideas of the "Chinese" than in historical terms like "mestizo" and the Hokkien *tsut-si-a*. It is Filipino ideas of mestizoness, however, that have changed over the past two to three decades, as third-generation acculturated Chinese Filipinos (including "pure Chinese"), now safely Filipinized, take on the attributes of mestizos whose "whiteness" (fair skin) becomes a highly valued and desirable asset. Moreover, this kind of mestizoness has strong generational, class, and spatial elements, since it pertains to third-generation or fourth-generation upper-class "Chinese" whose families have moved out of Binondo and into suburbs like Greenhills, Corinthian Gardens, and Grace Village (and the even more exclusive Forbes Park and Dasmariñas Village), and who matriculate at De La Salle High School, Xavier School, and Immaculate Concepcion Academy (ICA), through which they are most likely to socialize with their Filipino peers from similarly exclusive schools, such as the Ateneo de Manila. These "Chinese" who appear "mestizo"-like define themselves against both "Binondo Chinese" and new-migrant TDKs (Tai Diok Ka, "mainlanders," meaning new migrants), who have not undergone the same path of socialization into upper-class Filipino behavior or norms as their more "sosyal" upperclass counterparts have, even as third- and fourth-generation Binondo Chinese also seek to distinguish themselves from the GIs.[15]

Among middle- to upper-class "Chinese" who went to private schools and grew up watching Hollywood films and English-language television shows, a form of Americanization is part and parcel of their socialization as Chinese Filipinos. Those who can afford to send their children abroad for higher education do so, while private schools place a premium on acquiring proficiency in English rather than (and often at the expense of) Filipino, a fact that may help explain why there is more Chinese-Filipino literary production in English than in Filipino and other Philippine languages (see, for example, Hau 2000a).[16] This pattern of Anglo-Sinicization will be discussed in chapter 7. Suffice it to say that Filipino prejudice against brown skin is shared by Chinese Filipinos. Moreover, while the postwar era has eroded the social boundaries between middle- and upper-class Filipinos and Chinese and younger generations of Chinese have become more aware of their own historical and family legacies of ethnocentrism married to class biases,[17] crosscultural interactions are not always tension-free as "us and them" boundaries get redrawn in everyday life.

Although popular Filipino notions of the "Chinese" do not always concern themselves with blood lineage, this does not mean that the "Chinese" is completely free of the racialist taint of not being *kadugo* (of one's blood) or *kalahi* (of one's "race"). For this reason, the assertion of hybrid mestizoness is especially meaningful to "Chinese Filipinos" who are concerned to stress their double heritage. At the same time, their preference for using the English word "Chinese" as a "neutral" term of self-reference has to do with the fact that *Chinese* enjoys a regional/global currency that the locally oriented *tsinoy* and traditionally loaded *intsik* lack.

Mano Po holds up the crosscultural marriage as the emblematic representation and resolution of the historically entangled but fraught relationship between "Chinese" and "Filipinos." It is not content to argue that the intermingling of Filipino and Chinese cultures is a social fact; it seeks to make the commingling of cultures an incontestable genetic reality. Romantic love that defies the deep-rooted racial prejudices of both Filipinos and Chinese leads to the successful creation of a family unit composed of a Chinese father and Filipino mother (or, less frequently, Filipino father and Chinese mother) and their children. This foregrounding of the cultural mestizoness of the "Chinese Filipino" through the metaphor of biological mestizoness allows the "Chinese Filipino" to claim a "Chineseness" that is indissolubly tied to "Filipinoness" without making "Chinese" reducible to "Filipino." In effect, this enables the "Chinese Filipino" to be safely "Filipinized" without curtailing its ability to mediate, if not acquire, the external sources of social power created by the expanding "Chinese" regional and global economy. In *Mano Po*, the Go family fortune is founded on a Filipino-Chinese marriage, and the union of the third daughter and her Filipino police lover not only continues that crosscultural tradition but makes their offspring "natural" beneficiaries of the privileges and opportunities that accrue to their multiple claims of belonging.

To some extent, the resinification of mestizoness is rooted in the demands of the market. Women are the target audiences and female actors the main attractions of family dramas.[18] The *Mano Po* films were expensive to make, and they needed to recoup their big budgets by capitalizing on bankable stars, many of whom, in line with the traditional Filipino preference for light skin color, are mestizos. At the same time, these mestizos have to be coded securely as "Chinese" in the eyes of the moviegoers, hence the filmmakers' decision to resort to contrivances such as making them wear silk Chinese costumes or extensive eye makeup and prostheses. In *Mano Po 2*, the decision to cast Christopher de Leon was explained away in the film by having his character trace his ancestry to a British Army officer stationed in China.

The resinification of Chinese mestizoness allows the "new Chinese" to be internally differentiated from the other mestizo and Filipino elite while simultaneously laying down the conditions for a reconsolidation of elite symbolic capital and power (see the next chapter). "Chinese" mestizoness does not simply empower the "Chinese Filipino" to mediate between the Philippines, on the one hand, and America and Europe or the cosmopolitan west, on the other hand. The "Chineseness" of the "Chinese Filipino" now grants her access to the equally cosmopolitan but also specifically regional social capital produced by cultural and economic flows originating from East Asia. Even though the *Mano Po* films depict the Chinese culture of the past as being feudal, traditional, and backward, the emergence of China as an economic powerhouse and the association of "Chineseness" with "thoroughly modern 'Asian'" affluence (to use a phrase from Szanton Blanc [1996]) have made the "Chinese" an object of fascination and aspiration even for non-"Chinese" Filipinos. This has led even some ethnic Southeast Asian Chinese to selectively "resinify" themselves by restoring their Chinese surnames and acquiring a Chinese-language education (the notion of resinification/resinicization will be discussed in the final chapter). The decision of the mestizo scion of the polygynous Antonio Chan to take up Asian Studies in *Mano Po 2*, for example, attests to the elite's growing inclination to partake of the benefits and opportunities afforded by the growing significance of "Asia" as a region of economic growth. President Corazon Aquino's 1988 visit to Hongjian Village in Fujian Province, China, ancestral home of her great-grandfather, signaled the mestizo reclamation of their Chinese ancestry, even though the acknowledgement of Chinese roots has not completely become a social and political asset.[19]

The Limits of "Chineseness"

But if *Mano Po* underscores the potentials of "Chinese" identification with a changing, pluralist Philippine state and with regional capitalism, it also exposes the limits of this multiple identification.

Foremost among the limits is the mediation of "Chinese" dealings with the state and its various agencies and representatives by money. *Mano Po* shows how the Chinese attempted to overcome their vulnerability by relying on their own family for support, and on their money to circumvent state repression and exploitation. Money is the main currency for establishing "Chinese" connections with—or, more accurately, for "speaking" to— Filipinos, especially state officials; it may be considered a form of lingua franca by which the "Chinese" (Filipinos, too!) speak to the state. The *Forrest Gump* shots of the apolitical Go patriarch Don Luis hobnobbing with various presidents and government officials testify to the everyday Chinese survival tactic of forming *guanxi* relations with state representatives to ensure protection of their businesses and interests from the arbitrariness of the political and judicial systems. In *Mano Po*, when Philippine National Police director Dioscoro Blanco—a long time "protector" of the family— complains to Daniel Go (Tirso Cruz III) about his daughter Richelle's plan to testify in court and identify Blanco as the notorious "White Sky" involved in drug smuggling and pushing, Go hands him a check for P5 million with the words: *"Tanggapin mo ang pagpaumanhin ko"* (Accept my apologies). In *Mano Po 2*, Johnson (Jay Manalo), the son-in-law of murdered businessman Antonio Chan, pays the investigating detective P2 million to implicate

Chan's first wife, Sol, in the murder charges; but Sol's daughter, Grace, pays the same cop a bag full of money to expose this scam. When the cop protests that his life is on the line (*"Buhay ko ang nakataya dito*, ma'am"), she replies, while handing over the bag: *"Paniguro ng kinabukasan mo"* (Insurance for your future).

In *Mano Po*, the exchange between Vera and her sister Richelle's boyfriend, police officer Rafael (Richard Gomez), hinges on "Chinese" reliance on money to solve difficult problems, especially when the problem takes the form of the state and its claims, or, in this case, Vera's youngest sister Richelle's love affair with the cop, with whom she is working on a drug smuggling exposé. Here, Vera tries to get Rafael (Raf) to break off his relations with her sister.

VERA: *Wala ka ng perang mapapala sa kanya.* (You won't be able to milk her of any more money.)

RAF: *Alam mo, ang problema sa mga taong katulad mo na mayaman, ang tingin mo sa lahat ng bagay, may katumbas na pera.* (You know, the problem with rich people like you is that you think everything has a price.)

VERA: *Talaga namang ginagatasan mo kaming mga Chinese, eh.* (But you really do milk us Chinese.)

RAF: *Kung ganyan ang tingin mo sa amin, bakit naman dito ka pa sa Pilipinas?* (If this is what you think of us, why are you still in the Philippines?)

VERA: *Aminin mo na, talaga ngang pera lang ang tingin mo sa aming mga Chinese di ba?* (Admit it, you only think of us Chinese in terms of money, don't you?)

RAF: *Bakit ganyan ang tingin mo sa sarili mo? Dito ka na pinanganak, dito ka na lumaki, ang kabuhayan ninyo nandito na. Pilipino na rin kayo.* (Why do you see yourself this way? You were born here, you grew up here, you've made your livelihood here. You are also Filipino).

VERA: *Tinuring mo ba kaming kagaya niyo? Sa sampung kinidnap, ilan ang Chinese? O baka naman talagang nagkataon lamang na mas marami sa amin ang gusto ninyong kidnapin?* (Did you treat us just like one of you? For every ten kidnappings, how many are Chinese? Or is it just a coincidence that you want to kidnap more of us?)

RAF: *Lumaban kayo, magkaisa kayo...Ang problema sa inyo, wala kayong tiwala sa amin.* (Fight back, unite...The problem with you is you don't have faith in us.)

VERA: Five million, Mr. Rafael Bala.

RAF: *Sa ginagawa mong iyan, iniinsulto mo ang sarili mo.* (You insult yourself by doing that.)

This exchange discloses, among other things, a "nationalist" logic at work in a number of spectacular kidnapping incidents that victimize rich ethnic Chinese (see chap. 3). But it also reveals the two characters' fundamental ambivalence toward the nation. Raf's attitude, which oscillates between affirmation of the "Filipinoness" of the Chinese (*"Pilipino na rin kayo"* [You're already Filipino]) and resentment of the rich (*"mga taong katulad mo na mayaman"* [people like you who are rich]), reflects the tension within Filipino nationalism between the capacity for inclusiveness of the Filipino nation, on the one hand, and the exclusions generated by class that create deep divisions within the nation, on the other hand (as discussed in chap. 3). Vera's responses, which strongly negate Raf's (and the state's) good intentions, also lay bare the limits of nationalism by justifying Chinese lack of trust in the state authorities who have traditionally exploited the discourse of nationalism to fleece the Chinese. Her cynicism indicates the extent to which the Chinese—historically identified with money—have relied on money to speak and act for them, precisely because the nationalist rhetoric and practice of citizenship and belonging are not just inadequate to shield the Chinese against harassment but also often serve as the very instruments of extortion. In *Mano Po 3*, the daughter of anticrime crusader Lilia Chiong Veloso tells her aunt at the police station that the police were asking for money, and when the aunt confronts the police about fleecing the Chinese (*"Pinag-iinitan ninyo kami dahil Chinese kami"* [You're putting the heat on us because we're Chinese]), the irate policemen respond by saying that they are doing their job, and express their resentment of the rich (*"Paninindigan namin ito"* [We stand by this]). Lilia herself explodes when she hears the released kidnap gang leader, a policeman, declare brazenly his innocence on television.

While money has the capacity to transform ethnic Chinese into kidnap victims, it can also be used to pursue a brand of justice not often available in official courts. In talking to the authorities to try to find their father's killer in *Mano Po 2*, daughter Janet (Carmina Villaroel) asks her sister Grace (Judy Ann Santos): *"Magkano raw para may masabi sila?"* (How much does it take to make them speak?) Money can be the main instrument for exacting vengeance: when Lilia is feared missing, her son attempts to interrogate the chief kidnap suspect by offering money, and, when the suspect laughs it off, tells him: *"Kung may kinalaman kayo, alam namin kung saan ka matutunton*" (If you have anything to do with [her disappearance]...we know where to find you).

But if money can buy justice and protection not obtainable from the state, the roots of Chinese vulnerability also lie in the capacity of money to provoke popular resentment and retribution. When Antonio Chan is murdered, the family finds it hard to believe that the murder is a random act of robbery. Even the police begin their investigation by asking if Chan had fired or humiliated an employee. Class relations being so contentious in the Philippines, Chinese capitalists become vulnerable to a form of "nationalist" vengeance,[20] which crosses over class *ressentiment* into retribution aimed at redressing the shame and loss of dignity caused by humiliation or rejection. The threat and terror of state violence and popular vengeance expose the limits of "Chinese" belonging. In *Mano Po 3*, Lilia loses her first love Michael (Christopher de Leon) when the latter's family migrates to the U.S. to escape harassment by the state after Michael is detained for possession of anti-Marcos documents and involvement in the anti-Marcos movement.

Thus, however careful *Mano Po* may be in adumbrating the integration of ethnic Chinese into the Filipino nation, the fact that characters like Vera make the decision *not* to leave the Philippines (despite plans to relocate to Canada following the kidnapping trauma) indicates that, had the rescue operations ended in tragedy, the Go's may "choose" to leave after all, as millions of working Filipinos have done in light of the failure of the state to deliver welfare, security, and prosperity to the Filipino population. The situation of the second sister, Juliet Go-Co, whose husband plans to set up business in Shanghai, underscores the way in which "Chinese," like the capital with which they have become identified,[21] have the potential to create new channels of flows that may potentially breach and exceed the boundaries of the nation-state.

Filipino Identification with the "Chinese" Region

Like *Mano Po*, *Crying Ladies* knits together the multiple, conflicting strands of associations surrounding money and its identification with the "Chinese." But whereas *Mano Po* looks at Pinoy-Chinese relations from the perspective of the Chinese Filipino, *Crying Ladies* views Pinoy-Chinese interactions from the viewpoint of Filipinos. Not surprisingly, the *Crying Ladies* brand of happy ending provides an altogether different resolution of the problem of Chinese identification with money. Where *Mano Po* attempts to reterritorialize "Chineseness" by embedding the "Chinese" within the Philippine nation, *Crying Ladies* attempts to defuse the class tensions and nationalist resentment ignited by "Chineseness" by turning deterritorialized "Chinese" flows and connections into sources of Filipino self-advancement. In other words, whereas *Mano Po* puts a premium on the value of Chinese Filipino attachment to the Philippines, *Crying Ladies* suggests that the value of being Chinese Filipino lies precisely in its ability to mediate connections with the outside, especially the Philippines' economically better-performing East Asian neighbors, and in so doing provide capital and opportunities that Filipinos can tap. Like their mestizo counterparts, ethnic Chinese are now held up as models of entrepreneurship for their ability to parlay their (culturally mestizo) heritage and linkages into different kinds of capital—cultural, social, symbolic, and especially economic.

Crying Ladies follows three Filipino professional mourners hired by a young Chinese Filipino, Wilson Chua (played by the Chinese-Spanish mestizo

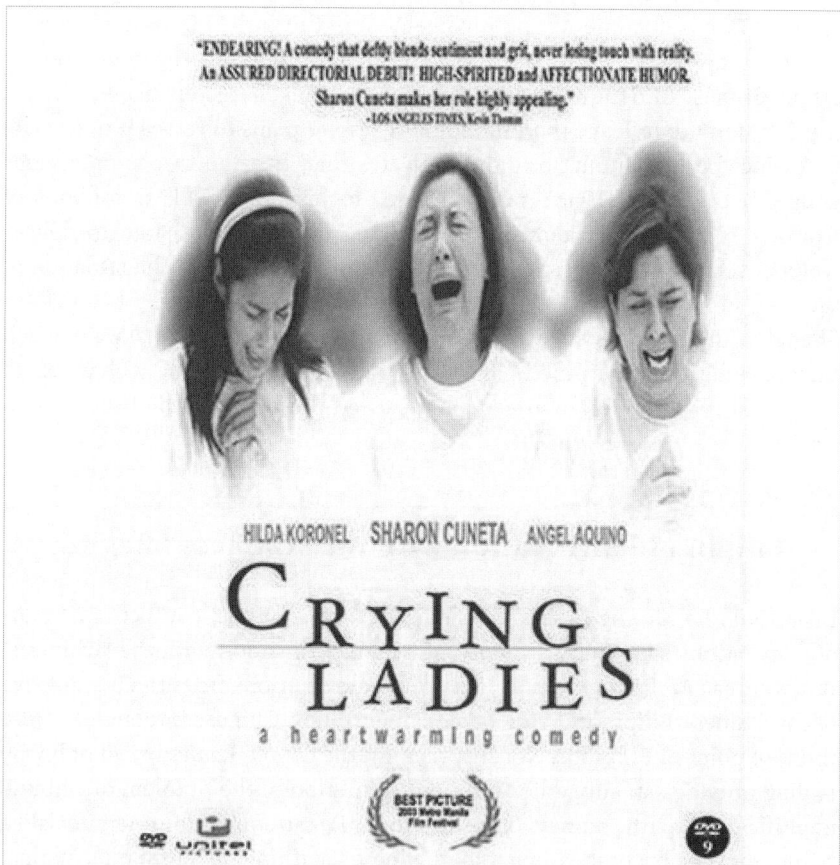

"ENDEARING! A comedy that deftly blends sentiment and grit, never losing touch with reality. An ASSURED DIRECTORIAL DEBUT! HIGH-SPIRITED and AFFECTIONATE HUMOR. Sharon Cuneta makes her role highly appealing." -LOS ANGELES TIMES, Kevin Thomas

HILDA KORONEL SHARON CUNETA ANGEL AQUINO

CRYING LADIES
a heartwarming comedy

BEST PICTURE
2003 Metro Manila
Film Festival

Crying Ladies

actor Eric Quizon), to work at his father's wake. The main protagonist, Stella (Sharon Cuneta), had once been jailed for estafa, and finds out that the dead man for whom she must cry was the one who had her jailed. Stella comes off as a trickster figure whose main preoccupation is with money, be it to obtain money or evade the obligations entailed by monetary exchange. The estafa case is an example of her attempt to escape monetary obligations by passing bouncing checks, but so is Stella's ploy of getting a free jeepney ride. Stella also exploits an ongoing workers' strike (directed at a corporation with the revealing name of El Rico, "The Rich") to masquerade as a striker and collect contributions from sympathetic bus passengers. Stella's laborious efforts to make money are mirrored in her predilection for gambling, the allure of which lies in its promise of generating money out of thin air through the machinations of luck (*suwerte*).

Here, money, or the threat of its absence, weighs heavily on Stella and her family. Stella's disillusionment with the ability of the state to provide services and a decent living is summed up in her frustrated exclamation at the repeated blackouts: "Brownout *na naman, anong klaseng gobyerno 'to!*" (Brownout again, what kind of government is this!) Her inability to give up her trickster ways and her perennial indebtedness from gambling and from constantly asking for *bale* (cash advance) from her Chinese employer (whose own business is not exactly flourishing) force her to relinquish her son to her former husband and his second wife, who plan to relocate to Cagayan de Oro (note the reference to gold) and offer the child a stable family environment and a future. Stella's need to earn a living forces her to leave her son under someone else's care; when a fire breaks out, Stella teeters on the brink of hysteria at the thought that her son may have been trapped alone in their house. Stella's attempts to apply for a job abroad as a cultural singer are thwarted by lack of singing talent and by the state because of a black mark on her National Bureau of Investigation (NBI) file. Not surprisingly, her thoughts are almost always of money—money problems even enter her subconscious in the form of an extended dream sequence in which Stella by sheer luck wins a slot as a contestant at a *Salapi o Salakot* TV game show, where she gets a chance to play for the million-peso prize money.

The gambling and tricksterisms she engages in are but small-scale versions of the speculative capital that is generated in such "legitimate" venues as the stockmarket and real estate. While gambling operates on the premise of magical accumulation, the odds against winning often end up impeding capital accumulation.[22] The magical qualities of capital, the ability of capital to multiply manifold, are spotlighted at the dead Chinese capitalist's wake—each day of the wake, a calligrapher writes down in Chinese characters the amount of donation in the tens of thousands of pesos from family friends of the dead man. Not only can money enable the dead Chinese's widow to buy grief (Wilson's mother at one point sharply tells Stella and her friends that they are being paid to mourn, not joke and laugh) to ensure her husband's safe passage to the afterworld, it allows the young Chinese-Filipino son to continue paying lip service to a dying tradition he no longer believes in. More, the death of the capitalist does not truncate capital accumulation, but inspires yet another round of accumulation. Professional mourning—now "subcontracted" to Filipinos because there is no more Chinese labor for hire and because the practice itself is dying out in the Chinese community—is a commodification of the ideology that seeks to marry wealth with virtue: those who are rich also have to earn virtue by being good and helpful, so that the outpouring of grief following their death assures them an easier passage to heaven. Money supplements private grief by securing the merit and virtue of the dead.

Stella's one-dimensional view of the dead man is complicated by the testimonials of the dead man's friends, but their positive portraits of the man are sealed off from her by her inability to understand Hokkien. The use of Chinese languages in the Philippine setting is one of the primary markers of "Chinese" alienness. Conversations conducted in Hokkien among "Chinese" in front of Filipinos have been known to elicit Filipino jokes about *"Binebenta na tayo"* (We're already being sold), remarks that derive their amusement/reproach value from the commonsensical identification of "Chineseness" with commercial and capitalist exchange.[23] *Crying Ladies*, like the *Mano Po* films, strives to render the "Chinese" scrutable by providing subtitled translations of the Hokkien dialogues. But the fact that these dialogues are translated (sometimes not accurately) into English rather than Filipino reinforces class difference in linguistic terms by linking Hokkien to the language of power and privilege in the Philippines and, in so doing, making the act of speaking Hokkien equivalent to "spokening in dollars" in their common allusion to money and exchange.[24]

Crying Ladies is at pains to defuse the potential antagonisms generated by class-coded ethnic difference, but it does so by distinguishing the "new Chinese" from the "old Chinese." Although the "Chinese" family's grief speaks to Stella across the chasm of their class differences, and moves her, class reconciliation in the film is mainly posited through Stella's deepening friendship with the dead Chinese's male heir, Wilson, whose business connections grant her access to Chinese money and, most important, connections.[25] Unlike his dead father, who can no longer speak for himself and whose good character and human frailties are spoken of in private and mainly in Hokkien, the culturally mestizo Wilson is "Filipino" enough to be able to communicate with Stella across the barriers of class, language, and ethnicity, but his added value for Stella inheres in his "Chinese" connections. The dead father remains as alien to Stella as the Philippine state itself: she knows him only as the intsik who had put her in jail and who, she hears, once had someone beaten up for failure to pay his or her debt. Her encounter with the son of the dead Chinese proves more rewarding: Wilson gives her a fat bonus and subsequently introduces her to a Japanese production company looking to hire karaoke video talents. Stella finally establishes herself as an award-winning video actress and presumably begins earning a decent living.

Crying Ladies tracks the socialization of Stella from trickster (whose attempts to conjure money are penalized as inappropriate by the system) into karaoke talent (whose wage-determined contract labor, now appropriate, buys her social respectability). Stella's trickster ways are attempts to evade the strictures of a state that has failed to alleviate the miseries of the majority of its population. (Similarly, her enterprising Filipino neighbor sidesteps Philippine laws prohibiting gambling by buying unclaimed cadavers and staging fake funerals as a front for gambling. Fake mourning and its commodified rituals have become a source of livelihood.) If the dead "Chinese" had once acted as an agent of her penalization by the state, his Chinese-Filipino heir becomes the agent of her socialization into the culture of chance and dream of upward mobility, all without recourse to state intervention. *Crying Ladies* makes the "Chinese" the exemplar of capital accumulation and the epitome of regional flows.[26] Stella's connections with Wilson Chua are vital to her social upliftment and legitimacy because it is Wilson's *guanxi* networking with fellow East Asian entrepreneurs, such as the Japanese videoke producer, that leads to Stella's discovery as an actress and delivery from the drudgery and inadequate living of manual labor. More crucially, this guanxi network enables her to circumvent the penalties of a permanent black mark on her NBI record which had long prevented her from being able to work abroad. In the fantasy world of equal parts individual luck and merit conjured up by *Crying Ladies*, a personal guarantee from Wilson is enough to persuade the Japanese producer to overlook Stella's estafa conviction and judge her not on the basis of the state's penalizing of her past actions but on her talent, potential, and "true" worth as a human being. Ironically, then, this form of meritocracy is dependent precisely on "Chinese" connections that have often been viewed as typical of East Asian capitalism, yet also stigmatized as "market corruption" because they bypass state regulation and legitimation.

Crying Ladies and *Mano Po* anchor their plots on the stereotypical identification of the "Chinese" with capital. Yet these films already stand at a distance from the nationalism of anti-Chinese films, such as *Maynila, sa Mga Kuko ng Liwanag* (discussed in chap. 3), not because Chinese ethnicity is no longer associated with capital (on the contrary, the identification is closer now than ever), but because the kind of commercial ethos that prioritizes capital accumulation and consumption has become a lot more pervasive, and organizes the lives of growing numbers of Filipinos who, through internal and international migration, find themselves living (and dreaming) in urban market-mediated environments. This growing Filipino identification with "Chineseness" is borne out in Philippine cinema most recently by the "Chinese-ization" of even Filipino superstars with strong *kayumanggi* (brown-skin) appeal (to use Bliss Lim's term [2009]). In 2011, the latest installment of the *Mano Po* franchise, *Hototay: Mano Po 7*, began production with Nora Aunor, the most iconic actress with mass appeal, in the starring role, while Robin Padilla, an action star also known for his brown-skinned "man of the masses" appeal, signed up for a reboot of the classic Chiquito starring vehicle, *Mr. Wong* (see chap. 2). (Tellingly, however, both films were subsequently withdrawn from the 2011 Metro Manila Film Festival owing to production delays and problems.)

Mano Po and *Crying Ladies* show that while Pinoy-Chinese relations are viewed differently by non-Chinese Filipinos (as opportunities for tapping "Chinese" capital and regional "Chinese" networks) and Chinese Filipinos (as opportunities for demonstrating "Chinese" embeddedness in the Filipino nation while also appropriating regional "Chinese" flows), these two seemingly opposite views are integral aspects of two mutually determining processes—the concomitant revaluation of both "Chineseness" and "Filipinoness." The imperative for integrating the Chinese into the nation is partly conditioned by the Philippine state's desire to utilize "Chinese" capital and connections in the region and beyond. The Chinese Filipino's perceived access to regional and global capital in turn adds to the social and cultural capital of being "Chinese" *and* "Filipino" in the Philippines. The Filipino now finds in either her "Chinese" ancestry or her "Chinese" neighbor a ready means of identifying with emergent, affluent "Asia," even as she or a member of her family is part of a diaspora that includes Chinese Filipinos. Growing regional identification on the part of the Philippine state, the "Chinese," and the "Filipino" does not erase nationness; it reinvents it.

But despite the growing visibility and desirability of "Chinese" entrepreneurial and social power embodied by the hybrid "new Chinese," the category "Chinese" itself remains deeply entangled with the issue of class, which defines its fraught relationship with the Filipino nation and which can potentially reactivate deep-seated ambivalence about, if not resentment of and violence against, alien capital/ists. Adopting the viewpoint of Chinese Filipinos who are particularly sensitive to the real and potential effects of this ambivalence, *Mano Po* attempts to resolve this issue

REGION   229

by providing a politically acceptable resolution that anchors the "Chinese"
firmly to the territorial bounds and narratives of the Philippine nation-
state. Even as it bolsters the commonplace view of the transnationality of
"Chinese" networks through its account of second daughter Juliet Go-Co's
husband's connections in Shanghai, the film opts to conclude by reaffirming
the rootedness of the Chinese Filipino within the Philippines, hence its
recourse to ending the story with eldest daughter Vera's decision to forego
her plan to move to Canada for her peace of mind following the traumatic
kidnapping of her sisters: "*Umalis man ako sa Pilipinas, sa ayaw't gusto
ko, dala ko pa rin ang Pilipinas. Kaya bakit ko pa aalisan ang 'di ko naman
lubusang matatakasan?*" (Even if I were to leave the Philippines, whether I
like it or not, I carry the Philippines with me. So why should I leave what I
cannot completely escape anyway?)

Cristina Szanton Blanc (1997, 272, 275) has commented on the Chinese-
Filipino unease with fully embracing the regional narratives and models
of Asian modernity (and mobility) propounded by emergent economies,
such as Malaysia or Singapore, noting that Taiwanese investments in the
Philippines have been resisted by both Chinese and non-Chinese who view
them as economic competition and quoting Chinese-Filipino members of
Kaisa para sa Kaunlaran as saying: "How can we emphasize our Chineseness
when we still need to make ourselves acceptable to a Filipino electorate?"[27]

This inability to enthusiastically embrace East Asian modernity may
also have to do with the kind of position occupied by the Philippines
within the region. Unlike the other countries, the Philippines has not
been privy to the kind of dramatic economic growth that shaped the myth
of the "East Asian economic miracle." A World Bank (1993) report, in
fact, omitted the Philippines from the list of Asia's "miracle economies."
As Aihwa Ong has argued (1999, 57, 72), discourses of Chinese capitalism
propounded in Singapore operate on the basis of an assumed "hierarchy
of moral and economic performances" that are coded as racial difference
between "Chinese" Singapore and "Malay" Southeast Asian countries,
such as the Philippines. This racial coding demonizes the Philippines
as a country whose economic underperformance is causally linked
to its politically "chaotic" democratic system of government, while
simultaneously legitimizing Singaporean-style authoritarianism for
engineering a high-performance economy. In his memoir, *From Third
World to First: The Singapore Story, 1965–2000* (2000, 299–305), Lee
Kuan Yew famously defined the Philippines as the Other of Singapore, "a
world apart from us, running a different style of politics and government
under an American military umbrella." Lee proceeded to elaborate on
the incompatibility between the American-style separation of powers in

government, on the one hand, and the "culture and habits of the Filipino people that had caused problems for the presidents before Marcos," a culture that he went on to characterize as "soft and forgiving" (304–5). In 2006, when a young voter opined that Singapore could benefit from greater freedom of expression, Lee invoked the political situation in Thailand and the Philippines: "You mean to tell me that what is happening in Thailand and the Philippines is binding the people, building the nation?" (*The Economist,* 2008)

Periodically buffeted by political and economic crises, the Philippines made the historic decision in the mid-1970s—around the time that LOI 270 sought to naturalize the "Chinese alien"—to export officially its labor, a sizeable percentage of which, heavily feminized and concentrated in domestic work and services, is based in countries in East Asia, such as Hong Kong, Taiwan, and Japan. Filipino efforts to partake of East Asian affluence are shadowed by the reality of Filipino workers—mainly female—providing the labor that shores up a number of East Asian economies, feminized labor that uncovers the underside of exploitation of foreign and native labor by state and private sector alike to underwrite the so-called Asian economic miracle. This asymmetry in economic relations between the Philippines and its more prosperous East Asian neighbors does not simply assume the form of a gendered division of labor and a division between skilled and "unskilled" labor (Hau 2004, 227–70), but takes on a racial cast in the contrast between "Chinese" employer and "Filipino" employee (see, for example, Constable 1997).

Not immune to the contagion of regional fantasies of capitalist success and consumption, the Philippine state has been largely unsuccessful in realizing its mission of national development. Under the administration of Fidel Ramos (1992–1998), the Philippines attempted to generate growth rates similar to those in the neighboring countries by initiating a series of financial liberalization programs in hopes of being able to benefit from the windfall of capital flows and investments sweeping through the region. With the Philippine state already so colonized by private interests that it had not been able to reinvent itself along the lines of the developmental state regimes in Japan, South Korea, and Taiwan, a combination of circumstance, happenstance, and structural constraints ensured in the 1990s that "[a]fter protesting vehemently that it is an East Asian economy, not a Latin American one, the Philippines returned to the region's ardent embrace by being swept into the Asian currency crisis" (Montes 1999, 263).

Seen in this light, the ongoing resignifications of Chineseness remain fraught with tension. The Philippines' position within the international capitalist order does not allow it to fully and uncritically embrace the regional discourse of urban middle-class consumption and economic growth. Moreover, the viability of the region depends on its ability to sustain economic growth and offer stability and prosperity (Shiraishi 2006, 268)—the yawning gap between the rich and poor and between urban and rural populations within and, equally important, between nations may engender social crises and rekindle nationalist sentiments, which the elite can capitalize on to protect its vested interests and which ordinary people can draw on in order to articulate their demands for social justice.

More recently, territorial disputes between the Philippines and an increasingly assertive mainland China have provoked nationalist backlash in both countries.[28] Ninety-nine percent of respondents to an online survey conducted by the mainland Chinese rabid-nationalist newspaper, *Global Times* (2011), called on China to take a tougher stance on its dispute with the Philippines over the Spratlys by meting out "substantive punishment" to the Philippines. In the Philippines, the backlash has taken the form of antimainland China rhetoric that has at times shaded off into anti-Chinese slurs against ethnic Chinese, particularly over the Internet. In his *Inquirer* column, Randy David (2012) expressed his concern that "A call to boycott Chinese products will no doubt catch attention, but it will do nothing more beneficial to our people than perhaps to stimulate discussion on the Chinese threat. It may revive the spirit of patriotism among our people by offering them a chance to validate this in their daily lives. But I don't know how one can prevent the complex sentiments it will unleash from sliding into a destructive form of racism. This is what I fear, more than the expected retaliation from our haughty neighbor." This concern appears legitimate in light of public comments, such as *Inquirer* columnist Jose Ma. Montelibano's (2012):

> When China suddenly, and irrationally, claims Scarborough Shoal
> (Panatag Reef) as theirs even though the shoal is less than 200 miles
> from the nearest Philippine shore and about 800 miles from the
> nearest Chinese counterpart shore, I did not know what to make of it.
> I say irrationally because the Philippines is already largely owned by
> Chinese-Filipinos, many of whom sourced goods, credit and capital
> from China. It did not seem useful, or even sane, for China to start
> provoking the Philippines when Chinese-Filipino businessmen, or
> Chinoys, dominate the Philippine economy.[29]

A letter published in the *Philippine Daily Inquirer* (Claver 2012) at the height of the Philippines-China standoff over Scarborough Shoal went so far as to demand that activist crime crusader Teresita Ang-See clarify her position on the issue:

> The Chinese community in the Philippines seems to be so quiet about the Scarborough standoff between the Philippines and China. Where before the Chinese community, through Teresita Ang-See, the outspoken anti-crime crusader and human rights advocate, would make her voice heard whenever political and social issues came to the fore, now it seems that her lips are sealed.
>
> The nation expects Ang-See to support the Philippine claim to Scarborough Shoal, after all she is a Filipino citizen and has lived in the Philippines most of her life or, perhaps, was even born here. Her comforting and wise words, often heard in the past for victims of kidnapping and heinous crimes, are very much needed at this time.
>
> It will show that she cares for her fellow Filipinos and Chinese Filipinos (Tsinoys) who want to resolve the problem as much as everyone does.
>
> Let's hear Ang-See's voice on the current PH-China standoff. Now.

Invoking issues of birth, territoriality, and citizenship ("after all she is a Filipino citizen and has lived in the Philippines most of her life or, perhaps, was even born here"), this letter calls for subjecting Chinese Filipinos to a loyalty test.[30] Chinese Filipinos like Daniel Ong (2012a; 2012b) have written thoughtful articles that draw on legal and academic sources to examine the territorial claims made by the Philippines and China over the Scarborough Shoal, but the ethnicity of their authors renders them vulnerable to being branded as "pro-China," given the uniformity of opinion and lack of informed debate in Philippine newspaper coverage of the issue.[31]

Rethinking "Chinese"

The figure of the "Chinese," like the dead capitalist in *Crying Ladies*, bears the embers of nationalist ambivalence and haunts the new orthodoxy of democratic pluralism and national integration. And the Philippines is not alone. In neighboring countries, such as post-May 1992 Thailand, post-Suharto Indonesia, and multiracial Malaysia, the conjuncture of growing urban middle classes, changing political cultures and economies, and political activism has laid the groundwork for the reinvention of the imagined communities of Thais, Indonesians, and Malaysians. Literature, cinema, and television have played crucial roles in undertaking these nationalist re-imaginings, not least in their attempts to resignify "Chineseness." These reinventions of Chineseness entail conscious interventions in refuting or recuperating longstanding stereotypes that correlate Chineseness with "otherness," with capitalism and communism.

Some, by embellishing the stereotypes, seek to reinvest them with positive meaning. In Thailand, the hugely popular TV drama *Lod Lai Mangkorn* (Through the Dragon Design, 1992), adapted from the novelistic saga—written by Praphassorn Sewikul and serialized in *Sakul Thai* magazine between 1989 and 1990—of a penurious Chinese immigrant turned multimillionaire and aired on the state-run channel, (re)claimed the entrepreneurial virtues of "diligence, patience, self-reliance, discipline, determination, parsimony, self-denial, business acumen, friendship, family ties, honesty, shrewdness, modesty" (Kasian 1997, 76) as "Chinese" in order to hold up the "Chinese" as a figure of emulation. *Lod Lai Mangkorn* rode the crest of a "cultural revolution" (Chang Noi 2009, 122–24) that began with the "rediscovery" and public proclamation from the 1970s onward by leading Thai figures, such as the academic Puey Ungphakorn and politician Kukrit Pramoj, of their Chinese ancestry. Historian Nidhi Eoseewong and

Lod Lai Mangkorn

journalist Sujit Wongthes reclaimed the pejorative *jek* (whose rough English equivalent is "chink") through their arguments about the contribution of the jek to Thai history and culture (222).

Kasian Tejapira (1997) argues that both the novel and the television adaptation of *Lod Lai Mangkorn* issued an explicit challenge against a Thai "official nationalism" that was based on the privileging of a majority Thai ethnic group, an idea that singled out the "Chinese" as the "archenemy" "Jew of the Orient" in King Vajiravudh's (reigned 1910–1925) own words and time and was "later consolidated, expanded and intensified" by the Prime Minister Plaek Phibunsongkhram (1938–1944; 1948–1957).[32] Prior to the twentieth century, cultural notions of Chineseness had been far less important in the eyes of the Chakri kings than the political fealty and economic utility of these "subjects" to the monarchical state. That preeminent symbol of Chineseness, the pigtail, as Kasian Tejapira (2001) has cogently argued, at first signified identification with the Qing Empire (an identification that was resisted by Ming loyalists). Later transformed into a marker of cultural nativism among the jeks, it was mainly viewed by the Thai state as a signifier for a specific administrative category, a specific tax value, and opium addiction. Only later, when Chinese republicanism (which culminated in the 1911 Revolution under Sun Yat-sen) came to be seen as a political threat to the state, did the Thai monarch Vajiravudh (Rama VI) actively propound a racial conception of Thai-ness that was opposed to Chineseness (Kasian 1997).

In recasting the immigrant merchant as a hero, *Lod Lai Mangkorn* spoke to, as well as articulated, a "pluralistic" view of the Thai imagined community that resonated with the interests and concerns of a new generation of middle-class Thais from a range of institutional settings (state, business, academia, and nongovernmental organizations) who had a "globalized outlook and broadly liberal-democratic political views," and were "well-educated (in the country or abroad) and multilingual (in foreign and local languages)" (87). These new urban middle classes had emerged out of "state-centralized and supervised national education system, together with the rapid, state-planned, capitalist economic development" under Sarit Thanarat in 1961, and included a sizeable number of *lookjin* who were born and raised in Thailand, worked in the most advanced sectors of both economy and culture, and possessed economic and consumer clout, while remaining outside the state (86). Like their Chinese-Filipino counterparts, these lookjin (*lukjin*) became politicized and were active in both militant and peaceful social movements, including the October 14, 1973, uprising, the communist armed struggle, and the May Democratic Movement of 1992 (87).

The end of the Thai Communist insurgency (which, like the Communist Party of the Philippines, had links with Communist China), coupled with market reforms in China, and Deng Xiaoping's visit to Thailand served to delink "Chineseness" from its associations with political (communist) radicalism and nationalist Other. King Bumibhol Adulyadej claimed Chinese ancestry, as did Prime Minister Kukrit Pramoj and, later, Thaksin Shinawatra. But it is worth noting that the revival of Chineseness in Thailand in fact preceded mainland China's increasing importance in the Thai economy. It was, in fact, the rise of the region now called "East Asia" as a growth center that led to a shift in the definition of "Thainess" to allow hitherto repressed Chineseness to come out (Kasian 2009a). Regional economic development had spurred the circulation of East Asian (particularly Japanese, Taiwanese, and Hong Kong) popular culture. The popularity of the Taiwanese TV miniseries *Judge Pao* (Bao Zheng) among Thai viewers in the 1990s was instrumental in making Chineseness "chic" (Pasuk and Baker 1996, 139–40).

Kasian (1997, 88) notes, however, that the inclusiveness of this plural notion of community remains to be tested against the reality of continuing exclusions of less affluent and disadvantaged groups (including Laotians, Malays, and indigent Thais) in a situation in which there exists a "real socioeconomic structural lack of community between the city and the countryside, between industry and agriculture, between Bangkok and the rest of the country, and between the awfully rich and the miserable poor." In recent years, these divisions have crystallized in the conflict between "red shirt" supporters of deposed Prime Minister Thaksin Shinawatra (who is of Hakka ancestry) and "yellow shirt" royalists. This conflict has seen the politicization of Thai Chinese on both sides of the divide, but without the politicization translating into the ethnicization of Thai politics (Kasian 2009b). Although "patriotic lookjins" have become politically conscious and active, taking to the streets as yellow shirts and red shirts, with media mogul Sondhi Limthongkul of the People's Alliance for Democracy proudly proclaiming his loyalty to the Thai king while calling on "patriotic Thai-born Chinese" (*lookjin rak chat*) to save the nation, the conflict itself has been represented by both sides in primarily socioeconomic or class—rather than ethnic—terms (ibid.).

In Indonesia, journalist and student activist Soe Hok Gie (1942–1969)[33] was the subject of Riri Riza's biopic *Gie* (2005, produced by Mira Lesmana), based on the activist's diaries and at the time of release the most expensive Indonesian film ever made after 1998. Unlike the rags-to-riches formula adopted by *Lod Lai Mangkorn*, *Gie* set out to explode a different stereotype of the "Chinese." While *Lod Lai Mangkorn* provided a corrective to the

Lebih baik diasingkan daripada menyerah terhadap kemunafikan.

GIE

A Film by Riri Riza

miles FILMS

Gie

image of the "Chinese" as "mafia villains, stingy, bloodsucking shopkeepers, and cultured buffoons" (Kasian 1997, 76), *Gie* targeted the idea of the "Chinese" as apolitical "material man" and Suharto crony by glamorizing a Chinese Indonesian who was an intellectual, an activist, and not rich.

In Indonesia and Malaysia, intermarriages between Chinese and natives had produced a stable "third culture" of *peranakan* and *baba*, whom Dutch and British colonial policies classified as "Chinese" and whom the colonial systems of social hierarchy, privileges, and incentives discouraged from assimilating into native society. Fresh waves of migration from China in the late nineteenth century created pressures to Sinicize on the part of the baba. As their political awakening preceded that of the successful anti-Manchu revolution in China, the peranakan worked through their modern identification as "Chinese" by means of active participation in Indies politics (Coppel 1976, 31). In the 1950s up to the mid-1960s (particularly 1963–1965), China and Indonesia under Soekarno's Guided Democracy enjoyed close relations that led to the coinage of the term "Pyongyang-Beijing-Jakarta Axis."[34] But Suharto viewed Communist China as the major foreign threat to his regime, and enacted a series of regulations to place ethnic Chinese of both Chinese and Indonesian citizenship under surveillance and to forcibly integrate the "Chinese." Since 2000, Chinese New Year (Imlek) has been officially celebrated in Indonesia, after decades of legal restrictions governing access to economic opportunities and Chinese-language education, use of Chinese names, and public observance of Chinese customs and ceremonies.[35] The bloody events of 1965–1966 that propelled Suharto to power victimized Indonesians and Chinese alike, but are remembered by ethnic Chinese elsewhere chiefly as anti-Chinese killings.

Soe Hok Gie's name had been linked with the Indonesian Socialist Party (Partai Sosialis Indonesia, PSI), which was established in 1948 as a splinter group of the Socialist Party. The PSI was banned by Soekarno under Guided Democracy because some of its leaders, with support from the American Central Intelligence Agency, had joined the regional rebellion of 1958–1959 against Jakarta. Educated in the University of Indonesia, Gie joined a youth organization that had ties with the PSI and became famous in 1965 for spearheading a movement among students to "stick to a moral political role, and not sell themselves to the military or the existing parties" (Anderson 2012). Although he was generally opposed to the Indonesian Communist Party (Partai Komunis Indonesia, PKI) and its subsidiary organizations, he courageously denounced the 1965–1966 massacres. His master's thesis, "Di bawah lentera merah" (Under the Red Lantern, published in 1990), looked at how the nationalist and socialist movements shaped the history of the Semarang branch of the Sarekat Islam, the first politically based nationalist organization in the Dutch East Indies; the thesis was dedicated to "all those who sacrificed themselves for the Revolution, no matter what their ideology" (Anderson 2012). His untimely death, by gas poisoning while mountain-climbing in Semeru in 1969, in contrast with the "success" enjoyed by many of the friends and cohorts who outlived him, made him a powerful figure of nostalgia for (lost) youthful idealism. This ambiguous allure of Soe Hok Gie would have an important bearing on his posthumous reputation.[36]

Gie's call for the Indonesian *mahasiswa* (student) to take a moral stance to gain a degree of autonomy from the factionalism of political parties was what attracted director Riri Riza to his subject (Abidin 2012, 136).[37] As Abidin Kusno (ibid.) writes: "For members of the post-Suharto generation, the retrieval of this figure serves various purposes. It allows people to come to terms with the guilt of past ignorance and responsibility to create a new subjectivity for the present and future generations." The romanticization of 1960s activism, as Ariel Heryanto (2008) also points out, had its political uses during the New Order era, when the short life of Soe Hok Gie provided a powerful counterculture image of the idealistic, uncompromising, and soulful Indonesian (85–86). But this mythologizing of the Chinese

Indonesian as a "morally 'pure,' intellectually superior, and politically ideal hero," a "model citizen" (85), does not sit well in a post-Suharto Indonesia in which nostalgia for the New Order coexists alongside a more generalized political apathy among the younger generation.

Moreover, Ariel Heryanto identifies two problems with the film. First, its valorizing of the anti-Communist Soe Hok Gie who joins an army-supported rally against the Communists and whose main interests are actually portrayed as lying outside of political activism (87) does not significantly depart from the language and stereotypes of the New Order itself. Second, its singling out of the ethnic Chinese is not successfully translatable onscreen, as seen in its choice of a Eurasian actor, the German-Indonesian mestizo Nicholas Saputra, for the starring role (86). Heryanto points to the persistence of "Chinese blood" as a dominant metaphor for thinking about Chinese ethnicity, and how this continues to play out in assumptions of the distinctiveness of "Chinese" and "indigenous," "whose co-existence can be in harmony or conflict" (90).

In the award-winning hit movie, *Sepet* (Slit-eyes, 2005), Yasmin Ahmad used the cross-cultural love story to reflect on the vicissitudes of multiracialism in Malaysia and expose the ways in which stereotypes of, and by, both Chinese and Malays manage and complicate race relations. An important indication of the relevance of East Asian cultural flows is the fact that the film tells the story of a well-to-do Malay girl named Orked whose passion for East Asian pop culture (including Wong Kar-wai's films) leads her to befriend and fall in love with a working-class Chinese boy named Ah Loong (who was named after martial arts icon Bruce Lee, but calls himself Jason), whom she first meets when she patronizes his pirated video compact discs stand in Ipoh in search of films featuring her favorite actor, the Japanese-Taiwanese Takeshi Kaneshiro. In the film, characters engage in frequent code-switching, speaking in a mix of languages—Malay, Cantonese, English, and Hokkien. Orked shares with Jason's friend Keong a taste for Hong Kong director John Woo's films, and her parents dance to Thai pop music. When Orked's parents find out about her relationship with Jason, they do not object to it. Orked learns about Jason's passion for writing poetry, and defends him against her Malay classmates in school. But the relationship becomes strained when Jason gets another girl pregnant, and Orked accepts a scholarship to study in London. Jason is badly injured in a road accident on his way to the airport, and the film ends with Orked on the phone, listening to the voice of Jason telling her they will meet again.

The film attracted both positive and negative reviews for its unconventional account of multiracialism in Malaysia. The film's use of *bahasa rojak* (code-switching between two or more languages on a Malay

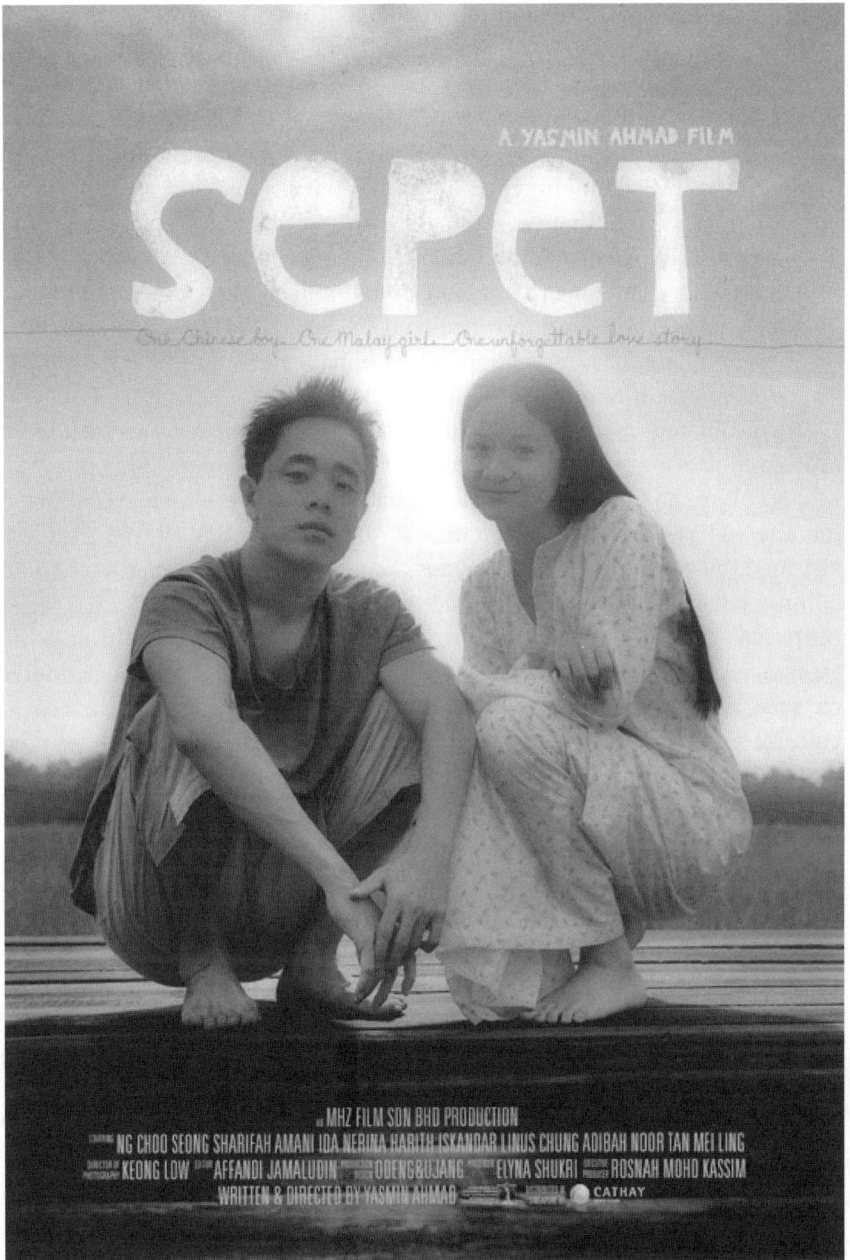

Sepet

base) and the scenes in which the audience learns that Orked was able to get a scholarship while Jason was denied one, despite his higher grades, attracted condemnation. On April 23, 2006, a forum called "*Sepet* and *Gubra* [its sequel] Mencemar Budaya" (Sepet and Gubra Corrupt Culture), sponsored by the "Fenomena Seni" (Arts Phenonema) program, was aired live over the TV channel owned by Radio Television Malaysia. Fifty-nine percent of its live audience voted to affirm the forum's position (Farah 2008). Film critic Akmal Abdullah, one of the panelists, stated that Malay Muslims find it confusing that a pious Muslim like Orked would fall in love with a Chinese "kafir" (infidel) criminal (*The Sun,* 2006).

The template for the creation of a national culture in Malaysia was set by the Ministry of Sports, Youth and Culture's National Culture Policy in 1971. Formulated in the wake of the bloody race riots in 1969—which were attributed to the lack of management of racial differences—this policy set Malay culture and Islam as the bases of national culture; although it allowed for the incorporation of elements of "other" cultures, it nevertheless affirmed the centrality of a "Malayness" equated with Islam in the national culture (Gabriel 2011, 355–57). In her study, Sharmani Patricia Gabriel (2011, 364) argues that *Sepet*'s articulation of "nationhood through its transracial images, while offering a challenge to the reigning hegemonies on race, constitute creative representations of the dynamic practices of cultural translation, exchange, and borrowings on the ground. These new textual and social principles of transracial solidarity and identification, especially visible since the 1990s, as people, consciously or not, translate themselves into a new cultural framework, were arguably bolstered by the climate of cultural liberalization that marked that decade." Gabriel links the production of these new transracial images to the growing "cultural complexity and racial 'incommensurability' of Malaysian realities" (358) as reflected in the rise of "interracial relationships" and the "hybrid" offspring of mixed unions, interethnic alliances in the political arena, and the expansion of an urbanized, English-educated, professional Malay middle class (356–57).

These Southeast Asian films, with their depictions of supposedly "Chinese" values, rituals and family, may not be completely purged of the (self-)Orientalizing (to use Dirlik's term [1997b, 45], based on Said 1979) impulse. But their main concern has been with how "Chineseness" figures and works (and can be refigured or reworked) in contemporary settings outside China. For them, the history of "Chineseness" begins not in (admittedly) politically charged representations of premodern or communist China, but in the passage to modern Southeast Asia and its particular entanglements; the filmic or telenovela narratives typically treat their protagonists' time in

China as a kind of sojourn, and focus on their lives in Southeast Asia. What *Mano Po* and *Crying Ladies*, and *Lod Lai Mangkorn, Gie*, and *Sepet* show is that allegedly "Chinese" values and experiences are nurtured less by "Chinese tradition" of "Chinese culture" than by specific geopolitical, social, economic, and cultural configurations that have taken root within the historical context of nation-building, capitalist transformation, and the American-mediated regional system in Asia.

If "Chineseness" is better understood as a kind of quasi-nature in which "Chinese" actively and/or passively take on the attributes of "Chineseness," this quasi-nature comes out of, and operates within, a mutating local, national, regional, and global force-field. The unstable dynamics of this force-field makes the interrogation of race and culture a far more difficult, yet also exigent, task than that of unmasking the "othering" of the "Chinese." David Harvey (1995, 423) has argued that the neoliberalist ideology of free market, sound money, and minimal state intervention (hitherto dominant until the Lehman Shock in 2008) relies on the "practical strategy" of affirming individual freedom and choice of variegated lifestyles, expressions, and cultural practices. This means that the same force-field that conditions and produces the freedom of speech, meeting, conscience, association, and the ideals of pluralism and multiculturalism also conditions and produces the freedom to exploit, to profit from the miseries of the many to the advantage of the few (36, drawing on Polanyi 1954).

Such conceptual and existential double-bind accounts for both the allure and ambivalence of "Chineseness." While *Crying Ladies* imagines a scenario in which class differences and the potential conflicts sparked by class disparity can be doused by the twinned discourses of meritocracy and chance, and *Mano Po* celebrates the cultural hybridity and enrichment wrought by national integration, the films cannot fully paper over "Chinese" vulnerability to state violence, popular vengeance, and the demand for social justice on the part of those, "Chinese" and non-"Chinese" alike, whose everyday lives give the lie to the fantasies of accumulation and consumer satisfaction peddled by the ideology of global capitalist triumph.

Notes

1   "Mano po" denotes the Filipino custom of showing filial piety by touching the elder's hand to one's forehead.

2   *Mano Po 6* also picked up the following awards: Best Supporting Actress (Heart Evangelista), Best Director (Joel Lamangan), Best Screenplay (Roy Iglesias), Best

Musical Score (Von de Guzman), the Gatpuno Villegas Cultural Award, and the Most Gender Sensitive Film Award.

3   "Chinese" films often have a mixed cast of actors from Hong Kong, Taiwan, and even Southeast Asia (Michelle Yeoh), and their financing also come form multinational sources. See chapter 7.

4   See Joel David's (2008) nuanced study of how the Marcoses exempted Filipino cinema from institutional repression, a fact that accounted for the high quality of film production in that era. David also argues that the recent digital boom enabled film production to flourish even though the film industry remained moribund (229).

5   A number of such *pito-pito* films—Jeffrey Jeturian's *Pila Balde* (Fetch a Pail of Water, 1999) and Lav Diaz's *Hubad sa Ilalim ng Buwan* (Naked Under the Moon, 1999)— have received international recognition, but director Lav Diaz, speaking in 2000, remained skeptical of the potentials of the low-budget film: "The idea that the 'pito-pito' is a source of promise for Philippine Cinema is a myth. The only reason Jeffrey [Jeturian] and I were able to make meaningful films within this type of production is that we fought [the studio] all the way. The 'pito-pito' is hell, from checks postdated to six months after the film shoot, to the lack of decent wages for the film crew— P100 to P150 [about U.S.$3] a day! It's very exploitative. Sometimes the shoot goes on for twenty-four hours straight, with no sleep. People collapse from exhaustion. Far from keeping Philippine cinema afloat, the 'pito-pitos' will make our industry sink to the very bottom. There is no redemption to be found in 'pito-pitos'" (quoted in Lim 2000).

6   Although *Mano Po* was well-received by the Filipino press, in terms of artistic and intellectual merit, it is not in the league of films by auteurs like Edward Yang and Hou Hsiao-Hsien of Taiwan's New Wave Cinema movement, Eric Khoo of Singapore, James Lee of Malaysia, and Apichatpong Weerasethakul of Thailand. The Chinese Question awaits an auteur who can do justice to its complexity.

7   See also Richard Chu's analysis (2011) of the *Mano Po* films and *Crying Ladies*, an analysis that situates these films in gender and long-term historical perspectives.

8   Ara Mina's character is loosely based on Mary "Rosebud" Ong (Flores 2002), who had worked as a "police asset" on antidrug trafficking operations but subsequently created controversy under the Arroyo administration when she turned state witness to accuse Opposition Senator Panfilo Lacson, former head of the Presidential Anti-Organized Crime Task Force (PAOCTF) under the Estrada administration (see chap. 2), of enriching himself on money obtained from drug smuggling, and of involvement in kidnapping for ransom activities. Under Lacson and Estrada, PAOCTF had claimed credit for several high-profile rescue operations involving kidnap victims, as well as for a substantial drop in the total number of kidnappings reported annually (Tiglao 1999). A *Far Eastern Economic Review* article (Sheehan 2001, 64) states that "to many in the Chinese-Filipino community Lacson remains a hero and a kidnapping-gang-buster. In 1999, they were overjoyed when then-President Joseph Estrada appointed Lacson as chief of police. Kidnapping rates declined, according to the Chinese-Filipino community, but when his protector, Estrada, was removed from office earlier this year [2001], Lacson went, too, and kidnappings started in earnest again." Lacson has been implicated in the extrajudicial killings of kidnapping suspects (members of an armed vigilante group that also doubled as a criminal syndicate called Kuratong Baleleng), while Mary Ong herself has been accused by Lacson's camp of involvement in a transnational

crime syndicate with connections to Hong Kong that engages in drug trafficking and kidnapping activities. *Mano Po*'s integrationist stance, which turns Ara Mina's character from black sheep into state witness, sanitizes a Philippine reality in which the line between state agents and criminals can be blurry and people are not so easily reducible to "hero" or "villain." S/Insp. John Campos, on whom the character of Rafael Bala was based, would have a falling out with his erstwhile lover Ong, and end up being murdered by persons unknown.

9   Taiwanese investments in the Philippines increased from P71 million in 1986 to P2.25 billion in 1988, making it the Philippines' biggest foreign investor that year (Baviera 1991, 117).

10   This is not to say that "Chinese" capital in the past was solely confined within one nation-state; the size of contemporary "Chinese" capital, however, dwarfs that of earlier "Chinese" capital, and the amount of investment abroad has also expanded.

11   On the concepts of deterritorialization and reterritorialization, see Deleuze and Guattari 1983. See footnote 6 of chapter 7.

12   "*Ethnic Chinese* are people with some measurable degree of Chinese parentage, who can speak and understand at least one Chinese dialect, who have received a minimum of Chinese-language education, and who have retained some Chinese customs and traditions enough to consider themselves and be considered by their neighbors as Chinese" (Kaisa para sa Kaunlaran 2005).

13   For a useful overview and critique of the "cultural and structural accommodation" that organizes the study of overseas Chinese, see Hodder 2005.

14   Dannhaeuser (2005) has also noted the same phenomenon of intraethnic competition among ethnic Chinese small- and medium-scale entrepreneurs in Dagupan.

15   Scholar Lisandro Claudio (2011a) recounts a telling anecdote: "When I was in high school in Ateneo, I remember how most Ateneo boys (including myself, he he) fetishized ICAns [students of the Immaculate Conception Academy]. If you were dating an ICAn and if you could penetrate the ICA/Xavier world, you were on top of the food chain. In fact, the Miriam girls complained about how difficult it was for them to compete with ICAns for the affections of Atenistas. Based on stories from my father's generation of Atenistas, I don't think the fetish was as intense during their time. Seems to me that the desire for the classic Kastila/mestiza/kolehiyala [Spanish/mestizo/college girl] was transferred to the 'new' mestiza in the form of the third- gen[eration] Chinese girl who was believed to have transcended old stereotypes about the Filipino Chinese. Oddly enough, it was the ICAns themselves who complained the most about the boorishness of the GIs (Genuine Intsiks) and Binondo Chinese." Claudio (2011b) adds that these ICAns are "sufficiently Filipinized, but Other enough to be the object of desire. *Kaya* [So] the Atenistas who dated ICAns were doubly *mahusay* [capable] because they were able to scale the 'Great Wall' either through persuading the Chinese parents or persuading the girl to keep it a secret from her family."

16   My high school once tried (admittedly without much success) to launch a speak-English campaign to encourage students to use the language during class hours (except for subjects that were taught in Filipino).

17   See the biting essay on Chinese anti-Filipino prejudice by Alessandra Gonzales (2000). Gonzales writes: "If we had been brought up in an impervious Chinese school, like my parents and some of my friends, we would naturally and inevitably

see things and people through haughty and suspicious slit eyes. Papa need not force us into thinking that Filipinos are inferior to us, that by their very nature, most of them are traitorous friends, husbands who have little sense of commitment, wives who are shallow and materialistic, business partners who will swindle you, incompetent employees, inconsiderate neighbors, lousy teachers, inefficient doctors and lawyers, and corrupt politicians, because a rigorous Chinese education and constant association with Chinese fossils who deem the *lan nang* superior to all would invariably inculcate in us most of these distorted assumptions. We would unwittingly be referring to Filipinos as *huanna* and saying things like, 'He's really nice, for *huanna*.' Or 'What? She's dating a *huanna*? Poor girl.' Or 'Thank goodness I'm not a *huanna*'" (263). The beauty of such generalizations is that if the word "Chinese" is substituted for "Filipino," so that it is "Chinese" who are traitorous friends, errant husbands, materialistic wives, lousy teachers, incompetent doctors, and even corrupt politicians, then the shoe also fits perfectly!

18   *Mano Po* showcases the participation of women in "Chinese" big business in the Philippines through its depiction of the Filipina matriarch and the eldest Chinese daughter-CEO. In *Mano Po 3*, the protagonist strong woman is a celebrated activist and anticrime crusader. But the emphasis on the dead patriarch and his disavowed eldest son in *Mano Po 2* and the subordination of second daughter Juliet in *Mano Po* points to the circumscribing of the "Chinese" family by patriarchal elements working in and through the highly personalized conflicts centering on romantic love, filial piety, and family duty. Even as the *Mano Po* films show the strong women characters defying patriarchal "Chinese tradition," their plots and characterizations continue to locate the ideals of passion and family within the orbit of male validation and heterosexuality. In *Crying Ladies*, which celebrates female bonding, the women's career and life trajectories are propelled by their connections to the male-dominated church, video production company, and film studio. See Chu 2011 for a nuanced critique of the gender dynamics in *Mano Po*.

19   The threat of "Chinese" alienness is still used as a weapon in political campaigns and economic competition. See Chap. 3.

20   For the link between nationalism and vengeance via the politics of translation and foreignness, see Rafael 2005.

21   In his review of *Mano Po 2*, critic Patrick Flores (2003) criticizes the film for perpetuating the "myth that all Chinese in the Philippines are wealthy and, therefore, prime targets of kidnapping syndicates" and for according "lavish exposure to the textures of custom, as if culture were simply a catalogue of exotic rituals and pageants. This culture is made to appear as the shackle of Chinese consciousness, a line of defense that protects them from the potentially hostile forces around them, but a scare tactic that is dated and retrogressive. In this respect, the concept of race figures as an important concern to the Chinese so that mixing or the infiltration of the Filipino is considered an impurity. It is for this reason that the most dramatically engaging characters in the film are the mestizos...."

22   For an illuminating discussion of gambling and its relationship to capital, labor, elite domination, and the state in the context of colonial Philippines, see Aguilar 1998.

23   In *Mano Po*, Rafael Bala's father expresses his reservations about his son's relationship with Richelle Go by pointing to such a discomfort when he tells Rafael: "*Kapag usap ng Intsik sa harap mo, maiilang ka*" (If Chinese were spoken in front of you, you will be put off). Public conversations in Hokkien may also provoke "ching-

chong-chang" mimicry which disrupts spoken Hokkien with onomatopoeic echoes that empty the language of its content while highlighting the discordant foreignness of its sound—a form of unsolicited participation in the absence of translation.

24 The linguistic identification of Hokkien with English works differently in the *Mano Po* scenes set in "feudal" China among the indigent "Chinese." In the "old" China scenes, English subtitles merely mark spoken Hokkien as the alien tongue of an alien culture. But when used in scenes set in the Philippines, they work to displace the potentially more disturbing alienness of the "Chinese" Tagalog of the elder generation of "Chinese." Because "Chinese"-accented, broken Tagalog risks provoking laughter or, worse, ridicule from the audience, Hokkien is quarantined from "Chinese" Tagalog by being rendered as written, and therefore safely unaccented and for the most part grammatically correct, English. Given the absence (or, more accurately, death) of the "Chinese" past and patriarch in *Crying Ladies* and the Chinese-Filipino characters' command of fluent Tagalog, Hokkien functions as an exclusive insider's language like English.

25 Although the film accords more attention to three female protagonists rather than to young Chinese Filipino, their stories unfold against the backdrop of the Chinese funeral. The Chinaman's wake serves as a catalyst for the transformation of the three women's lives and careers. The has-been actress (Hilda Koronel) receives much-needed validation from a fan, and the church worker (Angel Aquino) heeds her friends' advice and decides to give up her relationship with her adulterer boyfriend.

26 The presence in the film of a sympathetically portrayed Indian Filipino character named Khumar (Bebo Jiandani) is an important qualification of the popular conflation of Chinese ethnicity and capital, since Indian Filipinos are also routinely stereotyped as moneylenders (locally known as "5–6"). Moneylending had been a "traditional" occupation of Chinese mestizos and Chinese.

27 For a cogent critique of Taiwan's "moving southward" (*nanxiang*) policy toward Southeast Asia, see Chen 2010, 17–64.

28 A useful overview of the South China Sea and how it was perceived across time by various populations who lived in the vicinity is Tønnesson 2005. See also the more recent analysis provided by Thayer (2011).

29 As if aware that his facetious statement might be deemed offensive, Montelibano then adds that "I carry no rancor for China, or the Chinese. God knows how much Chinese blood has intermingled with our native strain, but I can safely say a lot. We are Asians, we have much more commonality than differences. And we are a small-sized country with a weak military capability if attacked by a superpower. There is no motivation for Filipinos to fight China."

30 Teresita Ang-See (2012) had, in fact, commented on the standoff in "Tsinoy Beats and Bytes," her column for the Chinese-Filipino fortnightly journal, *Tulay*.

31 See also Reynard Hing's (2011) nuanced take on China's soft power.

32 Vajiravudh made this comparison in his 1914 essay, written in English (discussed in Kasian 1997, 77). Objects of class resentment, the Jews and the Chinese, despite plenty of contrary evidence, were seen to be "different" and to resist being integrated into the state project of creating a "national culture." They were also viewed as purveyors of socialist ideas and activism in Europe and Asia. But there are important differences between the situation of the Jews and the Chinese. Unlike the "Chinese Question," the "Jewish Question" had often been conceived as a religious opposition between Christianity and Judaism. Moreover, unlike China, until the mid-twentieth century,

no extant territorial state acted as a frame of intellectual and practical reference for the Jewish diaspora. For more than two thousand years, Jews were forced to live in non-Jewish states, where they had to rely on the "protection" of often hostile rulers and governments. China, by contrast, was a powerful state, and accessible to Southeast Asia, a situation that allowed overseas Chinese to "return" as well as lend support to "China" (see chap. 7).

33   Gie was the younger brother of prominent Indonesian intellectual Arief Budiman.

34   See Liu Hong 2011 for an excellent discussion of the intellectual and cultural impact of this relationship in Indonesia.

35   For a good overview of the transformations and reinventions of Indonesian Chinese culture in the post-Soeharto era, see Kitamura 2010.

36   I am grateful to Ben Anderson, who had been a good friend of Gie, for sharing his impressions and memories of the man.

37   Abidin Kusno (2012, 140) argues that this notion of youth rising above politics was problematic because of the link between "Chinese" and communism. He also notes the occlusion of the "Chinese family" from the narrative of Gie's intellectual and political development.

6

F A M I L Y

On Chinese Lunar New Year of 2007, former chairman of the Ayala Corporation Jaime Zobel de Ayala delivered a speech at the opening of an exhibition in the family-owned museum. Touted as the biggest exhibition ever mounted by the Ayala Museum (Tejero 2008), *Chinese Diaspora: Art Streams from the Mainland* aimed "to celebrate the extraordinary achievements of syncretic Chinese cultures in Southeast Asia, achievements that significantly contribute to the formation and imagining of the nation in the present-day countries of Singapore and the Philippines, paying homage to their ultimate source—the ancient civilization of China" (Ayala Museum 2007). Addressing an audience that included Singaporean president S. R. Nathan, Zobel de Ayala alluded to the family lore that traced the ancestry of his great-grandfather, Domingo Roxas, to a "Chinese" with the surname of Lim (*Shijie Ribao* 2007).

Zobel de Ayala's public acknowledgment of his family's "Chinese" roots occurred more than ten years after then-president Corazon Cojuangco Aquino invoked her Chinese immigrant great-grandfather in a speech before the Federation of Filipino-Chinese Chambers of Commerce and Industry (Anderson 1998, 192). But, coming as the latest statement did from the patriarch of the country's most illustrious family, a family long admired for its Spanish-German mestizo ancestry, Zobel's remark is the culmination of a decade-long shift in Filipino elite self-definition and identification. The closet that had for more than a century hidden the "Chinese" ancestry of these mestizo elite from public view and imagination has been finally and fully opened. Whereas the Chinese mestizo was once considered a "special kind of Filipino" (Wickberg 1965, 31) and the ethnic Chinese can nowadays be viewed also as a "special kind of Filipino" (Hedman and Sidel

2000, 84), the Filipino mestizo is now amenable to being treated as a special
kind of Chinese!

As part of the exhibition, noted historian Ambeth Ocampo curated
Tsinoy: Mestizo Art of Colonial Times, which featured ivory and hardwood
santos (saints), furniture and jewelry created by "Tsinoy artisans and
representatives of the Chinese-Mestizo," artifacts that had hitherto been
"little known or traditionally regarded simply as nineteenth-century
Philippine colonial art" (Ayala Museum 2007). Another exhibit in this
series showcased the works of the "First Great Filipino Painter," Damian
Domingo. Appropriating the term "Tsinoy," the neologism popularized in
the late 1980s and 1990s by the Chinese-Filipino organization, Kaisa para
sa Kaunlaran, the Ayala Museum's project of highlighting not merely the
mestizoness, but the long-occluded *Chinese* mestizoness, of Philippine art
and culture belatedly affirms the historical and sociological "contributions"
of the "Chinese" to the formation of the Filipino nation.

But, more than simply a (self-)recognition of the "Chinese" as an
integral (and now safely "integrated") part of the Philippine nation, Zobel
de Ayala's speech was intended for, and addressed to, several audiences.
One, as briefly discussed above, is Filipino (including "Chinese Filipinos").
The other is Southeast Asian, and yet another is "mainland" Chinese. The
centerpiece of the *Chinese Diaspora* exhibit was *The Peranakan Legacy*, on
loan from Singapore's Asian Civilizations Museum, which showcased 200
artifacts, including jewelry, ceramics, garments and textiles, and other
"prestige goods" from the "gilded age" of the *peranakan*. This particular
exhibit was made possible by a memorandum of agreement that the Ayala
Foundation had signed with the National Heritage Board of Singapore. This
institutional alliance, in fact, has a wider symbolic resonance, since both the
Singaporean and Filipino elites—whose countries are of roughly the same
economic size—have staked claims to the terms "peranakan" and "Chinese
mestizo," notwithstanding the fact that the word "peranakan" was not
the most popular term used by the Singapore-based Straits Chinese (who
called themselves, and were also called, Baba, Nyonya, or Straits Chinese, or
Queen's/King's Chinese),[1] nor by historical scholarship on Singapore, and
notwithstanding the longstanding historical occlusion of "Chineseness" by
the Filipino mestizo elite.

Peranakan, derived from the Malay *anak* ("child"), has a long history of
usage. Eighteenth-century references to this word were basically made in
the context of discussions of family genealogies among people who would
come to be known as "Malays" (Yamamoto 2011, 9); peranakan in these
precolonial texts referred, among others, to *peranakan Minangkabau* and
the "mixing" of the people of Melaka with the Madjapahit Javanese (Nishio

2011, 54–55). Hiroyuki Yamamoto (2011, 9) has pointed out that "[a]s the *Melayu* concept began to evolve, many local inhabitants 'became Malay,' and the term "peranakan" came into use for those Malays who needed special mention regarding their origins."

Mestizos of native-white parentage, or ancestry, were called "Indos" in Indonesia, a term that also spread to Malaysia. Children of mixed parentage were and are still sometimes called *blasteran*, a term meaning "mixed" (and could be used to refer to animals!). Dutch people who were born and raised in the colony were called peranakan Belanda (Dutch). Indians and Arabs born and raised in the colony were also called peranakan. In all cases, the opposite of peranakan was *totok*, which referred to newcomers (new migrants) who were neither born nor raised in the colony. Peranakan were, in this sense, children of the Dutch East Indies colony. Buginese and Minangkabau who had migrated to places like Malaya were called peranakan because they did not grow up in the Indies.[2]

Claiming a "peranakan" or "Chinese mestizo" heritage is arguably a way for the elites of the Philippines and Singapore to leverage themselves as hubs of regional "Chinese" networks within Southeast Asia and the larger East Asian region (including mainland China). Singaporeans' appropriation in recent decades of "peranakan," a term historically associated with the locally born Chinese mestizos of Java, Indonesia, and with certain ethnolinguistic segments of the "Chinese" population found in the British Straits Settlements is instructive. An illustrated book called *Gateway to Peranakan Culture*, published in Singapore, happily conflates peranakan with "Babas, Nyonyas, Bibiks, Straits Chinese, Straits-born Chinese," arguing that "[t]he Peranakan community is unique to Southeast Asia. It has its origins in the interracial marriages that took place between immigrant Chinese and non-Muslim women such as Bataks, Balinese, and Chitty (descendants of old Hindu families) from Malacca, Penang, Trengganu, Burma, and Indonesia in the 16th century" (Lim 2008, 3).

In its current usage, peranakan refers to descendants of "Chinese" immigrants (predominantly Hokkien) who intermarried with non-Muslim "Malays" (Hardwick 2008, 38). The term is used by the *baba* (a word that originated as a term of respect from North India) (Khoo 1998, 24) as a term of self-identification, though it is not clear when the acculturated Chinese began to refer to themselves as either baba or peranakan (Tan 2000, 49).[3] Other terms, such as Straits Chinese/Straits-born Chinese and King's Chinese/Queen's Chinese, carry strong associations with the British colonial "Straits Settlements" (Hardwick 2008, 38, 39). By the early postwar era, "peranakan" and "baba" had taken on specific class and colonial connotations that linked them with a "corrupt and doomed antimodern identity weighed down by expensive tastes and archaic rituals" (44).[4] There were, of course, peranakan who migrated from the East Indies (for example, Sumatra) to Penang (Tan 2000, 50), but "baba" was the most popular term to denote Malay-speaking "Chinese" mestizos in Malaya and Singapore in the 1840s to 1880s (Purcell 1965, 249–51) and was strongly associated with Malacca, from which re-migration to Penang and Singapore occurred (Tan 2000). "Chinese" in Trengganu and Kelantan who did not initially call themselves "baba" or "peranakan" came to adopt these labels as a way to connect themselves to a broader collectivity of "Chinese" in Malaysia and Singapore (see, for example, Teo 2003, 50–51).[5] A possible incentive for using peranakan may have been the fact that, unlike the association of baba with the Hokkien, the term was not necessarily associated with any one Chinese topolect.[6]

An instructive example is the name-change of the Straits Chinese British Association, formed in 1900 by a number of prominent Straits Chinese "to afford facilities for the discussion of all questions relating to the social and moral welfare" of the community. Counting among its leading lights the "Anglo-Chinese" Lim Boon Keng (see chap. 7), the association lobbied for Chinese representation in the Executive Council. In the postindependence years (and on the eve of the separation between Singapore and Malaysia), SCBA changed its name in 1964 to the Singapore Chinese Peranakan Association, before settling on The Peranakan Association, Singapore, in 1966. But its official homepage continues to bill the association as "Your one-step resource site for everything Baba!" (The Peranakan Association 2011).

Connecting with Indonesia is clearly a factor in the Singaporean preference for "peranakan" over "baba," since Indonesian Chinese have made Singapore an important financial, intellectual, and home base, building second or third homes there, educating their children and working as academics there, and parking their assets there as a form of hedging against the political uncertainties in Indonesia, particularly in the wake of the 1965 abortive coup and 1997–1998 Anti-Chinese Riots.

Moreover, baba's strong association with Malacca touches on the culturally and economically intimate but politically sensitive relations between Singapore and Malaysia, and connotes a parochialism (perhaps too close to home!) that is not in keeping with Singapore's ambitions of establishing itself as a hub within the Association of Southeast Asian Nations (ASEAN), East Asia, and the world. The regionalization of "peranakan" as a term beyond its Dutch-Indies-Javanese and Straits Settlements referents coincides with both the rise of "overseas Chinese" studies and the so-called Chinese renaissance within the context of the East Asian "economic miracle," de facto regional economic integration, and the rise of mainland China (which will be discussed in chap. 7). In Singapore, Singapore Airlines' *kebaya*-wearing Singapore Girl ("You're a great way to fly"), first created in 1975, helped turn "Peranakan" into a brand name, whose cultural artifacts and imagery would make up, both materially and visually, the "national heritage" that the Singaporean state sought to "preserve" while also keenly promoting it as tourist attraction.

The idea of Singapore as a regional hub fits well within longtime Singaporean Prime Minister Lee Kuan Yew's ambitious proposal to create a global network of overseas Chinese business based on a specific vision of an international division of labor, with China as production base, Singapore and Hong Kong as financial centers, and North America and Europe as final consumption markets. His proposal became the blueprint for a series of World Chinese Entrepreneurs Conventions held in Singapore, Hong Kong, Bangkok, Nanjing, Vancouver, and Kobe, from 1991 onwards (Young 2003, 42–43).[7]

The promotion of a "peranakan identity" (rather than baba identity) is not just a project of the Singaporean state, but an offshoot of networking and dialogue among ethnic-Chinese organizations across the region and the world. This is evident in the networking activities of the Peranakan Association of Singapore, which has held annual Baba Conventions since 1988, in rotation among Penang, Malacca, and Singapore as a way of maintaining links across the causeway between Singapore and Malaysia. The regional networking and circulation of ideas, as Kataoka Tatsuki (2008, 34–35) has shown, have served as catalysts for an emerging consciousness in recent years of "Baba-ness" among the Phuket Chinese of Thailand, as evident in the circulation of the newly minted compound term "Baba-Peranakan" (35). The fact that neither the word 'baba" nor "peranakan" was used in Phuket and Malay is not the lingua franca of the Muslims of Phuket shows the recentness of this cultural self-labeling. The cultural politics of asserting regional solidarity that connects the Phuket baba to the peranakan of the neighboring countries of Indonesia and Malaysia is specifically directed against the hegemonic cultural influence of Bangkok. The director of the Baba-Peranakan Association explains this strategic use of the term "Baba-Peranakan":

"In Phuket we call ourselves Baba, whereas in Malaysia and Indonesia the term *peranakan* is more popular. I consciously use *peranakan* so that the people of Phuket might know this term. As migrants from the Straits Settlements, our culture has been much more influenced by Penang and Malacca than Bangkok. That is our unique distinctiveness, but recently cultural influence from Bangkok is undermining our cultural heritage. So we need to restore our pride in being Baba again. Use of the term Baba-Peranakan can connect us with the brethren in neighboring countries." (Quoted in Kataoka 2008, 36)

As for the Filipino elite, rediscovery of their "Chinese" roots is a way of claiming connection with an imagined regional and global ethnic-Chinese "bamboo network" which has taken center stage in academic as well as popular discourses of the economic dynamism of the region. Just as crucial, the exhibition's reference to the "mainland" explicitly links the "ancient civilization of China," the "ultimate source" of peranakan/mestizo syncretism and the so-called Chinese diaspora, to contemporary China's rise as economic and regional power. The mestizo-as-Tsinoy is not just a newly sinified or sinicized Filipino in the way that the Tsinoy-as-mestizo is a Filipinized Chinese, but (hopefully) a node as well in the network of the "Chinese diaspora" spread out across Southeast Asia and linked to "Mainland China" and beyond.

One important but unintended effect of this celebratory rhetoric of "Chinese" kinship and the use of family history to highlight national and regional connections among the elite has been to further increase the visibility—and vulnerability—of the ethnic Chinese population in the Philippines. While the museum's project of (re)claiming "Chineseness" dovetails neatly with state policies on "integration" and the advocacy of Chinese-Filipino organizations, such as Kaisa para sa Kaunlaran (discussed in chaps. 2 and 3), words like "peranakan" and "Chinese diaspora" carry far more ambiguous and ambivalent associations and implications for the ethnic Chinese than the largely positive meanings assigned by the museum's act of "paying homage." For ethnic Chinese in the Philippines, "peranakan" strongly recalls the 1997–1998 anti-Chinese riots that broke out in more than 100 cities in Indonesia—events widely covered in the Philippines by both the English- and Chinese-language press—and more generally a catalogue of Southeast Asian states' repressive measures and societal discrimination against the "Chinese."[8] Moreover, as discussed in the previous chapters, the "nationalism" of the (Chinese) mestizo elite had been instrumental in the political, economic, and cultural construction of the Chinese as "aliens." Experienced firsthand and passed on through family lore, memories of discrimination are not completely erased by the elite's belated public recognition of the "Chinese as Filipinos."

At the same time, however, discourses on the region have been successful in establishing a causal relationship between "Chineseness" and (regional) economic success through such concepts as "Chinese capitalism," "New Confucianism," and "Cultural China" (see the previous chap.). Although much criticized for their ethnocentrism and lack of self-criticism, such regional discourses have significantly revalued the place of the "Chinese" within and beyond the Philippine nation. Studies of overseas Chinese business and networks in the 1980s and 1990s, with their emphasis on the family firm as the main type of business organization in ASEAN countries, have been deployed for political and ideological affirmations of "Chinese" competitive advantage in business and its role in the economic growth and dynamism of the region (Pinches 1999, 16). Max Weber had expressed doubts about the ability of Chinese families strongly influenced by Confucianism to develop "modern" capitalist forms because family businesses imposed "kinship fetters" on economic development, but the economic boom in Southeast Asia in the 1980s and 1990s have recast the ethnic Chinese family businesses as the entrepreneurial engine in the region's economic development (Carney and Dieleman 2008, 50–51). Once derided as "clannish" trading minorities who "dominated" the economy, "Chinese business dynasties" centered on the family firm have become exemplary models of entrepreneurship whose businesses successes— achieved in spite of a difficult if not hostile environment—are now coded not just as contributions to national development, but as important agents of regional economic integration. The emergence of China as an economic powerhouse and the association of "Chineseness" with "thoroughly modern 'Asian'" affluence (Szanton Blanc 1996) have revalued the "Chinese" in the eyes of non-"Chinese" Filipinos. The irony is that despite the fact that the much-touted myths of "Chinese" capitalism and culture do not withstand serious scrutiny and the complexity of historical experience, these ideological constructions have been an enabling factor in the growing visibility and desirability of "Chinese" entrepreneurial and social power.

The Filipino Family

Apart from the popularity of regional discourses on "Chinese capitalism," an equally compelling reason for the positive revaluation of the "Chinese" over the past two decades is the crisis of legitimacy of the Filipino elite, one that has a bearing on the nature, status, and function of the family as the basic social and economic unit in the Philippines.

Kenji Koike's (2005) study of the Spanish-mestizo and Chinese-Filipino business families has underscored the importance of historical, social, political, and economic conditions rather than "ethnic background" in accounting for similarities, differences, and specificities in the business practices and cultures of these families. One notable difference between the Sy and Zobel de Ayala families concerns the role assigned to women in the management of the business. Despite the fact that the Ayala family owes its economic preeminence to Chinese-mestiza matriarch Margarita Roxas's business acumen in the nineteenth century, none of Zobel de Ayala's daughters is involved in the Ayala Group of Companies (Koike 1995, 61–62). The noninvolvement of daughters in the Ayala family business stands in contrast to the practices of the Chinese-Filipino taipans (among them real-estate and retail magnate Henry Sy), whose daughters routinely occupy executive positions in their fathers' companies (61). While it is not possible to generalize from these two families, we can nevertheless point out that what Zobel de Ayala and Sy do have in common is the fact that their families have not relied on political office to advance their economic interests. In this, they differ from another group of mestizo elite, represented by the Cojuangcos and Lopezes, two families (descended from Chinese mestizos) that have shaped Philippine political history through their access to the state. These families are the primary targets of nationalist critiques of the Filipino oligarchy.

Held up as the "basic unit of Philippine society" (Medina 2001, 12), the family is both a social fact and an ideological construct. As an institution, it is explicitly recognized by the state, through its 1986 Constitution, as "the foundation of the nation" (Philippines 1987, Article XV, Section 1). The Constitution declares that "The State recognizes the sanctity of family life and shall protect and strengthen the family as a basic autonomous social institution" (Article II, Section 12).

The assertive language of such an official promotion of the family belies the reality of the state's chronically limited resources and capacity. The state does have a say on what constitutes the "Filipino family": although the state allows polygamy among Muslim ethnic groups as part of its policy of integrating non-Christian communities, it has made the renunciation of polygamy a condition for Chinese acquisition of Filipino citizenship so as to discourage the formation of the transnational split-family.[9] But the state's upholding of the "Filipino family" does not signal the primacy of the state as an actor in the protection and strengthening of the family as an institution. Rather, its stance is revealing of its chronic dependence on the family to provide basic services to the Filipino population that the state itself is unable or no longer able to provide.

In the field of social sciences, the family figures as one of the most important units of analysis in studies of "particularistic ties" and their impact on Philippine politics. Drawing on anthropological works on networks of reciprocal relationships (mainly theorized as "alliances" based on kinship and ritual kinship), political scientists in the mid-1960s adopted a "patron-client" framework in analyzing Philippine politics (Landé 1965). The scholarly attention accorded to the political salience of the family was spearheaded by Simbulan (2005) and McCoy (1994), whose pioneering work analyzes Philippine political history through the "paradigm" of elite families.

Historical conditions and colonial legacies that account for the "absence of a strong, centralizing state" and the "lack of other competing institutions" (5) in the Philippines have made the family the main institution upon which Filipinos depend to obtain security, employment, capital, education, medical care, and emotional and psychological support (7; Kerkvliet 1995, 404). Abad (2005) found that Filipinos are acutely dependent on families and friends ("binding social capital"), but that social capital is highly asymmetrical since it is the privileged, educated, higher-income people who tend to bond more and trust more. Abad argues that the relative paucity of associational ties ("bridging social capital"), which are forged mainly by privileged adult males, has an adverse effect on the promotion of citizen participation and democratic governance in the Philippines.

Moreover, the elite family's concern with the transmission of "name, honor, land, capital and values to the next generation" (McCoy 1994, 7; Wolf 2001 [1966], 172–74) may also exercise "excessive claims on group membership" (Abad 2005, 9) that work against the national interest (for criticisms of the patron-clientelist perspective, see Kerkvliet 1995; and Quimpo 2005). Alfred McCoy (1994, 1) highlights the possible conflicts between the claims exercised by the family on the individual, on the one hand, and the "impersonal values" of the collective institutions charged with promoting the public good, on the other hand. This "negative" view of the elite family is further underscored by the fact that in the post-Marcos era, a mere sixty-three families controlled or exerted the most influence over the country's political and economic resources (Krinks 2002, 52–53).[10]

Family firms also figure as the dominant form of business organization in the country (Kondo 2008; Omohundro 1981). Quasi-familial relationships are integral to the organization and management of modern Filipino corporations. These corporations operate in a business environment that is markedly hierarchical, status-conscious, family-centered, and characterized by high unemployment, high mobility of professional labor, and the generally low level of public trust in individuals as well as institutions. Mindful of the "ideal" models of doing business propounded by globalized discourses of business management, these corporations have developed a hybrid management style that combines elements of *bata-bata* (lit., "child") patronage with the check-and-balancing potentials of meritocracy for purposes of relaying information, and monitoring and motivating managers and key employees.

The family firm functions as a device to reduce transaction costs, as a source of information, and as a reservoir of skill and finance (Corelli 2003, 30) within a particular Philippine business environment that is characterized by asymmetric information, political turbulence, economic uncertainty, and a legal system that is unable to secure property rights. But there exists the danger that the private interests of the family may overdetermine the rational management of the group, creating bias in the penalty system and difficulty in motivating and retaining competent workers who have no patrons (Kondo 2008, 280). Merito-patronage is a rational strategy for enabling companies to remain competitive within the particular socioeconomic contexts of Philippine capitalism. This system, however, has a downside as well, since it serves to further promote and perpetuate the Filipino elite's accumulation of wealth and political power.

Chinese families have been specifically criticized for their perpetuation of gender and other "traditional" social inequalities. Their exploitation of inequalities between men and women and between elder and younger generations of family members in pursuit of economic goals arguably underpins the kind of flexible capitalist accumulation that has been an essential ingredient of the resilience and success of the family firm in spurring East Asian economic development (Greenhalgh 1994; Yao 2002; Ong 1999).

Nevertheless, with some exceptions, ethnic Chinese families have largely avoided being tainted by the association of elite families with a "predatory" state (Sidel 1999). With "Chinese" private accumulation of wealth taking center stage as a highly visible component of Southeast Asian economic development, the ethnic Chinese's problematical relationship with the state and the politically dominant elite families has served to insulate them (though not completely) from the opprobrium heaped on the elite who have used the Philippine state to increase their family fortune and perpetuate their family names.

More crucially, the positive evaluation of the "Chinese" owes something to the shrinking of the state as a source of rents and the resources that are at its disposal (Asian Development Bank 2011).[11] The most important change in the Philippine economy over the last twenty years has been the increasing importance of remittances by overseas Filipino workers and migrants. The Philippines is the fourth-biggest recipient of remittances after China, India, and Mexico (Remo 2012). In 2011, record-breaking remittances accounted for 9 percent of the gross domestic product (*GMA News,* 2012). Remittances not only represent income that is harder for the state to capture, but also income that tends to be consumed in everyday life or saved for retirement—

hence, the higher growth in areas, such as retail, finance, and real estate development (a trend noted by Balisacan and Hill [2003, 13]), precisely the sectors in which a small number of Chinese Filipinos have succeeded in creating business empires that cater to a wide range of income groups, most especially in the middle- and lower-income spectrum (see, for example, Friedland 1988; Tiglao 1994;1995a; 1996). Ethnic Chinese, such as Henry Sy, have seen their family fortune surpass that of the traditionally dominant mestizo families. This has resulted in the integration, if not necessarily absorption, of a stratum of ethnic Chinese into the changing Philippine class structure, which is increasingly characterized by a small concentration of "new rich" and the creation of new middle classes (Pinches 1996, 103–33; 1999, 275–301).

Crisis and Reconsolidation of Filipino Elite Families

The positive view of the Chinese family as an engine of "Chinese capitalism" points to deep fissures in the ideology of elite domination in the Philippines. Michael Pinches (1999) has argued that the ideological leadership of the Filipino elite has come under pressure in recent decades because of the continued failure of the Philippines to lift itself out of its economic malaise. Scholars like Yoshihara Kunio (1995) have even blamed Filipino underdevelopment on the Philippine state's repression of the Chinese minority. To this extent, Chinese entrepreneurship has come to connote positive associations of dynamism and industry (Pinches 1999, 287), which the elite must perforce ideologically co-opt.

The shockwave generated in 1995 by the Metro Pacific Corporation— an Asian conglomerate chaired by a Filipino, Manuel V. Pangilinan, and an arm of the Sino-Indonesian Salim Group (founded by Suharto "crony" Liem Sioe Liong), which led a sixteen-member consortium that included Malaysian tycoon Robert Kuok Hock-Nien to outbid Ayala Land by bidding P30.2 billion for the 117-hectare chunk of Fort Bonifacio—demonstrated the "money power" of Southeast Asian Chinese capitalists now operating transnationally and in the Philippines. But lest this creates the mistaken impression that "Asian" capital signifies purely "Chinese" capital, we need only remember that ethnic Chinese tycoons in the Philippines and elsewhere have also formed profitable alliances with the Filipino elite in their business ventures, as did Henry Sy with the Ayalas, and John Gokongwei with the Lopezes (Tiglao 1990a, 70). In fact, when Metro Pacific ran aground during the Asian financial crisis, its Fort Bonifacio shares were eventually bought by Ayala Land in partnership with Evergreen Holdings (of the Chinese-Filipino-led Campos Group). Tycoons, such as Lucio Tan, Henry Sy, John Gokongwei, and George Ty, have developed linkages not only with Filipinos, but also with international partners in the U.S., United Kingdom, Japan, Taiwan, and China (Rivera 1995, 19–20)—countries that are part of an Anglophone regional system (discussed in the next chap.).

The line between "Chinese" and "Filipino" is no longer clear-cut, if it ever had been in the first place. All but one of the Chinese-Filipino tycoons were already Filipino citizens well before the 1975 mass naturalization of Chinese, and all but one are not members of the Chinese Chambers of Commerce, as the most successful Chinese-Filipino firms have been precisely the ones that have relied least on "Chinese" ties (Cariño 2001, 114). In other words, wealthy "Chinese" are able to move and mix to some extent in the highest Filipino social circles. Furthermore, a Chinese-Filipino tycoon like Emilio Yap (owner of *Manila Bulletin*) was able to foil the bid of the Malaysian state-linked (now state-owned) conglomerate Renong to take over the Manila Hotel by taking advantage of Filipino nationalist sentiments, which figured in the Supreme Court's decision to declare the Manila Hotel a "national patrimony" in 1997, and give preference to Filipino bidders.

Racist sentiments may continue to color elite evaluation of the Chinese middle class and new rich, who are derided for their "disloyalty"[12] and nouveau riche tastelessness, but the cultural authority interminably enjoyed and exerted by the old mestizo Spanish and Filipino elite can no longer be fully exercised over "Chinese" claims to an alternative (but not necessarily oppositional or subversive) modernity and aesthetics (Pinches 1999, 294–95; Ong and Nonini 1997). In light of the Philippines' deepening integration into the East Asian regional economy, the resinification of Chinese mestizoness among the Filipino elite is part of an ongoing process of elite reconsolidation of symbolic capital and power through the integration of the "Chinese" and, by extension, "Chinese" identification with East Asian capital, into the bounds of the Philippine official national imaginary.

The intermingling of Filipino and Chinese cultures through the successful creation of a family unit composed of a Chinese father and Filipino mother and their descendants, a historical and sociological fact, has now become an integral element of elite identity and self-identification. In some instances, even when no blood connection is claimed, mestizo elite families have cultivated their "Chinese" connections over decades through close business contact with the Chinese community and through the Chinese-language education of the sons. One such family, the Aboitizes, based in Cebu, are known for their "Chinese-style" of doing business (Flores 2004). The head of the clan, now in his early sixties, likes to tell the story of how, soon after finishing his studies in the U.S., he visited his grandfather and was berated by the old man for his inability to converse in Hokkien, the Philippine-Chinese lingua franca in which the Aboitiz grandfather was conversant, owing to the Aboitiz's close links with Cebuano Chinese families and businesses. Although the current patriarch came of age at the height of anti-Chinese nationalism, he has made sure that the next generation would receive Chinese-language (this time in Putonghua/ Mandarin, the lingua franca of "Greater China") training in Beijing and Taipei, in line with the increasing importance of the China market. Moreover, Cebu itself is touted as a model for the Philippine economy as well as Philippine-Chinese relations: Governor Emilio Osmeña—himself of Chinese mestizo ancestry—attributes Cebu's economic success to the fact that "Cebu society has assimilated its Chinese immigrant community...They [the Chinese] integrated well: Cebu has no Chinatown" (Tiglao 1991).

The claiming of Chineseness and Chinese connections by the mestizo elite is a symbolic affirmation of old and new alliances and linkages between the mestizos, the "Chinese Filipino," and the regional Chinese. Integration, however, has not fully eroded the ethnic boundaries that distinguish Chinese-Filipino from the Filipino elite, since the most affluent among Chinese Filipino families (particularly first-generation tycoons) have tended to marry among themselves (and occasionally with regional Chinese) rather than intermarry with elite Filipino families.

The irony is that while members of the mestizo elite are now highlighting their "Chinese" heritage and connections, the ethnic Chinese— even so-called pure Chinese—are in an important sense becoming more culturally mestizo. A degree of acculturation over generations has effectively turned the young Chinese into cultural *tsut-si-a,* whose mestizoness would be simultaneously a source of parental anxiety about the loss of Chinese culture and a cultural asset in its ability to claim Filipinoness while accessing and mediating regional East Asian capital and cultural flows (as discussed in the previous chap.). The younger generation of bicultural "Chinese" have taken on the attributes of the Chinese mestizos (Wickberg 1997, 177), precisely because the term "Chinese" is no longer defined by its problematic place within the nation, but by its additional revaluing as a signifier of both global and *regionally specific* capitalist development.

Regional Alliances with Mainland-Chinese Princelings

Moreover, elite consolidation is happening on a scale far beyond the Philippine nation-state. Ethnic Chinese tycoons in the Philippines are forming business alliances with the Filipino elite as well as East Asian—

Taiwanese, Japanese, Koreans, and other Southeast Asian—capitalists. Mainland Chinese are relative newcomers, but their presence is now being felt in the realms of politics and the economy across the region. Transformed from Communist antagonist outside the American-led Free Asia Cold War regional system into a global "superpower" and a key regional player, the mainland Chinese state has relied on economic and trade cooperation as the principal instrument of its international engagements (Shiraishi 2012), over and above its increasing militancy in the South China Sea.

Along with the expansion and diversification of its trade and investment, China's economic cooperation has undergone important changes since the 1990s. China started to provide economic and military assistance to Myanmar, Thailand, Vietnam, and other Southeast Asian countries toward the end of the 1990s as part of its neighborhood diplomacy. (Conversely, China is not above linking its trade flows either to its foreign policy agenda, thereby turning trade into a political weapon: Norwegian exports of fresh and frozen salmon dropped sharply following the announcement that Chinese dissident Liu Xiaobo would be awarded the Nobel Prize in 2010, and the banana and tourism industries in the Philippines took a beating during the Scarborough Shoal dispute [Chanco 2012].) More recently, it has deployed its economic cooperation as an instrument for natural resources procurement and export promotion. Its mode of assistance has also undergone change. Joint ventures emerged as an important vehicle for implementing projects in the 1980s, in which state corporations and state banks became important players in the 1990s. But these days, economic cooperation often means business collaboration in joint ventures in which trade and trade finance, investment, and official assistance (grant and concessional loans) are fused indistinguishably.[13]

This cooperation is underpinned by the increasingly blurred relationship between the mainland Chinese political and economic elite, most fittingly embodied by the princelings—children of high-ranking Communist officials who have greatly profited from going into business ventures through state-owned and private enterprises. It is this politico-business elite that has gone transnational, forging alliances with its counterparts elsewhere in the world, including the Philippines.

But this type of new alliance connecting the Filipino elite and Chinese Filipinos as well as Southeast Asian and Mainland Chinese elites is not without political risk. The Asian financial crisis accounted for a negative turn in critical evaluation of ethnic Chinese family businesses, which were blamed for their concentrated ownership, cronyism, weak governance, and "corruption" (Carney and Dieleman 2008, 51). Even though opinions improved as the Southeast Asian economies regained their footing after the crisis, the "dark side" of family business continually resurfaces in periodic charges of opportunism, lack of patriotism, capital flight, opaque transactions, and moral hazard.

In the Philippines, an instructive example is the scandal which involved President Gloria Macapagal-Arroyo's avowedly Chinese-mestizo husband, rival Filipino political elite, and mainland Chinese business. In April 2007, the Philippine government signed a deal with the mainland Chinese firm Zhong Xing Telecommunications Equipment (ZTE) to build a National Broadband Network for a total cost of U.S.$330 million. About two months later, a newspaper columnist published an exposé of Commission on Elections chairman Benjamin Abalos's connections with the ZTE deal. Jose de Venecia III, the son of the former House Speaker, and a major stockholder in the Amsterdam Holdings, Inc., a rival firm that had placed a bid for the project, revealed that the First Gentleman Mike Arroyo had told him to "back off" the deal. One of the consultants/liaisons involved in the deal, the Chinese mestizo Rodolfo "Jun" Lozada, was abducted by unidentified men, and only the media attention sparked by his wife's public appeal for information of his whereabouts saved him from possible "salvaging" (execution). Lozada blew the whistle on the deal, exposing the web of bribery and corruption connecting the ZTE Corporation and the Arroyo family that had led to a substantial "overhead" padding of the million-dollar deal.

This deal implicated not just rival Filipino political elite families, but also mainland Chinese firms. It is well-known among the Chinese community that both the Arroyo family and the rival political family of the de Venecias had connections with mainland Chinese "princelings" (taizi 太子), children of high-ranking Communist party and state officials who go into business by using their familial political connections (see Shimizu 2008, chap. 4), including no less than then-president and Chinese Communist Party Secretary-General Hu Jintao's son Hu Haifeng. These connections with Chinese princelings were largely overlooked by the media, which focused on Arroyo's husband. Criticism quickly took on a racial slant as ZTE Corp. came under criticism for fomenting "Chinese corruption," with Senator Miriam Defensor-Santiago accusing China of having "invented corruption."

It is a sign of how times have changed that Santiago had to apologize for her anti-Chinese "slur" (Uy 2007; Danao 2007). But by far the biggest beneficiary of this scandal was the Chinese-mestizo Lozada. Calling himself a "probinsyanong Intsik" ("chink"/Chinese from the province),[14] a derogatory term leveled at him in his school years (Aw 2008, 52), Lozada effectively appropriated the racially loaded label, not by foregrounding his mestizoness, but by recasting himself as the "Chinese" victim of the "racist" Filipino political elite. In so doing, Lozada "rekindled ethnic pride among local Chinese men and women, of different generations. Suddenly, people are referring to him as 'lan nang' (Minnan Chinese for 'one of us')... and digging into his Chinese origins" (Tan 2008). Lozada's plight became a national cause célèbre that politicized not just the Filipino public, but the proverbially "apathetic" ethnic Chinese, some of whom appeared in public wearing T-shirts that read "Probinsyanong Intsik." The Filipino political elite were blamed for the fact that, to quote one Chinese businessman, "American and European companies don't bid for our (Philippine) projects. They know there's just too much 'overhead' involved" (ibid.). But although public anger was directed mainly at the Filipino political elite, the scandal reveals not just the increasingly intimate links between Filipino and Chinese-Filipino elite, but the complication of these links by the growing presence in the East Asian region of mainland Chinese business (-cum-political) elite and the Chinese state itself as "national" players.

De Venecia's exposé cannot be said to have been motivated by a stricken conscience over the parlous state of the nation. The elder Jose de Venecia was himself embroiled in an earlier controversy over the Chinese-funded North Rail project for Luzon. The former Speaker of the House was alleged to have "brokered the entry" of the state-owned China National Machinery and Equipment Corp. into the project to rehabilitate the train line connecting Metro Manila to provinces in North Luzon. The project, initially estimated at U.S.$503 million, quickly ballooned to U.S.$2 billion amidst allegations of overpricing. Whistleblower Rodolfo Lozada had, in fact, explicitly drawn a parallel between the broadband deal and the North Rail project, since the broadband deal was to have been modeled on the "loan project à la North Rail" (*Philippine Daily Inquirer,* 2011b). And in a further plot twist following the aborted ZTE deal, President Gloria Arroyo would go on to endorse a U.S.$465.5 million cyber-education project involving a contract with the Tsinghua Tongfang NucTech Company, in which Hu Jintao's son Hu Haifeng had served as president (Buencamino 2007)!

The resinification of Chinese mestizoness among the Filipino elite provides ample proof that capital is no longer bound to the nation-state, but has become both globalized and, equally important, regionalized, transforming economies, societies, and even politics. The rise of middle classes and consumption regimes in East Asia has made the region a center of world economic growth, fueling fantasies of a life of plenty delivered by capitalist development. Southeast Asian countries like the Philippines, in hopes of being able to partake of this capitalist dream, have reformulated their policies to "attract" regional and global capital in the form of foreign direct investment.

Under Ferdinand Marcos, there was an attempt at creating a developmental state. But the kind of historical trajectory taken by the Philippines did not result in the creation of a developmental state (Walden Bello, et al. [2004], in fact, describe the post-Marcos Philippines as an "anti-developmental" state). Chronic political and economic instability and compromised institutions ended up scaring away much of the foreign direct investment, which flowed elsewhere to Thailand, Malaysia, and Vietnam. The Philippines instead opted to export its labor. The Philippines occupies both a strategic and vulnerable position in the regional order: Filipino domestic helpers are crucial to maintaining the life of plenty for the middle classes in Hong Kong, Taiwan, and Singapore, but—notwithstanding the trend toward increasing migration of Filipino professionals and other skilled workers—this labor is routinely devalued and vulnerable to manipulation, neglect, oversight, and abuse. Aspiring to the kind of economic growth its neighbors have experienced, the Philippines, because of its position in the regional order as labor, finds itself unable to fully embrace nor fulfill the promise of capitalist prosperity.

The ongoing redefinition of Chineseness is partly spurred by the desire (of both Filipinos and "Chinese") to partake of the dream of regional capitalist growth and prosperity. But Chineseness is also circumscribed by the impossibility of full identification with regional capitalism. "Chinese ethnicity" remains implicated in the conflation of "Chineseness" with money-as-capital. This conflation, however, has undergone revaluation in the post-Marcos era: Whereas Chinese identification with money had long been a source of nationalist opprobrium and the target of nationalist action, the past three decades have seen a resignification of "Chineseness" that is partly enabled by capitalist transformation that foregrounds, in an unprecedented way, the desire for money power without, at the same time, being able to resolve the inherent contradictions that continually generate economic and political crises in the Philippines. This accounts for both the potentials and limits of "Chineseness," and explains why "Chinese" identification remains fraught with ambivalence.

Moreover, the increasing presence and weight of the mainland Chinese state and economy have made the mainland Chinese politico-business elite important regional and global players who have had an impact on the fortunes and national consolidation of the Filipino elite. Not only are wealthy Chinese Filipinos now integrated (with varying degrees of social success) into the ranks of the Philippine elite. This national elite itself is also becoming increasingly embedded in transnational networks that connect it to Japanese, Taiwanese, Korean, Southeast Asian, American, European, and now mainland Chinese, companies and players (Shiraishi 2012). As the Chinese economy continues to grow, the transnational effects of the flows and movements of its people, capital, goods, and firms—including criminal networks—are bound to have an impact on the political economies of neighboring countries.

Economic and trade cooperation is the means by which "China provides export credits, concessional loans, investments, grants, technical assistance, and even labor for real-estate development, building presidential palaces and fertilizer plants, infrastructural projects (such as power plants, power grids, highways, bridges, port facilities), and other development projects" (Shiraishi 2012, 141). Chinese state corporations have been the key agents of China's economic cooperation, and have secured contracts from Southeast Asian governments for a variety of large-scale projects. Often run by "princelings," these state corporations have forged politico-business alliances with their national elite countparts in the Philippines, other Southeast Asian countries, such as Myanmar and Indonesia as well as in Africa. These crosscountry alliances have the potential to change the parameters by which the Philippines and other states define their national interests in economic terms, even as thorny issues of territory, sovereignty, American presence in the region, and the quest for resources (especially rich oil and gas reserves) have revitalized territorial disputes over the Spratlys, the Paracels, and more recently the Scarborough Shoal, which remain a bone of contention between the Philippines and mainland China.[15] How substantial the changes will be depends on the extent of elite circulation and competition within the partner country (as highlighted, for example, in the internecine conflict that sparked the ZTE controversy), how well integrated that particular state is within both the regional and global economy, and whether Chinese enterprises face competition from domestic and foreign enterprises in the terrain in which they operate (138–40).

In the Philippine case, intramural rivalry and competition among political families for contracts with Chinese state enterprises have lent a certain instability to the politico-business alliances forged by Chinese companies. Not only is it more likely that these alliances will shift, depending on which business connections are established between which Chinese princeling and which Filipino elite family, as shown by the musical-chairs arrangement that allows the Arroyos to link up with one Chinese company at one moment and with rival De Venecias' Chinese allies the next. These alliances are particularly vulnerable to public criticism and backlash, as under-the-table deals and lack of transparency in the bidding process are regularly exposed in the press, provoking public outcry and censure that erodes further the prestige and legitimacy of the Filipino elite families.

The "Chinese Family" in
Philippine Centennial Literature

How have Chinese Filipinos sought to make sense of these substantive changes in Philippine political economy, society, and culture in the wake of the rise of East Asia and mainland China?

"Chinese" inclusion within the Filipino national imaginary was highlighted in the 1998 government-sponsored celebration of the centenary of the declaration of Philippine independence. Chinese, along with other minority groups, such as Moros and indigenous peoples, were represented in the People's Parade on June 13, 1998. The Federation of Filipino-Chinese Chambers of Commerce sponsored five lion and two dragon dances to mark the festivities (Bankoff and Weekley 2002, 107). A float depicting Chinese participation in the independence struggle bore the slogan "Ang mga Tsinoy ay Pilipino rin" (The Chinese Filipinos are Filipinos, too) (136). Expo Pilipino, a national exposition in Clark Air Base, Pampanga—publicized as the "centerpiece" of the centennial celebrations"—carried a small display of the Parian (Chinese quarters from the Spanish period) to emphasize "the Chinese tradition and their influence on trade" (156). The media also spotlighted the achievements of Chinese like Ignacio Paua and Chinese mestizos like Telesforo Chuidian and Mariano Limjap (49).[16]

Among the activities sponsored by the state was a literary contest, the main attraction of which was its million-peso prize money. The winners of the Novel in English category came from the ranks of the Philippines' most prominent literati, including Eric Gamalinda (First Prize) and Alfred A. Yuson (Third Prize). This time, the winning novels had a wider thematic focus: marginalized millenarians and tribal minorities joined the dominant *ilustrados* on the literary stage. The question of literary merit aside, the decision to award the second prize to Charlson Ong's novel *An Embarrassment of Riches* (2000b), which takes as its main theme the Chinese and Chinese mestizo, also reflects the inclusionary spirit of the national celebrations.

But a close reading of the novel itself reveals a less-than-celebratory take not only on Philippine history and the fraught entanglement of the Chinese—and "Chinese family"—in the narrative of nation, but also the growing visibility of mainland Chinese elite players in the Philippine economy. The novel explores the intimate but fraught relationship between family and nation, offering nothing less than a deconstruction of conventional understandings of the "family" along with a different framework for understanding Philippine history and the Chinese's place and role within it.

In *Embarrassment*, Ong makes his Chinese-mestizo protagonist president, albeit briefly, of the fictional country of Victorianas (known as the "Little Philippines"). Born in the Victorianas to a Chinese father and Victoriana mother, Jeffrey Kennedy Tantivo is seventeen years old when his father, Carlos Tantivo, sends him to neighboring Philippines for higher education. In "enlightened Manila" (1), Jeffrey gets involved in student activism, and gains political experience from helping out in

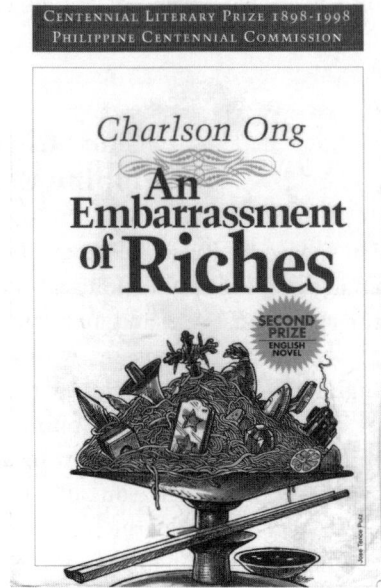

CENTENNIAL LITERARY PRIZE 1898-1998
PHILIPPINE CENTENNIAL COMMISSION

Charlson Ong

An Embarrassment of Riches

SECOND PRIZE ENGLISH NOVEL

Charlson Ong's Centennial-prize winning novel

Corazon Cojuangco Aquino's presidential campaign. His sister Jasmine had joined the Victorianas underground when Jeffrey was only four, and is now a ranking member of the Victorianas People's Liberation Army. Halfway through his sixth year abroad, in 1994, he learns that his father has died from cerebral aneurysm. His father's erstwhile business partner, a Spanish mestizo named Echevaria (who goes on to reinvent himself as the politically influential charismatic spiritual leader Mike Verano), sends Jeffrey the cremated remains and informs him that Carlos has lost his entire fortune in an ill-fated hotel venture as a "front" man for the dictator General Azurin. Jeffrey returns to the Victorianas three years later upon the death of the dictator to help manage the presidential campaign of his childhood friend, entrepreneur Jennifer Suarez Sy, whose retail and textile tycoon father—a mahjong buddy of Jeffrey's father—had built the giant mall, Megalomalla.[17] Jeffrey meanwhile receives conflicting reports from assorted acquaintances, family friends, and kinsmen concerning his father, and uncovers evidence that his father had been murdered. Although Jennifer wins the elections, her government immediately finds itself under attack from the opposition, funded by another of Carlos's Chinese mahjong buddies and a fellow former refugee from Indonesia, Alfonso Ong. Jeffrey finds out that Jennifer's spiritual adviser, Aldoux

Chang, has been doping her. Chang is also responsible for Carlos's "accidental" death and is in league with Ong, a timber tycoon who owns an island that doubles as a New Age "laboratory" for sheltering (and showcasing) tribal minorities and endangered animals and a twenty-first century model city and special economic zone. Ong eventually reveals that he is Jeffrey's real father. Jeffrey learns that Ong urgently needs a kidney transplant, for which Jeffrey is expected to be donor. He also learns that Ong's model city relies on the forced labor provided by a penal colony of transplanted (i.e., expatriated) mainland Chinese. Ong is busy concluding a deal with a high-ranking mainland Chinese, Comrade Lu, who plans to transfer his business base from China to Ong's private island, which turns out to have been developed using revenues from the lucrative drug trade in which Ong is involved. A coup supported by Ong and mounted by militant opposition forces overthrows Jennifer's government, and Jeffrey is asked to join the junta and serve as president. With the help of his sister Jasmine, Jeffrey smuggles a bomb hidden in his "father" Carlos's urn to the temple for a ceremony that is to be attended by his real father and other important officials. But at the last minute, fearing the death of innocents, Jeffrey throws the bomb into the river and takes the last flight, along with Jasmine's young son, out of Victorianas and into exile in the Philippines, just as his island country plunges into civil war.

Part satire, part domestic melodrama, part crime novel, and part political novel, *Embarrassment of Riches* begins, ironically, with the return of the native. The "native" turns out to be no native at all, but a Chinese-Victorianas mestizo who is technically stateless, since locally born children of Chinese fathers are not allowed to take Victorianas citizenship (in contrast to native-born Chinese, migrant Chinese with foreign passports can obtain citizenship through bribery). Jeffrey's father Carlos had obtained permanent residency, but this residency had been revoked by the government upon his death. Not only is Jeffrey stateless, but propertyless as well, since his father had apparently lost his fortune to Alfredo Sy, Carlos's erstwhile friend, fellow refugee, and Jennifer Sy's father. Even if there had been anything left to inherit, Carlos's failure to marry Jeffrey's mother had rendered Jeffrey illegitimate, unable to rely on his mother's Victorianas citizenship to protect his inheritance.

Family ties determine not only Jeffrey's legal status, but also his fate. The story unfolds around the mystery of Carlos's death, and a series of revelations that not only bring Jeffrey face-to-face with his father's killers, but lead him to the realization that everything he has known about himself and his family—his very sense of "who" he is and who his family members are—turns out to be false.

Jeffrey muses that "the search for happiness, if it should be undertaken at all, is always a personal, at most familial, rather than societal concern" (6–7), but Jeffrey's own actions and life trajectory stray from this injunction. Jeffrey has a strained relationship with Carlos, one based on guilt on one side and disappointment on the other. Carlos had wanted Jeffrey to study medicine in the U.S., "a badge of honor among Chinese Victorianos" (5), but Jeffrey is called back from Manila, the "first leg of our journey to the First World" (4), after his traveling companion and cousin Lorenzo's murder. Carlos cuts him out of the family business, but reluctantly gives in to a relative's advice to send Jeffrey back to Manila, where he then matriculates at the University of the Philippines. In Manila, Jeffrey dabbles in writing, publishing a number of articles for *Partisano Victoriano*, a small, "purportedly left-wing journal" edited by Jeffrey's friend Ignacio Manalo, and promptly incurs the wrath of the military, which burns all the copies it can find. This censorship turns Jeffrey into a dissident, much to his father's chagrin. Identifying with the Victorianas, Jeffrey finds himself unable to identify with China because of the Tiananmen incident.

But more than just flouting his father's wishes, the unfilial son differentiates himself from his father through his insistence on calling Victorianas "home":

> Our elders' frustration with our decreasing fluency in the Chinese
> language and increasing ignorance of most things Chinese, I surmised,
> had less to do with fears of our diminishing Chineseness much less any
> overwhelming sentiment for the mainland or Taiwan than with the
> possibility that some of us might have deluded ourselves into thinking
> that we had at last found a home. (7)

Carlos had an itinerant life, migrating to the Victorianas first from his native Fujian Province, South China, shortly before the Communists took over the mainland in 1949, and subsequently from Sulawesi and Jakarta, Indonesia, just before Suharto came to power on the heels of the 1965–1966 anticommunist (here also coded as anti-Chinese) riots. As one who has led a life of permanent exile, remigrating several times with plans, ultimately unfulfilled, to move from the Victorianas to First-World America, Carlos Tantivo[18] has lived in the shadow of political upheaval, defining his own life as one of "always staying one step ahead of the big one [i.e., revolution]" (6): "That is, collecting our payables, settling accounts and packing up with some to spare—leaving the place a bit better off than when one arrived" (ibid.) His fear that his children would be embroiled in the conflicts in Victorianas appears well-founded: Jasmine goes underground and becomes a guerrilla, while Jeffrey becomes a student activist and writer.

In an article, Jeffrey eloquently writes:

> [T]here is perhaps a nagging suspicion among our elders that we
> may have found another country. A country to live in and die for...
> that offers sustenance but demands commitment and sacrifice. A
> focus for youthful passions luring us away from more mundane and
> safer concerns of commerce and clan. A country that again dangles
> the promise of martyrdom which only ends in betrayals—all, that is,
> that an exile must at least partially abandon when he abandons home.
> "Never again" he tells himself and admonishes his children—"this is
> not our war, or yours, we fought ours many seasons ago so you may
> live in peace." At some point the migrant knows he must choose to live
> fully as a person without country if only to survive the vicissitudes *of*
> uprootedness. He bends with the wind and profits on cynicism. He
> says "no" to everything that forced him to leave home and family—war
> and patriotism. He dreams that his children will be citizens of the
> world. It is a pipe dream, of course, for one cannot love humanity
> without sympathizing with a neighbor brutalized by systematic
> oppression; because nationalism is only the concrete expression of our
> humanity in a particular historic context. This he knows. He knows
> in his hour of exile that his children are no longer his compatriots. He
> knows this dream of unbelonging is the last thing he must surrender
> with grace to time. (7–8)

Invoking the by-now familiar idea of the Chinese as "Jews of the Orient," Jeffrey attributes some of the characteristic traits associated with the "Chinese" to their existential condition of homelessness: "It is the homeless whose needs must dwell in the never-never land of ancestral glory and grandeur or in the imagined future of either borderless communism or the global multinational corporation" (Ong 2000b, 12).

Born on July 4, American independence day, the stateless, propertyless "Chinaman" Jeffrey feels that he "no longer owed allegiance to any clan or country" (12). And yet no sooner does he return to the Victorianas than he gets embroiled in the affairs of the nation. At the same time, he is caught in a family drama that climaxes in the revelation that the family he thinks he belongs to is not his family at all, and the friends he loves and trusts are not who they seem. Not only does he become involved in the messy fallout of his father Carlos's murder, but it turns out that Carlos is not even his father. Rather, his father is revealed as Carlos's friend, the Indonesian-Chinese refugee turned Chinese-Victoriano tycoon Alfonso Ong. Jeffrey becomes disillusioned with his childhood friend Jennifer Sy, a fellow Trekkie (a fan of the *Star Trek* television series) who gives a strong showing as a presidential candidate, but is crippled by the machinations of (and a drug habit induced by) her trusted spiritual advisor, the Chinese-mestizo Aldoux Chang, and Jeffrey's real father, Alfonso Ong.

The intimate relationship between family and nation is underscored not only in Jeffrey's fraught relationship with his erstwhile father Carlos, who, despite his professed noninvolvement in the affairs of the country, is eventually revealed as a "dreamer" (164) who wanted to establish a science and culture center on his share of the property on which Megalomalla was eventually built, and "who loved his adopted land deeply, if in silence" (294). The irony is that while Jeffrey's "father" Carlos had left him with neither inheritance nor legal standing in the Victorianas, he now stands to inherit not only his biological father's enormous fortune, but the ultimate political prize that this enormous fortune can secure: no less than the presidency of the country.

Torn between his adoptive father and his real father, Jeffrey then learns a number of unpalatable truths about his "real" father. Alfonso Ong's ambitious scheme of making half of his island a showcase high-tech twenty-first-century city and special economic zone is exposed as a scheme based on prison labor extracted from mainland Chinese, courtesy of a high-ranking communist Chinese military officer who moves his business interests and activities to Burias Island to escape the regulations of mainland China.

Ong's attempt to turn the other half of his island into a showcase for endangered wildlife (both animal and human) masks his darker personal motives. Ong reveals his identity to his real son because he is in need of a kidney transplant, and has in fact been harvesting kidneys from the indigenous people he has brought over to his island. Jasmine, reaffirming her sibling bond with Jeffrey in spite of the revelation that they are not related, tells him: "There's no such thing as blood, Jeffrey. He's not your father, you are nothing to him but a pair of kidneys. You won't inherit anything from him but his crimes." Among Jeffrey's first acts as president is to order a state funeral for Carlos Tantivo.

This intermeshing of family and state fortunes is played out in the history of the ruling Victoriano elite, whose dynastic ambitions, shifting alliances, and internecine rivalries recall the Philippine "anarchy of families" (McCoy 1994). The republic was established by Omay Policarpio, who as governor had teamed up with Vice-Governor Andronico Kawa to establish a constitutional committee with his and Kawa's sons as members. Barely after the Republic was founded, a civil war soon erupted between the two and involving the army. An illegitimate grandson of Policarpio, Artemio Azurin, seized power in 1984 and became dictator. Jennifer Sy's rival presidential hopefuls include Gelacio Kawa, grandson of Andronico; General Anthony Serrano, half-brother of her friend and Jeffrey's former sweetheart Isabela (now married to Jeffrey's friend Ignacio); and Agnes de Jesus, daughter of labor leader and "left-wing martyr" Aurelio "Fidel" Cuadra (Ong 2000b, 32). The periodic upheavals trigger the large-scale displacement of the population as Victorianos (including Chinese) flee the country. The novel ends with yet another coup d'etat that deposes the Sy/Tantivo government and sends Jeffrey back into exile in Manila.

In the novel, the Chinese have an ambiguous relationship with the nation and state. Alfredo and Jennifer Sy's Megalomalla, a "cradle-to-grave emporium" (27)—150 hectares, with 200 stores, including restaurants, cinema houses, offices, chapels, nurseries, a morgue, an emergency clinic, and a crematorium—and related enterprises (including low-cost housing and agribusiness) employ 50,000 people, thereby helping to "keep the economy afloat" (33). Jeffrey's father runs a petroleum products business. Corefugee from Indonesia, Alfonso Ong owns: (a) the country's biggest logging concession; (b) one-third of the country's foreign exchange; and (c) Burias Island. He plays kingmaker to his friend Alfredo's daughter Jennifer Sy, backing her presidential campaign while simultaneously undercutting it for his own purposes.

While a number of Chinese Victorianos have found their economic niche and flourished in the country, they are not invulnerable. President Azurin, whose mother is part Chinese, formulates a policy of promoting Chinese economic activity while blocking their access to citizenship. In a move recalling the action of Filipino president Ferdinand Marcos, Azurin orders the execution of a Chinese merchant on charges of drug dealing, even though it is widely believed that the Chinese had been fronting for him. In the final years of his regime, economic instability provokes public outcries "for the blood of Chinese merchants who are accused of inflating prices" (23). The business alliance between Alfonso Ong and Comrade Lu (a prescient scenario, since *Embarrassment* was published years before such alliances became publicly known) attracts condemnation from the anti-Chinese Libay, who would later emerge as the top warlord after the collapse of the Sy/Tantivo government. Libay, calling Jennifer an "alien whore" (332), is instrumental in fomenting rumors of government infiltration by foreign agents (306), and, once he assumes power, goes on to charge Ong with trying to turn Burias into a "trust territory of the Chinese" (423).

Four things stand out as principal achievements of *Embarrassment of Riches*. One is Charlson Ong's choice of a specifically Southeast Asian and more generally East Asian backdrop for the novel. Carlos Tantivo and Alfonso Ong first meet as refugees on the last boat from Indonesia just before the 1965–1966 massacres. Two sympathetically rendered Japanese characters, Yasunari Miyazawa and his nephew Charles, are among Jeffrey's friends. (The choice of the surname Miyazawa is telling, since Yasunari shares the same surname as Miyazawa Kiichi, whose career covered the years of Japan's economic miracle and the Plaza Accord that laid the foundation for East Asian regionalization.[19]) Explaining his motivations for writing the novel, Charlson Ong states:

> I started writing *Embarrassment of Riches* in 1994. At that time
> I intended to write a novel for the Philippine Centennial Year
> celebration although the contest had yet to be announced. I wanted to
> write a novel that would locate the Philippine imagined community in
> "south east Asia." Many significant Philippine novels in English—Nick
> Joaquin, [Wilfrido] Nolledo—trace nationhood to Spanish/Catholic
> colonization. This is inevitable, of course, and valid. We write under
> the shadow of [Jose] Rizal, as well. But I wanted to write the other
> story—that of Chinese emigration to the Nanyang that played a vital
> role in the formation of the nation states. In the Philippines, this led to
> the formation of the Sanglay[sic]/Ilustrado class at the turn of the last
> century and to the present Chinoy/Taipan. (Ong 2008)

Second is *Embarrassment*'s prescient handling of the rising China. Charlson Ong (2008) explains that "Historically, the mestizo (largely of Chinese descent) and the immigrant have tussled over economic turf. China's economic resurgence has revitalized this conflict. China's growth is both bane and boon to the local Chinese community, as well as the nation at large, and I believe that much of what will happen hereabout in the next decades will depend on how the local economic elite and business community—many of Chinese descent—will deal with China. Neither Spain, nor the U.S., or Europe or the Catholic Church will have as much impact on this country as will China. And yet there is really no strategic thinking, and very little artistic reflection, in this regard." The complex repositioning of the Filipino (mestizo) elite vis-à-vis the rising China and the connections now being forged between Filipino politicians and mainland Chinese princelings have already been discussed earlier in this chapter, while chapter 7 will address the question of how to think about the cultural ramifications of the rising China in Southeast Asia. Suffice it to say that in the novel, the mainland Chinese business venture in the Victorianas is built on a marriage of convenience between mainland Chinese and Chinese Victorianos and on the exploitation of mainland Chinese prison labor.

The third is Ong's decision to set his novel in a fictional country. The richly imagined details of history, people, and everyday life in Las Victorianas incite comparisons with the Philippines. Jeffrey Tantivo notes that it is not unusual for Europeans in Manila to confuse the Victorianas with Mindoro or other Philippine islands. The novel establishes the parallels by stating that the Victorianas were called the "Little Philippines," or "siao fei," by early Chinese settlers (Ong 2000b, 13), a clear homage to the historical Chinese appellation of Xiao Lusong (小呂宋 Little Luzon; Ming China used "Lusong" 呂宋 to refer to a polity on what is now the island of Luzon; in the sixteenth and seventeenth centuries, the term referred to the Spanish colonial Philippines).

In *Embarrassment of Riches*, the Philippines looms large in Victoriano history and imagination, the main difference being that this influence was not brought about by Philippine colonization of the Victorianas, but by their proximity and shared history. Nevertheless, the history of the Victorianas, while hewing closely to the general patterns of history in the Philippines, exhibits a number of crucial differences. Although the Victorianas, like the Philippines, was "discovered" and colonized by Spain, its relative insignificance as territory did not lead to the entrenchment of frailocracy; instead, treated with "benign neglect," it served as a rugged outpost where dissident Filipinos were exiled by the Spaniards. The British briefly occupied it (as they did the Philippines), and so did the Portuguese (who did not). Americans built some infrastructure, but the country proved to be of "little strategic value to the U.S. in its bid to open up China for Virginia tobacco and after the first eager waves of engineers, architects, and Thomasites, the number of Americans on the island dwindled to less that five hundred shortly before the outbreak of World War II" (17). And World War II? It "was a nonevent in the Victorianas," with the commanding officer and half the Japanese soldiers stationed in the country deserting the Japanese army and remaining in the country after the war.

As for population, the native Victorianos are classified as "Malays" ("but such ethnic categories have of late been questioned by contemporary anthropologists" [14]). The precolonial language, Sadagat, belongs in the "Malayo-Polynesian" family of languages, is similar to Bahasa and Tagalog, and survives in an "amalgamated form" known as Victoriano, with borrowings from Spanish, Portuguese, English, and Chinese. Victorianas have a Moro minority as well, and their Chinese, who make up 8 percent of the population, speak the "Xiamen dialect of southeastern China so that many Chinese terms in trading and cuisine have become part of the lingua franca" (ibid.).

A tongue-in-cheek, self-referential passage, conveyed through Jeffrey, tells the reader that "While such distinction may seem facile to those unaware of our histories, to my mind, it is the basic reason why, despite claims to the contrary, the Philippines and the Victorianas are quite separate nations" (15). A Jesuit historian in the novel calls the Victorianas a "shadow Philippines" (13), while Jeffrey himself prefers to describe the Victorianas as "a caricature of the gentle, if similarly unfortunate country [i.e., Philippines]" (14).

Setting the novel in a similar-but-different fictional country is an ingenious way of conjuring up the Philippines in the pages of the novel (where there are frequent comparative references to it), but most importantly in the reader's mind by means of a game of comparisons. Readers who are primed for comparison are not likely to miss out on the small but crucial differences between the Victorianas and the Philippines—to take one example, the Japanese occupation, a nonevent in the Victorianas but a traumatic one in the Philippines. A review of *Embarrassment of Riches* (Laurel 2003, 616) castigates Charlson Ong for downplaying colonization and the problems it has created in a novel that is supposed to be a memorial to the centennial of the Philippines' struggle for independence against Spain. This kind of critique, while valid in its own terms, is not the only way to read the novel, since its literal-minded approach to the objectives of the Centennial Literary Contest assumes that a novel can only ever be effective if it spells out (an unkind equivalent would be "spoon-feed") the "lessons" from Philippine history. Such prescriptions for "social relevance," when heeded by less-gifted writers, have played no small role in producing some of the most stultifying boring novels that do more damage to Philippine literature by turning readers off reading Philippine texts (if not reading altogether). *Embarrassment of Riches* explicitly deviates from the "standard" preoccupation of the Filipino novel in English: instead of simply retelling the pernicious legacy of colonialism, it focuses on hitherto unexplored dimensions (Nanyang Chinese and rising China) of the here-and-now, a century after the founding of the Philippine Republic, and forces readers to ask the question: to what extent must we claim responsibility for our own actions in the present, even if these actions are also partly informed by our past history?

Colonialism has been an important theme in Philippine writings in Filipino, and even in English.[20] Ong's novel, by bringing into play comparisons between the Victorianas and the Philippines, places the burden of interpreting Philippine history and contemporary realities onto the reader, whose attentiveness to details of similarity and difference between Victorianas and the Philippines compels him or her to piece together a mental portrait of the Philippines, its people, history, and current situation. In effect, it is the reader, not just the text per se, who undertakes the labor of *thinking about* "the Philippines" in the process of reading about the fictional country of Victorianas in *Embarrassment of Riches*.

The choice of a fictional country as setting also performs another function in the novel. By giving readers a "caricature of the gentle, if similarly unfortunate," Philippines, the novel invites readers to think about the civil unrest, the abject poverty, the social movements (among them the communist and El Shaddai movements), the political dynasties, the consumerism, the ubiquity of technomedia (which Jennifer cannily exploits for her political campaign), that beset the Philippines. "To spend one's early adulthood in my country is to be mired in a morass of poverty, power shortages, religious fanaticism, political charlatans, and inane movies that often erode whatever pride one has in a people that have survived five hundred years of foreign dominance and fifty more of local misrule and self-abuse to emerge as tolerant, peaceable and instinctively democratic as they are" (Ong 2000b, 9). "My country" here is the Victorianas, but it is also clearly the Philippines.

At the same time, the reference to Victorianas as a territorially proximate but geopolitically insignificant "shadow Philippines" has the paradoxical effect of presenting a loving, nostalgia-drenched view of the Philippines. Jeffrey elects to stay in Manila instead of moving on to America, "savor[ing] the aesthetic, technological and sensual pleasures" of the Philippine capital, even as its "coconut trees, fresh mangoes, crimson sunsets, brown women, cockfights, basketball fanatics, [and] political carousels...reminded me so much of home" (9). This nostalgia-drenched Philippines that is also a reminder of, indeed a stand-in for, Victorianas fuels Jeffrey's nostalgia for home precisely by keeping his "psychic ties to the motherland" tethered by dint of geographical proximity between the two countries.

Ong sidesteps Jose Rizal's "demonio de las comparaciones" (1887, 43), the proverbial *ilustrado* double consciousness that highlights the problems of the country by comparing it to other, better-off countries in the colonial metropole.[21] This double consciousness has been an important source of critical dissent aimed at upturning the assumed hierarchy between colony and metropole through liberation and revolution. *Embarrassment* retains the comparative perspective, but its choice of two countries from the periphery with parallel yet also intertwined histories evokes a different set of feelings from the ones engendered by the demon of comparisons between periphery and metropole. Whereas the patriotism incited by the demon of comparisons is stoked by a sense of oppression based on pride, humiliation, anger, and revenge, the Victorianas/Filipinas comparisons appeal to a different but no less powerful range of emotions—sympathy and solidarity. In the centuries of shared but differently experienced colonialism, each country has represented for the other an arena: whereas Victorianas had served as a place of exile for Filipino dissidents in the colonial era, the Philippines would serve a similar function for Jeffrey and for thousands of Victorianos fleeing repression and civil strife in their country. "Pin[ing] and poet[izing] for my country's deliverance," Jeffrey also helps out in the Aquino presidential campaign in the Philippines.

This capacity of empathy and solidarity to evoke a sense of nation as well as to render one attentive to the plight of similarly oppressed neighbors is what complicates Jeffrey's sense of himself as a "stateless and propertyless Chinaman": "I figured I didn't have enough at stake in any of this to risk life and limb for. Christ, I wasn't even a citizen of the republic!" (Ong 2000b, 82). He finds in his "father" Carlos's life experience all the ingredients of the dream of a cosmopolitanism that leads him to feel, upon his return to Victorianas following the end of the Azurin regime, that he "no longer owed allegiance to any clan or country" (12). But involved himself he did, just as Carlos had, in spite of his badmouthing of the Victoriano *huana* (huana/huanna is explained in the introduction). Driven into a second and perhaps permanent exile following the collapse of the government he briefly headed, he declares himself "a Victoriano; proud and true" (424) and vows to "speak for all of my people who drift in a sea of uncertainty. I live for all who keep vigil in the night of the world awaiting a certain daybreak" (425). These final words, echoing Elias's last words in Rizal's *Noli me tangere*, bring the Philippines and similarly oppressed countries to the forefront and the novel to a close.

The fourth achievement of *Embarrassment of Riches* is its somber disquisition on the limits of citizenship—in this case, noncitizenship. Ong's portrait of the Chinese-Victoriano Jeffrey Tantivo shows how a stateless "Chinaman"—who professes to be "torture-resistant. I confess to everything" (162)—nevertheless becomes politically involved in the affairs of the nation, at considerable risk to his personal safety. *Embarrassment of Riches* asks readers to imagine the unimaginable: that a stateless Chinaman might nevertheless risk life and limb for a country that he can neither completely embrace nor repudiate.

Charlson Ong's foregrounding of the issue of (non)citizenship is fortuitous, since it continues to have implications for Chinese in the Philippines. While considerable advances have been made in integrating the Chinese Filipino into the Philippine "imagined community," the gate of citizenship has remained the most important means for regulating and policing the Chinese. While kidnappings continue to take place, targeting both Filipinos and Chinese, Chinese Filipinos have been able to rely to some extent on their Philippine citizenship to make themselves heard and defend themselves both legally and publicly, even as citizenship has not spared them the everyday harassment and extortions that have victimized many other Filipinos (see, for example, *Tulay*, 2006b). But for Chinese Filipinos who are interested in politics, the issue of their (ancestors') citizenship is the weapon rival candidates use to bar them from running for office. Chinese-mestizo Alfredo Lim, former (now current) mayor of Manila, 1998 presidential hopeful, and a seasoned politician with a reputation for strong-arm tactics, once faced questions about his citizenship status as natural-born citizen (Baguioro 1998), while Jesse Robredo, a second-generation Chinese Filipino and a popular mayor of Naga City, Bicol, and later secretary of the Interior and Local Government, was disqualified from running in the 2007 mayoralty elections because of questions over his citizenship (Ronda 2007).[22]

But the most vulnerable elements among the "Chinese" are Chinese non-Filipino citizens and "paper sons" (Chinese who bought Philippine documentation) operating small businesses or as part of the informal economy of "illegal vendors" on the streets, on whom the state elements have preyed through period raids to root out "illegal aliens." A typical raid, say, of Plaza Miranda, Carriedo Arcade, and Carriedo Shopping Center in Quiapo, downtown Manila (*Tulay*, 1999), entails rounding up "Chinese" and bringing them en masse to the Bureau of Immigration detention center in Bicutan. Those who are able to present proof of their legal status through valid immigration and travel documents are released, while those who cannot are threatened with deportation.[23] Malls in or around Chinatown—especially Tutuban Shopping Mall, Divisoria Mall, and the newly built 168[24]—are a particular favorite raiding ground (Ang-See 2000, 8; *Tulay*, 2006a).[25]

Witnesses to a 1996 Tutuban raid claimed that BID agents used the criterion of "Chinese looks" to arrest people. Some of the raiders allegedly demanded P20,000–P30,000 from the arrested in exchange for their freedom. Of the eighteen people taken to the Immigration offices, eleven were released immediately for lack of evidence, and six of the remaining seven were freed after presenting proper documentation. The sole foreigner whose status remained in doubt was an Indian. The rather inflated figures that the government expected to earn have since been scaled down to a more modest sum of P1 billion (*Manila Bulletin*, 1996, 19). Furthermore, officers have been known to use Filipino when interrogating the people they round up, the idea being that a Chinese who cannot answer back in the same language automatically becomes a suspect.

These raids show that the discourse of official integration remains bound up with questions of "culture," a fact that also brings to light the tension between "us" Chinese Filipinos and "them" G.I.s (genuine intsik), with their *barok* (broken)-Tagalog/Cebuano, their "uncouth" ways, and their "China" orientation. In everyday life, the logic of civic conversion gets played out across generations, in neighborhoods, among siblings, and in some cases, even within oneself, between Filipinos and Chinese, and among Chinese themselves.

The "proof" of nationality and cultural integration demanded by the agents of the state serves as a ready means of separating "our" Chinese Filipinos from the TDKs and G.I.'s (genuine intsik), the "other" Chinese. This is not just a question of business, of making money off the "alien," even as the Filipino elite busy themselves with forging business alliances with their regional counterparts in East Asia, whether Japanese, Taiwanese, or South Korean, with mainland Chinese now constituting a latecomer but increasingly important partner. It constitutes proof of the fact that external and internal borders and boundaries continue to matter, that they have the power to make themselves felt in the everyday lives of those who remain "alien" even in the eyes of the now safely Filipinized Chinese Filipino. But they are also proof that the very act of living, even in the most basic imperative to survive, produces sentiments and attachments that are portable but not so easily containable, to be measured out in finite amounts to just one person, one group, one community, one people. These foreigners, by their very presence in Philippine life, prove that they can and have been able to make a "home" for themselves in a country where they may not always be welcome, a country they may not even think of as theirs, the way overstaying TNT (*tago-ng-tago*) Filipinos have done in America and elsewhere in the world. *Embarrassment* asks Filipino readers to experience what it would be like to learn to love a place where one "lives," even when one is unwanted. In the age of large-scale Filipino international migration, this experience is no longer unimaginable, but rather, commonplace for Chinese and Filipinos alike.

Notes

1   The National Museum of Singapore built a new "Straits Chinese Gallery" in 1987 to house its collection of "Peranakan material." A new Peranakan Museum was

established in 2004, on the heels of the growing popularity of peranakan material in auction sales between 1994 and 1998 and the growing nostalgia on the part of what the Museum calls the "Peranakan community" for the "loss of their world" (Peranakan Museum 2008, 10).

2 I thank Ben Anderson for explaining the nuances of the term "peranakan."

3 Women used "nyonya," a term that might have originated from Java and Sumatra.

4 In contemporary usage, *baba* is seen as less "westernized" and less "prosperous" than "peranakan." I thank Jafar Suryomenggolo for this information. Ben Anderson (2012) notes, however, that the key aspect of the British Malay baba is their being "'westernized' in an out-of-date way."

5 I thank Nobu Aizawa for his help in clarifying this issue.

6 I thank Ben Anderson for pointing out the salience of language issues.

7 This convention appears to have lost some steam, most likely because by 2004–2005, de facto regional integration of the East-Asia/Asia-Pacific region had created dense linkages among business people that made this kind of forum superfluous.

8 For years after the 1998 riots, video compact discs falsely claiming to be "documentaries" of the rapes committed during the riots were sold and circulated among overseas Chinese communities in Southeast Asia as well as in mainland China, Taiwan, and Hong Kong. The pornographic nature of these alleged atrocities strongly recalls the photographs taken by Japanese soldiers during the Nanjing Massacre.

9 The Chinese ideal of a patriarchal household resonates with the (mainly middle-class) Filipino ideal of *padre-de-familia* (lit., "father of the family," in which the father is the primary breadwinner and ultimate decision maker), even though the state has not actively propounded this norm.

10 "The official survey of incomes and expenditures in 1971 showed that the richest 10 per cent of the population received 56 per cent of all income while the poorest 30 per cent received 4 per cent. In urban areas (where the rich congregated), the proportions were, respectively, 81 and 7 per cent" (Krinks 2002, 40).

11 The total state revenue in 2011 was 13.4 percent of GDP at current market prices, compared to 16.5 percent in 2007; and 19.4 percent in 1997; and government collection of taxes has also declined in relative terms to 12.1 percent of GDP from a high of 17 percent in 1997 (Asian Development Bank 2011, 5). This trend indicates that the economy is growing faster than the state's extractive capacity.

12 No less than National Artist for Literature, F. Sionil José, raised the specter of anti-Chinese violence in a series of incendiary articles castigating "disloyal," "anti-Filipino Chinese" who "remit" their Philippine-earned money to China (1999a; 1999b; 2000). While Onghokham (chap. 2) saw in the Chinese mestizo a case of successful assimilation that could serve as a model for postcolonial Indonesia's *masalah cina* (Chinese problem), Jose (1999a) sees in Indonesia (as well as Malaysia) a final solution to the Chinese Question by virtue of the threat or actual fact of wholesale killing of unregenerate "Chinese" (from which he plans to exempt some of his Chinese friends): "Indeed, so many Chinese have become wealthy and they flaunt their wealth in their mansions, in their mausoleums at the Chinese Cemetery—nothing like it in all of Asia. There are no more Chinese junk peddlers, *sari-sari* store owners—their presence is pervasive in the most expensive watering holes. And perhaps, without their being aware of it, the natives look at them not only with envy but with growing resentment knowing that many of these entrepreneurs have salted

away the yolk of their fortunes to China or Taiwan. Is it possible that someday such Filipino resentment will erupt in bloody pogroms? This will, of course, be a tragedy but if it does happen, it is because the Chinese have willed it with their contempt for Filipinos, their continued loyalty to the Mainland." Ironically, Jose raises the specter of pogroms in order to support his argument in favor of "integration" of the Chinese. In 2000, Jose wrote: "In the event of hostilities with China, which is not impossible or even remote, then we must put them all in prison camps, seize or freeze their assets, and on the whole treat them as the enemy. In the meantime, all we can do is to beware of their presence, assure ourselves that they will not destroy us from within our ranks, and hope that those Chinese-Filipinos who are loyal to this nation can convince them to abandon their anti-Filipino beliefs."

13   The following discussion is indebted to Shiraishi 2012.

14   The label "probinsyano" also carries an urban bias, perhaps best exemplified by the Tagalog slang term, *promdi* (Filipinized contraction of the English phrase "from the province").

15   The disputes have provoked saber-rattling on both sides. For an overview of China's handling of territorial disputes both in the homeland and over offshore island, see Fravel 2008. Among the voluminous publications on this issue, see Bateman and Emmers 2009. Events of the past few years are happening at such a fast pace that it is too soon to offer any generalization about the impact of China's increasing military expenditure and decision to consider the South China Sea a "core nationalist interest." One need only recall similar incidents of saber-rattling over the Spratly Islands in the 1990s to realize that mainland Chinese responses are neither monolithic nor immutable.

16   Ignacio Paua, the only full-blooded Chinese general in the Philippine revolution, is generally lauded for his contribution to the Philippine revolution, but at the time of the Centennial celebrations, there was a debate in the newspapers over his role in arresting the Bonifacio brothers (Bankoff and Weekley 2004, 57n66).

17   A more modest, real-life parallel would be established more than ten years after *Embarrassment* was published, when Chinese-Filipino taipan Lucio Tan's daughter Vivienne, who ran for Congress in the May 2010 local and national elections. Although she successfully overcame a lawsuit seeking to disqualify her on grounds of her American citizenship, she lost out to Vincent "Bingbong" Crisologo, a member of the Crisologo political dynasty. I thank Charlson Ong for pointing out this parallel.

18   The surname Tantivo is derived from the Hokkien Tan Tibu, "tibu" meaning "pig," a reference to the fact that Carlos had once raised pigs for a Spanish priest.

19   The fact that George H. W. Bush vomited into Miyazawa's lap at a state dinner 1992, at which time the Japanese bubble had burst and recession had begun to set in, is replete with symbolic and narrative possibilities.

20   People who are likely to read Ong's novels would no doubt already be familiar with the works of F. Sionil Jose, whose Rosales saga represents one of the most sustained literary engagements with the impact and legacy of colonialism in the Philippines. Jose, though, has been criticized for his "anti-Chinese" remarks over the years. See footnote 12.

21   In a further homage to Rizal, Jeffrey is conscripted into planting a bomb in a temple during karma-cleansing rites, but at the last minute, like Rizal's Isagani, haunted

by the thought of innocent blood spilled, hurls his father's urn (in lieu of Simoun's pomegranate-shaped lamp) into the river.

22 Born to an ethnic-Chinese father and Filipino mother, Robredo would be hounded by disqualification cases filed against him in 1998, 2001, and 2004. Jojo Villafuerte, the man who filed the case with the Commission on Elections in 2007, is Robredo's cousin and nephew of Robredo's political opponent and uncle Luis Robredo Villafuerte Sr.

23 Actual initiation of deportation proceedings is often a last resort, if under-the-table "negotiations" fail to work out (Ang-See 2000). Biographical details of one such "illegal Chinese" who is part of the informal economy in Manila can be found in Uy 1999.

24 The shopping mecca for bargain-price goods, 168 has provided stiff competition against (Chinese-Filipino-owned) malls like SM and Robinsons. The periodic raid may have contributed to making 168 an "unsafe" place to shop, to the benefit of the big-time retail business owners.

25 The early twenty-first century has witnessed the revitalization of the Binondo-Divisoria area that forms the business core of Manila's Chinatown because of the influx of new migrants from China (Guéguen 2006). New residential apartments and condominiums have also transformed the landscape of Chinatown, though not always for the better, as old *bahay na bato* (wood-and-stone houses built during the Spanish and American periods) are torn down to give way to high rises.

7

"ANGLO-CHINESE"

Over the past three decades, territorial disputes notwithstanding, it has become "chic" (Pasuk and Baker 1996, 135) to be "Chinese," or to showcase one's "Chinese" connections in Southeast Asia. Leaders ranging from President Corazon Cojuangco Aquino of the Philippines to King Bhumibol Adulyadej, Prime Minister Kukrit Pramoj, and Prime Minister Thaksin Shinawatra of Thailand to President Abdurrahman Wahid of Indonesia and Prime Minister Abdullah Badawi of Malaysia have proclaimed their Chinese ancestry. Beyond elite and official pronouncements, popular culture has been instrumental in disseminating positive images of "Chinese" and "Chineseness," as discussed in chapter 5.

The term "re-Sinicization" (or "resinification") has been applied to the revival of hitherto devalued, occluded, or repressed "Chineseness," and more generally to the phenomenon of increasing visibility, acceptability, and self-assertiveness of ethnic Chinese in Southeast Asia and elsewhere.[1] The phenomenon of "re-Sinicization" marks a significant departure from an era in which "China" served as a model for the localization of socialism and propagation of socialist revolution in parts of Southeast Asia in the 1950s and 1960s, and Southeast Asian "Chinese" were viewed and treated as economically dominant, culturally different, and politically disloyal Others to be "de-Sinicized" through nation-building discourses and policies.

For want of a better word, the term "re-Sinicization" has served as an expedient signpost for the variegated manifestations and revaluations of such Chineseness. Its use, however, does not simply affirm the conventional understanding of Sinicization as a unilinear, unidirectional, and foreordained process of "becoming Chinese" that radiates (or is expected to increasingly radiate) outward from mainland China.[2] Since the "Sinosphere"[3] was inhabited by different "Chinas" at different times in history, the process of modern "Sinicization" cannot be analyzed in terms of a self-contained, autochthonous "China" or "Chinese" world, let alone an essentialized "Chinese" identity.[4] These "Chinas" were themselves products of hybridization and acculturation born of their intimate and sometimes contentious cultural, economic, and military contacts with populations across their western continental frontiers, most notably Mongols and Manchus, and with Southern Asia (India and Southeast Asia) across their southern frontiers.[5] This Sinosphere began to break down in the mid-nineteenth century. In their modern articulations, "China," "Chinese," and "Chineseness" are relational terms that, over the past century and a half, point to a history of conceptual disjunctions and distinctive patterns of historical hybridizations arising from the hegemonic challenges that the maritime powers of the "West" posed to the Sinocentric world. And in that world, social, economic, cultural, and intellectual interactions among many different sites were intense and largely enabled by the regional and global flows and movements of capital, people, goods, technologies, and ideas within and beyond the contexts of British and, later, American hegemony in East and Southeast Asia.

Without discounting China's important contribution to modern world-making (Liu 2004) over the past century and a half, this concluding chapter complicates the idea of "Sinicization" as a mainland state-centered and state-driven process of remaking the world (and the ethnic Chinese outside its borders) in its own image. Instead, it proposes to understand "Sinicization" as a complex, historically contingent process entailing not just multiple actors and practices, but equally important, multiple sites from which they, over time, have created, reinvented, and transformed received meanings associated with "China," "Chinese," and "Chineseness." Sinicization cannot be studied apart from the related concepts of re-Sinicization and de-Sinicization; taken together, they can best be understood as a congeries of pressures and possibilities, constraints and opportunities for "becoming-Chinese" that are subject to centripetal and centrifugal forces—as Wang Gungwu (2004, 224) has noted for the cultural context of territorialization and de/reterritorialization.[6] One crucial implication is that no single institution or agent, not even the putative superpower People's Republic of China, has so far been able to definitively claim authority as the final cultural arbiter of what constitutes "Chinese" and "Chineseness" or even, for that matter, "China."

Conceptual Disjunctions

From the mid-nineteenth century onwards, Qing China confronted a hegemonic challenge, not from across its continental borders to the west, but from the maritime world to its east. The Opium Wars and more crucially the Taiping rebellion—both manifestations in China's foreign and domestic relations of the explosive "clash of empires" (to use Lydia Liu's [2004] term)—were instrumental in the breakdown of the tribute-trade system in the east.[7] That system had hitherto been organized in terms of a China-centered tributary trade system along with what was called, in the late Ming and Qing periods, "mutual markets" (互市 *hushi/goshi*, in which traders could visit Chinese ports without accompanying a tributary mission), with two different dynastic regimes of "China" as its core state.[8] The ensuing century and a half has been characterized by the Chinese as a period of chaos (乱 *luan*), one that has borne witness to large-scale deterritorialization through outmigration from the mainland—a massive outflow of people that would only be reduced, and then only briefly, when Communist China was formally cut off from its non-Communist neighbors and the American-led world between the late 1940s and the mid-1970s.

From the late nineteenth century onward, "China" was incorporated into the international system. Rising nationalist sentiments made "Chinese/ness" an issue of paramount importance for "China" in its multiple discursive, territorial, and regime manifestations, and for the so-called Chinese in Southeast Asia (the principal region of immigration from the mainland) and their host states and societies. This created multiple disjunctions between territory, nation, state, culture, and civilization—key concepts in the study of modern politics—in the signifiers "China" and "Chinese/ness."

Not only is it problematical to equate or conflate the concepts of territory, nation, state, culture, and civilization when one talks about "China." The lack of an easy or necessary fit among territory, nation, state, culture, and civilization is further complicated by China's modern history of translating concepts from other languages (discussed in the next section), embedding thousands of foreign words in the Chinese language. Terms like "feudalism," "imperialism," "colonialism," "naturalism," and "modernity" not only carry with them the history of their usages and circulation in English, Japanese, German, French, and Russian, among other languages, but the history as well of their localization and (re)signification in the Chinese context. This complex history of global, regional, and local circulation and appropriation makes phrases such as "Han (Chinese) imperialism" and

"Han colonization of south and southwestern China" the subject of highly charged debates.

This is not to argue that the concepts of territory, nation, state, culture, and civilization are just abstractions that lack any referent in reality; on the contrary, modern Chinese history is an account of the prodigious time and energy expended, not to mention the blood-sweat-tears spilled, on determining, fixing, or challenging and changing the proper cultural, political, territorial, and civilizational referents of "China" (Duara 1997, 40). The fact that "China" was and continues to be a floating signifier (Levi-Strauss 1987 [1950], 63)—that is, its referents (i.e., what it refers to) are variable, sometimes indeterminate and unspecifiable—does not in any way suggest that "China" is purely a discursive construction; it only means that there is an irreducibly discursive dimension to ethnic-"Chinese's" relationship with "China." Taxonomic studies of ethnic "Chinese" political loyalty and orientations, and multiple manifestations of "Chineseness," can best be understood as attempts at making sense of the multiplicity of assertions, commitments, persuasions, declarations, and expressions generated by the floating signifier "China." They highlight the productive potential of the signifier "China" to be made to mean and do something, conditioning practices and claims made in the name of "China" and "Chinese."

Between the late nineteenth and the mid-twentieth century, there was a political disjunction as various entities and movements at various times—from late Qing provincial and central authorities, to reformers, such as Kang Youwei and Liang Qichao; to revolutionaries, such as Sun Yat-sen; and on to warlords, the Kuomintang, and the Chinese Communist Party—reached out to the "Chinese" in "China" as well as Nanyang (Southeast Asia) and elsewhere (Duara 1997; Godley 1981; Yen 1976). Motivated by imperatives of mobilizing human, financial, and affective resources, each of these appeals to the "Chinese" accomplished two tasks. It drew on or tapped different wellsprings of attachment to and identification with native place(s), ancestry, and origins; and it articulated competing political visions of community, people, nation, and state. Political disjunction meant that there was no easy or necessary fit between nation and state (Guo 2004). Different political movements, whose activities and mobilization sometimes took place outside of the territory of "China," targeted specific "Chinese" localities and communities and competed to capture the state and remake society in the image of their visions of the nation. "China"-driven Sinicization thus represents various attempts on the part of different "Chinese" regimes and actors to propound their notions of Chineseness and mobilize "Chinese" capital, resources, labor, and specific talents/skills for economic, political, and cultural objectives inside and outside the territorial boundaries of "China."

Such attempts to reterritorialize the "Chinese" in Southeast Asia were in some ways successful. They helped to create a new political, and more importantly, mobilizable entity called the *huaqiao*, a term that came into general use at the end of the nineteenth century but acquired its territorializing connotations only at the beginning of the twentieth (Wang 1992a, 6–7). But these efforts often came up short against competing deterritorializations and reterritorializations of "Chinese" and "Chineseness" that had taken place for at least three centuries in the colonial states of Southeast Asia—especially the Spanish Philippines, Dutch East Indies, British Malaya, and French Indochina. Their regimes promoted, cemented, and reinvented specific forms of "Chinese" identification and identities while curtailing or repressing others.

The "Chinese" had an important role in the Western colonies established in Southeast Asia. They were crucial agents and mediators in Spanish, British, Dutch, and French attempts to insert themselves into, to regulate and rechannel, the flows and networks of the regional maritime trade between China and its neighbors. Moreover, colonial states adopted different policies toward the "Chinese" as part of the divide-and-conquer logic of governing their resident populations. These policies had different consequences. The most salient feature of the colonial Southeast Asian state's treatment of the "Chinese" is the association of "Chinese" with commerce and capital (discussed in chap. 3), an identification that originated in the context of maritime trade and colonial economic enterprise but glosses over the existence of sizeable communities of Chinese laborers, especially in Malaya. (The Qing and Nationalist states also reinforced this historical conflation of ethnicity and commerce/capital by treating the huaqiao primarily as sources of financial "contributions" to underwrite state-led projects and undertakings and as sources of remittances to help shore up the economy in China.[9]) Such identification effectively conditioned the socialization of "Chinese" migrants as "material men" who played an indispensable role in the colonial economies. Reproduced and perpetuated through social relations of production that were characteristic of "Chinese" enterprise in the region (Chun 1989), this socialization enabled the "Chinese" to take advantage of the opportunities that were available in the colonial states and economies. But it also rendered them vulnerable to nationalist opprobrium that stigmatized "alien Chinese" as economically dominant and politically unreliable. "Chinese" participation in the national economies of Southeast Asia is significant and, more important, visible enough to lend credence to the myth of "Chinese" economic dominance. This myth is based on popularly disseminated statistics which, as Rupert Hodder (2005) has shown, are often problematical in their calculations: Chinese allegedly constitute 10 percent of the population of Thailand but command an 80 percent share of the country's market capital; in Indonesia, the share of market capital of this 3.5 percent of the population is supposed to be 75 percent; in Vietnam, 3 percent of the population are responsible for 50 percent of Ho Chi Minh's market activity; and in Malaysia, they constitute about one-third of the population, but they hold a share of between 60 percent and 70 percent of the country's market capital (Hodder 2005, 8).

This myth made the Chinese ready targets of nationalist policies aimed at disentangling the link between ethnicity and class through domestication of "cultural" differences (via assimilation and integration) and redistribution of wealth. Even though a combination of generational change and global/regional economic development has in recent decades produced sizeable urban professional middle classes that include not only "Chinese" but also non-Chinese Southeast Asians, economic regionalization has further cemented this identification of "Chinese" with capital. The crucial difference is that in the throes of economic and social transformation, postcolonial states and societies have generally revalued the identification of Chinese with capital in positive terms (see chaps. 5 and 6). The continuing identification of Chinese with capital is the source of "Chinese" assertive self-empowerment but also of continuing vulnerability to popular-nationalist resentment in contemporary Southeast Asia. Oscillating between these two poles, popular media portray Chinese as "heroes" of regional economic development and "villains" in times of economic crisis (and easy targets of violence, as in the case of Chinese Indonesians during the Asian crisis of 1997–1998).

Migration did not simply transplant "Chinese" and "Chineseness" to places outside China. These sites of immigration provided their own settings and cultural matrices for the invention, reinvention, and transformation of "Chineseness." Through the regional and global circulation of "Chinese" practices, ethnic Chinese learned about dragon dances and Chinese New Year celebration rites from each other's overseas communities. Some "Chinese" tested even the most expansive notion of Chinese "civilization" that defined Chineseness not in racial terms, but through written language and subscription to "Chinese" core values. Indeed, there were communities in Southeast Asia who called themselves or were treated by their states as "Chinese," but who neither spoke, read, nor wrote "Chinese," practiced "Chinese" customs or rituals, or looked "Chinese." The East Indies *peranakan* were classified by the Dutch as "Chinese," even though their culture exhibited pronounced hybridization of Javanese and other cultural elements that made them appear "un-Chinese" in the eyes of visiting Qing officials (Duara 1997). Until the early 1980s, to take another example, Kalimantan, Indonesia, had a community of stateless "Chinese" whom Indonesian government officials call *hitacis* (pronounced "hitachis," a word play on the Japanese appliance maker) or *hitam tapi cina* (black but Chinese).[10] Indonesian officials confessed to being unable to distinguish these individuals from native Indonesians,[11] whose sun-darkened skin and "Indonesianness" do not readily fit the accepted racial, linguistic, civilizational, and cultural criteria for Chineseness. This illustrates how "Chinese" and "Chineseness," in the hands and eyes of the Dutch East Indies colonial state and Indonesian postcolonial state, are rendered arbitrary by the exigencies and whims of the state and government officials.

The hitacis are not an exceptional case. What constitutes "Chinese" culture in the modernist sense of the term is continually enriched by the development of hybrid "Chinese" cultures that owe a great deal to the local histories of settlement and cultural contacts in social spaces outside the purview of the mainland state. The politicized huaqiao nationalism among "Chinese" immigrants and their descendants was a "peripheral" sort that was dependent and conditional on developments and contestations on the mainland. Physical and psychological distance from China gave it leeway to define its various "Chinese" cultures according to the pressures operating and opportunities open in the countries of residence (Wang 1981, 156–57).

At the same time, huaqiao activities had an impact on the mainland. Overseas Chinese support for the nationalist movement led Sun Yat-sen to call the huaqiao the "mother of the revolution" (*geming zhi mu*). Southeast Asian Chinese provided substantial financial support for "national salvation" activities against the Japanese in the 1930s and 1940s. Moreover, in the decades since the reopening of China, in deeply interactive processes, investment by ethnic Chinese from Hong Kong, Taiwan, Southeast Asia, America, and elsewhere has been crucial to the economic modernization of the mainland (Suryadinata 1995, 195, 208, 209–15). In the past decade, mainland China has emerged as the dominant trading partner of countries in Southeast Asia and East Asia more generally. It is Malaysia's biggest trading partner, Thailand's second largest, and the Philippines' third largest, with ASEAN being projected to become China's largest trading partner by 2015 (Bao 2012). China's deepening economic integration through trade and investment in East Asia and its Pacific partners (notably America and Canada) is also crucially mediated by ethnic Chinese living and working in and across the region.

To complicate the issue, during the first half of the twentieth century the mainland "Chinese" state was not unitary, weakened as it had been during the late Qing and the Republican years. Its reach and capacities were undermined by defeat at the hands of the British, French, Germans, Americans, Japanese, and Russians. In the twentieth century, the threat of dismemberment and secession loomed large as China was subject to decentralized rule by competing warlords, occupation by imperial Japan, and a civil war between the KMT and CCP. The enduring myth of historical continuity that rests on the ideal of a unitary state (Fitzgerald 1995) belies the reality of fragmentation of power and authority, with the state(s) serving as object(s) of intense competition among different forces.

Another disjunction arises from the modern state's fraught and contested inheritance of the territorial boundaries established by the Qing (with precedents in boundaries set by the Mongols and claimed by the Ming). While huge tracts of Mongolia were able to gain independence after the breakdown of the Qing Empire, territories such as Tibet and Xinjiang, which did not join the Chinese Republic, have been occupied and placed under the control of the mainland party state. They are now viewed as indivisible parts of China, a view that does not square with the opinions of Tibetan and Uyghur separatists. Attempts at promoting an inclusive nationalist discourse in the mainland coexist alongside a Han-Sinocentrism that defines "Chineseness" in exclusivist terms (Guo 2004).

The internal division of "China" was not the only significant disjunction. Equally important was the physical fragmentation around the edges of the Qing Empire, particularly the loss of Hong Kong to the British, and Taiwan to the Japanese. These geopolitical "splits" were to have crucial consequences during the Cold War era, when the mainland was "closed" to the American-dominated "Free Asia," and Taiwan and Hong Kong emerged as interlinked (but not necessarily overlapping) purveyors, respectively, of state-authorized and market-driven "Chinese" culture and "Chineseness" through the circulation of media and popular culture. In the post-Cold War era, the status of Taiwan remains a flashpoint as mainland China's integration into (and increasing importance in) the "East Asian" trade system has proceeded alongside its continuing exclusion from the hub-and-spokes security framework.

On the international front, Taiwan and Mainland China competed, with varying degrees of success, for the attention and support (if not loyalty) of overseas Chinese during the Cold War era (Oyen 2010). It is true that geopolitical identification of the mainland with socialism by noncommunist states in the region curtailed any means of direct contact between ethnic Chinese in "Free Asia" and "China." It is also true that for more than twenty years after World War II, emotional attachment to the place of ancestral origin did not necessarily translate into political (let alone economic) identification with the communist state.[12] Wang Gungwu (2004, 224) rightly notes the centripetal and centrifugal forces that have led to the creation of multiple cultural centers of Chineseness, and the inability of the current regime on the mainland to claim cultural authority as the sole legitimate representative of China and arbiter of Chineseness.

This does not mean, however, that these geopolitical sites of Chinese representations and contestations were totally discrete and mutually exclusive. Despite the "closing" of mainland China to Free Asia in the Cold War years, there existed some channels of communication among the authorities in the mainland, Taiwan and Hong Kong, and parts of the mainland. During the Cold War, for example, the Fujian and Guangdong Provinces continued to be linked, through small-scale migration and material inflows, to Hong Kong, Taiwan, Southeast Asia, Japan, and the United States. The opening of China after 1978 has seen further deterritorialization through large-scale migration from China as well as re-migration of ethnic Chinese from Northeast and Southeast Asia to mainly English-speaking countries of America and the British Commonwealth. Simultaneously, reterritorializations have occurred as the crisis of faith engendered by the retreat of socialism and socialist thought created a vacuum filled by versions of nationalist and Confucianist discourses propounded by diverse states, markets, communities, and individuals inside and outside China.[13] Various actors sought to fill the void through literature, mass media, such as newspapers, films, and television shows, and cybermedia, as well as regime sponsorships of Confucianism, Taiwanese cultural nationalism, and other undertakings.

"Sino-Japanese-English" Hybridization in the Age of Collective Imperialism

Conceptual disjunction is not the only characteristic feature of the modern term "China" and its attendant signifiers. A specific pattern of cultural hybridization has also been crucial to the emergence of modern "China" and its culture and politics. It has long been accepted that cultural inflows traditionally entered imperial China mainly through continental (particularly Inner) Asia and through the overland routes that brought Buddhism from India.[14] Several times in its history, "China" was ruled by non-Han: the Mongols, who incorporated China into their empire; and the Manchus, who presided over a multiethnic empire and cemented their legitimacy among the Han Chinese by selectively Sinicizing themselves (without, however, completely erasing their ethnic identification as Manchus) and acting as principal sponsors of state-propagated Confucianism (Huang 2011).

Rather than its lack of interest in exporting its institutions, social practices, and values (Kang 2010, 91), limits to the reach and might of the mainland state were instrumental in delineating its relations with neighbors to the east.[15] Its relations with Korea and Vietnam, with whom it shared borders, were historically organized in terms of a China-centered tributary system, periodically backed by military power, allowing for a flexible range of appropriations of—and acculturation to—things Chinese by neighboring states.[16] Even as Vietnam closely modeled its institutions and practices after China, it actively engaged in a form of appropriation that drew on "civilizational" notions shared among different polities in the East Asian region while abstracting the term for China from its geographical reference to the mainland.[17] This abstraction enabled the Vietnamese court and scholar-officials to enthusiastically adopt Confucian institutions and norms while simultaneously resisting political domination by the mainland state (Woodside 1971, 18–19, 21). Farther removed from China's reach, some polities in the region, such as Malaka and Butuan, sent tributary missions to China to secure economic benefits and accrue social prestige, without adopting wholesale Chinese institutions and social practices.

The hybridization that arose during the maritime period from the collision between China and the "West" entailed a different cultural politics. The flows of people and modes of transmission of new political and cultural ideas—as well as the new conceptions of community that entered and circulated in China from the West—ran through pathways and networks created in the East. Consequently, the making of "China" in the modern period is crucially mediated by two non-Chinese communicative spheres, Japanese and English (both British and American), which were created by the regional system in the East in which Britain, Japan, and the U.S. competed for dominance. Between the late nineteenth century and the 1930s, the formation of an East-based system of collective imperialism linked the territories and economies of China, Japan, and Southeast Asia, providing the bridges and avenues through which peoples, commodities, languages, and ideas moved into China.

This pattern of flows to, through, and from China is nested in a specific regional structure of power and wealth. Although western powers dominated the international order that provided the institutional framework for "forced free trade" in the region, the economic impact of the West on China was confined mainly to the littoral regions (Sugihara 2005a, 2, 8–9). It was intra-Asian trade, mediated by western collective imperialism, that penetrated China's hinterlands and connected China to the world market. In this sense, the impact of the West was principally mediated through intra-Asian regional links and connections among China,

Japan, and the various colonies in Southeast Asia. Chinese merchants and the development of colonial economies, underpinned in part by Chinese labor, played a crucial role in this connecting process (Sugihara 2005b). This regional system, rather than the "West" per se, played a central part in China-making and world-making. In its cultural matrix, Japanese was an important linguistic mode of transmission of western concepts, while English served as the de facto regional and commercial lingua franca.

The relationship between China and the so-called West was crucially mediated by the reconfigured relationship between China and Japan. Japan's victory over Qing China in the Sino-Japanese War of 1894–1895 was a spectacular reversal of traditional China-to-Japan unidirectional cultural flows. From the final years of the nineteenth century to the first half of the twentieth, the number of Chinese students who received their education in Japan surpassed the combined numbers of their compatriots in Europe and America (Lu 2004, 25, 39). These Chinese *ryūgakusei/liuxuesheng* (留学生) were key agents in the "translingual practices" that decisively shaped the very terms by which, for intellectual and political purposes, the "West" was discursively constructed and deployed in a China-West binary (Liu 1995, xviii, 17–19, 31–42). Through these practices, basic vocabulary, such as politics (*zhengzhi* 政治), economy (*jingji* 経済), and culture (*wenhua* 文化), entered the Chinese lexicon and circulated in China through "Sino-Japanese-English" translations in which not only Japan-educated Chinese and Japanese, but also western missionaries, played important roles.[18] In his study on sociology and socialism in China, Wong Siu-lun (1979, 5) estimates that more than half of the loan words in the Chinese language are from Japanese. Another scholar, Wang Binbin (2000, 164–65), has gone so far as to argue that 70 percent of the modern terms regularly used in the social sciences and humanities are imported from Japanese (ibid.). Some of these Japanese terms were neologisms first coined by western missionaries and subsequently re-imported to China via Japanese texts. Others were either neologisms rendered in *kanji* (Chinese character) form by the Japanese, or old classical kanji/Chinese terms that were assigned new and modern meanings by the Japanese, and then re-imported into China.

An early political form taken by these translingual practices was Asianism, for which Tokyo/Yokohama served as the main hub, with smaller hubs in San Francisco, Singapore, Siam, and Hong Kong. Here, a kind of Sino-Japanese kanji/hanyu communicative sphere helped create a network that linked, at different times, personalities such as Kim Okgyun of Korea, Inukai Tsuyoshi and Miyazaki Tōten of Japan, Sun-Yat-sen of China, and Phan Boi Chau of Vietnam (Shiraishi and Hau 2009; Hau and Shiraishi 2009). But it is also instructive to note that English became the second lingua franca of this Asianist network, connecting Suehiro Tetchō to Jose Rizal, and Sun Yat-sen and An Kyong-su to Mariano Ponce. Sun Yat-sen communicated with his Japanese friends and allies through Chinese (often in brush conversations, or *bitan/hitsudan*) as well as English. He switched completely to English when communicating with Filipino nationalist Mariano Ponce, as did Japanese activists like Suehiro Tetchō and Miyazaki Tōten.

In fact, along with his connections with Japan and Korea through the medium of written Chinese, Sun also exemplifies a specific kind of "modern Chinese" that first emerged in port cities such as Shanghai, Tianjin, Guangdong, and Xiamen, as well as sites of Chinese immigration in Southeast Asia and America. The "Anglo-Chinese" (to use a term by Takashi Shiraishi 2010[19]) were part of the British formal and commercial empire in the region in the nineteenth century. The reach and might of the British commercial empire could be felt even in non-British territories, such as Siam, Spanish Philippines, the Dutch Indies, and French Indochina in the nineteenth and early twentieth centuries. The extent of Spanish Philippines' dependence on trade with Great Britain (as well as the United States), mediated by British, American, and Chinese country traders, in the latter half of the nineteenth century provoked Spanish complaints that "From the commercial point of view the Philippines is an Anglo-Chinese colony with a Spanish Flag" (Recur 1879, 110, quoted in Wickberg 1965, 280).[20] As a consequence, English became the de facto regional lingua franca, although colonial states also imposed their own languages on the elites in their territories. The scale, however, was far smaller compared to the spread of English under American hegemony in the postwar and post-Cold War periods.

In Hong Kong and Southeast Asia, Anglo-Chinese—who, along with a smaller number of their Japanese counterparts, were often educated by Christian missionaries—staffed the bureaucracy and constituted the nascent middle classes of professionals (such as doctors) and scions of Chinese merchants. Educated in both Chinese and English and sometimes only in English, and interpellated as "Chinese" by the colonial policies of their respective domiciles, these Anglo-Chinese were proficient in local and colonial languages such as Cantonese, Hokkien, Malay, Javanese, Tagalog, Dutch, Portuguese, and French. Their multilingualism (and especially their proficiency in the commercial regional lingua franca) gave them the cultural resources to move across social and linguistic hierarchies in their polyglot colonial societies and beyond.[21]

These multicultural/hybrid Chinese include the Penang (Malaysia)-born Lim Boon Keng (林文庆 Lin Wenqing, 1869–1957), a doctor by profession who was educated in Edinburgh. He was an associate of Sun Yat-sen and later president of Xiamen (Amoy) University, and a key figure in the propagation of Confucianism in Singapore, Malaya, and the Dutch East Indies. Spurred by his exposure to English texts on China and Chinese classics, and the colonial dispensation that labeled him "Chinese," his attempt at creating a "modern Chinese identity" entailed the elevation of Confucianism to a national as well as a universal philosophy and religion comparable to, and on a par with, Christianity (Yamamoto 1995, 37–45; Li 1991, chaps. 2 and 3). His idea of an emergent Chineseness was not rooted in outward or physical signs of Chineseness (for example, costume or hairstyle), but rather in a personal code or morality that prepared the Chinese for progress. At the same time, as Wang Gungwu has pointed out, Lim's advocacy of Confucian education was complemented by his support for a modern curriculum that included the teaching of science. Famously delivered in English at his presidential address at Xiamen University (Wang 2003c, 166) on October 3, 1926, his vision of revivified Confucian teachings for the present time offered a distinctive platform for modernization in China. Despite differing sharply from the antitradition Chinese modernity envisioned by the Sino-Japanese hybrid Lu Xun, it was in some ways as modern as Lu's (176).

Two other exemplary Anglo-Chinese from opposite ends of the political spectrum are conservative Ku Hung-ming (辜鸿铭 Gu Hongming, 1857–1928) and May 4th activist Lee Teng Hwee (李登辉 Li Denghui, 1872–1947). Like Lim Boon Keng, Ku Hung-ming was born in Penang to a mother of Portuguese ancestry and to a Chinese father. He was educated in Edinburgh, but he also studied in Leipzig and Paris. Fluent in English, he studied Chinese, and became conversant in French and German. He translated Confucian and other classic texts into English, worked for the Qing government, and advocated a form of orthodox Confucianism that, counterposed to European civilization, proved to be unpopular even among Chinese (Wang 2011). Lee was born near Batavia (now Jakarta, Indonesia) and educated at the Anglo-Chinese School in Singapore and Yale University in the U.S. He founded the Yale Institute and taught at the Tiong Hwa Hwee Koan in Batavia, and later became the first president of Fudan University in Shanghai.[22]

The impact of political Asianism was limited and eventually curtailed by Japanese imperialism. It spurred the development of Chinese nationalism by providing Chinese nationalists with an identifiable enemy against which the Chinese people could be mobilized. Sino-Japanese-English translations arguably had a far more wide influence, especially on Chinese culture, politics, and military organization (Lee 1999, 315–21; Shih 2001, 4;

Lim Boon Keng

Ku Hung-ming

Lee Teng Hwee

Lu 2004). Such translingual practices transformed Chinese institutions and practices. Their political impact is readily apparent in the crucial role they played in the introduction of socialist thought into China, via translation from Japanese. Ishikawa Yoshihiro's (2001, 459–84) study reveals that, between 1919 and 1921, thirteen out of eighteen Chinese translations of texts by Marx and Engels, as well as other Marxist figures—including *The Communist Manifesto*—were based on Japanese translations. Writings by Japanese anarchists and Marxists, such as Kōtoku Shūsui, Ōsugi Sakae, and Kawakami Hajime, also were read in China, Korea, and Vietnam, and influenced the development of socialism in these countries (Dirlik 2008, 156). Where political surveillance of and crackdowns against Bolshevism restricted its transmission from Japan to China, Bolshevist thought, including its visual imagery, entered China via translations from English (many of them published in America) through the treaty port of Shanghai. The port city of Shanghai itself was a spatial representation of this Sino-Japanese-English hybridization: the British provided the policing and administration; the Japanese constituted the largest foreign contingent; and the gray zones created by the administratively segmented International Settlements enabled nationalists and communists from Asia and beyond to flourish, allowing figures such as Tan Malaka, Nguyen Ai Quoc (Ho Chi Minh), Hilaire Noulens, and Agnes Smedley (who communicated with each other in English, a lingua franca of the Comintern's[23] Far Eastern Bureau) to meet, mingle, and organize their respective political projects in the name of the nation and international solidarity (Onimaru 2011; this revolutionary cosmopolitanism is discussed in chap. 4).

Beyond mainland China, the Sino-Japanese-English cultural nexus was an enabling ground not only for the revolutionary movement in the Philippines, but also for the political awakening of the Indies Chinese, whose activities would provide models and inspiration for Indonesian nationalist activism. Tiong Hwa Hwee Koan (中华会馆), the first non-European modern social and educational association established in 1900, recruited staff from Chinese *ryūgakusei* in Japan to teach not only Chinese but also English (Williams 1966, 72). Its textbooks, which were published in Japan and later in Shanghai, had originally been designed for use by Chinese students in a Yokohama school run by a Yokohama Chinese; that school's opening had been graced by Sun Yat-sen and Inukai Tsuyoshi (74). The Indonesian writer Pramoedya Ananta Toer would memorialize the Chinese influence on Indonesian nationalism through the revolutionary Khouw Ah Soe—a graduate of an English-language high school in Shanghai. Although Soe does not publicly acknowledge this, he had in fact lived for some years in Japan before being sent to do political organizing among the Indies

Chinese. In *Anak Semua Bangsa* (Child of All Nations, 1980), the protagonist Minke learns from Soe about anticolonial struggles in the Philippines and China. In a little over one generation, this political awakening and educational trend would produce Anglo-Chinese Indonesians such as Njoo Cheong Seng (1902–1962), whose popular Gagaklodra series of martial-arts fiction features the eponymous half-Chinese, half-Javanese protagonist. Njoo typified a new breed of young Indonesian Chinese who were comfortable not only with Indonesian (and Dutch), but had some English as well. In imagining an Indonesian nationalism that was not incompatible with Chinese patriotism, he drew inspiration from both British and American literary traditions and popular cultures—especially American comics and Hollywood films (Chandra 2011).

Thailand offers another interesting case study of a different path of transmission of radical nationalism through the regional circulation of people and transmission of ideas. Communism came to Thailand not from the West, but via the East through Chinese and Vietnamese immigrants. Considered part of the Communist Party of Malaya, Thailand's communist party, which had been part of the Malayan communist party, was linked to the communist cells in Laos and Cambodia by Ho Chi Minh (Kasian 2001a). Although gifted Sino-Thais were able to obtain their education in England and, less frequently, in France, English education at the time was limited to Thai aristocrats, bureaucrats, and the nascent middle class. Sino-Thais received their education in China or in nearby Straits Chinese schools. The bilingual Thai-born *lukjin*, who were instrumental in translating socialist texts into Thai, bonded with their Thai counterparts in prison. During the American-led Cold War period, they achieved proficiency in English, enabling them, along with Thai radicals, to translate into Thai the English-language Marxist texts that were also circulating widely in America in the 1960s and 1970s. This pattern of increasing proficiency in the language of British and later American regional domination would be of great consequence in the post-Cold War period.

The Rise of the Anglo-Chinese under American Hegemony

Japan's primacy as a translingual hub was undermined by Japanese imperialism and its failed attempt to establish hegemony in the region. After its defeat, Japan was incorporated into the American-led "Free Asia" through a hub-and-spokes regional security system (anchored in the U.S.-Japan alliance and bilateral treaties between the U.S. and its Southeast

Asian allies) and a triangular trade system involving the U.S., Japan, and the rest of "Free Asia" that officially excluded (in the name of "containment") Communist China (Shiraishi 1997, 175–79).

Of equal import was the fact that for the first quarter century of this new regional arrangement, ethnic Chinese migrants faced a great deal of pressure from postcolonial nation-states in Southeast Asia to de-Sinicize. This pressure reached its apotheosis in the anti-Chinese discrimination practiced in Indonesia, which actively sought to erase all visible (and auditory) signs of Chineseness. Along with the postcolonial states in Malaysia and the Philippines, Indonesia aimed to regulate if not restrict the economic activities of ethnic Chinese through economic nationalism and affirmative-action programs favoring *bumiputera* ("sons of the soil"). While these de-Sinicizing policies and the absence of direct contact with mainland China succeeded in nationalizing the Chinese minority, erasing Chineseness by granting the Chinese Indonesian a form of second-class citizenship ironically reinforced and perpetuated the treatment of the ethnic Chinese as "alien" nationals.[24] The situation of the Chinese in the Philippines, however, shows how changing diplomatic and economic priorities led to shifts in state policies, as the reestablishment of diplomatic relations between the Philippines and China in 1975 (on the heels of the U.S.-China entente) paved the way for the mass granting of Filipino citizenship to large numbers of Chinese. The hitherto alien Chinese, through college education, were drawn into closer and more frequent social contact with Filipinos and came to identify themselves as "Filipino," thus facilitating their incorporation into both the national imaginary and the body politic (see chap. 2).

State-driven attempts at de-Sinicizing the Chinese and more recent market-driven re-Sinicization of the Chinese occurred with novel forms of hybridization. Anglophone education in the region and abroad and the acquisition of linguistic proficiency in English (or more accurately, englishes) became a widespread phenomenon that reached beyond the elite and professionals and scions of rich merchants of the earlier period to encompass the growing middle classes and urban populations. This hybridization also involves nationalization that incorporates elements and languages of Southeast Asia's indigenous cultures. The product and agent of this process is the "Anglo-Chinese" (and, in the case of the Southeast Asian Chinese, "Anglo-Chinese-Indonesian," and so on). The term "Anglo-Chinese" was originally applied to schools (sometimes western missionary-run) where sons (and later daughters) of ethnic-Chinese businessmen received the kind of education that prepared them for business and/ or professional careers. A version of the Confucian classics was taught in Chinese (国语 *Guoyu*), alongside English and practical subjects, such as accounting. Such "hybrid" schools were established in the Nanyang territories (mainly in the British colonies of Singapore and Malaya, but also in Indonesia and the Philippines), and in the port cities of Hong Kong, Tianjin, Guangdong, Xiamen, and Shanghai; some of their graduates went on to pursue higher education either in China or, more commonly, in England and America.[25]

A term that originated in the maritime-Asian world under British hegemony can thus be fruitfully applied to the contemporary regional context of the East Asian hybridization of Chinese under American hegemony. The crucial linguistic continuity from British to American English marked the transition from British to American hegemony and promoted the use of English as a regional and commercial lingua franca. What followed was the widespread dissemination of Hollywood films and, eventually, the Americanization of the bureaucratic elite and professional middle classes and their worldviews. Like their forefathers in this region, the Anglo-Chinese tend to have the following characteristics: they are at least bilingual (with English as one of their major languages); they receive a western-style education (which normally includes secondary or tertiary or graduate education in America or Britain);[26] they have some grounding in the school systems in their respective countries and intend to educate their children in the same way; they are well-versed in, though not uncritical of, "international" (mainly Anglo-American) business norms and values; and they have relied on their hybrid skills (whether linguistic or cultural) and connections to enter business, work as professionals, and accumulate social and cultural capital. One can also speak of comparable processes of Anglo-Japanization of Japanese, Anglo-Koreanization of Koreans, Anglo-Sinicization of Taiwanese, and comparable phenomena among segments of Southeast Asian middle and upper classes.

Far removed from the context of anti-imperialist nationalism that was the engine of "China"-driven Sinicization in the first half of the twentieth century, "re-Sinicization" is today more a component of, rather than an alternative to, ethnic Chinese Anglo-Sinicization. Now primarily market-driven, it is propelled as much by economic incentives for learning Mandarin Chinese and seeking jobs in a rapidly growing China and East Asian region as by the desire to learn "Chinese" culture in a more hospitable political environment. Rising China and Chinese immigration to the First World have spurred what Wang Gungwu (2004, 166) calls the new *huaqiao syndrome*, in which the mainland Chinese nation state is an increasingly important, but by no means the only, source of economic opportunities and cultural identification and validation. Contemporary Sinicization is recalibrating established routines. This process may entail a form of Sinicization that involves the Mandarinization of erstwhile provincialized/localized huaqiao identities, as the pressures and incentives among Anglo-Chinese to learn *putonghua* (as well as the simplified Chinese script) increase with China's economic rise. But it is not likely to happen at the expense of ongoing Anglo-hybridization, and may very well complement it. Moreover, the process of selective Anglo-hybridization involves not only ethnic Chinese, but also non-Chinese Southeast Asian elite and middle classes. It prepares the ground for the creation of an encompassing and inclusive cultural frame of reference and communicative meeting ground for interaction among the Southeast Asian middle and upper classes, and between these classes and their counterparts in other areas of the world. Along with fellow Anglo-hybrid elite in their respective countries, Anglo-Chinese parlay their proficiency in the global lingua franca and their familiarity with Anglo-American norms and codes into cultural, social, and material capital.

Ethnic Chinese were erstwhile subject to pressures to declare loyalty to their respective country of residence. During the Cold War, their lack of direct access to mainland China meant that the elder generation, who considered themselves sojourners, could no longer dream of returning to China. The younger generation grew up with the firm notion that their home was in the Philippines, Thailand, or other parts of Southeast Asia. "China" remained for them a geographical and symbolic marker whose image was now mediated by Taiwan and Hong Kong in the form of films, television programs, newspapers, and news reports. In the age of collective imperialism, and especially in conjunction with anti-Japanese nationalism, this condition of extended absence from the mainland had already created the phenomenon of "abstract" or "taught" nationalism among the so-called huaqiao (Wang 1981, 157). In the 1930s to 1940s, this type of nationalism inspired some of them to return to China during the Sino-Japanese war. In postcolonial Southeast Asia across the Taiwan straits, a bitter rivalry between two governments claiming to speak in the name of a legitimate "China" played out in Chinatowns across Southeast Asia, America, and elsewhere. This, despite the fact that younger generations, increasingly rooted in their countries of birth, looked to Southeast Asia for their identities. Some chose assimilation. Others, still identifying themselves as Chinese, practiced a form of abstract nationalism that enabled identification with (an often imaginary) "China" without necessarily supporting either the mainland or the Taiwanese state (Teo 1997, 111).

Moreover, Taiwan and especially Hong Kong emerged as hubs for the popular cultural dissemination of images of and knowledge about China, in the form of newspapers, books, movies, television shows, and pop music. This development was conditioned in large part by the potentials and restrictions inherent in the regional system created in America's "Free Asia." The example of Hong Kong cinema in the postwar period is instructive of how conceptual disjunction and historical hybridization influenced the development of the film industry. In the early postwar era, the production of Hong Kong films relied heavily on financing by overseas Chinese and pre-selling to distributors in Southeast Asia. Replacing prewar Shanghai as the "Hollywood of the East," Hong Kong had a preeminently regional cinema. Starting in the 1950s, during the Cold War, Taiwan emerged as the Hong Kong film industry's main market and a leading source of non-Hong Kong financing. Hong Kong's ability to capture the regional market of American-led "Free Asia" was made possible in part by Taiwan's ruling Kuomintang Party. By classifying Hong Kong films as part of its "national cinema," it promoted exchanges between Hong Kong and Taiwan (as well as "Free Asia" overseas Chinese communities). This made Hong Kong films eligible for consideration by Taiwan's film-awarding organizations, and offered incentives for import and production of Mandarin-language films through subsidies and preferential taxation (Law and Bren with Ho 2004, 291, 295). The intensification of indigenous nationalism in Southeast Asia in the late 1960s and 1970s had an adverse impact by restricting the circulation of Hong Kong films as well as Southeast Asian Chinese investment in the Hong Kong film industry. This led to a shift in focus from serving émigré-community markets to developing domestic along with national markets in the region and beyond. Hong Kong's regional émigré and overseas market in turn defined Hong Kong's film tradition, genres, and conventions. Mandarin and other Sinophone films of the 1950s (including Hokkien-language films produced by Chinese Filipinos) drew from the folk opera tradition and prewar Shanghai film conventions of featuring songs, historical themes and settings, and love and martial arts genres (Bordwell 2000, 66)— conventions on which even mainland Chinese filmmakers had to draw during the past decade when, in collaboration with their Hong Kong and Taiwanese counterparts, they began producing films for the international market.

Through the "Free Asia" regional system, Japan also became connected to Hong Kong and Taiwan. In line with the Sino-Japanese-English hybridization of modern China, Shanghai's film studios in the 1920s and 1930s were modeled not only after Hollywood, but also after Japan.[27] The postwar period witnessed an increase in popular culture flows from Japan (through film, music, *manga*, and *anime*) into Taiwan and Hong Kong. *Jidai-geki* (pre-Meiji historical drama) films from Japan, for example, inspired Hong Kong filmmakers to create their own swordplay movies. Taiwanese popular music has historical roots in Japanese *enka*,[28] with superstars such as Teresa Teng (邓丽君 Teng Li-chün, who has a huge fan base in China) cementing their domestic and international reputations by making it big in Japan, and going on to record songs not just in Mandarin, Cantonese, Japanese, and English, but also in Korean, Vietnamese, and Indonesian. Film technicians were trained in Japan, and Japanese talents were hired in Hong Kong. In the early 1950s, Japanese filmmakers initiated the establishment of the Southeast Asian Motion Picture Producers' Association and the Southeast Asian Film Festival. This move would eventually lead to the expansion of a regional film network under the designations of "Asia" and "Asia-Pacific" (Yau 2009, 169). Hong Kong films were shot on location

Teresa Teng

in Japan, Singapore, Malaysia, South Korea, Taiwan, and the Philippines; coproductions and talent inflows were initiated with Japan, South Korea, the Philippines, and Thailand (Law and Bren with Ho 2004, 203–10, 221); and from the 1970s onward, Hong Kong's domestic as well as other national markets (rather than just émigré-community markets) in Asia, America, and other areas became an important source of Hong Kong film revenues.

The reopening of China in the late 1970s marked the beginning of China's economic reintegration with the regional system. Hong Kong, Taiwan and ethnic Chinese entrepreneurs, professionals, and companies in Southeast Asia, America, and other regions played an important role in this process. In sharp contrast, on questions of security, China remains outside the U.S.-led hub-and-spokes system. A look at the cooperative and collaborative connections and networks in and around Hong Kong cinema reveals how the patterns and densities of regional exchanges have changed over time (Hau and Shiraishi 2012). Although China had opened and embarked on reform, in the late 1970s and early 1980s it was still in the process of being integrated into the regional system. The integration of "Free Asia" was already very much in place, as illustrated by the prominent presence of Taiwanese and the importance of Southeast Asian financing and distribution networks in Hong Kong films. Japanese inflows of money and talent peaked at the height of Japan's bubble years in the 1980s, when the country led the flying-geese pattern of regional development. As China became more integrated into the regional system and emerged as the locomotive of regional development after the Asian financial crisis of 1997–1978, mainland Chinese financing and talent inflows gained importance in Hong Kong films. Taiwanese actors/actresses have always formed an important contingent in Hong Kong films; in the 1990s, mainland actors came to constitute an equally important group that overtook their Taiwanese counterparts by the early 2000s.

Large-scale flows and exchanges between Hong Kong and China have resulted in a form of re-Sinicization, defined by Eric Ma (1999, 45) as "the recollection, reinvention and rediscovery of historical and cultural ties between Hong Kong and China." Despite the rise of cultural nationalism that has sought to articulate a uniquely Taiwanese national identity (entailing a reassessment of Japan's role in Taiwan's modernization), post-Cold War contacts and deepening economic ties with the mainland engendered a "Mainland Fever" in Taiwan that was fed by books, films, and music from and about mainland China (Hsiau 2000, 109). In the meantime, the "porous" nature of the regional system has enabled people and capital to go transnational (Katzenstein 2005, 18). This trend has become clearer in recent years through an increase in the "unclassifiability" of East Asians, such as the actor Takeshi Kaneshiro. He holds a Japanese passport, and his father is Japanese and mother Taiwanese. Conversant in Mandarin, Hokkien, Japanese, English, and Cantonese, he debuted as a singer under the Japanese name "Aniki" and gained fame first in Taiwan before appearing in Hong Kong and Japanese films.

The cultural impact of ongoing regionalization is far less understood and remarked upon. Japanization, which reached its peak in the 1980s and 1990s as Japan-led economic growth planted the seeds for regional economic integration, has now been subsumed under a broader process of East Asian regionalism and regionalization that has created variegated sources of cultural flows going well beyond Japan and Greater China. It is subject to interesting and novel recombinations, as when increasing numbers of mainland Chinese students opt to study in Japan rather than in America, Taiwanese manga artists begin publishing their works in Japan, mainland Chinese produce films using East Asian pop culture formats, Singaporeans follow Hong Kong and Taiwanese fashion trends, Filipinos fall in love with Taiwan's pop-idol band F4, and Japanese with Korean teledramas; Koreans learn English in the Philippines rather than in America or Britain. "Re-Sinicization" and Japanization are but two streams of this multi-sited, uneven process of hybridization (Katzenstein 2006, 4–14; Chua 2003; Qiu 2010).

Some Implications of Multi-sited "Chineseness"

The conceptual disjunctions and historical hybridizations that make "China" a floating signifier create multiple meanings of and identifications with "China," "Chineseness," and "Chinese culture/civilization." In *practice*, no single political entity/regime embodies or exercises ultimate authority on "China," "Chinese," and "Chineseness." Although its importance has greatly increased in economic and geopolitical terms, the mainland has so far not emerged as the preeminent cultural arbiter of Chineseness. Indeed, China is distinguished by a relative lack of soft power (Li 2008). Nor has the economic rise of China and the market-driven Mandarinization of "Chineseness" substantively reduced or simplified the multi-sited claims and belongings exercised by the ethnic "Chinese" in Southeast Asia.

What we see, instead, are multiple instances of cultural entrepreneurship that do not necessarily affirm the primacy of mainland China as the cultural center and arbiter of (Mandarin) Chineseness. An example is the Dragon Descendants' Museum, located northwest of Bangkok in Suphan Buri Province. A brainchild of former Thai prime minister (and himself Sino-

Thai) Banharn Silpa-archa, the museum was intended to commemorate the twentieth anniversary of the establishment of diplomatic relations between Thailand and China. Launched in late 2008, its celebration of "5,000 years" of Chinese history illustrates just how much ideas of China and Chineseness owe to the incorporation of a standardized version of Chinese history,[29] taught in Thai Chinese schools, into the narrative of "Chinese" contribution to the development of Thailand. More telling is its subscription to a version of Chinese history that is mediated by Taiwan's and Hong Kong's culture industries. One striking example of this Hong Kong/Taiwan pop-cultural mediation of Chineseness is the prominence accorded to the historical figure of Judge Pao (Bao Zheng), whom Thais came to know through the Taiwanese TV mini-series that was a huge hit not only in Taiwan, but also in Hong Kong and mainland China.[30] It was, in fact, the enormous popularity of the Judge Pao series among Thai viewers that made Chineseness "chic" in the 1990s (Pasuk and Baker 1996, 139–40).

Cultural entrepreneurs like Malaysia's Lillian Too (born in Penang) and Thailand's Chitra Konuntakiet (born in Bangkok) have turned Chineseness into a profitable business venture. Lillian Too has built her career on a curriculum vitae that emphasizes her MBA from the Harvard Business School; her position as the first woman CEO from Malaysia to head a publicly listed company, the Hong Kong Dao Heng Bank; and her self-reinvention as founder of the World of Feng Shui. Her Web site sells her English-language geomancy (*fengshui*) books, which target the "30 million English-speaking non-Chinese Asians" worldwide (Lim 2006). Educated in an elite school in Thailand before obtaining her master's degree in the United States, Thailand's Chitra Konuntakiet overcame her experience of anti-Chinese racism in school by becoming a successful columnist, radio personality, and novelist. Her books on Chinese culture (as filtered through her Teo-chiu upbringing)—*Chinese Knowledge from the Old Man, Chinese Children, Nine Philosophy Stories*, and most recently the novel *A-Pa*—have sold more than six hundred thousand copies to date.[31] Both Lillian Too and Chitra Konuntakiet propound notions of Chineseness that fall beyond the purview of state-sanctioned and mainland-originating discourses: in the case of Lillian Too, through access to a belief system that is not accorded official recognition in mainland China but is part of folk beliefs and practices in Taiwan, Hong Kong, Chinatowns elsewhere, and Mainland China; and in the case of Chitra Konuntakiet, through access to familial memories and ideas of Chinese customs and practices that were rooted primarily in her father's immigrant experience in Thailand rather than in received notions of Chineseness promoted by the mainland and Taiwan's China scholarship.[32]

Enforced for much of the twentieth century by the political turmoil on the mainland, "Chinese" migrants and their descendants' existential experiences of extended physical absence from their putative places of "origin" have meant that political contestation over the meanings of "China" did extend across the mainland and into Nanyang and Hong Kong. Yet there were important limits to the deterritorialization of these struggles, as illustrated by "the China factor" in the Hong Kong riots of 1967 (Bickers and Yep 2009, 11–12). Even when political and cultural movements succeeded in capturing the state, their ability to use the state to propound their vision of the "Chinese" nation remains constrained by the limited reach of the "Chinese" state. Through competing strategies of territorialization, deterritorialization, and reterritorialization, authorities and institutions impose constraints on ethnic Chinese, within both Chinese and non-Chinese territories. The spatial, political, cultural, and economic disjunctions that inform the different processes of Sinicization have lent an irreducibly "imaginative" dimension to "Chinese" identification without predetermining the practical consequences and outcomes of these identifications and projects.

Moreover, mainland China has not remained immune to the appeal of these different sources and centers of "Chineseness" (Wang 2004, 210–26). An important example of spirited debate on China's identity in the post-Maoist era is the one sparked by the controversial six-part TV documentary series Heshang (河殇River Elegy, 1988), which relied on the spatial metaphors of land-versus-sea to contrast the isolationism of so-called traditional Chinese culture, symbolized by the Great Wall, with the openness of the maritime-world "blue" ocean into which the Yellow River flows (Su and Wang 1991). Some enterprising companies have embarked on making films, set in China, that showcase China's regional connections and participation in shared urban regional lifestyles. One example is the successful mainland Chinese production of the East Asian romantic comedy genre Lian Ai Qian Gui Ze (恋爱潜规则My Airline Hostess Roommate, 2009) which deals with a Beijing-based flight attendant who falls in love with her roommate, a Taiwanese visual artist who creates a cute cat character modeled after Japanese anime. Another example is the persistence and continuing popularity of the traditional Chinese script, despite government attempts to impose and propagate a simplified system; traditional script continues to proliferate in China via the Internet, overseas news media, movies, books, and even shop signs (despite government prohibition). Thus it retains its usefulness as a means by which mainland Chinese can communicate with Taiwan and overseas Chinese communities (Guo 2004, 109). The Chinese government is even promoting the production of cartoon animation, drawing in part on the visual language and conventions of Japanese anime that were popularized through Taiwan and Hong Kong. One example of a successful venture is *Xi Yang Yang yu Hui Tai Lang* (喜羊羊与灰太狼 Pleasant Goat and Big Big Wolf), a television cartoon series produced by the Guangdong-based Creative Power Entertaining, whose 2009 movie version broke box office records for the Chinese animated film.[33] The cartoon series is now aired in thirteen Asian countries and regions (ChinaA2Z.com 2009).

By erasing their revolutionary past and in its place highlighting local and regional identities that carry traces of "traditional," or "folk" elements, and with the rise of regional/local identities, China's provinces in the hinterlands have sought to transform themselves into revenue-generating tourist attractions, thus challenging the "ultrastable spatial identity of Chineseness."[34] Nor have coastal provinces been remiss in self-promotion. Tourist-service companies in Xiamen, for example, have turned hybridity into a cultural asset as a way of attracting tourists from Taiwan, Hong Kong, and Southeast Asia, with which Xiamen has close historical connections. For example, a tourist brochure put out by the Xiamen Min'nan Tourism and Culture Industry Co. invokes international as well as local contexts to package Xiamen's attractions. Published in Chinese, English, and Japanese,

Pleasant Goat and Big, Big Wolf (courtesy of Creative Power Entertaining)

the brochure features a series of stage shows that celebrate, through song and dance, the heritage of "Magic Min'nan" (Southern Min) (Chen 2010). Min'nan is presented as a hybrid culture, a product of the historical position of Fujian as the "starting point" of the Maritime Silk Road, a "hotbed of reform" that played an important role in the reopening of post-Maoist China, and a "pioneer in the Western littoral of the Taiwan Straits." Alongside its ancient Yue (*Guyue* 古越) heritage, this brochure plays up Xiamen's shared cultural links with Taiwan and Inner Asia and its free-port access to the "West" and the world, thus laying simultaneous claim to western-oriented modernity and classical Chinese civilization (1).

Moreover, the highlighting of a hybrid South China culture with multiple traditions and connections rewrites the narrative of Chinese civilization, stressing its heterogeneity and, in particular, the openness and hybridity of the "south" as opposed to the "north" (Friedman 1994, 83–87). It affirms an idea first propounded by Fu Ssu-nien (傅斯年 Fu Sinian, 1896–1950) and Ku Chieh-kang (顾颉刚 Gu Jiegang 1893–1980) in the 1920s and 1930s (Wang Fan-sen 2000, 98–123) and revitalized during the past three decades by new archeological findings that prove the existence of a number of regional cultures (other than the one along the Yellow River in the Central Plains). These regional contacts formed a "core" which, by 3000 BC, linked a geographic area consisting of Shaanxi-Shanxi-Henan, Shandong, Hubei, lower Yangzi, the southern region from Poyang to the Pearl River delta, and the northern region by the Great Wall that would subsequently be called "China" (Chang 1999, 58–59). This idea of multiple sources and origins of Chinese civilization decenters the traditional claim of the Yellow River as the cradle of Chinese civilization without relinquishing altogether the idea of a civilizational "core."

The centripetal and centrifugal forces of territorializing and de/reterritorializing China and Chineseness thus define ethnic-Chinese attitudes and responses toward claims to cultural authenticity by mainland Chinese. The outcry in Hong Kong and Guangzhou against a proposal by the Chinese People's Political Consultative Conference Guangzhou Committee to increase the ratio of Mandarin-language to Cantonese content in Guangzhou Television's programming—an attempt to proscribe Cantonese-language coverage of the 2010 Asian Games—indicates that there are limits to how much restriction mainland authorities can impose on the use of local "dialects."[35] Sometimes derided as "culturally inferior" to their fellow "Chinese" on the mainland, some Southeast Asian Chinese have responded by claiming access, via their own local "Chinese" culture, to an authentic "ancient" China that survives through centuries-long, transplanted Chinese customs and rituals no longer practiced—or, for a time, proscribed by the government—in their places of ancestral origins in mainland China.[36] Negotiating between their self-identifications as "overseas Chinese" (huaqiao) and "ethnic Chinese" (*huaren*) has on occasion enabled Southeast Asian Chinese to lay claim to speaking, not in the name of China and Chinese unification, but as the voice of China itself. This happened, for example, in the coverage of Hong Kong's turnover and the Taiwan Question by the Malaysian Chinese newspaper *Kwong-Wah Yit Poh* (Guanghua Ribao 光华日报).[37] In other cases, the response may take the form of a compensatory gesture of defensive ethnocentrism against longstanding charges that overseas Chinese are uncultured and materialistic. An Internet document circulated by and addressed to the "49 million Hokkien-speakers" all over the world, for example, valorizes the Min'nan "dialect" as "the imperial language" of the Tang Dynasty and "the language of your ancestors."[38] Advocating a Han-Sinocentric approach while denying the equation of Chineseness with the state-promoted national language, Mandarin, the anonymous author appeals to "all Mandarin-speaking friends out there—do not look down on your other Chinese friends who do not speak Mandarin—whom you guys fondly refer to as 'Bananas.' In fact, they are speaking a language which is much more ancient and linguistically complicated than Mandarin." Mandarin is characterized as an alien tongue spoken by a non-Han minority, "a northern Chinese dialect heavily influenced by non-Han Chinese." In attesting to its ancient Chinese lineage, this argument is grounded in a comparison of vocabulary and pronunciation, not with other local Chinese "dialects" but with foreign languages, such as Japanese and Korean that were part of the "Golden Age" of the Tang China-centered Sinosphere. Such an argument conveniently overlooks the complex ways in which ethnic identity and differences were constructed during the Tang dynasty, and the fact that the ancestry, cultural practices, and geographic focus of the Tang elite were in large part already oriented toward Inner Asia and "barbarized" northern China (Abramson 2008, xxi). The above example is revealing of "pressures" brought to bear on Southeast Asian Chinese to learn and speak putonghua/Mandarin, when their "dialects" had long been the basis of their claim to a Chinese ethnic identity. This "Mandarinization" of Hokkien-, Teochiu-, or Cantonese-based "Chinese" identities, however, also constitutes proof of an internal contestation over what "Chinese" means, who can claim Chineseness, who counts as Chinese, and who can "represent" it.

Multiple cultural sites and centers of Chineseness produce different, at times competing, visions of Chineseness. Two opposing views are laid out in Shanghai-born and Hong Kong-based director Wong Kar-wai's *2046* (2004) and mainland China-based Zhang Yimou's *Hero* (2002). Set in 1960s Hong Kong, *2046* tells the story of a young author of erotic newspaper serials. Among the women with whom this writer falls in love is his landlord's daughter, whom he eventually helps to reunite with her Japanese lover. In this movie, Wong not only imagines the possibility of a Japanese-Chinese rapprochement, couched in the language of romantic love and family reconciliation—a vision that stands in stark contrast to the worsening of China-Japan relations owing to Prime Minister Koizumi Junichiro's 2001 and 2002 visits to the Yasukuni Shrine. More important, he lets his characters speak to each other in the language with which they are most comfortable, even though Cantonese, Mandarin, and Japanese are in reality mutually unintelligible. The lingua franca is not found in the movie, but rather *on* the movie, in the form of subtitles, the language of which varies from one market or set of audiences to another. In this way, the film evades the politically charged hierarchy of languages based on the assumed standard set by Mandarin or Putonghua that is audibly rendered in such films as Ang Lee's *Crouching Tiger, Hidden Dragon* (2003) and, more problematically, Zhang Yimou's *Hero*. Writes critic and scholar Gina Marchetti (2007, 7),

> In *Hero*, mainland Chinese director Zhang Yimou also takes a chance, through his proxy Nameless (Jet Li), that the world is ready for the return of the wandering hero. Nameless/Jet Li travels from the PRC to Hong Kong, to Hollywood and back again to China. *Hero* also repatriates Hong Kong's Tony Leung (as Broken Sword) and Maggie Cheung (as Flying Snow) as well as Chinese-American Donnie Yen (as Sky) who sacrifice themselves to maintain the Chinese nation-state. The diasporic Chinese from the far edges of the world symbolically capitulate to the central authority of the Emperor Qin (Chen Daoming)/Beijing/the PRC/Chinese cinema.[39]

Scholars who look at China from a broader, international perspective have generally been wary of subscribing to culturalist arguments in explaining both the rise of East Asia and of mainlad China. Wang Gungwu (1992b), for example, offers an important refutation of cultural essentialist arguments about "Chinese" economic success. Such scholars have highlighted instead the importance of the specific situatedness and locations of the "Chinese" in China, Southeast Asia, and beyond. Questions of "roots" and "routes" (Clifford 1997) are of paramount concern and have real consequences—including life-and-death ones—for the "Chinese" in Southeast Asia. In making sense of the historical construction of "China," "Chinese," and "Chineseness," in their modern articulations, their concern has been to emphasize the importance of both structure and agency.

Tu Wei Ming's (1994) notion of symbolic universes that make up "cultural China," and Jamie Davidson's (2008, 222) attempt to explain the restructuring of Southeast Asian countries by economic globalization as a form of "Chinese-ization" or becoming "structurally Chinese" of urban, middle-class, capitalist Southeast Asian societies are useful reminders that asserting the heterogeneity and historical variability of "becoming-Chinese" is the starting point, not the concluding statement, of any inquiry into questions and issues of "China," "Chinese," and "Chineseness." The propensity in overseas Chinese studies for taxonomic essays that classify ethnic Chinese according to their political orientations and loyalty is both an instructive symptom of the uneasy fit among the core concepts of territory, people, nation, culture, state, and civilization, and a valiant attempt to catalogue the various manifestations of their critical disjunctions. "Transnational" approaches that purport to move beyond the strictures of nation- and state-centered analysis to stress the "different ways of being Chinese" (Nonini and Ong 1997a, 26) or "deconstruct modern Chineseness" (Ong and Nonini 1997b, 326) offer nuanced case studies. Because they invoke "China" as a self-explanatory straw figure against which transnational or diasporic difference is *then* asserted, however, they overlook the broader implications of critical disjunctions and historical hybridization. William Callahan's sophisticated study of "Greater China" is rightly critical of binary thinking in China/West and center/periphery studies, advocating "an understanding of China and civilization in terms of popular sovereignty, heterotopia, and an open relation to Otherness" (Callahan 2004, 96). Yet Callahan's analysis is marked by aporia with regard to Japan's mediating role in "Chinese" modernity, be it historical or contemporary. This is apparent in his exclusion of Japan on methodological grounds. Although for Callahan it "is very important to regional economics and is crucial to a geopolitical understanding of East Asia, it is not included here, since Japan is peripheral to the transnational relations and theoretical challenges of Greater China" (xxix).

The "problem of clarifying what 'China' is" (Young 1999, 63; Chow 2009, x) is hardly novel. This chapter suggests that looking into the pressures and opportunities for "becoming Chinese" by colonial, "China"-driven, postcolonial (national), and market-driven processes of Sinicization in the region that we now call "East Asia" enables us to specify not just individual differences across time and space, but just as importantly, identify *patterns of differences*—or *differance* (Derrida 1982)—that are historically identified and lived as "Chinese" in China, Southeast Asia, and beyond. Among the most important of these patterns of differences is the identification of "Chinese" with commerce and capital in Southeast Asia; a comparable process happened also in Hong Kong and to the *benshengren* ("home-province" Taiwanese, as opposed to *waishengren*, "outer-province" Taiwanese who migrated from the mainland following the retreat of Chiang Kai-Shek from the mainland) in Taiwan. Another pattern of difference is the regional circulation of socialist ideas and creation of revolutionary networks in Southeast Asia. The historical incarnation of economic capital by "Chinese" bodies is a personification by which capital, and the "pragmatic" values, habits, and practices associated with it, are actively/passively/forcibly incorporated by living beings as "second nature." This process cannot be understood apart from the cultural matrices that embed two historical processes: Sino-Japanese-English hybridization after the middle of the nineteenth century; and the Anglo-Sinicization, regionalization, and globalization of the ethnic-"Chinese" in China and Southeast Asia, especially in the second half of the twentieth century.

Patterns of differences also account for the complexity and diversity of "Chinese" responses to, and perceptions, of power and authority in China and elsewhere, which range from enthusiastic accommodation with the mainland state on the part of so-called Red Capitalist taipans of Hong Kong, to militant challenges against the colonial state posed by the Communist guerrillas of Malaya, to hedging by Chinese-Filipino businessmen who contribute to the campaign coffers of all presidential candidates. "Chinese" identification with capital has meant a greater awareness of and sensitivity to the arbitrary exactions of the state and the vicissitudes of business. Anglo-Chinese who are safely nationalized and whose citizenships are not under question are under less pressure to be "apolitical" compared to earlier generations of "overseas Chinese."[40] Long distance nationalism, however, continues to shape overseas Chinese responses to mainland China.

The existence of multiple actors, acts, and sites of Chineseness foregrounds the importance of lived experiences in complicating commonsensical notions of "Chinese" identity. Civilizational notions of "Chineseness" continue to be haunted by race, nation, and territory. Cultural, political, and circumstantial ideas of "Chineseness" are often articulated as Han-Chinese ethnic identity; and Han-Chineseness as ethnic identity is, in turn, inflected by modern ideas of race (Dikötter 1992). Yet these ideas actually encompass older notions of patrilineal kinship that are concerned less with racial purity than with often mythical origins. The genealogy they construct is flexible and capable of transcending place, disregarding physical appearances, encompassing intermarriage and adoption, and incorporating diverse cultural practices, including "non-Chinese" ones (Ebrey 2003, 165–76).[41] Patrilineal kinship may be linked to the ideology of "Confucian culturalism" and its (ethnocentric) claims to absorb "outsiders" and Sinicize them. But as lived experience—and despite the pressures exerted by colonial, "China"-driven, postcolonial and market-driven Sinicization—becoming-Chinese is neither preordained nor unidirectional.

The cultural implications of the rise of China are far more complex than the naïve assertions behind a "Beijing consensus" that views China as remaking the world in its own image. "Sinicization" entails an interactive and dialogical process capable not just of blurring the lines between "self" and "other," but of transforming them across territorial boundaries and civilizational divides. Viewed in these terms, the phenomenon of "re-Sinicization" of the ethnic Chinese in Southeast Asia might be better understood not as recovery or revival (implied by the prefix "re-") of long-occluded Chineseness, but as *a* process of "becoming-Chinese" whose origins are traceable neither to the "core" nor to the "periphery" of so-called Cultural China, but to the vicissitudes of the broader phenomena of multi-sited state-, colony- and nation-, region-, and world-making out of which "China" and "Chinese culture" emerged.

Contrary to the idea that mainland China is currently remaking the region and the world in its image, parts of mainland China—particularly its urban, middle-, and upper-class populations in the coastal areas—are actually undergoing a form of Anglo-Sinicization that makes specific groups and communities more like the modern hybrid "Anglo-Chinese" that emerged, in the course of 150 years, out of the region we now call "East Asia" (which includes Northeast and Southeast Asia). These mainland Anglo-Chinese have more in common—in terms of lifestyle, upbringing, education, mores, and values—with urban, educated, middle-class "East Asians" than with the rural and impoverished peoples who remain rooted within China, East, and especially Southeast Asia, and beyond. This does not discount the possibility that mainland China's political and economic dynamics over the next few decades—especially if a Sinocentric order were actually to emerge and a power shift occur in China's favor, changing the rules and norms of doing business and politics, for example—might create pressures and incentives toward Sinicization that will be substantively different from the current phenomenon of Anglo-Sinicization. Compared to the processes discussed in this chapter, the evidence for this mainland-driven form of becoming-Chinese—such as the proliferation of simplified Chinese newspapers among overseas Chinese communities, the popularity of mainland Chinese popular culture (particularly historical dramas) among nonmainland Chinese migrant communities, de-Anglicization in Hong Kong[42]—exists to some extent; but its capacity to supplant other forms of becoming-Chinese remains debatable.[43]

This concluding chapter's main concern is to identify the broader historical patterns of hybridization and analyze how these patterns, arising from multiple sites and sources of creating "differences" that are lived as "Chinese," complicate the notion of Sinicization. The signifier "China" is the enabling as well as the delimiting condition of a politics of *identification*, which is not necessarily a politics of *identity* rooted in, as Rey Chow (1993, 24–26) has argued, the dominant myths of consanguinity and claims to ethnic oneness about "China." The challenge, then, is not simply one of retelling the various discourses *about* "China" and attempts by different agents to fix the meaning of Chineseness. Nor is it a simple issue of repudiating or resisting all claims to "Chineseness" in terms of origins or ancestry. Instead, the challenge is to understand how processes of territorializing and de/reterritorializing "China" and "Chineseness" regulate the complex interplay of proximity and distance in the geographical, political, economic, and cultural identifications among the "Chinese." This interplay allows migrants and their descendants—at certain times, in certain places, and under specific circumstances—to claim, and base their actions on, commonalities and/or differences with Southeast Asians, *other* "Chinese," and others. What is at stake in the rise of China and processes of "becoming-Chinese" is nothing less than how "Chinese-ness" is constituted out of forces both of its making and beyond its control, and what kinds of capacities, effects, possibilities, and limits structure these processes and the "Chinese's" "in/human condition" (Cheah 2006, 7, 10).

Notes

1   See the definition, among many such works, provided by Tjon (2009, 360).
2   See, for example, the critique of Chan and Tong (2001, 9); and Crossley, Siu, and Sutton (2006, 6–7); on resinification as an ideological activity of inventing unity through the production of "Chineseness," see Dirlik 1997a, 308.
3   Fogel 2009, 4, drawing on Matisoff 2003, 6.
4   See Souchou Yao's (2008, 7) cogent critique of the racialization of "Chineseness." Yao argues that ideas of Chineseness that replace "race" with "culture" and highlight the performativity of identity continue to be based on restrictive, boundary-making assumptions of "who" can *claim* to be Chinese. "It is culture *and* ancestry that makes one unambiguously Chinese; and this clarity is only possible when ethnicity takes on all the absolutism and essentialism of race." Yao argues that "We know that these appropriation, compromise, subversion, masking, invention of Chinese cultural things cannot unproblematically count as marker of Chinese identity: the simple point that using chopsticks and speaking Chinese wouldn't turn a German Jew or a Malaysian Tamil into a Chinese. It is mistaken to think that *re*invention makes no

reference to cultural and racial continuity." The case of Filipino mestizos claiming Chinese ancestry highlights the problematic nature of claims based on ancestry. Perhaps even more suggestive is the fact that many Southeast Asian Chinese base their claims to Chineseness on no other than the fact (a better word might be "fiction") of ancestry, given that many do not use chopsticks nor "speak Chinese"!

5   Shaffer 1994, 8–12. For a succinct discussion of the history of China's southward expansion and the impact of differing dynastic policies toward the southern frontier on Southeast Asia, see Sun 2010.

6   Territorialization, deterritorialization, and reterritorialization are routinely employed alongside "coding," "recoding," and "decoding" across a range of single- and co-authored texts written by Deleuze and Guattari (1983; 1987) to refer to particular instances of configuration, deconfiguration, and reconfiguration of "territory" understood in its spatial/physical, representational, social, psychoanalytic, economic, and political senses. I use these terms insofar as their emphasis on both fluidity and fixity of cultural flows and identities encourages critical thinking about, as well as beyond, the concepts of territory, nation, and sovereignty that inform studies of the "Chinese" in Southeast Asia.

7   See Wolters (1970) for a nuanced account of the tribute-trade system from the point of view of the mainland dynastic state in China as well as from the polities in what is now Southeast Asia.

8   The so-called tributary trade system, organized around tributary missions to "China" that were also accompanied by traders (and, in some states, established through military intervention), reached its zenith in the fifteenth century under the first Ming emperors. Qing emperors focused their energies on the north and northwestern frontier, adopting a policy of disengagement while encouraging maritime trade (see Sun 2010). Some states, such as Siam and Burma, continued to send tributary missions until the mid-nineteenth century. Tokugawa Japan and Qing China did not establish state-to-state relations, but Chinese traders could visit Nagasaki for trade. For a brief discussion of the reach and limits of the tributary trade system as concept and institution, see Shiraishi and Hau 2012, 122–66.

9   See the documentation by Zhuang Guotu (1989).

10   There are also Tjina Hitam in East Jakarta. I thank Ben Anderson for this information.

11   I owe this information to Nobuhiro Aizawa.

12   Following the Bandung Afro-Asian Solidarity Conference in 1955, mainland China renounced its Dual Nationality claims in an effort to improve relations with its Southeast Asian neighbors. However, Taiwan under Chiang Kai-shek was reluctant to give up its claims on the diasporic Chinese, leading to a divergence in policy between the Republic of China and U.S. policies on the overseas Chinese (Oyen 2010, 90–91). Taiwan's relations with overseas Chinese have been reconfigured in recent decades as attention has shifted to "overseas Taiwanese" rather than "overseas Chinese" among Taiwan policymakers, particularly the Democratic Progressive Party, in the Overseas Chinese Affairs Commission. Interest in and calls for "Taiwanization" do not normally include the "overseas Chinese." I thank Gregory Noble for the information on recent developments in Taiwan.

13   See, for example, Bell 2008 for a discussion of the Confucian revival in China.

14   The flows between China and other East Asian countries were not one-sided. Kanji used in Korea and Japan entered the Chinese vocabulary. An example is the term for

abalone 蚫/鮑, which may have originally come from Korea to Japan, and was then "exported" to China (Nihon Keizai Shimbun 2012).

15 The salience of maritime geography can be seen in the fact that, over a period of eleven years from 743 to 754 AD, the Chinese Buddhist monk Jianzhen (Ganjin) attempted five times to cross the East China Sea into Japan before succeeding on the sixth try. It was the Mongols' success in developing the capability to move large numbers of troops by ships that enabled them to reach Japan and Java, but even then, they were beaten back. Although maritime technology had developed sufficiently to enable, for instance, the movement of large numbers of troops at the time of Hideoyoshi's attempt to conquer Korea toward the end of the sixteenth century, insurmountable logistical problems made it practically impossible to sustain long-term military campaign and pacification. Only in the nineteenth century did advances in steamship technology make the large-scale movement of people a fact of life.

16 Reid and Zheng 2009; see also Giersch 2006, on Qing expansion into Yunnan, whose Tai elite also had relations with Burma and Siam.

17 Wang Gungwu (2011) offers a caveat on the use of the word "civilization": "although 'civilization' is a word introduced into China quite recently, there was an ancient consciousness derived from ideas that were eventually codified in the *Yijing*, *Laozi*, *Yinyang* writings, Confucian stress on ancestors and individual cultivation, down to the later Daoists, Buddhists and Neo-Confucians that together distinguished the peoples of East Asia. The ideas were drawn from the many kinds of ethnic and social groups who were within reach of the lands of eastern Asia, and who interacted and intermingled with one another over the millennia. For this, using the modern word 'civilization' may be misleading. The process involved was more important than the total content." See Kelley's (2005, 31–35) discussion of Sino-Vietnamese relations in terms of Vietnamese self-conceptions of their country as a "domain of manifest civility." The strong cultural identification with and acknowledgement of Vietnam's political subservience to China expressed in Vietnamese envoy poetry raise interesting questions about audience, intention, and reception that complicate (rather than simply affirm) commonsensical notions of "Sinicization." On the dynamism of acculturation and hybridization and their impact on Qing institutions and borderland societies along the Sino-Southeast Asian "frontiers," see Giersch 2006; and Shepherd 1993.

18 Liu 1995, especially the lists in appendices B, C, D, and E.

19 The term "Anglo-China" has been used to refer to the nineteenth-century "realm of economic, political and cultural exchange" with British Hong Kong as a capital (Munn 2009 [2001], 2). The use of "Anglo-Chinese" in this chapter highlights the importance not only of the territories under British and American colonial rule or commercial influence, but also of a specific pattern of hybridization that produced a certain type of "Chinese." "Anglo" refers primarily to linguistic proficiency acquired through Anglophone (which includes British, American, and other englishes) education in the region as well as in Britain, the U.S., Canada, Australia, and New Zealand.

20 On the transformation of Philippine economy in the nineteenth century, see the excellent study by Legarda (1999).

21 Lim and Ku were exceptionally gifted men of letters and published books in English. Not all Anglo-Chinese at the turn of the twentieth century could write in English

(a notable example of a bilingual who also wrote in English is Zhang Ailing/Eileen Chang [1920–1995], the celebrated Shanghai-born writer), but they nevertheless had reading and to a lesser extent speaking abilities in that language. It is instructive to note that China's foremost translator of the time, the Fujian-born Lin Shu (1852–1924), had no foreign languages himself, but instead relied on bilingual collaborators to translate Anglo-American (and to a lesser extent French) writings into literary Chinese.

22   I thank Wang Gungwu for his great help in identifying Ku and Lee as exemplary Anglo-Chinese.

23   I thank Bomen Guillermo for sharing this insight on the dominant language used in the Comintern, based on his research on the Comintern archive in Germany.

24   The situation in Suharto's Indonesia differs from the Sukarno era, when China's cultural diplomacy and the circulation of Chinese literary principles informed Indonesia's cultural politics, especially the discursive construction of a "national allegory" (Liu 2006).

25   The oldest Chinese school in the Philippines, the Anglo-Chinese School (whose name in Chinese—in the spirit of the hybrid, multivalent cultural upbringing of its students—was the Great Qing Chinese and Western School, Dai Qing Zhong Xi Xue Tang 大清中西学堂), was founded on April 15, 1899, by Tan Kong, the first Chinese consul to the Philippines. It is now called the Philippine Tiong Se Academy (菲律宾中西学院).

26   In some instances, owing to the vicissitudes of language policies, some Anglo-Chinese may be functional in English and their mother tongue (Malay, Tagalog, Hokkien, Cantonese) but not necessarily in Mandarin. The situation has changed as economic opportunities created by the rise of China have given Anglo-Chinese more incentives to learn Mandarin. Efforts to promote Mandarin in Singapore since the late 1970s, for example, have been successful, but at the expense of marginalizing non-Mandarin Chinese "dialects," such as Hokkien.

27   For an account of Japanese involvement in the wartime Chinese film industry, see Fu 2003.

28   Enka 演歌 itself is a hybrid musical genre. The "father" of enka, Koga Masao (古賀 政男 1904–1978), was born in Japan to Korean parents, and spent part of his childhood in Korea. The enka he pioneered combined elements of Korean traditional music and American church hymns. Strongly influenced by Korean music, Koga based his first song, produced in in 1931, on a Korean song. The origins of the Korean counterpart to enka, trot, predate those of enka ("The origin of enka from Korea," 2011).

29   The life-size display rooms are organized chronologically in terms of dynasties, but the Yuan dynasty (under Mongol rule) is not represented.

30   I thank Kasian Tejapira for his insights into the Dragon Descendant Museum's "strange" cultural politics of Chineseness (Interview with Kasian Tejapira, Bangkok, October 17, 2009).

31   Interview with Chitra Konuntakiet, Bangkok, October 19, 2009; see also Kupluthai 2008.

32   A more recent example is Yale University professor Amy Chua, whose article "Why Chinese Mothers are Superior" (2011) provoked fierce debates on the Internet over the merits (and demerits) of her self-proclaimed "Chinese" style of strict parenting.

The Anglo-Chinese Chua invoked her own upbringing by her parents, who were Chinese Filipino migrants to the U.S., as an inspiration.

33 I thank Allen Carlson for first alerting me to this *anime* series. In November 2009, the Chinese government established the China Animation Comic Group to promote animation production, technology, and marketing. Plans include the building of a national hub, China Animation Game City, in Beijing. The government also provides subsidies to Chinese animation companies (Hosaka 2010).

34 Oakes 2000, 668. See Friedman 1994; and Gladney 1994; on the reinvention of national identity in the post-Mao era.

35 Tellingly, among the songs sung at the protests that took place in Guangzhou and Hong Kong were a Cantonese song by the Hong Kong boy band Beyond, and a Cantonese adaptation of the theme song from the Japanese *anime*, *Dr. Slump* (Zhu 2010). A recent example of hybridization at work in *putonghua* itself is *geili* (literally, "to give force or power"; awesome, cool, exciting), whose antonym *bugeili* (boring, dull) was first popularized over the Internet by a Chinese-language dubbing of a Japanese anime based on the Chinese classic, *Xi You Ji* (Journey to the West), and quickly transmuted into the English "gelivable" and "ungelivable" and the French "guélile" ("Geili" 2010). The violent denunciation by Philip Fang Shun-shang (2011) of the Hong Kong people's alleged lack of patriotism is symptomatic of the continuing cultural recalcitrance of Hong Kong people in the face of pressures now brought to bear on reterritorializing Hong Kong as part of mainland China. Fang writes that "Generally, Hong Kong Chinese have no idea of their national identity and heritage, and are loath to identify with their brethren on the mainland. They would rather identify themselves with Taiwanese Chinese, Singaporean Chinese, Australian Chinese and American Chinese. They think they are superior. The mindset that fosters this superiority complex is no mystery; Hong Kong people worship money, power, and celebrity. Hong Kong creates no true wealth. It indulges in the culture of money making money." Fang then criticizes "The open defiance of the 'Gang of Four'—Anson Chan Fang On-san, Martin Lee Chu-ming, Jimmy Lai Chee-ying and Cardinal Joseph Zen Ze-kiun—and the Civic Party, headed by Audrey Eu Yuet-mee, only points to the urgency for the government and Legco to push through Article 23, under which many of their acts would be considered as endangering state security, that is, sedition. People must be made to understand they are Chinese citizens and subject to Chinese laws and sanctions."

36 I thank Francis Loh Kok Wah for providing information on the Penang Hokkien Chinese's "re-exporting" of rituals and ceremonies associated with ancestor worship back to their lineage/family associations in Fujian, China. See the valuable research by Liu Zhaohui (2005, especially 143–44).

37 Lee 2009, 57. I thank Shih Chih-yu for directing me to Lee's insightful analysis.

38 "Ancient Imperial Language of China—2,000 Years Ago," 2009.

39 Marchetti's critique (2007) cites Hong Kong-born and New York-based filmmaker Evans Chan's scathing analysis (2004) of *Hero*'s political subtext of legitimizing the authoritarian mainland Chinese state through the subordination of Greater China.

40 I thank Wang Gungwu for prodding me to think about the relationship between power and capital.

41 On a personal note, I can attest to this "flexibility" by pointing to my late uncle (husband of my father's younger sister), who was a "Bombay"-Filipino mestizo adopted and raised as "Chinese."

42   The leading Chinese-language dailies in Southeast Asia continue to use traditional Chinese script, although there are now newspapers that use simplified script. Mainland Chinese TV dramas are widely available on cable and are watched by overseas Chinese, but do not as yet command a wide following among non-Chinese Southeast Asians as Korean, Japanese, and Taiwanese dramas do.

43   Increased enrollment in Chinese-language programs of study in mainland China and the establishment of Confucius Institutes around the world are often taken as evidence of "Sinicization." It should be noted, however, that just as incentives to learn Mandarin have increased among Anglo-Chinese as well as non-Chinese, learning English—now mandatory from elementary grade 3 onwards in China—has become a big business in China, with well-to-do mainland Chinese sending their children abroad for English-language education (Thorniley 2010). Moreover, no power shift has (yet) happened in favor of China. In the absence of a significant social formation in which acquisition of Chinese language involves internalization of "Chinese" norms, regulations, and values on a scale that is comparable to what happened to Anglo-Chinese with English in the regional historical context of British and American hegemony, it is difficult to ascertain the degree to which "Sinicization" is actually taking place among people who are learning *Putonghua* (except on a limited, individual basis), and preparing the ground for the emergence of a Sinocentric order. It is instructive to note, for example, that Liang's (2010) call for making Mandarin the primary medium of instruction in publicly funded schools in Hong Kong remains rooted in the assumption of a multilingual Hong Kong in which Cantonese and English continue to be spoken. A proof of mainland-driven Sinicization would be if large numbers of people, whether ethnic Chinese or not, want to change their passports for a PRC passport, or *putonghua* becomes the regional lingua franca that is spoken even among non-Chinese, or Chinese norms (whether in business or politics) are accepted as legitimate in the region. So far the evidence seems to point in the opposite direction, with (Anglo-)Chinese professionals from the mainland as well as international movie stars, such as Jet Li and Gong Li, taking Singaporean citizenship and Zhang Ziyi taking Hong Kong citizenship mainly for the purpose of protecting their assets and properties. A notable contrary trend, however, is the fact that Hong Kong lawmakers have been under increasing pressure from the mainland government (which does not recognize Dual Citizenship, following its experience in Southeast Asia) to give up their foreign passports/nationalities.

WORKS CITED

Abad, Ricardo G. 2005. Social capital in the Philippines: Results from a national survey. *Philippine Sociological Review* 53:7–63.

Abidin Kusno. 2012. The hero in passage: The Chinese and the activist youth in Riri Riza's *Gie*. In *Film in contemporary Southeast Asia: Cultural interpretation and social intervention*, 130–46. Ed. David C. L. Lim and Hiroyuki Yamamoto. Oxon: Routledge.

Abinales, Patricio N. 2000a. From *orang besar* to colonial big man: Datu Piang of Cotabato and the American colonial state. In *Lives at the margin: Biography of Filipinos obscure, ordinary and heroic*, 192–227. Ed. Alfred W. McCoy. Quezon City: Ateneo de Manila University Press.

———. 2000b. *Making Mindanao: Cotabato and Davao in the formation of the Philippine nation-state.* Quezon City: Ateneo de Manila University Press.

Abramson, Marc S. 2008. *Ethnic identity in Tang China.* Philadelphia: University of Pennsylvania Press.

Acharya, Amitav. 2009. *Whose ideas matter? Agency and power in Asian regionalism.* Ithaca: Cornell University Press.

Agoncillo, Teodoro A., and Domingo Abella. 1978 [1990]. Becoming Filipino. *Turn of the century*, 8–21. Planned and produced by Gilda Cordero-Fernando and Nik Recio. Quezon City: GCF Books.

Agoncillo Teodoro A., and Milagros C. Guerrero. 1977. *History of the Filipino people.* 6th ed. Quezon City: R. P. Garcia Publishing Company.

Agpalo, Remigio. 1958. The political process and the nationalization of the retail trade in the Philippines. Ph.D. diss., Indiana University, U.S.A.

———. 1962. *The political process and the nationalization of the retail trade in the Philippines.* Quezon City: Office of the Coordinator of Research, University of the Philippines.

Aguilar, Filomeno V., Jr. 1998. *Clash of spirits: The history of power and sugar planter hegemony on a Visayan island.* Quezon City: Ateneo de Manila University Press.

———. 1999. The triumph of instrumental citizenship? Migration, identities, and the nation-state in Southeast Asia. *Asian Studies Review* 23, no. 3:307–33.

———. 2001. Citizenship, inheritance, and the indigenizing of "orang Chinese" in Indonesia. *positions* 9, no. 3:501–33.

———. 2005. Tracing origins: *Ilustrado* nationalism and the racial science of migration waves. *Journal of Asian Studies* 64, no. 3:605–37.

———. 2011a. Between the letter and spirit of the law: A history of Philippine citizenship by *jus soli*, 1899–1947. *Southeast Asian Studies* 49, no. 3:85–117.

———. 2011b. *Filibustero*, Rizal, and the Manilamen of the nineteenth century. *Philippine Studies* 59, no. 4:429–69.

———. 2012a. Book review: Richard T. Chu, *Chinese and Chinese mestizos of Manila: Family, identity, and culture, 1860s–1930s. Philippine Studies* 60, no. 1:134–38.

———. 2012b. Philippine citizenship by mass naturalization, a dictator's largesse? An interview with Benito Lim. *Philippine Studies* 60, no. 3: 319–415.

Ahmad, Aijaz. 1994. *In theory: Classes, nations, literatures.* London: Verso.

———. 1995. The politics of literary postcoloniality. *Race and Class* 36, no. 3:1–20.

Aizawa Nobuhiro. 2010. *Kajin to kokka: Indonesia no "china" mondai* (Ethnic Chinese and the state: Indonesia's "China" Question). Tokyo: Shoseki Kōbō Hayama.

Alba, Richard, and Victor Nee. 2003. *Rethinking the American mainstream: Assimilation and contemporary immigration.* Cambridge, Massachusetts: Harvard University Press.

Alejandrino, Clark L. 2003. *A history of the 1902 Chinese Exclusion Act: American colonial transmission and deterioration of Filipino-Chinese relations.* Manila: Kaisa para sa Kaunlaran, Inc.

Alvarez, Santiago V. 1992 [1927–1928]. *Ang Katipunan at paghihimagsik/Recalling the revolution: Memoirs of a Filipino general.* Trans. Paula Carolina S. Malay. Wisconsin: Center for Southeast Asian Studies, University of Wisconsin.

Amin, Samir. 1990. *Delinking: Towards a polycentric world.* Trans. Michael Wolfers. London and New Jersey: Zed Books.

Ancheta, Maria Rhodora G. 2006. The "King" of Philippine comedy: Some notes on Dolphy and the cinematic functions of Philippine cinematic humor as discourse. *Humanities Diliman* 3, no. 2 (July–Dec.): 74–117.

Ancient imperial language of China—2,000 years ago. n.d. Internet document, received Sept. 15, 2009.

Anderson, Benedict, R. O' G. 1991 [1983]. *Imagined communities: Reflections on the origins and spread of nationalism.* Rev. ed. London: Verso.

———. 1998. Cacique democracy in the Philippines. *Spectres of comparisons: Nationalism, Southeast Asia and the world,* 192–226. London: Verso.

———. 2008. *Why counting counts: A study of forms of consciousness and problems of language in* Noli me tangere *and* El filibusterismo. Quezon City: Ateneo de Manila University Press.

———. 2005. *Under three flags: Anarchism and the anti-colonial imagination.* London: Verso.

———. 2012. E-mail to the author, Jan. 25.

Andrade, Jeannette. 2006. Kidnapping cases in RP on the uptrend, police say. *Manila Times,* May 3, A3.

Ang, Alfonso O [Tu Yiban]. 2005. Rizal's Chinese overcoat. Trans. Daniel Ong. Rev. version of "Li Cha de Zhongguo wai yi," *Shangbao* (Chinese Commercial News), Feb. 14–18. http://joserizal.info/Reflections/rizals_chinese_overcoat.pdf, accessed Aug. 30, 2010.

Ang, Ien. 1998. Can one say no to Chineseness? Pushing the limits of the diasporic paradigm. *boundary 2* 25, no. 3:223–42.

Ang-See, Teresita. 1995. The many faces of the ethnic Chinese. *Manila Chronicle,* Nov. 19, 5.

_____. 1997a. *The Chinese in the Philippines: Problems and perspectives.* Vol. 1. Manila: Kaisa para sa Kaunlaran, Inc.

_____. 1997b. *The Chinese in the Philippines: Problems and perspectives.* Vol. 2. Manila: Kaisa para sa Kaunlaran, Inc.

_____. 2000. Preying on aliens. *Tulay,* Mar. 21, 8–9, 14.

_____. 2004a. *Chinese in the Philippines: Problems and perspectives.* Vol. 3. Manila: Kaisa para sa Kaunlaran.

_____. 2004b. The ethnic Chinese community in the Philippines and its unique position in Southeast Asia. *Chinese in the Philippines: Problems and perspectives* 3:37–51. Manila: Kaisa para sa Kaunlaran.

_____. 2004c. Ten scary years. *Tulay,* Jan. 13, 13.

_____. 2011. E-mail to the author, Oct. 9.

_____. 2012. Handshake better than fistfight. Tsinoy Beats and Bytes column. *Tulay* 24, no. 22 (Apr. 24–May 7). Internet document, http://kaisa.org.ph/tulay/tsinoy.html, accessed May 1, 2012.

Ang-See, Teresita, and Bon Juan Go. 1996. *The ethnic Chinese in the Philippine revolution.* Manila: Kaisa para sa Kaunlaran.

Angliongto, Jose L. 1969. *The sultanate.* Davao City: Eden Publishing House, Inc.

Apilado, Digna B. 2001. Nationalism and discrimination: Policies of the Revolutionary Government of 1898 toward the Chinese in the Philippines. Imperios y naciones en el Pacifico: Colonialismo e identidad nacional en Filipinas y Micronesia [Empires and nations in the Pacific: Colonialism and Identity in the Philippines and Micronesia], vol. 2, ed. Ma. Dolores Elizalde, Josep M. Frodera and Luis Alfonso, 173–86. Madrid Consejo Superior de Inestigaciones Cientificar.

Appiah, Kwame Anthony K. A. 1998. Cosmopolitan patriots. In *Cosmopolitics: Thinking and feeling beyond the nation,* 91–114. Ed. Pheng Cheah and Bruce Robbins. Minneapolis and London: University of Minnesota Press.

Appleton, Sheldon. 1960. Overseas Chinese and economic nationalization in the Philippines. *Journal of Asian Studies* 19:151–61.

Arcellana, Juaniyo Y. 2002. We have to know everything. *Starweek,* Dec. 22, 10–12, 14.

Arrighi, Giovanni. 1994. *The long twentieth century: Money, power, and the origins of our times.* London: Verso.

Arrighi, Giovanni, Takeshi Hamashita, and Mark Selden. 2006. *The resurgence of East Asia: 500, 150 and 50 year perspectives.* Oxon and New York: Routledge.

Arriola, Andrew K., and Grace C. Pe. 1989. *Discovering new horizons: Anthology of Chinese Filipino literature in English.* Manila: World News.

Asian Development Bank. 2011. The Philippines. Country Tables. *Key indicators for Asia and the Pacific 2011.* Internet document, http://www.adb.org/sites/default/files/KI/2011/pdf/PHI.pdf, accessed Aug. 3, 2012.

Austin, Carly, and Harald Bauder. 2010. *Jus domicile: A pathway to citizenship for temporary foreign workers?* CERIS Working Paper no. 81. Ontario: CERIS—The Ontario Metropolis Centre.

Aw, Olivia Limpe. 2008. A reluctant hero. *Asian Dragon* 2, no.1:52–54.

Ayala Museum. 2007. Chinese diaspora: Art streams from the Mainland. Web site press release. http://www.ayalamuseum.org/index.php?option=com_ayala_content&task=showpress&id=45, accessed Nov. 1, 2008.

Azcuna, Adolf. 1969. The Chinese and the law. In *The Chinese in the Philippines, 1770–1898*. 2: 75–95. Ed. Alfonso Felix Jr., presented by the Historical Conservation Society. Manila: Solidaridad Publishing House.

Baguioro, Luz. 1998. Dirty Harry may be barred from race. *The Straits Times*, Mar. 24, 19.

Bai Ren. 2007. *Lagalag sa Nanyang (Nanyang piaoliuji/Adrift in the Southern Ocean)*. Trans. Joaquin Sy. Quezon City: University of the Philippines Press.

Bai Ren [Wang Jisheng]. 1983. *Nanyang piaoliuji* (Adrift in the Southern Ocean). Guangzhou: Huacheng Chubanshe. First published in Hong Kong in 1983 as *Nanyang liulanger* (Orphan wanderer of the Southern Ocean) by South China Press.

Balibar, Etienne. 1991. Class racism. In *Race, nation, class: Ambiguous identities*, 204–16. Ed. Etienne Balibar and Immanuel Wallerstein, trans. Chris Turner. London and New York: Verso.

_____. 1994. "Rights of Man" and "Rights of the Citizen": The modern dialectic of freedom and equality. In *Masses, classes, ideas: Studies on politics and philosophy before and after Marx*, 39–59. Trans. James Swenson. New York and London: Routledge.

_____. 2004. *We, the people of Europe? Reflections on transnational citizenship*. Trans. James Swenson. Princeton: Princeton University Press.

Balisacan, Arsenio, and Hal Hill. 2003. An introduction to the key issues. In *The Philippine economy: Development, policies, and challenges*, 3–44. Ed. Arsenio Balisacan and Hal Hill. Quezon City: Ateneo de Manila University Press.

Bankoff, Greg, and Kathleen Weekley. 2004 [2002]. *Celebrating the centennial of independence: Postcolonial national identity in the Philippines*. Hampshire, England, and Manila: Ashgate Publishing Limited and De La Salle University Press.

Bao Chang. 2012. ASEAN, China to become top trade partners. *China Daily*, Apr. 20. Internet document, http://www.chinadaily.com.cn/cndy/2012-04/20/content_15094898.htm, accessed May 20, 2012.

Bateman, Sam, and Ralf Emmers. 2009. *Security and international politics in the South China Sea: Towards a Cooperative Management Regime*. Oxon: Routledge.

Baviera, Aileen San Pablo. 1991. Philippine-Taiwan Relations. In *China ASEAN relations: Political, economic and ethnic dimensions*, 112–26. Ed. Theresa C. Cariño. Manila: The China Studies Program, De La Salle University.

Ang Bayan. 1972. On the restoration of the legitimate rights of the People's Republic of China in the United Nations. *Ang Bayan* 4, no. 1 (Jan. 15): 3–4.

_____. 1977. Filipino people warmly receive Chinese friends. *Ang Bayan* 9, no. 13 (Sept. 15): 12–13.

_____. 1979. China acts to block Soviet aggression. *Ang Bayan* 11, no. 4 (Feb. 28): 7–8.

_____. 1980. October 1—China's liberation inspires peoples of the world. *Ang Bayan* (Oct. 31): 12–13.

Bayan Muna. 2001. Ad. *Shang Bao* (Chinese Commercial News), Jan. 7, 11.

Bayly, Susan. 2007. *Asian voices in a postcolonial age: Vietnam, India and beyond*. Cambridge, UK: Cambridge University Press.

_____. 2008. Vietnamese narratives of tradition, exchange and friendship in the worlds of the global socialist ecumene. In *Enduring socialism: Explorations of revolution and transformation, restoration and continuation*, 125–47. Ed. Harry G. West and Parvathi Raman. Oxford, UK: Berghahn Books.

Bell, Daniel A. 2008. *China's new Confucianism: Politics and everyday life in a changing society*. Princeton, NJ: Princeton University Press.

Bello, Walden, Herbert Docena, Marissa de Guzman, and May Lon Malig. 2004. *The anti-development state: The political economy of permanent crisis in the Philippines.* Quezon City: University of the Philippines Press.

Benton, Gregor. 2007. *Chinese migrants and internationalism: Forgotten histories, 1917–1945.* London and New York: Routledge.

Bhabha, Homi K. 1994. *The location of culture.* London and New York: Routledge.

Bickers, Robert, and Ray Yep. 2009. *May days in Hong Kong: Riot and emergency in 1967.* Hong Kong: Hong Kong University Press.

Blair, Emma H., and James A. Robertson, eds. 1903–1909. Relation of the insurrection of the Chinese. In *The Philippine Islands, 1493–1898* 29:208–58. Ohio: Arthur H. Clark, Company.

Blaker, James R. 1970. The Chinese in the Philippines: A study of power and change. Ph.D. diss., Ohio State University, U.S.A.

Blanc, Cristina Szanton. 1996. *Balikbayan*: A Filipino extension of the national imaginary and of state boundaries. *Philippine Sociological Review* 44, nos. 1–4:178–93.

———. 1997. The thoroughly modern "Asian": Capital, culture and nation in Thailand and the Philippines. In *Ungrounded empires: The cultural politics of modern Chinese transnationalism,* 261–86. Ed. Aihwa Ong and Donald M. Nonini. New York: Routledge.

Blanchetti-Revelli, Lanfranco. 2003. Moro, Muslim, or Filipino?: Cultural citizenship as practice and process. In *Cultural citizenship in island Southeast Asia: Nation and belonging in the hinterlands,* 44–75. Ed. Renato Rosaldo. Berkeley and Los Angeles: University of California Press.

Blanco, John D. 2009. *Frontier constitutions: Christianity and colonial empire in the ninteteenth-century Philippines.* Berkeley: University of California Press.

Bordwell, David. 2000. *Planet Hong Kong: Popular cinema and the art of entertainment.* Cambridge, Massachusetts: Harvard University Press.

Boxer, Charles R. 1950. A late sixteenth-century Manila MS. *Journal of the Royal Asiatic Society* (Apr.): 37–49.

Brubaker, Rogers. 1992. *Citizenship and nationhood in France and Germany.* Cambridge, Mass.: Harvard University Press.

Buan-Deveza, Reyma. 2011. Kim Chiu's challenges in "Binondo Girl." Abs-cbnNEWS. com, Apr. 11, http://www.abs-cbnnews.com/entertainment/04/11/11/kim-chius-new-challenges-binondo-girl, Aug. 30.

Buencamino, Manuel. 2007. Gung-ho or gung-Hu? *Business Mirror,* Oct. 16, A10.

Bulletin Today. 1973a. Tourism plan for Chinatown given support today, July 14. News clipping from Kaisa Heritage Center library.

———. 1973b. City Chinatown project to be launched Tuesday, Sept. 7. News clipping from Kaisa Heritage Center library.

Bureau of Immigration, Philippines. 2012. Dual citizenship. Frequently asked questions section. Internet document, http://immigration.gov.ph/index.php?option=com_con tent&task=view&id=163&Itemid=83, accessed Jan. 31.

Butler, Judith. 1993. *Bodies that matter: On the discursive limits of sex.* London and New York: Routledge.

Cabreza, Vincent. 2004. Filipino moviegoers "Asianized," notes screenwriter. *Philippine Daily Inquirer,* Entertainment section, Dec. 21, 1, 3.

Caldwell, Patricia. 1983. *The puritan conversion narrative: The beginnings of American expression.* Cambridge: Cambridge University Press.

Callahan, William A. 2004. *Contingent states: Greater China and transnational relations.* Minneapolis and London: University of Minnesota Press.

Cannell, Fenella. 1999. *Power and intimacy in the Christian Philippines.* Cambridge: Cambridge University Press.

Cariño, Theresa Chong. 1985. *China and the overseas Chinese in Southeast Asia.* Quezon City: New Day Publishers.

———. 1988. The Chinese in the Philippines: A survey of the literature. *Journal of the South Sea Society* 43:43–54.

———. 1998. *Chinese big business in the Philippines: Political leadership and change.* Singapore: Times Academic Press.

———. 2001. The Philippines. In *Chinese business in South-East Asia: Contesting cultural explanations, researching entrepreneurship,* 101–23. Ed. Edmund Terence Gomez and Hsin-Huang Michael Hsiao. Richmond, Surrey: Curzon.

Carney, Michael, and Marleen Dieleman. 2008. Heroes and villains: Ethnic Chinese family business in Southeast Asia. In *Theoretical developments and future research in family business,* 49–73. Ed. Phillip H. Phan and John E. Butler. Charlotte, North Carolina: Information Age Publishing, Inc.

Cense, A. 1955. Sanggalea, an old word for "Chinese" in South Celebes. *Bijdragen tot de Taal-, Land- en Volkenkunde* 111, no. 1:107–8.

Chan, Evans. 2004. Zhang Yimou's *Hero*—the temptations of fascism. *Film International,* no. 8 (Mar.). Internet document, http://www.filmint.nu/netonly/eng/heroevanschan.htm/, accessed Dec. 15, 2007.

Chan, Kwok Bun, and Chee Kiong Tong. 2001. Positionality and alternation: Identity of the Chinese of contemporary Thailand. In *Alternate identities: The Chinese of contemporary Thailand,* 1–8. Ed. Tong Chee Kiong and Kowk Bun Chan. Singapore: Times Academic Press.

Chanco, Boo. 2012. A bad case of "Sinositis." *The Philippine Star,* June 15. Internet document, http://www.philstar.com/Article.aspx?articleId=817240&publicationSub CategoryId=66, accessed June 20.

Chandra, Elizabeth. 2011. Fantasizing Chinese/Indonesian hero: Njoo Cheong Seng and the Gagaklodra series. *Archipel* 82:83–113.

Chang Kwang-chi. 1999. China on the eve of the historical period. In *The Cambridge history of ancient China: From the origins of civilization to 221 B.C.,* 33–73. Ed. Michael Loewe and Edward L. Shaughnessy. Cambridge, UK: Cambridge University Press.

Chang Noi [Pasuk Phongpaichit and Chris Baker]. 2009 [1996]. Cultural revolution in Thailand (Aug. 29, 1996). In *Jungle book: Thailand's politics, moral panic, and plunder, 1996–2008,* 121–24. Bangkok: Silkworm Press. Originally published in *The Nation,* Aug. 29, 1996.

Chang, Y. Z. 1937. Sangley, the merchant-traveller. In *Modern Language Notes* 52:189–90. Ed. H. Carrington Lancaster. Baltimore: The Johns Hopkins Press.

Cheah, Pheng. 1996. Mattering. *Diacritics* 26, no. 1:108–39.

———. 1997. Given culture: Rethinking cosmopolitical freedom in transnationalism. *boundary 2* 24, no. 2:157–97.

———. 1998. Introduction, part 2. In *Cosmopolitics: Thinking and feeling beyond the nation,* 20–41. Ed. Pheng Cheah and Bruce Robbins. Minneapolis: University of Minnesota Press.

———. 2001. Chinese cosmopolitanism in two senses and postcolonial national memory. In *Cosmopolitan geographies: New locations in literature and culture*, 133–69. Ed. Vinay Charwadker. New York: Routledge.

———. 2006. *Inhuman conditions: On cosmopolitanism and human rights*. Cambridge, Massachusetts: Harvard University Press.

Chen Hui-ying. 2010. Preface. *Magic Min'nan*, 1. Xiamen: Xiamen Min'nan Tourism and Culture Industry Co., Ltd.

Chen, Kuan-Hsing. 2010. *Asia as method: Toward deimperialization*. Durham: Duke University Press.

Chen, Richard. 2002. Straight out of *Joy Luck Club*. *Philippine Star*, Nov. 17, D4.

Chin, James K. 2010. Junk trade, business networks, and sojourning communities: Hokkien merchants in early maritime Asia. *Journal of Chinese Overseas* 6:157–215.

ChinaA2Zcom News. 2009. Chinese cartoon to land in international market. July 3, URL, http://news.chinaa2z.com/news/html/2009/20090703/20090703082238338604/20090 703082556451481.html, accessed May 8, 2010.

Chiquito, SLN. 2007. Movie celebrities then and now blog, Oct. 27. Internet document, http://movie-industry.blogspot.jp/2007/10/chiquito.html, accessed Mar. 20, 2011.

Chitra Konuntakiet. 2009. Interview with the author, Oct. 19, Bangkok, Thailand.

Chow, Rey. 1993. *Writing diaspora: Tactics of intervention in contemporary cultural studies*. Bloomington and Indianapolis: Indiana University Press.

———. 1998. Introduction: On Chineseness as a theoretical problem. *boundary 2* 25, no. 3: 1–24.

———. 2009. Foreword. *China abroad: Travel, spaces, subjects*, ix–xii. Ed. Elaine Yee Lin Ho and Julia Kuehn. Hong Kong: Hong Kong University Press.

Chu, Richard T. 2002a. The "Chinese" and the "*mestizos*" of the Philippines: Toward a new interpretation. *Philippine Studies* 50, no. 3:327–70.

———. 2002b. Rethinking the Chinese *mestizos* of the Philippines. In *Beyond China: Migrating identities*, 44–74. Ed. Shen Yuanfang and Penny Edwards. Canberra: Center for the Study of the Chinese Southern Diaspora, Australian National University.

———. 2010. *Chinese and Chinese mestizos of Manila: Family, identity, and culture, 1860s–1930s*. Leiden and Boston: Brill.

———. 2011. Strong(er) women and effete men: Negotiating Chineseness in Philippine cinema at a time of transnationalism. *positions* 19, no. 2:365–91.

Chua, Amy. 2011. Why Chinese mothers are superior. *Wall Street Journal*, Jan. 8. http://online.wsj.com/article/SB10001424052748704111504576059713528698754.html, accessed Mar. 5, 2011.

Chua, Apolonio. 1976/1977. Romantisayson ng probinsyano o Manila boy? (Romanticization of the country boy or Manila boy?). *Literary Apprentice* 49, no. 1:105–21.

Chua Beng Huat. 2003. *Life is not complete without shopping: Consumption culture in Singapore*. Singapore: Singapore University Press, National University of Singapore.

Chua, Yvonne T. 2000. The company he keeps: Many of the president's men have questionable pasts. *i: The Investigative Reporting Magazine* 6, no. 4 (Oct.–Dec.), http://pcij.org/imag/SpecialReport/cronies.html, accessed Aug. 30, 2011.

Chun, Allen. 1989. Pariah capitalism and the overseas Asia: Problems in the definition of the problem. *Ethnic and Racial Studies* 12, no. 2:233–56.

———. 1995. An oriental orientalism: The paradox of tradition and modernity in nationalist Taiwan. *History and Anthropology* 9, no. 1:27–56.

———. 1996. Fuck Chineseness: On the ambiguities of ethnicity as culture as identity. *boundary 2* 23, no. 2:111–38.

Claver, Peter B. 2012. Why is Teresita Ang-See silent on PH-China row? Letters to the editor section, *Philippine Daily Inquirer,* May 1. Internet document, http://opinion.inquirer.net/27907/why-is-teresita-ang-see-silent-on-ph-china-row, accessed May 1.

Clifford, James. 1997. *Routes: Travel and translation in the late twentieth century.* Cambridge, Massachusetts: Harvard University Press.

Co, Jacqueline. 1991. Kidnap-for-ransom leaves trail of terror. *Tulay,* Apr. 21, 6–7.

———. 1995. "Democracy" at work in crime. *Tulay,* Dec. 4, 7.

Communist Party of the Philippines. 1989. Background on China (June). Photostat MS.

———. 1990. Programme for a people's democratic revolution in the Philippines. App. 6 of Alfredo B. Saulo, *Communism in the Philippines: An introduction,* 196–209. Enlarged ed. Quezon City: Ateneo de Manila University Press.

Constable, Nicole. 1997. *Maid to order in Hong Kong: Stories of Filipina workers.* Ithaca: Cornell University Press.

Constantino, Renato, and Letizia R. Constantino. 1978. *The Philippines: The continuing past.* Quezon City: The Foundation for Nationalist Studies.

Cooper, Joshua Ramo. 2004. *The Beijing consensus.* London: The Foreign Policy Centre.

Coppel, Charles. 1974. The position of the Chinese in the Philippines, Malaysia, and Indonesia. In *Philippine-Chinese Profile: Essays and studies,* 69–88. Ed. Charles McCarthy. Manila: Pagkakaisa sa Pag-Unlad, Inc.

———. 1976. Patterns of Chinese political activity in Indonesia. In *The Chinese in Indonesia,* 19–76, 215–26. Ed. J. A. C. Mackie. Honolulu, Hawaii: University Press of Hawaii, Honolulu and Australian Institute of International Affairs.

———. 1983. *Indonesian Chinese in crisis.* Kuala Lumpur: Oxford University Press.

———. 2008. Anti-Chinese violence in Indonesia after Soeharto. In *Ethnic Chinese in contemporary Indonesia,* 117–36. Ed. Leo Suryadinata. Singapore: Institute of Southeast Asian Studies.

Corelli, Andrea. 2003. *The history of family business, 1850–2000.* Cambridge: Cambridge University Press.

Coronel, Sheila S., Yvonne T. Chua, Luz Rimban, and Booma B. Cruz. 2007. *The rulemakers: How the wealthy and the well-born dominate Congress.* Pasig City: Anvil Publishing, Inc.

Cristobal, Adrian E. 1965. From chink to Chinese. *Graphic* 32, no. 15 (Oct. 6): 12–14.

Crossley, Pamela Kyle, Helen F. Siu, and Donald S. Sutton. 2006. *Empire at the margins: Culture, ethnicity and frontier in early modern China.* Berkeley: University of California Press.

Cruz, Isagani R. 1996 [1995]. Ang panulaang Chinoy: Si Grace Hsieh-Hsing bilang makata (Chinoy poetry: Grace Hsieh-Hsing as poet). In *The Alfredo E. Litiatco lectures of Isagani R. Cruz,* 268–80. Ed. David Jonathan Y. Bayot. Manila: De La Salle University Press. First excerpted in *Kritika: Filipino Magazine,* Apr. 10, 1995, 23; and Apr. 17, 1995, 20.

Cruz, Isagani R., and Soledad S. Reyes, eds. 1984. *Ang ating panitikan* (Our literature). Manila: Goodwill Books.

Crying Ladies. 2003. Directed by Mark Meily. Motion picture, Unitel Pictures.

Cu Unjieng, Philip. 2004. Director Mark Meily: A mark-ed man. *Starweek: The Sunday Magazine of the Philippine Star,* Jan. 11, 8, 9, 11.

Cueto, Donna S. 1999. Erap's Sino pals said to push for foreign ownership of land. *Philippine Daily Inquirer,* Aug. 26, 2.

Cullamar, Evelyn. 1995. Huaqiao's long road to being Filipino. *Tulay,* Nov. 20, 8–9.

Cullinane, Michael. 1982. The changing nature of the Cebu urban elite in the 19th century. In *Philippine social history: Global trade and local transformations,* 251–96. Ed. Alfred W. McCoy and Ed. C. de Jesus. Quezon City: Ateneo de Manila University Press.

———. 2003. *Ilustrado politics: Filipino elite responses to American rule, 1898–1908.* Quezon City: Ateneo de Manila University Press.

Cushman, Jennifer W. 1989. The Chinese in Thailand. In *Ethnic Chinese in the ASEAN states: Bibliographical essays,* 221–59. Ed. Leo Suryadinata. Singapore: Institute of Southeast Asian Studies.

Daily Mirror. 1970. Nat. Case no. C-31, In the matter of the petition of Ng See Kui also known as Flaviano Uy Suy Cui alias Flavy to be admitted a citizen of the Philippines, petition published on Mar. 25.

Dalangin, Lira. 1995. The losing war against crime. *Sunday Times Chronicle,* Oct. 22, 1, 4.

Danao, Efren L. 2007. Miriam says sorry to Chinese. *Manila Times,* Sept. 28, A1, A2.

Dannhaeuser, Norbert. 2004. *Chinese traders in a Philippine town.* Quezon City: Ateneo de Manila University Press.

David, Joel. 2008. Awake in the dark: Philippine film during the Marcos era. *Philippine studies: Have we gone beyond St. Louis?* 227–43. Ed. Priscelina Patajo-Legasto. Quezon City: University of the Philippines Press.

David, Randy. 2012. The call to boycott Chinese products. *Philippine Daily Inquirer,* July 19. Internet document, http://opinion.inquirer.net/32863/the-call-to-boycott-chinese-products, accessed July 20, 2012.

Davidson, Jamie S. 2008. The study of political ethnicity in Southeast Asia. In *Southeast Asia in political science: Theory, region, and quantitative analysis,* 199–226, 352–54. Ed. Erik Martinez Kuhonta, Dan Slater, and Tuong Vu. Stanford: Stanford University Press.

Daza, Jullie Yap. 2003. VAT, an action movie. *Manila Standard,* Jan. 24. http://72.14.203.104/search?q=cache:2wAGiVrQCjMJ:www.manilastandardonline.com:8080/mnlastd/ContentLoader%3Fpage%3DjullieYapDaza_jan24_2003+%22Mano+Po%22+grossed&hl=ja&gl=jp&ct=clnk&cd=7, accessed Sept. 7, 2004.

De Leon, Francisco. 1970 [2000]. They never had a chance. *Manila Chronicle,* May 8. Rep. in *The case of the Yuyitung brothers: Philippine press freedom under siege,* 124–27. Comp. and ed. Rizal Yuyitung. Manila: Yuyitung Foundation, Inc.

De la Costa, Horacio. 1974. Chinese values in Philippine cultural development. In *Philippine-Chinese profile: Essays and studies,* 50–58. Ed. Charles J. McCarthy. Manila: Pagkakaisa sa Pag-unlad, Inc.

De Quiros, Conrado. 2001. Aliens. *Philippine Daily Inquirer,* June 18, A8.

Del Puerto, Luige A. 2005. Kidnapping not yet thing of the past, GMA told. *Philippine Daily Inquirer,* July 27, 1.

Deleuze, Gilles, and Felix Guattari. 1983 [1972; 1977]. *Anti-Oedipus: Capitalism and schizophrenia.* Trans. Robert Hurley, Mark Seem, and Helen R. Lane. Rep. ed. Minneapolis: University of Minnesota Press.

———. 1987 [1980]. *A thousand plateaus: Capitalism and schizophrenia.* Trans. Brian Massumi. Minneapolis: University of Minnesota Press.

Deng, Yingda. 1988. *Wo zai Shangzong sanshinian* (My thirty years in the Federation of Filipino-Chinese Chambers of Commerce). Manila: The Author.

Derrida, Jacques. 1982. Differance. In *Margins of philosophy*, 3–27. Trans. Alan Bass. Chicago: University of Chicago Press

———. 1994. *Specters of Marx: The state of the debt, the work of mourning, and the new international*. Trans. Peggy Kamuf. New York and London: Routledge.

Dery, Luis C. 2005. *When the world loved the Filipinos and other essays on Philippine history*, 3–15. Manila: University of Santo Tomas Publishing House.

Dian shi lianxu ju *Nanyang lei* ershi ri zai Jinjiang kaiji (*Nanyang Lei* TV mini-series begins shooting on the 20th). 2005. *Fujian Qiaolian*, Aug. 9. http://www.fjql.org/qldt/j1163.htm, accessed Sept. 7, 2006.

Diaz, Jess. 2006. 71 *Tsinoys* abducted this year. *Philippine Star*, Oct. 24, 1, 8.

Dikötter, Frank. 1992. *The discourse of race in modern China*. Stanford: Stanford University Press.

Ding Sheng. 2008. *The dragon's hidden wings: How China rises with its soft power*. Lanham, Maryland: Lexington Books.

Dirlik, Arif. 1997a. Critical reflections on "Chinese capitalism" as a paradigm. *Identities* 3: 303–30.

———. 1997b. Culturalism as hegemonic ideology and liberating practice. *The Postcolonial aura: Third world criticism in the age of global capitalism*, 23–51. Boulder: Westview Press.

———. 1999. Culture against history? The politics of East Asian identity. *Development and Society* 28, no. 2 (Dec.): 167–90.

———. 2008. Socialism in China: A historical overview. In *The Cambridge companion to modern Chinese culture*, 155–72. Ed. Kam Louie. Cambridge, UK: Cambridge University Press.

Dizon, David. 2011. Mindanao kidnappings on the rise: MRPO, Jan. 11. ABS-CBN News. com, http://www.abs-cbnnews.com/nation/01/11/11/mindanao-kidnappings-rise-mrpo, accessed Jan. 3, 2012.

Doeppers, Daniel F. 1994. Tracing the decline of the mestizo categories in Philippine life. *Philippine Quarterly of Culture and Society* 22, no. 2 (June): 80–89.

Dragnet. 1973. Motion picture. Directed by Luciano B. Carlos.

Du Ai [Cao Zhuanmei]. 1982. Wo de chuang zuo li cheng (My creative path). In *Du Ai Zixuanji* (Selected Works of Du Ai). Zhuhai: Huacheng Chubanshe.

———. 1985. *Fengyu Taipingyang* (Storm over the Pacific). Vol. 1. Guangzhou: Huacheng Chubanshe.

———. 1988. *Fengyu Taipingyang*. Vol. 2. Guangzhou: Huacheng Chubanshe (1991 ed. published in Beijing by Wenhua Yishu Chubanshe).

———. 1991. *Fengyu Taipingyang*. 3 vols. Zhuhai, Guangdong: Zhuhai Chubanshe.

———. 2002. *Fengyu Taipingyang*. 3 vols. Zhuhai: Zhuhai Chubanshe.

———. N.d. Biographical entry. In *Guangdong dangdai zuojia zhuanlie* (Biography of contemporary Guangdong writers). Guangzhou: Zhongshan University Press.

Duara, Prasenjit. 1997. Nationalists among transnationals: Overseas Chinese and the idea of China, 1900–1911. In *Ungrounded empires: The cultural politics of modern Chinese transnationalism*, 39–60. Ed. Aihwa Ong and Donald Nonini. New York and London: Routledge.

Dueñas, Michael. 1992. The kidnapping "industry." *Philippines Free Press*, Mar. 21, 34–36.

Dy, Aris S. 2003. Between two cultures. *Tulay Fortnightly*, Jan. 7, 16, 15.

Ebrey, Patricia Buckley. 2003. Surnames and Chinese Han identity. In *Women and the family in Chinese history*, 165–76, 247–49. London and New York: Routledge.

The Economist. 2008. Too much or too little? Nov. 26. http://www.economist.com/node/12672673, accessed Sept. 19, 2011.

Eder, James F., and Thomas M. MacKenna. 2004. Minorities in the Philippines: Ancestral lands and autonomy in theory and practice. In *Civilizing the margins: Southeast Asian government policies for the development of minorities*, 56–85. Ithaca and London: Cornell University Press.

Effendi, Wahyu, and Prasetyadji. 2008. *Tionghoa dalam cengkeraman SBKRI* (Chinese in the claws of SBKRI). Jakarta: Visimedia.

Emmerson, Donald K. 1984. "Southeast Asia": What's in a name? *Journal of Southeast Asian Studies* 15, no. 1 (Mar.): 1–21.

Entrala, Francisco Paula de. 1881. *Sin título: Novela de costumbres* (Without title: A novel of manners). Manila: Establecimiento tipográfico de Ramírez y Giraudier.

Etzioni, Amitai. 2007. Citizenship tests: A comparative, communitarian perspective. *The Political Quarterly* 78, no. 3 (July–Sept.): 353–63.

Fan, Philip Shun-sang. 2011. Brat in the family. *South China Morning Post*, Nov. 9. Internet document, http://www.scmp.com/portal/site/SCMP/menuitem.2c913216495213d5df646910cba0a0a0/?vgnextoid=a659bddd01383310VgnVCM100000360a0a0aRCRD&vgnextfmt=teaser&ss=Hong+Kong&s=News#top, accessed Nov. 11.

Fang Peng Cheng. 1988. Chinese-Philippine literature: A history and anthology. PhD diss., De la Salle University, Manila, Philippines.

Farah Azalea Mohamed Al Amin. 2008. Controversies surrounding Malaysian independent female director Yasmin Ahmad's first film, *Sepet*. Paper presented at the 17th Biennial Conference of the Asian Studies Association of Australia, Melbourne, Australia, July 1–3. Internet document, http://arts.monash.edu.au/mai/asaa/farahazaleamohamedalamin.pdf, accessed Feb. 1, 2012.

Faure, David. 1989. The lineage as a cultural invention: The case of the Pearl River Delta. *Modern China* 15:4–36.

Favell, Adrian. 1998. *Philosophies of integration: Immigration and the idea of citizenship in France and Britain*. Basingstoke and New York: Palgrave.

———. 2005. Assimilation/Integration. In *Immigration and asylum: From 1900 to the present*. Ed. Matthew Gibney and Randall Hansen. Santa Barbara, CA: Clio. Internet document, http://www.sscnet.ucla.edu/soc/faculty/favell/Clio.htm, accessed Jan. 18.

Felix, Alfonso Jr., ed. 1966. *The Chinese in the Philippines*. 2 vols. Manila: Solidaridad Publishing House.

Fichte, Johann Gottlieb. 1922. *Addresses to the German nation*. Trans. R. F. Jones and G. H. Turnbull. Chicago: Open Court.

Fitzgerald, John. 1995. The nationless state: The search for a nation in modern Chinese nationalism. *The Australian Journal of Chinese Affairs* 33 (Jan.): 75–104.

Flores, Patrick. 2003. The Chinatown conspiracy. *Manila Standard*, Dec. 30, B7.

Flores, Wilson Lee. 2002. Mano po: Can the inscrutable Chinese ever be understood by Philippine society? *Philippine Star*, Dec. 28. Rep. in Newsflash. Internet document, http://www.newsflash.org/2002/12/sb/sb002568.htm, accessed Aug. 30, 2011.

———. 2004. The top 10 most powerful families in the Philippines. *Philippine Star*, Apr. 17. Internet document, http://www.manilamail.com/features/PowerfulFamilies.htm, accessed Nov. 17, 2009.

_____. 2010. The secret father of President Sergio Osmeña & forefather of John Gokongwei, Jr., Gaisanos, Gotianuns. *Philippine Star,* June 20. Internet document, http://www.philstar.com/Article.aspx?articleid=585793, accessed Oct. 2.

Fogel, Joshua A. 2009. *Articulating the sinosphere: Sino-Japanese relations in space and time.* Cambridge, Massachusetts, and London: Harvard University Press.

Foster, Anne L. 2003. Models for governing : Opium and colonial policies in Southeast Asia, 1898–1910. In *The American colonial state in the Philippines: Global perspectives,* 92–117. Ed. Julian Go and Anne L. Foster. Durham: Duke University Press.

_____. 2009. Prohibiting opium in the Philippines and the United States: The creation of an interventionist state. In *Colonial crucible: Empire in the making of the modern American state,* 95–105. Ed. Alfred W. McCoy and Francisco A. Scarano. Madison: University of Wisconsin Press.

Foucault, Michael. 1980. Truth and power. In *Power/knowledge: Selected interviews and other writings 1972–1977,* 109–33. Ed. Colin Gordon. New York: Pantheon Books.

Fradera, Josep. 2001. La formación de una colonia: Objetivos metropolitanos y transacciones locales (The formation of a colony: Metropolitan objectives and local transactions). In *Imperios y naciones en el Pacífico* (Empires and nations in the Pacific), 1:83–103. Ed. Ma. Dolores Elizalde, Josep M. Fradera, and Luis Alonso. Madrid: Asociación Española de Estudios del Pacífico, Consejo Superior de Investigaciones Científicas.

Fravel, M. Taylor. 2008. *Strong borders, secure nation: Cooperation and conflict in China's territorial disputes.* Princeton: Princeton University Press.

Freud, Sigmund. 1975 [1917]. The taboo of virginity. In *The standard edition of the complete psychological works of Sigmund Freud,* 11:191–208. Trans. James Strachey. London: The Hogarth Press.

Friedland, Jonathan. 1988. Manila store wars. *Far Eastern Economic Review,* Dec. 22, 50–51.

Friedman, Edward. 1994. Reconstructing China's national identity: A southern alternative to Mao-Era anti-imperialist nationalism. *Journal of Asian Studies* 53, no. 1:67–91.

Friedman, Edward, and Mark Selden, eds. 1971. *America's Asia: Dissenting essays on Asian-American relations.* New York: Pantheon Books.

Fu, Poshek. 2003. *Between Shanghai and Hong Kong: The politics of Chinese cinemas.* Stanford, California: Stanford University Press.

Fuchikawa Hideo. 1934. Shina firipin tsūshō jō no "sangley" ni tsuite (On "sangley" in China-Philippine commerce). *Rekishi to chiri* 33, no. 4:336–47.

Fuller, Thomas. 2000. For youths in South, hostage-taking is about livelihood, not politics: In Philippines, a kidnapping industry. *International Herald Tribune,* Sept. 28. Internet document, http://www.www.iht.com/articles/2000/09/28/manila.2.t.php, accessed Aug. 27, 2007.

Furnivall, John S. 1991 [1939]. *The fashioning of Leviathan: The beginnings of British rule in Burma.* Ed. Gehan Wijeyewardene. Canberrra: Department of Anthropology, Australian National University. First published in the *The Journal of the Burma Research Society* 29, no. 1 (Apr. 1939): 3–137.

Gabriel, Sharmani Patricia. 2011. Translating Bangsa Malaysia. *Critical Asian Studies* 43, no. 3:349–72.

Gagelonia, Ding Guzman. 2009. Hayden Kho tags his frat brod, claims drugs caused his problems. "How things are, how they can be" blog, May 23. Internet document, http://midfield.wordpress.com/2009/05/23/hayden-kho-tags-his-frat-brod-claims-drugs-caused-his-problems/, accessed Aug. 30, 2011.

Ganito kami noon, paano kayo ngayon? (This is how we were then, how about you now?). 1976. Directed by Eddie Romero. Motion picture, Hemisphere Pictures, Inc., Philippines.

Gao, Qingyun. 1974. *Shangzong Niannian: Feihua Shanglian Zhonghui chengli ershi zhounian jinian tekan* (Federation Chronicle: Souvenir issue commemorating the 20th anniversary of the establishment of Federation of Filipino-Chinese Chambers of Commerce and Industry). Manila: Federation of Filipino-Chinese Chambers of Commerce, Inc.

Garcia Canclini, Nestor. 1990. *Hybrid cultures.* Minneapolis: University of Minnesota Press.

Genovea, Miguel. 1972. Chinatown signs are back, on mayor's orders. *Evening Express,* Nov. 9, 3.

Gie. 2005. Directed by Riri Reza. Motion picture, SINEMART Pictures, Indonesia.

Giersch, C. Patterson. 2006. *Asian borderlands: The transformation of Qing China's Yunnan frontier.* Cambridge, Mass.: Harvard University Press.

Gladney, Dru C. 1994. Representing nationality in China: Refiguring majority/minority identities. *Journal of Asian Studies* 53, no. 1:92–123.

Global Times. 2011. 99% shou fang wangyou renwei Zhongguo ying shizhixing di chengfa Feilubin (99% of Internet respondents think that China should mete out substantive punishment to the Philippines). Huanqiu.com, Sept. 28. Internet document, http://world.huanqiu.com/roll/2011-09/2043831.html, accessed Oct. 20.

GMA News. 2012. OFW remittances up 7.2% to new record $20.12B in 2011, Feb. 15. Internet document, http://www.gmanetwork.com/news/story/248122/economy/moneyandbanking/ofw-remittances-up-7-2-to-new-record-20-12b-in-2011, accessed June 10.

Go, Bernard C. 1974. The Pinsinos—facts and fancies. In *Philippine-Chinese profile: Essays and studies,* 230–40. Ed. Charles J. McCarthy. Manila: Pagkakaisa sa Pag-Unlad, Inc.

Go, Julian. 2008. *American empire and the politics of meaning.* Durham and London: Duke University Press.

Go, Kitty [Wu Shur Yuan]. 2005a. *When chic hits the fan: Celebrity and fashion confessions of a former magazine editor.* Philippines: Paradigm Software Systems, Inc.

———. 2005b. *Chic happens: An explosive celebrity and fashion insider account.* Philippines: Paradigm Software Systems, Inc.

Godley, Michael R. 1981. *The Mandarin-capitalists from Nanyang: Overseas Chinese enterprise in the modernization of China, 1893–1911.* Cambridge: Cambridge University Press.

Goldberg, David Theo. 2002. *The racial state.* Massachusetts: Blackwell Publishers, Inc.

Gomez, Edmund Terence, and Hsin-Huang Michael Hsiao. 2001. Chinese business research in Southeast Asia. In *Chinese business in South-East Asia: Contesting cultural explanations, researching entrepreneurship,* 1–37. Ed. Edmund Terence Gomez and Hsin-Huang Michael Hsiao. Richmond, Surrey: Curzon.

Gong Taoyi, ed. 2001. *Feilubin huaqiao kangri aiguo yinghun* (Philippine-Chinese martyrs of the anti-Japanese resistance). Beijing: Huawen Chubanshe.

———. 2002. *Feilubin huaqiao guiqiao aiguo danxin lu* (Philippine-Chinese returnee patriots). Beijing: Huawen Chubanshe.

Gonzales, Alessandra G. L. 2000. Fractured thoughts. In *Intsik: An anthology of Chinese Filipino writing*, 261–66. Ed. Caroline S. Hau. Pasig City: Anvil.

Grafilo, John. 1998. Erap goes after kidnappers. *Philippine Graphic*, Oct. 19, 17.

Granada, Ernesto O. 1970 [2000]. Kuomintang—government within a government. *The Manila Chronicle*, Apr. 27. Rep. in *The case of the Yuyitung brothers: Philippine press freedom under siege*, 104–5. Comp. and ed. Rizal Yuyitung. Manila: Yuyitung Foundation, Inc.

Greenhalgh, Susan. 1994. De-orientalizing the Chinese family firm. *American Ethnologist* 21, no. 4:746–75.

Guéguen, Catherine. 2006. Divisoria revitalized by new waves of migrants. *Tulay*, Sept. 19, 8–9.

———. 2010. Moving from Binondo to the "Chinese Villages" of the suburbs: A geographical study of the Chinese in Metro-Manila. *Journal of Chinese Overseas* 6:119–37.

Guerrero, Amadis Ma. 1970 [2000]. Family without a father. *Graphic*, Sept. 2. Rep. in *The case of the Yuyitung brothers: Philippine press freedom under siege*, 92–97. Comp. and ed. Rizal Yuyitung. Manila: Yuyitung Foundation, Inc.

Guerrero, Amado. 1979. *Philippine society and revolution*. 3d ed. California: International Association of Filipino Patriots.

———. 1988. Brief review of the history of the Communist Party of the Philippines: On the occasion of the 20th anniversary of its reestablishment. Mimeo. Dec. 26.

Guerrero, Milagros C. 1977. Luzon at war: Contradictions in Philippine society. Ph.D. diss., University of Michigan.

———. 1982. The provincial and municipal elites of Luzon during the revolution, 1898–1902. In *Philippine social history: Global trade and local transformations*, 155–90. Alfred W. McCoy and Ed. C. de Jesus. Quezon City: Ateneo de Manila University Press.

Gunsteren, Herman R. van. 1998. *A theory of citizenship: Organizing plurality in contemporary democracies*. Boulder: Westview Press.

Guo Yingjie. 2004. *Cultural nationalism in contemporary China: The search for national identity under reform*. London and New York: Routledge.

Hall, Stuart. 1996. New ethnicities. In *Stuart Hall: Critical dialogues in cultural studies*, 441–49. Ed. David Morley and Kuan-Hsing Chen. London: Routledge.

Hamashita, Takeshi. 2008. *China, East Asia and the global economy: Regional and historical perspectives*. Oxon and New York: Routledge.

Hardwick, Patricia Ann. 2008. "Neither fish nor fowl": Constructing peranakan identity in colonial and post-colonial Singapore. *Folklore Forum* 38, no. 1:36–55.

Harvey, David. 1990. *The condition of postmodernity*. Oxford: Blackwell.

———. 2005. *A brief history of neoliberalism*. Oxford: Oxford University Press.

Hau, Caroline S. 2000a. *Intsik: An anthology of Chinese Filipino writing*. Pasig City: Anvil.

———. 2000b. *Necessary fictions: Philippine literature and the nation, 1946–1980*. Quezon City: Ateneo de Manila University Press.

———. 2001. Too much, too little. *Philippine Daily Inquirer*, June 15, A9.

———. 2004. *On the subject of the nation: Filipino writings from the margins, 1980–2004*. Quezon City: Ateneo de Manila University Press.

———. 2011. "Patria è intereses": Reflections on the origins and changing meanings of *Ilustrado*. *Philippine Studies* 59, no. 1:3–54.

Hau, Caroline S., and Takashi Shiraishi. 2009. Daydreaming about Rizal and Tetchō: On Asianism as network and fantasy. *Philippine Studies* 57, no. 3:329–88.

———. 2012. Regional contexts of cooperation and collaboration in Hong Kong Cinema. In *Cultural collaboration in East Asian Popular culture*, 68–96. Ed. Nissim Otzmagin and Eyal Ben-Ari. Kyoto and Singapore: Kyoto University Press and National University of Singapore Press.

He Chuxiong. N.d. Daqibangbo de Zhongfei renming zhantou qingyi de songge—Du "Fengyu Taipingyang" yi, erbu (An epic of Chinese-Philippine comradeship: Reading *Fengyu Taipingyang*, pts. 1 and 2). Photostat MS.

———. 2002a. Zhongfei renmin bingjian kangji Riben qin lüezhe de shishi xingying xionglezhang—Ping sanjuanben changpian xiaoshuo "Fengyu Taipingyang." Pt 1. (Epic of Chinese and Filipino heroes struggling against the Japanese invaders: Critique of the three volumes of the long novel, *Fengyu Taipingyang*). *Shijie Ribao* (World News), July 2, 21.

———. 2002b. Zhongfei renmin bingjian kangji Riben qinlüezhe de shishi xingying xionglezhang—Ping sanjuanben changpian xiaoshuo "Fengyu Taipingyang." Pt. 2. *Shijie Ribao*, July 4, 21.

Hedman, Eva-Lotta, and John T. Sidel. 2000. Forget it, Jake, it's Chinatown. In *Philippine politics and society: Colonial legacies, post-colonial trajectories*, 65–87. London: Routledge.

Heidhues, Mary Somers. 2007. Remembering Ong from the sixties. In *Onze Ong: Onghokham dalam Kenangan* (Our Ong: Onghokham in memory), 231–35. Depok, Jakarta: Komunitas Bambu.

Hernandez, Amado. 1982 [1969]. *Mga ibong mandaragit* (Birds of prey). Quezon City: Progressive Printing Palace.

Hernandez, Salvador T. 1991. The man who fought to be called a Filipino. *Philippines Free Press,* July 6, 2,13–14, 30.

Heryanto, Ariel. 2008. Citizenship and Indonesian ethnic Chinese in post-1998 films. In *Popular culture in Indonesia: Fluid identities in post-authoritarian politics*, 70–92. Ed. Ariel Heryanto. Oxon and New York: Routledge.

Hindmarsh, D. Bruce. 2005. *The evangelical conversion narrative: Spiritual autobiography in early modern England*. Oxford and New York: Oxford University Press.

Hing, Reynard. 2011. China's soft power in the Asian context and the Philippines. Facebook, June 4. Internet document, http://www.facebook.com/notes/reynard-hing/chinas-soft-power-in-the-asian-context-and-the-philippines/10150266443460917, accessed June 5.

Hodder, Rupert. 2005. The study of Overseas Chinese in Southeast Asia: Some comments on its political meanings with particular reference to the Philippines. *Philippine Studies* 53, no.1: 3–31.

Holzberg, Niklas. 1995. *The ancient novel: An introduction*. Trans. from the German by Christine Jackson-Holzberg. London: Routledge.

Honig, Bonnie. 2001. *Democracy and the foreigner*. Princeton: Princeton University Press.

Hosaka, Tomoko A. 2010. Chinese version of anime catches the eye. *International Herald Tribune*, Mar. 30, 15.

Hsiao, Shi-ching. 1998. *History of Chinese-Philippine relations*. 2d ed. Quezon City: Bookman Printing House.

Hsiau, A-chin. 2000. *Contemporary Taiwanese cultural nationalism*. London and New York: Routledge.

Hu Yaohua. 1995. Yi dangnian, kangri qingyi bi haishen—Fang guiqiao nu zuojia Lin Bin (Remembering the past, comradeship in the anti-Japanese resistance is deeper than the ocean: An interview with woman writer Lin Bin). *Shijie Ribao* (World News), July 14, 11.

Huang, Mingde. 1957. *Feilubin huaqiao jingji* (Philippine Chinese economy). Taibei: Haiwai Chubanshe.

Huang, Pei. 2011. *Reorienting the Manchus: A study of sinicization, 1583–1796*. Ithaca: Cornell Southeast Asia Program.

Huang Weizong. n.d. Lun minzu wenhua de jian rongxing ji qidian xing zuojia—Du Ai (On the synthesis of national culture and its representative writers: Du Ai). Photostat MS.

Huang, Zisheng, and Sibing He. 1987. *Feilubin huaqiao shi* (A History of the Philippine Chinese). Guangzhou: Gunagdong Gaodeng Jiaoju Chubanshe.

Huynh Kim Kanh. 1982. *Vietnamese communism, 1925–1945*. Ithaca: Cornell University Press.

Ileto, Reynaldo C. 1989 [1979]. *Pasyon and revolution: Popular movements in the Philippines, 1840–1910*. 3d ed. Quezon City: Ateneo de Manila University Press.

———. 1998a. Orators and the crowd: Independence politics, 1910–1914. In *Filipinos and their revolution: Event, discourse, historiography*, 135–64. Quezon City: Ateneo de Manila University Press.

———. 1998b. The "unfinished revolution" in political discourse. In *Filipinos and their revolution: Event, discourse, historiography*, 177–201. Quezon City: Ateneo de Manila University Press.

Ishikawa Yoshihiro. 2001. *Chūgoku Kyōsantō seiritsu shi* (History of the formation of the Chinese Communist Party). Tokyo: Iwanami Shoten.

Iwabuchi, Koichi. 2004. Introduction: Cultural globalization and Asian media connections. In *Feeling Asian modernities: Transnational consumption of Japanese TV dramas*, 1–22. Ed. Koichi Iwabuchi. Hong Kong: Hong Kong University Press.

Jafar Suryomenggolo. 2011. E-mail to the author, Sept. 10.

Javellana, Juliet L. 1998. 230 crime groups identified by PNP. *Philippine Daily Inquirer*, Aug. 3, 1, 18.

Jensen, Khin Khin Myint. 1956. The Chinese in the Philippines during the American Regime: 1898–1946. Ph.D. diss., University of Wisconsin, Wisconsin, U.S.A.

Jiang Hua. 2001a. Kang zhan shi qi de Feihua wenxue. Pt. 1. (Philippine-Chinese literature during the wartime). *Shang Bao* (Chinese Commercial News), July 7, 7.

———. 2001b. Kang zhan shi qi de Feihua wenxue (Philippine-Chinese literature during the wartime). Pt. 2. *Shang Bao*, July 8, 7.

Jiang, Joseph P. L. 1974. The Chinese and the Philippine political process. In *Philippine-Chinese profile: Essays and studies*, 89–106. Ed. Charles J. McCarthy. Manila: Pagkakaisa sa Pag-unlad, Inc., Unity for Progress.

Jimenez-David, Rina. 2002. An unflinching look at Chinoy life. *Philippine Daily Inquirer*, Dec. 26, A7.

Jones, Gregg R. 1989. *Red revolution: Inside the Philippine guerrilla movement*. Boulder: Westview Press.

Joppke, Christian. 2003. Citizenship between de- and re-ethnicization. *Archives européennes de sociologie* 44, no. 3:29–58.

———. 2010. *Citizenship and immigration*. Cambridge and Maryland: Polity Press.

Jose, F. Sionil. 1999a. Chinese mischief. *Philippine Star*, Feb. 21, L-20.

————. 1999b. In a war with China, would our local ethnic Chinese be loyal to the Philippines? *Philippine Star,* Feb. 28, L-14.

————. 2000. Stanley Ho and the anti-Filipino Chinese. *Philippine Daily Inquirer,* Feb. 6, 7.

Jurriëns, Edwin, and Jeroen de Kloet, eds. 2007. *Cosmopatriots: On distant belongings and close encounters.* Amsterdam and New York: Rodopi.

Kaisa para sa Kaunlaran. 1989. *A Chinese general in the Philippine Revolution: Jose Ignacio Paua.* Manila: Kaisa para sa Kaunlaran, Inc.

————. 2005. Fact sheet no. 1: The Chinese in the Philippines: Some basic facts. Online, http://www.philonline.com.ph/~kaisa/kaisa_fact.html.

Kamio, Yoko. 1992–2003. *Hana yori dango* (Boys over flowers). Tokyo: Shueisha.

Kang, David C. 2010. Civilization and state formation in the shadow of China. In *Civilizations in world politics: Plural and pluralist perspectives,* 91–13. Ed. Peter J. Katzenstein. London and New York: Routledge.

————. 2007. *China rising: Peace, power and order in East Asia.* New York: Columbia University Press.

Karl, Rebecca E. 2002. *Staging the world: Chinese nationalism at the turn of the twentieth century.* Durham: Duke University Press.

Kasian Tejapira. 1997. "Imagined uncommunity": The lookjin middle class and Thai official nationalism. In *Essential outsiders: Chinese and Jews in the modern transformation of Southeast Asia and Central Europe,* 75–98. Ed. Daniel Chirot and Anthony Reid. Seattle and London: University of Washington Press.

————. 2001a. *Commodifying Marxism: The formation of modern Thai radical culture, 1927–1958.* Kyoto: Kyoto University Press and Trans Pacific Press.

————. 2001b [1992]. Pigtail: A prehistory of Chineseness in Siam. In *Alternate identities: The Chinese of contemporary Thailand,* 41–66. Ed. Tong Chee Kiong and Chan Kwok Bun. Singapore: Times Academic Press.

————. 2009a. Interview with the author, Oct. 17, Bangkok, Thailand.

————. 2009b. The misbehaving jeks: The evolving regime of Thainess and Sino-Thai challenges. *Asian Ethnicity* 10, no. 3:245–65.

Kataoka Tatsuki. 2008. The Baba culture in Thailand: Reconstruction of ethnic distinctiveness and cultural localization of the Hokkien descendants in Phuket. In *Chinese identities and inter-ethnic coexistence and cooperation in Southeast Asia,* 31–43. Proceedings of the Center for Southeast Asian Studies, Kyoto University, Global COE Program "In Search of Sustainable Humanosphere in Asia and Africa." Kyoto University and Netherlands Institute for War Documentation Joint International Workshop, July 4–5. Kyoto: Center for Southeast Asian Studies, Kyoto University.

Katzenstein, Peter J. 2005. *A world of regions: Asia and Europe in the American imperium.* Ithaca: Cornell University Press.

————. 2006. East Asia—Beyond Japan. In *Beyond Japan: The dynamics of East Asian regionalism,* 1–33. Ed. Peter J. Katzenstein and Takashi Shiraishi. Ithaca, New York and London: Cornell University Press.

Katzenstein, Peter J., and Takashi Shiraishi, eds. 1997. *Network power: Japan and Asia.* Ithaca: Cornell University Press.

Keane, Webb. 2006. Epilogue: Anxious transcendence. In *The anthropology of Christianity,* 308–23. Ed. Fenella Cannell. Durham: Duke University Press.

Kejia xiandai zhuming zuojia Du Ai [The celebrated Hakka writer Du Ai], *Kejia wenhua shuju ku* (Digital treasury of Hakka culture), Apr. 21, 2008. Internet document, http://sglyj.meizhou.gov.cn/modules/data/article.php?storyid=289, accessed June 22.

Kelley, Liam C. 2005. *Beyond the bronze pillars: Envoy poetry and the Sino-Vietnamese relationship.* Hawai'i: University of Hawai'i Press.

Kerkvliet, Benedict J. Tria. 1979. *The Huk rebellion: A study of peasant revolt in the Philippines.* Quezon City: New Day Publishers.

———. 1995. Toward a more comprehensive analysis of Philippine politics: Beyond the patron-client, factional framework. *Journal of Southeast Asian Studies* 26, no. 2:401–19.

Khoo, Boo Teik. 1995. *Paradoxes of Mahathirism: An intellectual biography of Mahathir Mohamad.* Kuala Lumpur and New York: Oxford University Press.

———. 2011. E-mail communication with author, Sept. 2.

Khoo Joo Ee. 1998. *The Straits Chinese: A cultural history.* Amsterdam: Pepin Press.

"Kim Chiu." 2011. *Wikipedia.* Internet document, http://en.wikipedia.org/wiki/Kim_Chiu. Last modified Aug. 31, accessed Sept. 6.

Kitamura, Yumi. 2010. *Minshuka go Indonesia ni okeru kajin bunka no dōtai (1998–2009)* (The dynamics of Indonesian-Chinese culture in Indonesia after democratization). Ph.D. diss., Hitotsubashi University, Tokyo, Japan.

Klöter, Henning. 2011. *The language of the sangleys: A Chinese vernacular in missionary sources of the seventeenth century.* Leiden and Boston: Brill.

Koike, Kenji. 1995. Changing ownership and management structure of taipans compared with Ayala Group. In *The Chinese-Filipino business families under Ramos government,* 35–65. Temario C. Rivera and Kenji Koike. Joint Research Program Series no. 114. Tokyo: Institute of Developing Economies.

Koizumi, Junko. 2006. Tai Chūgokujin shakaiken kyu no rekishisei to chiikisei—Reisenki Amerika ni okeru kakyo, kajin kenkyū to chiiki kenkyū ni kansuru ichi kosatsu" (A historical reappraisal of studies of overseas Chinese in Thailand). *Tonan Ajia Kenky* 43, no. 4:437–66.

———. 2008. Beyond the assimilation-sinicization framework: Studies of the Chinese society in Thailand Reconsidered from historical and local perspectives. In *Proceedings of the Center for Southeast Asian Studies, Kyoto University Global COE Program "In Search of Sustainable Humanosphere in Asia and Africa,"* 199–226. Kyoto University, and Netherlands Institute for War Documentation Joint International Workshop on Chinese Identities and Inter-ethnic Coexistence and Cooperation in Southeast Asia. Kyoto: Center for Southeast Asian Studies, Kyoto University.

Ang Komunista. 1971. Ping pong diplomacy 2, no. 4 (July 21): 1–3.

———. 1972. Issues in the ideological dispute between Maoism and the international communist movement 3, no. 1 (Jan.): 1–10.

Kondo, Mari. 2008. Twilling *Bata-bata* into meritocracy: Merito-Patronage management system in a modern Philippine corporation. *Philippine Studies* 56, no. 3:251–84.

Kostakopoulou, Dora. 2008. *The future governance of citizenship.* Cambridge: Cambridge University Press.

Kraidy, Marwan M. 2005. *Hybridity: Or the cultural logic of globalization.* Philadelphia: Temple University Press.

Krinks, Peter. 2002. *The economy of the Philippines: Elites, inequalities and economic restructuring.* London: Routledge.

Kiunisala, Edward. 1992. Kidnapping for ransom: A big business. Pt. 3. *Philippines Free Press*, Oct. 24, 10–11, 31.

———. 1993. Ka Hector: Rebel or common criminal? *Philippines Free Press*, Mar. 27, 2–3.

Kun Luo [Zeng Kun Luo]. 2003. *Nanyang lei: Jian nan sui yue* (Nanyang tears: The difficult years). Vol.1. Beijing: Zhongguo Guangbodianshi Chubanshe.

———. 2005. *Nanyang lei: Chun feng qiu yu* (Nanyang tears: Spring wind, autumn rain). Vol. 2. China: The Author.

———. 2009. *Nanyang lei: Xi yang xi xia* (Nanyang tears: The sun sets in the west). Vol. 3. China: The Author.

Kupluthai Pungkanon. 2008. Tales of the Father. *Daily Xpress*, Dec.29. Internet document, http://www.dailyxpress.net/2008/12/29/lifestyle/lifestyle_5242.php, accessed Apr. 26, 2010.

Kurlantzick, Joshua. 2008. *Charm offensive: How China's soft power is transforming the world*. New Haven: Yale University Press.

Lacaba, Jose F. 1970 [2000]. The case of the brothers Yuyitung. *Philippines Free Press*, May 9. Rep. in *The case of the Yuyitung brothers: Philippine press freedom under siege*, 23–37. Comp. and ed. Rizal Yuyitung. Manila: Yuyitung Foundation, Inc.

Lacara, Cesar Hernandez [Tatang]. 1988. *Sa tungki ng ilong ng kaaway: Talambuhay ni Tatang* (On the tip of the enemy's nose: Autobiography of Tatang). Metro Manila: Kilusan sa Paglilinang ng Rebolusyonaryong Panitikan at Sining sa Kanayunan (LINANG).

Lagustan, Nick A. 2009. The execution of Lim Seng. *Philippine Daily Inquirer*, Jan. 12. Internet document, http://opinion.inquirer.net/inquireropinion/letterstotheeditor/view/20090112-182765/Lim-Sengs-execution, accessed Aug. 30, 2011.

Lahirnya konsepsi asimilasi (The birth of the concept of assimilation). 1977. Jakarta: Yayasan Tunas Bangsa.

Lai Yuanyu. 2005. "Fengyu Taipingyang" yu Li Bingxiang yi jia (*Fengyu Taipingyang* and the family of Li Bingxiang). *Zhongshan Qiao Kan* 65, Sept. 1. Internet document, http://faob.zsnews.cn/QiaoKan_Showcontent.asp?id=649978, accessed Sept. 7, 2008.

Landé, Carl H. 1965. *Leaders, factions and parties: The structure of Philippine politics*. New Haven: Yale University Press.

Larkin, John. 1982. Philippine history reconsidered: A socioeconomic perspective. *American Historical Review* 87, no. 3:595–628.

Laufer, Berthold. 1907. The relations of the Chinese to the Philippines. *Smithsonian Miscellaneous Collections* 50:248–84.

Laurel, Herman Tiu. 2011. E-mail to the author, Oct. 31.

Laurel, R. Kwan. 2008. *Ongpin stories*. Manila: Kaisa para sa Kaunlaran, Inc.

———. 2003. A hundred years after the *Noli*: The three centennial novels in English. *Philippine Studies* 51, no. 4:599–643.

Lava, Jesus B. 2002. *Memoirs of a communist*. Manila: Anvil Publishing, Inc.

Law Kar and Frank Bren (with the collaboration of Sam Ho). 2004. *Hong Kong cinema: A cross-cultural view*. Lanham, Maryland, and Toronto and Oxford: The Scarecrow Press, Inc.

Lee Chin Chen [Li Zheng Xian/Steve Lee]. 2009. *Malaixiya Guanghua Ribao de Zhongguo Renshi—Zai Huaqiao yü Huaren Liang Zhong Shenfen zhi jian* (Malaysia-based *Kwong-Wah Yit Poh*'s Understanding of China: Between *Huaqiao* and *Huaren* Identities). Taibei: The Research and Educational Center for China Studies and

Cross-Taiwan Strait Relations, Department of Political Science, National Taiwan University.

Lee, Kwan Yew. 2000. *From third world to first: The Singapore story, 1965–2000*. New York: HarperCollins Publishers, Inc.

Lee, Leo Ou-fan. 1999. *Shanghai modern: The flowering of a new urban culture in China, 1930–1945*. Cambridge and London: Harvard University Press.

Lee, Ricardo. 1968. Huwag! Huwag mong kukuwentuhan ang batang si Wei-fung! (Don't! Don't tell Wei-fung any stories!). *Pilipino* (Dec.18): 1–3, 93–100, 106–8.

———. 2008. *Para kay B (o kung paano dinevastate ng pag-ibig ang 4 out of 5 sa atin)* (For B [or how love devastated 4 out of 5 of us]). Quezon City: The Writers' Studio.

———. 2011a. E-mail to the author, Aug. 10.

———. 2011b. E-mail to the author, Nov. 7.

———. 2011c. *Si Amapola sa 65 na kabanata* (Amapola in 65 chapters). Quezon City: Philippine Writers' Studio Foundation, Inc.

Lee, Rose Hum. 1960. *The Chinese in the United States*. Hong Kong: Hong Kong University Press.

Legarda, Benito J., Jr. 1999. *After the galleons: Foreign trade, economic change and entrepreneurship in the nineteenth-century Philippines*. Quezon City: Ateneo de Manila University Press.

Letter of Instructions 270. Apr. 11, 1975. Internet document, http://www.chanrobles.com/letterofinstructions/letterofinstructionsno270.html, accessed Sept. 22, 2011.

Levi-Strauss, Claude. 1987 [1950]. *Introduction to the work of Marcel Mauss*. Trans. Felicity Baker. London: Routledge.

Li Lijun 2001. Wo de fuqin Li Binxiang (Li Yongxiao) de yisheng (The life of my father, Li Binxiang [Li Yongxiao]). In *Feilubin huaqiao kangri aiguo yinghun* (Philippine-Chinese Martyrs of the Anti-Japanese Resistance), 14–19. Ed. Gong Taoyi. Beijing: Huawen Chubanshe.

Li Minjiang. 2008. Soft power in Chinese discourse: Popularity, prospect and parameter. *Chinese Journal of International Politics*, 1–22.

———. 2009. *Soft power: China's emerging strategy in international politics*. Lanham, Maryland: Lexington Books.

Li Qichang, ed. 1968. *Feilubin huaqiao shanju gongsuo jiushi zhounian jinian kan* (Souvenir issue of the Philippine Chinese Charitable Association's 90th Anniversary). Manila: Philippine Chinese Charitable Association.

Li, Yuanjin [Lee Guan Kin]. 1991. *Lin Wenqing de sixiang—Zhongxi wenhua de huiliu yu maodun* (The thought of Lim Boon Keng: Convergency and contradiction between Chinese and Western culture). Singapore: Singapore Society of Asian Studies.

Li Zhiyuan. N.d. "Gaoge fan faxi sidesheng lijin xingqu: Lun *Fengyu Taipingyang* de nü xingying xiongqun xiang suzao" (In praise of the anti-fascist victory anthem: On the portrayal of the heroines in *Fengyu Taipingyang*). Photostat MS.

Liang, Hongfu [James Leung]. 2010. Mandarin proficiency will aid Hong Kong. *China Daily*, June 3. Internet document, http://www.chinadaily.com.cn/opinion/2010-06/03/content_9925813.htm, accessed Mar. 22, 2011.

Liang Shangwan and Cai Jianhua. 1980. *Huaqiao kangri zhidui* (Overseas Chinese anti-Japanese troops). Hong Kong: Guangjiaojing Chubanshe.

———. 1996. *Huazhi huiyilu—Ji Feilubin huaqiao kangri youji zhidui* (Remembering Huazhi: On Philippine-Chinese anti-Japanese resistance troops). Hong Kong: All Directions Publishing.

_____. 1998. *The Wha Chi memoirs*. Trans. Joaquin Sy. Manila: Kaisa para sa Kaunlaran, Inc.

Liao, Schubert. 1964. *Chinese participation in Philippine culture and economy*. Manila: The Author.

Lim, Benito O. 1958. Fantasy of the maid. *Literary Apprentice*, 55–61. Golden Jubilee Anniversary Issue.

_____. 2001. The political economy of Philippines-China relations. In *China's economic growth and the ASEAN*, 271–301. Ed. Ellen H. Palanca. Makati City: Philippine APEC Study Center Network and Philippine Institute for Development Studies.

Lim, Bliss Cua. 2000. Festivals: Crisis or promise? New directions in Philippine cinema. *Indiewire*, Aug. 14. Internet document, http://www.indiewire.com/article/festivals_crisis_or_promise_new_directions_in_philippine_cinema#, accessed Sept. 17, 2009.

_____. 2009. Sharon's Noranian turn: Stardom, embodiment and language in Philippine cinema. *Discourse* 31, no. 3:318–58.

Lim, Carolyn. 2006. How Lilian Too creates the right space at the right time. *Wall Street Journal*, Oct. 2. Rep. in Lilian Too's Official Web site. Internet document, http://www.lillian-too.com/news_wsjoct06.php, accessed Apr. 12, 2010.

Lim, Catherine G.S. 2008 [2003]. *Gateway to peranakan culture*. 6th ed. (rev.). Singapore: Asiapac.

Lim, Paul Stephen. 1982. *Some arrivals, but mostly departures*. Quezon City: New Day Publishers.

Lin Bin. 2001a. Zhongguo xin wenxue he shi zoujin Feilubin de jikao (When did China's New Literature enter the Philippines? An examination). *Shijie Ribao* (World News), Feb. 17, 15.

_____. 2001b. "Daoguo jiqing" Houji—Feihua xiaoshuo sanwen xuanxu ("Memories of the archipelago": Preface to *Selections from Philippine-Chinese novels and essays*). *Shijie Ribao*, May 13, 15.

_____. 2001c. Kanri zhanzheng shi qi de Feihua wenxue wenhua huodong (Philippine-Chinese literary and cultural activities during the Sino-Japanese war). *Shijie Ribao*, May 22, 15.

_____. 2001d. Lao baoren Du Ai (Du Ai the veteran journalist). Pt. 1. *Shijie Ribao*, Aug. 4, 21.

_____. 2001e. Lao baoren Du Ai (Du Ai the veteran journalist) Pt. 2. *Shijie Ribao*, Aug. 7, 18.

_____. 2001f. Interview with the author, Sept. 30, Guangzhou, People's Republic of China.

_____. 2005. Letter to the author, Feb. 23.

Liu Hong. 2006. The transnational construction of 'national allegory': China and the cultural politics of postcolonial Indonesia. *Critical Asian Studies* (London) 38, no. 3 (Sept.): 179–210.

_____. 2011. *China and the shaping of Indonesia, 1949–1965*. Kyoto and Singapore: Kyoto University Press and National University of Singapore Press.

Liu, Lydia H. 1995. *Translingual practice: Literature, national culture, and translated modernity—China, 1900–1937*. Stanford: Stanford University Press.

_____. 1999. The question of meaning-value in the political economy of the sign. In *Tokens of exchange: The problem of translation in global circulations*, 13–41. Ed. Lydia H. Liu. Durham: Duke University Press.

_____. 2004. *The clash of empires: The invention of China in modern world making.* Cambridge, Massachusetts and London: Harvard University Press.

Liu Shiaoqi. 1952. *Internationalism and nationalism.* Beijing: Foreign Languages Press. Internet document, http://www.marxists.org/reference/archive/liu-shaoqi/1952/internationalism_nationalism/index.htm.

Liu, Zhaohui. 2005. *Chaoyue xiangtu shehui: Yi ge qiao xiang cun luo de lishi wenhua yu shehui jiegou* (Beyond peasant society: History, culture and social structure in a qiao xiang village). Beijing: Minzhu Chubanshe.

Liu, Zhitian. 1969. *Zhong-Fei guanxi shi* (History of China-Philippines Relations). Taibei: Zhengzhong Shuju.

Lo, Ricky. 2007. Body talk with Dr. Hayden Kho, Jr. *Philippine Star,* Oct. 12. Internet document, http://www.newsflash.org/2004/02/sb/sb005170.htm, accessed Aug. 30, 2011.

_____. 2008. The many faces of Katrina Halili. *Philippine Star,* Nov. 23. Internet document, http://www.philstar.com/funfare/exclusivesarticle.aspx?articleid=417687&publicationsubcategoryid=70, accessed Aug. 30, 2011.

Locsin, Teodoro L., Jr. 1970 [2000]. A Philippine Dreyfus case. *Philippines Free Press,* May 30. Rep. in *The case of the Yuyitung brothers: Philippine press freedom under siege,* 178–88. Comp. and ed. Rizal Yuyitung. Manila: Yuyitung Foundation, Inc.

Locsin, Teodoro M. 1952. The Chinese question. *Philippines Free Press,* July 12. Internet document, http://philippinesfreepress.wordpress.com/category/classic-articles/, accessed on June 24, 2001.

Lod lai mangkorn (Through the dragon design). 1992. TV drama. Premiered Sept., Thailand.

Lu Yan. 2004. *Re-understanding Japan: Chinese perspectives, 1895–1945.* Honolulu: Association for Asian Studies and University of Hawai'i Press.

Lua, Shirley O. 2001. Dragons becoming shrimps: Toward a Chinese-Philippine poetics. Ph.D. diss., De la Salle University, Manila, Philippines.

Ma, Eric K.W. 1999. *Culture, politics and television in Hong Kong.* London and New York: Routledge.

Majul, Cesar A. 1977. *Principales, ilustrados,* intellectuals, and the original concept of a Filipino national community. *Asian Studies* 15 (Apr./Dec.): 1–20.

Malay, Armando, Jr. 1984. Some random reflections on Marxism and Maoism in the Philippines. In *Marxism in the Philippines. Marx centennial lectures,* 45–93. Ed. Third World Studies. Quezon City: Third World Studies Center, University of the Philippines.

Malaya. 1998. Good guys win one. Oct. 27, 19.

_____. 2005. Kidnapping has stopped? It's news in Binondo. July 27, A1.

Malvezin, Laurent. 2004. The problems with (Chinese) diaspora: An interview with Wang Gungwu. In *Diasporic Chinese ventures: The life and work of Wang Gungwu,* 49–60. Ed. Gregor Benton and Hong Liu. London and New York: RoutledgeCurzon.

Manila Bulletin. 1971. Kidnappers "rule' Chinatown. Dec. 3, 1, 7.

_____. 1996. P1-billion immigration revenue eyed. Sept. 4, 19.

_____. 2002. Kris Aquino shines in "Mano Po." Dec. 23. Internet document, http://findarticles.com/p/news-articles/manila-bulletin/mi_7968/is_2002_Dec_23/kris-aquino-shines-mano-po/ai_n33288750/, accessed Mar. 3, 2008.

Manila Chronicle. 1995. BI now accepting applications for illegal aliens. June 1, 3.

Manuel, E. Arsenio. 1948. *Chinese elements in the Tagalog language: With some indication of Chinese influence on other Philippine languages and cultures, and an excursion into Austronesian linguistics by E. Arsenio Manuel.* Introduction by H. Otley Beyer. Manila: Filipiniana Publications.

Mao Dun. 1949. Preface to *Lusong pingyuan*. In Du Ai, *Zai Lusong pingyuan* (On the plains of Luzon). Hong Kong: Renjian Shuwu.

Marchetti, Gina. 2007. *Andrew Lau and Alan Mak's Infernal Affairs—the trilogy.* Hong Kong: University of Hong Kong Press.

Marcson, Simon. 1950–1951. A theory of intermarriage and assimilation. *Social Forces* 29, no. 1:75–78.

Marshall, Jane. 2008. CHINA: Record Numbers Studying Abroad. *University World News* 49 (Oct. 19). Internet document, http://www.universityworldnews.com/article.php?story=20081017100051628, accessed May 5, 2010.

Marx, Karl. 1977 [1867]. *Capital.* Vol. 1. Trans. Ben Fowkes. New York: Vintage Books.

———. 1978 [1844]. On the Jewish question. In *The Marx and Engels reader*, 26–52. Ed. Robert C. Tucker. 2d ed. New York: W. W. Norton & Company.

———. 1981. *Capital.* Vol 3. Translated by David Fernbach. London: Penguin Books.

Matisoff, James A. 2003. *Handbook of proto-Tibeto-Burman.* Berkeley and Los Angeles: University of California Press.

May, Glenn Anthony. 1980. *Social engineering in the Philippines: The aims, execution, and impact of American colonial policy, 1900–13.* Contributions to Comparative Colonial Studies 2. Westport, Conn.: Greenwood Press.

Maynila...sa mga kuko ng liwanag (Manila... in the talons of light). 1987. Directed by Lino Brocka. Motion picture, Cinema Artists, Philippines.

McBeath, Gerald A. 1973. *Political integration of the Philippine Chinese.* Berkeley: Center for South and Southeast Asia Studies.

McCarthy, Charles J. 1970. *Philippine-Chinese integration: The case for qualified jus soli.* Quezon City: The Tamaraw Press.

———, ed. 1974. The Chinese in the Philippines. In *Philippine-Chinese profile: Essays and studies*, 1–32. Manila: Pagkakaisa sa Pag-unlad, Inc.

McCoy, Alfred W. 1994. "An anarchy of families": The historiography of state and family in the Philippines. In *An anarchy of families: State and family in the Philippines*, 1–32. Ed. Alfred W. McCoy. Quezon City: Ateneo de Manila University Press.

McCoy, Alfred W., and Edilberto N. Alegre, eds. 1982 [2001]. *Philippine social history: Global trade and local transformations.* Quezon City: Ateneo de Manila University Press.

Meade, Edwin R. 1877. *The Chinese question.* New York: Arthur and Bonnell.

Medina, Belen T. G. 2001. *The Filipino family.* 2d ed. Quezon City: University of the Philippines Press.

Miller, J. Hillis. 2001. Derrida and literature. In *Jacques Derrida and the humanities: A critical reader*, 58–81. Ed. Tom Cohen. Cambridge: Cambridge University Press.

Milner, Anthony. 2002 [1995]. *The invention of politics in colonial Malaya.* Cambridge: Cambridge University Press.

———. 2008. *The Malays.* Chichester: Wiley-Blackwell.

Miyahara, Gyo. 1997. The status of the Chinese Filipinos in the 1950s, Cebu: An analysis of articles in two local newspapers. In *The ethnic Chinese as Filipinos. Part II.* Ed. Teresita Ang-See. *Chinese Studies Journal* 7:73–90.

_____. 2008a. Tojirareta shintai to creole no shintai no aida—Philippine Cebu ni okeru Chūgoku-kei jumin no shintai no politics to Higashi Ajia chiikikenkyū (Between the closed body and the creole body—Body politics of ethnic Chinese in Cebu, the Philippines and East Asian studies). In *Gendai Chūgoku no shakai henyō to kokusai kankei* (Social change and international relations of contemporary China), 205–22. Ed. Nishimura Shigeo and Xu Weidong. Tokyo: Kyūko Shoin.

_____. 2008b. Letter to the author, Sept. 19.

Mojares, Resil. 2011. The itineraries of Mariano Ponce. In *Traveling nation-makers: Transnational flows and movements in the making of modern Southeast Asia*, 32–63. Ed. Caroline S. Hau and Kasian Tejapira. Kyoto and Singapore: Kyoto University Press and National University of Singapore Press.

Montelibano, Jose Ma. 2012. Why, China, why? *Philippine Daily Inquirer*, July 20. Internet document, http://opinion.inquirer.net/32915/why-china-why, accessed July 21.

Montes, Manuel F. 1999. The Philippines as an unwitting participant in the Asian economic crisis. In *Asian contagion: The causes and consequences of a financial crisis*, 241–68. Ed. Karl D. Jackson. Colorado: Westview Press.

Mouffe, Chantal, and Ernesto Laclau. 1985. *Hegemony and socialist strategy: Towards a radical democratic politics*. London: Verso.

Movement for the Restoration of Peace and Order, and Citizens Action against Crime. 1996. Information packet provided at joint conference, Oct. 31.

Munn, Christopher. 2009 [2001]. *Anglo-China: Chinese people and British rule in Hong Kong, 1841–1880*. Hong Kong: Hong Kong University Press.

My Binondo girl. 2011. TV drama. Premiered Aug. 22. ABS-CBN, Philippines.

Mydans, Seth. 1996. Kidnapping of ethnic Chinese rises in the Philippines. *New York Times*, Mar. 17, 3.

Nazareno, Rocky. 2001. Rich Chinoys send kids to China amid kidnaps. *Philippine Daily Inquirer*, July 11, A1, A6.

Negri, Antonio, and Michael Hardt. 1994. *Labor of Dionysus: A critique of the state form*. Minneapolis: University of Minnesota Press.

New York Times. 2010. Geili. In "Schott's vocab: A miscellany of modern words and phrases." Nov. 18. Internet document, http://schott.blogs.nytimes.com/2010/11/18/geili/, accessed Mar. 5, 2011.

Nihon Keizai Shimbun. 2012. Higashi Ajia kōryū no shin shiten (A new perspective on East Asian flows). Aug. 18, 44.

Nishio Kanji. 2011. Statecraft and people-grouping concepts in Malay port-polities: Case studies on Johor-Riau and Riau-Lingga. In *Bangsa and umma: Development of people-grouping concepts in Islamized Southeast Asia*, 50–70. Ed. Yamamoto Hiroyuki, Anthony Milner, Kawashima Midori and Arai Kazuhiro. Kyoto: Kyoto University Press.

Nonini, Donald M., and Aihwa Ong. 1997. Chinese transnationalism as an alternative modernity. In *Ungrounded empires: The cultural politics of modern Chinese transnationalism*, 3–33. Ed. Aihwa Ong and Donald Nonini. New York and London: Routledge.

Nye, Joseph S., Jr. 2004. *Soft power: The means to success in world politics*. New York: Public Affairs.

Oakes, Tim. 2000. China's provincial identities: Reviving regionalism and reinventing "Chineseness." *The Journal of Asian Studies* 59, no. 3:667–92.

Omohundro, John T. 1981. *Chinese merchant families in Iloilo*. Quezon City: Ateneo de Manila University Press.

Ong, Aihwa. 1999. *Flexible citizenship: The cultural logics of transnationality*. Durham: Duke University Press.

Ong, Aihwa, and Donald M. Nonini. 1997a. Chinese transnationalism as an alternative modernity. In *Ungrounded empires: The cultural politics of modern Chinese transnationalism*, 3–33. Ed. Aihwa Ong and Donald M. Nonini. New York: Routledge.

———. 1997b. Toward a cultural politics of diaspora and transnationalism. In *Ungrounded empires: The cultural politics of modern Chinese transnationalism*, 323–32. Ed. Aihwa Ong and Donald Nonini. New York and London: Routledge.

Ong, Charlson. 1996. Mismanagement of grief. In *Conversion and other stories*, 35–48. Manila: Anvil Publishing, Inc. The story first appeared in the *Philippine Graphic* in 1995.

———. 2000a. A bridge too far: Thoughts on Chinese Filipino writing. In *Intsik: An anthology of Chinese Filipino writing*, ix–xv. Ed. Caroline S. Hau. Pasig City: Anvil Publishing, Inc.

———. 2000b. *An embarrassment of riches*. Quezon City: University of the Philippines Press.

———. 2006. *Banyaga: A song of war*. Manila: Anvil Publishing Inc.

———. 2008. E-mail to the author, Sept. 2.

Ong, Daniel. 2011. The nebulous "Chinese race" and "Malay race." Facebook entry, Sept. 13. Internet document, http://www.facebook.com/notes/daniel-ong/the-nebulous-chinese-race-and-malay-race/10150314284541165, accessed Sept. 13, 2011

———. 2012a. The myth that is Scarborough. Facebook, Apr. 22. Internet document, http://www.facebook.com/notes/daniel-ong/the-myth-that-is-scarborough/10150727420151165, accessed Apr. 23.

———. 2012b. Spanish maps and Scarborough: A case of false hope. Facebook, Apr. 25. Internet document, http://www.facebook.com/notes/daniel-ong/spanish-maps-and-scarborough-a-case-of-false-hope/10150734428991165, accessed Apr. 26.

Ong Hok Ham. 2005. *Riwayat Tionghoa peranakan di Jawa* (Peranakan Chinese history in Java). Ed. J. J. Rizal. Depok, Jakarta: Komunitas Bambu.

Onimaru, Takeshi. 2011. Living "underground" in Shanghai: Noulens and the Shanghai Comintern network. In *Travelling nation-makers: Transnational flows and movements in the making of modern Southeast Asia*, 96–125. Ed. Caroline S. Hau and Kasian Tejapira. Kyoto and Singapore: Kyoto University Press and National University of Singapore Press.

Ople, Blas F. 1958. Can the Chinese be integrated? *Sunday Times Magazine*, Sept. 28, 16–19.

The origin of enka from Korea. 2011. "Korean Sentry," discussion thread, Jan. 1–Mar. 28. Internet document, http://webcache.googleusercontent.com/search?q=cache:-PPiXdxmJAsJ:koreansentry.19.forumer.com/a/the-origin-of-enka-from-korea_post3789.html+Japanese+enka+Korean&cd=5&hl=en&ct=clnk&client=safari, accessed June 23, 2012.

Otmazgin, Nissim Kadosh. 2005. Cultural commodities and regionalization in East Asia. *Contemporary Southeast Asia* 27, no. 3:499–523.

Owen, Norman G. 1974. The principalia in Philippine history. *Philippine Studies* 22, nos. 3–4: 297–324.

Oyen, Meredith. 2010. Communism, containment and the Chinese Overseas. In *The Cold War in Asia: The battle for hearts and minds*, 59–93. Ed. Zheng Yangwen, Hong Liu and Michael Szonyi. Leiden and Boston: Brill.

Pablo, Carlito. 1997. Kidnapping worst in '96; 241 abducted. *Philippine Daily Inquirer*, Jan. 7, 1, 7.

Pacific Strategies and Assessments (PSA). 2012. *Philippines annual kidnapping report: Recapping 2011*. Internet document, http://www1.psagroup.com/psacms_kc_ph.nsf/b74a23deb4fb8520482575b50060d675/302483df3a83961548257a0e000f432e/$FILE/PSA%20-%20Philippines%20Annual%20Kidnapping%20Report%20-%20Recapping%202011.pdf, accessed Aug. 3.

Palanca, Ellen H. 1995. The 1990 top corporations in the Philippines. *Philippine Studies* 43, no. 4:547–74.

Parry, Benita. 2004. *Postcolonial studies: A materialist critique*. London and New York: Routledge.

Partido Komunista ng Pilipinas. 1980. Eighth Congress. Photostat MS.

———. 1996. *Communism in the Philippines: The PKP*. Vol. 1. Quezon City: Historical Commission, Partido Komunista ng Pilipinas.

Pasuk Phongpaichit and Chris Baker. 1996. *Thailand's boom!* Bangkok: Silkworm Books. See *Chang Noi*.

Pempel, T. J., ed. 2005. Introduction. In *Remapping East Asia: The construction of a region*, 1–28. Ithaca: Cornell University Press.

People's Daily.com. 2007. Chinese students in Japan look forward to Wen Jiabao's 'ice-melting' visit, Apr. 9. Internet document, http://english.peopledaily.com.cn/200704/09/eng20070409_364740.html, accessed May 5, 2010.

The Peranakan Association. 2011. A history of the Peranakan Association. Official Web site. Internet document, http://peranakan.org.sg/about/history-of-the-peranakan-association/, accessed Nov. 3.

Peranakan Museum. 2008. *Peranakan Museum A-Z Guide*. Singapore: Asian Civilizations Museum for the Peranakan Museum.

Philippine Chinese General Chamber of Commerce. 1936. *Feilubin Minnila Zhonghua Shanghui sanshi zhounian jinian kan* (Philippine Chinese General Chamber of Commerce Thirtieth Anniversary Commemorative Issue). Manila: Manila Press for the Philippine Chinese General Chamber of Commerce.

Philippine Daily Inquirer. 2001. Segregation. In Editorial, June 17, A8.

———. 2003. President ready to approve dual citizenship law. Aug. 20. Online, http//www.inq7.net/brk/2003/aug/20/text/brkpol_9-1-p.htm.

———. 2011a. Watchdog: 102 journalists killed in 2010. May 3. Internet document, http://globalnation.inquirer.net/news/breakingnews/view/20110503-334385/Watchdog-102-journalists-killed-in-2010, accessed Feb. 2, 2012.

———. 2011b. What went before: NorthRail Project. Sept. 2. Internet document, http://newsinfo.inquirer.net/51619/what-went-before-northrail-project, accessed Sept. 15.

Philippine Star. 1998a. '97 banner year for kidnappers. Jan. 1, 1, 12.

———. 1998b. Colombia tops world's kidnap league; RP 4th. Oct. 10, 1, 4.

———. 2001. Naturalization law to give gov't. P6.1 B. June 11, 2.

———. 2011. Kidnappings in Mindanao on upsurge again, Apr. 6. Internet document, http://www.philstar.com/Article.aspx?articleId=673574&publicationSubCategoryId=200, accessed Jan. 3, 2012.

Philippines, Republic of. 1987. *Constitution of the Republic of the Philippines*. Internet document, http://www.chanrobles.com/article2.htm, accessed Nov. 2, 2008.

Philippines Free Press. 1992a. Who will save us From the "law"? Sept. 5, 1–2.

———. 1992b. Why Chinese only? Oct. 3, 20.

————. 1993. Kidnapping—the growth industry. Feb. 27, 20.

Pinches, Michael. 1996. The Philippines' new rich: Capitalist transformation amidst economic gloom. In *The new rich in Asia: Mobile phones, McDonald's and middle-class revolution*, 103–33. Ed. Richard Robison and David S. G. Goodman. London: Routledge.

————. 1999. Entrepreneurship, consumption, ethnicity and national identity in the making of the Philippines' new rich. In *Culture and privilege in capitalist Asia*, 275–301. Ed. Michael Pinches. London: Routledge.

Polanyi, Karl. 1954. *The great transformation*. Boston: Beacon Press.

Political Review. 1971. Imperialist uses of the Sino-Soviet dispute. *Political Review* 1, no. 1 (Mar.): 4, 6.

Ponce, Mariano. 1965 [1912]. *Sun Yat-sen, the founder of the Republic of China*. Trans. Nick Joaquin. Manila: Filipino-Chinese Cultural Foundation. Originally published as *Sun Yat-sen, el fundador de la República de China*. Manila: Imp. de la Vanguardia y Taliba.

Pramoedya Ananta Toer. 1980. *Anak semua bangsa: Sebuah roman* (Child of All Nations: A Novel). Jakarta: Hasta Mitra.

Praphassorn Sewikul. 1992. *Lod lai mangkorn* (Through the dragon design). Bangkok: Dokya Press.

Purcell, Victor. 1965. *The Chinese in Southeast Asia*. Oxford: Oxford University Press.

Qiu Shu Ting [Kinnia Yau Shuk-ting]. 2010. *Zhong-Ri-Han dianying: Lishi, shehui, wenhua* (Chinese-Japanese-Korean Films; History, Society, Culture). Hong Kong: Hong Kong University Press.

Quimpo, Nathan Gilbert. 2005. Oligarchic patrimonialism, bossism, electoral clientelism, and contested democracy in the Philippines. *Comparative Politics* 37, no. 2:229–50.

Rafael, Vicente L. 1988. *Contracting colonialism: Translation and Christian conversion in Tagalog society under early Spanish rule*. Quezon City: Ateneo de Manila University Press.

————. 1999. Introduction: Criminality and its others. In *Figures of criminality in Indonesia, the Philippines, and colonial Vietnam*, 9–22. Ithaca: Cornell University Southeast Asia Program.

————. 2000. Taglish, or the phantom power of the lingua franca. In *White love and other events in Filipino history*, 162–89. Durham: Duke University Press.

————. 2005. *The promise of the foreign: Nationalism and the technics of translation in the Spanish Philippines*. Durham: Duke University Press.

Rama, Napoleon G. 1970 [2000]. Condemned! *Philippines Free Press*, May 30. Rep. in *The case of the Yuyitung brothers: Philippine press freedom under siege*, 166–75. Comp. and ed. Rizal Yuyitung. Manila: Yuyitung Foundation, Inc.

Ramos, Fidel V. 1992. Inaugural address: To win the future. *Philippines Free Press*, July 11, 10, 36–37.

————. 1993. The state of the nation. *Philippines Free Press*, Aug. 7, 8–9, 32, 47.

Recur, Carlos. 1879. *Filipinas. Estudios administrativos y comerciales* (The Philippines: Administrative and commercial studies). Madrid: Imprenta de Ramón Moreno y Ricardo Rojas.

Red, Isah V. 2005. *Mano Po* takes a comic turn. *Manila Standard*, Nov. 2. Rep. online, http://www.yehey.com/entertainment/movies/article.aspx?i=8449.

Regal Films. 2011. *Wikipedia*. Internet document, http://en.wikipedia.org/wiki/Regal_Films, accessed Sept. 2.

Reid, Anthony. 1988. *Southeast Asia in the age of commerce, 1450–1680, vol. 1: The lands below the winds.* New Haven: Yale University Press.

———. 2004. Understanding *Melayu* (Malay) as a source of diverse modern identities. *Contesting Malayness: Malay identity across boundaries,* 1–24. Ed. Timothy P. Barnard. Singapore: Singapore University Press.

———. 2010. *Imperial alchemy: Nationalism and political identity in Southeast Asia.* Cambridge, UK: Cambridge University Press.

Reid, Anthony, and Yangwen Zheng. 2009. *Negotiating asymmetry: China's place in Asia.* Singapore: National University of Singapore Press.

Remo, Michelle V. 2012. OFW remittances grew by 7.2% to $20.1-B in 2011—BSP. *Philippine Daily Inquirer,* Feb. 15. Internet document, http://business.inquirer.net/44695/ofw-remittances-grew-by-7-2-to-20-1-b-in-2011-bsp, accessed June 10.

Renacimiento Filipino. 1911a. Anarchist Chang King Ngok. *Renacimiento Filipino* 2, no. 60 (Sept.28): 445.

———. 1911b. Sino si Juan de Veyra? [Who is Juan de Veyra?] *Renacimiento Filipino* 2, no. 50 (July 14): 60–61.

Research Staff of Pagkakaisa sa Pag-unlad. 1974. The case against jus soli. In *Philippine-Chinese profile: Essays and studies,* 212–29. Ed. Charles J. McCarthy. Manila: Pagkakaisa sa Pag-unlad, Inc.

Reyes, Edgardo M. 1986. *Sa mga kuko ng liwanag* (In the talons of light). Manila: De La Salle University Press. Serialized in *Liwayway,* 1967–1968.

Reynolds, Craig J. 1995. A new look at old Southeast Asia. *Journal of Asian Studies* 54:419–46.

Rivera, Temario C. 1995. The Chinese-Filipino business families and industrial reform in the Ramos administration. In *The Chinese-Filipino business families under Ramos government,* 1–33. Ed. Temario C. Rivera and Kenjie Koike. Tokyo: Institute of Developing Economies.

Rizal, Jose. 1887 [1978]. *Noli me tangere.* Manila: Instituto Nacional de Historia. Originally published in Berlin.

———. 1891 [1990]. *El filibusterismo.* Manila: Instituto Nacional de Historia. Originally published in Ghent.

Ronda, Rainier Allan. 2007. Chinoys hit ruling vs mayor. *The Philippine* Star, May 10. Internet document, http://www.philstar.com/Article.aspx?articleId=397817, accessed Aug. 30, 2011.

Rush, James. 1991. Placing the Chinese in Java on the eve of the twentieth century. *Indonesia* (July): 13–24.

Said, Edward. 1979. *Orientalism.* New York: Vintage.

Salazar, Zeus. 2005. *Pangulong ERAP, pinunong bayan: Tungo sa hamon ng EDSA II, biograpiyang sosyopulitikal ang pangkalinangan ni Joseph Ejercito Estrada* (President ERAP, head of state: A sociopolitical and cultural biography of Joseph Ejercito Estrada). Vol. 1. San Juan, Metro Manila: RPG Foundation Inc.

Salterio, Leah. 2004. "Crying Ladies" RP entry to next year's Oscars. *Philippine Daily Inquirer,* Jan. 31. Internet document, http://www.inq7.net/globalnation/sec_sho/2004/sep/06-01.htm, accessed Feb. 22.

San Diego Jr., Bayani. 2008. Ricky Lee, man of letters. *Philippine Daily Inquirer,* Nov. 28. Internet document, http://showbizandstyle.inquirer.net/entertainment/entertainment/view/20081128-174791/Ricky-Lee-man-of-letters, accessed Nov. 7, 2011.

Sande, Francisco de. 1576. Relation of the Filipinas islands. In *The Philippine islands, 1493–1898*, 21–97. Ed. Emma H. Blair and James A. Robertson. Vol. 4 (1576–1582). Cleveland: Arthur H. Clark Company. June 7.

Santamaria, Carlos. 2012. We are all mestizos? Rappler.com, July 24. Internet document, http://www.rappler.com/nation/9143-we-are-all-mestizos, accessed July 26.

Santiago, Corazon Damo. 1972. *A century of activism*. Manila: Rex Bookstore.

Santiago, Erwin. 2012. Kantar Media-TNS Household Ratings (Jan. 20–23): *Walang Hanggan* zooms to no. 1 spot. *Philippine Entertainment Portal*, Jan. 24. Internet document, http://www.pep.ph/guide/tns/9684/kantar-media-tns-national-household -ratings-jan-20-23-walang-hanggan-zooms-to-no-1-spot, accessed Feb. 5.

Saspa, J. P. 1995. Welcome to kidnap town—again. *Philippines Free Press*, Sept. 9, 10.

———. 1996. Mastermind or fall guy? *Philippines Free Press*, Jan. 13, 5–6.

Schirmer, Daniel B., and Stephen Rosskamm Shalom. 1987. *The Philippines reader: A history of colonialism, neocolonialism, dictatorship, and resistance*. Boston: South End Press.

Schmitt, Carl. 1996 [1922]. *The concept of the political*. Trans. George Schwab. Chicago: University of Chicago Press.

Schuck, Peter H., and Rogers Smith. 1985. *Citizenship without consent: Illegal aliens in the American polity*. New Haven: Yale University Press.

Schumacher, John N. 1991. Recent perspectives on the revolution. In *The making of a nation: Essays on nineteenth-century Filipino nationalism*, 178–209, 252–62. Quezon City: Ateneo de Manila University Press.

Scott, William Henry. 1989. *Filipinos in China before 1500*. Manila: China Studies Program, De La Salle University.

———. 1994. *Barangay: Sixteenth-century Philippine culture and society*. Quezon City: New Day Publishers.

Seagrave, Sterling. 1988. *The Marcos Dynasty*. New York: Harper and Row.

See, Chinben. 1988. Chinese organizations and ethnic identity in the Philippines. *Changing identities of the Southeast Asian Chinese since World War II*, 319–34. Ed. Jennifer Cushman and Wang Gungwu. Hong Kong: Hong Kong University Press.

See, Chinben, and Teresita Ang-See, eds. 1990. *Chinese in the Philippines: A bibliography*. Manila: China Studies Program and De La Salle University Press.

See, Edna. 2003. *Mano Po*, through Chinoy eyes. *Philippine Daily Inquirer*, Jan. 31, A32.

Seno, Alexandra A. 2006. China's starring role in the Philippines. *New York Times*, Feb. 2. Internet document, http://webcache.googleusercontent.com/ search?q=cache:0eM6yfXIM20J:www.nytimes.com/2006/02/02/arts/02iht-fmlede3.html%3Fpagewanted%3Dall+Kris+Aquino+Mano+Po+Chinese+accent&cd =13&hl=en&ct=clnk, accessed Mar. 3, 2008.

Sepet (Slit eyes). 2004. Directed by Yasmin Ahmad. Motion picture, MHZ Film Production and Grand Brilliance, Malaysia.

Shaffer, Lynda. 1994. Southernization. *Journal of World History* 5, no. 1:1–21.

Shang Bao. 2001. *Shang Bao xiaoshuo xuan: Ershi shiji wushi dai* (Chinese Commercial News Anthology of Short Fiction: The 1950s). Manila: Yuyitong Jijinhui Chubanshe.

Shangzong mishuchang Zheng Yingda shumian tanhua (Written statement by Federation of Filipino Chinese Chambers of Commerce and Industry General-Secretary Zheng Yingda). 1961. In *Huaqiao shehui de luxiang* (Where huaqiao society is heading: A *Chinese Commercial News* series), 6–12. Manila: Yitong Chubansheinxing

Sheehan, Deirdre. 2001. Under siege. *Far Eastern Economic Review*, June 28, 62–64.

Shepherd, John Robert. 1993. *Statecraft and political economy on the Taiwan frontier, 1600–1800*. Stanford, Calif.: Stanford University Press.

Shi Yingzhou, ed. 1992. *Feihua wenyi* (Philippine Chinese literature). Manila: Feihua Wenyi Xiehui (Philippine-Chinese Literary Arts Association).

Shih, Shu-mei. 2001. *The lure of the modern: Writing modernism in semicolonial China, 1917–1937*. Berkeley, Los Angeles and London: University of California Press.

Shijie Ribao (World News). 1996. Yatai jinghe fenghui yu bangjia (APEC and Kidnapping). Nov. 11, 1.

———. 1997. Duzhe laisin Zhonggao Bannawei jie huaren (Letter from a reader reporting on the huaren of Banawe Street), July 13, 1.

———. 2001. Jiu yao san jiu hao gonghe lu "2000 nian xing zhenggui hualu" yuanwen (Original text of Republic Act no. 9139, "The Administrative Naturalization Law of 2000"), June 16, 11.

———. 2007. Yayela jiazu chengren you huaren xüetong (Ayala family acknowledges Chinese blood lineage), Feb. 15, 5.

Shimizu Yoshikazu. 2008. *"Chūgoku mondai" no uchimaku* (Inside story of the "China problem"). Tokyo: Chikuma Shinsho.

Shiraishi, Takashi. 1997. Japan and Southeast Asia. In *Network power: Japan and Asia*, 169–94. Ed. Peter J. Katzenstein and Takashi Shiraishi. Ithaca, New York: Cornell University Press.

———. 2006. The third wave: Southeast Asia and middle-class formation in the making of a region. In *Beyond Japan: The dynamics of East Asian regionalism*, 237–71. Ed. Peter J. Katzenstein and Takashi Shiraishi. Ithaca: Cornell University Press.

———. 2010. Shinshun sadankai: Ajia to ikiru Nihon (New Year Dialogue: Japan Living with Asia). *Kokusai Kaihatsu Journal* (Jan. 1): 14–21.

———. 2012. The rise of China and its implications for East Asia. In *Sinicization and the rise of China: Civilizational processes beyond East and West*, 120–49. Ed. Peter J. Katzenstein. London and New York: Routledge.

Shiraishi Takashi and Caroline Hau. 2009. "Ajia-shugi" no jyubaku wo koete–Higashi-Ajia kyōdotai saikō (Overcoming the curse of "Asianism": Revisiting the East Asia Community). *Chūokōron* (Feb.): 168–79.

———. 2012. *Chūgoku wa higashi Ajia wo dō kaeru ka? 21 seki no shin chiiki shisutemu* (How is China changing East Asia? The new regional system in the 21st century). Tokyo: Chūokoron.

Sidel, John T. 1999. *Capital, coercion, crime: Bossism in the Philippines*. Stanford: Stanford University Press.

Siklab. 1971. Why the Maoists lost in 'liberated Diliman.' Aug. 23, 2.

Simbulan, Dante. 2005 [1965]. *The modern principalia: The historical evolution of the Philippine ruling oligarchy*. Quezon City: University of the Philippines Press.

Skinner, G. William. 1957. *Chinese society in Thailand: An analytical history*. Ithaca, New York: Cornell University Press.

———. 1958a. The Chinese of Java. In *Colloquium on overseas Chinese*, 1–10. Ed. Morton Fried. New York: Institute of Pacific Relations.

———. 1958b. *Leadership and power in the Chinese community of Thailand*. Ithaca, New York: Cornell University Press.

———. 1960. Change and persistence in Chinese culture overseas: A comparison of Thailand and Java. *Journal of South Seas Society* (Nanyang Xuebao) 16, nos. 1–2:86–100.

_____. 1961. Java's Chinese minority: Continuity and change. *Journal of Asian Studies* 20: 353–62.

_____. 1996. Creolized Chinese societies in Southeast Asia. In *Sojourners and settlers: Histories of Southeast Asia and the Chinese*, 51–93. Ed. Anthony Reid. St. Leonards, NSW: Allen & Unwin.

Smith, Rogers. 2003. *Stories of peoplehood*. New York: Cambridge University Press.

Soe Hok Gie. 1990. *Di bawah lentera merah: Riwayat Sarekat Islam Semarang* (Under the red lantern: History of the Sarekat Islam in Semarang). Jakarta: Frantz Fanon Foundation.

Soliven, Max. 1997. By the way. *Philippine Star*, Oct. 28, 8.

Sosyal, Yasemin. 1994. *Limits of citizenship: Migrants and postnational membership in Europe*. Chicago: University of Chicago Press.

Spady, James G., Stefan Dupree, and Charles G. Lee. 1995. *Twisted tales: In the hip hop streets of Philly*. Philadelphia: Black History Museum UMUM/LOH Publishers.

Spivak, Gayatri. 1987. *In other worlds: Essays in cultural politics*. London: Methuen.

_____. 1988. Can the subaltern speak? In *Marxism and the interpretation of culture*, 271–313. Ed. Cary Nelson and Lawrence Grossberg. Chicago: University of Illinois Press.

Su, Xiaokang, and Luxiang Wang. 1991. *Deathsong of the river: A reader's guide to the Chinese TV series* Heshang. Ithaca: East Asia Program, Cornell University.

Sugaya, Nariko. 2011. Chūgoku-jin imin no 'datsu-Chūgoku-jin'-ka aruiwa 'shin'min'-ka: Supein-ryo Firipin ni okeru Chūgoku-kei mestizo kōryu no haigo ('Desinicization' or becoming-'subject' of Chinese migrants: Background of Chinese mestizos' prosperity in Spanish Philippines). In *Kindai Ajia no jiga-zo to tasha: Chiiki shakai to 'gaikoku-jin' mondai* (Self-portrait and other of modern Asia: Local societies and the problem of "aliens"), 17–37. Ed. Kishi Toshihiko. Kyoto: Kyoto University Press.

Sugihara, Kaoru. 2005a. An introduction. In *Japan, China, and the growth of the Asian international economy, 1850–1949*, 1–19. Ed. Kaoru Sugihara. Japan Studies in Economic and Social History. Vol. 1. Oxford and New York: Oxford University Press.

_____. 2005b. Patterns of Chinese emigration to Southeast Asia, 1869–1939. In *Japan, China, and the growth of the Asian international economy, 1850–1949*, 244–74. Ed. Kaoru Sugihara. Japan Studies in Economic and Social History. Vol.1. Oxford and New York: Oxford University Press.

The Sun. 2006. *Sepet* and *Gubra* draw controversy. Apr. 26. Rep. in Sisters in Islam homepage, http://www.sistersinislam.org.my/news.php?item.54.27, accessed Feb. 1, 2012.

Sun Ailing. 1996. *Lun guiqiao zuojia xiaoshuo* (On the novels of returned overseas Chinese). Singapore: Xinjiapo Yunnan Yuanyashe.

Sun, Laichen. 2010. Assessing the Ming role in China's southern expansion. In *Southeast Asia in the Fifteenth Century: The China Factor*, 44–79. Ed. Geoff Wade and Sun Laichen. Singapore and Hong Kong: NUS Press and Hong Kong University Press.

Suryadinata, Leo, ed. 1979 [1997]. *Political thinking of the Indonesian Chinese, 1900–1995: A sourcebook*. 2d ed. Singapore: Singapore University Press (issued under the auspices of the Institute of Southeast Asian Studies).

_____. 1993. The state and Chinese minority in Indonesia. In *Chinese adaptation and diversity: Essays on society and literature in Indonesia, Malaysia and Singapore*, 77–100. Singapore: Singapore University Press.

_____. 1995. China's economic modernization and the ethnic Chinese in ASEAN: A preliminary study, in *Southeast Asian Chinese and China: The Politico-economic dimension*, 193–215. Ed. Leo Suryadinata. Singapore: Times Academic Press.

_____. 1997. Ethnic Chinese in Southeast Asia: Overseas Chinese, Chinese Overseas or Southeast Asians? In *Ethnic Chinese as Southeast Asians*, 1–24. Ed. Leo Suryadinata. Singapore and New York: Institute of Southeast Asian Studies and St. Martin's Press.

Sy, Joaquin. 1979. Ah Tek, Pong at Chua: Ang Tsino sa panitikan (Ah Tek, Pong and Chua: The Chinese in literature). *Diliman Review* 28, no. 2 (Apr.–June): 57–65, 94–100.

_____. 1995. Tsinoy sa pulitika (The Chinese in politics). *Tulay*, June 5, 10–11.

Szanton Blanc, Cristina. 1996. *Balikbayan*: A Filipino extension of the national imaginary and of state boundaries. *Philippine Sociological Review* 44, nos. 1–4:178–93.

_____. 1997. The thoroughly modern "Asian": Capital, culture and nation in Thailand and the Philippines. In *Ungrounded empires: The cultural politics of modern Chinese transnationalism*, 261–86. Ed. Aihwa Ong and Donald M. Nonini. New York: Routledge.

Sze, Manchi [Shi Wenzhi]. 2011. *Jiefang tongnian/Pinalayang kamusmusan* (Childhood liberated). Trans. Joaquin Sy [Shi Huajin]. Manila: Kaisa para sa Kaunlaran, Inc.

Tam, Siumi Maria. 2006. Engendering Minnan mobility: Women sojourners in a patriarchal world. In *Southern Fujian: Reproduction of traditions in post-Mao China*, 145–62. Ed. Tan Chee Beng. Hong Kong: Chinese University of Hong Kong.

Tan, Antonio S. 1972. *The Chinese in the Philippines: A study of their national awakening*. Quezon City: Garcia Publications.

_____. 1981. *The Chinese in the Philippines during the Japanese occupation, 1942–45*. Quezon City: University of the Philippines Press.

_____. 1987. *The Chinese mestizos and the formation of the Filipino nationality*. Occasional paper. Quezon City: Asian Center, University of the Philippines.

_____. 1988. The changing identity of the Philippine Chinese, 1946–1984. In *Changing identities of the Southeast Asian Chinese since World War II, I*, 177–203. Ed. Jennifer Cushman and Wang Gungwu. Hong Kong: Hong Kong University Press.

Tan Chee-Beng. 2000. Socio-cultural diversities and identities. In *The Chinese in Malaya*, 37–70. Ed. Lim Kam Hing and Tan Chee-Beng. Selangor Darul Ehsan: Oxford University Press.

Tan, Michael. 2001. From Sangley to Chinoy. *Philippine Daily Inquirer*, Sept. 5. Internet document, http://pinoykasi.homestead.com/files/2001articles/08052001_From_Sangley.htm, accessed Nov. 2, 2011.

_____. 2008. Crying hero. *Pinoy Kasi* column, *Philippine Daily Inquirer*, Feb. 21. Internet document, http://opinion.inquirer.net/inquireropinion/columns/view/20080221-120381/Crying-hero, accessed Mar. 18.

_____. 2011. Intsik. *Philippine Daily Inquirer*, Jan. 28. Internet document, http://opinion.inquirer.net/inquireropinion/columns/view/20110128-317065/Intsik, accessed Feb. 13.

Tan, Samuel K. 1994. The Tans and Kongs of Sulu: An analysis of Chinese integration in a Muslim society. In *The ethnic Chinese—proceedings of the international conference on changing identities and relations in Southeast Asia*, 127–38. Ed. Teresita Ang-See and Go Bon Juan. Manila: Kaisa para sa Kaunlaran, Inc.

Tan, Susie L. 1993. Chinese language literature in the Philippines: Past and present. *Asian Culture* (June 17): 73–82.

_____. 1994a. Chinese language literature in the Philippines: Past and present. *National Book Review* (Jan.): 25–28.

_____. 1994b. Chinese language literature in the Philippines: Past and present. *National Book Review* (Feb.): 26–27.

Taruc, Luis. 1953. *Born of the people*. New York: International Publishers.

_____. 1967. *He who rides the tiger: The story of an Asian guerrilla leader*. New York: Praeger.

Taylor, Jeremy E. 2011. *Rethinking transnational Chinese cinemas: The Amoy-dialect film industry in Cold War Asia*. Oxon: Routledge.

Tejero, Constantino. 2008. Art of the Chinese diaspora. *Philippine Daily Inquirer*, Feb. 14. Internet document, http://globalnation.inquirer.net/features/features/view_article.php?article_id=49431, accessed Nov. 1.

Teo Kok Seong. 2003. *The peranakan Chinese of Kelantan: A study of the culture, language and communication of an assimilated group in Malaysia*. London: ASEAN Academic Press.

Teo, Stephen. 1997. *Hong Kong cinema: The extra dimension*. London: BFI (British Film Institute) Publishing.

Thayer, Carlyle A. 2011. Chinese assertiveness in the South China Sea and Southeast Asian responses. *Journal of Current Southeast Asian Affairs* 30, no. 2:77–104.

Thomas, Megan C. 2012. *Orientalists, propagandists, and ilustrados: Filipino scholarship and the end of Spanish colonialism*. Minneapolis and London: University of Minnesota Press.

Thorniley, Tessa. 2010. Battle intensifies for $2Bn English-teaching business in China. *Guardian Weekly*, July 13. http://www.guardian.co.uk/education/2010/jul/13/china-english-schools, accessed Mar. 5, 2011.

Tiglao, Rigoberto. 1990a. Class of taipans: The Chinese-Filipinos who are making the running. *Far Eastern Economic Review*, Feb. 15, 70–71.

_____. 1990b. Gung-ho in Manila. *Far Eastern Economic Review*, Feb. 15, 68–70.

_____. 1990c. The race to the top. *Far Eastern Economic Review*, Feb. 15, 70–71.

_____. 1991. Pioneer spirits. *Far Eastern Economic Review*, Nov. 28, 62.

_____. 1994. Strength in numbers. *Far Eastern Economic Review*, July 21, 60–61.

_____. 1995a. Mall mogul. *Far Eastern Economic Review*, Aug. 31, 50–51.

_____. 1995b. Caught napping. *Far Eastern Economic Review*, Oct. 12, 36.

_____. 1996. Tan triumphant. *Far Eastern Economic Review*, Sept. 26, 60–63.

_____. 1999. Crime buster. *Far Eastern Economic Review*, Dec. 2, 25.

Tilly, Charles. 1985. War making and state making as organized crime. In *Bringing the state back in*, 169–86. Ed. Peter Evans, Dietrich Rueschemeyer and Theda Skocpol. Cambridge: Cambridge University Press.

Times Journal. 1973. 'Chinatown Chinese'—A vanishing breed. June 13, 20.

Tjon Sie Fat, Paul. 2009. *Chinese new migrants in Suriname: The inevitability of ethnic performing*. Amsterdam: Amsterdam University Press.

Tønnesson, Stein. 2005. Locating the South China Sea. *Locating Southeast Asia: Geographies of knowledge and politics of space*, 203–33. Ed. Paul H. Kratoska, Remco Raben, and Henk Schulte Nordholt. Singapore and Ohio: Singapore University Press and Ohio University Press.

Tope, Lily Rose. 1993. The Chinese margin in Philippine literature. In *Philippine post-colonial studies: Essays in language and literature*, 73–81. Ed. Priscelina Patajo-

Legasto and Cristina Pantoja-Hidalgo. Quezon City: University of the Philippines Press.

———. 2000. Writing Chinese diaspora in English. In *Intercultural relations, cultural transformation, and identity: The ethnic Chinese. Selected papers presented at the 1998 ISSCO conference*, 301–7. Ed. Teresita Ang-See. Manila: Kaisa para sa Kaunlaran, Inc.

Trocki, Carl A. 1999. *Empire and the global political economy: A study of the Asian opium trade, 1750–1950*. London: Routledge.

Tu, Wei-ming. 1991. Cultural China: The periphery as center. *Daedalus* 120, no. 2:1–32. Rep. in 1994 as "Cultural China: The Periphery as Center." In *The Living Tree: The Changing Meaning of Being Chinese Today*, 1–34. Ed. Tu Wei-ming. Stanford: Stanford University Press.

Tulay. 1987. Our credo. *Tulay*, June 12, 1.

———. 1992. Order of battle: Kidnap-for ransom gang members wanted. *Tulay*, Nov. 8, 6–7.

———. 1994a. Tsinoys: Responding to change and challenge. *Tulay*, June 6, 12–13.

———. 1994b. BID raids Tutuban Center. *Tulay*, July 4, 6.

———. 1995. ABB expresses brotherhood with Tsinoys. *Tulay*, Feb. 6, 8.

———. 1996. Act with integrity. *Tulay*, Apr. 1, 3.

———. 1998a. Kidnap watch—an update. *Tulay*, Jan. 6, 4.

———. 1998b. Police, community unite vs. kidnapping. *Tulay*, Oct. 20, 16–15.

———. 1999. BI intensifies anti-illegal aliens campaign. *Tulay*, May 18, 5.

———. 2000. Chinese triad's hand in RP kidnaps seen. *Tulay*, Feb. 1, 4.

———. 2006a. 168 Mall in Binondo raided. *Tulay*, Mar. 21, 7.

———. 2006b. Extortion cases on the rise. *Tulay*, Mar. 21, 4.

———. 2007. Kidnapping incidents (1993–2006). *Tulay*, Feb. 6, 4.

———. 2008. 2007 marks all-time low in kidnapping incidents. *Tulay*, Jan. 8, 4.

Tulfo, Ramon. 1998. Who is to blame for PAL closure? *Philippine Daily Inquirer*, Sept. 24, 17.

United Daily News. 1973. Chinatown's development will trace Chinese influence on Filipino. *United Daily News*, Sept. 17.

United Nations Office on Drugs and Crime. 2011. *Global study on homicide*. Vienna: United Nations Office on Drugs and Crime.

"Urban legend #1: Robinsons' snake." 2007. "Not-so-recent Manila" blog, Oct. 17. Internet document, http://not-so-recent-manila.blogspot.com/2007/10/urban-legend-1-robinsons-snake.html, accessed Nov. 2, 2011.

Uy, Veronica C. 1999. Illegal Chinese find RP greener pasture. *Tulay*, July 20, 10, 11.

———. 2007. Chinese Embassy, Filipino-Chinese group slam Santiago "slur." *Philippine Daily Inquirer*, Sept. 27. Internet document, http://globalnation.inquirer.net/news/breakingnews/view_article.php?article_id=91094, accessed Apr. 8, 2008.

Valencia, Teodoro F. 1970 [2000]. The fight for Yuyitungs is not yet over. *The Manila Times*, May 7. Rep. in *The case of the Yuyitung brothers: Philippine press freedom under siege*, 134–36. Comp. and ed. Rizal Yuyitung. Manila: Yuyitung Foundation, Inc.

Villanueva, Marichu A. 2007. Kidnap politics. *Philippine Star*, Jan. 26. Internet document, http://www.philstar.com/Article.aspx?articleId=381786, accessed Mar. 30, 2010.

Villanueva, Robert C. 1993a. Big trouble in little China. *Philippines Free Press*, May 8, 14–15, 47.

_____. 1993b. The Chinese near exodus. *Philippines Free Press,* July 3, 38–39.

_____. 1994. Secrets of the Federation. *Philippines Free Press,* Jan. 8, 23–24.

Viva.com. 2011. Heart Evangelista speaks up, July 21. Internet document, http://www.viva.com.ph/index.php?option=com_content&view=article&id=2696:heart-evangelista-speaks-up&catid=1:news&Itemid=2, accessed Aug. 30.

Von Brevern, Marilies. 1986. Three Filipino-Chinese businessmen. In *The turning point: Twenty-six accounts of February events in the Philippines,* 174–82. Manila: Lyceum Press, Inc.

_____. 1988. *"Once a Chinese, always a Chinese?" The Chinese of Manila—tradition and change.* Manila: Lyceum Press, Inc.

Waldinger, Roger. 2001. Strangers at the gates. In *Strangers at the gates: New immigrants in urban America,* 1–29. Ed. Roger Waldinger. Berkeley and Los Angeles: University of California Press.

Wang Binbin. 2000. Gezai Zhongxi zhi jian de Riben: Xiandai Hanyu zhong de Riyü 'wailai yu' wenti (Japan between China and the West: The question of Japanese-imported terms in the Chinese language). In *Shouwang Linghun:* Shanghai Wenxue *suibi jingpin* (Vigilant Spirit: Essays from the *Shanghai Wenxue*). Ed. He Xiongfei. Shanghai: Zhonghua Gongshang Lianhe Chubanshe.

Wang Fan-sen. 2000. *Fu Ssu-nien: A life in Chinese history and politics.* Cambridge, UK: Cambridge University Press.

Wang Gungwu. 1981/1992a. The limits of Nanyang nationalism, 1912–1937. In *Community and nation: Essays on Southeast Asia and the Chinese,* 40–57. Singapore: Heinemann.

_____. 1992b. The origins of hua-ch'iao. In *Community and nation: China, Southeast Asia and Australia,* 1–10. New South Wales: Association of Asian Studies in Australia and Allen and Unwin.

_____. 1992c. A short history of the Nanyang Chinese. In *Community and nation: China, Southeast Asia and Australia,* 11–39. New South Wales: Association of Asian Studies in Australia and Allen and Unwin.

_____. 1992d. Trade and cultural values: Australia and the Four Dragons. In *Community and nation: China, Southeast Asia and Australia,* 301–13. New South Wales: Association of Asian Studies in Australia and Allen and Unwin.

_____. 2003a [1958]. *The Nanhai trade: The early history of Chinese trade in the South China Sea.* New ed. Singapore: Times Academic Press.

_____. 2003b. The culture of Chinese merchants. In *China and the Chinese Overseas,* 203–20. Singapore: Eastern University Press.

_____. 2003c [1991]. Lu Xun, Lim Boon Keng, and Confucianism. In *China and the Chinese overseas,* 163–84. Singapore: Eastern University Press.

_____. 2003d. Merchants without empires: The Hokkien sojourning communities. In *China and the Chinese Overseas,* 87–111. Singapore: Eastern University Press.

_____. 2003e. Political Chinese: Their contribution to modern Southeast Asian history. In *China and the Chinese Overseas,* 144–62. Singapore: Eastern University Press.

_____. 2003f. The study of Chinese identities in Southeast Asia. In *China and the Chinese Overseas,* 221–47. Singapore: Eastern University Press.

_____. 2004. Cultural centres for the Chinese overseas. In *Diasporic Chinese ventures: The life and work of Wang Gungwu,* 210–26. Ed. Gregor Benton and Hong Liu. London and New York: RoutledgeCurzon.

_____. 2011. E-mail to the author, Jan. 10.

Wang Hui. 2011. *The politics of imagining Asia*. Cambridge, Mass.: Harvard University Press.

Weber, Max. 1947 [1913]. The fundamental concepts of sociology. In *The theory of social and economic organization*, 87–157. Trans. A. M. Henderson and Talcott Parsons. New York: Free Press.

Weightman, George H. 1959. The Philippine Chinese: A cultural history of a marginal trading community. Ph.D. diss., Cornell University, U.S.A.

Wha Chi. 1982. *The souvenir issue of the 40th anniversary of the Philippine Chinese anti-Japanese guerrilla forces*. Manila: Wha Chi.

Wickberg, Edgar. 1964. The Chinese *mestizo* in Philippine history. *The Journal of Southeast Asian History* 5, no. 1:62–100.

_____. 1965. *The Chinese in Philippine life, 1850–1898*. New Haven: Yale University Press.

_____. 1992. Notes on contemporary social organizations in Manila Chinese society. In *China, across the seas/The Chinese as Filipinos*. Edited by Aileen S.P. Baviera and Teresita Ang-See, 59–64. Quezon City: Philippine Association for Chinese Studies.

_____. 1997. Anti-Sinicism and Chinese identity options in the Philippines. In *Essential outsiders: Chinese and Jews in the modern transformation of Southeast Asia and Central Europe*, 158–83. Ed. Daniel Chirot and Anthony Reid. Seattle: University of Washington Press.

_____. 2006. Hokkien-Philippines familial transnationalism, 1949–1975. In *Reading Chinese transnationalisms: Society, literature, film*, 17–36, 190–92, 212–15. Ed. Maria N. Ng and Philip Holden. Hong Kong: Hong Kong University Press.

Williams, Lea E. 1966. *The future of the overseas Chinese in Southeast Asia*. The United States and China in World Affairs Series. New York: McGraw-Hill Book Company.

Willmott, Donald E. 1961. *The national status of the Chinese in Indonesia, 1900–1958*. Ithaca: Southeast Asia Program, Cornell University.

Wilson, Andrew. 2004. *Ambition and identity: Chinese merchant elites in colonial Manila, 1880–1916*. University of Hawaii Press.

Winarta, Frans H. 2008. No more discrimination against the Chinese. In *The ethnic Chinese in Indonesia*, 57–74. Ed. Leo Suryadinata. Singapore: Institute of Southeast Asian Studies.

Wolf, Eric R. 2001 [1966]. Kinship, friendship, and patron-client relations in complex societies. In *Pathways of power: Building an anthropology of the modern world*, 166–83. Eric R. Wolf with Sydel Silverman. Berkeley: University of California Press.

Wolters, Oliver W. 1970. *The fall of Srivijaya*. Ithaca: Cornell University Press.

_____. 1999. *History, culture and region in Southeast Asian perspectives*. Rev. ed. Ithaca: Cornell University Southeast Asia Program.

Wong Kwok-Chu. 1999. *The Chinese in the Philippine economy, 1891–1941*. Quezon City: Ateneo de Manila University Press.

Wong Siu-lun. 1979. *Sociology and socialism in contemporary China*. London: Routledge and Kegan Paul.

Woodside, Alexander Barton. 1971. *Vietnam and the Chinese model: A comparative study of Nguyen and Ch'ing civil government in the first half of the nineteenth century*. Cambridge, Massachusetts: Harvard University Press.

World Bank. 1993. *The East Asian miracle*. Washington, D.C.: The World Bank.

Worsley, Peter. 2002. *Marx and Marxism*. Rev. ed. London: Routledge.

Wu, David Yen-ho. 1991. The construction of Chinese and non-Chinese identities. *Daedalus* 120, no. 2:159–79.

Xin Mei. 2006. *Afraid to be Chinese*. New Manila: Milflores Publishing Inc.

Xu Chengjian, Xu Chengyan, and Xu Chengliang. 2001. Shenqie huainian jingai de fuqin Xu Li [Xu Jingcheng] (Cherishing profoundly the memory of our beloved father Xu Li [Xu Jingcheng]). In *Feilubin huaqiao kangri aiguo yinghun* (Philippine-Chinese martyrs of the anti-Japanese resistance), 6–13. Ed. Gong Taoyi. Beijing: Huawen Chubanshe.

Xü Xuan. 1972. Qiaoshe wang na li qu? (Whither huaqiao/overseas Chinese society?) *Huaqiao Zhoukan* (China Weekly, Sunday Magazine of the Chinese Commercial News]), Special New Year Issue 44, no.1 (Jan. 2): 3–4.

Yamamoto Hiroyuki. 2011. Introduction. In *Bangsa and umma: Development of people-grouping concepts in Islamized Southeast Asia*, 1–13. Ed. Yamamoto Hiroyuki, Anthony Milner, Kawashima Midori, and Arai Kazuhiro. Kyoto: Kyoto University Press.

Yamamoto Nobuto. 1995. Lim Boon Keng ni okeru 'Kindai teki Chūgokujin' no sōzō –'Shinpo' no jidai ni okeru shoki Nanyō kajin nationalism kenkyū shiron (Lim Boon Keng and the creation of the "Modern Chinese": A preliminary study of Early Nanyang Chinese nationalism in the age of "progress"). *Hōgaku Kenkyū* 68, no. 5:27–66.

Yang Yi. n.d. Du Ai zai Zhongguo xiandai xiaoshuo shishang de diwei (Du Ai's place in the history of the contemporary novel). Photostat MS.

_____. 2000. Lingnan wentan Nanyang feng (Nanyangism in Lingnan literary circles). In *Chen chuang jian xia: Yang Yi xueshu suibi zixuan ji* (Window at dawn cuts through the red clouds: Yang Yi's academic essays, as selected by the author), 201–5. Fujian: Fujian Jiaoyu Chubanshe.

Yao, Souchou. 2008. Being essentially Chinese: What is it to us? In *Chineseness unbound: Boundaries, burdens and belongings of Chineseness outside China*. Asia Research Institute Asia Trends, 11 Sept. 11. Singapore: Asia Research Institute.

_____. 2002. *Confucian capitalism: Discourse, practice and the myth of Chinese enterprise*. London: RoutledgeCurzon.

Yap, Gloria C. 1970. Philippine Chinese fiction in English. *Kinaadman* 1:29–47.

Yau Shuk-Ting, Kinnia. 2009. The early development of East Asian cinema in a regional context. *Asian Studies Review* 33:161–73.

Yen, Ching-hwang. 1976. *The overseas Chinese and the 1911 revolution, with special reference to Singapore and Malaya*. Kuala Lumpur: Oxford University Press.

Yoshihara, Kunio. 1985. *Philippine industrialization: Foreign and domestic capital*. Quezon City: Ateneo de Manila University Press.

_____. 1995. *The nation and economic growth: The Philippines and Thailand*. Kuala Lumpur: Oxford University Press.

Young, Ken. 1999. Consumption, social differentiation and self-definition of the new rich in industrialising Southeast Asia. In *Culture and privilege in capitalist Asia*, 56–85. Ed. Michael Pinches. London and New York: Routledge.

Young, Robert. 1995. *Colonial desire: Hybridity in theory, culture and race*. London and New York: Routledge.

Young Rok Cheong. 2003. Chinese business networks and their implications for South Korea. In *The Korean diaspora in the world economy*, 31–55. Ed. C. Fred Bergsten and Inbom Choi. Washington: Institute for International Economics.

Yu, Henry. 2001. *Thinking Orientals: Migration, contact, and exoticism in modern America*. Oxford and New York: Oxford University Press.

Yu Zhanggeng [Rizal Yuyitung, writing under the nom de plume Xi Ning]. 1961a [originally published 1952]. Huaqiao shehui de luxiang (Shangbao Congshu: Where huaqiao society is heading). In *Huaqiao shehui de luxiang* (Where huaqiao society is heading: A *Chinese Commercial News* series), 35–49. Manila: Yitong Chubansheinxing.

———. 1961b. Shi tuibian de shihou le—Muqian huaqiao chujing de zhongxin guji (It's time for change: Reappraising the current unfavorable status of the huaqiao/ overseas Chinese). In *Qiaoshe luxiang de lunzhan* (Where Huaqiao/Overseas Chinese Society is Heading: A Debate), 32–42. Manila: Yitongchubansheyinxing.

Yu Zhanggeng [Rizal Yuyitung], ed. 1997. Xin bu xin you ni: Wo de Tangshan mama shi moluo houyi (Believe it or not: My Tengsua/Chinese mother is of Moro ancestry). In *Zhonghunyipo: Yu Yitong lieshi yü Huaqiao Shangbao* (Yu Yi Tong the martyr and the *Huaqiao Commercial News*), 25–30. Manila: Yu Yitong Jijinghui.

Yun He, ed. 2000. *Dongnan Ya huawen wenxue daxi: Feilubin juan* (Anthology of Southeast Asian Chinese literature: The Philippines). Gen. ed. Yang Jiaqing. 10 vols. Xiamen: Lujiang Chubanshe.

Yung Li, Yuk-wai. 1996. *The huaqiao warriors: Chinese resistance movements in the Philippines, 1942–45.* Quezon City: Ateneo de Manila University Press.

Yuyitung, Quentin [Quintin]. 1966. A Chinese view on Philippine-Chinese tensions. *Solidarity* 1, no. 1:33–36.

Yuyitung, Rizal, ed. 2000. *The case of the Yuyitung brothers: Philippine press freedom under siege.* Manila: Yuyitung Foundation, Inc.

Zaide, Gregorio M. 1970. *Rizal, Asia's first apostle of nationalism.* Manila: Red Star Book Store.

Zhu, Danting. 2010. Yue chang yue you ai—he ku bao dong gua (Singing in Cantonese for love of Cantonese: Why bother to speak Putonghua). *Nan Fang Du Shi Bao* (Southern Metropolitan Daily), *Nandu Daily*, July 12. Internet document, http://gcontent.oeeee. com/9/ad/9adeb82fffb5444e/Blog/89a/b53716.html, accessed Mar. 5, 2011.

Zhuang Guotu. 1989. *Zhongguo fengjian zhengfu de huaqiao zhengce* (The policies of China's feudal government concerning the overseas Chinese). Xiamen: Xiamen Daxue Chubanshe.

Zhuang Zhongqing. 2001. Mao Dun yu biaoxian Nanyang shehui de wenxue (Mao Dun and the literary depiction of Nanyang society). *Xiamen Ribao* (Xiamen News), May 2, 7.

Zialcita, Fernando Nakpil. 2009. Preguntas acerca de la identidad Filipina (Questions concerning Filipino identity). In *Repensar Filipinas: Política, identidad y religión en la construcción de la nación filipina* (Rethinking the Philippines: Politics, identity and religion in the making of the Filipino nation). Ed. María Dolores Elizalde Pérez-Grueso. Barcelona: CSIC-Casa Asia Edicions Bellaterra.

Zulueta, Lito B. 1995. Pinoy taipans: The secret of their success. *The Sunday Chronicle*, Nov. 19, 1, 4.

———. 1998. Industry of fear and greed. *METRO*, Jan.–Feb., 48.

———. 2002. MMFF: Why the Metro filmfest should be abolished. *Philippine Daily Inquirer*, Dec. 31, A22.

INDEX

A

Aalog-alog (TV series), 47n2

Abalos, Benjamin, 261

Abdullah, Akmal, 240

Abella, Domingo, 13

Aboitizes, 258–59

ABS-CBN Film Productions, Inc., 206

Absorption, 98, 111–12, 141, 257

Acculturation, 5, 82, 99, 109, 259

Activism, political, 100, 123, 232, 238

Administrative Naturalization Law (RA
    9138), 89n24, 114, 171n38

Adulyadej, Bhumibol: Chinese ancestry, 235, 283

Agence-France Press, 91

Agoncillo, Teodoro, 13, 30

Aguilar, Filomeno V., 26, 66, 70, 72

Aguinaldo, Emilio, 33, 69

Ah Tek (fictional character), 129–30

Ahmad, Yasmin, 238

Aizawa, Nobuhiro, 109

Ako Legal Wife: Mano Po 4 (film), 203, 205

Alay Puso Feeding Center, 172n45

Alba, Pia (fictional character), 18

Alejandrino, Casto, 193

Alex Boncayao Brigade (ABB), 160

Alien Chinese, 75, 110, 121, 141, 154, 160, 230, 299; and
    alienating capital, 170n30; stigmatization, 287

Alien Legalization Program (ALP), 161

Alien Social Integration Act (ASIA, 1995), 156, 161,
    164, 165; residency status to aliens, 171n38

Alienness, of Chinese, 150, 194

Aliens, Illegal, 277

Amalgamation, 94, 98

America, 6, 16, 67–68, 99, 100, 113, 251, 278, 289, 291,
    293, 298, 300, 301, 304, 305; Chinese immigration,
    294; and Free Asia, 7, 35, 59, 75, 97, 101

American Central Intelligence Agency, 237

American Chamber of Commerce Journal, 30

American hegemony: Anglo-Chinese, 298–305

Ampatuan, Andal, Sr., 162

An Kyong-su, 294

Anak Semua Bangsa, 298

Anderson, Benedict, 19

Anderson, Gerald, 47n2

Anderson's Command, 173

Ang, Charlie "Atong," 125

Angliongto, Jose L., 39, 55, 87n2, 97

powerhouse, 34–35, 37, 42, 214, 219, 253; as trading partners, 289–90
Malaka: tributary mission to China, 292
Malay, Armando: on Marxist-Leninist legitimacy, 194
Malaya. *See* Malaysia
Malayness, 61, 240
"Malays," 61, 248, 273
Malaysia, 29, 213, 263; *baba*, 12, 236, 250–51; *blasteran*, 249; Bumiputera, 27–28; Chinese labourers, 287; Chinese population, 7, 51–52, 288; communist guerrillas of, 313; Confucianism, 295; East Asian region, 213; economic nationalism, 299; emergency in, 37; ethnic Chinese, 27, 48n15, 97, 299; Hong Kong films, 303–4; and mainland China, 289; Ministry of Home Affairs, 28; multiracialism, 238; national culture, 240; pop culture, 205; refugees, 44; urban middle class, 232
Malolos Congress, 67
Malolos Constitution of 1899, 33, 70
Manchus, 95, 284, 291
Mandarin, 11, 28, 185, 216, 259, 300, 302–3, 305, 310–11, 318n26, 320n43
Manglapus, Raul, 124
Manila, 21, 66; British occupation, 64–66; Catholic Chinese, 88n11; Chinese mestizos, 67, 73; Chinese-owned shopping malls, 139, 281n25; kidnapping, 144, 163; Wha Chi, 176–77, 183–85, 190–92, 201n35; Young Communist League, 199n10
Manila Hotel, 258
Manila Post, The: on Chinese, 141
Manila Press Club, 91
"Mano po," as gesture, 47n3
Mano Po (film), 2–3, 41, 45–46, 136n33, 203, 204; Chinese capital, 210; Chinese culture, 241; Chinese identification, 220; Chinese mestizoness, 217; Chinese themes, 207; Chinese-Filipino attachment to the Philippines, 224; Chineseness and Filipinoness, 228; crosscultural marriage, 218, 219; cultural hybridity,

241; expense, 219; filial piety, 241n1; integrationist message, 208–9; and Kaisa Para sa Kaunlaran, 208; plot, 227; public conversation in Hokkien, 244n23; reliance on money, 220–23; women in Chinese business, 244n18
Mano Po 2, 219: ethnic Chinese integration, 223; Chinese capital, 210; domesticating alien Chinese, 213; *My Home* (film), 203, 205; patriarch in, 244n18
Mano Po 3: extortion, 222–23; *My Love* (film), 203, 205; woman in, 244n18
Mano Po 5: *Gua Ai Di* (film), 203
Mano Po 6: *A Mother's Story* (film), 203; awards, 241n2
Manuel L. Quezon University, 109
Manuel, E. Arsenio, 10
Mao, Dun, 181
Mao, Zedong, 97, 195, 197; on patriotism, 200n17
Maoist Chinese Communist Party, 193, 201n38
Maoist propaganda, 92
Marcos, Ferdinand, 62, 91, 96, 263: on drug dealing, 271
Marcos regime: Chinese naturalization, 168n11; Chinese-Filipinos in business, 170–71n33; kidnappings, 162
Maritime geography, 317n15
Maritime Silk Road, 309
Maritime trade, 148, 287, 316n8
Market Stalls Act of 1946, 30
Martial Law of 1972, 97, 122
Marx, Karl: commercial capital, 149, 150; merchant labor, 151; commodity exchange, 145, 146
Marxist theory, 151
Maryknoll College, 111
Mass media, 212, 291
May Democratic Movement (1992), 234
May Fourth Movement, 184
Maynila sa Mga Kuko ng Liwanag, 1975 (film): 40, 129–31; anti-Chinese, 227
McBeath, Gerald, 114
McCarthy, Charles, 111–12
Meily, Mark, 205
Melayu concept, 249

S

305, 313: re-Sinicization, 314; films, 240; indigenous nationalism, 178, 302; interracial marriages, 249; and Mainland Chinese alliance, 260
Southeast Asian Chinese: local "Chinese" culture, 309–10
Southeast Asian Film Festival, 303
Southeast Asian Motion Picture Producers' Association, 303
Southwest China: Han colonization, 286
Spain, 67: ancestry, 23; Civil Code, 70
Spanish colonial period, 67; on Chinese immigration, 148; Chinese traders, 148; revenues from Chinese, 171n37
Spanish mestizos, 25, 67, 133n13
Spanish Philippines, 287, 294
"Special Visa for Employment Generation," 211
Specific Characteristics of Our People's War, 195
Spivak, Gayatri Chakravorty, 27, 50n26
Split-family system, 72; transnationalization, 254
Spratly Islands, 34, 143, 264, 280n15
Squadron, 48, 190–91
Squadron, 8, 176
State corporations: politico-business alliances, 264
Stock market, 225
Straits Chinese British Association, 250
Straits Chinese Gallery: Peranakan material, 278–79n1
Straits Chinese/Straits-born Chinese, 249
Straits Settlements, 104, 249–50, 251
Suehiro, Tetchō, 294
Suharto: on Communist China, 236–27
Sukimura, Kim Chan (fictional character), 47n2
Sukubangsa (ethnic group), 105
Sultanate, The (novel), 39, 46, 55, 76–87
Sun, Ping, 176
Sun, Yat-sen, 184, 198n4, 286, 289, 294, 297
Sunico, Hilario Chanuangco Santos, 18
Surat Bukti Kewarganegaraan Republik Indonesia (SBKRI), 28
Surat Ganti Nama, 28
Surplus value, 151

Suryadinata, Leo, 105
Switzerland, 100
Sy family, 254
Sy, Charlene Mayne, 163, 168n8, 170n24
Sy, Chen (fictional character), 1
Sy, Henry, 171n34, 257, 258
Sy, Yuan, (fictional character), 1
Sycip, Alexander, 163

T

Tagalog, 273, 294
Tai Diok Ka (TDKs), 13, 218
Taipans (tycoons), 39: fortunes, 154
Taiping rebellion, 285
Taiwan, 2, 8, 11, 24, 34, 58, 122, 213, 214, 230, 263; culture, 215; inflow, 291; diasporic, 316n12; Dragon economies, 147; film industry, 205, 302; folk beliefs/practices, 306; Hong Kong films, 303–4; and Mainland China, 290; New Wave of Cinema movement, 242n6; popular cultural dissemination, 301; popular music, 302; populations, 215
Taiwanese, 260, 264: Anglo-Sinicization, 300
Taiwanization, 316n12
Tambunting, Ildefonso, 65, 67
Tan, Dante, 125
Tan, Kong, 318n25
Tan, Lucio, 171n34, 258
Tan, Michael, 10
Tan, Robbie, 206–7
Tan, Vivienne, 280n17
Tan Malaka, 297
Tang Dynasty: "Golden age," 310; Min'nan "dialect," 310
Tangren, 216
Tangshan, 216
Tantivo, 280n18
Tariff system, 31
Taruc, Luis, 199n12. Born of the People, 190–91
Tatalon Free Clinic and Immunization Projects, 172n45
Tejapira, Kasian, 202n43, 234, 235

KYOTO CSEAS SERIES ON ASIAN STUDIES
Center for Southeast Asian Studies, Kyoto University

The Economic Transition in Myanmar after 1988: Market Economy versus State Control, edited by Koichi Fujita, Fumiharu Mieno, and Ikuko Okamoto, 2009

Populism in Asia, edited by Kosuke Mizuno and Pasuk Phongpaichit, 2009

Traveling Nation-Makers: Transnational Flows and Movements in the Making of Modern Southeast Asia, edited by Caroline S. Hau and Kasian Tejapira, 2011

China and the Shaping of Indonesia, 1949–1965, by Hong Liu, 2011

Questioning Modernity in Indonesia and Malaysia, edited by Wendy Mee and Joel S. Kahn, 2012

Industrialization with a Weak State: Thailand's Development in Historical Perspective, by Somboon Siriprachai, edited by Kaoru Sugihara, Pasuk Phongpaichit, and Chris Baker, 2012

Popular Culture Co-productions and Collaborations in East and Southeast Asia, edited by Nissim Otmazgin and Eyal Ben-Ari, 2012

Strong Soldiers, Failed Revolution: The State and Military in Burma, 1962–88, by Yoshihiro Nakanishi, 2013

Organising Under the Revolution: Unions and the State in Java, 1945–48, by Jafar Suryomenggolo, 2013

Living with Risk: Precarity & Bangkok's Urban Poor, by Tamaki Endo, 2014

Migration Revolution: Philippine Nationhood and Class Relations in a Globalized Age, by Filomeno V. Aguilar Jr., 2014